Microprocessor systems:
Software & Hardware Architecture

MICROPROCESSOR SYSTEMS

SOFTWARE AND HARDWARE ARCHITECTURE

Edited by STEPHEN EVANCZUK,

Microsystems & Software Editor, *Electronics*

Library of Congress Cataloging in Publication Data
Main entry under title:

Microprocessor systems.

Articles originally published in *Electronics*
magazine.
Includes index.
1. Microprocessors. I. Evanczuk, Stephen
QA76.5.M521955 1983   001.64   83-19969

ISBN 0-07-606876-5   (pbk.)

ISBN 0-07-019756-3   (casebound)

Electronics

McGraw-Hill Publications Company
1221 Avenue of the Americas
New York, NY 10020

CONTENTS

FOREWORD

For many years, the computer industry's primary concerns were to keep data-processing shops supplied with large central-processing units tied to acres of mass storage devices like disk and magnetic-tape drives. With the invention of the microprocessor chip, the industry found a growing market in smaller commercial applications and, increasingly, in personal computers and work stations.

Although the entrepreneurs who first explored the design of these early microprocessor-based systems used relatively simple techniques, current microsystems have turned to highly sophisticated software and hardware techniques to squeeze performance out of these systems that can measure up to large general-purpose mainframes. For the mostpart, the appearance of this new generation of microprocessor-based systems is due to the appearance of a new breed of design engineer: the systems-integration expert.

Once the domain of mainframe experts, systems design has turned into a formal discipline in academia and an accepted design procedure in the industry. Backed by a semiconductor industry that is constantly finding new ways to boost performance and function of chips, systems designers have, in turn, responded to that industry's need for product definition by suggesting new ways to partition function into silicon. Simultaneously, the software industry has dug deeply into its bag of tricks to bring forth systems software of a level surpassing some of the most time-honored mainframe software.

These six chapters highlight the major milestones that have led to this new era of microsystems. Divided into the major subsystems of concern to a systems designer, they examine trends in systems software, new microprocessor chips, memory, peripheral controller subsystems, networks, and special-purpose chips for math and digital signal processing.

In order to patch readers back into the source, each article includes a dateline indicating the original issue of Electronics magazine in which the article originally appeared.

-Stephen Evanczuk

1.
SOFTWARE

As computers edge into a broadening range of applications, industry is attending more closely to the software that drives these systems. Previously unrelated branches of companies are now cooperating in a software design process that includes more than the traditional issues of feasibility and performance.

Designers, besieged by more severe demands on their time, look for a software package that is easy to design, implement, and maintain. Marketing managers, concerned with return on investment of scarce engineering resources, look for a package that fits a wide segment of the marketplace.

Consequently, software engineers and corporate executives alike are closely watching issues in software standards and market share. Not suprising, then, is the increased discussion on topics in operating systems and languages. Translating the functional capability of the underlying hardware into a set of software routines, the operating system in a computer acts to bend the power of the hardware to the user's needs. As long as a designer is careful to use that set of operating system routines—and avoid hardware-specific code—programs can execute in the operating-system environment regardless of the type of hardware.

The articles in this chapter highlight the major trends in software—spanning issues from operating systems to languages and data-base managers. Although it is difficult to tag an evolving, dynamic industry like the software industry, these articles do spotlight the significant trends pushing the development of new software systems and applications.

Bell Labs' Unix operating system spreads powerful new wings

Software vendors breed enhanced versions of the Unix operating system for machines ranging from microsystems through supercomputers

In a software industry still testing its wings in a mass market, Bell Laboratories' Unix operating system is soaring toward the lead. Hatched by the labs' Ken Thompson and Dennis Ritchie [*Electronics*, Oct. 20, 1982, p. 108], this highly sophisticated system software has migrated from a research and development environment to a commercial market in which it is expected to gross more than $5 billion by 1986 in the microsystem area alone.

That huge market appeal derives from Unix's potential for leading the computer industry out of the wilderness of program incompatibility. By now, many Unix variants have been developed for radically different hardware systems; but, because they adhere to the fundamental organization of the "vanilla" Unix system, the new flavors remain remarkably compatible across architectures. Applications written for machines running one Unix flavor should therefore be able to run with very little change on machines running others, to the delight of overworked programmers.

Indeed, much of the success of the Unix operating system can be traced back to these same software engineers. Encountering it in the universities, where it is very popular, they learn as students to appreciate its utilities for program development. Then as graduates, they bring their liking for it into industry, persuading software-development managers to use the operating system in house, even if the final product is not directly related to it.

Thus pulled by the marketplace and pushed by programmers, Unix system software will clearly be around in one form or another for a long time. Although those forms will change, the articles presented in the series beginning in this issue suggest the major characteristics the Unix variants will have in common as they reach toward the market.

by Stephen Evanczuk
Software Editor

Berkeley 4.2 gives Unix operating system network support

Virtual memory support lets larger processes execute;
improved file system speeds access to data

by Bill Joy, *Sun Microsystems Inc., Mountain View, Calif.*

☐ Linked together in networks that share resources like disks and printers, high-performance personal work stations will meet the needs for cost-effective computing in the 1980s. But creating special-purpose operating systems for each of these different computing nodes would exact a heavy toll on already overburdened programming resources. By using a single operating system such as Bell Laboratories' Unix on all nodes, designers can greatly reduce the cost and complexity of creating a distributed computing environment.

Version 4.2 of the Berkeley Software Distribution of Unix meets the challenge of integrating this network of work stations and peripherals with new and existing computers by means of enhancements like virtual-memory support, faster file access, the creation of such network services as file systems and printing, and interprocess communication supporting a multiwindow interface.

Early versions of the Unix operating systems used swapping and ran on machines like the PDP-11 (see "Evolution of the Unix operating system,"), whose memory-management hardware could support only simple segmentation. With the migration of even the largest application programs to smaller superminicomputers and now to microcomputer-based work stations, virtual memory is needed on the smallest machines.

Replacing pages

Virtual-memory support in Unix 4.2BSD allows very large processes to be run, for the system moves pages to and from secondary storage as needed. Its secret is a global page-replacement algorithm, which helps minimize the amount of memory used by each process by retaining the set of the pages it has most recently used. Consequently, several large processes, whose size is greater than the available main memory, can be run concurrently. Moreover, processes as large as 16 megabytes can be run under 4.2BSD on a VAX/11 superminicomputer or a Sun work station—a desktop computer based on the MC68010—even when those machines are not equipped with that amount of physical memory.

Benchmarks have shown that the addition of virtual-memory facilities to the Unix 4.2BSD system greatly increases the number of users a single time-sharing system can support. On a personal work station like Sun's,

virtual memory not only increases the size of programs that can be run—it also greatly improves system responsiveness. Rather than preloading an entire large program when it is invoked, the paging facilities allow the individual page frames to be loaded into physical memory only as they are needed. As each is loaded, the page-replacement algorithm selects a less recently used page to be replaced with the new page.

If 4.2BSD is to be run on a machine without virtual-memory management, the system can still take advantage of page-level memory mapping to place individual pages in scattered locations in memory, even if the machine does not support the restartable instructions needed to remedy attempts to access nonresident pages (page faults). Thus it has been possible to run the system on the MC68000 microprocessor, which does not support virtual memory, before the MC68010 processor with virtual-memory support was available. When paging is not used, however, the delay in starting processes increases, and fewer processes can be run concurrently.

Fast file access

Traditional 16-bit Unix systems provide an elegant hierarchical file system—but one with low performance. On a disk drive with a 1-megabyte-per-second transfer rate, the available throughput on large file transfers is no better than 50 kilobytes/s because of the poor layout of the blocks on the disk. Though that rate is more than sufficient for time-sharing applications consisting of program development and text processing, it is inadequate to meet the needs of large applications or to implement network file systems. Unix 4.2BSD contains a new file-system implementation, one that uses better data structures and algorithms to improve performance.

In earlier versions of the Unix operating system, the file system kept free blocks on a linked list. When a file system was created, this list was sorted, with the blocks interleaved in the free list for fast access. Interleaving the blocks of a disk file is a common technique for efficiently transferring data from disk to memory. Without interleaving, the system delay in preparing for the next logical block would result in the disk drive's head overshooting that block on the disk, so that another complete disk rotation would be needed before the head was positioned correctly. But with interleaving, the system delay overlaps with the time the disk takes to skip an interleaved block before reaching the one it needs to access.

In earlier versions of Unix, the system attempted to read only 512 bytes from the disk in a single transfer operation. Larger transfers would take two or more input/output operations. Over time, as files were created and removed, the free list became scrambled. Successive

blocks allocated to a file were located far apart on the disk, so that many seek operations were needed to read a typical file.

Unix 4.2BSD solves the file-system performance problem by evincing a greater understanding of disk geometry—it places consecutive data blocks and related indexing information in neighboring areas on the disk. Thus files in a directory are nearly always stored on a single

Evolution of the Unix operating system

The Unix operating system was born in the early days of minicomputers, through the efforts of a research group at Bell Laboratories [*Electronics,* Oct. 20, 1982, p. 108]. And it gained widespread acceptance shortly after it was adapted to Digital Equipment Corp.'s 16-bit PDP-11 minicomputer and made available at nominal cost to universities and research laboratories.

It deserved its popularity, for it supported a set of features unusual for a minicomputer operating system in the early 1970s, the time it was introduced: a hierarchical file system, compatible file, device, and interprocess input/output, a powerful programmable command interpreter, support for the initiation of asynchronous tasks, and a rich and easily extendable set of programming tools. Today, this set of features is considered so important that most vendors of operating systems equip them with similar features in order to be able to call them "Unix-like."

The most widespread versions of Unix are based on the PDP-11 version. System III and System V from Western Electric, commercial systems such as Xenix, and the Unix look-alikes, such as Idris and Coherent, are all based on and function like Unix version 7, released in 1978. The primary areas of application for this system are in text processing and program development.

Bell Laboratories subsequently ported Unix to the VAX 11/780, a 32-bit computer with virtual memory hardware and then in 1979, another group, at the University of California at Berkeley, added virtual memory management to this system. The Berkeley version was released as 3BSD (the abbreviation for the third Berkeley software distribution for Unix) to other VAX/Unix sites. This system and its successors have been the primary system used on the roughly 1,000 VAX/Unix systems outside Bell Laboratories.

When the Defense Advanced Research Projects Agency was looking for new hardware to replace the PDP-10 minicomputers widely used in the research community, it chose the VAX line as among the primary machines. But instead of staying with the vendor-supplied VAX/VMS operating system, the agency decided to fund further development of the 3BSD system, with the aim of turning it into a portable system that could be used on a wide range of hardware in further research projects.

Unix 4.2BSD (described in the accompanying article) is the result of that project. It embodies a number of enhancements not present in other versions. These include foreground-background job control, automatic reboot after system crashes, and a powerful new symbolic debugger. No other current version of Unix has all these facilities.

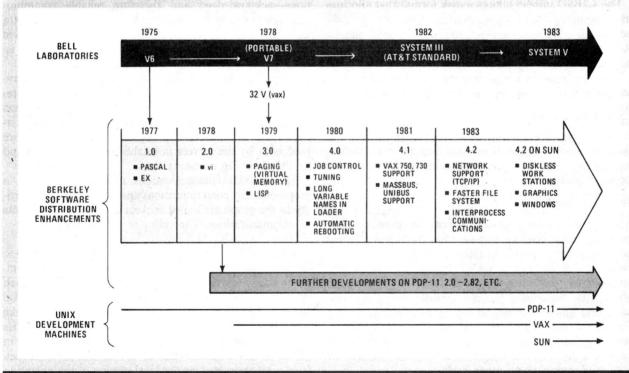

track, or cylinder, of the disk, eliminating most of the seek time when this information is accessed. Furthermore, storing the data blocks of a file in larger contiguous chunks (several kilobytes rather than 512 bytes) results in a higher data-transfer rate due to reduced system overhead. If it is impossible to place consecutive blocks together, they are located so as to minimize rotational and positioning delay.

On the older Unix file systems, reading a 32-K-byte file into system memory from a disk was a repetitive process, consisting of 64 seek operations to a new cylinder and 64 transfers of 512 bytes each. On average, a seek took about 30 milliseconds, plus another 8 ms of average rotational latency once the disk head was on the correct cylinder. In the worst case, this entire operation consumed roughly 2.5 s (see figure opposite). Even if an average of two consecutive blocks in the file did happen to be properly interleaved as a result of the way the free list was sorted, the time might still only be cut in half—to about 1.5 s.

In the 4.2BSD file system, most data is stored in 4,096-byte blocks, with one smaller block per file storing any residual data. Reading a 32-K-byte file now requires reading only eight records. Further, these records are likely to all be on the same cylinder. Even if they are on two different cylinders, the time to read the file is on the order of 0.125 s, still better than 10 times faster than the lucky 1.5 s under the older file system.

Unfortunately, some newer I/O architectures, such as the American National Standards Institute's proposed Small Computer System Interface, hide the details of the block layout on the disk from the system. They map bad blocks on the disk by slipping, in effect, the rest of the blocks on the disk to create a logical map that is free of bad blocks—a solution that makes it very complicated for the system to develop an accurate model of the disk.

The 4.2BSD instead adopts a disk format that allocates one or more extra sectors per track for bad spots. This technique is used in the VAX family's newer disk formats, like that of the DEC R80 disk-drive family, to localize the effect of the bad sectors on disk geometry.

This way of increasing throughput when accessing files does not alter the programmer's view of the storage medium. Today, the file-system performance closely matches that the best obtainable with current disk technology. Future evolution in Unix file-system facilities will likely be aspects of the file system that are unrelated to performance—for instance, replicating files to improve their availability.

Communications

The original Unix operating system was created before local networks became a common technology. It has facilities merely for exchanging information over dial-up lines, and some versions include support for some minicomputer-to-mainframe communications in the remote-job-entry style. But it is notably lacking in interprocess communications facilities. The "pipe" facility of earlier Unix systems provides only a byte-stream capability between processes on a single machine; it does not generalize to message-oriented communications and communications with processes on other hosts.

Instead of defining a new local-network architecture, Unix 4.2BSD introduces a network-protocol support subsystem. Different networking architectures can be supported in the system, much as different disks can be supported by different drivers in a traditional operating system. Just as the read, write, seek, and format operations are common to all disk-drive controllers, the communications subsystem abstracts the properties common to all communications systems and provides its users with them, hiding the details of the specific network protocols internally. Unix 4.2BSD builds its communications services on top of external low-level networking facilities. Consequently, this version of Unix is more dependent on external network facilities than are other operating systems that define their own network protocols. On the other hand, 4.2BSD is more flexible in adapting to new networking environments.

The 4.2BSD system could have been built without networking support in the kernel; instead, it could have used network server processes that would have been accessed by other applications through the native Unix interprocess communication. Furthermore, these processes could have run the networking hardware directly. However, this approach was rejected because the overhead incurred in context switching in current hardware architectures significantly reduces network throughput. Moreover, the approach adopted avoids introducing a new networking protocol for Unix and, instead, keeps the operating system open to existing and future networks and protocols.

One- or two-way contact

Unix 4.2BSD provides name spaces in which processes may contact each other to send unidirectional datagrams—unacknowledged and therefore unreliable messages—or set up bidirectional virtual-circuit connections—acknowledged and therefore reliable communication streams. The system does not interpret the data sent in datagrams or along circuits, but instead leaves data-conversion, -representation, and -transformation issues to the application-program level.

The 4.2BSD's facilities are designed to support a server model of local network services. Here, network resources either respond to single requests with datagrams or establish more long-lived services using virtual circuits. The communications facilities described here are used both by the servers in establishing the services and by the clients in accessing them.

The 4.2BSD communications model is based on a graph-oriented communications space, in which the vertices in the graph are called sockets and are the endpoints of communications. The call:

S = SOCKET(DOMAIN, TYPE)

creates a socket, returning a descriptor S to which communications-oriented operations may be applied. Much like Unix file descriptors, the socket descriptor may also be manipulated, for example, using the DUP call to make a duplicate of it or the CLOSE call to destroy it. The argument DOMAIN specifies the application sphere in which communications are to occur, and it is chosen from a set supported by the local version of the operating

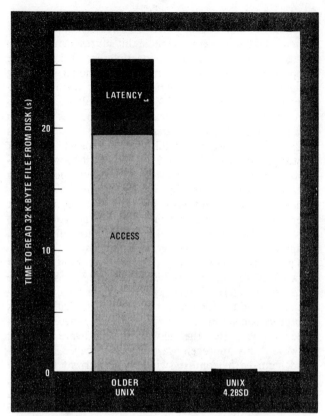

Less overhead. In Unix 4.2BSD, files are stored as blocks of 4,096 bytes—a length that requires much faster access and latency than do the 512-byte blocks of older Unix systems. Interleaving physical blocks on the disk makes disk-data access more efficient.

system. The operations are interpreted by the domain's implementer to be as independent as possible of the domain's particular characteristics. The 4.2BSD release supports both an internal Unix communications domain and an external communications domain for Xerox's Internet protocol. Other domains likely soon to be implemented would support the Xerox Network Systems (XNS) family of protocols and the emerging European Computer Manufacturers Association (ECMA) protocols.

Network sockets

Each different type of transport semantics defines a socket type. The initial 4.2BSD release defines two primary socket types: SOCK_DGRAM, a datagram interface, and SOCK_STREAM, a virtual circuit. Both servers and clients make sockets.

When a server makes a socket, it needs to give it a name that other processes can use to contact the service. A socket's name is used either when sending a message to a socket or when establishing connections between sockets for the exchange of more than one message. An address is given to a socket by the call:

BIND(S, NAME).

In the Unix domain, NAMEs are Unix file system path names, while in the Internet domain they are pairs, consisting of a 32-bit Internet address and a 16-bit Internet port number.

Simple datagram-based network services may operate by creating sockets and sending and receiving datagrams with the SENDTO and RECVFROM calls:

SENDTO(S, MSG, TO)
RECVFROM(S, MSG, FROM).

SENDTO arguments include a socket S, from which the datagram is to be sent; a message MSG, composed of an array of bytes to be sent; and the address of the recipient TO. The datagram can be received at a socket that has been given the TO address with BIND. The address of the socket from which the datagram is sent will be available at the receiving socket as FROM.

In the simplest useful server-client relationship, a server creates a socket and binds it to a well-known name. A client wishing to contact the service then creates a socket and executes a SENDTO call to send a message to this server. The server receives the message with a RECV-FROM and can send a response by using the address FROM. The 4.2BSD communications subsystem will assign a NAME to a socket used to send a message if none has been assigned to it with BIND. Thus there is always an address to which the reply may be sent.

A connection-based network service is established by creating a socket, binding it to an address, and then issuing the calls:

LISTEN(S, BACKLOG)
CLIENT=ACCEPT(S, FROM).

LISTEN tells the system to queue connections to the server on socket S, while BACKLOG is the maximum number of connections that are allowed to be queued simultaneously. The server operates by removing connections from this queue and servicing them. Connections are removed by the call:

S=ACCEPT(Q, FROM)

which returns a socket descriptor.

This model of connection queuing assumes that the connections are established before they are accepted; there is no chance for a server selectively to refuse a connection before the ACCEPT. Consequently, the CON-NECT-CONFIRM message of some transport protocols is sent when the connection is queued. CONNECT-REFUSE is sent either if there is no room in the queue or if the addressed server is not active.

With this type of model, the domain-independent primitives demand no detailed knowledge of the mechanisms of establishing a connection that are passed through at the CONNECT/ACCEPT interface. If a complicated protocol is required for the establishment of a connection in a particular communications network, it can be done by mapping connection acceptance to an initial step of this protocol and by establishing additional connections in the application processes.

The ACCEPT call may be issued repeatedly to remove multiple entries from the connection queue. A client that wishes to contact a server creates a socket and specifies the server name in a CONNECT call:

CONNECT(S, TO)

where TO specifies the server address.

After a connection is established in this way, the usual

Unix read and write calls can be used on the circuit. Remote log-in and file-transfer services are easily constructed from the circuit facilities.

Communications-oriented programs often have to multiplex several simultaneous I/O activities. In Unix 4.2BSD, they can do this in one of two ways. Either they can use a select mechanism to choose a set of I/O activities that can be done synchronously without blocking, or or they can opt for an interrupt-driven programming style, where a software interrupt is delivered when input becomes available or when output on a formerly blocked channel becomes possible again.

Practical proof

Experience has shown the performance of the local-network facilities in Unix 4.2BSD to be excellent. On processors of the VAX 11/750 or 10-megahertz MC68000 class, it has achieved a protocol overhead as low as 1 ms per packet, under the stream-based protocol, and packet-processing rates of nearly 1,000 packets per second, for datagrams. These rates are two to five times faster than other implementations of the Transmission Control Protocol/Internet Protocol (TCP/IP) on similar processors.

Although the 4.2BSD addresses the transport protocol issues in local networking and provides facilities for building network services, those services now provided with the system are still under development. Several

groups are working on printer, file server, and mail protocols, but clear standards have yet to emerge. Unix 4.2BSD is well prepared to adopt any protocol, and applications written for it it can easily participate in the development of new protocols.

Present and to come

Currently, Sun Microsystems is building network services on top of Unix 4.2BSD running on its MC68010-based work stations. By using 4.2BSD for basic facilities like remote command execution and remote log-in, designers can concentrate on the details of the network services, such as a network disk service, which allows a number of diskless work stations to be run off a disk server node. Sun work stations and VAX computers all running 4.2BSD can be used in a mixed environment to provide a wide range of computing facilities tied together with an Ethernet local network.

The interprocess communications facilities of the 4.2BSD system aid the construction of good user interfaces. The Sun Window System, which allows multiple processes to use the bit-mapped display and provide concurrent access to overlapping screen windows, allows the construction of communication multiprocess applications. These processes communicate with each other and with window-system facilities, such as the window manager and the menu manager, using the Unix communications domain. □

Unix variant opens a path to managing multiprocessor systems

Inter-CPU messages coordinate separate processors; offloading file management speeds application processing

by Paul Jackson, *Convergent Technologies, Santa Clara, Calif.*

□ A prominent example of the benefits that come from fine-tuning Bell Laboratories' Unix operating system is MegaFrame, a system that overcomes several key bottlenecks impeding performance. In standard Unix, these hindrances involve the file system, management of processes and memory, and communication with terminals and other peripherals. Dealing with such obstacles is the subject of intensive efforts on the part of many systems software designers (see "Shortcomings of the standard Unix operating system").

The MegaFrame system (Fig. 1) is a multiprocessor system composed of separate sets of MC68010 and

iAPX-186 processors. One set, which performs the duties of the central processing unit of a conventional architecture, handles all application-related tasks including process and memory management. Another set takes care of all file management, and the third set handles communications with peripheral devices. The high degree of independence enjoyed by each application processor means that adding extra processors gives an almost linear increase in the processing power of the system. The Unix kernel in each application processor provides user programs with an interface compatible with the Unix System V. MegaFrame replaces the hardware-specific aspects of

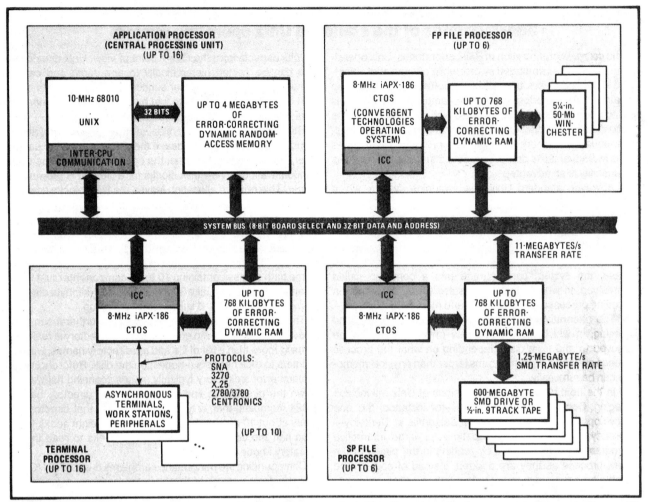

1. Distributed system. Modified Unix handles application programs running in MegaFrame's application processor. Communications and file handling get a hand from separate terminal processors and file processors, respectively, which run a real-time executive called CTOS.

System V, such as drivers for Digital Equipment Corp. disks, with software for the MegaFrame hardware.

To improve the management of memory by the CPU, the MegaFrame system has adopted portions of the virtual-memory code from the Berkeley version of Unix (see the previous article), converting the Unix kernel from a swapping system into a virtual-memory system. On each memory reference, the memory-management hardware sets a page-accessed bit on the page being referenced. If the reference was for a write operation, the hardware sets a page-modified bit.

When accessing a page that is not in main memory, the memory-management hardware generates a page fault into the application processor so that the paging software can find the needed page out on disk. By clearing the access bit and checking the length of its reset time, the paging software can find those pages in memory that have not been used recently. These unused pages are put on a free list, where they become available for reuse when a page fault results in a new page being brought in from disk.

Another Berkeley concept, called the vfork, allows the Unix kernel to create subprocesses without an unnecessary copy to and from disk. Executable object modules on disk typically are compiled so that they can be direct-

ly paged as needed from disk. Such demand-paged memory management eliminates the need to read a full copy into memory before they can run.

By using segments and pages, the memory-management hardware supports virtual memory. It keeps track of when a 4-K-byte page is accessed, modified, or not present. Pages are grouped into segments having 16 pages, or 64-K bytes, each. Protection circuits in the memory-management hardware enforce read, write, execute, and privileged (kernel-only), access on each segment. Any one process can have 64 segments, or 4 megabytes, of virtual memory. The pages and segments are not visible to user applications, which see a simple 4-megabyte virtual-address space.

Cross talk

For the processes running within this virtual-memory environment, the Unix kernel sends file-system and communications requests to the appropriate specialized processor using what is called an inter-CPU-communication (ICC) facility. The ICC data structures and the procedures that use them are the major MegaFrame addition to Unix and control all routine interactions between the application processors and the outside world. ICC messages are also available to Unix user processes as an

Shortcomings of the standard Unix operating system

The complex organization of Bell Laboratories' Unix operating system is a two-edged sword: while offering sophisticated services to users, the underlying software structures also detract from its performance. For example, one attraction is Unix's multitasking capability, in which multiple processes like disk input/output and communications may exist simultaneously in memory and share the processor. As long as the individual tasks do not require substantial memory, this capability is an advantage.

However, standard Unix is a swapping system, which means that if it must move any part of a user's process out to disk because it exceeds main memory, then it copies the entire process out. This tactic can prove to be a disadvantage when a user wishes to execute a number of concurrent processes, each requiring a swapping operation. In this case, the system can degrade into a condition called thrashing, in which its resources are totally consumed in moving processes between disk and memory.

The alternative to this swapping procedure is demand paging, in which individual pages of a process may be moved to and from disk, depending on what the process needs currently. Also, programs larger than physical memory can be run easily.

In the next few years, new versions of Unix will include paging. Some research versions—for instance, the one developed by the University of California at Berkeley— already have it. The start-up time for large interactive programs can be reduced by reading in the pages of the new process as they are needed, instead of copying the entire process into memory before letting it execute.

Unix itself freely uses its multiple-process capability. In fact, its interactive command interpreter, or shell, encourages users to create numerous short-lived processes; indeed, some applications using the shell can create several processes per second. The shell creates processes in two steps. First, it makes a copy (through the fork operation) of itself, then it overlays itself (through the exec operation) with the new process.

On a busy system, the kernel frequently makes a wasted copy of the shell (of its writable data area, more exactly), going from the memory to the swap disk and back again when creating it. Performance can be much improved by providing the shell (and other programs that create many processes) with a special form of process creation that obviates the unnecessary disk copy.

Although management of disk I/O for swapping is not traditionally one of Unix's strong points, the file-management capability of this operating system is one of its most helpful aspects from the user's point of view. Unix directories can be nested hierarchically to any depth and can contain both files and further subdirectories. More data or text can be added to any file just by writing to it, and more files and directories can be created at any time.

Still, in this user-friendly side of Unix lie some of its performance problems. Because the user never has to say how long a file might become, the operating system has to randomly allocate new disk blocks for a file that is growing larger. This random allocation leaves the file's blocks scattered about the disk. Similarly, since the user never specifies a limit on directory size, the directory blocks also end up scattered about the disk as the directory grows. Each component in a path name typically requires two to four disk seek operations to evaluate. A large file system may have some path names containing 10 to 15 components. Just to open such a file could take 30 disk seeks, a 30-kilobyte disk-to-memory transfer, and substantial processing.

The file system's performance degrades further if some directories are allowed to grow fairly big. A directory is really nothing more than a list of file and subdirectory names, with pointers to their headers (i-nodes) on the disk. Referencing a member of a directory typically means scanning halfway down the directory to find the name. If the directory has 1,024 members, then a typical reference to that directory costs about 10 disk seeks and block reads: eight seeks to read half the directory and one or two seeks to read the directory i-node.

Compounding the performance problems due to disk I/O, on many Unix systems every character read from or written to a terminal causes a separate interrupt of the central processing unit. If several users are active in a screen-oriented editor that frequently repaints the screen, character interrupts become a major source of processor overhead. Some Unix systems use a form of direct-memory-access hardware to allow several characters to be transmitted for each interrupt. Alternatively, some systems use input buffers that are polled off the 60-hertz line clock to avoid input interrupts (though the polling is not free either).

Often these efforts at performance improvement have the side effect that the XON-XOFF (transmission enable and disable) protocol no longer works reliably. Many peripheral devices such as printers use this protocol to control their input. As the buffer nears its limit, such a device will send the XOFF back to the host in an attempt to suspend transmission. When the device has more buffer space, it sends XON to resume input from the Unix host. Buffering terminal I/O can delay the XOFF and cause loss of data.

---

improved form of interprocess communication.

As important as the ICC facility is the communications exchange mechanism, which allows for the efficient passage of ICC messages among processors and between processes on a single machine. Together, these two facilities ease communication among the various types of processors in the MegaFrame system.

The ICC message format (Fig. 2) is compatible with the Convergent Technologies' operating-system (CTOS) ker-

nal—a real-time distributed executive that runs on Mega-Frame's file and communications processors. A fixed-length portion of the ICC message contains a request code used to route the message and determine what service is being requested, counts of the number of request and response data areas, the size in bytes of the control information (a part of the variable-length portion), a place for the error return code, and a field called the response exchange. The variable-length portion contains the control information and for each request or response data area, a pointer to that area, and a 2-byte field for that area. CTOS constrains the total size of all the data areas to be less than 2.5-K bytes.

To send an ICC message, the Unix kernel (or user process) fills in the request code specifying the desired service and pointers to the outgoing request data and response data areas. For example, the kernel might request a file processor to open a file. In the initial request, the kernel supplies a path name, identification of the user process that requested the open operation, and a data-return area. If the user is not allowed to open the file or if there is no file with the given path name, then that file processor will return an error code. If the request to open succeeds, then the file processor will place file information in the response data area for use in subsequent reads and writes.

Routing requests

After filling out the message structure, the kernel calls a routine to send it. This routine examines the requested service type to determine to what processor it should be sent. Although some requests are always sent to a specific processor, other requests are sent to one of a family of processors, depending on which is least heavily loaded. Sometimes another processor has already announced to the system that it is the serving unit for a specific service type. System tables containing the routing information for each service type are maintained in shared memory.

The sending routine places a 40-bit pointer (8-bit board address plus 32-bit memory address) in the input request queue of the serving processor. Since the input request queues are shared data structures, additions to these queues are guarded with a test-and-set instruction. This indivisible instruction guarantees that only one processor is adding to a given queue at a time. The sending processor notifies the serving processor that it has a message address on its queue by issuing an interprocessor interrupt across the system bus.

On answering the interrupt, the serving processor removes the 40-bit pointer from its request queue and uses it to read the request from the sending processor. This request is passed off to the serving process, which performs the requested work and issues a response. This response consists of a return status message (either a success or an error code) and perhaps some response data. The serving processor copies the status and response data back into the sending processor's memory, places the request's 40-bit address on the response queue of the sender, and interrupts the sender. On answering this interrupt, the sender removes the pointer from its response queue and returns the status and data to the requesting process.

Since messages and their associated data items come in a variety of sizes, the kernel uses a dynamic memory-allocation scheme called a heap. This scheme manages a pool of memory by allocating free sections of memory on request and putting the memory back in the pool when it is freed.

In order to realize the ICC communication mechanism, MegaFrame processors need access to information about the other processors in the system. For this reason, each

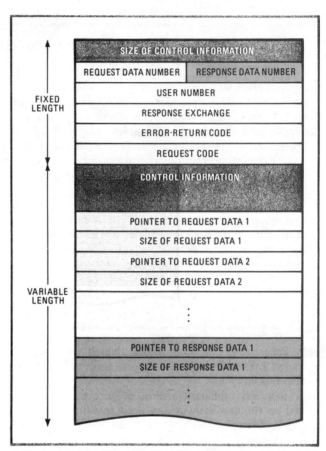

2. Communicator. MegaFrame's inter-CPU-communication (ICC) message is the basis for all communication between processors. A fixed-length portion handles request and status, and the variable-length portion holds input/output data.

processor on the system bus has a standard descriptor block (Fig. 3) in shareable memory that is always accessible using a 2-byte offset located at address $1F8_{16}$. As well as holding some key ICC data structures, this block contains several elements used to initialize and configure the system automatically. Descriptor blocks allow any processor to send to and receive from any other processor, even if they are running different operating systems with otherwise different memory layouts.

ICC pointers

The ICC data structures in the descriptor block are the headers for the response and request queues and the common lock byte for these queues. The two headers each contain four offsets of 2 bytes each. The offsets are all relative to the base of the descriptor block and provide the get pointer, put pointer, and pointers to the bottom and top of their queue. The response and request queues each contain several 5-byte slots where the 40-bit address of a request or response can be entered.

One of the MegaFrame's satellite file processors, designated the master, contains a descriptor block with a map showing which processor slot in the system handles each of the active request codes. This master file processor is also connected to the MegaFrame front panel, as it is responsible for initializing the system. At system initialization, the master processor establishes another table in

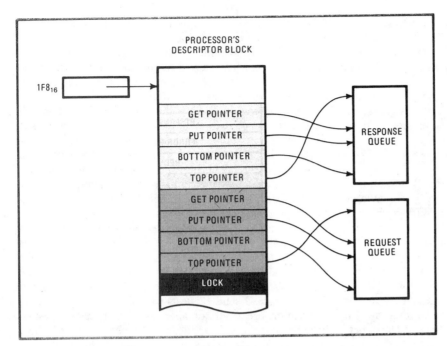

PROCESSOR'S
DESCRIPTOR BLOCK

1F8₁₆

GET POINTER
PUT POINTER
BOTTOM POINTER
TOP POINTER
GET POINTER
PUT POINTER
BOTTOM POINTER
TOP POINTER
LOCK

RESPONSE
QUEUE

REQUEST
QUEUE

3. To the point. Processor communications revolve around a processor descriptor block which can always be found at location 1F8₁₆. Separate pointers indicate the beginning of a message queue area, its end, the next available slot for new messages, and the slot for getting the next message. A lock byte coordinates multiple accesses.

each processor's descriptor block, which indicates the preferred byte ordering of each processor active on the system bus.

In this way, different makes of processors may be placed on the bus without any need to worry about the particular format used for byte addressing. For example, Intel (and DEC) processors place the upper byte of a 16-bit word in the higher address, whereas Motorola (and IBM) processors place the upper byte in the lower address. The ICC mechanism automatically swaps certain fields when they are transferred across processors by using the proper byte ordering.

Message exchanges

Key to the success of a multiple processor configuration is an efficient communications exchange mechanism. In MegaFrame, the mechanism is to pass ICC communications between different processors and between processes on a single machine through message exchanges. Each process has one or more of these exchanges that are used to queue requests and responses destined for that process. Messages are queued on an exchange using doubly linked lists called link blocks, each of which points to one request or response and contains some flags and status for that message. An exchange contains the head and tail of a potentially empty linked list of link blocks, as well as a flag indicating if it is free or allocated.

A request sent out by a process (either by the kernel to a file or terminal processor or by a user process to a remote service, such as file management or communications) is queued on the response exchange it indicates. When sending a message, the kernel always uses the first (default) response exchange assigned to that process. The user process can allocate and use additional exchanges if it wants, but the kernel will not.

Pointers to all of a process's exchanges are maintained by the kernel. Once a message has been sent out, the copy of it in kernel memory must be left unaltered until the response comes back. When a process terminates, any

outbound request left sitting on one of its exchanges is designated as a zombie. When a response is returned to a zombie, the response and the link block can be deleted. Furthermore, if the exchange then becomes empty, it can also be deleted.

If there is a service process running on an application processor that accepts certain request codes, then at start-up that process tells the kernel what request codes it services. The kernel specifies in the master file processor that each of these request codes should be sent to its slot, and it also specifies in a local table that these request codes go to the exchange that is specified by the server process.

As an added aid to performance, the separate processors for file management in the MegaFrame system function as more than just disk controllers. They accept commands from the Unix system software to read, write, open, close, and randomly seek in any named file and perform path-name searches. Therefore the system bus and application processors never notice a high percentage of the file system's activity. As more disks are added, more file processors are also added, always providing ample processing power for managing the file system.

File processors

In the MegaFrame system, two types of processors handle file management activities. One type, called an FP processor, handles 5¼-inch removable and fixed Winchester disk drives. Each FP unit manages up to four drives of 50 megabytes each. With the maximum of six allowed FP processors, the system handles up to 1.2 gigabytes of mass storage from the FP subsystem. In addition, the other type, called an SP processor, handles up to six 600-megabyte Storage Module Drive or nine-track ½-in.tape drives. Each of the six allowed SP processors manages up to six drives, for a total of 21.6 gigabytes of mass storage from this file-management subsystem.

The powerful Unix file system invites intensive use, and the easy creation of processes (which are loaded

11

from disk) further invites a high level of file-system activity. Therefore, the file manager consumes the major portion of Unix's resources and is heavily shared between processes—so that moving it to specialized processors requires major internal changes to the software.

To obtain a balanced multiple-processor architecture, much of the file system's overhead must be removed from the application processors. But it is not obvious how to do this.

Hashing it out

MegaFrame adopts the Unix System V solution of reducing the cost of searching for members of a large directory by using a hashing technique. With hashing, a special algorithm calculates the address of a directory entry on the basis of the value of the desired member itself. MegaFrame hashes the members of a directory so that the desired directory block can be found without scanning half (on the average) of the other blocks.

Once the Unix file system locates a file and reads the necessary blocks into memory, the operating system maintains a pool of active disk blocks in main memory. This buffer pool is essential to good performance, and the blocks in it are often being shared among several processes at once. Consequently, although it would seem beneficial to provide each application processor with its own buffer pool, this solution could introduce inconsistencies in the file system, since two application processors would occasionally each update its own copy of the same block in disk storage.

Some key insights solved these problems. The Unix kernel accesses its file system in two essentially different ways. Some commands, such as those that open a file or create a directory, provide a path name as an argument and mostly involve searching and modifying directories. Also, portions of the directory structure are often being both read and written by multiple processes simultaneously. Accesses such as these all involve searching through a potentially large number of disk blocks in order to return what is typically a small amount of information, such as the status of a newly opened file. These accesses, involving a large amount of shared data and producing a small result, were candidates for offloading into file processors.

Other operations, such as reading and writing a file, loading in an executable file, and paging to and from disk, all involve the contents of a single file. Typically only one or two closely related processes in the same application are accessing a given file at the same time. Furthermore, each file access involves the direct transfer of an entire block of data to or from user memory. These accesses were candidates for being retained in the application processors.

Splitting the file system

These considerations suggested that control of the directory structure and evaluation of path names should be moved to the file processors, but that once a file was opened, the buffering of reads and writes would still be handled locally in the application processors (Fig. 4). The Unix kernel's standard buffering routines are kept, but the interface to the disk is replaced by a special disk driver that uses ICC requests to the file processors to obtain and return disk blocks.

Thus the MegaFrame system moves the Unix routines that search path names and manipulate directories to the file processors. Conflict between Unix files is reduced by keeping all the processes running on behalf of one user (or, more precisely, during the same log-on session) all on the same application processor. This strategy means that two processes in the same application that are exchanging large amounts of data by the file system—a frequent occurrence using the standard Unix interprocess-communication mechanism—often manage to transfer the data just using the buffer pool local to the application processor.

Occasionally, though, processes on separate application processors do read and write the same files. When this happens, the file processor that owns the shared file controls all accesses to it. In this case, the separate processors do not maintain a local buffer for the shared file, but instead send requests for data to the controlling application processor for all reads and writes. A permanent process on each application processor services these requests, ensuring consistent updating of the file.

Auxiliary processors such as the MegaFrame's file processors relieve application processors of a great deal of system-related overhead. Furthermore, through separate processors handling communications tasks, the MegaFrame is able to adjust the loading on the system's application processors dynamically.

Switching data

Until now, systems with many users have often used a separate data switch or concentrator that allows more terminals to be connected than were active at any one time. The architecture of the MegaFrame provides this data switching automatically. As users sign on to the system, the communications processor will dynamically switch them to the least loaded application processor. The switching is entirely transparent to both the end user and the application software.

MegaFrame uses two types of telecommunications processors. One handles up to 10 asynchronous terminals at speeds up to 19.2 kilobaud, while another manages multi-function work stations and office-automation products. Both types of communications processors handle a wide range of communications protocols including Systems Network Architecture, X.25, and 2780/3780 protocols. As many as 256 intelligent terminals can be connected to the MegaFrame system using as many as 16 processors.

The asynchronous terminal software polls each line at 500-microsecond intervals. This polling rate allows simultaneous input bursts from each terminal line at 19.2 kilobaud, without data loss. Since the XON-XOFF (transmission enable and disable) protocol is handled right in the polling loop, an XOFF stops output within a single character.

Besides this high rate of transfer between external terminals and the communication processors, Megaframe enhances throughput with a flexible buffering strategy between the communication and application processors that eliminates the high interrupt overhead of I/O in most Unix systems. On the input side, it reduces interrupts to

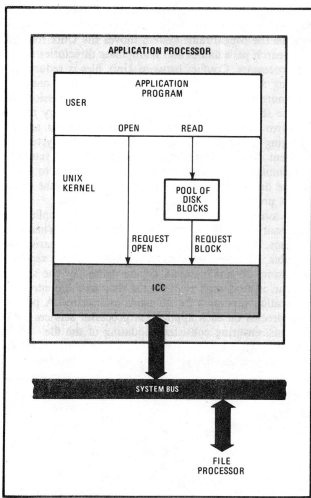

4. Pooled blocks. In MegaFrame's file management scheme, application processors maintain a working pool of disk blocks locally, although new data is retrieved by means of an ICC message across the system bus to a file processor.

a maximum of 60 per second, even from a 19.2-kilobaud line supplying 1,920 characters per second. On the output side, which usually has the most traffic, it completely eliminates additional interrupts.

When the Unix kernel in an application processor has some characters to be transferred from a process to a terminal, it places them on an output queue shared with a terminal processor. The terminal software polls terminals for input and polls these queues for characters to be sent. Should an output queue become full, the Unix kernel uses its timer mechanism to resume stuffing characters in the output queue when it is nearly empty. A 256-byte output queue will empty in 133 milliseconds on a 19.2-kilobaud line, in 8.533 seconds on a 300-baud line.

Doing housekeeping

Unix System V supplies an improved printf, as it is called. Printf is the function most often used in application programs to write to the terminal. The improved printf, which MegaFrame uses, performs buffered writes instead of single character writes, reducing the number of kernel calls that the application must make.

The Unix kernel running on each application processor

handles input and output to character-oriented devices like terminals, communications lines, and printers in much the same way as the single-processor version of Unix does. The only significant changes are in the terminal's device-driver software and in the terminal processors. Unix already has a flexible mechanism for installing new device drivers while preserving as much common code as practical. By using this mechanism, the MegaFrame provides improved performance with minimal change to the kernel.

The application processors use the standard ICC message to request input from a terminal processor. This request includes a pointer to a buffer, the buffer's size, and a timeout. Buffer size and device timeout are selected from a table based on the baud rate of the terminal line. For a 19.2-kilobaud line, the buffer is 128 characters and the timeout is 60 ms. These specifications provide seemingly instantaneous response to the terminal user, while still efficiently buffering input from another computer, even at full speed. Slower speed lines get proportionately smaller buffers and slightly longer timeouts.

Managing incoming data

When a terminal processor polls a terminal and finds an input character, it places the character in a local buffer. A background process on each terminal processor moves the characters from the input buffer to the buffer that is provided in the next read request to that terminal port. Once the provided buffer is full or the timeout has expired, the read is returned to the requesting application processor. Any parity or framing errors are noted in the error return code that is sent with the returned data. An application processor sees one interrupt for each returned read request.

On the output side, the application processors take advantage of the polling architecture of the terminal processors to avoid all additional interrupts. Each terminal port has a circular output buffer in the shareable memory of its terminal processor. Usually, the application processor's terminal-device driver just inserts characters into the proper output buffer.

Because multiple processors may be writing to the same terminal at the same time, adding characters must be synchronized. To send out one or more characters, a processor sets a lock byte (using the indivisible test-and-set instruction), adds the character(s) to the buffer, increments the buffer's input pointer past what was added, and clears the lock byte.

If the output buffer for a terminal port reaches its maximum of 256 characters, then the device driver sets an internal software timer to resume copying to the output buffer at a later time. The amount of delay is set to allow the output buffer to just empty before copying into it resumes. This setup ensures continuous output to the user with a minimum amount of overhead for the application processor.

The terminal processors handle the hardware aspects of each port, such as parity, data clocking, and start/stop-bit generation. The application processors can query and alter the hardware setting of any port, using ICC requests. They can also enable or disable the XON-XOFF protocol, for both the input and output side. □

Unix-like software runs on mini- and microcomputers

Multiuser operating system uses same file formats and system calls, runs programs without modification

by P. J. Plauger and M. S. Krieger

Whitesmiths Ltd., New York, N. Y.

□ The Unix operating system has quietly revolutionized the way software is developed by proving itself an excellent workbench for a broad class of applications. Though it was first developed on rather small minicomputers, current versions of Unix can run on machines that support 50 or more simultaneous users. Until recently, larger-scale microcomputers have been barred from exploiting its benefits.

In response, Whitesmiths Ltd. has developed its own implementation of the Unix operating system for both mini- and micro-computers. Called Idris, it is a separate system that has been designed from the ground up—not just an adaptation of the existing Unix system—and hence requires no additional licensing from Western Electric Co. And unlike other operating systems modeled on Unix, Idris looks identical to the original when run on Digital Equipment Corp.'s PDP-11 or LSI-11 systems. Programs that operate under Unix have a high probability of running without modification when moved to Idris, or vice versa (Fig. 1).

As 16-bit microcomputers become more available, the long-felt need for decent development systems will become even more acute, and Idris is an answer. There is a broad gap between computers too big for operating systems such as Digital Research's CP/M and those too

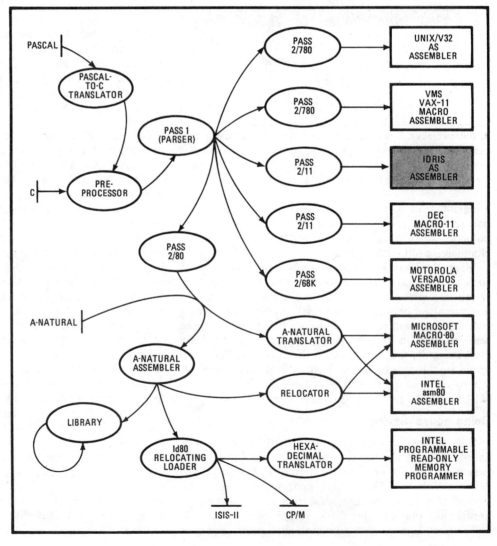

1. Software system. The various programs shown convert high-level language statements into a form compatible with the various assemblers listed on the right. The path traced in color shows the transformations that a C program undergoes with Idris.

A short history of Unix

It all began with Kenneth Thompson's and Dennis Ritchie's frustration with the operating systems available in 1969. The Murray Hill Computer Center for Bell Laboratories was running a General Electric 645 mainframe under the Multics operating system, which was one of the first multiuser interactive systems. Before Multics, however, only batch-oriented operating systems—typically using punched cards and producing printouts—were available. Following in the batch-processing tradition, a major emphasis of Multics was isolating users from one another with several layers of protection to ensure that they did not inadvertently alter each other's disk files. Since sharing files among a well-organized team of programmers was the emerging software project style at Bell Labs, Thompson (right) set out to build a better system. The final result—Unix—was not written all at once, however, but rather evolved in response to more immediate needs.

One of Thompson's ambitious software projects that spurred him on toward Unix was his Space Travel program, which simulated the movement of the major celestial bodies in the solar system. A little-used Digital Equipment Corp. PDP-7 with an excellent display processor was a natural for rewriting Space Travel, especially since it cost $75 to run the program on the GE machine.

The project served as a painful introduction to how difficult program development can be with a computer lacking an adequate operating system. Initially, programs for the PDP-7 were developed on the 645 and carried to the DEC machine on paper tape. But Thompson soon tired of that, first implementing a rudimentary operating system and, finally, an assembler for the PDP-7, both of which were written entirely in assembly language. That adventure set him thinking about the kind of file system that would by its nature encourage cooperative programming projects. As he implemented these ideas, the name Unix was suggested as a play on the name of the soon-to-be-abandoned Multics system.

Thus, Unix was born in the mind of Ken Thompson and continued evolving into its current form in response to its increasing use within Bell Labs. For example, the patent department's interest in Unix resulted in extensive word-processing capabilities being built into the system. As Unix grew, however, its lack of a high-level language became the limiting factor that spurred Thompson to write the language B just before the whole system was transported to one of the first DEC PDP-11/45s ever made. Several utilities were written in B, but it soon became evident that an interpretive language without structures or data typing would not be suitable for rewriting Unix.

Finally, the maintenance headaches became so splitting that Dennis Ritchie wrote C in order to shape Unix into a more manageable form. "One of my primary goals was to eradicate explicit machine dependencies like the Nuxi problem," comments Ritchie, inverting the two syllables of Unix in comic reference to the PDP-11 technique of storing the least significant byte of 16-bit words first.

C evolved along with the whole Unix project, making possible the addition of multiprocessing and the transportability of Unix to other machines. Now one of the most respected structured programming languages around, C is largely responsible for the widespread use of Unix in many multiple-user processing systems.

Currently, Thompson is working on a microprogrammable chess-playing machine with discrete logic components spread over nine large wrapped-wire cards and supervised by an LSI-11. Ritchie is working on network communication problems, but both do all their programming in C and under Unix. "Unix is light years ahead of everything else," notes Thompson, who sounds as though he is still thinking in terms of space. **-R. Colin Johnson**

small for Unix. And with the seventh edition of Unix, which must be stuffed into a PDP-11/23, that gap has widened considerably.

The Idris market lies between these two extremes. There seems to be a large contingent of people who feel that Unix is an excellent operating system, but not large enough. Idris is committed to the notion that Unix is excellent, except it is not small enough.

Idris is a multiprocessing system that manipulates a sophisticated hierarchical file system and multiple input/output devices. Yet only about 60-K bytes of memory are needed for a machine with the code space efficiency of a PDP-11 to hold the resident code plus the largest pass of the C compiler. At least half a megabyte of secondary storage is also required for a reasonable collection of commands and for swapping; but a megabyte is really needed to give one user a comfortable storage area. Idris performs best, however, with a Winchester drive and one or more extra banks of memory.

When a program is being moved between two operating systems, even if both are provided by the same vendor for the same piece of hardware, certain peculiarities invariably spring up. Hardware-dependent system calls are the most obvious difference, since the services made available to a user rely on existing system components such as disk-controller protocols.

The organization of files on disks, conventionally called file systems, differs markedly among systems. This is hardly surprising, given the lack of standards for file-system formats; but it is distressing to find most file systems so poorly documented and idiosyncratic that only the original hardware configuration can read and write acceptable disks. Even more surprising is the fact that magnetic tapes are often incompatible with various systems, making it impossible to produce media in different formats on a single system.

Idris shares two important characteristics with Unix that address those problems: it recognizes the same

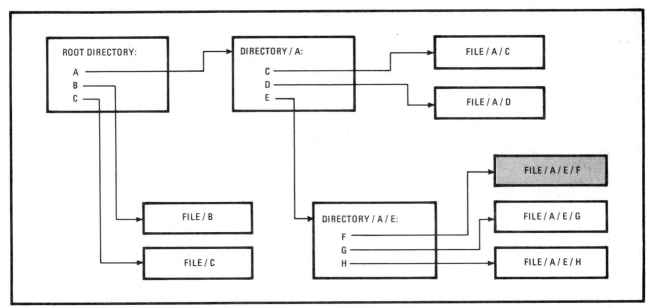

2. Hierarchical file structure. A file can be a program, data, or another directory, all originating from the root directory whose name is "/" on all systems. The file named /A/E/F shows its origin by indicating that it is referred to in directories /A/E, /A and /.

system calls, and it manipulates the same file formats. On the PDP-11 and LSI-11, in fact, the in-core images—the binary form of data and programs—of executable files are almost always bit-for-bit–identical between Idris and Unix. On other Unix-like systems, the matchup occurs at the library level, where a set of functions written in the high-level language C performs the necessary transformations to maintain the same external characteristics across implementations.

Inherent differences

Internally, however, there are substantial differences between Idris and Unix. For one, Idris has its own process-priority scheme and its own mechanisms for sharing memory effectively among multiple processes.

On small machines, Idris can run with no memory management hardware at all, which is impossible for standard Unix; a battery of software checks keeps system integrity high even in the absence of hardware memory protection schemes. Idris makes no attempt to maintain shared-text files, which pay off only on large memory configurations, and it is also much more restrictive than Unix in letting dynamic memory-allocation requests dictate how processes will grow in size.

These differences seldom affect the user, but they let Idris effectively use much smaller hardware configurations than Unix. On the PDP-11 family, the Intel 8086, or even on the Motorola 68000, both memory-managed and non–memory-managed hardware can be equally well supported. On an LSI-11/03 with 64-K bytes of memory and double-density diskettes, Idris will support a full multiprocessing environment. This flexibility stems from the fact that Idris has been carefully partitioned to isolate dependencies on memory management hardware (if any) to a few small modules; there is no preoccupation with the PDP-11 style of memory management.

Idris has approximately 40 system calls identical to those defined in the sixth edition of Unix. Half are concerned with process control—spawning new processes, communicating among them, and setting and testing various process attributes—and the other half perform input/output and related control functions.

Unlike many systems, both Idris and Unix have no secret system calls. Though some of them can be performed only by a privileged user, the style in which all processes are written is not affected.

The fundamental control program, called the shell, which corresponds to a command line interpreter or master control program in other systems, is simply another (nonprivileged) process. The shell provided with Idris is a streamlined counterpart of the sophisticated command interpreter evolved on later Unix versions.

Nearly all processes under Idris are initiated by a command made by a logged-in user to the shell. The shell prompts for a text line with a $ (the prompt can be changed by each user) and then reads lines of the form:

$ ECHO HELLO WORLD!

This command calls for the shell, after being passed the three string arguments ECHO, HELLO, and WORLD!, to execute the file ECHO as a program. ECHO is sought and, if found in the proper format, executed. The supplied version of ECHO simply types its arguments to the standard output, usually the user's terminal, and exits.

Such a function is more useful than may be at first apparent. For example, redirecting the standard output:

$ ECHO HELLO WORLD! > FILENAME

causes ECHO to write its line of output to the file called FILENAME instead of the terminal. It is just as easy to append more data to an existing file or to redirect the standard input from the user's terminal to a file of commands.

How the shell runs a program under Idris or Unix is quite interesting. After it reads and parses, or recognizes, a command line, it executes the fork system call. The fork creates a new process—one that is identical to the original right down to the files it has opened. The

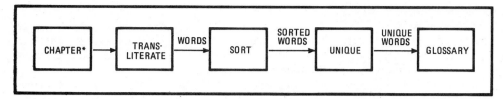

3. Pipelines. Programs may be linked with what are called pipes. Illustrated is a series of programs that convert a text file into an ordered list of unique words—a glossary.

child, or new process, instantly executes the specified program in the command line. The parent, or original, waits until that child has terminated execution, reporting its exit status back to the parent. The child image is lost for good after the program has been successfully executed, which is why the original shell chose to fork in the first place.

With this scheme, an arbitrary tree of processes can be set up, and considerable information can be passed up and down the tree. An additional mechanism called a pipe lets one program pass data to another program as if it were writing to a file and thereby communicate data to another process, which reads the data as if from a file. Such pipelines are easily manipulated, and the shell facilitates stitching together several simple utilities into a powerful new mechanism.

Thus, any program can run any other program, and many separate small programs can be encapsulated under user control. Since the shell is just another process that reads and writes standard output, it is easy to execute a script of commands previously stored in a file; no special submit facility, or spooling mechanism, is required. Command scripts may accept arguments and perform conditional and looping statements just like a compiled program; so the shell is, in a very real sense, an interpreter for a very high-level user-oriented language.

Device independence

Like Unix, Idris easily interfaces processes with disk files and I/O devices. Device independence receives much lip service, but is seldom attained in practice. Idris comes much closer to that goal than most operating systems by using a hierarchical file system structure and by minimizing the internal structure of files, even when files are actually physical devices.

A file system is simply a logical data structure imposed on a contiguous collection of disk data blocks. The blocks are standardized across devices at 512 bytes, but the logical data structure contains information in its header on how many blocks it comprises, so that a broad class of secondary storage devices can support the same structure.

Up to 65,536 blocks may participate in a single Idris file system. Large disks are partitioned into multiple file systems of up to 32 megabytes apiece; conventional diskettes can be formatted as 250-K-byte file systems with the same format.

File systems constructed under Unix on the PDP-11 may be freely interchanged with those written under Idris. Moreover, Idris supports this standard across different machines, regardless of native byte-order or address size—something the Unix community has failed to do. Thus the file systems written on removable media become a true *lingua franca* among diverse machine architectures.

Each file system contains a "root" directory that can lead to an arbitrary number of files and/or subdirectories (Fig. 2). A file is located by its path name, as in ABC/DEF/G or ABC/G. The former identifies the file G in subdirectory DEF of directory /ABC (the difference between directory and subdirectory being academic), while the latter path name identifies a different file G in /ABC. There are no limits to the structural depth of the directory that may be constructed.

To navigate through this potentially huge name space, each Idris process keeps track of the current directory in which it is operating. Files in this directory are referred to by family name, as in G; files in other directories are reached by path names that start at the root ABC/DEF/G or by local navigation from the current directory DEF/G. If the current directory were ABC, both of these path names would identify the same file. Thus, many different users may reuse the same file names with little fear of collision and without the cost of writing a long qualifier for each file reference.

Physical I/O devices are accessed by making special entries in this directory structure. The entries have names just like any other disk file, but cause devices to twitch when addressed.

It is also possible to mount a file system on a physical device, so that all the files appear as a subtree hanging off the existing directory structure. As a result, an essentially unlimited amount of data can be placed simultaneously on line, without requiring any one process to know about more than one directory entry. For most applications, even the 32-megabyte limitation on an individual file system is thus largely irrelevant, since the boundaries in the directory structure are nearly invisible once file systems are mounted.

Uniform files

Nearly all operating systems make a sharp distinction between binary files to be fed to programs and text files destined for users. Idris treats all files the same—as ordered sets of 8-bit bytes. Programs that handle text expect a file to contain zero or more lines, where each line consists of zero or more arbitrary characters terminated by an ASCII linefeed or new-line character. No information stored in the file attributes promises this line structure, however, and many programs work very well without it.

Even physical devices emulate these simple standards as much as possible. Reading an interactive terminal, for example, delivers at most one line of text after character delete and other editing have been performed. Each line is invariably terminated by a new-line character, even if the particular terminal encourages the use of ASCII carriage return instead. Similarly, writing a new-line–terminated line to any terminal causes insertion of carriage returns and delays as appropriate.

As a result, the vast majority of programs are written to read standard input as a text file and write standard output as another text file. Each program is debugged, and often used to advantage as a separate package that interacts with a terminal. Later it can be redirected to files or pipelined to other programs with no changes, greatly simplifying program development.

Software tools

In addition to its operating system facilities, Idris has a powerful group of software tools that can be used either separately or as part of a pipeline (Fig. 3). These tools include a context-sensitive editor, a runoff facility for formatting text, file comparators for source-code control and automated testing, a program for finding text patterns within files, a sort program, encryption and decryption tools, and programs for copying or moving files or subtrees of files. Over seventy tools are currently available with Idris, and together they encompass the functions most widely used at Unix installations.

Similar tools are found in many operating systems; however, in Idris, they have been designed to work together, often in ways never envisioned by the system implementers. Little or no need exists for the many traditional packages built atop other systems—packages with names like source-code control system, word processor, data-base management system, or report generator. All such functions are applications of the standard Idris tools.

A prime example of this system integration can be found in producing a glossary for a set of files named chapter 1, chapter 2, and so on. This task reduces to a shell one-liner that assembles the chapters into a single stream, translates the white space between words into new lines, sorts the resulting word list, discards multiple entries, and then writes the unique entries onto the file glossary:

```
tr "\ t" −t"\n" chapter* | sort | uniq > glossary
```

Software tools such as these make Idris powerful: good system calls and a flexible file system merely provide a hospitable environment. No single enterprise is likely to duplicate the extensive set of tools that has grown up under Unix; but Idris already encompasses many of these valuable facilities, and it can support most Unix-based tools as well.

Most operating systems are written in machine-dependent assembly language. The authors of the Unix system have avoided this pitfall, however, and it has been successfully transported by Bell Labs to several machines. Whitesmiths has followed Unix's lead by writing Idris as much as possible in the highly portable C language. Dependencies on individual machines or memory management styles are kept isolated to a small portion of the resident program (see table below), so that large portions of Idris come up very quickly once a small piece of it is redone.

Transporting Idris

In many ways, the hardest part of transporting Idris is writing a code generator for the C compiler that is targeted to the new machine. Along with this, an existing assembler must be modified for the new instruction set, and a runtime package must be written. That package includes those operations not easily executed by in-line code, such as floating-point arithmetic on computers without floating-point hardware and the forty-odd system calls described earlier. It is also desirable to replace the disassembler portion of the standard debugger with functions that can interpret the new instruction set in object files and core images.

Once this is finished, the resident program is reworked to reflect the target-interrupt structure, memory management architecture, and device peculiarities of the recipient system. Initially, handlers must be written for a console device and at least one disk drive. Most of the resident program modification is done in C, and, all in all, only a small portion of the resident program need be touched.

Utilities can then be moved across—presumably unchanged, although there are always a few surprises when working with a new code generator, on a new machine, or on a machine with different byte-order from any of its predecessors.

For all the preparation that has gone into Idris, Whitsmiths still budgets a minimum of two senior programmer-years to move C and Idris to a new machine. This is a large investment compared with the time required to rewrite an interpreter for a pseudo-code–type machine; but the payoff is the dramatically better efficiency and execution speed resulting from using a true compiler tailored to the target environment. However, it is only a small investment compared with what has been made by others who have attempted to transport operating systems, and it is trivial compared with the effort needed to rewrite most systems. □

PROJECTED IDRIS SYSTEM PARAMETERS						
Machine	Master/slave hardware	Mapping hardware	Program relocation	Instruction and data space	System area access	Pointer size
LSI-11	no	no	software	no	direct	2
8080	no	bank switch	software	no	copy in/copy out	2
PDP-11	yes	yes	hardware	maybe	copy in/copy out	2
8086	no	yes	hardware	yes	copy in/copy out	2
68000	yes	no	software	no	direct	4
VAX-11	yes	yes	paged	no	paged	4
IBM/370	yes	yes	paged	no	paged	4
UNIX VERSION 6 AND 7 SYSTEM PARAMETERS						
	required	required	required	option	paged	2−4

Punching in for real-time jobs in industry, R&D, and offices, operating systems use special software structures to squeeze better-than-ever performance out of 16-bit microprocessors

by Stephen Evanczuk, *Software Editor*

☐ A special class of operating systems is hard at work in the I6-bit microsystem world. For controlling environmental processes, acquiring data at high speed, or even handling transactions at a commercial bank, these operating systems contain mechanisms that enable them to respond rapidly to external events and that differentiate them from the more familiar general-purpose operating systems.

In fact, all the operating systems for 16-bit microprocessors respond in a reasonable period of time. But the general-purpose, or developmental, operating systems like CP/M, Bell Laboratories' Unix, and MS-DOS are intended for standard programming activities like editing, compiling, and file management. As such, they lack certain software structures needed for reliable control of processes producing data at a high speed.

Real-time operating systems tend to fall into two general categories—multipurpose and embedded, reflecting the type of hardware they run on. Multipurpose real-time systems are typically built around full-fledged microcomputer systems with terminal, keyboard, plenty of system memory, and mass storage. Furthermore, in process-control or data-acquisition applications, some special-purpose hardware is usually included in these systems to serve equipment or high-speed data input operations. Besides the familiar applications for research and development, transaction-processing environments are an example of situations needing multipurpose real-time systems.

No doubt the largest class in volume because of their growing use in consumer items, embedded systems are minimal hardware systems, often just one-chip microprocessors that control limited parts of a larger system. Programmers ordinarily employ a special development system to create the software, which is loaded into the target system for use and ideally is never seen again.

To meet the needs of these two classes of applications, real-time operating systems come in three flavors for 16-bit microprocessors. Serving multipurpose real-time systems, one type—discussed in the first part of this report —includes all the software development support found in their general-purpose counterparts. Furthermore, many can be stripped of the layers needed in the developmental environment and placed in programmable read-only memory for use in an embedded system.

For those who swear by Unix, the group of Unix-based operating systems discussed in the second part may mean no need to swear at it in real-time applications. A growing number of vendors are starting to convert this admittedly non–real-time operating system into versions that can be used to handle external processes. Although the industry is cautious, if not downright skeptical, of real-time versions of Unix, the fact that C—the language of Unix—is so highly regarded for use in real-time applications may help swing this group into the forefront.

The potential for distributed-control systems based on embedded microprocessors hinges largely on the availability of high-performance real-time operating systems that can be plugged into the application with the same ease as an integrated circuit. Called silicon software, these operating systems discussed in the last part have been designed to be stored in read-only memory. Providing a fixed set of system calls, they present programmers with a consistent set of high-level commands to perform the low-level functions usually built from scratch.

Building system-level software from scratch has long been the hallmark of real-time programmers, even a mark of honor. Fortunately, however, the increased acceptance of ready-made operating systems using well-understood algorithms (described in the first part) is helping to replace this software "random logic" with rather more standardized packages.

On still another level, the unique responsiveness and throughput demonstrated by real-time operating systems is a truly user-friendly feature. For this reason, these systems should find their way into less obvious real-time applications, such as transaction processing, word processing, and personal work stations for office automation.

OS real-time Algorithms star in multipurpose systems

☐ Whatever environment it finds itself in, the function of an operating system is the efficient management of shared resources by a number of users, whether these are human beings accessing a computer through terminals or programs vying for a single central processing unit. In fact, the degree of sophistication of an operating system is reflected by the number and types of physical resources it manages and by the fineness of control it exercises in their management. And operating systems targeted for control of the external environment must wrestle with the most demanding resource of all—time. The degree of care with which such software is designed to manage time is what determines its suitability for the real-time environment.

Schedulers and queues

Two critical aspects of the real-time environment are the random nature of physical events and the simultaneous occurrence of physical processes. Consequently, interrupt handling and multitasking are primary attributes of a real-time operating system. In fact, it might be argued that the mechanism for handling multitasking—the scheduler—is the heart of the operating system. The rest of the operating system lies atop this kernel and serves the specific demands of the application environment.

In particular, the lists, or queues, and their managers that surround the scheduler are constructed to deal with the different physical resources supported by the operating system. Thus, one queue may contain those tasks (processes, or programs in the course of being run) that are ready to execute on the processor, another queue may be tasks waiting for access to input/output hardware, and another queue may contain tasks waiting for some specified event to occur.

In any multitasking operating system, the scheduler uses the queues as input. Its output, on the other hand, is a single task that has been activated and allowed to execute on the central processing unit. The scheduling algorithm in large part defines the operating system.

In one system, the scheduler may simply select a task on a first-come, first-served basis, allowing it to run until completion or until some specified period of time has elapsed. This type of relatively primitive algorithm was commonly used in mainframe computers running simple batch-oriented operating systems.

In a slightly more sophisticated operating system that can be used interactively through terminals, the scheduler may select tasks on a round-robin basis and permit each of them to run for a specified period of time (Fig. 1). Once the task exceeds its time slice, it is placed at the end of the queue and forced to wait until all other tasks have had a chance to execute.

Round-robin scheduling with equal time slices is adequate if every task is no more important than any other task. However, if some are considered to possess a higher priority, then a more sophisticated scheduling algorithm must be used—one that recognizes that some tasks are more important, but that no task should be excluded from using the CPU.

One solution is the use of several queues, where the length of the time slice is related to the priority of elements in the queue. In this case, the scheduler would allow all tasks in each queue of a different priority to execute on the CPU, but lower-priority tasks would be given less time.

A further refinement permits higher-priority tasks to suspend a running task. This technique, called preemptive scheduling, is an important feature for real-time environments, in which the delayed execution of a high-priority task could have disastrous results, rather than simply disappointing the user.

In scheduling algorithms, tasks may exist in a number of logical states, depending on their readiness to run. In the Versatile Real-Time Executive (VRTX) from Hunter

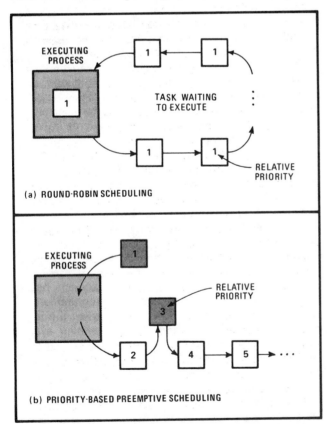

1. Priorities. In round-robin scheduling (a), tasks (or processes) take equal turns executing, while a higher-priority task will supersede a lower-priority one in priority-based preemptive scheduling (b). Most schedulers employ some combination of these techniques.

& Ready Inc., Palo Alto, Calif., for example, tasks are driven through four possible states by external events, by other tasks and system utilities, or by their own system calls (Fig. 2). For example, an executing task may delete itself—in which case it enters a dormant state—or may cause itself to be blocked either explicitly through a call to suspend itself or implicitly through a call to perform some I/O function. On the other hand, once suspended, a task may reschedule itself through a system call, or an external real-time event may bring the task back into the ready queue.

Recognizing the importance of scheduler design, at least one software vendor has made it easier for real-time users to build systems around a prepared kernel. United States Software of Portland, Ore., is offering a basic scheduler that assembles into less than 100 bytes of object code for the target microprocessor.

Furthermore, in anticipation of real-time systems targeted for specific application areas, U. S. Software supplies a list of design notes detailing extensions to the basic kernel.

Another use for queues

In addition to having queues serving the scheduler directly, most systems use them as the preferred means of associating a task with a required resource. For example, one capability commonly found in real-time operating systems is the ability to suspend a task for a specified period of time. Typically, the operating system contains a special queue for this function. Each element in the queue is a task in a suspended state. Associated with each task is a counter that contains the number of clock ticks remaining until it should be reactivated.

For example, in iRMX-86 from Intel Corp., Santa Clara, Calif., the counters keep track of the incremental time remaining with respect to the previous element in the queue, rather than the total time remaining before

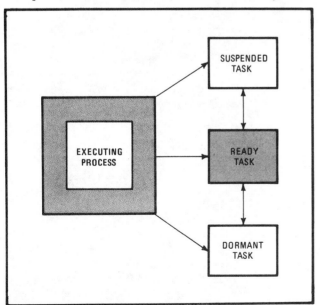

2. Task states. As one task (or process) runs, others may be in various states of readiness. In Hunter & Ready's VRTX, for example, tasks can be ready (able to run immediately), suspended (waiting for a resource), or dormant (deleted by a system call).

the task may be reactivated. Thus at each clock tick only the counter in the element at the head of the queue need be decremented, rather than every counter in every queue element. This method takes longer to insert new elements into the queue and so requires slightly higher overhead for insertion than when the total time is maintained by each counter; however, that overhead is more than offset by the time saved by updating only a single counter.

Real-time environments pose a special set of problems for resource allocation. Besides all the more familiar problems of scheduling, a real-time operating system must maintain reliable behavior under extremes of load when it is driven by a high rate of external stimuli. From the system user's point of view, the system must maintain a predictable level of response and throughput.

In an interactive environment, users sitting at terminals measure response as the time the system needs to react to a keystroke. In general, system response is the time that the system needs to detect and collect data from some external stimulus. Throughput, in an interactive environment, is seen as the number of users able to utilize the installation simultaneously. In a more general real-time environment, throughput is the rate at which the system is able to collect, process, and store data.

In fact, although response and throughput share some common software elements, operating-system designers will invariably find themselves forced to make choices that will tend to optimize one at the expense of the other. Often, the interrupt-handling requirements of a real-time operating system force this choice.

Interrupt processing is hardware and software integration at its most demanding (see "Handling hardware interrupts,"). To handle interrupts, operating systems often place layers of software between the user and the microprocessor in order to allow different levels of performance and capability.

Intel's RMX-86 is a typical example of distinct levels of software used to perform basic interrupt processing. At the lowest level, an interrupt handler works intimately with the hardware to execute some operation, such as sending a message character by character to a printer. Code for interrupt handlers is kept compact and simple, since system interrupts are disabled during their operation. The higher level, called the interrupt task, works at a priority associated with the particular hardware it services. Interrupt tasks act as interfaces between application tasks, working with specific interrupt handlers to complete execution of operations dealing with external devices. RMX makes this interrupt-handling mechanism available to application programs through a special set of system calls.

Protection and communication

Once the interrupt software has completed its function, tasks that use the data are indistinguishable from any other task in the system as far as the operating system is concerned. Unless special care is taken, conflicts could still arise between two separate tasks that might need to use the same resource, such as the same location in memory. MP/M-86, for example, employs a special queue, called a mutual exclusion queue, that contains a unique message representing the shared resource. In or-

der to use the resource, a task must first capture the message, much as a node in a token-passing network must first obtain the token before being at liberty to transmit.

Per Brinch Hansen[1] identified such shared resources as key elements in multitasking systems. Sections of code that access critical resources are called critical regions. The simple expedient of ensuring that only one task at a time is allowed in a critical region guarantees that multiple tasks may share the same critical resource without fear that its integrity may be compromised when two of them attempt to access it simultaneously (Fig. 3).

This concept of the mutual exclusion of tasks from critical regions is implemented in a structure called a monitor, in which critical regions are gathered in one section of code and protected from use by more than one task at a time. The MSP operating system from Hemenway Corp. of Boston explicitly supports mutual exclusion through monitors in its internal structure.

Furthermore, user-written routines needing monitor protection are provided with four functions in MSP that are implemented using hardware traps for rapid access: Entermon, Exitmon, Wait, and Signal. Entermon and Exitmon serve as monitor entry and exit points, respectively, performing required housekeeping functions. Entermon disables system interrupts and preserves all registers, while Exitmon reverses these actions. Wait and Signal, on the other hand, work in tandem to control access to a critical resource. Wait queues up tasks needing an unavailable resource. Signal releases them from the queue when the resource becomes available.

Wait and Signal are examples of an intertask communication mechanism, called semaphores, found in most real-time operating systems. As noted, these commands simply queue up and release tasks needing a critical resource. Such a resource may be an I/O device, a memory location, or simply a go-ahead signal that synchronizes a pair of tasks. For example, task A may execute only after task B has completed. In this case, task A would begin with a Wait (flag) command, where the flag is used as an associated variable. Task B, on the other hand, would end with a Signal (flag) command. In this way, task A would be blocked until task B had executed its Signal command at the end of its processing. But exchanging simple go–no-go signals is not sufficient for many multitasking environments.

For longer messages, real-time operating systems offer extensive intertask communication facilities called mailboxes. Mailboxes are essentially semaphores with storage. As such, tasks needing data from another task will wait until the other has loaded the mailbox with the information. Intel's object-oriented RMX-86 transfers any of the defined objects in the system through mailboxes. Hemenway's MSP, on the other hand, provides a buffer of fixed size that may be used without restriction on its contents, as long as the 256-byte buffer is not exceeded. With its Multibus message exchange (iMMX) extension to RMX for

Handling hardware interrupts

Underlying the special software of a real-time system is th assumption that the hardware itself can respond in a coord nated fashion to external events, or interrupts. In fac microprocessors contain subsystems whose sole functic is to deal with interrupts in a way that eases integration the interrupt-handling software.

All modern computers integrate interrupt-handling har ware and software at a very low level of design. When a us accesses a microprocessor through a terminal, the san hardware interrupt facilities come into play as when, f example, an analog-to-digital converter sends data to th same type of microprocessor. The software response, o the other hand, depends on the type of operating syster but both real-time and general-purpose operating system must take some action, like read in the data value or th character.

Examining the details of a simple keyboard task illu trates the complex nature of real-time processing. It als serves as a vehicle for introducing some of the bas vocabulary in this field.

A standard software subsystem in a microcomputer sy tem, called the keyboard monitor, is responsible for workir with the hardware interrupt system to detect a characte collect it, and effect some action based on the inp character. When a key is struck on a terminal, the corr sponding byte is converted into a serial stream of bits th are passed from the terminal to a universal asynchronou receiver-transmitter. Once it receives the full character, th UART generates a hardware signal, or interrupt, that no fies the processor. Since interrupt management is a cor mon activity, processors contain special hardware to r spond to this signal.

Although the details may vary from one particular micr processor to the next, the result is the same for all. When interrupt-request line is asserted, the processor ceases current processing and places values from its intern registers into system memory. Typically, the process status and instruction-address registers are saved in th system stack, a last-in, first-out buffer located in son portion of system memory. As the figure shows, the proce sor responds to the original interrupt-request signal issuing a signal of its own, called an interrupt acknowledg

The peripheral hardware that originated the interru detects the interrupt-acknowledge signal on the system b and responds by returning the memory addresses of bo the interrupt-handling subroutine and the new process status. Typically, the new processor status will provide f disabling any further interrupts. This latter action is a simp precaution, preventing a single external stimulus from cau ing a continuous series of interrupts that will eventua result in an overflow of the system stack.

Such an interrupt mechanism, called a vectored interru allows the speediest identification and reaction to an inte rupt. (An alternative interrupt mechanism used by earli processors, called a device-polling interrupt, simply forc the processor to switch to a defined address in memo containing software that polled each peripheral device ur the device that generated the interrupt was discovered.)

this point in the interrupt-handling task, all the activity was exclusively in hardware, but nevertheless resulted in extensive processor activity and bus traffic due to multiple accesses of system memory and the involved peripheral-device controller.

Consequently, it is not surprising that the time for hardware to set the processor to handle the interrupt—the hardware-interrupt latency—should be several processor cycle times in length. In general, hardware-interrupt latency is not a fixed number, but will lie within some range, since the processor will need a variable length of time to complete its current instruction and to initiate the interrupt-acknowledge signal. For example, if a processor is involved in a lengthy floating-point operation, several microseconds could elapse before the interrupt is acknowledged.

Once the processor has reached the interrupt-handling subroutine, the contents of only a minimal set of its internal registers have been preserved. However, before the real work of the subroutine may commence, the contents of other registers and variables shared by independent sections of the operating system must be preserved. The time needed to perform this action is called the context-switching time. Only after the software context is switched is the system ready to begin handling the special requirements of the device that originated the interrupt. The period of time between the occurrence of the external event and this state is the total interrupt-response latency.

In real-time operating systems, interrupt-response latency is usually a specified value—around 100 microseconds in very high-performance systems based on 16-bit microprocessors. Designers often bypass the constraints imposed by response latency by including special-purpose hardware to boost system response to external events.

Throughout all this time, system interrupts are still disabled. However, now that the context switch has taken place, the keyboard handler is free to transfer the character from the UART. Deciding where to put the character is important in terms of system throughput and overall efficiency. When it is put in some specified location in system memory, system interrupts must remain disabled; otherwise, if the handler attempted to service a subsequent interrupt, the new character would overwrite the character already in the location, but not yet fully processed.

In general, there are two methods for handling this problem. In the first method, the character is simply placed on the system stack and referenced through the relevant pointer. In an alternative method, the character is placed in a block of memory that has been reserved just for the handler and is called a context block. In this case, the character is referred to by using a specified offset from the base of the context block. Each time the keyboard handler is called in response to an interrupt, one of these context blocks is reserved from available system memory. Setting up a context block and switching the processor to it in a context switch accounts for a significant fraction of the time that is needed to respond to an interrupt.

Software code, such as the UART handler in this example, that does not contain any memory locations for variables is called reentrant because the processor may asynchronously enter it, be called away by an interrupt (even one that results in another call to the same piece of code), and return without loss of data or context. If the code is not already resident in system memory, another routine causes a copy of the code to be read from storage into memory. With reentrant code, only a single copy of the program or task need be resident at any time. Each context block, or logical copy of the task, is called an instance of the task.

Multiple instances of a task help explain some of the confusion associated with performance figures reported as a result of benchmarks. In examining benchmark figures, it should be clear just what the values are that are being reported. Total interrupt latency generally includes hardware interrupt latency, the time to create an instance of a task (plus the time to call in the task into memory if not already resident), the context-switch time, and an additional period needed to execute a variable amount of code that causes the data to be read from the peripheral registers. Creating a new task means either calling in a new task and creating a context block for an instance of it or just creating a new instance of a task already existing in memory.

Once the handler in the UART example reads in the character from the receiver buffer, it will reenable interrupts. The time between entry to the interrupt routine, when interrupts were disabled, until the time when interrupts are reenabled is an important factor in determining the effective latency of system response.

This dead time must be minimized, or the system will remain deaf to external stimuli for unacceptably long periods of time. In fact, the length of time that system interrupts are disabled is one of the criteria for determining the usefulness of an operating system for real-time applications. The longest period during which interrupts are disabled is a direct measure of the responsiveness of the system. Because of the weight of disabled interrupts on total system performance, modern microprocessors use a number of hardware-interrupt levels, or priorities, that disable interrupts at or below the priority level of the device originating the interrupt.

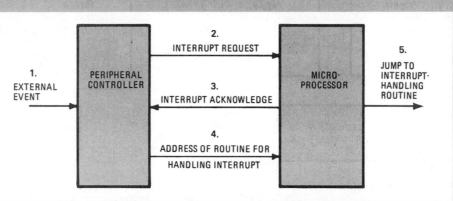

multiprocessor-based systems, Intel replaces the concept of a mailbox with that of a software port connecting different tasks, whether they exist on the same or different physical processor.

Unlike memory-intensive software development systems, real-time environments find less need to support a virtual address space. In fact, the increased system overhead is less than desirable, because the designer seeks to minimize response latency. A useful feature, however, that can be found in some real-time operating systems is a set of system calls responsible for dynamically allocating and deallocating memory.

For example, in the ZRTS system from Zilog Corp., which comes in different versions for the Cupertino, Calif., firm's segmented Z8001 and nonsegmented Z8002, a set of three system calls provides for dynamic allocation and deallocation, as well as information on the status of memory allocation. The system call for memory allocation allows application programs to specify the attributes of the memory block to be allocated and returns a name referring to the created structure.

Besides similar system calls, Intel's RMX adds some calls suited to its context-based architecture. In RMX, each task lies within the context of a job environment that bounds the scope of tasks within it (Fig. 4). As such, each task is allowed to draw from the memory pool of its job. In case more memory is required than that initially allocated to the job, a pair of system calls provides for querying the system on the size of the job memory pool and for dynamically changing it.

Dynamic memory allocation and deallocation is a relatively advanced concept that exacts some overhead during runtime. However, the alternative—static allocation before runtime based on expected requirements—may be less suitable for applications in which the real-time environment is relatively unpredictable.

In real-time operating systems, disk-file management is treated as just another asynchronous task possessing a particular set of critical resources—mass-storage devices. In real-time environments, file-management utilities have to meet not only the requirements of general-purpose systems but some additional demands.

In terms of system response, a requirement of real-time operating systems in heavily loaded systems is the ability to conduct asynchronous I/O operations. In such an operation, the calling task simply queues up the I/O request, then immediately returns as if the task were completed in zero time. When the I/O request is fulfilled, the operating system switches the processor to a separate routine whose address is supplied when the original asynchronous request was made. This completion routine then may continue any processing that may be required following the I/O request.

System throughput depends heavily on the efficiency and performance of the I/O subsystem. Peripheral controllers with direct memory access and the ability to move the disk's read-write head without necessarily performing data transfer can significantly reduce the overhead associated with data movement.

Reducing overhead

System software can also contribute to reduced overhead by providing a simple disk organization when high throughput is needed. One of the simplest structures is a file consisting of an unbroken series of disk sectors, such as the contiguous file in Hemenway's MSP or the physical file in Intel's RMX. By ensuring that the next block of data will be written to the next physical sector on a disk, the operating system can reduce the delay caused by head movement on the disk.

In their use of an I/O interface that is common to all system device drivers, MSP and RMX attack another important aspect of system design, though one not necessarily tied to their utility in real-time applications. In MSP, a basic I/O routine called Iohdlr serves for all operations by accessing a special block of information in memory. RMX, on the other hand, uses a number of device-independent system calls to handle communication with peripheral devices.

Next to multiprocessor-based software systems, real-time software systems are the most difficult to debug. Again, the cause is the distinguishing feature of real-time operating systems—precise management of time. Standard debugging tools for single-user general-purpose op-

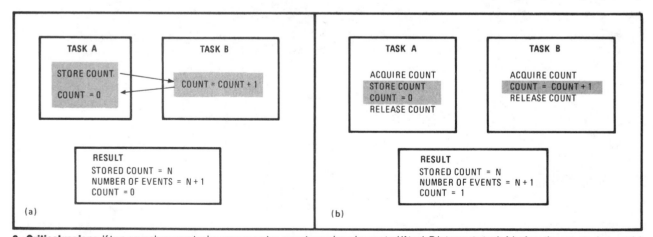

3. Critical regions. If two asynchronous tasks use a counter, events can be miscounted if task B interrupts task A before the counter is reset (a). Forcing the tasks to acquire a counter before using it (b) ensures synchronization through the critical regions (tinted).

4. Job context. In Intel's RMX, all jobs exist within the context of another job. A directory defines the objects that are known to other objects in the same context. For example, all three jobs may use mailbox R_M since it is in the system's root-job object directory.

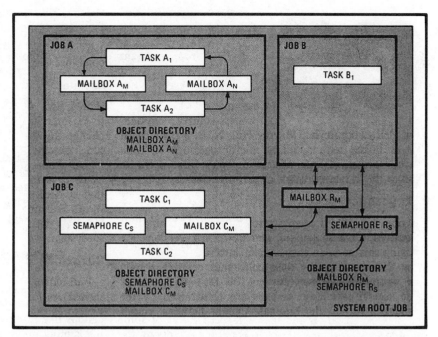

erating systems generally disable all system interrupts in various phases of the debugging routines. Since the object of a real-time software system is asynchronous involvement with the task under control, this effect makes standard debugging tools useless.

Ideally, debugging real-time software would use performance-analysis tools and troubleshooting aids built into the operating system itself. Unfortunately, the processing overhead and additional memory requirements imposed by such a technique make this an unpopular notion in the design of an operating system. However, some systems do provide some means for run-time error handling. The exception handlers in RMX, for example, are procedures that are associated with each task when it is created. If a task attempts to use a system call but encounters an error, called an exception, the operating system invokes the associated exception handler to allow some graceful recovery from the error.

Although the technique in VRTX is not true exception handling, Hunter & Ready's silicon-software system does include a mechanism to build run-time debugging software. A special location in the VRTX configuration table causes a user-defined routine to be called whenever a context switch is performed. By recording information about the task as well as the processor, such a routine can be used to create a list, called a trace, of the history of task execution.

Because real-time systems often include special-purpose hardware, the accepted technique for debugging user-written routines uses the classical approach of collecting data before and after passing through a suspect region, along with a logic analyzer to monitor timing of traffic through critical regions.

Intel offers some relief to this problem through the iRMX debugger In particular, the debugger allows the user to work with individual tasks without interfering in the operation of other tasks, as well as to monitor the activity of the system as a whole without disturbing it. The debugger recognizes data structures in the RMX kernel, so the user may examine system objects. In addition, Intel's crash analyzer brings mainframe debugging power to microprocessor-based applications using RMX.

Zilog's ZRTS configuration language offers another level of support to the development of systems targeted to specific hardware complements. By defining the details of the hardware, a system designer can configure ZRTS to particular systems.

Reference
1. Per Brinch Hansen, "Operating System Principles," Prentice-Hall, Englewood Cliffs, N. J., 1973, p. 84.

Designers tune Unix for real-time use

☐ With an eye on the growing momentum of Bell Laboratories' Unix, real-time system designers have endeavored to squeeze this complex operating system into the rigid confines imposed by the demands of real-time environments. Although Unix brought advanced system ca-

pability to mini- and microcomputers, the original intent was to provide a hospitable software-development environment, rather than to include the features considered necessary for real-time uses.

Until now, data-acquisition systems employing unmod-

ified Unix typically used dedicated microprocessors to buffer a central computer from constant random activity caused by external events. For example, in the Conceps process-control system from Bell Laboratories, Murray Hill, N. J., a Unix-based host is linked with auxiliary microprocessors. In each microprocessor, software derived from Unix software handles the low-level details of real-time activity (Fig. 1).

Unix goes real-time

Appearing in all shapes and sizes, Unix-compatible executives, Unix lookalikes, and new Unix versions are bringing this popular environment into real-time applications. However, unlike their colleagues creating totally new operating systems designers of
these second-generation systems are constrained by the boundaries set by the original. Caught between Unix's complex organization and the high-speed needs of some real-time applications, they have opted for preserving the basic architecture. Still, for intensive data-acquisition applications, vendors like VenturCom, Cambridge, Mass., and Masscomp, Littleton, Mass., add on dedicated hardware like high-speed peripheral controllers to link devices into the main system without losing the generality of the Unix software architecture.

For microprocessor-based dedicated systems, memory-

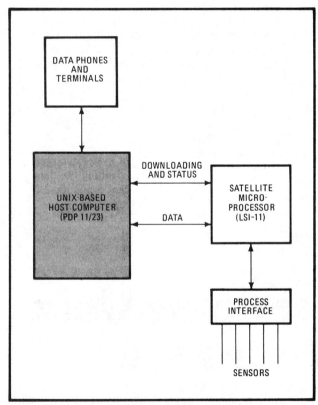

1. Satellite processing. In Bell Labs' Conceps system, separate microprocessors handle low-level details of process control. Yet another processor—a host computer that runs the Unix operating system—is in charge of coordinating these satellite machines.

resident kernels like the C Executive bring a measure of Unix compatibility to even dedicated systems. Offered by JMI Software Consultants of Roslyn, Pa., the C Executive combines support of an extensive C-language run-time library with many of the features considered important in real-time applications. Although not directly supporting shared data in its multitasking architecture, the executive's intertask-communication facilities include data exchange through a queuing mechanism. As befits a real-time executive, the task-scheduling algorithm allows higher-priority tasks to preempt lower-priority ones. Because it is intended primarily for embedded systems—that is, dedicated microsystems that do not have disks—the C Executive is totally contained in system memory and does not support the extensive Unix file-management subsystem.

Controlling real-time tasks

Full-blown Unix lookalikes, on the other hand, find themselves forced to deal with some of the very internal structures that aided Unix's rise in popularity. For applications like program development where regular scheduling is more important that instant response, scheduling is aided by Unix's manipulation of the priority levels of tasks (or processes, in Unix's preferred terminology). For real-time applications, however, the slight uncertainties this feature introduces could destroy the synchrony of timed events controlled by the system.

Consequently, one enhancement commonly found in the real-time offshoots is the addition of some mechanism to ensure more precise control of real-time tasks. A technique that sits well within Unix's task-oriented (that is, process-oriented) design is the definition of a real-time class of tasks (or processes). This class earns special rights in the operating system, such as a guarantee that each task will not be swapped out of memory, but remain locked in and ready to respond more rapidly to events.

VenturCom's Venix, for example, defines a real-time priority level. The scheduler allows tasks running at this level to maintain control of the processor for as long as necessary. In contrast, Regulus from Alcyon Corp. of San Diego, Calif., speeds response to real-time events through the use of 32 user-defined priority signals.

Better I/O handling

In addition to its scheduling algorithm, Unix's method of handling input/output operations needs improvement to perform well in real-time applications. Aiding total system response, the asynchronous I/O procedure in Venix supplements the conventional synchronous procedure in Unix, in which the requesting task must be suspended until the I/O operation is completed (Fig. 2). By placing asynchronous requests at the head of the I/O request queue, Venix's manager lets real-time tasks issue a write request, for example, and immediately continue processing, assured that the request will be honored next.

Concentrating instead on improving what happens when I/O requests have been completed, Masscomp's enhanced version of Bell Labs' Unix System III adds a modified signal called an asynchronous signal trap. Similar to the concept of completion routines in other operat-

Going Forth with alternatives

Few nightmares evoke the feelings of dread experienced by a programmer who must alter code that has been developed by another programmer—worse yet if the code is all assembly language for an embedded system. Fortunately, system developers are seeing the light of day and are specifying one of the commercially available real-time operating systems, so programmers now are dealing with a set of well-defined software calls for system functions. Still, for the true diehard who feels restricted by using someone else's system or the developer trying to eliminate all processing overhead caused by the operating system, alternatives do exist.

For straightforward, yet high-performance, process-control applications, the use of a finite-state machine as the controller is an easily implemented technique. A finite-state machine is simply some device that produces a defined output state based on its input state. For example, a microprocessor may read some input register, access a table in memory using this input as the address, and send out the value contained in the accessed location. In such a system, a value could be created with a single indirect move instruction in a microprocessor using a memory-mapped input/output scheme. Clearly, using a microprocessor this way would allow only a relatively small number of states.

Besides this hardware approach, the software alternatives include the interpreters for high-level languages, such as Forth and concurrent versions of Pascal, that are appearing in the read-only memory of single-chip 8-bit microcomputers. For example, the CDP1804P complementary-

MOS single-chip microcomputer from RCA Corp.'s Solid State division, Somerville, N. J. contains a core interpreter for Micro Concurrent

Pascal (mCP) from Enertec Inc. of Lansdale, Pa. Based on Per Brinch Hansen's Concurrent Pascal, mCP contains all the constructs necessary for real-time applications, such as shared data, monitors, interrupt handling, and task queuing and switching. RCA also provides a ROM that extends the core interpreter to include full multitasking support. Software for this microsystem is developed using an RCA cross-compiler available on various host machines.

In parallel with the use of modified high-level languages like mCP, Forth interpreters are on the verge of appearing as single-chip microcomputers like the CDP1804 or the RF1/12 from Rockwell International Corp.'s Newport Beach, Calif., Electronic Devices division [*Electronics*, Jan. 13, 1983, p. 41]. After its development in the 1960s for real-time applications, Forth gained a slow acceptance among system developers. But with the inception of Forth standards committees and the spread of interpreters into more systems, this stack-oriented language is rapidly attracting the attention of larger houses.

Forth is a threaded language in which basic procedure calls, or words, are used to build up more complex words. Because of the threading, programs tend to be very compact. Once the programmer gets used to reverse-Polish notation, program development is simply a matter of building up the system dictionary with the words needed for the particular application.

---

ing systems, the AST mechanism allows tasks to perform operations that were contingent on the completion of a separate real-time operation. For example, by issuing an AST when it has completed its work, a read task is able to notify another task that a buffer has been filled. The other task is then free to initiate whatever calculation

may be needed to make use of this new data.

Besides such modifications improving Unix's response to asynchronous events, Masscomp upgraded the system's throughput by adding support for contiguous files to the file-management system. In this way, large amounts of data may be written at a high speed to

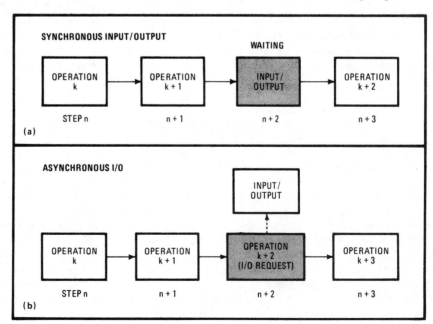

2. No blocking. In synchronous I/O, execution of a task blocks, or waits, until the data transfer is completed (a). Since I/O is handled independently, a task need only request an I/O operation and continue on to the next operation.

consecutive disk sectors. Since other disk accesses are locked out in this mode, the disk head will be positioned correctly, thereby eliminating unnecessary and time-consuming movements.

In addition to these I/O add-ons, Masscomp boosted intertask communication capability by enlarging the Unix standard intertask communication mechanism, called pipes, to allow tasks to transfer buffers. In an alternative approach, Charles River Data Systems of Natick, Mass., allows tasks in its Unix-like Unos system to share data directly. A number of independently constructed software tasks may use a common set of locations in memory to transfer data between themselves or to perform some sequence of calculations. However, whenever asynchronous tasks share some common re-

source, their use of the resource could result in corrupted data—unless some mechanism coordinates their activities, such as the monitor concept described on page 108. Unos provides a mechanism called event counts to help avoid these conditions.

Event counts are integer values that are a nondecreasing count of the number of times some particular event has occurred. By using an event count associated with some task that produces shared data and another event count for a task that consumes the shared data, programmers may ensure the correct sequencing of asynchronous data-producing and -consuming tasks. Similarly, event counts serve as primitive operations for emulating the synchronization function that is provided by semaphores and the mutual exclusion that is furnished by monitors.

 # Chips come to aid of embedded systems

☐ Storing machine instructions in read-only memory is hardly a new concept in microprocessors. If supporting software totally breaks down, Digital Equipment Corp.'s LSI-11, for example, resorts to a basic keyboard monitor stored in a special ROM that is logically placed in the input/output address space. Using a primitive on-line debugging technique stored in the same ROM as the monitor, a software designer may read and alter memory locations and initiate a bootstrap loading operation from storage—a common provision in computer systems.

From these primitive beginnings, however, ROM-based software has evolved into complete operating systems in memory, engendering the term silicon software. Complementing hardware for distributed-processing architectures, such silicon-software systems signal a migration of application software into dedicated microcomputers previously considered unable to gain full systems capability. For developers of dedicated microcomputers embedded in some larger real-time system, silicon software spells the end of the need to reinvent the wheel to carry out the fundamental functions of a real-time operating system.

Extending the microprocessor

Functionally, silicon operating systems extend the microprocessor's instruction set to include system-level instructions that perform operations on software structures, like queues and tables, rather than on hardware registers. Application-program developers are then presented with a virtual machine—one that is perceived by the programmer as different from the actual host processor. In these virtual operating-system machines, their instruction set includes a well-defined set of system calls as well as the basic machine instructions of the host microprocessor. For example, with systems like VRTX and RMX, the virtual microprocessor has a special set of instructions for handling interrupts (see Table 1).

For system developers, however, the problems in developing reliable silicon software extend beyond resource

protection, timing, and communication problems (see pp. 106–111). In fact, the development problems extend beyond the purely logistical exercise of maintaining a separate ROM-based instruction store and one for variables that need to be placed in system read-write memory. Treading a fine edge between the full function of a general operating system and the fine-tuned performance of special-purpose software, silicon systems need to balance the need for a wide range of system functions with the requirement that they squeeze into a minimal amount of ROM.

Flexibility for expansion

Still, once a system meets a reasonable compromise between capability and size, it should not irrevocably lock the user into accepting its choices. For example, many real-time applications require some custom peripheral-device drivers and system-level functions. Consequently, the program should provide a mechanism for logically incorporating user-written extensions to the operating system, such as the user-defined pointers in the VRTX system from Hunter & Ready, Palo Alto, Calif.

In VRTX, a configuration table (Table 2) in system random-access memory allows specification of a custom routine that is to be executed whenever the system is initialized. For even more delicate control of system operations by custom software, a trio of pointers in the table specifies user-written routines to be accessed whenever a task is created or deleted or whenever a context switch is performed. Hunter & Ready also includes a location in this baseline configuration table for its anticipated file-management extensions to VRTX.

The 80130, an RMX-86 kernel in silicon from Intel Corp., Santa Clara, Calif., generalizes this approach through an index table containing pointers to system routines. If circumstances require the replacement of an existing system routine, the index-table pointer is merely altered to indicate the address of the new routine. In an

TABLE 1: SYSTEM CALLS FOR HANDLING INTERRUPTS	
Instruction	**Description**
Versatile Real-Time Executive (VRTX)	
UI-POST	deposit message from interrupt handler
UI-EXIT	exit from interrupt handler
UI-TIMER	timer interrupt
UI-RXCHR	receiver-ready interrupt
UI-TXRDY	transmitter-ready interrupt
iRMX-86	
RQSETINTERRUPT	assign interrupt handler
RQ$RESET$INTERRUPT	deassign interrupt handler
RQGETLEVEL	return number of highest-priority interrupt level currently being processed
RQ$SIGNAL$INTERRUPT	signal from interrupt handler that event has occurred
RQ$WAIT$INTERRUPT	wait for occurrence of event
RQ$EXIT$INTERRUPT	relinquish control of the system
RQ$ENABLE	enable hardware to accept interrupts
RQ$DISABLE	disable hardware from accepting interrupts

TABLE 2: VRTX CONFIGURATION TABLE	
Table Entry	**Entry Description**
sys-RAM-addr	system beginning address
sys-RAM-size	system memory size
sys-stack-size	system stack size
user-RAM-addr	starting address for available memory in initial partition
user-RAM-size	size of initial partition
user-block-size	size of memory block for dynamic allocation
user-stack-size	size of stack for user tasks
user-task-addr	address of first user task
user-task-count	maximum number of tasks
sys-init-addr	address of user-supplied initialization routine
sys-tcreate-addr	address of user-supplied routine accessed when a task is created
sys-tdelete-addr	address of user-supplied routine accessed when a task is deleted
sys-tswap-addr	address of user-supplied routine accessed when a context switch occurs
[RESERVED]	address of Hunter & Ready future extensions to VRTX

embedded system, this new routine could be placed in ROM along with application software.

Now that programs in ROM have matured into silicon systems, the development of software for embedded systems may now follow a more hospitable development cycle. The particular method used to create embedded systems will, in general, fall into one of two paths represented by the two major camps.

On one hand, kernels in silicon from systems such as RMX-86 or the MSP from Hemenway Corp., Boston, Mass., for the 68000 or Z8000 are self-contained subsets of the full operating system. Consequently, software programmers may use the full development version of the same operating system as that in the eventual target to create the application package. On the other hand, development of application programs around the ZRTS system from Zilog Corp., Cupertino, Calif., or Hunter & Ready's VRTX for the Z8002, iAPX-86 family, or 68000 relies on the use of a separate development system to create software for the target microprocessor, since this software does not have development versions.

Two approaches

The significance of these two approaches as usual depends on the intended application. Hunter & Ready views VRTX as a set of processor-independent building blocks that programmers use to construct application packages for embedded systems. As such, the programmers employ the same development systems that they might use to build application code, but now with the benefit of a sophisticated set of ready-made system-software components.

In playing its part in Intel's systematic drive toward providing an integrated environment around the iAPX-86 family, the 80130 holds the anchor position in an interlocked set of components. Able to function independently of the upper layers of the operating system, it provides a hardware base for the rest of RMX-86. Serving as a viewport into this system-software base for the central processing unit, Intel's universal run-time and development interfaces offer the mechanism for software portability needed for the next stage in the company's plan to grow into higher-performance microprocessors, such as the 186, 286, and 386.

While interlocking with the software in this way, the 80130 also must play its role in the complementary relationships being established at the hardware level. As such, it includes on-chip hardware support for system-level functions, including timers, interrupt controller, bus control, and bus interface.

Meanwhile, Intel's plan for software-in-silicon becomes evident as it gathers the other pieces of the puzzle, such as the 82730 text-coprocessor chip, the 82586 local-network coprocessor, and the 82720 graphics processor chip. Similar to the 80130 software connection, the 82720 graphics part interlocks with the rest of the system at the software level through its support of another well-defined software interface—the virtual device interface. Yet to come are pieces for voice I/O support, as well as some level of hardware support for data-base access. □

Multitasking operating system backs real-time uses on 16-bit processors

Layered architecture, accessible through system calls, also supports the software development environment

by Robert J. Oberg, *Hemenway Corp., Boston, Mass.*

☐ Emboldened by the near universal acceptance of high-performance microprocessors, system designers are pushing these low-cost machines into real-time application environments at a rate that software engineers are hard pressed to match. In the face of this exploding demand for software, designers are recognizing the critical role that a real-time operating system plays in enhancing productivity while maintaining the degree of performance and reliability demanded by the application.

The Multitasking System Program is such an operating system. By supplying all the essential ingredients needed for both development and execution of real-time software routines, it provides a powerful base for building real-time application packages.

Out of the pool of operating systems, microcomputer users will generally draw from one of two broad categories. A disk operating system, or development system, is generally optimized for the services needed for program development—such as file managers, editors, assemblers, compilers, and linkers. On the other hand, a real-time operating system is optimized for handling on-line external processes within strict timing constraints. Typically, the functions of a real-time operating system are embedded in the application code, possibly being stored in read-only memory in the target system.

The Multitasking System Program presents the designer with a hierarchical structure that serves as both development and run-time support of real-time application programs (Fig. 1). At the center of this layered architecture is the hardware, including microprocessor, memory, input/output devices, mass storage, and other special-purpose hardware components needed for the particular task.

Each successive layer wraps the lower levels with a further level of sophistication, thereby creating an in-

creasingly powerful virtual machine. But unlike many operating systems, where application programs can only address the outermost layer, the multitasking system program gives users access to all layers of the system through over 70 system calls.

Kernel is key

At the heart of the Multitasking System Program, a compact set, or kernel, of five optimized routines supplies the key services needed in a real-time multitasking environment—those of task scheduling and synchronization and real-time clock management. Four routines (Entermon, Exitmon, Wait, and Signal) form the basic mechanism for ensuring task synchronization. The interrupt service routine, Timday, responds to a clock interrupt every 1/20 second, at which time tasks are switched and a real-time clock is updated.

Ensuring reliable synchronization of tasks proves to be of fundamental importance in designing a real-time operating system. In most real-time application programs, several tasks, or processes, that execute concurrently often need to share the same resource, such as a memory location or hardware peripheral. When such a resource is subject to modification by more than one task, it is called a critical resource. Unless some means is made available to ensure that only one process at a time utilizes the critical resource, errors may occur, depending on the timing of the different tasks' access to the resource.

For example, suppose that in some data-acquisition system two tasks have to use the same counter to keep track of some event. One task, called acquire, increments the counter whenever it observes the event. The other task, called report, prints the value contained in the counter and resets it to zero, as illustrated in Fig. 2. These tasks can be repre-

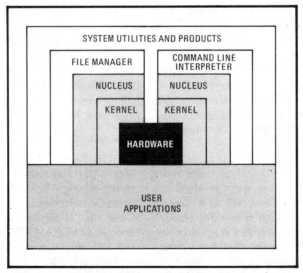

1. Layered architecture. At the core of the operating system, the nucleus and kernel provide the essential services for a real-time environment, yet are accessible from the application and system utility levels through system calls.

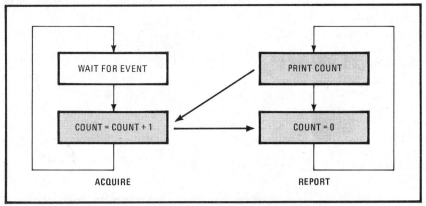

2. Lost events. In the scenario indicated by the arrows, a race condition can cause events to be misrecorded. After "count" is printed, an interrupt to the acquire task increments the count variable. Before this most recent event is printed, the variable is reset to zero.

sented by the following lines of pseudocode:

```
ACQUIRE: Do Forever
              Wait until Event has occurred
              Count = Count + 1
         End

REPORT: Do Forever
             Print Count
             Count = 0
        End
```

In the manner that the two tasks, acquire and report, share the variable called count in this example, problems can occur. Suppose that the acquire task has increased count to the value 4 and that the report task prints that value. Furthermore, suppose, as is likely to happen in a real-time environment, that another event occurs so that the report task is interrupted just after the print count statement but before it can set the count variable to 0. In this case, the acquire task increases count to 5, control is returned to the report task, and the variable count is reset to 0, with the effect that the interrupting event goes unreported.

This problem, known as a race condition, arises whenever two or more tasks share a critical resource, such as the variable count, and generate errors that depend on the timing of execution of the different tasks. Race conditions pose a significant problem in the programming of systems using concurrent tasks—such as operating systems and real-time applications—because the errors they cause depend on timing behavior that is often not reproducible.

But the method for avoiding this bane of programmers relies on enforcing the mutual exclusion of tasks from those sections of code—called critical sections—that access a critical resource. Thus only one task at a time is allowed in a critical section. A further important characteristic of an operating system that handles mutual exclusion is that no task is indefinitely prevented from entering its critical section.

Though various implementations of mutual exclusion are available, the basic mechanism calls for a task to assert some type of lock when it enters a critical section and to release the lock when it leaves. While the lock is asserted, no other task may enter a critical section.

The lock itself may be either some hardware mechanism—such as the disabling of hardware interrupts on a single-processor configuration—or some software mechanism—such as a busy wait, where a set of instructions continually tests some global status bit that is modified within a critical section. Either mechanism may be satisfactory for very short critical sections, but when a task may have to spend an appreciable time in its critical section, such locks are intolerable. An extended disabling of hardware interrupts cannot be allowed for real-time applications, and lengthy busy waits inevitably tie up a central processing unit, significantly degrading system performance.

A better solution for lengthy critical sections is a wait and signal mechanism. The effect of executing a wait command is to remove a task from the run state and place it on a wait queue, where it does not execute or consume CPU cycles. Later—which may be an arbitrarily long time—a signal for the waiting task is issued by some other task when the critical resource that caused the original wait is freed. This signal causes the waiting task to be placed on the ready queue and scheduled for execution by the CPU.

The Multitasking System Program uses the concept of a monitor to establish a structured means for mutual exclusion and task synchronization. In a monitor, as introduced by C. A. R. Hoare[1] and elaborated by Per Brinch Hansen,[2] all the critical sections of code for a particular set of shared data is collected into one place. Each critical section becomes an entry point to the monitor. Whenever one of the entries is invoked, exclusive access to the shared data is automatically provided. Thus the enforcement of mutual exclusion is implicit—the programmer need only invoke the entry.

In the multitasking operating system the routines Entermon and Exitmon implement this exclusion by disabling interrupts (in the case of Entermon) and enabling interrupts (in the case of Exitmon). Monitors are the fundamental synchronization construct in this operating system and may be used to build other synchronization primitives, such as mailboxes and semaphores.

Task scheduling

As implied previously, any task can exist in one of three states under the Multitasking System Program operating system (Fig. 3). A task in the run state is the one currently executing on the CPU. A task in the ready state is one that is capable of executing when the processor becomes available. Finally, a task in the wait state is one that will not be ready until some resource has become available or some event has occurred.

Task scheduling—the control of the flow of tasks through the various states—is performed on a priority basis in the Multitasking System Program, taking into account both resource availability and processor sharing through time slicing. Every task under the program is assigned a priority that may be changed dynamically. A queue manager links tasks into the ready queue in order of priority, with higher-priority tasks first. Tasks of the same priority, on the other hand, are round-robin scheduled on a first-come, first-served basis.

In any case, the currently executing task will continue to run until either the current time slice expires or the task is blocked while waiting for some resource. Thus if a task is unable to keep the CPU fully occupied, it is placed in a wait state and the next task at the head of the ready queue is immediately scheduled without waiting for the next time slice.

Nuclear layer

The next layer of the Multitasking System Program, the nucleus, can stand alone in ROM and can form the basis of a customized operating system. In particular, the nucleus uses monitors to protect essential resources, including the console, line printer, and system tables. With its task-control primitives, the nucleus provides the means to start, stop, suspend, and wake up tasks, as well as calls to get task status and set task priority.

Through memory-management routines, the nucleus supplies the means to access common system data areas and to allocate and deallocate memory in 2-kilobyte blocks. For I/O support, this layer contains basic device-independent I/O routines and a buffer-pool manager that grants and reclaims space from system memory for I/O request blocks and buffers.

Finally, for communication between tasks, the nucleus comes up with basic mailbox services. On the other hand, for communication with the user, this layer contains command-parsing primitives. These basic routines simplify common parsing tasks, such as retrieving a token from a string and expanding wild-card file names.

At the next layer of the operating-system architecture, a file manager provides a powerful set of file-handling and I/O operations. As with the nucleus, the programmer may access all the functions in this layer through system calls. Particularly well suited to the demands of both development and run-time support, the file manager supports sequential, contiguous, or random files.

Sequential files, specified through a linked list representation, can be dynamically allocated, expanded, or deleted as needed. On the other hand, the minimum head movement incurred in using contiguous files ensures fast access, but at the cost of less flexibility and the requirement to compress the files to reclaim space after deletion. Random files give rapid access to individual records in a file, without the need to search sequentially through it.

Within the restrictions of the type of file supported by a physical device, all system calls are device-independent in the multitasking program. Physical devices are linked to the system through entries in a system table that specifies the address of the corresponding device-driver routine. In the standard release, the program supplies drives for the console, line printer, teletypewriter, and floppy disk. Extra physical devices may be added as needed by programmers by writing an appropriate device driver and placing the proper entries in the system tables.

Thus far, all the aspects of the operating system that

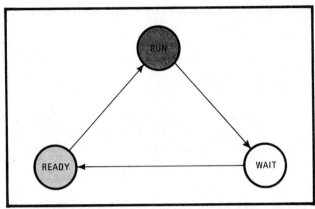

3. Three states. Under the Multitasking System Program, a task will cycle through the three possible states: wait, until an unavailable resource is freed; ready, until the processor is available; and run, until blocked by an unavailable resource or the expiration of its time slice.

have been described are passive. The various routines are resident in memory and will respond quickly and efficiently to a request for services. Nevertheless, on their own these routines do no processing. Even task scheduling enabled by the time-slice mechanism is driven by interrupts from an external timer. As a result, the Multitasking System Program may be embedded in a target system for efficient support of real-time applications.

On the other hand, the command-line interpreter is an active task that reads a command from the console and executes the command by transferring control to the inner layers of the operating system or loading and executing a transient (nonresident) routine, as appropriate. In fact, this interpreter may be killed as a task to stop it competing with application tasks for time slices.

Top level

Just above this layer is the final layer of operating-system–supplied functions. The systems utilities and products layer adds the final elements of functional capability needed to make the multitasking program an operating system suited to program development as well as to real-time support. As in conventional development-type operating systems, the program offers a powerful file-handling utility, called the peripheral interchange program, for file copying, concatenation, and translation among the various devices on the system. In addition, this layer includes a resident text editor, a macro-assembler that produces relocatable object code, a linker for combining relocatable object modules, and a library manager to ease the cataloging of separate object modules.

An additional pair of utilities—locate and task builder—produce an absolute binary module or relocatable task image, respectively. Tasks, as constructed by task builder, are not fixed to absolute addresses but are dynamically relocated into available space, depending on the availability of memory. Two or more instances of such a task may be run concurrently by a user simply by issuing the run command for each task to be executed. □

References
1. C. A. R. Hoare, "Monitors: An Operating System Structuring Concept," Communications of the ACM, Association for Computing Machinery, New York, Oct. 1974, pp. 549–557.
2. Per Brinch Hansen, "Operating System Principles," Prentice-Hall Inc., Englewood Cliffs, N. J., 1973.

Real-time operating system puts its executive on silicon

A software component as standard as a TTL device, this kernel runs identically on three 16-bit microprocessors

by John Tinnon, *Hunter & Ready Inc., Palo Alto, Calif.*

□ The invasion of real-time applications by 16-bit microprocessors would be advancing much faster if standard operating-system software were available. As things are, programmers find they can spend up to 60% of their time on just writing the basic mechanisms needed to support a real-time system's multiple concurrent tasks.

These support mechanisms are, however, common to all real-time systems, so they are a prime candidate for time-saving standardization—especially in the form of silicon software components, which are as easy to use as hardware. The Versatile Real-Time Executive, or VRTX (pronounced "vertex"), is just such a silicon software family. Read-only-memory chips containing VRTX are already available for the three most popular 16-bit microprocessors, the 68000, the 8086 and 8088, and the Z8000. A fourth version for National Semiconductor's 16000 is under development.

Prepackaged real-time multitasking executives, also called operating-system kernels, are nothing new. Vendors of single-board computers have been supplying them for several years. But unlike VRTX, these earlier executives are designed to run only on a specific target board and require a particular host system for development. Also unlike VRTX, they generally do not permit custom designs unless the user is willing to buy the source code and modify it extensively.

VRTX offers interrupt-driven task scheduling, intertask communications and synchronization, dynamic as well as static memory allocation, real-time clock support, and character input/output. It is also compact and fast, occupying only 4-K bytes of memory and taking only about 100 microseconds to switch tasks (Table 1).

Supplied in two 2716 ultraviolet-light–erasable programmable read-only memories, this operating-system kernel is a true silicon software component. Like an Ada package, it serves as a building block out of which larger systems can be constructed. And unlike executives supplied on disk that require modification in order to adapt to a particular hardware configuration, it makes no assumptions about the board on which it will be running.

In effect, it simply adds 22 high-level instructions to the processor's existing repertoire (Table 2). Being written entirely in position-independent code, it can be located anywhere in the user's address space and as a result can easily be retrofitted to an existing design. Its interface with the target board is an external configuration table that may occupy as few as 28 bytes of main system memory.

More than that, this silicon kernel was designed from the start to reach beyond the microprocessor board. A uniform mechanism exists for supplementing it with both user-defined system calls and user-defined interrupt handlers. As a result, it is possible to add not only simple, device-dependent interrupt handlers but also more complex logical functions, such as administering a file structure.

Task management

The basic logical unit controlled by VRTX is the task, which is a logically complete execution path through user code that demands the use of system resources. A task is not the same as a program, which is merely a section of code, whereas several tasks may share the same code.

The user may write as many as 256 unique tasks to run under VRTX. He or she assigns each task a priority

TABLE 1: PERFORMANCE DATA FOR VRTX REAL-TIME EXECUTIVE FOR THREE MICROPROCESSORS*			
Operation	**Execution time (μs)***		
	VRTX/8002	**VRTX/68000**	**VRTX/86**
Create a task	128	144	191
Send message (with task switch)	129	143	173
Send message (without task switch)	53	59	111
Receive message (task waits)	110	130	133
Receive message (message waiting)	32	38	66
Maximum time interrupts are off (no time slicing)	$13 + 6n^{\dagger}$	$14 + 7n^{\dagger}$	$16 + 8n^{\dagger}$

*Clock rate is 8 MHz. †n = number of tasks.

TABLE 2: THE 22 VRTX SYSTEM CALLS FOR CONTROLLING USER'S TASKS

Task control

Task create	creates a ready-to-run task with the specified priority and start address plus (optionally) an identification number
Task delete	deletes a specified task from the system
Task suspend	suspends a specified task by setting its status as suspended
Task resume	resumes a previously suspended task by resetting its status as ready-to-run
Task priority	changes the priority of a specified task
Task inquiry	obtains the ID number, priority, and/or status information about a particular task

Communication and synchronization

Post message	sends a message from one task to another via a specified mailbox location
Pend for message	receives a message via a specified mailbox location either from another task or from an interrupt handler; if no message is immediately available, the calling task is suspended until a message is received

Character input/output

Get character	receives the next input character from the designated I/O device
Put character	transmits the next output character to the designated I/O device
Wait for character	suspends the calling task until a specified character is received from the designated I/O device

Clock management

Task delay	suspends the calling task for a specified number of clock intervals
Get time	obtains the current value of the system clock
Set time	sets the current value of the system clock
Time-slice	enables round-robin scheduling among tasks of equal priority

Memory management

Get block	allocates a block of memory
Release block	de-allocates a block of memory

Interrupt interface

Post from interrupt	sends a message from an interrupt handler to a task via a specified mailbox location
Exit from interrupt	invokes a task rescheduling upon completion of interrupt handling
Timer interrupt	used by an interrupt handler to signal expiration of a clock interval
Receiver interrupt	used by an interrupt handler to signal receipt of an input character
Transmitter interrupt	used by an interrupt handler to signal its readiness to transmit an output character

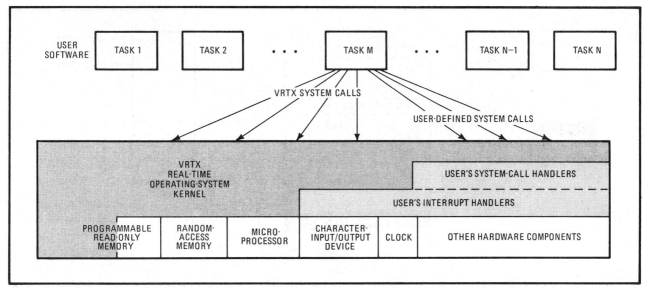

1. VRTX architecture. The real-time multitasking executive, VRTX, provides 22 system calls that can greatly simplify the embedded system programming of 16-bit microcomputers in real-time applications. The user supplies his own interrupt handlers and device drivers.

level, and VRTX allocates control of the processor sequentially to the highest-priority task that is ready to execute. The kernel supports as many as 256 levels of priority. It employs an event-driven, round-robin scheduling algorithm and, if a clock is present, also permits task delays to occur.

Tasks may create other tasks, and they may delete, suspend, resume, and change the priority of themselves or other tasks. They may also need to send messages to one another. Two simple system calls, SC_POST and SC_PEND form a completely general mechanism for communication and synchronization. Tasks can send or receive 2- or 4-byte values to or from any memory location (which may, of course, be pointers to large data structures). If a location is empty, a task trying to receive will remain pending until a message arrives.

These communication and synchronization mechanisms are similar to the corresponding mechanisms in Data General Corp.'s Real-Time Operating System (RTOS), a widely used minicomputer operating system. The approach obviates the need for complex predefined entities (or objects) such as mailboxes, semaphores, message headers, and exchanges. It also makes mutual exclusion and resource locking easy to perform. For instance, resource locking can be implemented simply by arranging for all the tasks trying to use a resource to remain pending at the same location; as each task finishes with the resource, it sends a message to that location waking up the next task.

Real-time support

A real-time system must by definition respond quickly to external interrupts. Under VRTX, user-supplied interrupt handlers can adjust the scheduling of critically important tasks to unexpected events.

By analogy with the intertask communication mechanisms just mentioned, the UI_POST command allows an interrupt handler to post a message to a waiting task upon the occurrence of a significant event. The UI_EXIT command forces immediate rescheduling after the inter-

rupt handler finishes. These two commands serve as a general interface between VRTX functions and device-dependent service routines.

Like the microprocessor itself, the silicon software kernel makes no assumptions about the interrupt structure that the user will choose to implement. The Z8000 uses a data structure called the new program status area (NPSA) to define the addresses of user-supplied interrupt-service routines. Aside from requiring that system-call traps be routed through VRTX, the user is completely free to use the NPSA directly to specify the entire interrupt structure. Similarly, VRTX/86 uses 32 vectors from the interrupt vector table leaving all other interrupt vectors to the user. VRTX/68000 uses trap 0 in the exception vector table. The kernel occupies a position that is hierarchically above the interrupt service routines, as shown in Fig. 1.

Going by the clock

Many VRTX applications will require a real-time clock and at least one character-oriented I/O device such as a terminal. Therefore, support for these devices is fully integrated into VRTX. The user need supply only a small hardware-dependent interrupt-servicing routine for each such device. VRTX, in turn, will manage all the logical operations needed to supply user application tasks with a full repertoire of associated clock management and character I/O commands. It is important to realize, however, that this kernel has been designed to operate quite satisfactorily independently of these devices—even the clock is not essential.

The VRTX commands to support character I/O and a clock fall into two categories: calls from user tasks and calls from interrupt handlers. For the clock, VRTX recognizes four user calls (SC_GTME, SC_TIME, SC_TDELAY, and SC_TSLICE) and one call from the clock service routine (UI_TIMER). Employing the first two calls, user tasks can get the value from the clock counter and set a new value for the counter. The remaining two user calls implement task delays and round-robin scheduling. The

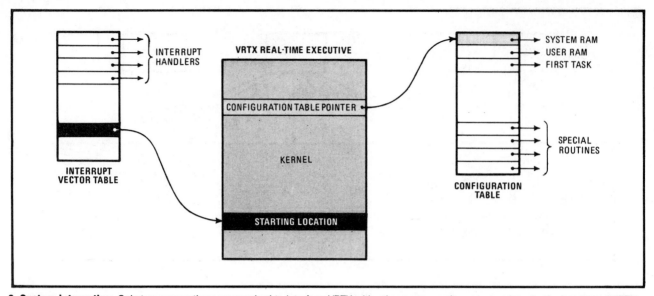

2. System integration. Only two connections are required to interface VRTX with other system software—a pointer to the location of VRTX, and a pointer with the location of the configuration table that resolves all the hardware dependencies of the host environment.

UI_TIMER call, issued from an interrupt handler, simply notifies VRTX that a time interval has expired.

For character I/O, VRTX supplies three user calls (SC_GETC, SC_PUTC, and SC_WAITC) and two calls from interrupt handlers (UI_RXCHR and UI_TXRDY). The first two implement standard system-call get-character and put-character functions. The third user call allows a user task function as a "watchdog" for a particular character (for example, CONTROL-C). The two calls received from interrupt handlers will implement the necessary handshaking functions.

Managing memory

One of the basic functions provided by a real-time executive is memory management. VRTX supports dynamic as well as static allocation of memory blocks. In dynamic allocation, the two system calls allow user tasks to get and release blocks of memory. A separate stack is provided for each task.

The Z8000 status lines can distinguish among four address spaces for system code and data and for user code and data. Similarly, the 68000 distinguishes among supervisor program and data and user program and data. The kernel has been carefully designed to ensure complete compatibility with boards that actually effect such a separation. Of course, nothing precludes the use of VRTX with designs that do not utilize separate memory spaces. In addition, VRTX/86 is also compatible with the 8086 segmented memory architecture.

The user-supplied configuration table along with simple, device-specific user-supplied interrupt handlers interface VRTX with its environment. The table is VRTX's window on the rest of the board. It occupies 42 bytes on the 68000, 32 bytes on the 8086, and as little as 28 bytes on the Z8000. With it, the user can specify all the parameters needed by the kernel for a configuration.

One location in VRTX points to the base of the configuration table, and one vector in the interrupt vector table points to the VRTX starting location. These two pointers are the only links between the silicon kernel and the rest

of the board. Values in the configuration table specify the start of system RAM and of user RAM, the length of user memory, the maximum number of tasks, and the location of any special routines that the user might wish to be invoked whenever a task is switched, created, or deleted, or the system is initialized. Figure 2 is a diagram of the relationships among VRTX, the configuration table, and the interrupt vector table.

Users who may want to add system calls to support special I/O devices have only to add a one-word pointer to the configuration table. Entries in this table can also be made to specify user routines for initializing special devices at system start-up or saving the state of custom devices on task switches. For example, if the user has a floating-point processor in the system, it will be necessary to save its registers on a context switch. Almost no other operating systems, even the user-configurable ones, give the designer the option of easily adding user save routines and initialization routines to the system scheduler. When VRTX was designed it was realized that easy extendability would be a key requirement for silicon software components, so these hooks were included.

Hooks and handlers

Next on the list of future silicon software components to be developed by Hunter & Ready is a file handler. This component will manage disk files—reading, writing, allocation, and so forth—in a manner similar to Unix. It will be hierarchically structured and will include schemes for fast access, possibly using what are called Indexed Sequential Access Methods. In addition, it will be supported by a library of hard- and floppy-disk drivers also cast in silicon. Together, they will enable users to implement a sophisticated file system by selecting from a catalog of standard components. In fact, VRTX already has the hooks installed to allow the file handler to be grafted onto existing designs without sacrificing throughput. Beyond the file handler are component data-base managers, network interfaces, and communications packages. □

Standard software interface boosts program portability

With stock operating-system routines and formats, programs may be easily fitted to new applications

by Al Hartman, *Intel Corp., Santa Clara, Calif.*

☐ The patchwork era of microsystem software is ending, as the programming philosophy of compatibility gains strength. Among the standardization techniques that will write *finis* to software incompatibility is the concept of a standard software interface (see figure).

Such an interface, consisting of standard system calls and shared code- and data-storage formats, allows conforming operating systems and user programs simply to plug into new hardware configurations. In fact, with the intervention of an adapter program, even nonstandard operating systems can be used, as can any compiler, assembler, utility, or application that uses the standard interface or that can be adapted to it.

No longer will writing a program that is to run under several distinct operating systems require a maddening duplication of effort involving subtle and arbitrary differences in handling similar items. Rather, such file-, memory-, and device-management operations will be standardized for true software compatibility.

A standard software interface tends to increase the available software base from which users may choose. The portability of operating systems, system software, and application programs is increased, lowering software development costs. Adoption of a software-interface standard creates a ready market in which software producers and consumers alike can participate to their mutual benefit.

With the Intel family of microprocessors, software writers are encouraged to use the software interface component called the Universal Development Interface (See Table 1). The UDI may be implemented for any microprocessor, since it is not specific to any one instruction set. In fact, the set of UDI primitives has been adapted by one customer to the VAX minicomputer from Digital Equipment Corp. However Intel's major thrust is in the proliferation of software for the already large base of 8088, 8086, iAPX-186, and iAPX-286 users.

Freedom in standardization

Designers conforming to UDI are free to choose operating systems, system software, or application programs provided by any source that conforms to that software interface. The chaotic custom-software marketplace, which spawned a cottage industry almost overnight, sometimes cannot meet the cost, functionality, and reliability requirements for newer microprocessors. With UDI, quality software for all common applications is becoming available, because proven programs can be

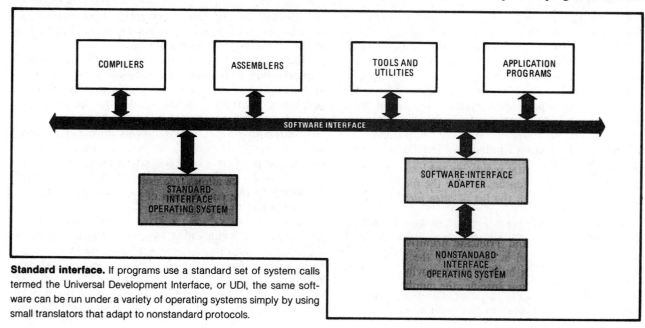

Standard interface. If programs use a standard set of system calls termed the Universal Development Interface, or UDI, the same software can be run under a variety of operating systems simply by using small translators that adapt to nonstandard protocols.

TABLE 1: SOFTWARE COMPATIBLE WITH UNIVERSAL DEVELOPMENT INTERFACE	
Operating systems	High level languages
Isis	Pascal
iRMX-86	Fortran
CP/M-86	Basic
MP/M-86	C
MP/NET-86	Cobol
Xenix	PL/M
MS/DOS	Jovial
Oasis*	Ada**
*under negotiation	**under development

TABLE 2: STANDARD PRIMITIVES OF THE UNIVERSAL DEVELOPMENT INTERFACE	
Name	Type of service
Allocate Free Get size	Memory management
Delete Rename Change extension Attach Create Open Close Detach Get status	File management
Read Write Seek Truncate	Input/output operations
Trap exception Get exception handler Decode exception	Exception handling
Trap control-C Special Get argument Switch buffer	Command interpretation
Exit Get time Get system ID Overlay	Miscellaneous

quickly transfered from one processor type to another.

The UDI consists of 27 primitives (see Table 2) for memory and file management, input/output operations, exception handling, and command interpretation, as well as some miscellaneous functions. These primitives provide a standard interface with sequential programs and can be implemented for single- or multitasking operating systems. Few assumptions are made about the form of the user's command language, and virtually any style of command syntax is possible when the UDI is implemented. Almost any operating system can be adapted to this interface. In addition, a standard format for 8086 object-code modules allows interchangeability regardless of the source of the modules.

As one of the memory-management services, a free block of memory can be obtained for a task using the Allocate primitive, with the desired size as an argument. The Free primitive returns a block of memory to the available pool, and the Get-size primitive provides the actual size of a given memory segment. As with all of the operating-system primitives, the memory-management primitives return an exception code to the caller indicating either no exception or one of several error conditions.

Managing the files

For file management, primitives exist to create or delete connections to files, to attach or detach files to and from a program, and to open or close files for input, output, or updating. Also, files may be renamed and have their type and status changed.

The Attach operation searches a directory for a file, verifies file-access privileges, creates a file control block, and returns an internal pointer for future file references. The Open operation verifies access for write or update privileges and allocates file buffers. The Detach operation scratches the pointer indicating the location of a file, and the Close operation deallocates the file buffers and removes its name from the list of open files kept by the operating system.

I/O and positioning operations on an open file include Read, Write, Seek, and Truncate primitives. A simple byte-stream I/O model is assumed in the design of the UDI rather than using built-in block-moving operations. A Read or Write request specifies the number of bytes to be manipulated. A Seek operation specifies a byte displacement from the current file position or from the beginning or end of the file. And the Truncate operation cuts off the file at the current position.

The exception-handling primitives are Trap exception, Get exception handler, and Decode exception. The Trap exception designates user routines to gain control if the operating system detects an exception. The Get-exception-handler primitive returns a pointer to the current exception handler. To aid in providing user diagnostic information, the Decode-exception operation translates an exception code into an error message for display at the terminal or in a listing file.

Other aids to user interaction are the command-interpretation primitives. The Trap-control-C primitive establishes a user routine that will gain control when the user types "control-C." What is called the Special primitive selects terminal input in either a line-edited mode (where the program system interprets editing characters, such as delete or rubout) or in a transparent mode (where the program interprets editing characters its own way). This choice allows free usage of editing characters according to the conventions of different operating systems or application programs.

No particular command syntax is enforced, but the first word of a command is frequently the file name of the invoked program. Arguments following this may be read using the Get-argument primitive, which allows any reasonable argument delimiter, including blanks. By use of the Switch-buffer primitive, the command interpreter may be used to read commands that are found in locations other than in the standard console input file.

UDI also provides several miscellaneous primitives. Exit relinquishes control to the operating system, while providing it with a completion code for the program. Get time provides a data and time message for a console display or file stamping. The Get-system-ID primitive provides an operating-system identification message, also for a console or listing display. Finally, to support overlaid programs, the Overlay primitive loads an over-lay from a one-level overlay program. An overlaid pro-gram is a single program file containing an overlay directory at its beginning.

Representing information

Object-module formats are standard ways of repre-senting the binary information that will be executed on a processor. Intel has versions for the 8086, 286, 8085, and 8051 microprocessors, because different types of infor-mation need to be represented for each.

First of all, OMFs are a way of representing the inter-dependency between the modules that need to be linked together to form an executable program. Having a stan-dard way of representing data objects that will be passed among procedures and standard ways of calling them is a necessity for modern languages that allow separate compilation of modules.

One common approach is to follow program compila-tion with what is called a linking loader. Using a stan-dard format allows the language translator to produce the same type of modules that are produced by the linkage utilities. In this way, standard libraries of mod-ules can be built up, any one of which may be passed to a linker, loader, debugger or other system utility in a compatible fashion.

What is more, debugging information like data types and symbolic names can be stored in object-module formats by each of the system utilities and used by any of them. Thus debugging can be much more sophisti-cated than would otherwise be possible. For instance, whenever the linker resolves variable references between modules, it can perform type checking to make sure that both modules are using the same type of data. This check can flush out errors that would be very difficult to find at debugging or execution time.

Also, memory-segment information is included so that modules can be assigned to the same segments whenever possible. This arrangement can speed up the execution of programs to the point where they will run faster than equivalent programs written on a machine with linear addressing, such as the 68000.

For the 286 with on-chip memory management, the protection information (read-only, system-only, and so on) is stored in an OMF so that it is accessible to the operating-system language translators, linkers, loaders, and debuggers, and to other system-level tools. Because this protection information is easily accessible to the system software, it can be well hidden from the applica-tion programmer, thereby eliminating the need to under-stand the underlying architecture.

Also, the object-module format makes it easy to add new features without introducing incompatibilities, because the specific storage mechanisms are very flexi-ble. For instance, when the 8087 numeric coprocessor was introduced, a new data type—the 80-bit long-real—was easily integrated into the object-module format. Also, the PL/M-86 compiler has recently been updated to produce the same kinds of debugging information that the Pascal-86 compiler does, without introducing incom-patibilities. Thus access to PL/M is opened to debuggers such as Intel's new Pscope, which allows debugging within the high-level language itself rather than resorting to assembly language. □

Silicon operating system standardizes software

All the basic functions for real-time multitasking programs,
including software subroutines and hardware timers, fit on the 80130

by C. McMinn, R. Markowitz, J. Wharton, and W. Grundmann, *Intel Corp., Santa Clara, Calif.*

☐ Silicon software, an inherently ambiguous phrase, refers to the solid-state realization of standard programs. It is the midpoint in the migration of microprocessor software into microcode and, as such, it exhibits the characteristics of both. Like software, it must be reconfigurable if it is to endure the fast-changing world of microprocessor technology, and like hardware, it must capitalize on this technology to reduce hardware and software costs and to provide increased system performance.

Recognizing this need, Intel Corp. has designed a set of silicon operating-system primitives that provides all of the basic building-blocks needed to write real-time multitasking software. These building blocks have been carefully chosen to include the functionality needed today as well as to allow reconfigurability for tomorrow. But the 80130 is not just software, since it also includes on chip all the other hardware components necessary to make the system work without additional external logic (Fig. 1). It is designed to be closely coupled to either the 8086 or 8088 16-bit microprocessor, creating the iAPX 86/30 and 88/30 two-chip sets.

These two-chip operating-system processors, as they are called, were specifically developed to remove the burden of designing multitasking operating-system primitives from the application programmer by providing a well-defined, fully debugged set implemented directly in the hardware. The application programmer no longer has to write the program that processes and coordinates a number of events. Instead, he or she can write several programs, each of which has only to process a single event and uses the common multitasking primitives for coordination. In essence, the handling of multiple, concurrent, asynchronous events has been localized entirely in these primitives, freeing the application programmer to concentrate on his or her own program and allowing an application to be developed faster and with reduced software costs.

The primitives support an event-oriented design that entrusts the application to separate concurrent tasks, rather than burdening a single program with the complex dependencies inherent in random real-time events. Each event can be processed by a separate task or along with closely related events in a common task. External events and interrupts are processed by the interrupt-handling primitives directly from the on-chip interrupt controller subsystem as they occur in real time. Multiple tasks and multiple events are coordinated by the scheduler, whose preemptive, priority-based scheduling algorithm and system timers organize and monitor the processing of each task to guarantee that events are performed in their order of importance. The 80130 also provides primitives for intertask communication—by mailboxes—and for mutual exclusion—by regions—both of which are essential

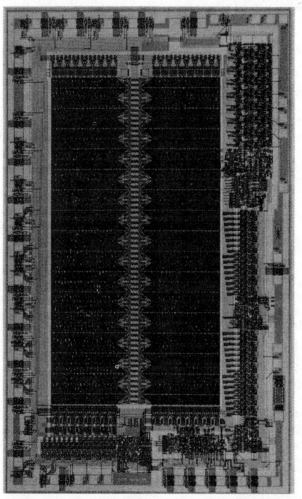

1. More than memory. Though the die of the 80130 is mostly occupied by the 16-K-byte kernel control store, it also includes an interrupt controller and two 16-bit timers for operating-system use, plus a bit-rate generator for the user's convenience.

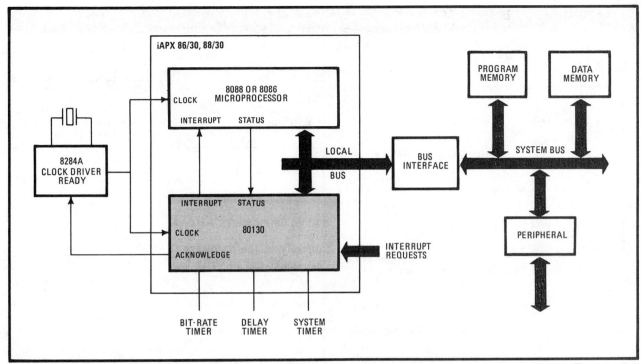

2. Intimate contact. The 80130 is closely coupled to the 8086 or 8088 processor, in effect extending the instruction set. The two used together form the iAPX-86/30 or 88/30 operating-system processors. With an 8087 arithmetic processor, they form the 88/31.

functions for multitasking applications.

From the application programmer's viewpoint, the 80130 extends the base of the 8086 architecture by providing more than 30 operating-system primitive instructions (see Table 1), making the 80130 a logical and easy-to-use extension to an 8086 or 8088 system.

The 80130 replaces approximately 10 large- and small-scale integrated circuits in a system. It sits directly on the local bus of the processor and runs with both the 8086 and 8088 at an 8-megahertz clock rate. This guarantees that, regardless of the speed of the remaining memory in the system, these time-critical operating-system primitives will operate at the maximum bus bandwidth.

The chip has also been designed to be compatible with the iRMX-86 operating system and, as such, has been thoroughly tested against a wide range of text software available for this product.

The 80130 primitives were chosen after much analysis both because they are useful in many applications today and because they will continue to be useful primitives, if not standard machine instructions, in future processors. The 80130 kernel implementation is simple and efficient yet powerful enough to be a highly versatile architectural building block.

Architectural details

The 80130 is connected directly to the local bus of the 8086 and 8088 processor (it automatically detects whether the 8086 or 8088 is present), with address decoding, buffering, and bus-demultiplexing logic contained on chip (Fig. 2). The 80130's firmware is memory-mapped to any 16-K boundary in the processor's 1-megabyte address space. The control registers are mapped into the input/output space; they are aligned on

any 16-byte boundary within the space.

Internally, the 80130 firmware consists of two sections: an operating-system unit and a control unit (Fig. 3). The former consists of a 16-K-byte operating-system–kernel control store complete with an operating-system timer and a delay timer; a bit-rate generator; and 8259A-compatible programmable interrupt logic.

The first timer generates the fundamental real-time clock period in the system. It is set to 10 milliseconds initially but can be modified by the system designer. The delay timer supports the kernel timing function by indicating the next event. Both these timer resources are reserved for use by the kernel.

The bit-rate generator, which has a range of 75 to 768 kilobits per second, is provided as a user resource. The 80130 interrupt logic vectors eight independent priority levels, one of which is reserved for the operating-system timers. Optional external slave interrupt controllers (8259A) can expand the number of user-programmable interrupt levels to 57.

Individual treatment

The 80130 interrupt logic goes beyond that of an 8259A interrupt controller. First, it allows the eight interrupt inputs to be individually programmed as level- or edge-sensitive (whereas the 8259A requires all to be programmed alike). Second, the 80130 has an output line that can be used in conjunction with the 8289 bus arbiter to reduce interrupt latency by localizing interrupt response to a single board in a multiboard system. An additional advantage is that the system bus remains available to other processors during an interrupt.

The 80130 supplements the 8086's basic architecture with five new objects, or system data types—jobs, tasks, segments, mailboxes, and regions.

TABLE 1: PRIMITIVES USED IN 80130 OPERATING SYSTEM FIRMWARE

Category	Primitive	Description	Category	Primitive	Description
Job	Create job	Creates a job partition including memory pool, task list, and stack area.	Interrupt	Enable	Enables an external interrupt level.
Task	Create task	Creates a task with the specified environment and priority and puts it in the ready state. Checks for insuffcient memory available within the containing job.		Disable	Disables an external interrupt level.
				Get exception handler	Reads the location- and exception-handling mode of the current operating system exception handler for a task.
	Delete task	Deletes a task from the system as well as from any queues in which it is waiting. The task's state and stack segment are deallocated.		Set exception handler	Establishes the location-and exception-handling mode of the current OSP exception handler for a task.
	Suspend task	Suspends a task (changes its status to suspended) or increases the task's suspension count by 1. A sleeping task may also be suspended and will then awaken suspended unless resumed.	Segment	Create segment	Allocates dynamically an area of memory of a specified length in 16-byte paragraph units up to a maximum of 64-k bytes (for example, for use as a buffer). Returns a location token for the segment allocated.
	Resume task	Decreases the suspension count of a task by 1. If the count is at that point reduced to 0, the task state is made ready or if it was suspend-asleep, it is put back to asleep.		Delete segment	De-allocates the memory segment indicated by the parameter token.
				Enable deletion	Allows the system data type value indicated by the location token to be deleted.
	Sleep	Puts the task in the asleep state, a number of 10-ms units may be specified.		Disable deletion	Prevents the system data type value indicated by the location token from being deleted.
	Set priority	Changes the task's priority to the value passed in the primitive.	Mailbox	Create mailbox	Creates a mailbox with the specified task queueing discipline. Returns a location token.
	Set interrupt	Assigns an interrupt handler to a level. The task that makes this call is made the interrupt task for the same level, unless the call indicates there is no interrupt task.		Delete mailbox	Deletes a mailbox, and returns its memory. If tasks are waiting for the mailbox, they are awakened (their state is made ready) with an appropriate exception condition. If messages are waiting for tasks, they are discarded.
Interrupt	Reset interrupt	Disables an interrupt level. Cancels the interrupt handler, deletes the interrupt task for that level if assigned.		Send message	Sends a message segment to a mailbox.
	Get level	Returns the number of the interrupt level for highest-priority interrupt handler currently in operation (several interrupt handlers could be operating).		Receive message	A task is ready to receive a message at a mailbox. The task is placed on the mailbox task queue. The task may optionally wait for a response indefinitely, or a number of time intervals (generally 10 ms long), or not at all. When complete, the primitive returns to the task the location token of the message segment received.
	Exit interrupt	Completes interrupt processing and sends end-of-interrupt signal to hardware.	Region	Create region	Creates a region data type value, specifying a queuing discipline. Returns a token for the region.
	Signal interrupt	Invokes the interrupt task assigned to a level from that level's interrupt handler.		Delete region	Deletes a region if and only if the region is not in use.
	Wait interrupt	Makes the interrupt task state suspended pending a signal interrupt from an interrupt handler. Used by an interrupt task to signal its readiness to service an interrupt.		Accept control	Gains control of a region if it is immediately available, but does not wait if it is not available.
				Receive control	Is the same primitive as accept control but the task that performs it may elect to wait.
				Send control	Relinquishes a region.

The 86/30 operates by creating, manipulating and deleting individual system objects. When an object is created, the 86/30 returns its name to the creating task. This name is referred to and used as an abstract data type, called a token. The token is a highly efficient way of accessing the 86/30 address space. Referring to a segment object, for example, causes a 16-bit address to be loaded into one of the processor segment registers, which can then be used to directly address a paragraph (16-byte unit) anywhere in the 1-megabyte address space. Task creation is also accomplished in this manner and requires only the specification of a priority, a task private data segment (if needed), a task stack, and a task program starting address.

To take full advantage of multiprogramming, the operating system must provide each application with a separate environment—that is, separate memory and tasks. This isolation both protects independent programs from interfering with one another and allows the application programmer to work without regard to the other application programs in the system. The 80130 supports multiprogramming with the job data type. The creation of a job requires the specification of a large number of parameters and is normally done only when the system is being initialized.

Interrupt-driven

In multitasking systems, there are two common techniques for deciding which task is to be run at any given moment. Time slicing runs tasks in rotation and is the technique used in time-sharing systems. Priority-based scheduling, on the other hand, compares assigned task priorities to decide which task is to be run next. Further, priority-based systems are usually preemptive—in other

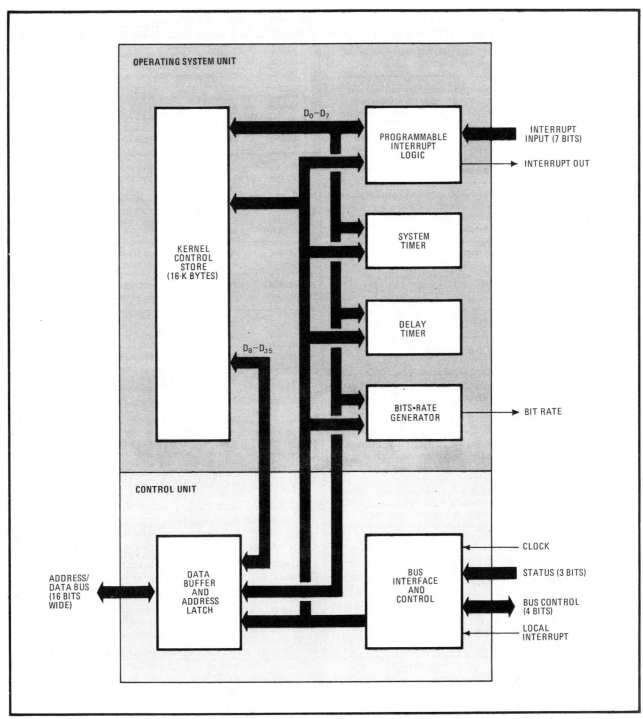

OPERATING SYSTEM UNIT

KERNEL
CONTROL
STORE
(16-K BYTES)

D_0-D_7

D_8-D_{15}

PROGRAMMABLE
INTERRUPT
LOGIC

INTERRUPT
INPUT (7 BITS)

INTERRUPT OUT

SYSTEM
TIMER

DELAY
TIMER

BITS-RATE
GENERATOR

BIT RATE

CONTROL UNIT

ADDRESS/
DATA BUS
(16 BITS
WIDE)

DATA
BUFFER
AND
ADDRESS
LATCH

BUS
INTERFACE
AND
CONTROL

CLOCK

STATUS (3 BITS)

BUS CONTROL
(4 BITS)

LOCAL
INTERRUPT

3. Inside view. The silicon operating system is realized in the 80130 pictured here in the form of firmware containing the operating-system kernel, plus the two timers, interrupt-handling logic, and other support hardware necessary to handle complex multitasking applications.

words, a higher-priority task is executed as soon as it is ready to run, rather than only after the current task has run to completion of a time slice.

The 86/30 supports preemptive, priority-based scheduling. The built-in scheduler performs all task-scheduling functions and controls the transition of tasks among the five possible operating states. Tasks that may be executed are in what is called the ready state. The one with the highest priority will be running, while all those of lower priority remain ready.

The 86/30 hardware timer facilities support time-outs

with the asleep state. Tasks can put themselves into the asleep state in one of two ways. They can wait for a predefined number of 10-ms time periods (or for some other user-defined value if 10 ms is not appropriate for the application), or they can wait for a message that a shared resource, such as an I/O device, has by now been made available.

Tasks can also make themselves or other tasks enter the nonready state called suspended. A task may be suspended more than once, and suspensions are cumulative, requiring the task to be resumed for each suspension. A task marked asleep can also be suspended. It will then be put in the special state that requires both the time-expiration condition and the suspension condition to be met before it again becomes ready.

The 80130's preemptive-scheduling algorithm ensures that the highest-priority task that is in the ready state will receive the processor and that a task that is running will continue to do so until a higher-priority interrupt occurs (including a time-out interrupt) or until it relinquishes the resources that would allow a higher-priority task to make the transition to the ready status. Each task is given a priority-and-interrupt level relative to every other task and interrupt when it is created, but task priority may also be altered dynamically.

The 80130 maps external interrupts directly into internal task priorities, using the interrupt control logic included on the chip.

Two methods of interrupt management are supported for each level. The first is the interrupt handler. It can be used for time-critical interrupts or for interrupt processing requiring a small amount of work—for example, entering an input character into a buffer. While executing in the interrupt handler, a task will be restricted to calling a very limited set of operating-system primitive functions: enter-interrupt, get-level, signal-interrupt, and exit-interrupt.

The second method, the more general interrupt task, can be used when there is more processing work to be done. This interrupt task is an ordinary 80130 task, but one that cannot be suspended. Its processing of an interrupt begins with execution of the interrupt handler for that level. It is the handler that fields the time-critical portions of the interrupt and then optionally invokes an interrupt task.

Segments, mailboxes, and regions

The 80130 also provides a free-memory manager that allocates memory to requesting tasks dynamically. This manager operates within the pool of memory resources allocated by the create-job function of the containing job. When a system object is created, the memory manager allocates the required memory; when the value is deleted, it de-allocates it. This operation is implicit, and a separate create-segment call is not required. Two related kernel primitives are provided to enable or disable the deletion of individual system objects. When a value is deleted, its memory is automatically recovered for the job memory pool. When a value is created, the deletion function is enabled, so that the disable-deletion primitive must be executed to "lock" it in memory and remove it from the available memory list.

The technique used to facilitate communication and synchronization is a mailbox, a system data type designed to pass this information reliably and efficiently between tasks. Mailboxes support both priority and first-in, first-out queues. If the receiving task is of a higher priority than the sending task, receipt of a message can cause preemptive rescheduling of the sending and receiving tasks.

One of the most difficult problems to solve in a multitasking system is mutual exclusion. Mutual exclusion is absolutely essential to a multitasking system, for

Data-type class	Primitive	Execution speed* (μs)
Job	Create job	2,950
Task	Create task (no preemption)	1,360
Segment	Create segment	700
Mailbox	Send message (with task switch)	475
	Send message (no task switch)	265
	Receive message (task waits)	540
	Receive message (message waiting)	260
Region	Send control	170
	Receive control	205

TABLE 2: EXAMPLES OF THE PERFORMANCE OF OPERATING-SYSTEM PROCESSOR PRIMITIVES

*in the 8-MHz iAPX 86/30 configuration

it guarantees proper processing whenever two tasks require the exclusive use of a memory or I/O resource like a disk drive. Without mutual exclusion, the higher-priority task would immediately gain access to the shared resource, even if the lower-priority task is already in the process of modifying the information.

The 80130 solves the problem of mutual exclusion with the region object. It provides for both code regions and data regions, and both may be protected from simultaneous access by multiple tasks. If one task is in a region when another higher-priority task requests control (with receive-control), the task currently in the region will be run at the higher priority of the requester until it relinquishes the region via send-control. At that point a scheduling preemption will occur.

The performance of several 80130 primitives is given in Table 2. These times are shown for an iAPX 86/30 implementation at 8 MHz and rival those of similar functions in today's high-end minicomputers, being an entire order of magnitude faster than those of the previous generation of microprocessors. Indeed, many of these primitives operate faster than the basic multiply and divide operations of the last generation of machines.

Configuration plus

In addition to placing the 80130 in his system, the 86/30 user must supply a configuration and initialization area adjacent to the kernel store. A working area of approximately 1,500 bytes for use as the kernel stack will also be allocated in system random-access memory as part of the system initialization process.

The configuration process for the 80130 is simplified by the use of the iAPX 86/30 and 88/30 Operating-System–Processor Support Package. This software package, which runs on Intel development systems, includes optional user parameter validation code, system initialization software, and the 80130 interface library. This library and the 80130 design itself provide position independence for the 80130. All accesses to the 80130 are indirect, made through an on-chip jump table at an address supplied by the interface library. With this arrangement, the 80130 can be located on any 16-K-byte boundary in the user's address space. The on-chip jump table also ensures that if the primitives are changed, the user-to-program interface remains identical. □

Electronics/March 24, 1982

Operating systems hold a full house of features for 16-bit microprocessors

Standard software packages often satisfy application needs as well as presenting a wide range of options to the original-equipment manufacturer

by R. Colin Johnson, *Software Editor*

☐ In the six years of its existence, the 16-bit microprocessor has made little impression on the commercial scene, despite considerable success in industrial applications. On the one hand, it has suffered from a dearth of appropriate software. On the other, 8-bit devices, fortified by their libraries of hard-won programs, have been firmly entrenched in all of the likely markets.

The arrival last fall of IBM Corp.'s Personal Computer—the first to be based on a 16-bit chip—signals a change of attitude. Possibly for the first time, the majority of new microsystems to bow this year will use 16-bit processors. The development hinges on the recent availability of a number of standard 16-bit operating systems—that software soul essential to every computer, without which it would be unable to communicate with its users, march data to and from mass-storage units, or even display the results of its calculations on either terminals or printers (see "What does an operating system do anyway?").

These standard systems include the programmer-oriented Unix and its imitators; the business-oriented, user-friendly Oasis-16; the real-time MP/M-86 and CP/M-86 (virtually a clone of CP/M-80) plus their concurrent and networking flavors; the Personal Computer's MS/DOS; the Pascal-derived UCSD p-System; and such newcomers as Hemenway's single-user multitasking operating system, MSP (Table 1).

Filling the bill

Traditionally, operating systems have been written in house by the hardware manufacturer himself, but the complexity of the job has given rise to a demand for standard software systems that could be adapted to different hardware configurations. Some of these were developed in house to solve the problem of incompatibility between computers within a particular company. Most, however, have been written by the burgeoning software-house industry to serve the proliferating personal computer.

The result is that several standard operating systems now exist for the original-equipment manufacturer who has decided that time-to-market constraints have made it more economical to purchase a software pack than to roll his own. Into the bargain, the adaptation of such a system to a computer often gives its users access to a substantial amount of application software already written for it. So the question for the OEM becomes: what should he know about the systems available in order to make the most intelligent choice for the applications he envisages for his microsystem?

There is no one operating system that can fill the needs of all users and applications. In fact, each operating system itself was designed to solve some specific problem, or at least to do it better, more cheaply, or faster than competitive systems. The aim here is to present the salient features of the standard operating systems available for the current 16-bit microprocessors—the 8086, 68000, Z8000, and 9900 (recently updated to microcomputer status as the 99000).

Proprietary operating systems that are designed to run only on a particular manufacturer's computer setup will not be considered here—examples are the operating systems that run on the development systems marketed by the manufacturers of the microprocessors themselves, such as Texas Instruments' Txds, Motorola's Versados, Zilog's Zeus, and Intel's Isis. These are often quite good operating systems, but are designed to produce code that is set to then be run on an application-specific target machine, often with the assistance of a real-time kernel. Still, some of them could be repackaged and enhanced—as Intel is doing with its iRMX-86—so that they could serve as the stand-alone resident operating system for the emerging 16-bit microsystem market. But that development is still down the road.

As areas like office automation grow, there will be an increasing demand for the standard operating system that can handle the execution of many programs simultaneously, each accessing common data bases and serving many users over local networks. Other operating systems have been designed specifically to be cast in silicon to execute programs in real-time environments (see "Defining silicon software,").   However, practically all operating systems can be used to execute single-user application programs, including all of those discussed below. The best choice of an operating system that will be used to execute only application programs is based on the availability of those programs and the user-friendliness of the system.

Many of those application programs, of course, are being written on computers that are running operating systems primarily designed for just that task—program development. Indeed, it is this category of operating systems that is the most prevalent—all of them also doubling as application-execution vehicles. In the last few years, tremendous advances have been made in this area, especially with regard to the invention of sophisticated software tools designed to streamline the program-development process—like screen editors, data-base managers, and more recently application generators (programs that write programs).

From laboratory to user

One of the premiere examples of an operating system optimized for program development by professional programmers is the multiuser interactive Unix from Bell Laboratories in Murray Hill, N. J. Designed from the beginning to be a productive environment for programmers, Unix was developed by Bell Labs' Kenneth Thompson and Dennis Ritchie out of frustration with the primitive batch-oriented program-development tools with which they were shackled. Thompson concentrated on the structure of Unix, while Ritchie wrote the high-level C language in which the entire system is now implemented. In fact, the main task in bringing up the whole Unix system on a microprocessor is the implementation of a C compiler for it. Microsoft Inc. of Bellevue, Wash., has done this for the Z8000, 68000, and 8086, while renaming the package Xenix. Table 2 lists this and

TABLE 1: 16-BIT OPERATING SYSTEMS AT A GLANCE								
Company	Location	Name	Processors				Real time	Details
			8086	68000	Z8000	9900		
Western Electric	Greensboro, N.C.	Unix	●	●	●		no	program-development tool only, written in C
Digital Research	Pacific Grove, Calif.	CP/M	●	*			yes	some real-time, compatible multitasking, multiuser, and network operating systems, written in PL/M and assembly language
SofTech Microsystems	San Diego, Calif.	UCSD p-System	●	●	●	●	no	interpreted p-code, portable and small, written in Pascal
Microsoft	Bellevue, Wash.	MS-DOS	●				no	IBM Personal Computer DOS, embedded graphics, written in assembly language
Phase One Systems	Oakland, Calif.	Oasis-16	●				no	adaptable to a wide range of users, extensive file management, written in C
Hemenway Associates	Boston, Mass.	MSP		●			yes	multitasking, mailbox intertask communication, written in assembly language

*under development

What does an operating system do anyway?

The operating system of a computer is the nucleus of its software. It is cognizant of all the hardware resources of the computer and how to transfer information among them, as well as how to run users' programs.

Thus it is the operating system that gathers commands from the user's terminal and interprets them. It knows the locations of all the disks, printers, tape drives, and other input/output devices in the system. It also contains the protocols necessary to make these devices work. When a user types a command to dump a disk file on the printer—or when such a request is made in a program—it is the operating system that initiates the process that starts up the motor on the disk drive, guides the head out to the proper sector, reads the information, and transfers it to the printer port at the right speed.

In multitasking computers, the operating system has the further responsibility of scheduling just when each task is to run according to some predefined priority. Moreover, in real-time systems it must respond to external events as cues to when certain tasks need to run.

---

other Unix implementations plus its look-alikes.

However, the Unix interface with the user's hardware configuration is not as clean as in operating systems separating that interface physically into an input/output code segment for the device drivers, interrupt handlers, and so on. Source code costing over $20,000 from Western Electric is required in order to implement Unix on a specific computer system, which even then will require more twiddling—commonly called maintenance—if extra devices are added later.

Copy a winner

Unix's good features have by now become so popular that virtually all new operating systems emulate them. Among them are device-independent input/output calls that allow any I/O device to be utilized without changing any of the statements in the program itself. In other words, an output statement can utilize the printer, dump to a disk file, or even direct a data stream to another program, all under console control. The terminal operator has only to respecify what is to be defined as the output device before running the program. The same kind of flexibility can be exercised over input statements, permitting data to be collected from the console during program development and later taken from disk files or any other input device.

A related feature is called pipes. In essence, pipes direct the output of one program to the input of another program without the necessity of creating cumbersome intermediate disk files. They encourage modular program development by permitting program fragments to be fully coded and debugged independently of one another. While they are being developed, their inputs and outputs can be defined from the console; but afterwards the pipes can be permanently installed in the software system so that the entire program runs sequentially and with little, if any, performance penalty.

As a program-development safeguard, before any program is executed, Unix performs what is termed a fork. This is a replication process that stores duplicates of the code, data, register values, open files, and all other relevant information before execution. In this way, if the program goes haywire, a copy of the complete environment has been kept so that no effort will have to be wasted on rewriting destroyed programs.

It is what is called the shell, however, that is the most visible part of Unix. The shell is the program that interacts with the user via the console. It utilizes a very concise vocabulary that allows one command after another to be strung together so that the results of their operations can be fed to succeeding commands.

Even the file structure of Unix is very programmer-oriented. Because of its hierarchical structure, file names and directory names can be treated in an analogous manner. A directory file is merely a list of program files, data files, and other directories. In this way the whole file structure can be traced back to an original root file. Moreover, any file in the system can be located by specifying its path name: that is, a list of directory names separated by delimiting slashes and terminating with the desired file's name. As a result, many files can have the same names—so long as they are listed in different directories—and the programmer is not continually forced to invent new names, nor do directories have to be related to specific, physical mass-storage devices.

Now that version III of Unix has been released, it has also become as cost-effective as its competitors. Unix III

TABLE 2: UNIX AND LOOK-ALIKE OPERATING SYSTEMS				
Processor or computer	Company	Name	Bell Laboratories version	Original implementation
Z8000	Interactive Systems	Unix		
	Zilog	Zeus		
	Onyx	Onix		
	Microsoft	Xenix		
	Plexus Computers	Unix		
	Mark Williams	Coherent		
68000	Microsoft	Xenix		
	Technical System Consultants	Uniflex		
	Whitesmiths	Idris		
	Mark Williams	Coherent		
	Lucas Films	Unix		
8086	Mark Williams	Coherent		
	Microsoft	Xenix		
Z80	Cromemco	Cromix		
	Morrow Designs	μNIX		
	Whitesmiths	Idris		
LSI-11 and PDP-11	Whitesmiths	Idris		
	Microsoft	Xenix		
	Mark Williams	Coherent		
6809	Technical System Consultants	Uniflex		
C/70	BBN Computer	Unix		
470	Amdahl	UTS		
3200	Wollongon Group	Unix		
	Perkin-Elmer	Unix		
VAX	Whitesmiths	Idris		

Defining silicon software

That buzzword, silicon software, is floating about the industry these days with a wide degree of variance as to just what it may refer to. For instance, a Basic interpreter in a read-only memory is certainly software in silicon but counts as true silicon software to very few.

To be precise, the term should be used only in reference to programs and subroutines that reside in silicon but are analogous to hardware components in the following important respects. Like a NAND gate, these components should not have to be modified. Further, the user should not have to know the internal workings of the device—just its capabilities and input/output protocols. Nor should the device assume that its external environment is fixed, like a particular board or system configuration. This rules out both the Basic interpreter mentioned above and monolithic operating systems that assume a fixed hardware environment or must be modified by the user to adapt to one.

Silicon software is really a component that complements a microprocessor by in effect extending its instruction set. Thus a set of floating-point math routines relieves programmers of having to code them themselves. Motorola Inc. of Austin, Texas, has just such a set of routines cast in silicon for its 68000 and 6809 microprocessors.

But more significant areas are those in which routines cast in silicon offer a modular yet interconnected set of primitives that lowers the level of programming skill needed. An example is those operating system primitives cast in silicon that allow the programmer to use a micro processor as if it had a built-in operating system.

Intel Corp. is offering such a solution—the iRMX-8 silicon operating system. Called the 80130, it solves hard ware dependencies by including the timers and counters real-time system needs on one and the same chip. Th Santa Clara, Calif., company also plans to offer CP/M in similar configuration.

This way of extending the instruction set of a micropro cessor promises to help alleviate the software enginee shortage of the 1980s exactly as large-scale integratio relieved the hardware engineer shortage of the 1960s—b lowering the level of the design skill required.

However, this path is fraught with peril, and a great de of care must be taken so as not to paint a design into corner. Software in silicon should never have to b changed. Therefore it must be broken down into parts th may be fitted together in different ways to solve the large possible array of problems, just as the 7400 TTL serie can provide the answer to a multitude of hardware prob lems. For instance, operating-system kernels in silico must allow for the addition of new peripheral devices the basic computer—The VRTX kernel from Hunter Ready Inc., Palo Alto, Calif., does this by referencin external tables that identify the location of user-define system calls. The kernel must also give users access to th routines it contains, which VRTX does, so that hardwar

---

is a package that includes not only an enhanced Unix operating system, but also a collection of utilities called the Programmer's Workbench that have won almost as much acclaim as Unix proper.

Unix, however, is not appropriate in all environments. First and foremost, it does not function in real time, for it does not include the mechanisms necessary to guarantee a minimum response time to external inputs. It cannot, therefore, be used in process-control environments and cannot even handle high-speed data transfers from remote devices without hardware buffering.

Unix is also no operating system for the computer-shy. Its command shell assumes a user sophistication that could spell disaster for the novice. Moreover, there is no mechanism to lock records to prevent more than one user from accessing them simultaneously. Also, an inadvertent system crash can destroy the hierarchical file directory, rendering important information—like accounts receivable—inaccessible. These inadequacies are well known, of course, and can be remedied by custom shells and file-protection enhancements made by the OEM. But without them, Unix remains an excellent program-development tool only.

Kind to people

In sharp contrast with Unix is an operating system whose major emphasis is on creating a user-friendly and highly protected business environment. Developed by Phase One Systems Inc. of Oakland, Calif., Oasis-16 has only recently been made over for the 8086, having originally been written for 8-bit Z80 systems.

Despite its orientation toward the less sophisticated office user, Oasis-16 offers facilities similar to those of Unix for program development—its system calls are functionally identical to Unix's. However, it adds a sophisticated job-control language that equips each user signing on the system with the equivalent of a custom shell. In contrast, Unix presents all system users with the same command language.

When a novice signs onto Oasis-16, his or her password can cue the system to present a console environment that lets that person perform one specific task only, thereby protecting the system from illiterate users. For example, it is possible for a data-entry program to be set up to be cued when one password is used, a word processor to be cued on another, and a full-access system-level shell to be made available to a trusted user.

Oasis-16's file structure is particularly well-thought-out for business applications. It employs a three-tier hierarchy with sequential, random, indexed-sequential access and unsorted but keyed files. Also, whenever a user gains access to a record, it is automatically locked—that is, no other user may have access to it.

Other built-in conveniences for the business community include an extensive help facility. This, like the cumbersome manual it replaces, can be used at any time to obtain information on just what certain commands mean, as well as just which of them are currently available as options at that particular point in a program. Also, all error messages are automatically generated with the cursor positioned upon the offending keystroke and with an explanation as to why that stroke is illegal and what can be done to fix it. Currently, Basic and C are the only languages available for Oasis-16, but Cobol is expected

specific conditions can be met. For example, when a task switch is made, the registers of any coprocessors in a system must be saved. The silicon operating system that allows the user to augment its assortment of routines may be updated to take advantage of the new devices as they become available in the marketplace.

Other silicon software candidates include data-base management systems and file managers for disk-based operating systems. Hunter & Ready plans one of the latter, to be complemented by a library of parts that will drive popular disk-drive-controller boards and chips.

One area already seeing an influx of preprogrammed silicon devices is data-communication protocols. But most of these are showing up on the read-only memories of single-chip microcomputers such as the Z8 from Zilog of Campbell, Calif., and Mostek Corp.'s 3870 series. Both Mostek of Carrollton, Texas, with its new 68200 chip—a 68000-like 16-bit microcomputer—and Texas Instruments of Dallas, with its 7000 series and 99000 series of 8- and 16-bit microcomputers, are promising whole catalogs of preprogrammed components. The silicon software in some of these parts will be so vast that TI plans to call them "intelligent memories," rather than microcomputers. Mostek plans 68200 parts that will perform the second and third levels of the seven-level Ethernet network protocol and will interface directly with the company's controller for the first level, the 68590.

later this year.

Inspired by Unix but designed to be more appropriate to the business market is the MP/M-86 operating system from Digital Research Inc. of Pacific Grove, Calif. (Table 3). MP/M-86 is the multiuser descendant of MP/M-80, the *de facto* standard of the 8-bit arena. However, MP/M-86 is unlikely to achieve a similar degree of dominance in the 16-bit arena, for there are other reputable software vendors out there today, unlike when CP/M was written in 1973 by Gary Kildall, now president of Digital Research, in frustration at the lack of any operating systems for the 8080 microprocessor.

Broadening the user base

MP/M-86 can be adapted to any disk-based system using an 8086 as its main engine and is currently being adapted to the 68000 under contract with Hitachi, whose alternate-sourcing agreement with Motorola has led it to initiate negotiations with several U. S. software houses.

Like Unix, MP/M-86 is a multiuser, multitasking operating system. MP/M-86 also has an OEM-configurable shell called the Terminal Message Processor. Thanks to this configurability, a custom shell can be produced that goes a long way to protecting the integrity of the system from the nontechnical user. However, most will go with the standard TMP for its similarity to CP/M.

Several features of the file system of MP/M-86 make it more suitable than Unix to business users. To prevent catastrophic information losses, the file structure uses multilevel directories rather than Unix's tree structure, and records are automatically locked for a more convenient and safer method of sharing data bases.

Unlike Unix, MP/M-86 has a real-time kernel that can be either interrupt-driven or dependent upon device polling. In the former and faster case, it requires from 400 to 600 microseconds to switch between tasks and disables the interrupt system for 150 μs. Thus it is not suitable for systems requiring a faster response than this. It does, however, use a pipe-like interprocess communication system that is faster and more flexible than Unix (which, after all, has less need of speed, being a time-sharing system). By using memory-resident queues, rather than disk files, as buffers for information, it is possible to pass data among processes much more quickly.

MP/M-86 can comfortably support approximately eight users on a 10-megahertz processor if each is running only one task. It partitions a maximum of 1 megabyte of memory into a variable number of segments that can range in size from 16 bytes to 1 megabyte. This partition size, however, is fixed at system-generation time. When a task makes a request to the operating system, it finds the number of contiguous free segments that best fit the calling task. If no contiguous space is large enough, then the task is delayed until one becomes available. To date, MP/M-86 supports no hardware memory-management units, though a version for the upcoming iAPX-286 with on-chip memory management is already in the works.

There does not exist as yet anything approaching the flexibility of Unix III's Programmer's Workbench as utilities to assist in program development for MP/M-86. But many application programs are becoming available, since Digital Research is adapting several popular 8-bit languages for execution under MP/M-86, including Pascal/MT and C-Basic.

The one or the many

So far, only multiuser operating systems have been discussed. However, the most common operating system is the kind designed to handle single-user, single-processor configurations. In many cases, this sort of operating system is entirely adequate.

Digital Research's CP/M is perhaps the most widely used of this type of operating system, and the company has high hopes that CP/M-86 will become just as prevalent in the 16-bit arena as CP/M-80 is in the 8-bit one. Consequently its appearance to the user was designed to be practically identical to that of its 8-bit predecessor. Moreover, it uses the same file structures as CP/M-80, making it much easier for programs to be updated to 16-bit status and to use common data bases.

The 8086 version of CP/M does, however, take advantage of the increased address space of that 16-bit processor, permitting up to 1 megabyte to be accessed. No hardware memory-management schemes are supported, since Digital Research prefers to wait till the 286 version of the 8086 (with on-chip memory management) is released. However, Intel is releasing a board that plugs into its micromodule bus, and Microsoft will utilize that board to give its Xenix-86 hardware memory-management support—and Digital Research might choose to follow suit.

CP/M requires only about 12-K bytes of memory to run in, as opposed to the over 50-K bytes needed by Unix. A

TABLE 3: COMPARISON OF TWO MULTIUSER OPERATING SYSTEMS		
	UNIX	**MP/M-86**
Software	large array of flexible system tools	small collection of system tools oriented toward development of application software
	extensive text processing	
	few end-user applications as yet	large array of end-user application software already on the market and written in high-level languages
Languages	C — system language	PL/I — application language
	Xenix: 　　Cobol 　　Basic interpreter	also from other vendors: 　　Pascal 　　Cobol 　　Fortran 　　Basic
Implementation	written in C	written in PL/M and optimized assembly code
	large but very flexible if source available	
		small, peripheral-independent
	no plan for peripheral independence	
		no need for source to add, modify drivers
	needs source to add or modify device drivers	
Support	all support must be supplied by OEM (Western Electric supplies only the source)	fully supported, OEMs add only drivers
Orientation	research and development	application and end user
Timesharing	multiterminal, multitask per terminal	multiterminal, multitask per terminal
Real-time control	not suitable due to large dispatch time	real-time kernel using device polling and interrupt flags
Process communication	PIPES — limited to character I/O between two processes; uses a fast disk file as a buffer; pipes are opened and closed as a standard file	QUEUES — variably sized messages written to and read from any number of processes; buffer maintained in memory; each queue has a name and is created, opened, read, written and deleted like disk files; queues optimized for message size; messages by value or address
File system	tree-structured directory	multilevel directory
	standard I/O	disk files as virtual consoles
User interface	programmer-oriented	end-user-oriented
	utilities can be connected through a single command	utilities must be executed sequentially

limitation is that it is a very minimal program-development tool, offering nowhere near the productivity factors of Unix, Oasis, and MP/M-86.

Unique to Digital Research is the fact that it offers a whole family of compatible operating systems for 8086-based machines. These include single-user plus single-tasking, single-user plus multitasking, and multiuser plus multitasking systems. Finally, a pair of networking operating systems—CP/NET-86 and MP/NET-86—will shortly hit the market, making it possible for separate microsystems to share expensive peripherals and files with both 8- and 16-bit microsystems and to link up with larger host machines.

A better mousetrap?

Another 8086-only operating system that was designed to emulate the CP/M-86 product is MS/DOS, which was written under contract to IBM Corp. by Microsoft for the Personal Computer. Like CP/M, MS/DOS is a single-user operating system designed primarily for running prepackaged application programs but also for developing small programs. Microsoft has rewritten compilers for all of its languages—Basic, Pascal, Fortran, and Cobol—for MS/DOS, so that any programs already written in those languages can be adapted to run under MS/DOS. For a specific OEM, the company has also adapted its languages to run under CP/M-86, but will not sell these adaptations directly to end users; nor will it support those copies sold by the OEM.

Like CP/M, MS/DOS consists of three parts: the basic Disk Operating System (DOS), the Command Processor (user interface), and a Basic Input/Output System (BIOS). Unlike CP/M-86, the BIOS is not linked into MS/DOS on the disk, so that updates of it can be made without having to perform a complicated system-generation procedure. Instead, a new BIOS is shipped to the customer, who merely dumps it on his system disk. The linking of the three parts of the operating system is done at run time.

An enhancement to CP/M is date-stamping of files so that newer versions can be easily identified. Also, the size of disk files is specified in the exact number of bytes, rather than in increments of 128 bytes, and file directories can be listed in several different abbreviated formats for users' convenience. Also there is no need to log in disks, as CP/M requires. MS-DOS keeps the disk directory in memory for fast access, but checks to make sure that a disk is still in place before it makes an access. Nor are code segments restricted to 64-K bytes as in CP/M-86.

Even error recovery is user-friendly. A copy, called a template, is made of each command line before it is executed. A bad command is redisplayed along with a statement, in English, as to why it is in error, plus suggestions as to how it can be fixed. The command can then be edited (Table 4) so that the whole line need not be retyped in the process.

Especially worth noting are the several graphics capabilities that Microsoft built into MS-DOS in order to take care of IBM's contractual specification of graphics statements in its version of Microsoft Basic. Later this year, those graphics routines will be moved from the DOS into the BIOS portion, so that other manufacturers with dif-

ferent types of hardware can take advantage of that capability added to Basic.

(As it happens, Digital Research also·plans to embed graphics capabilities in its BIOS for CP/M-86, perhaps utilizing the rich set of so-called core routines specified by the Association for Computing Machinery/Siggraph Graphics Standards Committee in 1979.)

Later this year Microsoft will release a second version of MS-DOS. It will include Unix-like pipes, a background task capability for simultaneous printing and processing, plus an OEM-configurable BIOS. At present, the BIOS can be configured only by Microsoft itself. Version 2 will also move one step closer to compatibility with Xenix by supplying the utilities that are necessary to compile

TABLE 4: EDITING FUNCTIONS FOR COMMAND LINES	
MS-DOS Command	Function
Copy one character	copy one character from the template — copy of bad command line — to the new line
Copy up to character	copy all characters from the template to the new line up to the character specified
Copy template	copy all remaining characters in the template to the new line
Skip one character	do not copy (skip over) a character in the template
Skip up to character	do not copy (skip over) the characters in the template up to the character specified
Quit input	void the current input; leave the template unchanged
Insert mode	enter insert mode
Replace mode	exit insert mode (toggle from insert); default
New template	make the new line the new template

programs on Xenix but to execute them under MS-DOS.

The single-user operating system to which it is easiest to transport 8-bit software is one that was originally developed by the University of California at San Diego but is now owned and sold by SofTech Microsystems of San Diego, Calif., under the name of the UCSD p-System. Its compatibility with 8-bit programs is due to the system's use of an intermediate code called p-code, into which all its high-level languages are compiled. Whenever a new processor is introduced, the p-System can be implemented on it simply by writing an interpreter that translates p-code into the new processor's native code. This is a far easier task than rewriting all the high-level languages in the native tongue of the new processor. The penalty, of course, is the reduced execution speed of interpreted code in comparison with compiled code. So far, the UCSD p-System is available for the 8086, 9900, 68000, Z8000, and IBM's Personal Comput-

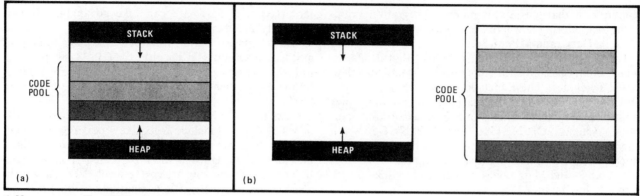

1. Memory map. The UCSD p-System can organize memory according to the microprocessor on which it is running. In all cases, it maintains a stack and heap that grow from upper and lower memory toward each other. The code pool can be between them (a) or in its own space (b).

er. Also Texas Instruments has just signed a contract with SofTech to distribute the p-System with its whole range of micro- and mini-computer systems.

The user interface with the p-System displays the user's current command options along the bottom of the display at all times, and all commands can be abbreviated to single keystrokes. It is also possible to configure the system to come up running an application program, so that novice users do not have to learn how to use the operating system. An integral screen-oriented editor is included, as well as a background printer-spooler.

The p-System supports Fortran and Basic, in addition to the Pascal in which it is written. An interesting by-product of the whole system's being in p-code is that the upgrading of one part of the system is inherited by the rest. For instance, version IV includes the ability to embed the native code of the processor being used within interpreted p-code. In this way critical portions of programs can be put in native code for higher speed, while the rest of the program is left in p-code for the memory space savings that results. This feature is available on all the languages since it has been implemented at the p-code level. The source code of the high-level languages simply includes delimiters indicating the segments to be translated into native code by a utility program that is run by the user before execution.

Processor-independent

The main-memory–management scheme is especially well-thought-out. It is designed to be processor-independent, so that the architectural features of present or future processors may be exploited. It supports dynamically relocatable code and data segments that may or may not occupy separate memory spaces. A stack area (Fig. 1) grows downward from high memory and is used in the conventional manner to store process activation records and variables under evaluation. A heap (an indexed pile of temporary data) grows from lower memory upward and contains the dynamic variables that are managed by the routines that interpret the p-code. In machines that support separate code and data spaces, code is kept in a separate space (Fig. 1b), whereas in machines that support only a single space (Fig. 1a) code is stored between the stack and the heap. In either case, code is swapped into memory dynamically using intelligent algorithms, so that programs are unlimited by main

memory size except with regard to their execution speed.

However, it is often the case that the single user would like to run more than one program simultaneously. The classic example of this is printing out a file—there is nothing more frustrating than waiting for a slow line printer to finish printing before continuing work. In a multitasking system, though, the user can start one task, like printing, and then continue with his or her work without having to wait for the printing to finish.

This sort of foreground-background processing has been a feature of minicomputer operating systems for years. In fact, under many operating systems the user can run many more than two programs simultaneously from the same terminal, and so may start a compilation, print out a file, send another message file over a modem to a remote site, and still be able to use a word processor to edit or compose a new file, all simultaneously. All of the multiuser operating systems discussed have this capability, but very few single-user ones do. One of these exceptions is a new version of CP/M-86 called Concurrent CP/M-86, featuring prioritized multitasking.

Concurrent CP/M-86 is actually a stripped-down version of MP/M-86, with all the routines that were needed only for multiusers pulled out and a new OEM-configurable screen formatter put in. The OEM can configure the system to display the separate tasks running in individual windows or on overlapping pages or in the same way that MP/M-86 does—by executing a status command that merely notifies the user which tasks are running.

A new operating system configured for single-user multitasking with both the 68000 and Z8000 is MSP from Hemenway Associates of Boston. It uses the status command style for task identification and includes all the facilities necessary for real-time intertask communications as well. Tasks can start and stop each other, as well as pass information among themselves, by using a real-time clock and what is called the mailbox method. (In this method, tasks leave messages for each other at a given memory location, which they always check for "mail" before carrying out any operation.)

Like Concurrent CP/M-86, tasks are arranged by priority so that the user can dedicate more processor time to more important ones, as well as suspend, resume, and kill them. MSP also has gleaned many of Unix's best features, like standard I/O, but has a more highly protected file system and fits in only 16-K bytes. □

Electronics/May 8, 1980

C language's grip on hardware makes sense for small computers

Versatile structured syntax also permits adjustment of program portability, length, and speed of execution

by M. S. Krieger and P. J. Plauger
Whitesmiths Ltd., New York, N. Y.

☐ Minicomputer and microcomputer programmers often start out short on memory space and machine speed, and so take it as axiomatic that assembly language must be used to program their small machines. But there are obvious productivity gains to be had from structured high-level languages, gains that are at least as important in microprocessor work as they are in mainframe work. And high-level languages offer the possibility that machine-independent code can be written, leaving the software investment less at the mercy of any one hardware vendor.

How can the benefits of a high-level language be realized without paying penalties in code space and execution time? One solution is to pick the right language and use it on several different computers, while paying careful attention to both efficiency and portability. Whitesmiths Ltd. chose the language C, developed at Bell Laboratories and used widely throughout the Bell System, as the best tool for writing large quantities of software for small computers.

In the past year, two to three programmers have delivered over 30,000 lines of documented code that supports C programming on microprocessors and minicomputers. Compilers are currently available for Digital Equipment Corp.'s LSI-11, PDP 11/04, 11/34, and 11/70, and VAX-11/780; Intel Corp.'s 8080 and 8085; and Zilog Inc.'s Z80. Intel's 8086 and 8088 microprocessors are also supported, but as emulations of their simpler precursors, and are not yet used to full advantage. Support for Motorola Inc.'s MC68000 is currently being readied as well.

All PDP 11–based code makes use of the extended instruction set and the floating-point processor whenever possible, but versions of the code are also available that use neither or only one of these hardware options. This assortment represents a broad range of hardware capable of supporting identically the same program.

Along with the C compiler comes an extensive library of portable routines, including functions for performing formatted and random input/output on a variety of operating systems, including RT-11/RSTS CP/M, CDOS, RSX-11M/IAS, ISIS-II, VMS, and UNIX/Idris.

The C language

C was developed by Dennis Ritchie at Bell Laboratories, Murray Hill, N. J., about 10 years ago; compilers for C on the PDP 11 have been operational since the early 1970s. C is not machine-dependent, so programs can be freely transported from machine to machine with the not unreasonable expectation that they will run correctly without modification. Furthermore, there are no committees meeting to determine a standard C; rather, Appendix A of "The C Programming Language," by B. W. Kernighan and D. M. Ritchie (Prentice-Hall, 1978), serves to define C.

The language mirrors the abilities of many different processor architectures and produces particularly efficient code as a result. The need to break into assembly language for efficiency's sake is exceedingly rare. For example, the UNIX operating system, which served as initial host and testbed for C, has been rewritten almost completely in C over the past several years. UNIX is not

Pointer arithmetic in C

One of the C programming language's unique advantages is that it permits extensive manipulation of pointers—variables that can be used as machine addresses. Languages such as Fortran implicitly pass pointers on subroutine calls (on a call-by-reference basis), so that changes are made to the original variable and not just to a temporary copy. Pascal permits only pointer assignment and copying; modification must take the form of subscripting, as in the Fortran array references.

In C, the statement:

```
int a [10], i, *p;
```

declares an array of 10 integers called a, an integer i, and a pointer to integer p. Thereafter, the following statements can be written:

```
p = &i; /* p now points at i */
*p = 3; /* i is assigned 3 */
```

More importantly, consider the traditional loop for clearing 10 elements of the array a in Fortran:

```
      do 100 i = 1,10
      a(i) = 0
100 continue
```

This can be written in C as:

```
for (i = 0; i < 10; + +i)
   a[i] = 0;
```

or, using pointers:

```
for (p = a; p < &a[10]; + +p)
   *p = 0;
```

Note that + +i adds 1 to the integer i, but + +p adds 2 to p on a computer with 2-byte integers. Pointers are adjusted by multiples of the size of the objects pointed to.

Pointer arithmetic frequently leads to more efficient programs—an important consideration in operating systems and microcomputer applications. In the program above, the inner loop using pointers, *p = 0, is much more efficient than a [i] = 0, which requires a multiplication and an addition before the assignment can be made. The standard method in C, for instance, of copying a null-terminated string is to use source and destination pointers and to write:

```
cpystr(s, d)
   register char *s, *d;
   {
   while ((*d + + = *s + +) != '\0');
   }
```

On an LSI-11, the move loop in this function body takes only 4 bytes of code; on VAX it takes 5 bytes.

The danger in using pointers is that program errors cause wild storage overwrites that are very hard to debug. It is also easier to write programs that are hard to read, as the last example suggests. C, however, seems to provide just enough checking of pointer usage to catch the worst offenses, but not enough to interfere with flexible use.

---

only a well-designed and reliable system, but is at least as efficient as systems operating on comparable hardware.

UNIX has been transported to at least three other computers, and Whitesmiths Ltd. has developed a smaller operating system, called Idris, with most of the external characteristics of UNIX, also written mostly in a highly portable version of C. Idris currently supports several simultaneous users on an LSI-11, with reasonable response.

C provides the usual control-flow statements (if-then-else, while, for, and case) found in most modern structured programming languages. It provides both simple and complex data types, and new types may be created through a definition facility called typedef.

Extensive data types

Among C's simple data types are bit fields, characters, short and long integers, pointers, and short and long floating-point quantities. Complex objects are built from the simple types, or from other complex objects, by repetition (array of), sequencing (struct), and alternation (union). The words in parenthesis are the names of the associated types.

The major advantage of this full set of data types is that any construct that arises in system programming, including hardware control registers, can be represented in C. Furthermore, if the hardware can be addressed in memory, as on the PDP 11 Unibus, then it can be directly manipulated from within a C program. It is significant that all input and output drivers provided

with the UNIX system are written exclusively in C.

C functions are called by value. Simple data objects passed to functions have their values passed rather than their addresses, making it impossible to accidentally overwrite the original. Since the value of a pointer may be passed, calls by reference are also provided.

All C functions are recursive; it is an easy matter to automatically declare variables local to a function, so that a fresh set of them is allocated on the stack for each call. If a local variable is known to be heavily used, the programmer can request that it be held in a register, and, up to the limit of machine resources, the compiler will accommodate the request. Judicious use of registers can dramatically reduce the size and execution time of a program.

C programs are generally represented as sequences of data objects and function bodies within multiple files. Data objects may be global to all program files, local to a specific program file, or local to a specific range of code within a function. Static data, even complex structures, may be initialized at compiling time. The language itself does not provide a controlled storage class, but that is provided by the library functions alloc and free, which administer a run-time heap. The language also has no input/output statements; once again, ample facilities are provided by the portable library.

C has a richer-than-usual set of arithmetic operators, but confines its operands to scalars (integers, floating-point numbers, and pointers), so that code explosion is minimized. For example, a whole array will never be implicitly copied by what looks like a simple assignment.

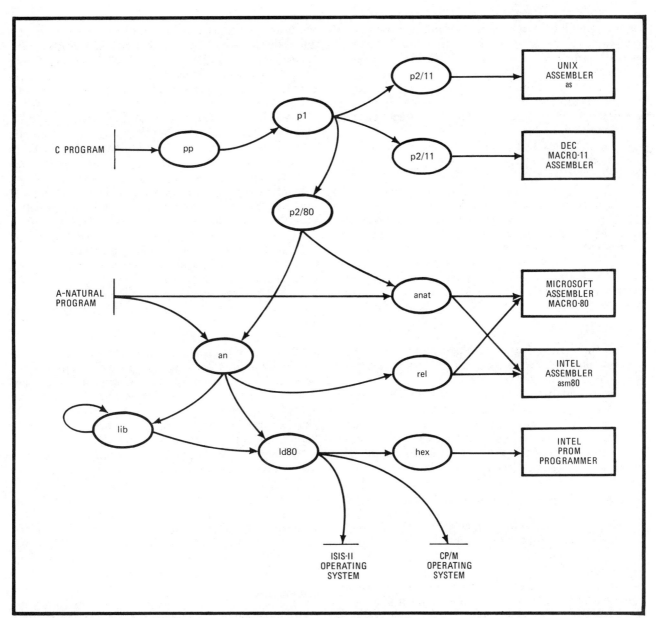

1. Translation. Each bubble represents a separate program that does part of the translation of an application program in C or A-Natural into a number of different forms. Output can be fed directly to standard operating systems or assemblers used with PDP 11s and 8080s.

One method of improving object-code efficiency is to use one of the many assigning operators of C. The value of variable y is added to the doubly dimensioned array a (represented as a [i] [j] in C) by:

a [i] [j] + = y;

This is the same as a [i] [j] = a [i] [j] + y except that the elaborate expression on the left side of the first expression need be evaluated only once, effecting a much tighter code sequence.

Mixed-mode expressions are widely permitted in C, since all meaningful type conversions are defined. The following are all valid C statements:

double d;
char c;
int i;
int *p; /* p is a pointer */

p = i; /* pointer gets integer */
c = d; /* character gets double floating */
i = d; /* integer gets double floating */
d = c; /* double floating gets character */

A pointer may not be multiplied by seven, however (an operation not likely to be useful); but the programmer is explicitly permitted to assign an absolute machine address—which looks like an integer—to a pointer, a very useful license for low-level handlers. (See "Pointer arithmetic in C,")

By judiciously relaxing its type checking in certain places such as this, C permits code that must normally be written in assembly language to be intermixed with normal data manipulations. That way, maintaining mixed code in two different languages can often be avoided, and the data manipulations at least can be kept readable.

It is difficult to say precisely how efficient the code

produced by the C compiler is. The best indicator is that the output of the compiler can typically be pared down by 15%, with relatively little effort, in the hands of an experienced assembler programmer. With considerable rethinking and rearrangement, that same programmer can often gain an additional 15% saving in memory requirements. The same savings apply to execution time, as a general rule.

Note that this is not the same as saying that an assembler programmer will always beat the C compiler by 30%. Even ignoring the tremendous savings in coding time gained from writing in a higher-level language, the much higher error rate that comes with assembly language programming must also be considered. Compilers are not as inventive as humans, but they do not get tired.

Whatever the true cost of using C, Whitesmiths has found that it is more than repaid in lower programming costs. And since software costs are large and growing, while read-only memory and microprocessor costs are small and shrinking, the benefits can only increase.

Portability

It is important to write machine-dependent code only with malice aforethought, keeping trickery isolated to a minimum number of program files. This takes planning, standards, and discipline—three things that many people have tried in vain to legislate through compilers with stringent checking. C does not really attempt to perform this testing because no matter how persnickety a compiler is, programmers can still write bad programs unless they adopt a style and standards not easily enforced by the machine. Since this added discipline is unavoidable, it may as well be used to supplement a simpler and more flexible language. (The only real justification for this approach, however, is that it works.)

Those 30,000 lines of code mentioned earlier break down into 3,000 lines of assembler support for two machines, 4,000 lines of system-dependent C for five systems, 11,000 lines of machine-targeted C, and 13,000 lines of highly portable C. Machine-targeted C refers to programs such as code generators and assemblers; code that can run on any computer that supports C but whose output is eventually useful only on one machine—an 8080 cross compiler based on PDP 11, for instance.

Note that three quarters of this code is portable in the usual sense of being able to run unchanged on multiple systems, and that nearly half is truly indifferent to its environment. Applications programs should fit almost exclusively into this last, most portable category.

Machine-independent C is written with no knowledge of the hardware or operating system on which it will run; it calls on the portable C library for all input and output. In addition, certain known pitfalls are avoided, such as assuming that integers are a given size, or that bytes within an integer occur in a given order. This style is not hard to master, but does require constant attention to avoid lapses.

System-dependent C is used by systems programmers to write operating systems or interfaces to operating systems. The RSX-11M library, for instance, includes a function called emt, which permits an arbitrary system call to be generated via the standard emulator-trap

hardware mechanism on the PDP 11. Needless to say, any code that uses emt is necessarily tied to RSX-11M or one of its ilk. But writing in C makes the code easier to write and to maintain. Other functions permit synchronous or asynchronous system traps and Fortran IV function calls.

Machine-dependent C is used by systems programmers to write those parts of an operating system that talk directly to the hardware. In addition to the numerous PDP 11 examples that benefit from Unibus addressing, there are the 8080 functions, like in(port) and out(port, data), that permit arbitrary input and output from a C function. Hence, even on the 8080, I/O drivers can often be written purely in C.

The point is that by rigorously factoring code into these three categories, one can keep a remarkable quantity of the software for any application highly portable, to reduce the amount of code that must be written when moving to a new machine. The implementer can thus obtain the cross product of applications programs and machines.

A simple example of this cross-product effect is Whitesmiths' e program, a text editor used to enter and edit programs and ordinary text (including this article). Written in machine-independent C, e relies on the system-dependent interface to talk to any of a variety of operating systems. It consists of approximately 2,000 lines of C code, and was originally implemented on a PDP 11 under the Idris operating system.

By simply cross-compiling the C code for the 8080, e was moved to an 8080 running CP/M. By recompiling e on the PDP 11 running under RSX-11M or RT-11, the editor was made available for those systems as well. The very same tool is thus present on a variety of systems. The user avoids having to learn new editors often and the editor can be made available to diverse users. The result is a very popular utility that runs on several operating systems, and it can be made to run on many more.

C translation

A C program can be processed in many ways, depending upon the output desired. Each of the bubbles in Fig. 1 is a separate Whitesmiths program that does part of the translation process; the square boxes represent the standard assemblers and operating systems used with PDP 11s and 8080s. A C program is first preprocessed (by pp) to include parameter files and to define manifest constants. For instance, if the file x.c contained:

```
#include "file.h"
#define EOF -1
. . .
```

then file.h would be included in the input stream, and any subsequent occurrences of the manifest constant EOF (end of file) would result in its value being taken as -1. The resulting stream of data is fed to passl (pl) which performs all remaining semantic checking and produces a flow graph with imbedded expressions for subsequent code generation.

For the PDP 11, a code generator (p2) produces either UNIX assembler code or MACRO-11 for the various operating systems of Digital Equipment Corp.; a similar

A natural assembly language

The output of Whitesmiths Ltd.'s 8080 code generator is A-Natural, a narrative assembly language that is easier to read and write than conventional assembler code. It features uniform register names and simple operator notation, plus a precedence-free left-to-right translation:

a = *bc + *hl → *hl

is A-Natural for the 8080 instructions:

```
LDAX   B
ADD    M
MOV    M,A
```

Note that the leftmost operand in the A-Natural expression is used repeatedly across the line, making it easy to express multiple operations on an accumulator. The above example could have been written:

```
a = *bc
a + *hl / answer in a
a → *hl / move answer into *hl
```

The following two sample functions are the only ones in A-Natural needed in the portable ISIS-II interface, reflecting the two places where C code is not sufficient. The first is ihdr.8:

```
/   ihdr.8
/ copyright © 1979 by Whitesmiths Ltd.
/ startup code for C under ISIS
public start
public isis.
start:
    sp = &stack / put the address of stack (in iend)
                     into sp register
    call _main / call the main C function
```

```
sp ← bc / put the completion code onto the stack
call exit. / exit from C environment
isis.:        / isis interface packed with ihdr
    c = *(hl = 2 + sp) / system code from stack
    de → sp = ʌ (hl + 1 + 1) / cb address from stack
                            / first save de
    call isis / address of isis found in iend.8 (40)
    sp → de / restore de
    bc = (hl = 4 + sp) / get return code
    ret
```

The second function is iend.8:

```
/   iend.8
/ copyright © 1979 by Whitesmiths Ltd.
/ system parameters for C
public isis
public _memory
public stack
isis: = 0x40 / isis system is found at hex 40
stack: = 0xf600 / isis default stack at hex f600
_memory.: / iend should be loaded last and _memory.
          will point to the beginning of usable memory
```

When loading or binding a C program to run under ISIS, ihdr.8 is placed first and iend.8 is placed last. Thus, ihdr will be entered at the start of a program; it will call the user's C main program, and exit. The isis interface is packed with ihdr. It too must be written in A-Natural assembler language, since the ISIS calling sequence is not compatible with that used with C. The iend.8 function includes only those constants that must be known to ihdr or other C functions. In particular, '_memory.', a constant known to the C interface, must be loaded statically as the last data location.

---

pair of generators talks to either VAX/VMS or VAX/UNIX. The output of the 8080 code generator is always A-Natural, a narrative assembly language developed by Whitesmiths (see "A natural assembly language," above).

A-Natural code is either translated (anat) into an existing assembler language or assembled (an) into relocatable binary code for use with the Whitesmiths librarian (lib) and loader (1d80). The output can then be executed on an existing 8080 system, or used to program read-only memories for free-standing applications.

Thus, a C program can be compiled and tested on a PDP 11 under, say, RT-11, then transported to an 8080 for final checkout. Even free-standing code can be largely checked out in a more hospitable environment, with suitable machine-level stubs, before being unleashed.

Popularity contest

The widespread adoption of UNIX among universities has bred a generation of C enthusiasts that are only now coming into the labor force in real numbers. And since C has become a *de facto* standard programming language in the Bell System, now in use on upwards of 1,000 small and large computers, it is probably going to be around for a while.

This is a safe bet even given the popularity of Pascal and the strong government backing of Ada. The former is a much smaller language than C that must inevitably be extended to be useful outside its original sphere of discourse: expressing student programs in a teaching environment. Pascal implementations tend to be either nonstandard or nonportable.

Ada, on the other hand, is a much larger language than C and requires many services that are usually considered part of the operating system. Since no operating system currently exists that can support Ada without change, it will be some time before anywhere near the full language is available. And even the simplest use of Ada may well call for more run-time baggage than most small computers can support.

Regardless of the eventual success of these competing languages, C is here now and growing fast. Implementations are springing up on the newer microprocessors and minicomputers, and ever greater quantities of C code are appearing in the marketplace. C compilers have been announced for the Motorola 6800, the Zilog Z8000, and the Intel 8086, among other popular machines. Whitesmiths plans at least two—possibly three—new code generators in the next year.

It is ironic that the ability to write very machine-dependent code with C has encouraged its portability. By filling the gap between assembly language and traditional high-level languages, C has succeeded in wooing numerous converts from both camps. □

Electronics/December 4, 1980

High-level language takes on most of real-time system software

Pascal extension can handle operating system functions like peripheral device drivers and data sharing

by Cynthia Fulton and Richard Whiffen, *Enertec Inc., Lansdale, Pa.*

☐ Operating systems for microprocessors and minicomputers can be written in a derivative of Pascal that combines the ease of high-level language programming with the efficiency of the assembly language approach. Designed for the purpose, Micro Concurrent Pascal (mCP) responds to the demands of multitasking by adopting a highly structured approach to protecting shared data areas.

Standard high-level languages perform tasks sequentially and provide no facilities for real-time responses to interrupts or even bit-level manipulation. They therefore make it cumbersome to handle the real-time concurrent events of a multitasking operating system. For this job, assembly language has been the traditional choice, despite the difficulty of debugging, maintaining, and modifying programs written in it. But a simpler means of system implementation has become necessary as the growth in the variety of microprocessors has caused a corresponding increase in the variety of assembly languages.

Basically, a mCP program takes over the multitasking and device driver functions of a conventional operating system, leaving just the scheduling functions behind in what is called a kernel. This kernel and a mCP interpreter are written in the assembly language of a given microprocessor. But the mCP programs can be run on any suitably equipped microprocessor.

Concurrent Pascal

Micro Concurrent Pascal is a modification of Concurrent Pascal, which was developed by Per Brinch Hansen on the basis of the ideas of Niklaus Wirth, C. A. R. Hoare, and E. Djikstra. Concurrent Pascal can handle multiple processes that run independently but share data and communicate with each other. In other words, it is designed for system programming. Yet as a superset of Pascal, it also satisfies the requirements for application programming.

Concurrent Pascal is more modular than its parent, Pascal, and even better suited for top-down structured design. It adopts and enforces that philosophy on the programmer even more heavily than Pascal does—an important asset in the real-time programming world of the operating system, where process scheduling and resource management are critical. Its structured nature also makes it easy to divide a large software project among a team of programmers. Like Pascal, Concurrent Pascal offers the programmer not just the standard data types (integer, real, character, and boolean) but also user-defined data structures with strong data-type checking by the compiler to prevent programmer errors in this area.

Concurrent Pascal differs from Pascal in making use of processes and monitors. These processes and monitors are system component types—that is, the programmer defines their make-up and format, later creating specific

TABLE 1: HOW MICRO CONCURRENT PASCAL DIFFERS FROM SEQUENTIAL PASCAL	
Constructs added	**Description**
Processes	the system components that execute code
Monitors	shared-data structures plus the routine that processes call to operate on that data
Device monitor	variant of a monitor through which processes communicate with peripheral devices; it permits the writing of device drivers directly in mCP
Class	a monitor that can be accessed only by a process that is specified at compilation time
Delay	a statement used to stop execution of a process until some external event such as an interrupt occurs
Continue	a statement used to restart a process stopped by a delay statement
Queue	a variable type used with delay and continue statements to determine when a process should execute (similar to a semaphore)
DOIO	a statement permissible only in a device monitor that causes execution to wait for an interrupt
Initial	a statement that creates instances of system component types (variables, processes, monitors, etc.)
Structured constants	memory-saving feature that allows fixed constants to be initialized and used in place of variables or immediate values
Constructs deleted	**Description**
Recursion	recursive routines are not allowed
Dynamic heap	all memory allocation is done at compilation time; no POINTER data types or NEW procedures are allowed
Standard input/ output	standard Pascal I/O routines do not appear since users are now expected to be able to write their own custom versions easily

TABLE 2: DEVICE MONITOR FOR A UNIVERSAL ASYNCHRONOUS RECEIVER TRANSMITTER	
PROGRAM	COMMENTS
UART WRITE	THIS ROUTINE WRITES A LINE TO A MICROCOMPUTER'S 8251 UART.
CONST	DEFINE SEVERAL CONSTANTS.
LINELENGTH = 72;	LENGTH OF LINE IS 72 CHARACTERS.
NUL = '(:0:)';	A NUL IS ALL ZEROS.
TBE BIT = 2;	TRANSMITTER-BUFFER-EMPTY IS BIT 2.
REQ_TO_SEND = #26;	REQUEST-TO-SEND INITIATED BY 26_{16}.
WAIT_TO_SEND = #27;	TERMINATE REQ_TO_SEND BY 27_{16}, THEN WAIT.
TYPE	DEFINE SYSTEM COMPONENT TYPES.
LINE = ARRAY [1 . . LINELENGTH] OF CHAR;	LINE IS A 1-BY-72 ARRAY OF CHARACTERS.
UART_WRITE = DEVICE_MON (CTRL_WORD,	UART_WRITE IS DEVICE MONITOR: CTRL_WORD AND
DATA_WORD: ADDRESS;	DATA_WORD ARE ADDRESS OF UART'S CONTROL AND
SELECTOR: INTEGER);	DATA REGISTER; SELECTOR IS INTERRUPT NUMBER.
PROCEDURE ENTRY WRITE (MESSAGE: LINE);	WRITE A MESSAGE OF TYPE LINE TO UART.
VAR I: INTEGER;	DECLARE COUNTER VARIABLE I.
BEGIN	ENTER BLOCK THAT TRANSMITS A LINE.
REPEAT UNTIL (INN (CTRL_WORD) AND TBE_BIT) 〈〉 0;	TEST UNTIL TRANSMITTER BUFFER IS EMPTY.
OUT (REQ_TO_SEND, CTRL_WORD);	MAKE REQUEST-TO-SEND ACTIVE.
OUT (WAIT_TO_SEND, CTRL_WORD);	THEN DE-ACTIVATE
DOIO;	AND WAIT FOR CLEAR-TO-SEND INTERRUPT.
I: = 1;	SET CHARACTER COUNTER TO FIRST CHARACTER.
WHILE (MESSAGE [I] 〈〉 NUL) AND (I 〈= LINELENGTH) DO	CHECK FOR NUL OR COUNTER 〉 72
BEGIN	AND SEND MESSAGE.
OUT (ORD (MESSAGE [I], DATA_WORD);	TRANSMIT ITH CHARACTER.
DOIO;	WAIT FOR CLEAR-TO-SEND INTERRUPT.
INC (I);	THEN INCREMENT CHARACTER COUNTER.
END;	CONTINUE SENDING MESSAGE.
END;	EXIT WRITE PROCEDURE.

instances or variables of these component types.

Processes are application programs written to communicate through monitors instead of a conventional operating system. They represent system activities, and several of them may run simultaneously and are continually operative. For example, a typical Concurrent Pascal program would contain a process for the real-time clock, an operator process representing possible operator actions, and other processes as needed to represent various other system tasks (see "The basics of Micro Concurrent Pascal,").

Role of the monitors

A monitor is the only means through which the processes can communicate with each other. It is an area of shared data and a group of procedures and functions that can operate on that shared data. Different processes gain access to data in a monitor by calling a procedure or function resident in it and thereby operate on and share its data. For instance, the process for a time-of-day clock might call a procedure in a monitor to write the time into that monitor, making it available for access by another process—for example, one that prints the time of day on a user's program listing.

Data protection is enforced by the language itself. Only one process at a time may be executing code within a monitor—the kernel code implementing the procedure call ensures that. If a process calls a procedure in an active monitor in which another process is executing code, that process is blocked until the current one exits or delays. Delay and continue statements, permissible only within monitors, enable processes to be blocked and resumed, respectively. They serve much the same purpose as the traditional semaphores—flags that are set before entering a routine to signal that it will be in use.

Monitors further support structured design by isolating data formats. Since the logical organization of a shared data structure is known only to its monitor, only procedures within that monitor need be modified to operate on updated data formats. If interfaces to external processes are preserved, then no code outside of the monitor is affected by changes in the data representation within it. In other words, Concurrent Pascal correctly assumes that it is safer to communicate via calls to monitors than via shared data structures, which would require all routines that use that data to be changed so as to recognize updated versions.

Micro Concurrent Pascal

In concept and general implementation, Concurrent Pascal is an excellent language for the dedicated real-time application programming that can take over many of the functions of the operating system. But it does have limitations. It requires that all processes be declared at compilation time, and it is therefore not a suitable language for timesharing operating systems, in which the

The basics of Micro Concurrent Pascal

The high-level language called Micro Concurrent Pascal has been designed to handle system as well as application software. It takes over two key functions of the operating system of a microprocessor-based system—its data-sharing and device-driver capabilities. To implement them, mCP employs software modules called monitors. The mCP application programs, or processes, used to read and write devices like a time-of-day clock and a user's terminal, communicate with one another only through a shared-data monitor and with their associated hardware through the device monitors. Shorn of all but its scheduling functions, the operating system is called a kernel. The kernel is written in assembly language and is accompanied by an interpreter.

The two diagrams refer to a simple microprocessor-based system that allows a time-of-day clock to be set and read from a user's terminal. The first illustrates the conventional distribution of software functions between an assembly language operating system and application programs written in Pascal. The second shows the redistribu-

tion of functions made by the Micro Concurrent Pascal approach.

A possible sequence of events in the mCP system might be as follows. The clock interrupts the microprocessor (not shown), alerting the kernel, which promptly transfers system control to the clock process. This process first uses the clock device monitor to find out the time and then puts the information in the shared-data time monitor. In performing these two tasks, the process uses the interpreter to turn its compiled mCP statements into executable machine code.

The clock data might in this way be routinely updated by the system every second. Meanwhile, the operator of the terminal may at some point ask for the time. As before, the kernel deduces that the microprocessor has been interrupted by the terminal and transfers system control to the terminal process. That process collects the current time from the shared-data time monitor and passes it on to the terminal via the terminal device monitor for display to the user.　　　**-R. Colin Johnson**

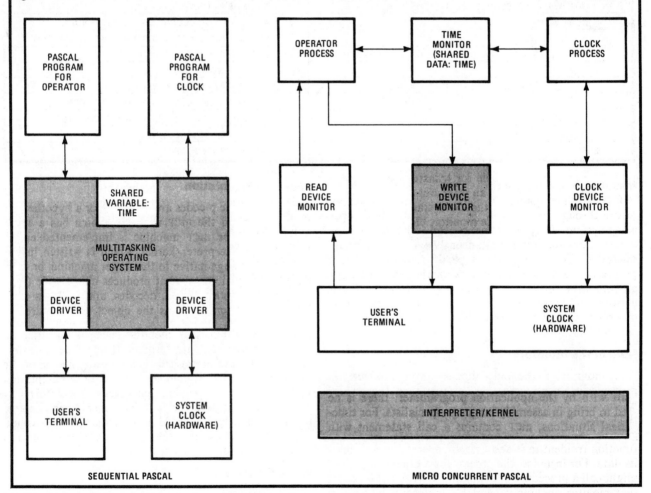

number of operator processes varies. mCP at present also has this limitation, though a version that allows processes to be created and destroyed dynamically is under development.

The mCP language is derived from Concurrent Pascal, but specifically tailored for mini- and micro-computer

use (Table 1). The most important extension (and one of the primary goals) of mCP was to adapt the language for writing device drivers—routines designed to communicate with peripherals. Thus the task of writing device drivers and other system-level software need no longer be viewed with foreboding because the mCP language

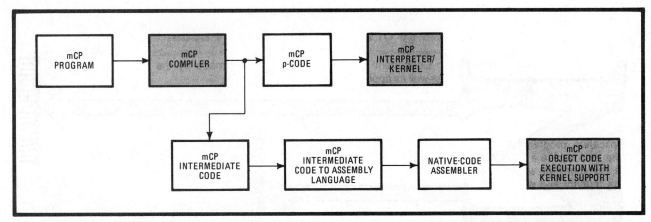

1. Two routes. In one method of implementing a mCP program, the p-code statements are decoded by an interpreter at run time. Alternatively, another intermediate code may be translated into assembly language and then native object code for direct execution.

includes extensions that allow all of this low-level software to be developed very conveniently.

A system implementation language should provide a means for realizing the architectural potential of a microcomputer, including its interrupt facilities. So mCP introduces a construct called a peripheral device monitor, a variant of a normal monitor, as a major means to this goal. Table 2 is an example of a device monitor.

In mCP, as in Concurrent Pascal, peripheral device operation and the interrupt service routines associated with it are considered a single process. A process calls a device monitor in the same manner as it calls a normal monitor, except that a symbolically determined interrupt is associated with each device monitor. The kernel contains a table of addresses that shows the whereabouts of the device monitor corresponding to each external interrupt; this table is responsible for transferring control to the monitor whenever such an interrupt occurs. Another language construct, called the DOIO statement and permissible only within a device monitor, blocks the process that called it until the associated interrupt has occurred. At that point, the currently running process is blocked and the process waiting for the interrupt is resumed. The interrupt table is the only part of an entire real-time application program that must be coded in assembly language—all the rest can be written in mCP.

Devices that do not generate interrupts and instead must be polled—checking a bit to see if the device is ready—are handled by additional language constructs for addressing hardware directly and manipulating data bits. Consequently, peripheral communication can be dealt with by the application programmer; there is no need to bring in assembly language specialists. For time-critical situations, mCP contains a call statement with which assembly language subroutines can be called upon by monitors and device monitors.

Still other constructs in mCP reduce memory requirements. The most important of these, as far as the programming language itself is concerned, is the recognition of the size of an integer by its type declaration and structured constants. String-manipulation intrinsic routines are also included in mCP as a space-saving modification since these functions do not require special subroutines. Other features that reap minor improvements include the address data type, hexadecimal constants,

and a default clause in the CASE statement.

mCP is implemented via a compiler and an interpreter with the option of also producing directly executable object code. The mCP compiler is a series of stand-alone programs written in sequential Pascal, accepting mCP programs as input and generating pseudo-code (p-code) as output. The mCP compiler will run on any host system that has a sequential Pascal compiler. Currently it is available on Hewlett-Packard, Digital Equipment, and Data General minicomputers as well as IBM mainframes. The mCP p-code may either be interpreted or used to generate pure object code for most popular microprocessors. A single p-code statement translates into several statements in assembly language. This makes mCP p-code comparable to, if not smaller in size than, pure assembly-language code.

mCP implementation

At present, the p-codes are designed for a hypothetical computer, called the mCP machine, which has a stack architecture. The mCP machine is implemented either via the mCP interpreter/kernel, which is written in the assembly language native to the target machine, or by a second compilation step that produces object code (Fig. 1). The interpreter fetches, decodes, and executes each p-code instruction, whereas the object code is directly executable.

Currently interpreters are available for Z80, 8080/85 and 1802 microprocessors, and others for the 6809, 68000, Z8000, and 8086 are nearing completion. This affords program transportability to both existing and future microprocessors. Since all data references and jumps are relative, the p-code output by the compiler is relocatable anywhere in the memory of the target machine. The p-code was also designed to reside in ROM since it does not modify itself.

The kernel is responsible for multiplexing the microprocessor among concurrent processes and giving processes exclusive access to monitors. Process switching, process synchronization, and machine-dependent details such as interrupt recognition and vectoring are all handled by the kernel. Thus the kernel directs the activity of the microprocessor, allowing the user to concern himself only with algorithmic manipulations of data. The kernel is typically about 512 bytes long. □

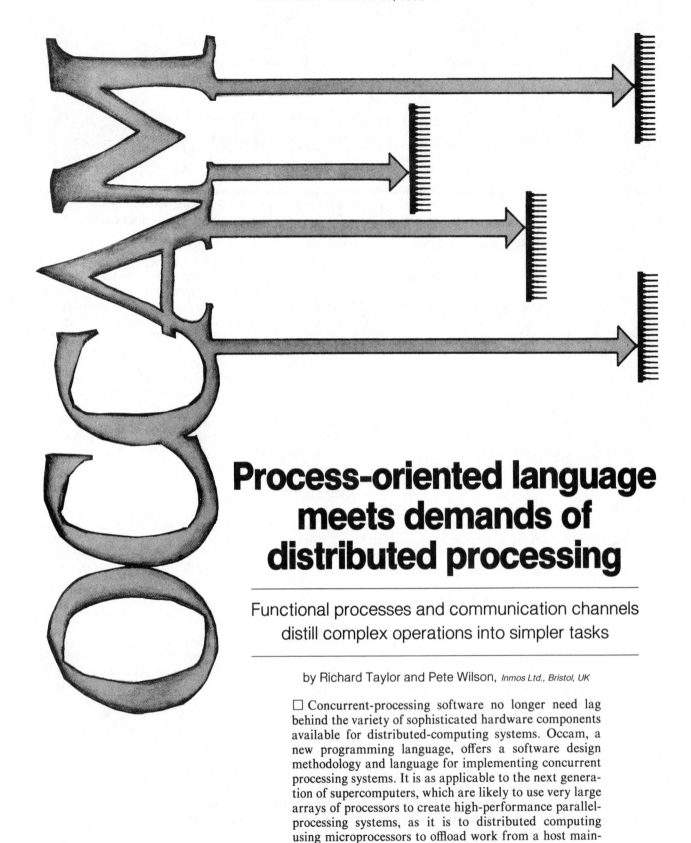

Process-oriented language meets demands of distributed processing

Functional processes and communication channels
distill complex operations into simpler tasks

by Richard Taylor and Pete Wilson, *Inmos Ltd., Bristol, UK*

☐ Concurrent-processing software no longer need lag behind the variety of sophisticated hardware components available for distributed-computing systems. Occam, a new programming language, offers a software design methodology and language for implementing concurrent processing systems. It is as applicable to the next generation of supercomputers, which are likely to use very large arrays of processors to create high-performance parallel-processing systems, as it is to distributed computing using microprocessors to offload work from a host mainframe computer.

Occam gets its name from the medieval postulate known as Occam's razor, which holds that entities should not be multipled unnecessarily. Put another way, the argument is to reject complex propositions in favor of simpler ones whenever possible. The new language's name reflects the decision that its design would be bound by Occam's razor, that concurrency can be expressed by a few relatively simple software constructs.

Although system designers and many application programmers must routinely incorporate features of concurrent processing in their work, they have been forced to design and implement software systems with sequential programming languages. Occam resolves this paradox by introducing a few simple constructions built around a pair of structures that logically mirror the important functions of concurrent systems: parallel processing of independent activities and communication between these parallel activities.

A process—the fundamental working element in Occam—is a single statement, group of statements, or even a group of other processes and is responsible for handling one prescribed activity. Functionally, then, it is a group of statements (or processes) that share the same context. For an Occam compiler, a group of contiguous lines of code, whether statements or processes, indented at the same level share the same context.

On the other hand, a channel is the fundamental communication element that allows concurrent processes to communicate with each other. Connecting exactly two of these processes, a channel is an unbuffered structure and allows information to pass in one direction only. It can be considered a synchronization device, allowing two processes to transfer information. Thus, a channel behaves as a read-only element to a receiving process and a write-only element to a transmitting process. The transmitter can write only when the channel is empty, while the receiver can read only when the channel is full. Writing fills the channel, and reading empties it.

In Occam, concurrency goes right down to the lowest level of the language. Individual statements are processes that can run in parallel with each other. Language statements are grouped together by constructors that allow individual statements or groups of statements to be executed in parallel or in sequence, or for one out of a set to be selected for execution depending on some logical condition. Along with a looping mechanism, these constructors complete the major control structure recognized by the Occam compiler (see table). By retaining simplicity with this fundamental set of constructs, the language ensures that its own structure is not a barrier between a designer's view of a problem and the problem's representation in Occam.

Hardware mirror

Processes communicate with each other by sending and receiving messages. Occam provides a channel to link them, just as a data path links a pair of hardware units that communicate with each other. In fact, the simple model of processes and communication for Occam corresponds exactly to the behavior of real electronic systems, setting the language apart from attempts others have made to capture the concept of the process.

Two pieces of equipment that wish to communicate asynchronously often employ a handshaking protocol. Thus they have a means of transferring the data between themselves, together with a means of signaling whether or not they are ready for communication.

When the sender wishes to transmit a value to the other, the receiver may not be prepared, so the sender will hang up until the other indicates that it is ready. When the receiver is ready, the data value is transferred and both sender and receiver resume their respective tasks. A similar situation arises if the receiver was prepared to receive before the sender was ready.

Two concurrent Occam processes communicate in exactly the same way. The process that is prepared to transfer the value hangs up until the other is ready; and after the transfer, each continues its own way. The processes may actually be multiplexed onto a single physical processor, in which case the operation of hanging and resuming will be handled by calls to a run-time system. (Here, though, the required operations are simpler than the usual semaphore implementations commonly used in multitasking operating systems.)

In hardware, the unbuffered handshaking transfer is not always good enough. Often, peak data rates can cause a mismatch between the sender and receiver, despite the fact that they both can achieve the same average throughput rates. In this case, a simple first-in-first-out buffer between the two pieces of hardware will smooth out such peaks and valleys in throughput.

In Occam, the same options are available in software (Fig. 1). Naturally, the FIFO buffer will be a process rather than hardware memory, but the Occam FIFO is really no more than a description of the function of the hardware buffer and is similarly interposed between the two original processes. Rather than the two processes communicating directly, the sending process will send data to the FIFO process, which will in turn hand it on to the receiving process.

Simple structure

The notion of simplicity begins in Occam with the fundamental definitions that underlie its structure. Besides a basic assignment process—such as setting one value equal to another, as in A:=B—Occam defines only two additional primitive processes, input and output. The channel in Occam—an entity defined by the keyword CHAN, as in "CHAN link"—is the central element in both of these processes.

In an output process, some value is sent through a channel to an input process that also recognizes the channel. Thus, the output process link!A, would use the named channel "link" to send the value A. At the other end of the channel, an input process, link?B, would accept the value and store it in some location called B.

To control the order of execution of such processes, Occam identifies three fundamental mechanisms—sequential (SEQ), parallel (PAR), and alternate (ALT)—besides the conventional WHILE and IF constructions. Statements or processes contained within the context of SEQ or PAR are executed in sequence or in parallel, respectively. ALT, on the other hand, causes one and only one statement or process to be executed. Which one of several statements in the ALT context is executed depends on a guarding condition: an input process or a logical statement. The ALT construction, although simi-

OCCAM SYNTAX		
Keyword	Example	Comments
SEQ	SEQ in?char out!char SEQ i=[0 FOR 100] sum:=sum+array[i]	sequential block of processes do this first . . . then this FOR loop to sum elements of an array
PAR	PAR out1!'A' out2!'B' PAR i=[0 FOR 100] array[i]:=0	parallel block of processes do this . . . and this simultaneously replicator creates 100 parallal processes initialize array simultaneously
ALT	ALT in1?char out!char in2?char out!char ALT i=[0 FOR 10] inputs[i] ?char out!char	alternate block get character from either in1 and output it or in2 and output it select one of 10 inputs for an array of channels and output char from the one active channel
WHILE	WHILE x>0 SEQ in?x out!x	keep on looping on this set of instructions read then write until 0 is read
IF	IF x<0 x:=−x	traditional conditional return absolute value
VAR	VAR char: VAR array[100] :	declare a variable named "char" declare an array of 100 elements
CHAN	CHAN in: CHAN inputs[100] :	declare a channel named "in" declare an array of channels
BYTE	char:=array(BYTE i)	access i^{th} byte of an array
PROC	PROC echo(CHAN in,out)= WHILE TRUE VAR x: SEQ in?x out!x: (example of use) CHAN kb[32] : CHAN pr[32] : PAR i=[0 FOR 32] echo(kb[i],pr[i])	define an abstraction called "echo" make process go on forever declare a variable execute sequence get input when ready output when ready declare keyboard channels and their associated printer channels echo in parallel for all the terminals

lar to a parallel IF, differs in that one choice must be made. The process will not continue past the ALT until at least one of the guarding conditions is true. Thus,

```
ALT
    keyboard1?char
        screen!char
    keyboard2?char
        screen!char
```

will accept the first character typed on either keyboard and send it to the screen. (This scenario might apply in some type of game program, for example, where the first to react wins some advantage.) On the other hand,

```
SEQ
    keyboard1.input?char
    keyboard1.output!char
```

would echo a character—repeat it by writing back to the keyboard what was just read from it. In a multiterminal environment, PAR could be used to echo, say, two terminals in parallel:

```
PAR
    VAR char:
    SEQ
        keyboard1.input?char
        keyboard1.output!char
    VAR char:
    SEQ
        keyboard2.input?char
        keyboard2.output!char
```

This example of the use of PAR illustrates an additional pair of principles of Occam. The various primitive constructions may be combined, such as parallel sets of sequentially executed statements or processes, and indenting identifies the context of a statement for the compiler, as opposed to the use of additional keywords to muddy the clarity of the language. More significantly, this use of PAR demonstrates how an Occam program is able to mirror the concurrent nature of hardware. Thus, unlike sequential languages that force designers to invent tricks to match the concurrent nature of hardware, Occam meets the demands of implementation of concurrent systems with just a few constructions.

Designing with Occam

Occam is not just a language for implementing concurrent systems, but is also intended as a design tool. In its design-aid role, it is capable of describing a design all the way from an abstract high-level description down to a compilable program—all with the same notation. In fact, with some care, a program representing a high-level design description can be compiled and even executed. With such techniques, designers gain insight into design flaws and omissions while the design is still at a high level, permitting much easier and less costly change. Furthermore, the ability to use Occam to describe the hardware aspects of a system design lightens the burden of integrating software with hardware.

Occam's support of system design is well illustrated in a simple example of a small process controller. A combination alarm clock and teamaker is a simple consumer item that can soften the blow of a wake-up call with a freshly brewed cup of tea or coffee.

Starting with a diagram of the subsystems that form the beverage maker (Fig. 2a), the design at this level would look like a network of boxes, representing the functional unit, connected by labeled lines, representing the interactions between the subsystems. A designer can map this diagram directly into an Occam program with

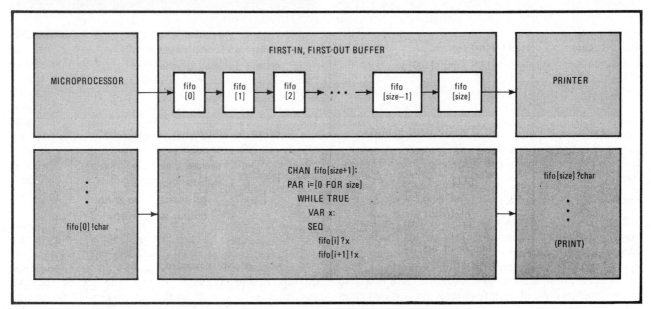

1. Hardware analog. Executed in parallel, three Occam processes simulate a microprocessor passing data to a printer through a first-in, first-out buffer The processes directly correspond to their hardware counterparts.

Creating an Occam compiler

In designing and implementing an Occam compiler, the major considerations are the choice of processes and channels, the multiplexing of these processes on the processor, and the mechanisms for communication between an Occam program and the external world. With the choice of the UCSD p-system as the first target system, dealing with these factors did not prove to be difficult. UCSD Pascal supports the concept of processes directly, although for synchronization it uses its own construction of semaphores, rather than channels. Consequently, an Occam process is a p-machine process, while a channel in this language is a word shared between two processes with two associated semaphores, namely channel-in and channel-out (below, left).

But arranging for process to communicate is only half the battle; the processor must be shared fairly among all the processes that are ready to run. In the present p-system implementation of Occam, arranging for this multiplexing is accomplished by inserting switch operations inside all loops (below, center). Switch is really a pair of Pascal statements: "wait switch-in," followed by "signal switch-out."

One more process called switch is needed, taking the form shown below, right. The switch process is executed between each slice of each of the user's Occam processes. Since each process then signals and waits in turn with the shared semaphores, this has the effect of a round-robin scheduler.

Access to the host's screen, keyboard, and filing system is easy to arrange. The outside world is represented to an Occam program as a set of channels that are mapped onto the facilities of the host computer. Two predeclared processes—write-text-to and read-text-from—allow Occam programs to read from and write to arbitrary files or devices.

This initial Occam compiler us simply an evaluation kit, giving a low-cost introduction to the concepts of concurrency to those used to thinking in terms of sequential programming. Occam programs using it are restricted to running on a single processor, and at a speed limited to the interpretation of p-code.

Programming microprocessors to utilize Occam to its full advantage will require using more sophisticated tools. A complete design package including an editor, compiler, and debugging aids will be available for 8086- and 68000-family processors.

```
    channel?variable
becomes
    WAIT channel-in;
    variable: = contents(channel);
    SIGNAL channel-out;
and
    channel!variable
becomes
    contents(channel): = variable;
    SIGNAL channel-in;
    WAIT channel-out;
```

```
WHILE TRUE
SEQ
    . . .
becomes
WHILE TRUE
SEQ
    . . .
    SWITCH
```

```
WHILE TRUE DO
    BEGIN
        SIGNAL switch-in;
        WAIT switch-out;
    END;
```

processes replacing the boxes and channels replacing the lines (Fig. 2b). At this stage, the design merely identifies some processes and channels, but does not yet specify the detailed tasks associated with each process.

Although not yet complete, the Occam program would indicate the control flow of the subsystem. As a designer adds detail for each subsequent level of the subsystem design, the specific tasks of each process would become more clearly defined. The increased detail will provide a further check on the validity of the overall design. When all the details are filled in, the designer has not only a complete specification of the system, but also a complete compilable program.

Facilitating team work

This example of the design methodology that the language brings to system design is applicable for more general problems and is well suited to the team-oriented approaches to design. Starting from a high-level functional description of the system, a design team establishes the specifications of each functional process and channel. From that point, the team members are free to work independently on different processes, assured that their individual contributions will interact properly with the completed system.

The various design trade-offs that make up a complete system, such as number of processors and number of input/output devices, will generally mean that design will iterate toward a solution agreeable to the team as a whole. Because of the direct mapping of the Occam representation onto the physical architecture, these iterations are completed relatively painlessly. As a bonus, the parts of the system that can proceed in parallel are clearly identifiable with the PAR construction. This identification furnishes a very simple method for the same program to be executed on a number of different hardware topologies, which may be single- or even multiple-processor systems.

Occam's use in this way as a system description language, not just a programming language, rests on two bases. First, all the parts of a real system of course exist simultaneously, or concurrently. This fact is represented directly in the language through the use of the PAR construct around a collection of processes. Sequential languages, on the other hand, cannot represent this physical reality. By their nature, they must call the

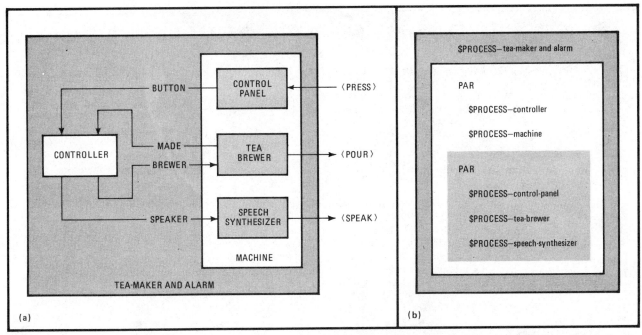

2. Hierarchical design. In Occam, each level of concurrent hardware processing (a) maps directly into a set of processes (b) sharing the same PAR context. Here the machine components, tinted in (a), share the same level of concurrency, tinted in (b).

individual parts of the system one after the other, discarding each in turn as execution of the program proceeds to the next call.

Secondly, the meaning and form of Occam's elements—the primitive processes and their associated constructs—have been carefully defined in logical terms so that Occam programs may be reasoned about formally. This feature improves the likelihood that individual designers will understand the actual properties of their systems and leaves the door open to future possibilities of formal program proving.

Although such abstract properties make Occam an object of interest to language theorists, its concrete capabilities bring a practical design and implementation tool to microprocessor system designers. Because of the simplicity of its world view, it is entirely suitable for programming currently available microprocessors. In addition to its ability to capture all the software elements of a system in a single unified view, it has a run-time memory and performance nearer those of assembly-language programs than is the case with typical high-level languages like Pascal.

Implementing Occam

When implementing Occam on a microprocessor, the main decisions to be made are how to represent the two fundamental structures—the process and the channel—and how the processor is to be multiplexed among the processes.

In an implementation on an MC68000, each process is represented by a small area of storage called the process base. Here, housekeeping information provides the necessary data for manipulating the process and the process's local variables. All of the bases for processes that can be executed are built up into a simple queue, with the head of the queue being the process that is currently active.

Multiplexing the processes onto a single physical processor is the task of the run-time system. Handling the various housekeeping chores needed to effect this operation, the run-time system is similar to the kernel of an operating system and can be implemented for a typical microprocessor in less than 100 instructions. For most machines, the most difficult aspect of the run-time system is the interrupt-handling software subsystem.

Most languages balk at the problems imposed by interrupt handling. Typically, programmers are forced to sidestep the problem by resorting to assembly-language routines that capture the data and queue it up for processing by background tasks written in the high-level language. Occam allows a more consistent approach, however, because its structures that are designed for multiprocessing can be used for multitasking functions like interrupt handling.

Handling interrupts

In an Occam system, a processor with an interrupt levels is modeled as $n+1$ processor-type processes multiplexed onto one real processor. Each modeled processor has its own scheduler and population of processes, and communication between these $n+1$ virtual processors is accomplished by message passing. The conventional interrupt routine awaiting an interrupt becomes a process in the appropriate virtual processor, handling some hardware channel. An interrupt signal will then cause the real processor's interrupt-handling hardware mechanism—along with some software support from the run-time system—to switch to the execution of the process handling the hardware channel.

For concurrent operations outside the realm of interrupt handling, the run-time system will include a simple scheduler. With interrupts handled properly, a round-robin scheduler that can perform timeslicing will often be adequate.

On the razor's edge in performance

Parallel architectures represent a means for duplicating the high performance mainframe computers with a large number of processors, each individually much lower in performance and cost. The systolic array processor, developed by H. T. Kung at Carnegie-Mellon University [*Electronics*, June 2, p. 46], represents one such technique. In these processors, data values are continuously pumped through an array of simple processing elements. Since each processing element operates in parallel on the same values, they can speed up a computational processes while keeping bus transfer rates low.

Occam proves to be well suited to designing and simulating systolic arrays. For example, a systolic processor used to perform matrix multiplication would consist of a two-dimensional array of elements. One matrix enters the array from the left, while the other matrix enters from the top. As data values from the two matrices pass through each processing element, they are multiplied together and accumulated. When the two matrices have passed through the array, each processing element will have accumulated a word of the final matrix.

A program in Occam that describes the action of a processing element would combine the serial sequence of parallel data movement and multiplication, followed by parallel data movement (below, left).

Each processing element—"mult"—has two input channels—up and left—and two output channels—down and right. After first receiving the two input values—a and b—the values are multiplied and accumulated. Only after this step has completed are the two values passed "down" or to the "right." Because the array consists of parallel elements, these input and output processes may occur simultaneously.

The whole array of processing elements and all the connecting channels can be described by one Occam program that uses the "mult" process (below, right). This example shows how arrays of vertical and horizontal channels can be declared in the language and connected up to arrays of "mult" processors created by using the parallel replication command.

```
PROC mult
  (CHAN up,down,left,right) =
VAR r,a,b:
SEQ
  r: = 0
  SEQ i = [0 FOR n]
  SEQ
    PAR
      up?a
      left?b
    r: = r + (a*b)
    PAR
      down!a
      right!b:
```

```
CHANS vertical [n*(n + 1)]:
CHANS horizontal [n*(n + 1)]:
PAR i = [0 FOR n]
  PAR j = [0 FOR n]
    mult(vertical[ (n*i + j],
         vertical[ (n*i) + j + 1],
         horizontal[ (n*i) + j],
         horizontal[ (n*(i + 1)) + j] ])
```

On a processor not explicitly designed for process support, excessive use of parallelism in programs will exact a performance penalty due to the scheduling overhead costs. This penalty will be not be more than the cost of equivalent operations in an industry-standard kernel. Thus the benefits of expressing the whole design in one form—as an Occam program—are not lost.

Bypassing operating systems

By using Occam, implementers may avoid an operating system. The work that an operating system does in supporting concurrency and communication is handled better and more naturally, thus simplifying design and implementation. In fact, the utilities that an operating system offers are better represented as Occam processes.

The language is not limited to use in traditional architectures. Designers wishing to explore new parallel architectures that exploit the strengths of very large-scale integration will find it to be an ideal notation for describing their systems. With Occam as a design and programming language, standard microprocessors can be easily assembled into a multiprocessor system, such as a systolic processor (see "On the razor's edge in performance," above). In such a machine, each processing element consists of a microprocessor, some memory chips, some connecting logic elements, and parallel I/O chips. As an example, a 68000 could be used with four 6821 peripheral interface adapters. The two ports in each PIA would be used to implement two channels in the systolic array—the A port for output and the B port for input—with the control lines used as usual to effect the handshaking.

Such relatively small multiprocessor arrays foreshadow future complex systems such as the fifth-generation supercomputers expected to implement knowledge-based, or expert, systems. These architectures have been viewed as consisting of a very large number of interconnected elements, each with local processing and storage capabilities. Much doubt has arisen concerning whether the current state of the art actually provides the conceptual tools needed to comprehend the behavior of such systems, let alone the algorithms needed to make them work. Such languages as Prolog deal with the application-level task of encoding knowledge and reasoning rules for the expert system. Occam is ideal for the other, more hardware-oriented task of understanding how to make the processors cooperate optimally.

Besides providing a design language for high-level descriptions of the behavior of these systems, Occam furnishes programmers with a highly efficient means to implement complex software systems because of its close relationship to the underlying hardware base. However, its system-level capabilities do not exclude its use in writing application programs. Any complex function may be programmed as a process and used just as functions or procedures are used in a sequential language. In this respect, Occam is similar to the languages C and BCPL. □

Computer graphics needs standards as a foundation for future growth

Software and interface standards must pave the way for successive generations of VLSI to transform the face of computer displays

by Miles Lewitt and Bruce Cohen
Intel Corp., Hillsboro, Ore.

☐ Computer terminals are coming alive with graphics, displaying colorful images as varied as Disney animation or circuit schematics. But this transformation will be realized to its fullest extent only if computer graphics standards are generally adopted to enable different manufacturers from different countries to work in concert. New applications of computers are emerging even now, thanks to graphics, and more traditional applications are undergoing a metamorphosis as computer graphics comes into its own.

The advantages of mixing graphics and computers are obvious, from easier and friendlier user communication to the more immediate transmission of information that can be achieved only by pictures. Industry experts believe that by 1985 most computer-based systems will have some sort of graphics capability.

The technology and the recognition of computer graphics' advantages are over 20 years old. It is coming of age only now, however, because of the advent of the very large-scale integrated circuits that have made the requisite hardware affordable. VLSI presents the system designer with the opportunity to build graphics systems lower in cost, higher in performance and density, and with more reliability than ever before.

However, systems that are not designed to allow the incorporation of future technological advancements risk rapid obsolescence. Therefore, designers are challenged to create systems that can remain competitive by easily assimilating successive generations of VLSI

The widespread use of graphics will be hastened by timely acceptance of standards. Although the recent level of activity in graphics standards has heightened, the industry still needs wider participation, an understanding of the task's importance, and a spirit of cooperation.

In the last decade, many organizations and individuals have worked on standardizing computer graphics interfaces. Professional groups such as the Association for Computing Machinery have advocated and worked on the development of standards. Also, equally intent on realizing that goal, standards agencies such as the American National Standards Institute and the International Standards Organization have formed technical committees to develop graphic standards.[1,2]

On the move

Each of the groups working on graphics standards has been motivated differently, but all seek a standard interface for computer graphics. Portability is the prime need. For example, in application software, graphics users want their software to be portable from one host computer to another and from one operating system to another. Besides releasing users from a sole-source trap, portability also slows the obsolesence of software by allowing it to run on successive generations of computers. For the vendors of the hardware, it increases the available market for their products.

Another aspect of portability is device independence, or display portability. This allows a graphics application program to use any of a number of different display devices without "knowing" about each device's individual characteristics. Even similar technologies are not a prerequisite for the displays. For instance, a pen-plotter

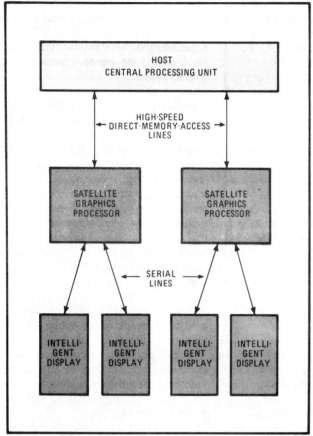

1. Spread it around. A typical distributed graphics system today will probably have graphics functions in at least three levels of hierarchy. The application packages may be in the host, imaging, or viewing functions in satellite graphics processors and in device drivers and display controllers in intelligent display units.

and a raster-scanned cathode-ray-tube terminal could work with the software equally well. Device independence lets a graphics system be tailored for its application environment without a major effort aimed at rewriting existing software.

A third aspect of portability is image portability. Identical pictures reproduced on different devices should look as much alike as possible. Image portability makes a graphics system less hostile to someone with no computer expertise.

Standards for communicating and storing images are as important as those for generating them. If a standard exists for representing the contents of a picture, then the picture can be sent from one place to another by any means or be stored for a while and played back on a different device.

Two trends in the advancement of graphics systems architecture in the last few years have been distributed systems and the development of specialized subsystems. Graphic computations that a decade ago would have been performed in a host computer directly controlling a graphics display can now be done in a satellite processor. This processor can in turn be connected to an intelligent display device (Fig. 1).

Without a standard interface with graphics functions, each step in the development of distributed architectures

has required the development of new software to allow the parts of the system to talk to each other. New generations of VLSI graphic-display controllers will result in yet another raft of software changes unless standards are adopted. With such standards in hand, systems can be upgraded by replacing an old generation of chips with a new generation having the same interface.

The great controversy

The graphics standard effort in the U. S. over the last 10 years has been intensive, but it is only now beginning to produce standards that the industry is likely to adopt. Great controversy has surrounded all attempts at standardization because standards must serve many application areas and system technologies.

In the mid-1970s, the Special Interest Group on Graphics (Siggraph) of the ACM worked to develop a standard that would provide both two- and three-dimensional graphic functions that could be implemented with different levels of functionality, from simple to more sophisticated, in order to serve both large and small systems. In 1979 the Siggraph group called the Graphics Standards Planning Committee decided to hand over this proposed standard, called the GSPC Core, or simply Core, to ANSI to be developed into an American national standard. The ANSI X3H3 technical committee formed for this purpose included many of the Core developers. Attempts by vendors to market Core implementations designed to the 1979 Siggraph document have resulted in a number of interfaces—all, unfortunately, mutually incompatible to some degree.

Many graphics manufacturers and users have implemented the proposed Core standard anyway under the assumption that something approaching a standard is better than none at all. However, in what may be a breakthrough, the X3H3 committee on computer graphics voted overwhelmingly last October to seek formal approval of the European-developed Graphical Kernel System as a U. S. standard for device-independent graphics software. The executive committee of Siggraph is now investigating alternate methods of obtaining a recognized standard for the Core interface to provide standardization for the many users of existing Core packages.

GKS, a 2-d graphics interface, is similar in function to Core—which in addition encompasses 3-d graphics—but it is somewhat different in philosophy. Core was developed for a number of applications—computer-aided design and manufacturing being the main ones—in which the representation of an image is controlled by the user.

For example, employing a Core graphics software system, a user could set a line's color to be red and its style to be dashed. However, GKS's designers chose to emphasize distinguishability over control of representation. This means that GKS can ensure that two lines that must be distinguished will be represented differently but that the user may not be able to control how they differ. For instance, though the user can draw a red-dashed triangle and a blue solid-line circle with a Core system, he or she may try the same thing with a GKS system but the system may render these as a black wide solid-line triangle and black dashed thin-line circle.

Another difficulty for GKS is that many systems origi-

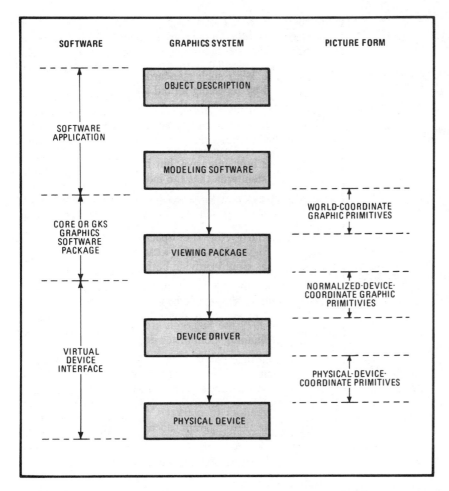

SOFTWARE	GRAPHICS SYSTEM	PICTURE FORM

OBJECT DESCRIPTION

SOFTWARE APPLICATION

MODELING SOFTWARE

WORLD-COORDINATE GRAPHIC PRIMITIVES

CORE OR GKS GRAPHICS SOFTWARE PACKAGE

VIEWING PACKAGE

NORMALIZED-DEVICE-COORDINATE GRAPHIC PRIMITIVIES

VIRTUAL DEVICE INTERFACE

DEVICE DRIVER

PHYSICAL-DEVICE-COORDINATE PRIMITIVES

PHYSICAL DEVICE

2. Pathway to pictures. From a description of an object in application software to a picture of that object on a display screen or on paper, a particular set of steps and processes are becoming the standard procedure in graphics systems.

nating in the U. S. are up and running with Core as a basis. However, one major difference is currently being ironed out, as work is under way in Europe to extend GKS to cover 3-d functions. Moreover, the ANSI X3H3 committee has expressed interest in helping or even leading this effort so that users who switch from Core to GKS will not lose functionality.

The Core task group of X3H3 is working on a much-extended standard called the Programmer's Hierarchical Interactive Graphics Standard (PHIGS). This standard is aimed at very sophisticated computer modeling applications employing graphics for realistic representations of objects. Though its development has just begun, the future of PHIGS may be brighter than that of Core because of its greater sweep.

With GKS as the likeliest candidate for a widespresd standard now, ANSI effort remains directed at making it an American standard and expanding it into a family of standards. Because it interfaces with only one level of the graphics hierarchy, the viewing-package level that turns the computer model into a picture (Fig. 2), the X3H3 committee is also working on the Virtual Device Interface (VDI) and Virtual Device Metafile (VDM) standards proposals, which address the interface at the device level. VDM, which ANSI will present to ISO for consideration as an international standard, is scheduled for public review in mid-1983. It deals with file-format standards for storing and transmitting a picture in terms of device-level primitives in the form of coordinates. VDI, the standard

for converting the output of the viewing package into the physical-device primitives, will follow in six to nine months.

In addition, X3H3 is writing a standard for a Programmer's Minimal Interface to Graphics. PMIG is at the same level of the hierarchy as Core, but it is compatible at a minimal level with GKS. It is intended for use by programmers with little or no graphics expertise, in application areas such as business graphics or graphic arts. The draft American GKS and PMIG standards are scheduled to be available for public review by the middle of 1983.[2]

Then again, just to complicate the matter further, the intense interest in videotex, the interactive communication of text and graphics between central data bases and terminals, has resulted in a number of standards for the encoding of that information. The North American Presentation Level Protocol Syntax, the most ambitious yet, grew out of the Canadian Telidon system. Telidon, adopted by AT&T and enhanced as a standard for the transmission of text and graphic information, rose again as the North American standard.

The videotex and teletext working group of the ANSI X3L2 technical committee on character codes, in cooperation with the Canadian Standards Association working group on videotex, has developed a technical specification with the AT&T standard as a baseline.[3] The document was accepted as a preliminary standard by CSA and was published for public review by ANSI in January 1983.

Some companies have already started investigating the possibility of expanding the functionality of the NAPLPS standard. Because one of the design goals for the standard was that the interface be extensible, it should be easy for users to add such functions. Those extensions that are the most widely applicable will no doubt present a good case to be added to the standard at a later date.

The primitive state

Graphics interface standards have been proposed at several levels of the hierarchy of a graphics system (Fig. 3). Application software deals with descriptions of the geometry and topology of the objects to be displayed. These objects are described in world coordinates which are the usual X, Y coordinates in 2-d space or the X, Y, Z coordinates in 3-d space.

In CAD applications, these descriptions would be of real objects, such as gears and bearings in 3-d space

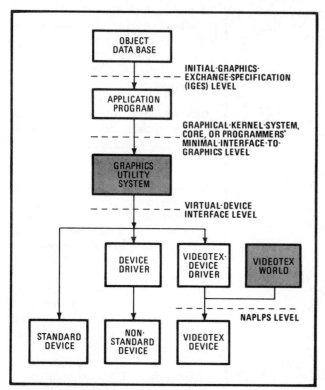

3. Standards hierarchy. Current and proposed graphics standards specify interfaces at four levels of hierarchy in a typical graphics system. The IGES is a communications file structure for the exchange of data in computer-aided design systems. Other standards to which the hierarchy applies are GKS, CORE, PMIG, VDI, and NAPLPS.

using a standard set of high-level graphic primitives. In a business application, the description might be of points and lines on a chart, with the world coordinates as the units used for the chart.

The graphic primitives in world coordinates are transformed by the viewing package into a lower-level set of primitives expressed in what are called normalized or virtual-device coordinates, that is, coordinates for an idealized device. This transformation produces image data that is ready for a display device. For a particular device, a device driver will transform the virtual-device coordinates into commands for that device. If the world-coordinate space is 3-d, the viewing package might perform a perspective projection onto a viewing plane.

The proposed Core and GKS standards are examples of standard interfaces with the viewing package, which changes the description of a picture into a picture. Because of the standards' relatively high level in the system hierarchy and their inclusion of 3-d capability (in development for GKS), they are or will likely be extensively used in CAD and other sophisticated applications.

At the next level down, the virtual-device interface standard is intended as a single standard supporting as many types of graphics devices as possible with the same set of functions. The devices can range from pen-plotters to raster-scanned displays to microfilm recorders. The design philosophy of VDI is a balance between the simplicity desired for a low-level interface to allow it run efficiently in a variety of environments and the sophistication required to adequately support the expected range

of higher-level graphics packages, that is, those that employ GKS or other higher-level standards. Its companion standard, the virtual-device metafile, or VDM, is being developed in parallel with VDI. The VDM is a standard means of storing or transmitting pictures.

Because VDI and VDM provide device-independent interfaces for display, storage, and transmission of graphic information, they do not exploit any one display technology to its full potential. Raster-scanned display, where dots are displayed line by line and appropriately turned on or off, is becoming the most widely used technology for graphic display because of the low cost of television-based displays and the use of VLSI—the cost per bit of VLSI memory continues to decrease and the performace and functionality per dollar of VLSI central processing units keeps going up. This trend is expected by most observers of the industry to continue in the next few years. It would therefore seem advantageous for the industry to adopt a standard interface especially suited to raster-scanning graphic information.

The NAPLPS is such a standard. It provides a common means of interchanging graphic information either by communication lines like telephones or satellites or by computer storage media such as floppy disks or magnetic-tape cartridges. It is designed for raster graphics devices and standardizes several methods of compressing the descriptions of graphic and pictorial information for efficiency. NAPLPS trades an easy method of modifying images plus a simple interface with interactive graphics systems based on other standards for efficient transmission and closeness of fit to raster devices.

Pulling together

A key element of Intel's strategy for graphics products is to adopt NAPLPS and VDI standards as the interface with functional graphics units. In conjunction with Digital Equipment Corp. and Tektronix Inc., Intel has announced its support for these graphics standards. After the original announcement, 12 additional companies have joined with Digital Equipment Corp., Intel, and Tektronix. Representing a wide range within different parts of the communications, computer, and graphics fields, they are Digital Research Inc., Graphics Software Systems Inc., Hazeltine Corp., ICL Ltd., ISSCO Graphics Inc., Mannesmann Tally Corp., Microsoft Inc., AEL Microtel Ltd., Norpak Ltd., Westinghouse Electric Corp., Xerox Corp., and Precision Visuals Inc.

The goals of the original three companies with regard to these graphics standards are:
■ To ensure that the standards are technically sound.
■ To assist in the rapid completion and adoption of the standards by contributing additional resources to support the ANSI committees.
■ To encourage other vendors to adopt these graphics standards, for the success of the standards will depend on the breadth of product support they receive. □

References
1. "Draft proposed American National Standard for the Virtual Device Metafile," ANSI X3H33 Virtual Device Interface Task Group, American National Standards Institute, Dec. 1982.
2. B. Shepherd, "Graphics Standards Status Report," Siggraph Computer Graphics, August 1979.
3. "Draft Standard, Videotex/Teletext Presentation Level Protocol Syntax (North American PLPS)," ANSI X3L2.1 Videotex Standing Task Group and CVCC/CSA Working Group on Videotex, June 1982.

Unix-based data base fits 16-bit systems

Multiple access methods boost performance in relational data-base management system

by Nicolas C. Nierenberg, *Unify Corp., Portland, Ore.*

☐ Scores of different brands of business "supermicrocomputers" are hitting the market. Based on the new generation of 16-bit microprocessor chips and using Bell Laboratories' Unix operating system, they magnify the need for both system and application software.

In particular, data-base–management systems will be essential both as a tool for end users and as a working foundation for program developers. One such system, called Unify, backs an innovative user interface with a unique high-performance architecture designed for just this new class of computers.

Software engineers who are creating programs for these machines are now faced with three choices. Programs can be adapted downward from large minicomputers running the Unix operating system, adapted upward from 8-bit personal computers running non-Unix software, or developed specifically for those computers running Unix. Since these business computers are based on 16/32-bit microprocessors, they have certain characteristics of both the 8-bit personal computer and also the 32-bit minicomputer.

On the face of it, therefore, drawing software from each environment is appealing. A closer look, though, indicates the disadvantages that such hybrid software may inherit from its 8- and 32-bit ancestors. Programs from the smaller systems will be deficient in such 16-bit system features as multiuser capability. On the other hand, software from the larger systems will be oversized for the smaller working environment of most 16-bit personal computers. Consequently, the best approach is to design software specifically for these machines.

In the case of the Unify data-base–management system, the design process had three primary objectives: Unify was to serve as a base for application development; it had to have rapid response and occupy as little system memory as possible; and it would have to be easily used by people who were not professional programmers.

Program support first

In its main function as a foundation for application development, Unify would be expected to interact with many end users through menus, screens, and reports—all of which would be designed once and then used repeatedly. In addition, a typical application program would require the support of high update rates, of the kind found in transaction systems for application programs written for insurance-claim processing, inventory control, accounting, and customer-contact and engineering-update tracking. The eventual end user of these applications should become aware of the existence of Unify only when performing an *ad hoc* query or when creating new screens or reports.

To provide this functional capability, the system would have to present a flexible user interface that could be modified to suit a particular application. Furthermore, to meet the demands of complex applications for sophisticated users and programmers, Unify would need powerful programming interfaces.

Of importance to applications that utilize a data-base management system is the latter's ability to respond interactively to users' queries, summarizing and distilling the information it has collected from the daily transac-

1. At your service. In the Unify data-base–management system, user interaction passes through a menu handler (shaded), as well as directly through the host-language interface in application programs. The Unitrieve data-base kernel (black) manages the actual access that is made to the physical data-base volumes.

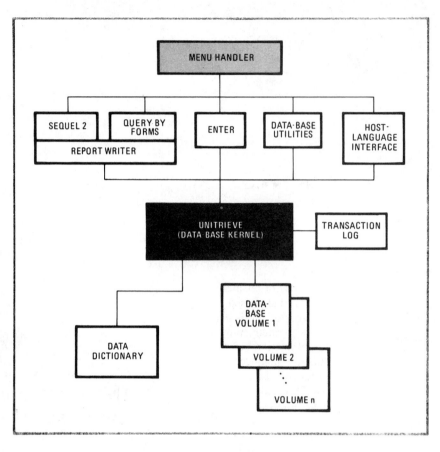

tions. For this reason, Unify had to provide powerful query capabilities aimed at both technical and nontechnical users.

Since few supermicrocomputers will be associated with a professional data-processing staff, various other people will be forced into the role of application developers. Besides their inexperience with data-base systems, many of these people will be neither able nor willing to write conventional programs. Consequently, the Unify tools for designing data-processing procedures must be as straightforward as possible. In fact, Unify should itself be a Unify application, so that it utilizes the same user interfaces as the final application. Users should be able to create various "obvious" parts of applications (such as menus, data-entry screens, reports, and updates) simply by configuring the various Unify utilities instead of having to develop conventional programs.

In transaction applications, the data-base–management system responds to external events, such as requests made by users in real time. In fact, it should respond at least as fast as do application programs written without a data-base–management system. More specifically, it should complete simple requests within 2 seconds, even with two or more users and with data files of more than 100,000 records.

Besides fast response time, a data-base–management system like Unify should not occupy more than 100 kilobytes of storage. Many of the new 16-bit personal computers are, after all, delivered with as little as 256-K bytes of system memory. In contrast, some earlier systems required at least 750 kilobytes to function in a single-user mode—and Unify is multiuser.

The third and last of the chief design goals—ease of use—dictated the adoption of the relational data-base model. Current implementations of such data bases have been plagued by performance problems, to such an extent that some designers have questioned whether the relational model is practical for transaction systems. As a result, the design of Unify extends current relational implementations and uses modifications where necessary to provide the required response time in a reasonable amount of memory.

Over and above these performance problems of the conventional relational–data-base–management system model, the Unix operating system throws in its own stumbling blocks to efficient data-base management. For

example, the Unix file system was not designed to be efficient with large files. In fact, the operating system often imposes two or three additional, or hidden, disk accesses in order to read a specific disk block. Since disk accesses are a critical aspect of data-base performance, this factor alone would have doubled response time unless Unify provided some alternative.

Unix lacks a general interprocess communication mechanism. This deficiency prevented the use of typical data-access optimization strategies, such as buffer pooling or reading disk blocks before they are actually needed. Overcoming these problems required innovative ways of working with Unix so that its many advantages would not be lost to applications needing high performance.

The solutions

Providing an environment powerful enough for the creation of complex applications, yet simple enough for nonprogrammers, is a challenge in any situation. Further constraining the system to 100 kilobytes of memory while maintaining rapid response adds another level of complexity to the design. Yet Unify (Fig. 1) meets these design objectives through a number of features, including a modular architecture, a menu handler, high-level query interfaces, a relational model, predefined relations, multiple on-line and programming access methods, reduced file overhead, and a run-time performance optimizer.

As one approach to satisfying the 100-kilobyte limit, Unify is segmented by function into a number of separately executable utility modules—data-dictionary update, data-base creation, data-base modification, and query (Fig. 2). This setup naturally means that data-base

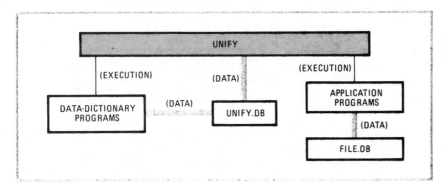

creation is not available from query but, given the assumptions listed above concerning Unify utilization, it is more than justified by the memory savings. This utility-program approach mirrors the implementation of the Unix system, which also prefers a few small interacting programs to having a single very large all-purpose utility.

A utility of particular importance to the data-base design process is Unify's menu handler. All the data-base utilities—such as data-base design maintenance, create data base, and reconfigure data base—may be selected by number or name. The menus are kept in the data dictionary and can be modified easily. The data dictionary also contains a matrix of each user's starting point in the menu hierarchy and the programs to which he or she has access. Each menu node also has associated on-line help documentation.

When Unify is first installed, the menus allow access to 28 programs. If the system were not menu-oriented, the user would be forced to memorize or look up numerous command sequences. Instead, the menus present the user with a simple list of options broken down by category. Once a utility is invoked, the user continues to interact in a structured full-screen mode. Designing a data base means just filling in the names and characteristics of tables and columns. Modifying a data-base design means just tabbing to the entry to be changed and replacing it. This style of interface reduces the knowledge needed to create and modify data structures.

Because menus may be modified and new functions easily added, menus also serve as the interface to application programs developed using Unify. All these programs can be registered with the menu handler and placed into an application hierarchy, with access assigned to each user according to individual need.

One important function supported by the menu system is Unify's high-level interface for data entry and query by forms. Using two Unify utilities, ENTER and SFORM, users create data-entry screens for Unify tables without programming. Because ENTER is fully integrated with the menu handler, forms users are limited to those combinations of update privileges (add, inquire, modify, or delete) specified by the system designer. Users can also employ these forms to query the data base by entering desired values into the fields on the screen.

Alternatively, Unify offers a Sequel query processor that is a substantial subset of the query and data-manipulation portion of IBM's Sequel language—an extremely powerful relational calculus that is the basis for IBM's relational data-base product, SQL/DS. Sequel is much more powerful and easier to use than relational algebras that employ separate select, project, and join operators. Results from either Sequel or ENTER queries can be passed to the Unify report processor, which creates formatted reports according to nonprocedural specifications provided by the user.

Relational model

Of course, it would be of little use to allow this type of easy access to the design tools if the data model itself were difficult to understand. For this reason, Unify employs the relational model, with its relatively simple structure, rather than more cumbersome network or hierarchical models.

Unify extends the relational model in two important ways. First, it allows for the specification of a record key—a set of values unique to a table and contained in one or more columns of just one of its rows. Only one row in any table can contain a particular set of values in its key column(s). (Extra secondary keys can be specified, but these do not affect the data base's logical structure.) Second, Unify allows for the specification of links between tables. In a pure relational–data-base system, tables are laid out independently of one another and integrated only when a user specifies a join—a logical operation that combines information in the tables. With Unify's links, on the other hand, a user who knows that columns in two or more distinct tables are logically related can specify that relationship to the system.

For example, a value—a customer number—might appear as column entries in both customer and order tables. If, as in this case, the user knows that these columns in the separate tables are logically related, the columns can be tied together. The result is that only customer numbers that are stored in the customer table may be stored in the order table. Thus invalid data is kept out of the data base without its being necessary to carry out specific logic checks in each application program. Additionally, this "pre-join" greatly increases the speed of any subsequent join operations that involve these two columns.

Logical and physical links

The specification of links between tables has physical as well as logical ramifications. Unify uses this specification of the data-base structure to implement an access method that is unique among relational data bases. In this access method, relative row pointers reduce the number of disk accesses by a factor of two or three for some operations.

Figure 3a represents the pointers maintained by Unify when the user specifies a relationship between columns in two different tables. These pointers are completely trans-

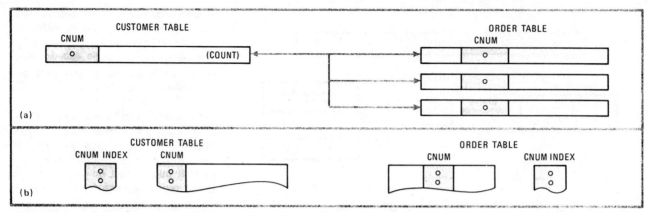

3. Linked up. Unify lets user specify links between tables of data, as when a value in the customer table and order table are known by the user to be related (a). Conventional relational implementations maintain separate tables, as well as adding overhead for indexes into the tables.

parent to the user and are updated when the information in the columns is changed. One pointer runs from each row in the order table to the related row in the customer table. This pointer is used when the join sequence starts with the order table.

A second set of pointers begins in the customer table and brings together a list of related order rows. These pointers are used when the join sequence starts with the customer table. They are also used when selecting those order-table rows that contain a particular customer number. Associated with the pointer in the customer table is a count of the number of related order rows. This count is extremely useful in searches where several columns are specified, for it enables Unify to select the shortest possible search path.

For comparison purposes, the conventional approach is illustrated in Fig. 3b. Here two indexes (B trees, typically) are built—one for the cnum column in each table. This approach can be used with Unify by not specifying the link and by building two B trees. However, it uses at least twice the disk space of the pointers even in the best case (a 2-byte integer key). More importantly, it requires a B-tree search for each row of the join operation. The B-tree search can be up to 10 times slower in comparison with the use of pointers, when disk accesses and central-processing-unit utilization are taken into account.

Experiments have also shown that update of the links is only about 10% slower than update of the B trees. Join operations without either of these two approaches—using linear search—would be prohibitively slow. Consequently, the links are viewed not as more overhead but as a tradeoff with indexes.

Access methods

Equally important to Unify's link access method is the way Unify selects the most efficient of its three access methods—key, link, or B tree—for a given retrieval. This optimization is dynamic and can vary from search to search on the same data base.

Unify performs this optimization by evaluating the columns specified and the access methods available, based on a defined set of criteria. Scores are assigned and the best approach is accepted. The choices are listed in order from best to worst:

■ An exact match on each one of the columns that

make up the primary key of the table (hashing.)
■ An exact match on a column that is in a pre-specified relationship. If several columns fit, then the one with the shortest list is chosen. (If the list is long relative to the number of rows in the table, then this may not be chosen if any of the three following choices appears to be better.)
■ An exact match on a B-tree column.
■ A numeric range on a B-tree column.
■ An inexact match on a B-tree column where the first characters are specified.

As an interesting note, a single column may have more than one access method applied to it, depending on the search criteria. For example, the primary key of record is always hashed, but the user may also build a B tree on it. If the key is specified precisely, then the hash method will be used, but otherwise the B tree will be utilized.

Because the Unify kernel itself performs these optimizations, they are independent of the way the query is written. Thus a Sequel query may operate in a completely different way, depending on how the physical access methods are configured or how the data base is loaded. The only difference perceived by the user is the length of time the system takes to respond.

Software developers building complex applications can select whatever level of access they desire through Unify's multilevel programming interface. At the highest level, the programmer is kept completely independent of the access methods used to fulfill the request. At the lowest level, the programmer may specify not only the access methods to be used but also how they are to be used.

UNISEL, the highest-level routine, optimally searches tables on the basis of criteria specified for various columns in the table. The programmer is free to mix criteria, such as exact, greater than, less than, ranges, and string-pattern matches. In addition, he or she can specify that the contents of a column must match the key of another table previously selected. If more complex computational or algorithmic tests are needed to complete a selection, UNISEL also allows for the specification of a user-written subroutine to perform the other tests.

UNISEL takes these inputs and selects an optimal

4. Speaking volumes. When, for example, Unify data volumes are laid out over two physical disk drives, the data base starts on the first disk and continues on the second. If this structure is not desired, the data base can reside in a single Unix file.

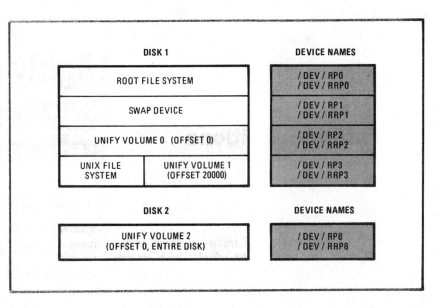

search strategy based on the physical access methods available. The rows that pass the criteria are returned in a specified sequence for processing by the program.

In cases where the programmers wish to direct the operation more precisely, they can access the B trees, hash keys, and links directly. Of course, programs using this option will be affected by changes in the physical configuration of the data base.

Once the desired rows have been selected, Unify allows the programmer to read and write them at the column level. To a considerable extent, this technique insulates programs from changes to the logical structure of the data base, as opposed to other techniques that require the entire record to be read or written. In addition, this low-level access capability greatly reduces the buffer space needed for data input/output operations.

At the system level, one of the Unix system's limitations *vis-à-vis* data-base management is its file system. Although work has been done recently to remedy this weakness, much block scattering and indirection (multiple physical reads for one logical read) still occur on large files. In addition, Unix has a tendency under some circumstances to allow files to be contaminated. For these reasons, Unify uses a specially designed file system, which can (at the user's discretion) run on portions of the disk outside conventional Unix file-system space. Tests have shown that this technique improves Unify's performance by over 40% compared with the standard Unix file-management scheme.

Figure 4 illustrates how the Unify file system is laid out on disk. In this case, the data base begins with two volumes on portions of the first disk and continues with the entire second disk. Up to eight disk extensions can be specified. These specifications are optional—without them, Unify resides in a single Unix file.

Within the Unify volumes, the rows of the tables are arranged as arrays within large segments. The block offset of each segment is kept in memory, so that, if the row number, the number of rows per segment, and the row length are known, a row can be read with one disk access. Additionally, since rows are stored contiguously, a great many of them can be read in a single disk request. Using this technique, sequential search speeds of 700 records a second have been observed.

In the conventional approach, each table is a separate Unix file within an ordinary Unix file system. Using this technique, most Unix systems restrict the size of the data base to a single Unix file system. Also, they lack control over block placement, so that the disk head travels excessively even on sequential access. Finally,

the Unix file system imposes an average overhead of two disk accesses, in addition to any indirection imposed by the data-base system itself.

An extra benefit of using raw disk files is the speed at which backup and recovery can be done. Unify utilities perform these operations using multisectored raw I/O at a fraction of the time needed by other systems.

Rapid row replacement

To provide the response time needed for multiuser online operations, Unify stresses run-time performance in other areas besides disk organization—in certain cases even at the expense of data compaction and dynamic change. The two key areas are fixed versus variable physical row lengths and dynamic reconfiguration.

Unify uses fixed physical row lengths both for direct computed access to rows (as discussed above) and for improved free-space recovery. With fixed row lengths, a newly inserted row can always take the place of a previously deleted one. In systems where row length is not guaranteed to be a certain size, all the rows in an arbitrary area, or page, must be deleted before the space can be reused. Since an entire page is rarely freed at random in reasonably stable data bases, compression runs are inevitably needed to reclaim space available on partially deleted pages. Consequently, direct row access and elimination of compression runs more than make up for the extra space needed for fixed-length rows.

Some data-base–management systems are also able to add tables and columns dynamically. Unify, on the other hand, requires a reconfiguration process to accomplish this. Although the ability to modify the logical data structures dynamically may be desirable, its benefits are outweighed by the penalties associated with it. For instance, since such data-base–management systems scatter data over the disk, they require the user to execute a lengthy process—the performance maintenance run, which reorganizes the data—in order to avoid performance degradation. During the life of a typical application, this requirement takes the system off line frequently, whereas Unify requires no maintenance runs to avoid performance degradation. □

Highly portable language protects software bankroll

Mainsail unfurled reveals itself to be
a general-purpose structured language
that is machine-independent for
easy adaptation to the latest computers

by Clark R. Wilcox and Gregory A. Jirak
Xidak Inc., Los Altos, Calif.

☐ Taking dead aim at the goal of portability, a general-purpose programming language incorporates source-level features that permit it to be moved from one machine to another with a minimal retargeting effort. Mainsail offers all the features of a modern structured language in a single package that runs identically on all computer systems.

The rapid proliferation of increasingly powerful and inexpensive computers has outstripped programmers' abilities to supply each with its own software. Economic considerations are beginning to dictate that software be written so that it can be easily moved among many computers with little or no alteration.

The traditional preeminence of hardware in the design and selection of computing systems is now giving way to the realization that software can have a value and lifetime greater than any particular hardware environment. The subordination of software to hardware for so many years has resulted in programs that are molded in conformance to the underlying hardware and operating-system environment and hence become useless in its absence. The binding of software to specific computing systems in turn binds the users. This ploy, in fact, has been exploited by hardware vendors to lock users into a particular product line.

Even software packages marketed to run on different computer systems are often substantially modified or rewritten from scratch for each system, giving rise to needless incompatibilities that plague both users and implementers. A software vendor has much to gain from a programming system that can be quickly moved among a variety of computers.

Portable software

Portable software means different things to different people, and is indeed a matter of degree rather than an absolute. For example, there is conceptual portability, in which the problem solved by the software is the same even if done in different languages. At the language level, there is standardized portability, wherein a program is written in a standard language like Fortran or Cobol. Finally there is source-level portability that utilizes a language, such as Mainsail, appearing in precisely the same form on all computing systems, so that the same program source code is simply recompiled for different target systems (see "A portable run-time system,").

Unfortunately, so-called standard languages are seldom realized identically in different computing systems. Even if two implementations are essentially identical, there are still potentially significant differences in the program-development tools, which are not usually a part of the language definition. Incompatible linkers, loaders, debuggers, text editors, and the like conspire to decrease the effectiveness of standardized portability. As a result, the difficulty of moving, say, a Fortran program from one computing system to another can be more difficult than rewriting the program.

Mainsail strives to be a sufficiently rich environment for the development of large, sophisticated software packages that can be run on many different computer systems. For instance, Intel Corp. is now using Mainsail in its computer-aided-design efforts because these extremely large and sophisticated programs are too valuable to be tied to a particular computer system.

At the same time, support is provided for isolating those parts of a system that must be rewritten, either for ultimate efficiency or for inherent machine dependencies. The system encompasses a complete language definition, a compiler, an expandable set of code generators, a comprehensive run-time system, a source-level debugger, program-monitoring tools, a full-screen text editor, and other utility programs.

The user perceives the same program-development and -execution environment, no matter what computer system is used. A low-cost development machine can be used to write and completely debug portable software packages, compile them into target code for many different computers, and even put the generated code onto distribution media in the proper target-machine formats.

The language syntax and semantics are independent of the underlying hardware and operating system. Every feature described as part of the language is supported in every implementation. This includes compile-time features, such as compiler directives, macroinstructions, and conditional compilation, that are not considered part of many other languages' definitions and hence often vary among implementations.

Language design

The Mainsail language specification is more than a blueprint for various enhanced versions, as is the case for Pascal. Since machine-specific extensions have no place in a portable language, all the facilities required to write sophisticated software systems are provided, some of which are usually considered part of the operating system rather than part of a language specification. For example, Mainsail has a completely self-contained notion of modularity, including linking and loading, and a file model that is identical across all machines and operating systems.

Mainsail is not itself an operating system, such as UCSD Pascal, but rather interfaces with existing operating systems. The host operating system provides the underlying file system and the input/output links with peripheral equipment like terminals. In fact, these components could be written in Mainsail to provide a simple, portable, single-user, single-language operating system for use on personal computers.

To achieve the goal of portability across a wide range of computers, it is of utmost importance to minimize the time required to fit the language to a new system. From the outset, all its components were designed with the intention of facilitating the movement to new computing environments as the need arises.

The compiler was carefully crafted to allow any host machine to generate code for any target machine (see "A compiler that promotes portability,"). For example, all evaluation of compile-time expressions is carried out on string representations of the data, so that the same results will be obtained no matter what host machine is in use.

Care also was taken to provide a code-generation environment that does as much as possible in a target-independent manner, yet retains the ability to generate code for essentially any target machine. The portable run-time system provides everything except the final interface to the host operating system for file and I/O support. Because the language was developed in parallel with the compiler and run-time system, it benefited from feedback concerning the features that are necessary for complete portability.

In addition to the language, compiler, and run-time support, all other phases of program development are provided by Mainsail. This provision eliminates the need to learn new editors, debuggers, and other utilities when moving among machines. As far as interaction with the language is concerned, the programmer need not even know what computer system is being utilized.

The various components of Mainsail work together to unify the program-development process. When the compiler detects a syntax error, it can automatically invoke the text editor to fill the screen with the source text and put the cursor at the point of the error. The user can fix the error, then give a command to the editor to continue the compilation.

Similarly, the debugger can use the editor to show single-step execution, with the cursor moving over the

A portable run-time system

Mainsail necessarily depends on an implementation strategy that minimizes the retargeting effort required to move software to a new machine or operating system. The cornerstone of this strategy is moving the entire software system to a new target environment simply by recompilation. This easy move is largely made possible by the inclusion in the language of low-level features allowing even the essence of the run-time system, like the storage-management algorithms, to be machine-independent.

The run-time system is a collection of modules managing the execution environment, such as the input/output interface and memory allocation, and also provides the user with a predefined set of utility procedures. The source text for the Mainsail run-time system consists of three parts: machine-independent, machine-dependent, and operating-system-dependent.

The machine-independent part accounts for the vast majority of the code. It utilizes compile-time features to incorporate the second and third parts into the portable source text.

For each computer, the machine-dependent part contains constant definitions describing machine resources such as the word size and a handful of procedures that could not be expressed in a machine-independent manner. So it contains those aspects of the implementation outside the realm of the code generator.

For each operating system, there is a file containing the portion of the runtime system dependent on the operating system. This file contains macroinstruction definitions and procedures for interfacing with the host operating system. The actual calls to the operating system usually require some use of assembly language, but it is limited to code to set up parameters for system calls, make the call, then prepare the results for the return to Mainsail.

All such assembly code is in a single part of Mainsail called the boot, which obtains control from the operating system to start execution. This is the only part of Mainsail that is statically linked in accordance with host system conventions and that can be linked with foreign code.

To make the language as self-contained as possible, portable routines are provided for mathematical operations, such as trigonometric and logarithmic functions in both single and double precision. Routines are also provided to convert among the string and internal forms of floating-point values. Mainsail provides portable versions of all the standard routines, but in such a manner that they can be replaced with machine-dependent versions for added efficiency.

A compiler that promotes portability

The Mainsail compiler consists of three parts. The first pass processes the source files to build an intermediate representation, which is then set up by the second pass for processing by the target-dependent code generator. The first and second passes are entirely independent of the target machine, except for a small top-level module that provides some target-dependent information like the size of each data type and the name of the target code generator.

Each code generator, of course, knows about its target machine, but is portable so that any host machine can be used to generate code for any target machine. The output of the code generator is typically position-independent binary code ready for execution, though early code generators produced assembly language. Thus far, all of the Mainsail code generators are operating-system independent. For example, the same code generator is used for the VAX minicomputer, whether it is running the Unix or VMS operating system.

The intermediate form is a tree structure for each procedure, using Mainsail records for the nodes of the tree (the tree is temporarily stored on a file between passes). The nodes of the trees correspond to the language's statements and operators—it is not broken down into a more primitive form. In fact, the original program structure can be regenerated from the intermediate representation.

Each code generator is a member of the class that consists of a fixed set of code-generation procedures. Since it is handed a tree for an entire procedure, it is free to scrutinize the entire tree before generating code, thereby allowing procedure-wide optimization techniques.

Writing a new code generator requires from one to four months, depending on the complexity of the target machine and the validity of the assumptions made by the code's target-independent part of the code generator. The machine-dependent and operating-system-dependent parts of Mainsail can be developed in parallel with the code generators. Since they usually require less time than the code generator, a new implementation can be ready for testing in a couple of months.

Any machine that supports the Mainsail development tools can serve as the host in a new project. For example, the VAX minicomputer utilized both a hard-wire and DEC-net connection to a PDP-10, and an IBM implementation used a VAX in California as a host connected to an IBM 3033 in Arizona.

source text as each statement is executed. The user sets breakpoints by issuing a command to the editor to set one at the current cursor position.

The distinction between the compiler, editor, and debugger is thus fuzzy because each consists of many modules, some of them shared by the others. Together they form an environment identical in all implementations. Each such component is similarly available for incorporation into user packages.

Storage management

To avoid machine dependencies and at the same time provide a more flexible program environment, Mainsail was designed to bind neither code nor data to specific memory locations and in fact can move both around during execution (Fig. 1). Program code can be loaded into and executed out of any memory location, and all data is allocated dynamically and can be moved at any time by the storage allocator. Furthermore, there is a complete separation of code from data, with the code portion read-only (except possibly for debugging breakpoints) so that it can be placed in shareable libraries or burned into read-only memories.

All procedures can be invoked recursively, with all modules and data structures like arrays, strings, and records allocated and deallocated dynamically. An interesting side effect of this totally dynamic approach is that the generated code contains no memory addresses and hence is not affected by the size of an address. Base-displacement addressing is used for all memory references, so there is no need to adjust addresses in the code when the module is loaded.

Mainsail partitions the available memory into pages, which need have no relationship to host-machine pages, if such exist. The number of pages used starts out small and increases dynamically, so that large core images—

the storage area allocated to a program—are created only as necessary, which is advantageous for some non-paged operating systems.

Mainsail's runtime system allocates control pages at one end of the available memory, and chunk (Fig. 2), string, and static (I/O buffers, primarily) pages at the other. If control and data pages meet in the middle of the memory, more pages are obtained from the operating system (the core image increases), and the control pages are moved to the new high end of memory to make more room in the middle.

The Mainsail string data type involves no declaration of a maximum length; instead any string may grow or shrink as needed. A string variable's descriptor consists of its current length (number of characters) and a starting address. The storage area for characters is allocated as needed in a separate area of memory called the string space. The characters that make up the string are never altered, in contrast to other software systems that store their strings in arrays.

Mainsail uses the storage-reclamation technique called garbage collection to reclaim all chunks no longer accessible and to compress string space by squeezing out characters no longer being used. A garbage collection automatically occurs whenever there is insufficient string space for an operation. The user can invoke or suppress garbage collections, but this level of control is rarely needed.

Dynamic modules

Mainsail uses an innovative approach to modularity that provides portability and flexibility far beyond the usual notion of static modules supported by other programming languages. Unlike statically linked systems that combine separately compiled program components into an amorphous code image, modules retain their identity during execution. Mainsail's more robust notion of a module enables portable formulation of all phases of program development from separate compilation, to intermodule communication, to debugging facilities communicating with the user in terms of modules and procedures rather than of memory addresses.

As in other structured languages, a module consists of a collection of data and procedures, some of which may be made visible to other modules. They cannot be statically nested—a module cannot contain within itself another module. Facilities are provided for sharing compiled declarative information among many modules, thereby avoiding error-prone redundant specifications and the overhead of recompilation of such information for each module.

A module's internal structure is hidden, with only the interface fields visible from the outside. These fields can be either data or procedures, so that, especially with respect to implementation, a module is like a record that can also have procedure fields.

In Mainsail, modules can be referenced by pointers and thus incorporated into data structures. For example, a record field can point to a module, an array can consist of module references, and modules can be used in general programming strategies that have previously been available only in interpreted languages like Lisp.

Unlike most languages, Mainsail modules are not combined into a program image before execution. Instead, the run-time system automatically brings modules into memory during execution and dynamically provides for intermodule access. Mainsail does not use machine-dependent linkers, thereby providing an identical program environment across all machines. A side effect of this self-contained loading and linking mechanism is the lack of restriction on the length of an

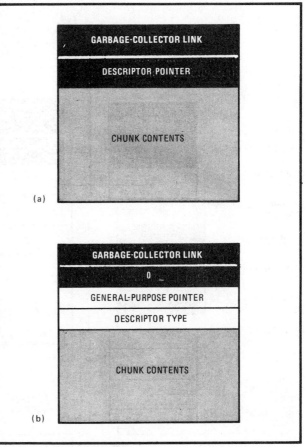

2. Chunks. These general-purpose storage units called chunks (a) contain a location for linking them together during garbage collection (a way of reclaiming unused or inactive storage space), followed by a pointer to the chunk's descriptor. A descriptor (b) indicates self-description with a null pointer field.

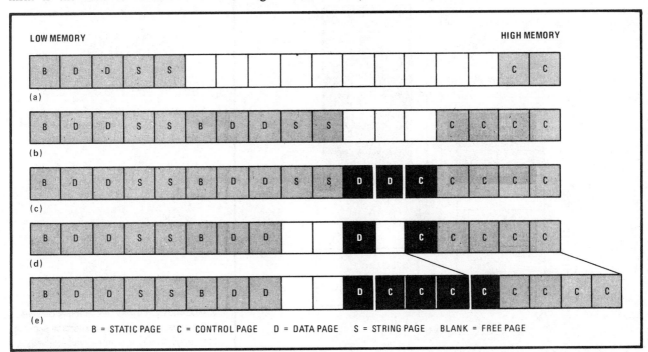

1. Paging through memory. At program initiation, Mainsail loads the first module's code and data (a) into high and low memory respectively. During execution, more pages are dynamically allocated (b) for other called modules until the memory is full (c). Unused pages are then deleted (d) and the core image is expanded (e) to make room. Thus paged memory management is a feature of the language itself.

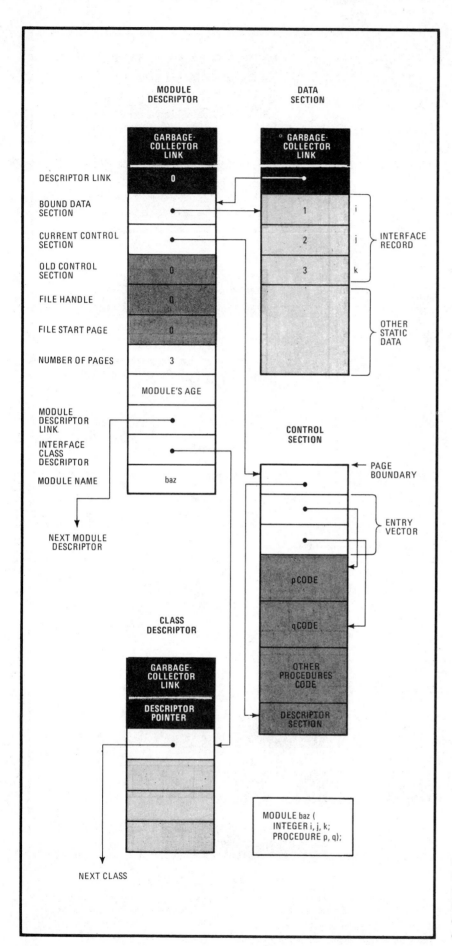

MODULE
DESCRIPTOR

DATA
SECTION

GARBAGE-
COLLECTOR
LINK

GARBAGE-
COLLECTOR
LINK

DESCRIPTOR LINK — 0

BOUND DATA
SECTION

CURRENT CONTROL
SECTION

OLD CONTROL
SECTION — 0

FILE HANDLE — 0

FILE START PAGE — 0

NUMBER OF PAGES — 3

MODULE'S AGE

MODULE
DESCRIPTOR
LINK

INTERFACE
CLASS
DESCRIPTOR

MODULE NAME — baz

1 — i

2 — j

3 — k

INTERFACE
RECORD

OTHER
STATIC
DATA

NEXT MODULE
DESCRIPTOR

CONTROL
SECTION

PAGE
BOUNDARY

ENTRY
VECTOR

pCODE

qCODE

OTHER
PROCEDURES
CODE

DESCRIPTOR
SECTION

CLASS
DESCRIPTOR

GARBAGE-
COLLECTOR
LINK

DESCRIPTOR
POINTER

NEXT CLASS

MODULE baz (
    INTEGER i, j, k;
    PROCEDURE p, q);

3. Modularity reigns. This module, declared in the upper left box, has an interface section that only allows the three variables—i, j, k,—to be visible outside of the module. The control section contains the code, and the class descriptor, the format of the interface.

identifier for interface fields, which specify global data and procedures.

Each module can contain an initial and a final procedure. The initial procedure is automatically invoked when the module is first allocated, and the final procedure is invoked when it is deallocated. This gives each module a chance to initialize itself and an opportunity to clean up after itself.

The ability to bring any module into play at any time provides a natural setting for an interactive environment utilizing modules as building blocks. In a statically linked language, in contrast, the debugger would have to be linked into every debuggable core image; every display module would have to be linked with the editor; and all code generators would have to be linked with the compiler—or else separate core images would have to be created for each combination. The editor could be invoked only if it had been linked with the user program. To get around such cumbersome linkages, other languages must rely on the operating system, thereby undermining portability by going outside the language.

Virtual code space

A working set of modules is kept in memory, subject to its availability. If there is insufficient room for an incoming module, those least recently accessed are automatically removed from memory until there is sufficient space. Upon return from an intermodule procedure call, Mainsail will automatically swap in the calling module if it is not in memory.

Thus the user is provided with a completely general and automatic overlay facility. No such mechanism is provided for data, because efficient detection of data absent from a module requires hardware support.

The user need never specify all modules in a program, because new ones can be dynamically brought into play at any time during execution. A program is best viewed as an open-ended collection of modules, and there is no imposed structure on the relationships among modules—each is considered equal to all others and can access any other symmetrically.

A module can reside either in a file by itself or in a module library, which is a collection maintained in a single file by the portable Mainsail module librarian. The language locates a new module by first checking all open module libraries; if unsuccessful, it forms a file name from the module name and tries to open the file and obtain the object module from it.

If there is no such file, or if Mainsail detects that the file does not contain the desired module, then the user is interactively asked to provide it. As an extreme example, the programmer could at this point recursively enter the executive level of Mainsail, use the editor to write the required module, compile it, and then continue execution with the newly compiled module.

Mainsail allows the declaration of a module's interface fields to be separated from the body of the module (Fig. 3). This declaration may be provided in a manner independent of any module body, so that it serves solely as an interface specification.

During execution, any conforming module can be brought into memory to implement the interface specification. The name of the module can be specified by a string variable, so that, for example, the program can read from a terminal which module is to be accessed for the next operation.

The first pass of the compiler is independent of the target machine, but one of many target-dependent code generators is used for a particular compilation. All code generators conform to a fixed interface specification—in Mainsail terms, all code generators belong to the same class—and that class is all that is known to the compiler's first pass.

The top-level compiler module, which is target-dependent, specifies which code-generator module to use. When the compiler first accesses a field of the code-generator class, the run-time system automatically fetches the proper module. The text editor obtains the proper display module in a similar manner.

During execution, a module consists of execute-only code and data allocated separately from the code. A module can have multiple instances of its data, each sharing the same code. For example, a module implementing a symbol table can be used to maintain any number of such tables by creating a new and separate instance of the data for each one. Thus, a single structure can serve any number of customer modules in which each customer's data is automatically kept separate from the others' entries.

Standard I/O

Many languages' failure to achieve source-level portability is at least partly due to inadequate specification of I/O tasks. There is either a total lack of standard I/O routines or an overly simplistic approach that results in incompatible implementations of the language attempting to fill in the gaps.

To provide compatibility, the Mainsail file I/O is stream-oriented. Text files are a stream of characters, and data files are a stream of storage units that may represent any mixture of data types. Repositioning by relative character or storage unit, interspersed by sequential reads and writes, accomplishes random access. Details of various file systems, such as buffering, block size, and the like, are hidden from the user. A Mainsail file variable is a pointer to a record. The file record contains machine-independent information about the file, as well as a pointer to the file's device module, which handles the operating system interface.

The device-module field is an example of how modules can be incorporated into data structures. Device modules are, of course, dynamically brought into memory to handle the input and output. This approach naturally allows the user to contribute his own device modules by simply writing one conforming to the device module class, and then prefixing relevant file names with the name of the device module.

Such user-specific device modules can perform a wide variety of nonstandard processing, all without alteration to the text of the program that does the I/O. Device modules have been written to communicate over networks, thereby enabling all programs to transparently access files remotely, even on networks for which such support is not usually specified via file-name syntax. □

Ada, the ultimate language?

Software components, so portable that they would be bought
like hardware modules, can customize Ada for any task

by R. Colin Johnson, *Microsystems & Software Editor*

☐ Augusta Ada Byron, Countess of Lovelace (1816–1852) and the
daughter of the poet Lord George Byron, is credited with being the
first programmer because of her work on Charles Babbage's Difference
Engine. The forefather of the computer, the machine was designed to
calculate entries in logarithm tables. It is a special tribute that the
high-level language Ada was named for the first programmer, since its
principal designer, Jean Ichbiah, sees Ada as the last computer
language. In fact, he holds that Ada will "become the predominant
language of the 1980s" and will maintain that position until it is
replaced by "automatic program generators by the year 2000."

The concept that guided Ichbiah in achieving Ada's design goals as
laid down by the United States Department of Defense is that of the
software component [*Electronics*, Dec. 18, 1980, p. 39]. Analogous to
hardware components, the software components envisioned by Ichbiah
would be selected from a catalog and joined in any combination by
virtue of their compatibility with a common bus. Actually, the bus is
realized by an Ada compiler itself, which allows the various software
components to be "plugged" into it. The place they are plugged into is
the program library; any program becomes the bus controller and
hence may use the facilities that an installed component provides—just
as any module plugged into a hardware bus is available for use by any
bus controller.

Ichbiah picked up the concept of software components from M.
Douglas McIlroy, head of the Computing Techniques Research department of Bell Laboratories' Computing Research Center in Murray
Hill, N. J. He is fond of quoting MacIlroy's statement: "I would like to
see components become a dignified branch of software engineering. I
would like to see standard catalogs of routines classified by precision,
robustness, time-space requirements, and binding time of parameters."

Meeting the goal

The design goal laid out by the Department of Defense was to
produce a language that not only could be used in all programming
environments—business, scientific, and so forth—but that also would
set new standards in reliability, maintainability, and readability [*Electronics*, Sept. 25, 1980, p. 56]. What has emerged from this charter is a
language that contains the best features of Pascal, Algol, and PL/1
while adding real-time multitasking—all under the guiding influence
of the software component.

Software components enable Ada to be customized for a specific
application without making the extended version incompatible—extensibility without incompatibility was, in fact, a key goal. Most other
languages are quite different. Pascal, for instance, exists in many
different versions that include unique, incompatible extensions. Ada's
designers have taken great pains to maximize Ada's extensibility
without sacrificing portability—the ability to run on many different

Eponym. The programming language Ada is named
after the first programmer, Augusta Ada Byron (1816
–1852), who worked with Charles Babbage.

machines. The software component permits the extensions themselves to be moved easily to new machines. Thus software components could very well revolutionize the industry, bringing the art of computer programming one step closer to a science.

Ada is also the first computer language to be fully standardized before commercial compilers were written for it. Most languages were designed for a specific purpose, like scientific calculations, where standardization was not an issue. Ada, however, was designed to be universal and standardized from the very beginning. In fact, the standardization committees of both the American National Standards Institute and Europe's International Standards Organization are now reviewing Ada's final specification document (see "The DOD moves for standardization"), which became available in July 1980. What's more, the Defense Department intends to enforce standardization by vigorously defending the use of the Ada name only for compilers that have passed its rigorous validation procedure. Thus, as with the qualification of a hardware part, each Ada compiler will be tested for correctness, as well as for complete compatibility with the original specification; if it does not pass, the DOD will not allow use of the name Ada.

With a validated compiler, users of different computers will be able to run the very same programs—not just similar, but identical. And as noted earlier, this ideal portability does not limit the language, since extensions may be added to any of those same programs—without introducing incompatibility—by plugging software components into the Ada bus.

The language

Ada has inherited much of its structured design from Pascal but with the addition of many constructs that expand its applications domain. It has the basic control statements and strong typing of Pascal, the block structure of Algol, and the exception handling of PL/1, to which it adds extensive real-time control facilities, as well as the concept of a software component.

An integral part of the Ada language is the program library that acts as the repository of those software components. The usefulness of the program library is that it allows programmers to concentrate on writing the main programs rather than on debugging their internal subroutines—thereby promising increased productivity for programmers. Placing components in the program library connects them to the software bus—that is, an Ada compiler.

Ada is customized for the application at hand by including in the library those software components that define the data types and valid operations that are needed to solve a specific problem. On any given system, these components will be cataloged in the program library, which resides in a mass-storage device. The components consist of separately compiled modules that can be used by any authorized program to perform

LIBRARY PACKAGES CATALOG: PAGE 201							
Name	Special data types	Overloaded operators				Other packages called	Details
		+	−	*	÷		
Vectors	vector, direction, velocity	✓	✓	✓	✓	math_for_physics matrix_operations	
Matrix_ operations	n_tuple, index	✓	✓	✓		multidimensions	"−" stands fo inversion
Weather	temperature wind_velocity humidity	✓	✓			vectors statistics	
Business_ manager	dollars, cents, territory, salesman	✓	✓			gen_ledger, inventory, accts_payable, accts_receivable	helps manager as keep track o salesmen's com whereabouts
Statistics	variance, mean, std_dev	✓	✓	✓	✓	recursive_functions matrix_operations	basic stati or multiva
Calendar	time, data, week, day, month	✓	✓			temporal_math	supersedes by adding re

1. Hypothetical software catalog. Library components, called packages, extend the capabilities of Ada. Special data types, like vectors, and the valid operations on those types, like vector addition, can be overloaded into the normal operators (+, −, *, /).

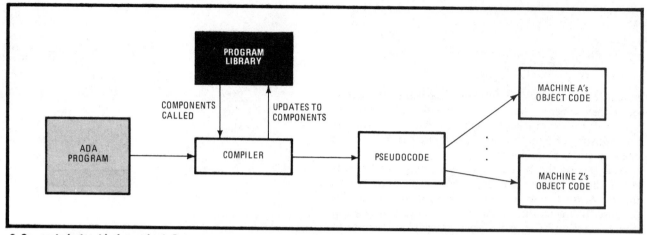

2. Separate but not independent. Components called by a user's program are linked to it at compilation time, and any updates to the library are done then. Most Ada compilers use an intermediate psuedocode that can be translated into the object code of any computer.

operations that would otherwise require separate subroutines. They are more than just subroutines, however, since they extend the capabilities of the language into specific application areas (Fig. 1). For instance, a vector package would define a one-dimensional-array data type that enables the normal plus and minus signs to add and subtract vectors.

In the library

The library is a collection of compiled units that are separate and largely independent of each other. The library file is submitted each time a program is compiled (Figs. 2 and 3); it is consulted and possibly updated by the compiler. Components that are called in by a program are linked to it at this time; also, new components or alterations to old ones are added to the library. Some library units will need periodic updating, like the system calendar that gives users access to the time and date. Most compiler projects are opting for compilation into a pseudocode that can be predefined for some imaginary machine. It is then a relatively simple step to translate this code into the native tongue of the target computer.

The library modules may be linked to a program by use of the "with" clause. For instance:

   with VECTORS;

allows the program to use the vector data types and functions that are defined in that module. The programmer is free to use any of the modules that have been contributed to the library, and with a validated compiler users can acquire additional units from outside software houses, several of which are already gearing up to offer components. The vision of a software catalog for the Ada language that is continuously being expanded raises the hope that the science of software has truly come of age.

Inside the packages

Within the primary software component, called the package, resides Ada's universality. Subroutines, called procedures, as well as several other program fragments, may be stored in the library as well, but the advantages of the package will cause it to become the basic type of component. A package encapsulates a group of related subroutines and data types into an isolated environment

and thus can extend the capabilities of the language while maintaining tight control over its proper use. To that end, a separate interface portion of the package (Fig. 4) includes a specification of all the subprograms, functions, and variables that are accessible to the user.

The implementation, called the body, which contains the algorithms that perform the actual operation, can be hidden from the user of the package. Hiding is accomplished with the "body separate" clause, a feature that will enable software houses to supply the implementation portion in object-code form only, so as to protect their products. The hidden portion may use its own private data types and need not be the same from installation to installation so long as the interface portion is identical. This variability allows easy updating of software components without making past investments obsolete, since both the original and the updated version will perform properly. Presumably, however, the new package will execute the program faster, use less memory, or be optimized in some other way—perhaps by taking advantage of new hardware that has recently been added to the system. In this way, software components can be created by software houses and sold with the same kind of reliability assurances as hardware products. With a validated compiler serving as the system bus, the interface specifying its proper use, and the implementation hidden, software packages will likely be offered with guarantees of correctness—a most welcome advance in software engineering.

Overloading operators

Ada is unique in that a single operation can be expanded, or overloaded, so that it takes on different meanings depending on its context. For instance, the multiplication operator can be overloaded by adding a definition for vector multiplication. Then, whenever it is placed between two variables that are vectors, the compiler will ascertain from the context that vector multiplication is desired and will perform it. This process can be extended to subroutines as well, allowing several different procedures to have the same name. Each procedure is then invoked whenever the name is called with arguments of that procedure's respective type.

With generic procedures, on the other hand, variables

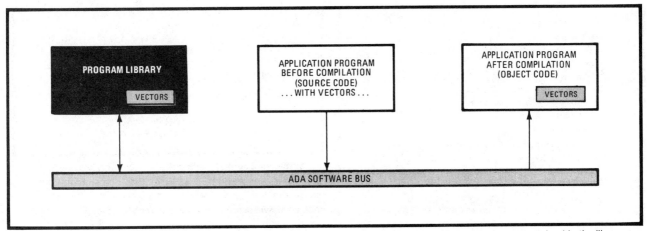

3. Software bus. Ada acts as a software bus into which both the user's programs and the software components contained in the library are plugged. Application programs that use "with" statements inherit new data types and operations during compilation.

of different types can make use of the same subprograms. These procedures may be stored in the library with their attendant variables left untyped. Then, at compilation time the variables that will access the procedure are specified and the generic procedure is appropriately recompiled.

Subprograms themselves can be either functions (that is, those returning one value only) or procedures. For procedures, the separate declaration part specifies the variables to be passed, designating them as inputs to the procedure, outputs from it, or both (Fig. 5). Furthermore, Ada also contains the statements that have become the familiar hallmarks of structured programming: BEGIN . . . END, IF . . . THEN . . . ELSE, LOOP, and CASE.

Real-time capabilities

A significant amount of the Ada compiler is devoted to the real-time concurrent programming environment. Task units are defined separately for each asynchronous process that is to be controlled, but execution is concurrent. Several mechanisms are provided by which tasks may communicate as well as keep track of external-world events like time.

Like packages, a task uses an interface portion that is separate from its implementation, or body. The interface portion of a task enumerates the entry declarations indicating how the task is activated. The task body includes the sequence of statements that perform the task at hand.

A rendezvous mechanism allows tasks to communicate with each other; one task acts as the server by containing an entry statement, and the other acts as the caller by using the name of the task's entry point. For instance, a task to write a line to a printer might contain in its interface the declaration:

    entry PUT;

This declaration indicates that using PUT causes entry to this routine and is then followed by a task body that contains the statement:

    accept PUT (L : in LINE);

This statement says that the code following it will put a line on the printer after accepting and storing it in local variable L of type LINE. The calling task will have a corresponding line like:

    PUT ("HI THERE")

which will transfer the character string "HI THERE" to the task at the point where the accept statement occurs.

When execution reaches the accept statement, the server waits till the calling task reaches its PUT statement. Conversely, if the caller reaches its PUT statement before the server reaches its accept, then the caller will wait. In this way, a rendezvous is accomplished, either server or caller waiting for the other until both reach their respective lines referring to PUT.

Since many tasks may be operating in parallel and many of them may contain identical PUT statements, each entry declaration has a corresponding queue that stores the order in which the respective routines called the server task. They are processed first in, first out so that no callers will be locked out. The statement:

    N := PUT'COUNT

will assign the number of waiting callers on the PUT task to the variable N, enabling a caller to determine what its position is in the queue.

Data types

Ada's strong typing is inherited from Pascal as a means of increasing the reliability of programs. At both compilation and execution times, extensive checking of types is done to ensure that no invalid assignments are made. For instance, the variables HEIGHT and WIDTH can be declared to be of type INCHES, whereas variable AREA is declared to be of type SQUARE INCHES. Then:

    function "*"(HEIGHT : INCHES; WIDTH : INCHES)
        return SQUARE INCHES;

requires that all multiplication of inches times inches have results in square inches, and the compiler will check to make sure that this rule is adhered to. This is in strong contrast to most languages, which do not allow user-defined data types, so that no such checking is even possible. All variables that are used in a program must have their types declared, along with any operations on

87

```
package CALENDAR is
   type TIME is
   --define a data type called TIME
      record
         YEAR : INTEGER range 1901 .. 2099;
         MONTH : MONTHS_NAMES;
         DAY : INTEGER range 1 .. 31;
         SECOND : DURATION;
      end record;
   --define an enumeration data type called MONTHS_NAMES
   type MONTHS_NAMES is (JAN, FEB, MAR, APR, MAY,
         JUN, JUL, AUG, SEP, OCT, NOV, DEC);
   function CLOCK return TIME;
   --overload the "+" and "−" operators
   function "+" (A : TIME; B : DURATION) return TIME;
   function "−" (A : DURATION; B : TIME) return TIME;
   function "−" (A : TIME; B : TIME) return DURATION;
end CALENDAR;
--end of interface portion
package body CALENDAR is separate;
```

4. A predefined package. One package that will be supplied with all validated compilers is a calendar that works with a real-time clock. The plus and minus signs must be redefined for temporal calculations so that, for instance, a time minus a time yields a duration.

```
procedure QUADRATIC_EQUATION (A, B, C, : in REAL;
                    ROOT_1, ROOT_2 : out REAL);
--enter the equation's coefficients and return its roots
   RADICAL : REAL
--now find the equation's roots
begin
   RADICAL : = (B**2) − (4.0*A*C);
   ROOT_1 : = (−B + SQRT(D))/(2.0*A);
   ROOT_2 : = (−B − SQRT(D))/(2.0*A);
end QUADRATIC_EQUATION;
```

5. Typical subroutine. The procedure subroutine lets any number of arguments pass between it and the calling program. The quadratic equation solver shown requires three coefficients ($Ax^2 + Bx + C$) as inputs and two outputs corresponding to the roots.

them that do not result in the same type (like inches times inches yielding square inches).

A type, then, is not only a set of values, but also a set of valid operations on those values. If a violation of these rules occurs, it will always be detected: incorrect type assignments at compilation time, and incorrect value assignments at execution time. It should be noted, too, that types are not the same just because their values can be; for two variables to be of the same type they must be explicitly declared as such.

Several types are predefined: integer, real, floating-point, character, boolean, array, string, enumeration, record, and access. Others may be defined explicitly by the user or may be built up from the predefined ones.

With the enumeration type, the specific values of a variable can be listed—for example:

```
type DAYS_OF_WEEK is
   (SUN,MON,TUE,WED,THU,FRI,SAT);
```

This enumeration restricts variables of the type DAYS_OF_WEEK to the seven strings specified. A subtype may be derived from this one by limiting its range—for instance, by:

```
type WEEK_DAY is DAYS_OF_WEEK
   range (MON .. FRI)
```

which restricts WEEK_DAY data types to the normal weekday range.

Record types allow different but related values to be grouped together and called by a common name. For example:

```
type DATE is
   record MONTH : MONTH_NAME
          DAY : INTEGER range 1 .. 31
          YEAR : INTEGER range 0 .. 2000
   end record;
```

permits variables of type DATE to be assigned values like WWII := (SEP, 1, 1939). If any attempt is made to assign values outside the specified range (like the thirty-second day of the month) a constraint error will be raised at execution time. In addition, elements of a record type can be accessed by dot notation, so that, say, WWII.MONTH picks out SEP as the month in which World War II started.

Imposing restrictions

A type may have its proper values and operations restricted in any way defined by the user by including what are called discriminants. These impose certain conditions to be checked by the compiler at both compilation and execution time. The example:

```
type SQUARE_MATRIX(I : INTEGER) is
   array (I,I) of REAL;
```

restricts the values of type SQUARE_MATRIX variables to ones that are really square by using the single discriminant I for both its dimensions. Even more complex data structures, called composition types, can be built up as well. For example, two square matrixes can be combined in a single record if they are assigned thus:

```
type DUAL_SQ_MATRIX (I : INTEGER) is
   record
      LEFT : SQUARE(I);
      RIGHT : SQUARE(I);
   end record;
```

That defines a DUAL_SQ_MATRIX to consist of a left and right portion, each of which is a square matrix as previously defined.

Once a type has been defined, objects (variables) may be declared using the notation:

```
MAT_2 : SQUARE_MATRIX
```

which now restricts the values that variable MAT_2 can take on to be square matrixes.

Exception handling

Ada has the ability to recover from execution time errors in a manner similar to PL/1. Whenever an error is encountered, an exception is raised, several of which are predefined, like CONSTRAINT_ERROR and NUMERIC_ERROR. To prevent execution from stopping when the exception is raised, a handler may be added by the user.

```
task DISK_HANDLER is
--define two entry points for data to and from the disk
   entry READ_DISK (A : out TRACK);
   entry WRITE_DISK (B : in TRACK);
end;
--end of interface portion
task body DISK_HANDLER is
begin
   loop
      select
      --either read or write
         accept READ_DISK (A : out TRACK) do
            GET_FROM_DISK (A);
         end;
            --external subroutines perform the reads and writes
      or
         accept WRITE (B : in TRACK)
            SEND_TO_DISK (B);
         end;
      else null;
      --if no reads or writes are waiting,then continue
      end select;
   end loop;
      --repeat
end;
```

6. Multitasking. The disk handler lets any program write or read a track of the disk, but not both simultaneously. "Select" and "or" statements allow only one alternative at a time. The "else null" clause causes exit from the select segment.

For example, to prevent a numerical error from being raised when a division by zero is performed, the following function may be used:

```
function " ÷ " (U,V : REAL) return REAL is
   begin
   return U/V;
   exception
      when NUMERIC_ERROR = >
            return REAL'LARGEST
   end;
```

Now, whenever two real numbers are divided with an out-of-bounds result, rather than causing the program to crash, the exception handler returns the largest value representable on the machine.

Current projects

Already, the race to produce Ada compilers is on. Many universities have experimental versions, but they are not intended for industrial users. At a conference held by the Association for Computing Machinery in Boston in December 1980, many companies said that they have programs in Ada ready to go as soon as compilers become available. General Electric, for instance, has Ada programs in hand that control one of its microwave ovens. Many are also working to ready test and validation programs for these compilers.

The first commercial compilers to appear will be for microprocessors. TeleSoftware Inc., a new company in San Diego, Calif., headed by Ken Bowles, the creator of UCSD Pascal, is working on a first quarter 1981 release of a compiler for a subset of Ada that runs on the Microengine from Western Digital Corp., Newport Beach, Calif. It also plans to be the first clearinghouse for software components and undertook the compiler project to get started. In fact, Western Digital, part owner of TeleSoftware, is producing an Ada Microengine employing special microcode optimized for Ada. This compiler will also work with systems based on the S-100 bus now that the WD chip set is available for the bus [*Electronics*, Jan. 13, 1981, p. 290]. Others are reportedly working on implementations for the 68000 and the Z8000 microprocessors, though these are certainly a good way off.

Intel Corp., Santa Clara, Calif., will be offering an Ada-based microprocessor chip set in the near future, called the iAPX-432, that mirrors the structure of the language in its hardware. The iAPX-432 has been designed from the ground up with Ada in mind. In fact, Ada is its system implementation language, and the first validated compiler may well be from Intel, which appears to have a head start here, too.

The first Department of Defense contract for a compiler was granted by the Army to SofTech Inc. The Waltham, Mass., company has been asked to produce a full Ada compiler for Digital Equipment Corp's VAX-11/780. Preliminary versions of the compiler should be ready in 1981, though the validation process will probably hold up final delivery till 1982.

The other major DOD effort comes from the Air Force, which has granted three preliminary contracts to Texas Instruments, Intermetrics Inc., and Computer Science Corp. It will choose one of these companies to develop a full Ada compiler for IBM computers next year.

The designer of the language, Jean Ichbiah has formed his own company, named ALSYS, in Paris, which is currently working on a front-end compiler for CII-Honeywell Bull's and Siemen's computers.

Many implementations will compile Ada source statements into an intermediate code that can then be translated into the machine code of the target computer. Several manufacturers will be looking at these compilers as possible front ends for their own implementations. Joseph Rowe, vice president of research and development at the Harris Semiconductor Group's Minicomputer division, believes that "Ada will replace Fortran," and consequently the Melbourne, Fla., company is one of those already working on test programs to help evaluate compilers as they become available. Another minicomputer effort, for Data General's machines, is being undertaken by Application Software of Johannesburg, South Africa. And Westinghouse Electric Corp.'s Defense and Electronic Systems Center in Baltimore is working on an Ada–to–Fortran-77 translator for Sperry Univac, Burroughs, IBM, Honeywell, DEC, and Control Data computers.

However, most of the major minicomputer and mainframe manufacturers appear to be holding back from full-fledged compiler projects. Those with major defense contracts are training programmers, but they are not committing the funds necessary to write a full Ada compiler and validate it. Says Mary Van Duesen, editor of the Ada Implementor's Newsletter, "All of them will eventually go to Ada, it's just a matter of whether they take the first or second wave of customers." □

Multiuser microprocessor systems get a data-base manager

Sophisticated hardware and software control disk resource while managing data base and files

by Eugene Lowenthal, *Intel Corp., Austin, Texas*

☐ Yet another mainframe support tool is migrating to the microprocessor environment: the data-base processor. It is being introduced at a time when the industry is recognizing that microprocessor-based multiuser systems now have the power and capacity to support the complex, large problems that have been the exclusive domain of mainframe computers. However, these small microprocessor-based systems have outstripped the capabilities of available support software.

In particular, there is a vacuum to be filled with respect to sophisticated data-base management systems capable of supporting shared access to data by multiple terminals, programs, and applications. The iDBP 86/440 data-base processor [*Electronics,* March 24, 1982, p. 44] is the first of a family of such systems that will be designed to fill that vacuum.

In addition to controlling a shared disk resource for the host computer or computers, this microprocessor-based peripheral system offers comprehensive data-base and file management. Consequently, the designer who integrates the iDBP into an end product can focus on the application—without concern for the mechanics of data-storage techniques.

The iDBP is a building block for the product designer, rather than an end-user system. Intel's objective for

data-base machines (and the systems business in general) is to provide high-level building blocks for system integrators and value-added resellers. Thus the iDBP will not appear as an end product, but as a subsystem incorporated within a total system offering developed by Intel's customer. Consequently, the design of the 86/440 accommodates interfaces with a wide spectrum of hosts.

A building block for OEMs

The iDBP will be designed into minicomputers, small-business computers, networks of small computers and work stations, and integrated office systems. Only in rare instances will it be appropriate to connect it to a large mainframe or an isolated single-user system (work station, personal computer, and so on.)

The 86/440 is particularly well suited for integrated office systems. It fills the large gap between software developed for managing text in word-processing systems and that developed for managing records in data-processing systems. Storage-management facilities for office networks must marry both disciplines. In fact, no meaningful integration of word and data processing can be undertaken until there is a common mechanism for managing and relating both record-oriented data (for data processing) and stream-oriented data (such as text,

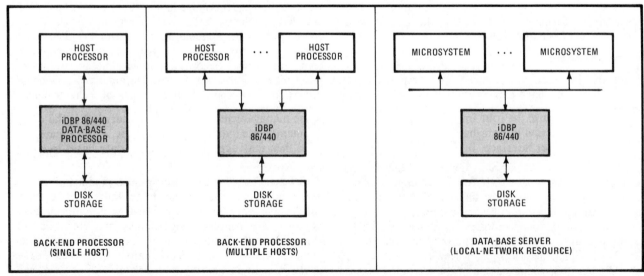

1. Building block. The iDBP can be connected to a host processor as a back-end processor (left), as a data-base server for a network of microsystems (right), or as an embedded system transparent to users. This versatility makes it a high-level building block.

digitized voice, digitized images, graphics representations, and the like). The iDBP provides this common mechanism for a system to which it is attached.

An important design consideration was to provide a general-purpose building block that could be incorporated into a variety of original-equipment-manufacturer systems (Fig. 1). The iDBP can serve as a back-end processor dedicated to a single host, possibly integrated within the host enclosure—a superintelligent controller.

Adaptable to many different hosts

It can also serve as a back end that is connected to multiple hosts, possibly of different brands—a multiport back end. This configuration is the only efficient way that applications running on different computers can share data, particularly in a heterogeneous configuration of machines.

Finally, it can be a special node in a network. There it is a data-base server, which is a shared network resource that allows all users access to a common pool of information on disks.

The 86/440 is designed to handle large data bases, having files that are individually hundreds of millions of bytes long—but not those that are measured in billions of bytes. It is currently oriented to commercial and office applications, rather than number-intensive scientific uses. Also, the flexibility designed into the host interface is not present in the disk interface. The iDBP supports a broad but specific class of storage devices.

In addition, it does not support transparent distributed data bases. Data transfers from one unit to another, if desired, are initiated not by the 86/440, but by the host to which it is attached. Likewise, the consolidation of data from multiple iDBPs to satisfy a global query is also the responsibility of the host.

In designing the data-management software, the first question was the choice of data-base definitions and manipulation languages. A relational interface was chosen because it accommodates extremely high-level data-manipulation commands, including those that can operate on entire sets of records in a single step. This is in marked contrast to the typical navigational interfaces, which are lower level and require that individual records be addressed only one at a time. The net effect of using the higher-level interface is a dramatic reduction not only in the size and complexity of applications programs, but also in traffic between the host and iDBP.

Division of labor

By its very nature, the iDBP imposes a division of labor whereby the function of data-base management is separated from the user interface. In the distributed environment for which it is intended, other machines—the hosts—contain the software and hardware that provide the bridge between the user and the data-base processor. Since a bridge must be developed in any case, there is no requirement that the relational nature of the 86/440 must be apparent to the end user if there are good reasons for doing otherwise.

If, by virtue of technical preference or past history, the designer is committed to providing a network or a hierarchical style of data-base management in his product, he

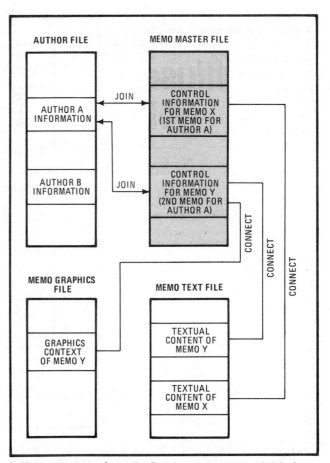

2. Heterogeneous elements. Data-base managers ordinarily focus on either records—data processing—or strings—word processing. The iDBP allows mixing of both using join commands—relating like elements—and connect commands—relating unlike ones.

or she can superimpose it over the relational personality of the iDBP. In fact the iDBP has some special features just to support these nonrelational styles. Chief among these are data-base pointers, which allow records to be addressed by location as well as content, and list-processing primitives, which allow structures of records to be built and accessed by means of such pointers. These mechanisms are completely in violation of the formal rules of the relational model. However, they can simply be ignored if the iDBP is designed into a purely relational end product. The point is that iDBP itself need not be purely relational because the customized host software will act as a filter between it and the user.

Another important departure from traditional data-base management (relational or otherwise) is the ability to manipulate individual files. That is, a user creates files and then may aggregate them into data bases to exploit interfile relationships.

However, a given file need not belong to any data base if there are no relationships with other files. Conventional data-base management, in contrast, starts from the notion of an inclusive data base and does not readily accommodate the existence of unincorporated files.

More importantly, these files do not have to consist of records. That is, a file need not be described in relational terms, and its structure, if any, is not known to the iDBP but is interpretable only by software in the host. For

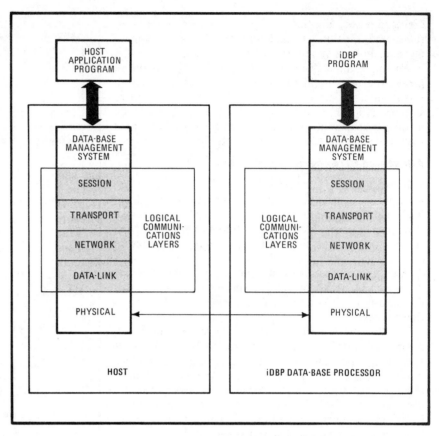

3. High-level communications. The strategy of using a multilayered protocol for the host-to-iDBP interconnection provides great flexibility for the OEM in choosing a specific interface. It also ensures the necessary framework for reliable communication among concurrent tasks executing in the iDBP and its ensemble of hosts.

example, the file might contain a document, a Cobol source library, an array of graphics vectors, or a store-and-forward message queue.

It is important that the iDBP accommodate such arbitrarily structured files because it will be used in small systems where separate subsystems for data bases and files would be too expensive. In local-network environments, data-base servers will also have to manage both data bases and individual files. What's more, the iDBP offers some special extensions to the relational model, which allow these files to be searched, manipulated, and even integrated within a data base.

An unstructured file is treated simply as a string of bytes. Individual substrings can be retrieved and updated, and there is an extremely versatile pattern-search capability for isolating substrings that satisfy the search criteria.

The most radical departure from strict relational principles, however, derives from the unique ability to establish relationships between structured and unstructured files. Fields within records of one file can refer to substrings in other files. Just as the Join—a relational operator command—creates a new file by concatenating records from two source files, the iDBP's Connect operator creates a new file by concatenating records with substrings. For example, a file each of whose records controls a single memorandum in an electronic mail system can connect to one file that contains the textual body of a given memo, connect to another that contains each memo's graphics content in digital representation, and be joined to yet another file of information about the author of the memo (Fig. 2).

The simple ability to interrelate record-oriented infor-

mation with stream-oriented information under a common data-base discipline will change the way designers perceive the necessary solutions in a number of significant application areas, including office automation and computer-aided design. For the first time, they will be able to think of the organization, access, and control of their information in data-base terms. The cost of developing these applications will diminish dramatically as a consequence of this capability.

Although the iDBP does have a number of unusual features, in most respects it offers the same facilities found in mainframe data-base management systems. Among these are:

■ An integrated data dictionary and directory.
■ Coordination of concurrent access by multiple users.
■ Recovery mechanisms that include save-restore, roll-forward, and automatic roll-backward.
■ File-paging algorithms to minimize disk input/output operations.
■ Data-base security and integrity mechanisms.
■ Performance options like hashing and indexing.
■ Data independence, so that the exercise of any performance option will not require changes to the database design or application software.
■ Integrated sorting and merging.
■ Macroinstructions—the ability to define, catalog and invoke frequently used command sequences.

The emphasis on application sophistication clearly differentiates the iDBP from the very simple data-base management systems that are well-suited to personal computers or small-business computers. The 86/440 addresses the more demanding needs of multiuser and network environments. Its capabilities are commensurate with the computational power and storage capacity of such systems.

The challenge in designing the iDBP's interface to the hosts it serves was to select a single strategy that would most easily accommodate a very wide range of system environments. The strategy had to be independent of the host. It also needed to support a spectrum of iDBP roles, from back end for a single host to data-base server for hosts in a heterogeneous network.

The interface's architecture

The answer is a multilayer communications architecture (Fig. 3), such that the full protocol would be used in a network environment and a compatible subset could be configured for the simpler back-end (point-to-point) applications. However, even in the simplest case of a host-iDBP pair, the functionality of the interface must be rich enough to support multiplexing several concurrent dialogues on a single line. This requirement arises from the multiuser nature of the 86/440; that is, several processes in a host can be communicating with corresponding processes in the iDBP on one party line.

The interface also must support reliable delivery of information in both directions, through data-integrity checks and error-recovery mechanisms. This capability is particularly important when the iDBP is used in applications where it is remote from the host.

The communications architecture is typical in that the session, transport, network, and data-link layers are responsible for providing these generic communications services. The layer for data-base management, however, is unique to the iDBP. At this level, the host transmits groups of commands to define access or control files, and the data-base processor returns groups of responses (data and status).

The ability to aggregate commands and responses serves two important purposes. First, communications overhead is minimized because throughput is affected more by the number of transmissions than by the size of each message. Secondly, entire "programs"—sequences of data-base–management commands—can be swallowed up and executed by the iDBP. To complement this capability, branching (if, then, else) and looping instructions have been added to the command set. When decision making and loop control can be offloaded to the 86/440, the traffic on the interface drops dramatically.

Another important benefit of a layered communications framework is the flexibility that derives from the independence of the various layers of the protocol from one another. In particular, new data-link or physical layers can be incorporated as required without modifying the higher layers. So, for example, Ethernet, RS-232-C, IEEE-488, or even a highly customized channel interface can be implemented without reworking the overall communications approach. This partitioning of the protocol is reflected in the modularity of the software and hardware in the iDBP's communications subsystem.

The 86/440 employs a multiprocessor organization (Fig. 4). Several microprocessors execute the complex software and firmware routines that provide the product's functionality. The standard Multibus is the internal high-speed bus used by each processor to communicate with other subsystems and the global memory resource. From a mechanical standpoint, the product is available in several packaging levels, ranging from a board set to a fully enclosed system that is appropriate for applications in the office.

An 8086 configuration

The heart of the system is a processor subsystem constructed around an 8-megahertz 8086, which executes the software of the data-base management system and the operating system. This microprocessor resides on a printed-circuit board that also has the bootstrap read-only memory, diagnostic ROM, RS-232-C diagnostic port (for local or remote service), and 128-K bytes of random access memory. The 8086 can access a 512-K-byte memory board across the Multibus. An additional 384-K-byte memory board can be configured to increase the size of the buffer pool and support more users. All of the RAM modules have error-detection and -correction circuitry to ensure data integrity.

An iDBP can have one to four disk controllers, where each controller is a pc board whose main element is an 8089 I/O processor. Each of these units can handle up to four drives, for a system maximum of 16. For backup and recovery purposes, the system may also be configured with a single 8089-based tape controller for ¼- and ½-in. start-stop drives.

The foundation of the communications subsystem is an 8086-based board that implements the network, transport, and session layers of the host interface proto-

Software-house acquisition buys data-base expertise

The data-base processor for microprocessor systems was an ambitious undertaking, breaking new ground on several fronts. Data-base machines as a class represent new technology, but the iDBP 86/440 was particularly challenging because the paramount design goal was to package mainframe data-base features in a low-cost microprocessor-based vehicle.

Furthermore, it was necessary to extend the notion of data-base management as it applies to conventional data processing, because data processing as such represents only part of the work load for small systems. The iDBP was designed to address the data-manipulation requirements of new applications like those found in office automation.

Although the iDBP development effort did not begin in earnest until late 1979, the product reflects the result of intensive research and development that had been in progress since 1974 at the firm—it was then known as MRI Systems Corp. Over the years, the research emphasis shifted from large back ends (for the system 2000 DBMS) to small systems supporting the relational model of data-base managers. This investment in fundamental groundwork was an important factor in Intel's decision to acquire MRI in 1979 and proceed with the implementation of iDBP. —R. Colin Johnson

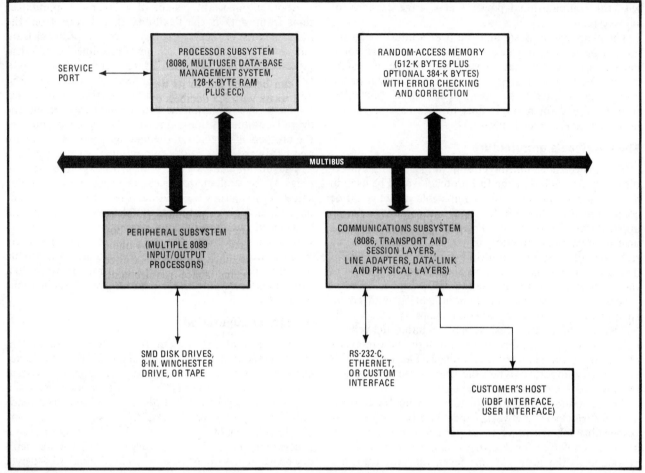

4. Multiprocessor. Several Intel processors organized around a multibus are used in the iDBP. The 8086 main processor in the system is supplemented by another 8086 for protocol handling with the host and by 8089s for communication with mass storage.

col. This board incorporates a dedicated bus with taps for up to eight line adapters, each of them a small pc board with sufficient logic and firmware to implement the data-link and physical layers of the protocol.

Off-the-shelf line adapters will be available to support the RS-232-C electrical interface with asynchronous, synchronous, SDLC (synchronous data-link control), and HDLC (high-level data-link control) lines. Each line-adapter board can drive two channels at speeds up to 50 kilobits a second. Hence, as many as 16 hosts can be connected to a single iDBP using these common RS-232-C–based protocols.

An Ethernet interface is also provided to support local-network implementations. Special links may also be designed as required to accommodate the idiosyncrasies of various host network and channel architectures.

Future directions

Planned software upgrades are aimed at enhancing the capabilities and performance of the data-base manager. What's more, special attention will be paid to the data-management requirements of the automated office and automated design and engineering workbench applications. Key to success in this effort will be a growing understanding of the kind of data objects that are manipulated in these realms, as distinct from those found in traditional data processing.

The hardware strategy is to move from a single product (like the iDBP 86/440 to a family of application-compatible data-base processors covering a range of prices and performance. The next product in the family will focus on the low end—an entry-level iDBP supporting 5¼-in. hard-disk drives for small hosts or networks. Also, research has begun on techniques for implementing data-base logic at the chip level to reduce the cost of building blocks further.

The needs of the high end are also being addressed. Plans are in place to develop a data-base processor based on the new iAPX-286 microprocessor, with more system memory, and an intelligent disk controller. Ultimately, there will be systems organized around 32-bit microprocessor architectures.

In addition to research and development directly related to the evolution of the iDBP product line itself, there is also the potential to incorporate the technology within other Intel products. For example, work has begun on a data-base work station, which would function as a satellite in a large data-processing installation. The work station would permit its operator to spin off subsets of a central data base for local inquiry and report generation by means of a friendly interface. It would bridge the gap between a mainframe data-base management system such as Intel's system 2000 and its own microcomputer-resident data-base manager. □

Bringing greater portability to application programs

This software system's use of an intermediate code lets it run on any small-computer system

by Mark Overgaard, *SofTech Microsystems Inc., San Diego, Calif.*

☐ The old adage "divide and conquer" is taking on a new meaning in software engineering as the modular development of software takes hold. In the design of the UCSD Pascal-based p-System, for example, optimal portability was achieved by an approach that emphasized partitioning. The latest iteration, version IV, continues the emphasis on a modular architecture separating machine-dependent routines from the rest of the software system.

The result is true object-code portability across a wide range of small-computer systems, enhanced in this case by software development tools that encourage compilation in the form of discrete modules. What's more, a sophisticated form of virtual addressing carries this modularity over into program execution as well, maximizing main-memory utilization of small computers.

The issue of software portability is looming ever larger as the small-computer market and the demand for application programs expand. The production of the needed software is complicated by the fact that there is no unanimity in the industry about the best host processor to use in these computers. The 8080 and its derivatives are very popular, but so is the 6502. The newer 16-bit processors, like the 8086 and 68000, are also gaining significant market penetration. Furthermore, as minicomputer manufacturers enter the personal-computer market, microprocessors with minicomputer-compatible instruction sets are also important (for example, the 9900, LSI-11, and MicroNova).

p-System portability

A result of this potentially bewildering array of mutually incompatible hardware is heightened awareness throughout the industry of the benefits of software portability. The reason is that portability allows the same software to be sold across a broad market of ordinarily incompatible hardware systems. This feature allows development efforts to concentrate on the functional improvement to software products, and not on wasteful attention to the logistic difficulties of concurrent maintenance of several versions of a product customized for particular brands.

The portability of the p-System can be understood with the help of a schematic of its architecture (Fig. 1). The architecture has been chosen to isolate application programs and most system components from the details of the host computer and to reduce the effort involved in adapting the p-System to new host configurations.

Most p-System programs are represented entirely in p-code—that is, object code consisting of instructions for the p-machine, or pseudo-machine, an idealized computer architecture optimized for high-level–language execution on small host machines. This p-code is executed by a p-machine emulator written in the native code of the host computer. Object p-code may originate from any of the p-System source languages (UCSD Pascal, Fortran-77, and Basic). As long as a program has no native-code elements, it is isolated entirely from the host computer and can be executed without recompilation and indeed without modifications of any kind on any host hardware supporting the p-System.

It is sometimes necessary, for reasons of performance or access to low-level facilities, to translate part of an application program into the native instruction set of the host. These portions of a program interact directly with

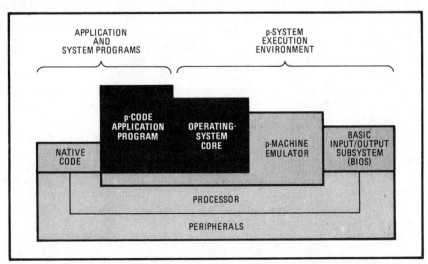

1. Partitioning for portability. The p-System has three principal subsystems: the hardware, the execution environment, and the application and operating-system programs. The deeper tint indicates p-code components; the lighter, native-code components.

```
Unit SimpleGraphics;

Interface

        Procedure PrintScreen;
        Procedure PutDot (xcoordinate, ycoordinate : integer);

Implementation

        ┌─────────────────────────────────────────────────┐
        │  Segment Procedure PrintIt;  begin . . . end;   │
        │  Procedure PrintScreen;  begin PrintIt end;     │
        │  Procedure PutDot;  begin . . . end;            │
        └─────────────────────────────────────────────────┘

End.
```

2. Separation of powers. A unit (a modular program element) can contain an embedded segment routine. Only the public interface declarations are available to users of these units; the private declarations appear after implementation, within the box.

Object-level portability means that the application developer can reduce the development time necessary to turn out a program serving more than one of the processor types supported by version IV—the 6502, 6809, Z80, 8086, 9900, 68000, and LSI-11. Identical object code could be shipped to a customer with any of these machines, and that code could be developed on any of the host computers.

For the user, software investment could be preserved as machines are replaced. What's more, one application program could run on a variety of computers. In fact, if these computers share a disk subsystem, they could even execute the same copy of the software.

To simplify the logistics of software development and distribution, the Universal Medium has been developed [*Electronics*, June 30, 1982, p. 51]. It permits software distribution to most small computers using 5¼-inch soft-sectored floppy disks as a mass-storage medium.

To realize the Universal Medium concept, the software developer must provide the application in a standard format on a diskette. The user must have a diskette containing the p-System operating system and a utility program that temporarily reconfigures the system's programmable disk-controller circuitry so that it can read the format used on all Universal Medium diskettes. As a result, the application object code may be read into the system's main memory and then written out to mass storage in the format that is native to the system. The Universal Medium's merger of the p-System's object-level portability with a standard diskette format should significantly improve the efficiency of the small-computer software marketplace.

Segments and units

The two programming facilities that are probably the most important aids for the development and execution of capable applications are the unit construct, which supports separate compilation of program components, and the segment-routine construct, which supports partitioning of these components into overlayable segments that need to be present in main memory only when they are being used.

The segment routine was the first of these two improvements to be incorporated in USCD Pascal. This construct facilitates the running of programs that are simply too big to fit in the available memory on a small host computer. Using it, USCD Pascal programmers can designate the overlayable partitions of a large program.

A segment routine is a collection of source code whose declaration is immediately preceded by the special word, "segment," that signals the special nature of the routine that follows. The addition of segment does not change

the host processor and possibly even with the peripherals.

Input/output facilities of the p-System are partitioned to improve the portability of the system and its programs. In some cases, almost no adaptation is needed to install the p-System on new hardware.

When the p-System is installed on new host hardware, there may be several levels of adaptation. The simplest possibility is catering to a new type of console terminal. In this case, the screen-I/O component of the operating system must be modified so that requests, say, to clear the screen or home the cursor are implemented appropriately for the chosen terminal. For most terminals, this adaptation is primarily a matter of modifying tables and possibly writing a few lines of Pascal code. The effort involved is usually a matter of hours.

Another possibility is that the host processor is unchanged in the new configuration, but that the peripheral complement or interface protocols are different. In this case, modification of the basic I/O subsystem (BIOS) is necessary. If software drivers for the new devices already exist and are easily integrated, this task may not be large. The total effort here is usually measured in days or weeks.

Finally, if a new host processor is introduced, the p-machine emulator must be reimplemented, along with a BIOS for each target-peripheral environment. The effort required for one of these implementations has ranged from six man-weeks to nine man-months, depending on the experience of the implementer and suitability of the host for p-machine emulation.

Fortunately the level of difficulty involved in each of these degrees of adaptation has an inverse relationship with the likelihood that an adaptation will be needed. Relatively few processor types account for most of the small-computer systems being sold, and for most of these, p-machine emulators have already been written. There are many more I/O configurations, but the effort involved in an adaptation at this level is not great. Variations in console terminals between I/O configurations that are otherwise identical are very common; customizing the p-System to one of these is very simple. Finally, and most importantly, properly written application programs can be moved between version IV p-System installations in p-code form, with no change or recompilation whatsoever.

the meaning of the code, but it may affect the time that is needed for its execution and the amount of memory space that it occupies.

These effects stem from the fact that the corresponding object code is bundled together in what is called a code segment that needs to be present in main memory only when it is being actively executed; at all other times, it may reside on disk. If a code segment is not present in main memory when the corresponding segment routine is activated, there may be some delay as it is read in from disk. The nonsegment routines in each program or module are also bound together as a code segment, which also needs to be present in main memory only when it is being executed.

Benefits of the unit

The original motivation for adding the unit construct to UCSD Pascal was to provide a way of ensuring that libraries of service routines preserve the strong data-type security that is characteristic of Pascal. As realized in version IV of the p-System, the unit construct serves this need well and also provides other benefits.

A unit is a group of routines and data structures, usually related to a common task area. A program or another unit can access these facilities by naming the unit in a simple "uses" declaration. Such a program or unit is called a client module.

A unit consists of two parts: the interface part, which can declare data items and program-routine headings that are public—made available to any client module—and the implementation part, containing the routines as well as any private declarations. These private declarations are available only within the unit, and not to client modules. Units may be compiled separately from their client modules.

A sample unit, called SimpleGraphics, is outlined in Fig. 2. It provides a very simple dot-matrix–oriented graphics facility to its clients. There are only two primitives defined in the interface section: one prints the contents of the entire screen on the system printer; the other puts a dot at a particular coordinate position on the graphics screen of the host computer.

Within the box is the private section of Simple-Graphics where the definitions of the two interface routines, PrintScreen and PutDot, are provided. The definition of PrintScreen is simply a call to the segment routine, which contains the code to transmit a graphical image to the printer. The code will be present in main memory while a print operation is going on, but it may be absent otherwise. The implementation of these two routines can cater to a wide range of graphics and printer equipment while preserving the interface with any client programs that use SimpleGraphics.

First of all, the unit facility does achieve its original objective of supporting strongly typed library routines. In the implementation, the source code of the interface section of a unit is stored by the compiler with the object code it produces for the unit. When a client module uses a unit, this interface text is found by the compiler and essentially recompiled in the context of the client. Thus all the type declarations made in the unit and used in its variables and in the parameters of its routine are known

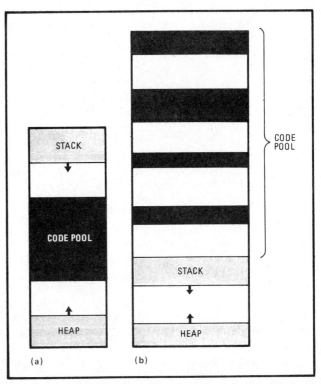

3. Memory-allocation alternatives. Dynamic memory management in version IV of the p-System supports two types of main-memory organization: one in which the system's code pool is unified with the stack and heap data areas (a) and one in which it is separate (b).

and can be checked when the unit's facilities are invoked by the client.

A unit can also encapsulate a computational idea; that is, it can hide from its clients the detailed implementation mechanisms by which the idea is realized. The details of an implementation can be changed over time without making client modules obsolete. Alternatively, several distinct implementations sharing the same interface can serve the cause of different hardware configurations and thus promote application portability.

TurtleGraphics, for example, is a graphics package that is considerably more sophisticated than Simple-Graphics. Variants of this unit have been created for both the Apple II and the IBM Personal Computer. These variants share the same interface with client programs, but the implementations are quite different, because the graphics facilities of the underlying hardware are different.

Dynamic memory management

Segmenting the units of large programs into overlays does overcome the difficulty of too small a main memory, but it raises a new problem of managing the contents of that memory to provide the room for the shifting needs for data and the instructions. Version IV of the p-System provides two answers: internal or external code pools, both dynamically managed.

The internal code pool (Fig. 3a) can expand, contract, or shift in response to the needs of the program for stack and heap space for the data. The p-machine architecture requires that a segment be in main memory when it is being executed. In addition, when an intersegment transfer of control occurs, both segments involved must be present during the transfer.

Much more space is usually available for the code pool than is necessary to meet these minimum constraints. In this case, as many as possible of the most recently used segments are retained. It is also possible for a program to lock segments into memory during a particular period of its execution.

The other possibility is an extended memory configuration (Fig. 3b), in which the "external" code pool is entirely separate from the data area containing the stack and the heap. The architecture of this facility is such that a wide range of host memory organizations can be accommodated, including large virtual address spaces (as in the 68000) and small ones (as in the LSI-11/23). Support of large virtual spaces is compatible with two addressing styles: segmented (as in the 8086 or Z8000) or linear (as in the 68000).

The dynamic and automatic management of code segments in the p-System is a real boon to application-program developers. Very large application programs can be built with much less concern for main-memory constraints than is necessary in other widely available software environments. The same program can run in a 64-K-byte Z80 environment and in a 128-K-byte 68000 environment. There will be performance differences, but the p-System will automatically adjust its management

of the segments of the program to exploit the memory resources of the host. Consequently, its developer need not abandon the 8-bit market in order to exploit the larger address spaces available with 16-bit machines.

The current p-System can manage only one data area and only one code pool. When they are separate, each of these areas can be larger than 64-K of the host's fundamental addressing units (generally 8-bit bytes or 16-bit words). Therefore on a byte-addressed processor like the 8086, the maximum space for code and data that can currently be used by the p-System is 128-K bytes. In spite of this restriction, the compactness of p-code and the sophistication of the p-System's dynamic code-segment management combine to make very substantial application programs highly feasible (perhaps even more feasible than in other software environments that can service a larger physical memory because of the p-System's swapping in and out of code segments).

Most programming environments require the use of a link editor to resolve references between separate compilations and to build a single coherent code file containing the host program and the separately compiled components. In version IV, however, no link editing of separately compiled high-level–language components is required to execute the program using them.

Units in version IV are compiled so that it is unnecessary to bundle them together when forming a program;

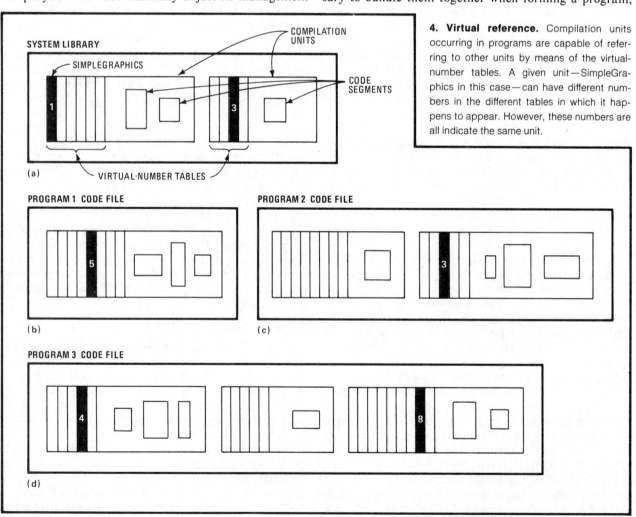

4. Virtual reference. Compilation units occurring in programs are capable of referring to other units by means of the virtual-number tables. A given unit—SimpleGraphics in this case—can have different numbers in the different tables in which it happens to appear. However, these numbers are all indicate the same unit.

Version IV of the p-System in action

Portability, memory management, and modularity all add up to an architecture that is a good foundation for the effective development and execution of application programs. Equally important for both the user and the programmer are the operational capabilities of version IV of the p-System. The capabilities described below are those accessible to both user and programmer; those described opposite are accessible only to the programmer.

The facilities used by both programmer and non-programmer all share a common user-interface approach: a prompt line is maintained at the top of the console screen indicating the current state of the p-System and the options available. Selection from those options is made with single-character commands.

Programs are invoked by name or by shorthand single-character commands for important utilities. Commands to redirect console input/output to disk files or other serial devices are also provided. In addition, a monitor facility can capture typed input so that a console session can later be recreated.

Peripherals are accessed logically. Some of the peripherals (like terminals and printers) can serve as a source or destination of serial streams of bytes, usually ASCII characters. Storage peripherals (like diskettes or Winchester disks) are also supported and can contain directories of named files. A file-handler utility supports housekeeping activities involving these files and peripherals.

The principal text editor requires a cathode-ray-tube console, although another can use a hard-copy terminal. The screen-oriented editor maintains the cursor in the text file being edited and a window showing the current status of that area of the file on the terminal screen. Commands are provided for moving the cursor, finding and replacing textual patterns, inserting and deleting text, and so forth. User-specified left and right margins can be automatically enforced by the editor, and new margin requirements can easily be applied to existing text.

Text files can be printed with the aid of a transfer operation in the file handler. In addition, a print spooler is available to queue files for printing in the background while text editing or other console-intensive operations are going on. Finally, there are text formatters that interpret embedded commands in text files and produce formatted output on a variety of printers.

---

rather, they may be called in as needed by means of a virtual-reference scheme. Each unit contains a table indicating the names of the other units it references and the virtual numbers it uses to refer to them. When a program is invoked, the operating system searches these unit-reference tables and locates the units to which they refer. Then tables are built in main memory to allow calls or other reference between units to reach the correct actual destination, even though virtual numbers are employed.

Figure 4 is an example of using the tables in a suite programs that share access to a library of units. One of the units is SimpleGraphics (in color in each program), and different virtual numbers are used in the various environments to designate this unit.

The p-System places an upper limit of 255 on the number of segment routines declared within a unit plus the number of other units referenced virtually. Thus a program may consist of a extensive network of units.

The support for dynamic linking of separate compilations can aid the application-program developer in several ways. First, no link editing is required when one or more modules of such a program is changed. Assuming that changes are not made to the interface sections of units, the program can be reexecuted as soon as the modified units are recompiled. Second, a single copy (on disk) of the object code of a unit can be shared by multiple programs that use it.

For many large and interactive small-computer application programs, the performance of p-code is fully acceptable. One reason is that the p-machine instruction set has been optimized for compactness. This can mean that the p-code version of a large program requires less I/O activity to support overlaying and may therefore be more responsive than the same program translated entirely into native code. In the p-System, all major programming tools are distributed in p-code, including compilers, assemblers, native-code translators, and a highly responsive screen-oriented editor.

Native code

When native code is required, there are two ways to generate it. First, the native code can be produced automatically by a code-generator program that takes p-code as input and produces equivalent native code for programmer-designated performance-critical sections. Alternatively, it is possible to handwrite native code in assembly language.

No matter how the native code is produced, its execution can be interleaved with p-code execution. That is, a program can have both native and p-code components,

| | | High-level-language source | |
| TRADEOFFS IN APPROACHES TO PROGRAM IMPLEMENTATION | | | |
Factor	Hand-crafted assembly language	Automatically generated native code	p-code
Initial implementation cost	high	low	low
Action to move to distinct processor	reimplement	retranslate from p-code	none
Execution time	fastest	fast: factor of 5 to 10 over p-code	slow
Space requirement	smallest	largest: 50% to 300% over p-code	small

Development tools aid the programmer

All of the capabilities described opposite are crucial to the success of the programmer. For instance, much of the time of a software developer is spent on manipulating natural-language text—and conveniently the screen-oriented editor used for that work is also capable of program editing, for a special mode eases the production of pleasantly indented source text. In addition to these capabilities, version IV of the p-System contains a number of facilities that address the needs of programmers.

Three languages are supported: UCSD Pascal, Fortran-77, and Basic. All three compilers produce p-code as output and share conventions for invocation, syntax-error handling, and so on. Also, interlingual separate compilation is supported for all combinations of languages. The most frequent use of this facility is for access to units written in UCSD Pascal from Basic and Fortran-77.

System utilities also make use of the separate compilation support in the p-System to augment the computational primitives available to programmers. These programmatic utilities are intended to be embedded in, and invoked programmatically from, an application system. Some of them even include related utility programs that are invoked from the console, for example:

■ Turtlegraphics, which allows application programs to produce two-dimensional graphics displays (monochrome or color) by controlling the activities of a fast-moving "turtle" cursor as it carries a "pen" about a graphics display. Automatic scaling and translation of the coordinate system are supported. Turtlegraphics can be adapted to most microcomputer graphics environments. Application-program clients' modules can be made independent of the details of the underlying graphics facilities.

■ KSAM80, a file-management system that supports efficient sequential and keyed retrieval of data records in p-System files. One primary together with one or more alternate keys are supported; these can be fixed or variable in length.

■ Xenofile for CP/M, which permits p-System application programs to read and write data on CP/M-organized disks. Primitives available include analogs of most of the file-related CP/M system calls.

Assemblers for 6502, 9900, 6809, 68000, 8086, Z80, 8080, Z8, and PDP-11 are available and share common directives and expression syntax. Machine-instruction syntax is as close as possible to that of the principal manufacturer of the target processor. Macroinstruction definition and conditional assembly are supported. Any of these assemblers can run on any p-System, regardless of the host processor in the development system.

When an assembly-language routine is referenced from a high-level compilation unit, a link-editor program is used to install the assembly-language object code into the main code segment of the compilation unit. The unit then is available for dynamic linking at program-invocation time (as has been detailed within the body of the article). All p-System languages can reference assembly-language routines in this way.

Assembly language can also be intended for standalone use, outside the usual p-System environment. In this case, separately assembled components are link-edited together and then processed by a utility that discards the p-System code-file superstructure and prepares a simple memory image. This facility is used, for example, in building p-machine emulators.

and frequent transitions back and forth between the two modes of execution are likely.

The choice among p-code and the two approaches to native code for a particular portion of a program requires an analysis of tradeoffs among several factors (see table). The result of these considerations is that, when native-code generation is available for particular processor, handwritten assembly language is very rarely used and then only when there is a requirement for low-level access to the host hardware that simply cannot be accomplished from a high-level language.

The use of executable p-code as input to p-System native-code generators has several implications. The code-generation step can be skipped entirely during program development, when execution speed is not as important as improving programmer productivity. Also, the p-code to be translated can come from any of the p-System high-level languages. To boot, application programs can be distributed in portable p-code form and optimized by end users with their native-code generators. A software house can even mark the sections to be translated into native code with special delimiters, making the process automatic.

There is another important boon to the ability of the p-System to support a mixture of p-code and native code within a single program. In the typical program 80% of the execution time is spent on 10% of the code. It is therefore useful to be able to optimize the speed of that

crucial portion while at the same time preserving the compactness of p-code for the remainder.

The p-System currently serves the stand-alone work station primarily. It will be necessary eventually to provide better facilities for data- and resource-sharing among work stations. For instance, many organizations already own several different computer systems and need to share expensive peripheral resources (like large disks) among local clusters of these machines. In addition, application programs for computers often need shared access to data from multiple work stations (as, for instance, in a multioperator data-entry operation).

Future evolution

These needs are to be met by integrating local-network support into the p-System, while preserving its single-user orientation. Just as the p-System is portable across many kinds of host computers, this local-network support will be adaptable to various physical network media—like Ethernet, Wangnet, and Omninet.

The first step in p-System local-net activities is a prototype based on Corvus Systems' Omninet medium. Most of the processor types supported by the software have already been attached. The portability of the p-System is proving valuable in this heterogeneous local-network environment because it promotes the effective homogeneity on which distributed application programs necessarily depend. □

Object-oriented languages tackle massive programming headaches

By encapsulating data and the procedures that manipulate them,
languages like Ada restrict data access to authorized routines

by Kevin C. Kahn, *Intel Corp., Aloha, Ore.*

☐ A monumental shift is under way in computer programming, as its practitioners move to associate data structures with control procedures in discrete modules. While the move is in some respects a logical extension of structured programming, it still represents a radical departure from conventional programming methods that will profoundly affect the way users interact with computers. An overview of this new methodology, called object-oriented programming, underscores the major implications for both programmer and user.

The new emphasis in programming is largely a result of new demands occasioned by the spread of computers. The difficulties already inherent in designing software increase whenever real-time, asynchronous events require computer interaction with the real world. Add to these requirements the need for fail-safe systems such as those used to control and navigate airplanes, and dreams of developing and maintaining reliable software turn into nightmares.

Faced with these challenges, programmers are pressed against the outside limits of present programming tools. Research aimed at overcoming these difficulties has shifted the view of the programming task itself. No longer is the major concern program control flow—a program's data structures have become paramount.

Adding structure

Early work in structured programming concentrated on bringing clarity and discipline to program control flow—the ordering of processes or functions that manipulate data. More recently, work has concentrated on applying the same level of discipline to the organization of the data itself. The result is a new design methodology that modularized data handling as well as procedures: object-oriented programming.

Using objects, as will become clear, provides a natural approach to programming because it reflects the way in which humans interact with their world. Among lan-

iAPX-432 cooperates in object-oriented processing

Just as object-oriented programming supports a natural transference from a system designer's thought processes into a piece of software, the iAPX-432 microprocessor supports the resulting software structures with a hardware base tailored for handling objects. Like any computer, the 432 processor provides basic data types and instructions such as integer addition, character manipulation, floating-point multiplication, and logical operations. In addition, its architecture gives an extra measure of higher-level support through the direct recognition and manipulation of what are called system objects.

Of the several types of system objects, some reflect the structure of a program and contain information about its processing state. First, there is the processor object, unique to each processor in a system, containing processor-status information, as well as reference information for the process currently being executed. Also, each process in a system is assigned a process object, which holds scheduling information and serves as a reference for the context currently being executed.

Continuing this hierarchical structure, a context object—one for each activation of a procedure—contains housekeeping information, including the instruction pointer for this context, the stack pointer for the context, and a return link for the calling context. Each context object serves as a reference for both instruction objects and data objects that can be accessed by the context itself. The instruction objects contain only instructions and are the only type of object that a processor will use as a source of instructions to be fetched and executed.

Because most errors in programs quickly lead to an attempt to violate another program's address space, the 432 helps make software easier to debug by trapping addressing errors before any damage can occur. This capability-based addressing limits the address space of each process to only those specific objects it has the need to access.

To perform this task, each 432 object contains a list of references—access descriptors—that describe which other objects an object may access and the operations it may perform on them. Whenever a process attempts to gain access to an object, the hardware first checks to ensure that the process has a valid access descriptor. If valid, the access descriptor is translated into a physical address. Otherwise a fault occurs and the operating system is notified. Because of this protection, programs may be independently modified without fear of damaging critical portions of the system.

guages, Ada embodies the present ideal for object-oriented languages, just as the Intel iAPX-432 is a microprocessor that supports that ideal in silicon (see "iAPX-432 cooperates in object-oriented processing,").

One of the earliest techniques for dividing the programming burden was the subroutine, which isolated the function it performed from all others and could be called into service whenever that function was needed. The subroutine enabled the programmer to limit the scope of his work to a single function at a time within the larger programming task. It also was an important step in reducing the complexity of programs by eliminating the need to reprogram common functions.

Traditional modularity

Supplementing this approach was structured programming, which arranged the control flow of an algorithm in order to clarify a program's structure and meaning and thereby to ease program development. In terms of clarity, this approach was the most useful when it insisted upon one-entrance, one-exit, top-down programming; in other words, each section of code—each module—had one entrance point and one exit point that flowed logically to the entrance point of another module. The confusing use of go-to instructions interspersed throughout a module—providing multiple exit points to numerous sections of code—was eliminated with this approach, making program logic much easier to follow.

Constructing code in such a way that it could be reduced to a list of subroutine calls whose logic was easily followed meant a great step forward in program clarity, but it still ignored the task of managing the complex data structures. So long as a program's routines retained global access to data, they tended to interact by means of shared data, often in undisciplined ways.

A consequence of this situation is that, while it is possible in a traditional modular program to isolate the particular routine that performs a specific function, the data associated with that particular routine is not isolated from routines in other modules. Such a form of interaction between program modules and data violates the principle of module integrity. The most obvious practical consequence occurs in program debugging and maintenance. When the data output by a program is erroneous, it is difficult to isolate the offending routine because the data is shared or manipulated by so many of them (Fig. 1).

Early programming languages supported the traditional procedural approach to modularity. Fortran's Common declaration, for example, provided global data storage: any routine that required the data could access it. In a Fortran program that uses the Common declaration extensively, the programmer could fail to grasp the relationships among a piece of data and the program's various routines, regardless of how small and well-structured they may be. Cobol and PL/1 suffer the same shortcomings.

Recently, languages like Pascal have advanced the ideas of data structuring and typing. Pascal also embodies all the flow-structuring primitives developed for structured programming. Nevertheless, it does little to improve the data modularity of a program. Any variable that must exist throughout the entire run of a Pascal program must be declared at the outermost level of the program and is therefore globally accessible to any of the program's procedures.

Difficult error isolation

The Pascal programmer finds it difficult to identify and control the many possible manipulations that apply to a particular data structure. Because it is difficult to determine which procedures modify or access the data structures, the programmer still has a hard time isolating errors, particularly those occurring during the ongoing maintenance of a program.

D. L. Parnas described in 1972 the essential features of an alternative approach to modularization that

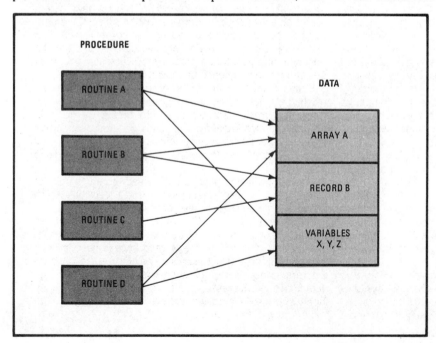

1. Lack of discipline. When program routines (left) have global access to shared data (right), it is difficult to determine just where data errors originate because it is difficult to isolate the offending routine.

encompassed both control and data structures. Using this approach—object-oriented programming—a module is designed to encapsulate a small set of software design decisions. Such decisions generally defined one or a few data structures and the ways they could be manipulated. Included within this module are decisions about data layout and formatting, as well as algorithm choices.

By this definition, a module is not a single subroutine or data structure, but rather an interrelated collection of procedures and data: the encapsulation of a single major design decision. Such a module provides a service or function to the outside world through its prescribed interface; the means of achieving that service or function—the data structures and algorithms that are used—are neither visible nor usually accessible.

The interface defines the module to the outside world. It may provide the user with a set of procedures that manipulate the module's internal data structures and may include constants or variables that the user can access, as well as the data-type definitions that he or she must know. Among the data types may be some whose structure is delineated only within the internal coding of the module, and they are accessible only to the module that creates them.

Logical encapsulation

Programming structures of this sort, which remain inscrutable to all but their creator, are said to be logically encapsulated because from the user's point of view, they are black boxes without internal structure. It is fitting that such encapsulated data structures should be termed objects, because they are used much like objects in the real world: that is, they have specific visible properties and certain uses, but their inner workings are of little concern.

In addition, the modules that contain these data structures can themselves be thought of as objects for other modules to use. This conceptual approach to programming provides a unified view in which a program consists of a network of objects that use one another to perform the desired application.

Object-oriented programming shares with control-oriented modular programming the ability to contain a given algorithm within one procedure or a small set of procedures. In the object-oriented approach, however, these procedures are clustered to operate upon a common data structure. Thus, for any major data structure it is immediately apparent what procedures may affect it.

Any errors in the data structure must have been caused by one of these procedures, since access to its inner details is restricted to the procedures of the defin-

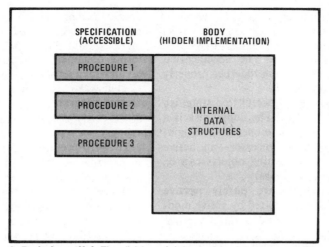

2. Body beautiful. The division of Ada modules into an accessible specification and a separate hidden body allow access to the services provided by the module, while shielding the details of implementation from unauthorized manipulation by the user.

ing module that reads and writes to that data structure. By the same token, any changes to the design of the data structure will affect only the procedures within the module defining it.

An analogy can be made between the hidden data structures within a programming module and the pattern of bits recorded onto a floppy disk used for data storage. A floppy disk can be used by a word-processing machine to store text in a way that leaves the patterns of data storage internal to the disk entirely invisible to the user. The person using the word processor need have no familiarity with its internal workings nor with the format of data storage on the floppy disk in order to use them.

Similarly, in programming it is useful to be able to pass over how to accomplish an operation in order to focus on the module or object that performs the desired operation. This approach makes program design primarily a question of deciding what are the major tasks to be accomplished and setting about building the objects that will do each of these tasks.

Programming languages have naturally evolved to support this view of programming. Simula, Smalltalk, Mesa, Clu, Alphard, Model, and others embody language constructs to express and enforce this sort of modularization. Ada, of course, is firmly rooted in this methodology.

Ada permits the definition of a module called a package, which has two parts: a specification and a body (Fig. 2). The specification of the package serves as an interface, or a contract between the user and the developer of the package. It describes the access that a user has to the services provided by the package, specifying the procedures that may be called, the parameters that they expect, and other information relevant to the use of the module.

So long as the specification or contract is upheld, changes can be made on either side of the interface, that is, by the developer or the user. This flexibility frees users from needing to understand how all the parts of the system are implemented.

The body of the package provides the details of the algorithms and data structures that compose the service provided by the package. These details are completely inaccessible to the user of the package. They may, however, be changed in any manner by the package designer so long as they continue to provide the service defined by the specification.

The Ada compiler ensures that calls to the module and the implementation provided in the package body agree with the specification of the module. An important consequence of this package structure is that, once the specification of a package has been agreed upon, development can proceed in parallel with that of other packages or modules that will use it. The specification ensures that the modules will function together properly when they are finally integrated.

When talking about objects, it is useful to distinguish between active and passive objects. The floppy disk is a passive object because it performs no operation without being acted upon by the word processor—an active object. In the same way, programming objects can be either passive (data) or active (routines).

Encapsulated data structures are purely passive objects that are defined and manipulated by active modules that understand their internal structure. A purely active programming object would be a collection of procedures that operate on internal data structures to provide desired outputs. Many programming objects are hybrid in form, combining properties of both active and passive objects.

Active and passive objects

The usefulness of understanding the active and passive object types comes in pursuing further definitions that occur in object-oriented programming. Some of these are easily explained and grasped by analogy.

To return to the word-processing example, the floppy disk is an object that may have a limited and well-defined set of operations performed upon it by the agent defining it (the word processor), but may not otherwise be used. Inserting the disk into a machine other than the word processor would be meaningless.

The owner can, of course, give the disk to anyone else if he wishes, and that person may in turn put the disk into the word processor along with a request that it perform a specific operation, so long as it is one of the specific operations defined for the use of the disk.

For its part, the word processor need not keep track of the disk at all, because the two objects exist independently, except when it is necessary for the processor to perform a specific operation using the disk. Furthermore, should the manufacturer find a better way of storing documents on the disk, it need not change the way in which a person uses the word processor.

The word processor corresponds to what object-oriented programming calls a type manager. The class of objects that a type manager controls is called—not surprisingly—a type. If the word processor manages a type called word-processor-disk, then an individual disk that it manages is called an object of the type known as word-processor-disk type.

A given version of a form letter kept on the disk is an instance of the form letter. A different instance of the same form letter could occur when the letter is being sent to a different person, which corresponds to a different context in which the form letter is called.

As a programming example, suppose a programmer wishes to create a task or process in an operating system such as the iAPX 432's iMAX. He or she wants to create the process in order to run some program as an independent unit in a computer system. In this case, it is a process type manager that would perform operations upon objects of the type known as process.

One such operation would be Create, which would take some parameters about the process being created—such as the name of the program to be run—and return a process object to the calling routine (Fig. 3). This process object is a data structure that contains all the information needed to run the process: its priority, the current value of its instruction pointer, its storage location in memory, etc.

None of this internal structure, however, would be accessible to the user of the process. The program that called to have the process created could pass the pointer to·the process object along to other routines if it needed to, but it could not directly manipulate the process object itself.

Instead, it would call other operations in the process-

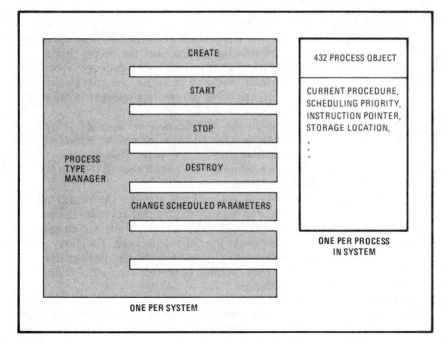

3. Just the type. A process type manager (left) establishes a process object (right) when asked to do so by some object in the system. The process type manager can be called upon subsequently to manipulate or control the process object.

4. Sample code. An Ada specification for a telephone directory (a) is a general format of procedures and data structures that can be turned into a specific implementation, such as a very small directory that uses a simple array of names and numbers (b).

```
package Telephone_Directory is

    type telephone_number is . . . ;

    type subscriber_name is . . . ;

    not_found: exception;

    function Find_number (name: subscriber_name) return telephone_number;

    procedure Add_number (name: subscriber_name; number: telephone_number);

    procedure Delete_number (name: subscriber_name);

    . . .

end Telephone_Directory;
(a)
```

```
package body Telephone_Directory is

    type directory_item is

      record

        name: subscriber_name;

        number: telephone_number;

      end record;

    directory: array (1 . . 100) of directory_item;

    directory_count: range 0 . . 100;

    function Find_number (name: subscriber_name) return telephone_number is

    begin

      for i in 1 . . directory_count loop

        if directory (i) .name = name then return directory (i) .number; end if;

      end loop;

      raise not_found;

    end Find_number;

    . . .

end Telephone_Directory;
(b)
```

type-manager module to do such things as start or stop the process, change its scheduling priority, or destroy the process object when it was finished running. Process objects and other passive objects have an outside representation because their data structure exists independently of—or outside—their type managers. A process type manager that uses an outside representation of a data structure in this way is exactly analogous to a word processor, which keeps its data structures outside itself on disks.

An active object that is self-contained performs all its defined operations upon internal data structures and therefore need not manifest an external data object. A real-world example of such an object is a simple pocket calculator, which performs a well-defined set of operations. Its internal structure, while clearly essential to the correct performance of its operations, remains inaccessible to the user.

In programming terms, a particular calculator is an object of some type, say, a four-function calculator. The type manager is the manufacturer that built it, who probably provides only the Create operation and perhaps a repair operation for four-function calculator objects. The buyer may give it to anyone, but it will still perform only its specified functions.

A similar example of an active object in programming would be a module that maintains a telephone directory (Fig. 4). Such an object would be of the type telephone directory and would consist of a set of procedures together with some internal data structures. Such a module would provide procedures for adding a person's name and phone number to the directory and retrieving the phone number for a given person. It might also have other procedures that update phone numbers, keep track of additional numbers for a person, and so on. However, the internal structure of the directory would not be visible to the user of the module.

This last point is important, because it might be necessary at some time to change the implementation of the module and such a change should not affect its users. For example, a simple array of names and numbers might be quite adequate if a small number of names were kept in the directory, but if the list grew too large, it might be better to switch to some more exotic structure. That change must remain invisible to the user; and

so long as the interface is undisturbed, it will.

Furthermore, the programmer will find that the object-oriented modularization will simplify his task because all the routines that operate on the data would be in a single known location. By contrast, with a conventional approach to modularization, such a major change would require locating every routine in the program that accessed the directory. Even if only a few routines in the original design of the program accessed the directory, maintenance or enhancement of the program may have added unexpected references to the directory structure. It is because of such hidden program references that massive data reorganizations are feared by program development groups.

Active objects have an inside representation because their data structures are maintained inside the module that provides the operations of the object. One such directory object might be needed for each department within an organization. In such a case, a telephone directory manager would be responsible for creating new instances of telephone directories as needed.

Most objects are really hybrids in that it is difficult to classify them as purely active or passive. The telephone directory objects just mentioned are active when viewed as directories, but passive from the point of view of the telephone directory manager that creates new ones. □

2.
CPU
ARCHITECTURE

Through their design of single-chip central-processing units, microprocessor designers can rightly lay claim to sparking the revolution in information technology that is putting inexpensive, yet powerful computers in homes and on office desks. From the earlier 8-bit CPU designs, semiconductor manufacturers have taken giant strides in creating new types of chips. Even though the boom in 16-bit microprocessors has not yet played out, a new generation of 32-bit processor chips is beginning.

Accompanying this new generation of design, alternate architectures for microprocessors are beginning to share the limelight. By concentrating on the specific requirements of particular application areas, designers are able to construct hardware structures that closely match the needs of the environment. For the software engineer, this means direct support in hardware for functions that once had to be built up out of a cumbersome series of software instructions. Although the use of special-purpose CPU architectures is still gaining momentum, the end of the war for more bits—signalled with the arrival of 32-bit microprocessors—will bring on the first skirmishes between chip vendors seeking to expand vertically into special applications markets.

In this chapter, technical articles mark the major milestones in the manufacture of new microprocessors. Beginning with articles on 32-bit microprocessors, this chapter reviews the current crop of 16-bit machines and ends with a look forward at the parallel architectures that will form the basis of the next generation of computer systems.

32-bit processor chip integrates major system functions

On-chip cache feeds six-stage pipeline for high throughput software-protected with paged memory management

by Don Alpert, Dean Carberry, Mike Yamamura, Ying Chow, and Phil Mak, *Zilog Inc., Campbell, Calif.*

☐ The once-distinct boundaries between micro-, mini-, and mainframe computer architectures have been fast eroding in the face of advances in very large-scale integrated-circuit design. Now, a 32-bit processor chip, the Z80,000 central processing unit, breaks down the last of the barriers to concentrating mainframe power in an integrated-circuit chip. In addition to the extra functional capability and performance gained with full 32-bit address and data formats, the 1.5-million-instruction-per-second Z80,000 boasts a 32-bit pipelined processor with both virtual memory management and cache memory—all on a single IC.

Through a variety of selectable options—such as segmented or linear addressing, size of address space, organization of translation tables, and method of protecting input and output—designers gain the ability to tune the power of the Z80,000 to the unique demands of specialized applications. In keeping with its flexible architecture, the Z80,000 allows system designers to choose the memory data width, access time, and bandwidth needed for the particular cost and performance objectives (see "The ins and outs of Z80,000 processor performance,"). Likewise, its external interface supports low-cost systems spanning the performance range from dedicated controllers to superminicomputers. In addition, the processor, which will be available in the spring of 1984, is compatible with Zilog's complete line of Z8000 support, including compilers, the ZRTS real-time operating system, Bell Laboratories' Unix operating system, and numerous peripheral components.

Upwardly compatible with the Z8000, the Z80,000 advances the cause of on-chip computing on several fronts, with enhancements to the addressing range, register file, addressing modes, instruction set, and exception handling. With its 32-bit logical addressing, the Z80,000 is capable of directly accessing 4 billion bytes in each of four address spaces, for a total addressability of 16 billion bytes. These address spaces include separate instruction and data partitions in both the system and normal operating modes.

Two bits in the flag-and-control word allow programmers to select among three modes of address representation for accessing this huge memory space—compact, segmented, and linear. For programs with an address space of less than 64-K bytes, the compact 16-bit address results in very dense code and efficient use of the base registers. The second type of addressing, 32-bit segmented addressing, leaves two options in the hands of designers. By using bit 31 of the address, programmers can select either a segmented address with a 15-bit segment number and 16-bit offset or one with a 7-bit segment number and 24-bit offset. Thus, for example, a system may be designed that can accommodate up to 32,768 segments each of up to 64-K bytes in size.

During address calculations the segment number is unchanged; only the offset is affected. Many applications benefit from the logical structure of segmentation by allocating individual objects such as a program module, stack, or large data structure to separate segments.

Finally, the CPU also supports 32-bit linear addressing, permitting uniform and unstructured access to 4 gigabytes of memory. Many applications benefit from the flexibility of linear addressing by allocating objects at arbitrary positions in the address space.

Two methods of input/output addressing further extend the flexibility of the Z80,000. In one method, the CPU maps data memory references to I/O ports through the memory management mechanism. This technique affords user programs protected access to I/O. The second mechanism—particularly useful when memory management is turned off—uses privileged instructions dedicated for I/O. Whichever method is used, the external interface generates I/O status and timing for the references.

With 16 32-bit general-purpose registers, the Z80,000 enjoys the largest register file of any microprocessor. Its architecture also includes a 32-bit program counter, a 16-bit flag-and-control word, and nine other control registers. Further adding to the part's flexibility is the unique overlapped organization of the register file, which uses the first 16 bytes as accumulators for byte data. The same portion of the register file is also used for the first set of eight word-length registers as well as the first set of four long-word–length registers. This organization makes it possible for bytes to be manipulated conveniently, especially for byte-stuffing operations, while leaving most of the register file free to hold addresses and other data. Two of the registers in the file are dedicated to holding the stack pointer (SP) and frame pointer (FP) used by call, enter, exit, and return instructions.

The program counter and flag-and-control word form the program status registers, which are automatically saved for traps and interrupts. The bits in the flag and control word are used to indicate operating modes, masks for traps and interrupts, flags set by arithmetic and logical instructions, and process state. The remaining control registers are used for memory management and system configuration.

Change of address

In addition, the Z80,000 supports nine general addressing modes with most instructions. These modes are register, direct address, indirect register, index, base, immediate, base index plus displacement, program counter relative, and program counter relative plus index. The last three are used in segmented operation only. The other, general addressing modes allow operands to be located in a register, in the instruction, or in memory. The index register used in index, base index, or relative

---

The ins and outs of Z80,000 processor performance

Although a pipelined architecture and cache memory boost the performance of the 32-bit Z80,000 microprocessor chip, they also complicate the measurement of its performance. Breaking out instruction processing time into the sum of three components—execution, pipeline, and memory delays—is the best approach.

The execution time for an instruction is the number of cycles required to execute the instruction when all memory references hit in the cache and translation-lookaside buffer (TLB), and there is no interference from other instructions in the pipeline. The average execution time depends on the execution time of individual instructions (below, left) and on the frequency distribution of op codes and addressing modes. Common instructions, such as loading a register with a word operand specified by a base-register-plus-displacement addressing mode, execute in one processor cycle (two clock cycles). The same load instruction requires 10 cycles on Zilog's Z8002, 12 on Motorola's MC68000, 17 on Intel's 8086, and 10 on National's NS16032 when there are no wait states. The average instruction execution delay for the Z80,000 is 1.3 processor cycles.

Pipeline delays are caused by several types of dependencies among instructions. The most significant delays are for branch instructions, such as unconditional jump, conditional jump, call, return, and so on. When a branch is taken, a gap develops in the flow of instructions through the pipeline while the branch target instruction is fetched. Unconditional branches create a gap of two processor cycles. Conditional branches cause a delay of three processor cycles when the

branch is taken but no delay when it is not. The average branch delay is 0.5 processor cycle per instruction.

Another significant pipeline delay occurs when an instruction modifies a register that is required for an address calculation by either of the next two instructions. When this occurs, the address calculation must wait one or two processor cycles until the instruction modifying the register has executed. The average register interlock delay is 0.2 processor cycle per instruction.

Several other minor causes of pipeline delays together average 0.2 processor cycle. The average pipeline delay caused by branches, register interlocks, and other causes is 0.9 processor cycle per instruction.

Memory delays are caused by misses in the cache and TLB. This delay depends on the memory system used with the CPU. Considered here are three memory systems that might be used with the Z80,000. Memory 1 has a 16-bit data path, a cycle time of three processor cycles, and no burst transfers; memory 2 has a 32-bit data path, a cycle time of three processor cycles, and no burst transfers; memory 3 has a 32-bit data path, a cycle time of three processor cycles, and burst transfers.

When the processor fetches an instruction or operand that misses in the cache, a delay of three processor cycles is required to access main memory. The effectiveness of the cache is measured by its hit ratio (h)—the fraction of

Z80,000 INSTRUCTION EXECUTION TIMES IN PROCESSOR CYCLES	
Instruction	Number of cycles
Load long word, register to register	1
Add long word, memory to register	1
Compare word, immediate to register	2
Multiply long word, memory to register	20
Divide long word, register to register	36

Z80,000 CACHE PERFORMANCE			
Memory configuration	Memory 1	Memory 2	Memory 3
Memory cache performance			
Hit ratio	0.62	0.75	0.88
Misses per instruction	0.65	0.42	0.21
Delay per instruction	1.9	1.3	0.63
Translation-lookaside-buffer performance			
Hit ratio	0.98	0.98	0.98
Misses per instruction	0.04	0.04	0.04
Delay per instruction	0.78	0.56	0.56

index addressing mode can be either a word or long-word value. Although the most frequently used memory addressing modes may be encoded compactly, longer encodings that span the entire address space are used in the less frequent cases.

Programmers will directly benefit from the architecture of the Z80,000, since the instruction set is oriented toward the compilation of programs written in high-level languages, such as C and Pascal. Working on 8-, 16-, and 32-bit operands, the instructions handle binary arithmetic, logical, and signed and unsigned multiply and divide operations, as well as string operations, such as move, compare, search, test, and translate. Other instructions manipulate bit fields such as are necessary for packed records and video graphics. Four instructions—call, enter, exit, and return—handle procedure linkage. Enter and exit specify the registers to save and restore using a bit mask. Enter indivisibly establishes the new activation

record and initializes an exception handler, making possible asynchronous traps for supporting Ada.

Performance booster

Floating-point instructions find a performance boost through the use of the Z8070 arithmetic processing unit. This coprocessor complies with the complete P754 standard proposed by the Institute of Electrical and Electronics Engineers for floating-point arithmetic, including single-precision, double-precision, and double-extended-precision representation. When the coprocessor is not present in the system, the CPU traps floating-point instructions for emulation by a software package. The Z8070 also handles arithmetic on packed binary-coded decimal strings.

In addition to handling floating-point exceptions according to IEEE P754, the Z80,000 includes extensive facilities for other forms of run-time error detection and

ords fetched that are found in the cache. To determine the average delay caused by cache misses, it is useful to compute the average number of misses per instruction, μ. On average, 1.4 instruction words and 0.3 operand word are fetched per instruction executed. Therefore, the average number of cache misses per instruction is given by $\mu = .7(1 - h)$. The average delay per instruction due to cache misses is 3μ. The resulting values for cache hit ratio and misses and delay per instruction for the three memory systems are shown in the table (right) on the facing page.

The delay due to TLB misses depends not only on the memory system, but also on the number of levels of translation tables. The delay in processing a TLB miss is $(5+T)*N$, where T is the number of processor cycles for an aligned 32-bit memory reference and N is the number of levels in the translation tables. The calculation of average TLB miss delay is similar to cache miss delay, but operand stores can also cause a TLB miss because the page table entry is needed to store the operand in physical memory. On average, 0.15 operand word is stored per instruction. The TLB hit ratios and the misses and delays per instruction (with two-level translation tables) for the three memory systems appear in the table to the right on the facing page.

Now that the components of average instruction processing time have been determined, performance can be calculated. The results (below, left) indicate the average instruction processing time is from 3.4 to 4.9 processor cycles, depending on the memory system. This corresponds to a performance range of 1.0 to 1.5 million instructions per second with a 10-megahertz central-processing-unit clock and 600-nanosecond memory cycle time. By comparison, a Z8000 executing the same workload with the same clock speed and memory cycle time executes 0.7 MIPS. Zilog will also introduce parts rated at clock speeds up to 25 MHz, which with 240-ns memory cycle time will have a performance of 2.5 to 3.7 MIPS.

The performance of the Z80,000 CPU cited here has been evaluated for a workload of 15 nonsegmented programs used by the Zilog Z8000 microcomputer system. The programs (listed in the table below) are written in C and run in normal mode under Zilog's Zeus version of the Unix operating system.

Z80,000 PROCESSING PERFORMANCE

Memory system	Million instructions per second	Instruction processing time (T_I)*	Execution delay (T_E)*	Pipeline delay (T_D)*	Memory delay (T_M)*
16-bit bus (no burst)	1.1	4.9	1.3	0.9	2.7
32-bit bus (no burst)	1.3	4.0	1.3	0.9	1.8
32-bit bus (burst)	1.6	3.4	1.3	0.9	1.2

*$T_I = T_E + T_D + T_M$ (T = time in processor cycles)
Z80,000 at 10-MHz, 600-ns memory cycle time, with 98% translation-lookaside-buffer hit ratio, and with two-level translation tables

PROGRAM WORKLOAD USED FOR Z80,000 PERFORMANCE EVALUATION

Program	Use
C1	C compiler parser
C2	C compiler code generator
C3	C compiler optimizer
C4	C compiler lister
CPP	C compiler preprocessor
DIFF	file comparison
ED	line editor
GREP	pattern searching
LS	file directory listing
NM	load module name listing
OD	octal dumping of core images
PR	format for line printer
SED	stream editor
SORT	sorting
VI	screen editor

software debugging. For debugging, programmers may use breakpoint instructions and the single-instruction mode of operation. Supplementing floating-point exception traps are other traps for dealing with integer overflow, out-of-bounds array subscripts, and attempted execution of reserved codes. Operating system traps for system calls, privileged instructions, memory-access violations, and page faults keep user programs out of the realm of system-level functions. When the CPU detects an exception—whether a trap or interrupt—the program counter and flag-and-control word are saved on the system stack. The CPU then fetches a new program counter and flag-and-control word from a table in memory.

A bit in the flag-and-control word selects distinct operating modes for system and application software. Only system mode programs are privileged to execute I/O instructions and modify registers controlling memory management and interrupts. This privileged mode, called the system mode, is further protected from the user, or normal, mode by a separate stack pointer. The memory management mechanism further protects the operating system from damage by user programs and protects user programs from other users. Thus, sensitive portions of the operating system are usually executed in system mode. Programs executing in normal mode can request that services be performed in system mode through the system call instructions and trap.

Memory management at hand

Through its on-chip memory management features, the Z80,000 eases the operating system's task of handling a 4-gigabyte address space while taking into account protection and address translation. The CPU does this by implementing a paging translation mechanism similar to that used in mainframes and superminicomputers. The memory management mechanism divides the logical address space into 1-K-byte pages, and the physical address space into 1-K-byte frames. Since a logical page address can be mapped to any physical frame address, memory allocation becomes quite simple.

Through cooperation between the operating system and the Z80,000, the logical addresses generated by a program are translated to the physical addresses used to access memory. Once the operating system creates translation tables in memory and initializes pointers to the tables in CPU control registers, the Z80,000 automatically references the tables to perform address translation and access protection. Further assisting the operating system in implementing virtual memory, the CPU separately marks pages that have been referenced and those that have been modified. Software correction of the program counter or other registers is unnecessary, since the CPU automatically recovers from address translation traps to allow instruction restart.

Reduction in parts count is only one of the advantages gained by integrating memory management with the processor. Memory access is faster because the CPU generates physical addresses, thus eliminating the delay of an external memory-mapping circuit. Also, locating the memory management functions on the same chip as the processor allows translation errors to be detected before the actual memory access is performed. This simplifies recovery from memory faults and improves performance.

Ready reference

A special on-chip buffer, called the translation-lookaside buffer (TLB), holds the information needed to translate the 16 most recently used pages. During the address calculation, a logical address is presented to the TLB for translation. If the logical page address matches an entry in the TLB associative-tag memory—a TLB hit—the corresponding physical frame address is read from the TLB data memory. Only if the logical page address does not match any valid TLB address tag—a TLB miss—does the CPU reference the tables in memory to perform the translation, and the missing entry replaces the least recently used entry in the TLB.

Figure 1 illustrates the four fields in the logical address that are used by the address translation mechanism to load a missing entry into the TLB. The translation process begins by selecting one of four table descriptor registers in the CPU, depending on the address space for

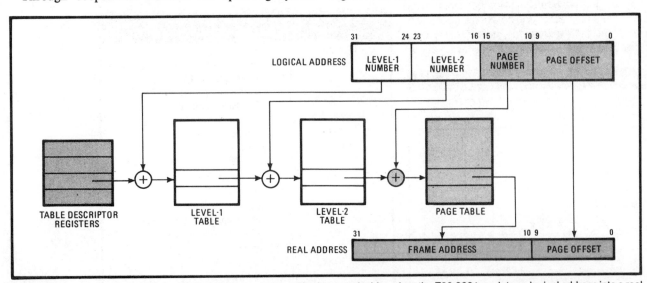

1. Translator. The multiple fields in a logical address point to entries in several tables when the Z80,000 translates a logical address into a real address to load the translation-lookaside buffer. Only the tinted portion of this process is needed when 16-bit addresses are used.

the reference: system instruction space, system data space, normal instruction space, or normal data space. The table descriptor register points to the beginning of the level-1 table in memory. The L1-NO field in the logical address is used as an index into this table to select the level-1 table entry.

This entry in turn points to the beginning of the level-2 table entry, which in turn points to the beginning of the page table in memory. The PAGE-NO field in the logical address is used as an index into this table to select the page table entry. The 4-byte page table entry contains the page frame's physical address and is concatenated with the page offset to complete the translation from logical to physical address.

A logic 1 in bit 31 in the page-table entry indicates memory-mapped I/O. The CPU then uses I/O status and timing for the reference. In this way, the address translation process allows systems to be given protected access to memory-mapped I/O devices.

Access protection information (see table above) is encoded in a 4-bit field at any level of the translation process. During this translation process, the protection information is selected from the first table descriptor or table entry that has a protection code different from 1000_{16}, ignoring subsequent protection fields. The operating system can choose to associate the access rights with a segment or an individual page. Proprietary code can be protected from unauthorized duplication by allowing execute access but not read access.

Several options allow the number of levels and the size of tables to be reduced. When memory address spaces are not separated, two or more of the translation-table descriptor registers can be loaded with the same value so that tables are common for the different address spaces. Furthermore, the table descriptor register can specify that either or both of the level-1 and level-2 tables should be skipped during the translation process. Skipping level-1 tables is useful for 24-bit addresses. For 16-bit addresses, both level-1 and level-2 tables can be skipped. The table size can be reduced by allocating only 256, 512, or 768 bytes for the translation tables, with the remaining table entries assumed invalid. The tables can also be allocated efficiently

Z80,000 PROTECTION-FIELD ENCODING		
Code	System mode	Normal mode
0000	na	na
0001	re	na
0010	re	e
0011	re	re
0100	e	na
0101	e	e
0110	r	na
0111	r	r
1000	next	next
1001	rw	na
1010	rw	r
1011	rw	rw
1100	rwe	na
1101	rwe	e
1110	rwe	re
1111	rwe	rwe

na	no access
r	read access
w	write access
e	execute access
next	use protection field of the next translation table or no access

for downward-growing stacks.

Compatible with the Zilog Z-bus, the external interface of the Z80,000 CPU includes extensions to increase bandwidth and simplify system design. Besides supporting both 16- and 32-bit memory data paths, the data path width and number of wait states can be separately programmed for two regions of memory. For example, one portion of memory could use a 16-bit path with several wait states for bootstrap read-only memory and the other portion could use 32-bit path with no wait state for dynamic random-access memory.

The Z80,000 bus runs at a frequency 1/2 or 1/4 that of the CPU clock inputs. Thus, the standard 10-megahertz CPU would generally use a 5-MHz bus. Alternatively, a 20-MHz CPU could use the same bus timing by selecting a scale factor of 1/4 rather than 1/2. Cache memory in the CPU (see "On-chip cache keeps data flowing through the pipeline,") helps to decouple the processor performance from the memory access time.

Since a 68-pin leadless chip-carrier is used for the Z80,000 CPU, address and data are time-multiplexed through a shared set of 32 pins. All transactions begin with an address strobe that verifies the validity of the address, status (specifying the type of transaction), read-write, and data-transfer size (8, 16, or 32 bits). Following the address, the data-strobe line is asserted during the data-transfer portion of the transaction. The slave device uses two signal lines in order to encode any of four possible responses:

■ The transaction has been successfully completed.

■ The CPU should wait in order for the transaction to be completed.

■ The CPU should retry the transaction because of a transient error has been detected.

■ An irrecoverable error has been detected.

The output-enable and input-enable lines can be used to

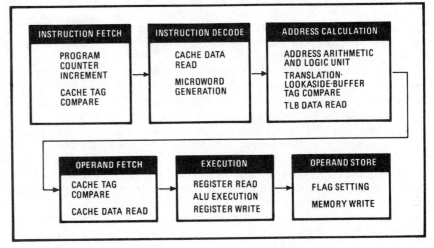

2. Pipes. Six stages of pipelining boost performance in the 32-bit Z80,000 central processing unit. Since accesses to external memory would not be fast enough to keep the pipe full, the Z80,000 uses on-chip cache store in order to buffer the pipeline.

INSTRUCTION FETCH	INSTRUCTION DECODE	ADDRESS CALCULATION
PROGRAM COUNTER INCREMENT / CACHE TAG COMPARE	CACHE DATA READ / MICROWORD GENERATION	ADDRESS ARITHMETIC AND LOGIC UNIT / TRANSLATION-LOOKASIDE-BUFFER TAG COMPARE / TLB DATA READ

OPERAND FETCH	EXECUTION	OPERAND STORE
CACHE TAG COMPARE / CACHE DATA READ	REGISTER READ / ALU EXECUTION / REGISTER WRITE	FLAG SETTING / MEMORY WRITE

On-chip cache keeps data flowing through the pipeline

Pipelined architectures can enhance the throughput of a system, but they need a ready source of data to keep them full. In the Z80,000 32-bit microprocessor chip, the pipeline may require two memory fetches during each processor cycle, one during the instruction fetch stage and one during the operand fetch stage. Since main memory references typically require three processor cycles, the pipeline would be idle most of the time if all references had to access main memory. Helping speed memory access in the Z80,000 is an on-chip cache that can be accessed every clock cycle to buffer most of the memory fetches—typically 90% of instruction fetches and 75% of operand fetches.

The cache holds copies of the most recently referenced memory locations. On each memory fetch reference, the central processing unit examines the cache to determine if the data at that address is available on chip, an occurrence called a cache hit. If so, then the data is read from the cache, and there is no external transaction to fetch from main memory. If not—a cache miss—then the CPU generates an external transaction to fetch from memory, and the data is entered into the cache. The pipeline stage requesting the missing data must wait until the external reference is complete, although other pipeline stages can continue to operate.

The cache stores information from main memory in blocks of 16 bytes. Each block is associated with a 28-bit tag that holds the most significant bits of the main memory address for the block. There is a validity bit associated with each 16-bit word in the cache. The

cache has 16 blocks, providing 256 bytes of storage.

When a block miss occurs, the least recently used (LRU) block is replaced by the missing block. When a cache miss occurs on an instruction fetch, then the CPU fetches the missing instruction from memory and prefetches the bytes following in the block using a burst transaction. If the memory does not support burst transaction, the CPU does not prefetch instructions into the cache. When a cache miss occurs on an operand fetch, then the CPU fetches only the missing data from memory. Missing operands are prefetched only for string instructions. This selective use of prefetching makes the most effective use of main memory bandwidth.

On operand store references, the data is written to memory—a process called write-through. If the store reference hits in the cache, then the data is also written into it. If the store reference misses in the cache, then the cache is unaffected. The write-through storage mechanism ensures that main memory holds the most recent value stored at any address. In cases where multiple processors may share writable storage, the address translation tables allow individual pages to be marked noncacheable.

Unlike the Motorola MC68020, which will cache instructions only, the caching mechanism of the Z80,000 can be selectively enabled for instruction fetches and operand fetches. Particular applications for the Z80,000 may choose to cache only instructions, but caching data along with instructions typically improves performance by some 20%.

---

control the direction of the buffers on the multiplexed address and data lines.

Burst transfers are another feature of the Z80,000 interface. During a bus transaction, the CPU can issue multiple data strobes following a single address strobe. This increases the effective bus bandwidth when transferring data in a block of consecutive memory locations. A transaction with a single data strobe and no wait states requires three bus clocks. However, with burst transfers, a transaction with four data strobes and no wait states requires six bus clocks, resulting in twice the bus bandwidth of the single transfer transaction. With a 5-MHz bus clock (10-MHz CPU clock), 32-bit data path, and four data transfers per transaction, the bandwidth is 13.3 megabytes a second.

A two-wire handshake, burst (BRST) and burst acknowledge (BRSTA), controls the number of transfers in a burst transaction. The CPU asserts BRST as long as it can handle data, while memory asserts BRSTA as long as it can. Either the CPU or the memory can terminate the burst transaction. If the memory terminates the burst, then the CPU initiates another transaction to transfer the remaining data. It is the system designer's choice whether the memory supports burst transfers. The burst transfer protocol used by the CPU for the on-chip cache is appropriate for interleaved memory systems or for memory systems designed with "nibble-mode" RAMs.

The 32-bit Z80,000 CPU can also serve as the heart of a multiprocessor configuration involving coprocessors, slave processors, tightly coupled multiple CPUs, and loosely coupled multiple CPUs. Coprocessors, such as the Z8070 arithmetic processing unit, assist the CPU in executing a single instruction stream by performing complex operations with special hardware. As a result,the Z80,000 and Z8070 combination at 10 MHz is capable of executing more than 600,000 floating-point operations per second in the form of single-precision vector inner-product calculations.

Master, slave, equal

Slave processors, such as the Z8016 direct-memory-access transfer controller or Z800 I/O processor, perform dedicated functions asynchronously to the CPU through a shared local bus controlled by the CPU. The CPU grants the local bus to a slave processor using the two-wire bus-request/bus-acknowledge handshake.

Tightly coupled multiple CPUs execute independent instruction streams and communicate through shared memory or peripherals located on a common bus. This common, or global, bus is controlled by an arbiter external to the CPU. A control register in the CPU specifies a region of the physical address space used for the global bus. Before performing a transaction on the global bus the CPU uses the two-wire global-request/global-acknowledge handshake with the external arbiter.

Loosely coupled multiple CPUs generally communicate through a multiported peripheral, like the first-in, first-out Z8038. The Z80,000 CPU's I/O and interrupt facilities can support loosely coupled multiprocessing.

Pipelined

The Z80,000 CPU is designed as a six-stage, synchronous pipeline (Fig. 2). Instructions pass sequentially through every stage of the pipeline, with the possible exception of the operand storage stage. The various stages of the pipeline can be working simultaneously on different instructions or different portions of a single complex instruction.

All pipeline stages can operate in a single processor cycle, which is composed of two clock cycles, ϕ_1 and ϕ_2. The pipeline allows simple instructions, such as register-to-register load and memory-to-register add, to be executed at a rate of one instruction for each processor cycle, leading to a peak performance of the CPU of 5 million instructions/s with a 10-MHz clock. In practice, the actual instruction rate is about one third of the peak rate because of three sources of delay: some instructions are too complex to be executed in a single cycle, interference between instructions causes delays, and main memory accesses force the pipeline to wait.

The instruction-fetch stage of the pipeline increments the program counter and initiates the instruction fetchings. The instruction-decode stage receives and decodes the instruction to determine the instruction length and to set up control of the address calculation stage. This latter stage has a port to the register file and an adder dedicated to address arithmetic. During a processor cycle the address-calculation stage can handle one immediate operand or generate one operand address in memory. Address translation also occurs during the address calculation stage. The operand-fetch stage initiates memory fetch references for operands and receives the date in a holding register.

Instructions are executed at the execution stage. This stage has two 32-bit data paths to the register file and a 32-bit ALU. Byte, word, and long-word ALU operations from register to register or from memory to register are performed in a single processor cycle. The ALU incorporates special-purpose hardware for speeding multiplication and division.

The operand storage stage sets the condition flags and stores data in memory. However, unlike other pipeline stages, operand store requires several cycles in order to perform the memory reference for storing data. This does not seriously degrade performance, however, because most instructions do not store results in memory, and the store operation can usually overlap with the execution of other instructions. □

Ada determines architecture of 32-bit microprocessor

Its use of the high-level language makes the chip set easy to program for multiuser, multifunction applications like office systems

by Justin Rattner and William W. Lattin *Intel Corp., Aloha, Ore.*

☐ Generation after generation, microprocessors increase in sophistication. And the time and cost of developing new applications for them escalates also, till by now skilled system designers and programmers are in very short supply.

Anticipating this critical situation, Intel Corp. undertook to develop a microcomputer system that can be made to handle complex, software-intensive applications in much less time and at much lower cost than has been usual. The project encompassed nearly all aspects of computer technology and resulted in the development of a new semiconductor process—high-performance MOS, or H-MOS—a new package with a high pin count—the quad in-line package or QUIP—and three of the largest integrated circuits in history (see "A history of the Aloha project,").

Its crowning achievement thus far is a 32-bit microprocessor—the iAPX 432—that has a major new architecture, a new operating system (iMAX), and one of the first compilers for Ada, the Department of Defense's new standard programming language.

As the first 32-bit microprocessor designed specially for multiuser applications, the two-chip general data processor (GDP) is a significant milestone in computer technology (Figs. 1 and 2). Together with the single-chip interface processor (IP) shown in Fig. 3, it was designed to serve the kind of cooperative, multifunction applications typified by future office information equipment and distributed data-processing systems. Similar systems are also envisioned for use in computer-aided design and factory automation.

Cooperative multifunction applications share four important characteristics. They are large in scale and broad in scope, requiring mainframe computing power. They are software-intensive, each discrete function or service requiring considerable programming. They are expected to evolve over time, so the design must allow for future software enhancement and increments in performance. Finally, they are applications where the failure of the computer system can have serious conse-

quences to human life or the cost of doing business, so that long-term dependability of both hardware and software is essential.

Those characteristics of cooperative multifunction applications guided the 432 designers to its major goals. The breadth of computing power required, in terms of both function and performance, includes support for multiprogrammed and virtual memory operating systems; as such, ultimate performance for fully configured systems was to be that of a mid-range mainframe.

Further, it was decided that the long-dreamed-of incremental performance capability—adding power to a 432-based product already in the field simply by plugging in additional GDPs and IPs—would gracefully accommodate planned or even unplanned growth in computational power over the life of an application. The goal of increased programmer productivity was met by supporting a comprehensive methodology for modular software development, served by using Ada as the 432's native tongue. And finally, to ensure high hardware and software dependability, the 432 includes extensive hardware fault detection and software-protection mechanisms.

Transparent multiprocessing

Through careful attention to multiprocessing issues in the definition of both its system organization and its architecture, the 432 successfully implements the long-sought-after idea of transparent multiprocessing for general-purpose computation. This simple but important concept means that the number of data processors in a 432 system can be increased or decreased without software modification. It is even possible to start or stop a processor at any time without informing, let alone damaging, a single piece of software. More importantly, neither the operating system nor the application programs need rewriting to exploit an increase in the number of processors.

A principal challenge in the development of any multiprocessing system is the design of the interconnection

1. Instruction decoding. One of the two chips that make up the general data processor, the 43201 is the instruction decoder. It contains more than 100,000 devices on a single die, making it one of the densest VLSI circuits to have been fabricated so far.

2. Microexecution unit. Decoded instructions from the 43201 are executed by the 43202, which has over 60,000 devices on chip. Its unusual horseshoe-shaped data bus can be discerned from the photograph. The device is housed in a 64-pin quad in-line package.

structure that ties the processors and memory subsystem together. The 432 approach to this problem is unusual: rather than define a standard bus, the 432 simply defines a standard way for processors to communicate with memory and each other. This frees the designer to choose his own bus structure, optimizing the cost/performance ratio of the application. All 432 processors are compatible with the interconnect protocol.

The main goal of the interconnect protocol is to reduce bus use. For that reason, it puts requests and replies in separate packets, so that the first need not monopolize the bus while waiting for the second. For example, a processor generates a request packet in order to access memory but expects a reply packet (Fig. 4) from the memory system only if the request specified a read cycle. The result is that the processor ties up the bus only long enough to transmit a packet to the interconnect; sometime later a reply packet will be returned, if necessary, to the requesting processor. In the interval, other processors may be active on the interconnection.

For still greater efficiency, the protocol defines packets as variable in length. A single request or reply may transmit from 1 to 16 bytes of information. Fewer individual storage accesses need be made to obtain long operands, and designers using the 432 can improve system performance by widening the interconnect's bus.

Communication between processors is one of several additional functions supported by the interconnect protocol. Because of the packet format, a processor can send an attention signal to one processor or broadcast it to several processors simultaneously. Upon receiving a signal, a processor examines an interprocessor message area defined in memory. The message previously deposited there by the sending processor will instruct the receiving processor as to the desired course of action. Typical

interprocessor messages can direct either one or a set of processors to start, stop and redispatch.

Many bus structures can be designed to meet the 432 packet protocol. A simple, single bus interconnect implemented in discrete logic is shown in Fig. 5. On this bus, the packets are demultiplexed as they leave the processors. The separate address and data lines are interfaced to a static memory subsystem in the conventional way. Up to four processors can be supported without serious contention by this simple interconnect.

A conventional mainframe often offloads onto a minicomputer all responsibility for low-level device control and data transfers. The 432 general data processor (GDP) uses an attached input/output processor in the same way. Device driver execution, device interrupts, direct-memory-access channel initialization are all handled within the I/O subsystem.

Offloading I/O chores

A typical I/O subsystem is built around a Multibus or other standard microprocessor system. A standard microprocessor, such as an 8086, is connected to the bus along with memories and peripheral devices to form a complete, attached I/O processor.

The GDP is connected to the microprocessor-based I/O subsystem by the 432 interface processor (IP). Under software control, a group of programmable, associative memories in the IP called window registers can be programmed to map a subsystem's address space into the 432's. The mapping operation is totally transparent to the attached I/O processor, so that both read and write

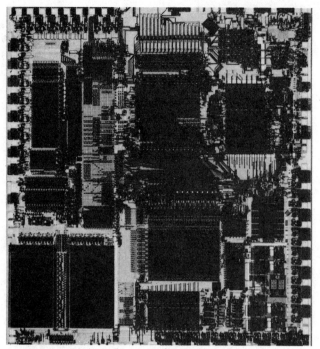

3. Input/output support. The single-chip interface processor, 43203, offloads the general data processor of the tasks involved in communicating with input/output devices. It includes 65,000 devices and can emulate many of the general processor's instructions.

cycles on the subsystem bus can proceed normally.

All communication in the 432's central system is based on messages and not interrupts. The IP receives those messages sent to an I/O subsystem and holds them in its window registers while signaling the I/O processor with an interrupt. The I/O processor then fetches the message through the IP window.

Communication in the opposite direction is slightly more complex. Since conventional interrupts do not exist in the central 432 system, the IP must give the attached processor the ability to send messages in the same way as a 432 data processor. The IP looks like a memory-mapped peripheral to the I/O subsystem as the latter writes commands to the IP registers. In passing those messages into the central system the microprogrammed logic of the IP emulates many of the same functions found in the high-level instruction set of the 432 data processor. Among the available commands is one to send message. Consequently a 432 data processor cannot detect any difference between messages sent by an IP and those sent by another data processor.

Multiple I/O subsystems may also be used to incrementally increase I/O processing power much as multitple data processors increase processing power for general computation. By multiprocessing both I/O and data, the 432 serves many more applications than existing microcomputer systems can and meets the major goal of incremental, field-expandable, processing capability.

On chip

The processing units of the 432 are designed to exploit very large-scale integrated H-MOS technology to the full. The two-chip 43201/2 GDP, whose microphotographs appear in Figs. 1 and 2, contains 160,000 transistors.

Over 100,000 devices are on the 43201 alone. The single-chip IP in Fig. 3 holds roughly 65,000 transistors. Each of the three 432 chips is housed in a 64-pin QUIP, as shown in Fig. 6 [*Electronics*, Jan. 4, 1978, p. 130], and each dissipates less than 2.5 watts of power from a single 5-volt supply. Two-phase clocking at 8 megahertz yields the nominal 125-nanosecond microcycle time.

These complex components could not have been developed without several advances in design techniques and tools. Among these was the use of regular logic structures and wiring topologies.

This technique, developed almost simultaneously at Intel by Sam Schwartz and at the California Institute of Technology by Carver Mead, dramatically reduces the number of randomly drawn transistors. Creating a structured integrated circuit design is hard but gets easier with practice. The micrographs reveal a general increase in geometric regularity from the earliest of the chips to be developed, the 43201, to the latest, the 43203.

Both the GDP and the IP are microprogrammed and rely on high-performance microarchitectures to minimize microprogram size. The two-chip GDP contains a 4-K-by-16-bit microprogram ROM, and the IP contains a 2-K-by-16-bit ROM. The physical size of the IP's microprogram ROM is further reduced by having 2 bits stored in each ROM cell, a technique developed for the 8087 numeric data processor [*Electronics*, Oct. 9, 1980, p. 39] and improved upon in the 432.

The last two entries of Table 1 mention two of the more interesting functional capabilities of the 43201 and 43202. The address generator on the 43202 is responsible for mapping or translating 432 logical addresses into the physical addresses used to access the memory system. To accelerate the translation process, the address generator maintains a cache of recently used addresses, so that a new entry automatically replaces the one least recently used.

The silicon operating system is largely in microcode with some simple hardware assistance. Consequently the execution time for a typical operation like "send message" is five times faster than for a highly tuned minicomputer operating system and 20 to 30 times faster than for the best mainframe operating system.

Table 2 describes the allocation of microcode in the 43201/2 data processor and provides one of the most

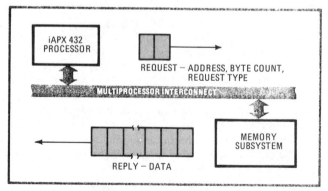

4. Quantized memory requests. Since memory is shared by several processors, requests to access it are optimized by being quantized into packets. A processor controls the bus just long enough to make a request and receives a reply only if the request was to read.

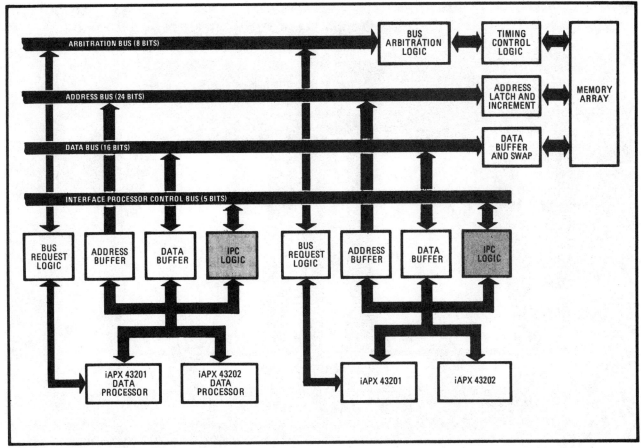

5. Many bus structures. Illustrated is the minimal bus structure consistent with the iAPX 432 architecture. Many other configurations are possible as long as they adhere to the quantized packet protocol of the 432. For example, a faster bus might use wider data paths.

important clues to the functional power of its microarchitecture: only 6% of the total microprogram is required to implement the basic instruction set. The low percentage is due to the close match between the basic instruction set and the microinstructions. Many instructions can be executed by just a single microinstruction. These microinstructions emerge directly from the instruction decoder located on the 43201 and therefore do not take up space in the main microprogram ROM.

Virtual addresses

Virtual addressing, another important 432 function, uses only 7% of microprogram space on the 43201. This percentage is kept small by a little extra hardware, in the form of back-up copies of certain key registers. When a requested memory segment is not in RAM, microcode can restore the machine to the state it was in when the requesting instruction started. System software can then bring the missing segment in from secondary storage and execute the instruction afresh. The entire operation is transparent to the executing program.

Table 2 also shows that a large amount of microcode is devoted to the silicon operating system. Many of the high-level 432 instructions, such as send message, are included in this total. Equivalent functions, programmed in the instruction set of a typical microprocessor, would take four to eight times as many bits.

All 432 components are designed to operate in two modes so that highly fault-sensitive systems can be built

from them. In the master mode, a component operates normally. But in the checker mode—a feature never before found in a microprocessor—all the pins that would normally operate as outputs reverse themselves to function in a special input mode. Instead of asserting output data, they sample the states of their signal lines. The sampled data is compared internally, by an exclusive-OR gate built into each output stage, with the data that would have been asserted in master mode. A mismatch on any pin indicates an error.

A fault-sensitive unit is formed, as shown in Fig. 7, by simply wiring together two identical 432 components. One chip is placed in the master mode and the other in the checker mode by asserting the checker-mode pin. Any error signal asserted by the checker is routed to a special input on the master. In operation, the master and checker stay in lock-step synchrony. Any disagreement apparent at the output pins of the master is flagged immediately by the checker and freezes the operation of both units.

Longer and shorter

The instruction formats are designed to simplify and to reduce the size of code. Consequently, instructions vary in length and have from zero- to three-operand references. The operand addressing modes are modeled after the structures found in high-level languages like Ada to support scalar, vector, and record data types. These correspond roughly to the base-plus-displacement,

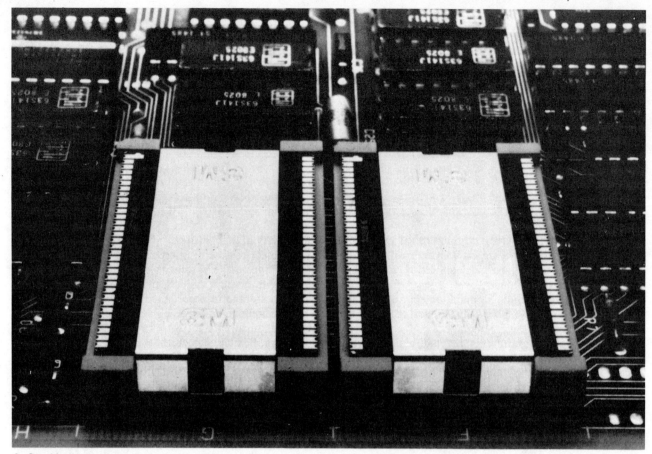

6. Quad in-line package. To house the 432 devices, a more reliable package was developed. The QUIP combines a leadless chip-carrier with a socket that has four staggered rows of pins on 100-mil centers. A metal clip helps dissipate heat, and test points are easily accessible.

base-plus-index, and base-plus-displacement-plus-index addressing modes, respectively, found in conventional machines. Instructions also never refer to a register, since registers can be hard to manage during compilation. Instead, operands may come either from memory or from the hardware-supported expression-evaluation stack. Any mix of memory or stack-based operands is allowed. Lastly, the instructions may start and end on any bit boundaries. Naturally, branch instructions are designed to branch to a bit location, too.

With instruction formats such as these, the most frequent statements of a high-level language like Ada compile to single 432 instructions. Some examples are shown in Fig. 8, along with the corresponding instruction lengths (in bits).

An object orientation

The 432 has an object-oriented architecture. Objects provide an identical framework for everything from a simple piece of data, like a byte, to a message being sent to another processor. They are responsible for most of the facilities found in the 432 architecture, including basic computation, language run-time environment, resource management, interprocess communication, and protected addressing.

A data object supports basic computation. It is simply a linear, logical address space from 1-K to 64-K bytes in length. Any type of binary data can be stored in a data object, and a given element within the object is accessed

by specifying its byte displacement from the starting address of the object. The complete logical address of a single data item, as found in the operand fields of a typical instruction, contains both the displacement and the program's local name (or nickname) for the data object. This short, local object name selects the much longer access descriptor, which indicates the location of the object's full name (or absolute address). The local name often runs as few as 6 bits in an operand reference.

More than ordinary

Just as data objects support basic computation in the 432, more complex objects are used to support higher-level functions. The hardware knows from their descriptor-type code that they contain more than just ordinary

TABLE 1: EXECUTION TIMES OF THE iAPX 432 32-BIT MICROPROCESSOR		
Functional unit	Typical operation	Execution time at 8 MHz (μs)
Variable-precision integer arithmetic unit	32-bit integer multiply	6.25 (16 μs on IBM 370/148)
Microprogrammed floating-point arithmetic unit	80-bit floating multiply	26.125 (38.5 μs on IBM 370/148)
Barrel-shift unit	32-bit field extract	1.875
Address generator with associative cache of least recently used addresses	32-bit memory access	0.75
Silicon operating system	send message	80.875

TABLE 2: ALLOCATION OF MICROCODE IN THE iAPX-43201/2 DATA MICROPROCESSOR		
Function	Bits	Percentage
Basic instruction set	3,680	6
Floating-point arithmetic	11,680	18
Run-time environment	6,400	10
Virtual addressing	4,800	7
Fault handling	2,640	4
Silicon operating system	26,400	40
Multiprocessor control	8,640	13
Debug services	1,280	2
Total	64-K	100

data and uses that knowledge to implement many functions carried out by software on conventional machines. The hardware-recognized objects are referred to generically as system objects.

System objects include domain objects and context objects. Both of these primarily support the run-time environments of high-level languages.

A domain object represents the addressing environment of a program module. Contained within the domain object are all the access descriptors for both the module's instruction objects and its data objects. The domain also contains links to other domains and thus is part of a network of domains representing a completely linked but still modular program.

A domain is actually composed of two parts—public and private—that are analogous to the interface and body portions of an Ada package ·

The public part contains the links to the objects defined by a module's interface specification, while the links to other objects not defined in the interface but used to implement the module are located in the private part. Only objects whose links are found in the public part of a domain object can be accessed from other connected domains.

Context objects support the dynamic allocation of memory every time they are activated. A context is created dynamically when a procedure is called and is deleted dynamically when the procedure returns. Since a new context is created for every activation, contexts directly support shared, recursive, and re-entrant procedures. Their second major function is to provide each procedure activation with a data object for its local data and an operand stack for expression evaluation.

The remaining 432 system objects support the hardware-based operating system services called the silicon operating system. A data structure representing an individual GDP is called a processor object. There is one processor object for each physical GDP in a 432 system.

Some more objects

An object representing an independent concurrent program or task is called a process object. Processes may be scheduled to run on a processor and thus represent a claim on some part of the system's total processing resources. A process object contains, among other things, the priority of that process.

An object representing a portion of the allocatable or free storage in the system is called a storage resource object. Many such objects may exist in a system to partition storage in accordance with claims and grants. Through storage resource objects, new objects are created dynamically for software by the hardware.

A very flexible object that is used to support the buffered transmission of messages between processes, or programs, is called a port object. Port objects also support the scheduling and dispatching of processes on multiple processors in a multiprogrammed fashion. Ports are able to serve both functions because scheduling and dispatching is modeled as sending a message (the process object) to a process (the processor). In practice, the message is nothing more than an access descriptor. Since an access descriptor can reference any object, the send instruction can be used to send any object and, hence, any complex message. A message might be a data object containing a string of text or a complex object including executable code and perhaps representing an important system resource. Objects, therefore, present a consistent framework in which both processes and processors may communicate conveniently.

Object addressing

Objects are stored in pieces of the address space called segments. Simple objects can be stored by a single segment, but complex ones may occupy many of them. Important information about each object, including its type and location in physical memory, is found in its object descriptor. An object is always addressed via this descriptor, the location of which is indicated by an access descriptor (Fig. 9).

Length information is used to protect the object from out-of-range addresses, and presence information, along with other data in the object descriptor, is used to implement virtual memory. To simplify storage management, all object descriptors are grouped in a central table. Naturally, the object table is an object, too, and its object descriptor is contained within itself.

To select or refer to an object requires a 32-bit access descriptor that contains the identity of the object it references. Each access descriptor also contains other information to help control access to the object to which it refers. Different access rights can be represented by different access descriptors for the same object. This fact

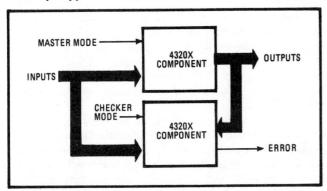

7. Error-checking mode. Each 432 chip has a checker mode as well as a master mode. Two devices can be wired in parallel and one put in the checker mode to duplicate all the operations of the master and signal an error when it detects a discrepancy.

119

A history of the Aloha project

The iAPX 432 32-bit microprocessor has been in gestation for over six years, a third of that time in Santa Clara, Calif., and the remainder in Aloha, Ore. There its development eventually became known as the special systems operation, or SSO, with Jean-Claude Cornet as director. But its shroud of privacy led some to think SSO stood for "secret systems operation."

In the beginning the 432 was called the 8816, then the 8800. It had to be given a number because at Intel, "as soon as you give something a number, it is instantly perceived as this little thing with side-brazed connections coming out of it," jokes principal engineer Justin R. Rattner (see photo). By November of 1975 the endeavor had coalesced into a working unit under William W. Lattin. He remained 432 program manager until April of last year, when he moved over to another Intel division.

The original idea was to "do something interesting" with very large-scale integration, but with Schottky TTL performance. The team looked at and then discarded a double-diffused MOS process and a modified charge-coupled-device structure, before it finally came up with a short-channel technology that could squeeze 100,000 transistors onto a single chip yet still support future geometry reductions. It was the birth of the high-performance MOS, or H-MOS, process.

After some preliminary design work, the group presented prospective users with a specification. "They were responsible for our emphasis on multiprocessing," says Rattner. "It was the No. 1 thing they wanted." Back then, the notion of software objects as a way of simplifying programming barely existed. "But suggested mechanisms began to get very ad hoc," he adds. "Every new feature seemed to involve a different machine facility, a different hardware unit."

Early one Saturday morning Rattner woke up convinced software objects were the solution. "I wrote for about six hours and called George Cox [a staff scientist], and that Sunday morning we met at Intel to start working out the details," he recalls.

Then came the hardware design, which "made extensive use of regular logic cells and wiring topologies, very much along the lines of the work done at Cal Tech" by Carver Mead, who had begun consulting on the project in 1975. "We knew we couldn't just randomly wire 100,000 transistors," so computer-aided design and simulation tools had to be designed.

Portions of the chips' architecture were implemented directly in silicon—so intimately that they have no logic-gate equivalent. "We looked at each function, but instead of drawing a logic diagram and figuring out a gate implementation, we asked if there was a way to do it with MOS transistors directly," says Rattner. For the processor's control store, the team adapted a read-only memory cell designed for the 8087 numeric processor that stores 2 bits [*Electronics*, Oct. 9, 1980, p. 39]. Without tricks like the ROM cell, "the chips couldn't have been built."

Rattner feels the modular design methodology was "a spectacular success." At least one of the chips, the complex execution unit, "could have been shipped in sample quantities the first day out of fab," he says, adding that all in all, "productivity was five, six, seven times that of some other Intel projects."

The SSO now employs over 100 engineers designing follow-on board computers and design aids for the 432 family. Many of them have worked with minicomputer or larger machines in the past, as also has marketing manager Dave Best.

The project "cost a bundle," says Best, adding that "it was the largest investment in a single program that Intel has ever made—larger even than the magnetic stuff," the bubble memories.

-John G. Posa

is the basis of the 432's need-to-know protection system: in order to refer to an object, a program must contain an access descriptor for it; a program may only access an object according to privilege rights encoded in the access descriptor it holds.

Access descriptors are found only in a special type of segment called an access segment. This protects the integrity of access descriptors by preventing them from being treated as ordinary data. Only certain instructions are permitted to move or manipulate access descriptors.

Selective entry

An access descriptor selects one of the 2^{24} entries in the object table, and each entry can specify a single-segment object of up to 2^{16} bytes. That gives a system-wide logical address space of $2^{40}-1$ trillion—bytes of information. At any instant, however, the logical addressing environment of a program is restricted to 2^{16} objects of up to 2^{16} bytes, or 4 gigabytes. The instanta-neous addressing environment is represented by four access segments, each of which is limited to 2^{14} access descriptors.

To implement the 432's two-level addressing architecture efficiently, each processor contains a buffer or cache of the most recently used object addresses. Cache data made stale by a software alteration of an object descriptor (which is a relatively infrequent occurrence) can be flushed by the operating system through interprocessor communication.

The key computing resources of the 432, unlike conventional systems, are controlled by hardware-defined system objects rather than by user-supplied software. This difference dramatically changes the way resources are managed by, and ultimately the structure of, the entire system.

For each type of system object, the hardware automatically handles some part of the operations that can be carried out on an object. Some of the operations are

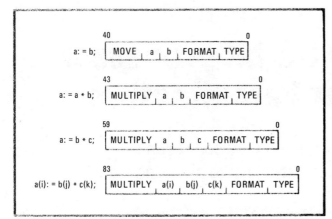

8. Variable-size instructions. Since users are not expected to program the 432 in assembly language, its instructions are not aligned on convenient byte boundaries but instead can be any length of bits. The statements illustrated compile to single 432 instructions.

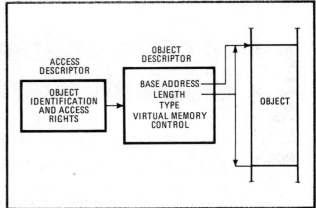

9. Address calculations. All memory requests are calculated via a two-level operation in which an access descriptor points to an object descriptor and the object descriptor in turn indicates the location and size of the desired memory contents (called an object).

available as instructions, while others are involved only when the hardware determines, independently of any particular instruction, that the operation is needed, such as fetching an absent memory segment. Software is responsible for providing the remainder of the operations defining the complete interface to the object.

This organization presents an important hardware-software tradeoff, involving just which operations should be put into hardware and which would be better left to software. In the 432, the decision to put an operation in hardware is based on one of three factors. First, the timing of an operation may be critical, affecting overall system performance in a fundamental way. Second, an operation may be security-critical, affecting the integrity of the protection system and the isolation of important information. Third, its reliability may be critical, affecting the ability of the system to function correctly in delicate programming situations.

The software part of the object management function is still by no means trivial. Software is largely responsible for creating new objects and disposing of old ones.

Generally speaking, objects work to remove the traditional barriers between the operating system and the application environment. The packages that make up iMAX are tools with which the user may build an application. If the iMAX package for a particular service is not quite right, the user is free to replace it with a package of different design.

Ada: implementation language

Ada, the Department of Defense's new standard programming language, is an ideal systems implementation language for the 432. The goals established for Ada's design were very like those set for the 432 since the language's designers drew upon the same body of research. The ultimate goals of both Ada and the 432 are increased programmer productivity, increased software reliability, and low software life-cycle costs.

Ada is inspired by the Pascal language and has much in common with it. But it differs from Pascal, and moves far beyond the older high-level language, in its support for large-scale, modular software. While several attempts have been made to repair this deficiency in Pascal, none has been widely accepted or used. Ada makes these efforts obsolete.

Through its "package" construct, Ada provides a natural way to put together large programs based on object-oriented modularization. A package defines an object and the operations that can be done on it. Following the object-oriented view further, a package restricts access to an object as specified in a separate interface portion and thus succeeds in hiding the details of its implementation.

Ada turns out to be an ideal language for the 432 not only because they embody the same idea of modularization but because many Ada constructs map directly onto the hardware. For example, the Ada package construct is directly supported in the 432 architecture by the concept of a domain object and Ada subprogram activations become contexts in the 432 architecture.

In those cases where the hardware of the 432 goes beyond Ada's built-in constructs, Ada's definition allows for a special machine-access package. Any 432 instruction or feature can be accessed via this package, eliminating the need for a 432 assembler. Ada is thus the only language used to write the iMAX executive and programmers are not ordinarily expected to require machine access. Hence even systems programmers will use Ada, resorting to direct machine access only rarely.

Ada and the 432 architecture cooperate to provide complementary checks on a program's design. Ada checks data types and interfaces during compilation, and the 432 subsequently rechecks them at run time in order to catch errors missed or possibly caused by the compiler. The 432 architecture also provides those checks on interfaces and data types that in Ada can only be made during execution.

Finally, Ada is the basis of the 432's integrated programming system. This software development system is built around Ada to provide separate compilation of programs with fully checked interfaces as well as link-time checking of module version numbers. The latter capability ensures that old versions of programs will not sneak back into a system. A symbolic source-level debugger lets the application programmer debug programs in Ada rather than 432 machine language. □

Electronics/April 7, 1983

Two chips endow 32-bit processor with fault-tolerant architecture

With a bus interface unit and a memory control unit, a distributed-processing system can reconfigure and repair itself

by C. B. Peterson, R. C. Duzett, D. L. Budde, D. G. Carson, M. T. Imel, C. A. Jasper,
D. B Johnson, R. H. Kravitz, C. K Ng, D. K. Wilde, and J. R Young, *Intel Corp., Aloha, Ore.*

☐ Silicon bodyguards that protect a microsystem from hardware-induced errors are now a reality. The iAPX 43204 bus interface unit and the 43205 memory control unit are two highly complex integrated circuits that bring fault-tolerant distributed processing to the iAPX 432 32-bit microprocessor family.

The new MCU and BIU are hardly stern, inflexible wardens of a single right path to reliability; in fact, they offer modular configurability with three levels of fault-tolerance capabilities. These sentinels can ward off the system crash that can occur with the failure of just one component in a distributed-processing system.

Companion pieces

The new ICs work with the existing 432 three-chip set: the iAPX 43201 instruction decoder, the 43202 microcode generator, and the 43203 interface controller. This trio has mechanisms that help the system integrator build more reliable and fault-tolerant software for such applications as transaction processing, industrial automation, and communication systems.

There are three aspects to hardware fault-tolerance in the 432 system—error detection, error confinement, and error recovery. The MCU and BIU base the implementation of each of these on the concept of confinement boundaries. This approach of preventing an error from propagating provides fault-tolerance capability ranging from a simple, basically reliable system to a continously computing system that replaces its defective parts.

The fault-tolerant mechanisms implemented in the MCU and BIU offer error-detection capabilities that can isolate and confine single-point failures anywhere in the distributed system. Furthermore, system-wide error re-

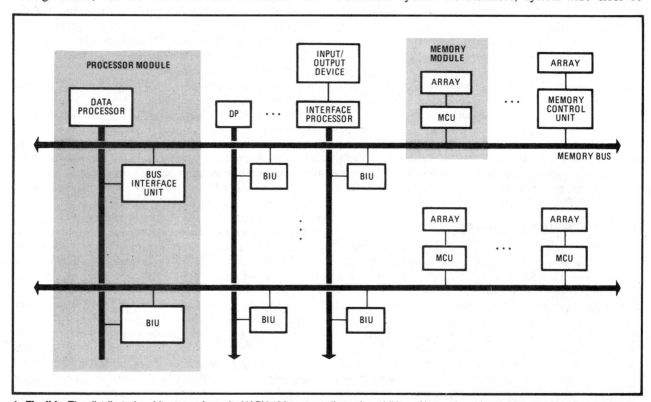

1. Flexible. The distributed architecture of a typical iAPX 432 system allows the addition of bus or input/output bandwidth. More processing power or memory may also be had in a system that is made fault-tolerant with the aid of new memory-control and bus-interface chips.

porting specifies the type and location of a hardware failure and initiates the appropriate recovery action. As the recovery begun by these chips is immediate, software execution continues from the point of hardware failure.

There are still other benefits to the designer concerned with fault tolerance. For example, system software is notified after the hardware recovery so that statistics may be gathered and a longer-term recovery policy may be implemented. Simply put, while hardware faults are corrected by hardware, software still controls the system operation and ultimate configuration.

Dense chips

Recovery procedures provided by the chips include access retry, system-module reconfiguration, access rerouting on other backplane buses, and a host of simpler bit-correction schemes for soft errors. To perform all these functions, the chips need to form the interconnection between processors and memory and provide the memory control for the iAPX 432 central processing units. Consequently, they need lots of transistors in a small die size. This capability is only possible if there is a very high level of integration, comparable to some of today's microprocessors. The MCU is 340 mils squared and contains 84,000 transistors, while the BIU is 285 mil² and contains 65,000 transistors.

A look at a typical iAPX 432 system topology provides the basis for understanding the fault-tolerance phi-losophy of the MCU and BIU (Fig. 1). The topology is modular and flexible in configuration. A data processor (an iAPX 43201 instruction decoder plus a 43202 microcode generator) or an interface processor (an iAPX 43203) and its associated BIUs are considered to be a processor module. Similarly, an MCU and its array of memory chips are considered a memory module. Processor modules, memory modules, or memory buses can be modularly replicated to tailor system performance, resources, or fault tolerance for specific applications.

As mentioned, several levels of fault-tolerance capability are available with the MCU and BIU. The base-level capability provides a highly reliable distributed system with features such as bus parity, error-correction code across memory arrays, and access retry. In the base-level design—known as a self-healing system—the down time after a system crash due to a hardware failure is measured by the time needed to reinitialize and run a diagnostic program that localizes the error and reconfigures the system to disconnect the faulty module or backplane bus. Any software that was interrupted in the hardware crash must be restarted.

A second level of fault tolerance available from the MCU and BIU provides almost 100% detection and isolation of any single-point failures in the distributed system by implementing confinement boundaries. Any communication across the interface of a module or bus is checked for consistency using detection mechanisms such as func-

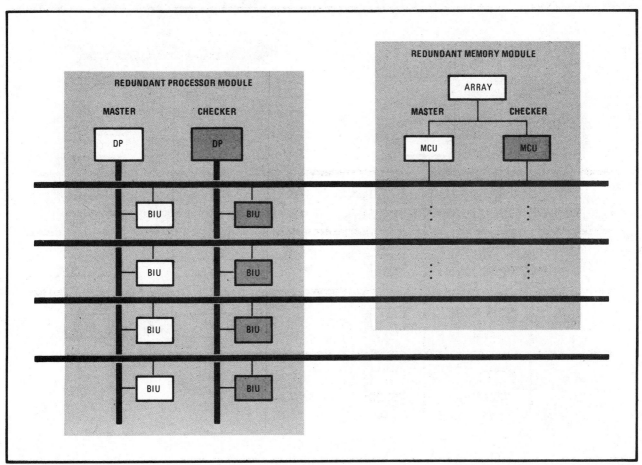

2. Check it out. Proper processor and memory operation may be almost guaranteed by using the MCUs and BIUs in redundant modules. The checker's function is to listen for disagreement between itself and the master and to report such an occurrence to the system software.

tional redundancy checking and parity.

Functional redundancy checking is implemented with module redundancy (Fig. 2). Here, two modules form one logical module, with one of the physical modules denoted as the master and the other as the checker. The checker acts only as a listener and checks for disagreement between itself and the master. If a disagreement is detected, the checker MCU or BIU issues an error report to the other units. Whenever a master and checker disagree, the module shuts itself down.

Self-checking modules

A hardware failure in a second-level system of this type is immediately caught because the modules are self-checking. This capability is in contrast to the base-level system where a failure may produce an error that might potentially be ignored and possibly propagated into some permanent data base. Though the system may still crash as it will in a base-level system, the crash is in a controlled manner with erroneous information confined.

Since all the MCUs and BIUs record the error type and location, a diagnostic program can readily assess what the exact error was that caused the crash. The operating system can also elect to implement some long-term recovery policy. Since reconfiguration software can be run from an input/output subsystem, the system could restart itself after a crash due to hardware failure. The original software is then restarted. Clearly, this type of system forms a more sophisticated and comprehensive self-healing system than the base-level system.

A third level of fault-tolerance capability provides recovery from any single-point failure in the distributed system. This capability is achieved with yet another level of modular redundancy supplied by the MCU and BIU in systems that have already implemented the second-level capability (Fig. 3). The third level is realized by allocating two master-checker module pairs of the same type whenever it is desirable in the system and marrying them. With the marriage concept, one master-checker pair is denoted as primary, the other pair as shadow. Each one acts as a hot backup for the other, and together they form one logical module.

No down time

Recovery in a system of this type occurs immediately as the failed module's spouse switches in and as all outstanding accesses are retried. Since recovery is immediate, software continues to run after the recovery as though a failure had never occurred. Of course, a module with a failed spouse is now unprotected from another failure. However, operating-system software can bring about some longer-term recovery, such as allocating another spouse as a shadow.

The concept of confinement boundaries lies behind the ability of the MCU and BIU to provide multiple-level hardware error detection and recovery from any error detect-

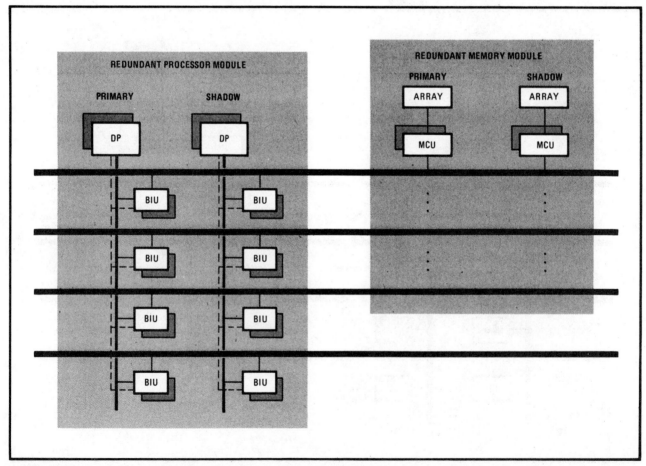

3. A double check. If recovery from any single-point hardware failure in a distributed iAPX 432 computer system is needed, the MCUs and BIUs may be configured to control master-checker module pairs of the same type. Each member of the chip pair has the job of backing up the other.

ed. In this approach to fault-tolerance, a system is divided into a group of adjacent nonoverlapping sections. The key idea is that any information flow across a section boundary is checked at the boundary for correctness. If incorrect information is detected, the invalid information is not propagated to an adjacent section. Recovery from a permanent failure in a confinement area can be implemented by replacing the failed confinement area with a duplicate area (Fig. 4).

Checking the correctness of information across confinement boundaries is implemented by placing detection mechanisms at any interface that crosses a confinement boundary. These detection mechanisms are not required in a data processor or a memory array since information crosses a confinement boundary only at an MCU or BIU. Confinement of errors is supplemented through the use of an error-reporting network that informs all MCUs and BIUs in the system about an error.

An example of confinement-boundary operation is the flow of a memory access issued by a data processor. First, it issues a memory read request to the bus. Detection mechanisms in the associated BIU check for consistency of the issued request on the bus. In the second step, the request is checked for correct propagation down the bus by the MCU in the memory module. Then the memory module checks that the reply message is correct as it is issued to the bus. Finally, the BIU verifies correct transmission back to its processor.

Detection of errors

The MCU and BIU must be able to take care of the two categories of hardware faults, active and latent. Active faults are those that can be observed immediately using detection mechanisms because they occur in circuitry that is either presently active or frequently active as a part of usual system operation. In contrast, latent faults are failures that occur in portions of the system not usually exercised. Some examples of areas where latent faults may occur include infrequently accessed memory locations, detection and reporting mechanisms, and recovery and other hardware resources that are infrequently used. Latent fault coverage is achieved by periodic testing of these areas.

Mechanisms provided for detecting active faults include functional redundancy checking (FRC), bus parity, error checking and correction (ECC), buffer checking and consistency checking on duplicated error-report lines. FRC detection mechanisms are found along module boundaries where information flows out of the module.

Latent fault detection coverage is provided by extensive diagnostic and on-line testing facilities that are software-controlled in the MCU and BIU. Periodic testing for latent faults allows recovery action to be enacted if a failure has occurred and thereby prevents the possibility of compound faults. An example of a compound fault could be the existence of a serious failure in a module's error-reporting logic coupled with the sudden detection of an FRC error by the same module.

An extensive set of software facilities is supplied for the detection of latent faults. These facilities range from special commands issued from software to automatic functions like array scrubbing. For instance, the command to test detection mechanisms is issued by system software to each MCU or BIU one at a time. This test forces errors at the FRC hardware, the buffer-checking mechanisms, and bus parity bits. If all detection circuits signal an error, then a report of no error is issued on the error-report network. If any one of the circuits fails to signal an error, then a module error is reported.

An example of an automatic latent-error detection is the array-scrubbing mechanism that detects and corrects soft errors in a memory array. This mechanism virtually guarantees that a double-bit error in one memory location due to accumulation of soft errors will never occur.

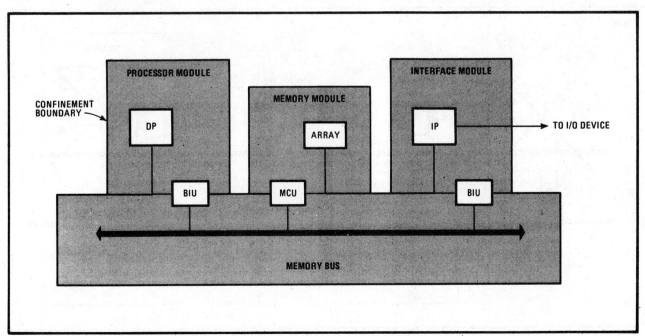

4. Quarantine. The error-detection mechanisms built into the bus interface and memory control unit do not allow errors to leave the component within a confinement boundary. The errors are both trapped and reported to all BIUs and MCUs.

The scrubbing operation is performed on memory as part of the refresh cycle. When memory is read by the MCU during a refresh operation, the data and ECC check bits are checked for consistency. Any single-bit errors are corrected, and all errors are reported.

Report and confine

Error confinement depends on both the detection already discussed and the subsequent restriction of the faulty information to its area of origin. In some cases, confinement also requires isolating the hardware that is the source of the faulty information. To perform these chores, the MCU and BIU error-report message contains an error-type indication, the identification of the module that detected the error (module ID), the identification of the bus on which the reporting node resides (bus ID), a parity bit, and the classification of the error as transient (recover on retry) or permanent.

The error-report network that transmits the messages is also fault-tolerant and broadcasts any error report to all MCUs and BIUs in the system. This network is implemented with serial communication lines. In fact, two redundant error-report lines parallel each memory bus in the central system.

Each processor module contains an error-report line that will broadcast a report on one memory bus to all the other memory buses. With this configuration, the network will continue to function properly as long as a memory bus has at least one functioning report line and there is at least one processor module that can propagate the error report to the other buses.

The broadcast of an error report is performed in three phases. In the first phase, an MCU or BIU issues an error report onto the report lines that parallel its memory bus. In the next phase, all BIUs on that memory bus propagate the error report to the associated units in their module. In the last phase of the error-report broadcast, all BIUs rebroadcast their error reports on all buses.

Arbitration for use of the error-report lines is a two-part procedure. The first order of arbitration is a first-come, first-served allocation. Once an MCU or BIU observes a report being broadcast, it will not issue a new report during the current reporting period.

The second order of arbitration occurs if two modules issue a report at the same time. In this case, priority allocation is implemented with bit-by-bit arbitration based on the message content. Since the error-report lines are open-collector–driven, a lower-priority message will eventually fail to pull a connecting line low while the higher-priority one does. Upon observing that the error-report line is pulled low by another node, an MCU or BIU reporting a lower-priority error will withdraw. Since error type is one of the first fields in a message, collision resolution is won by an error type with the higher-priority code.

With these procedures, the contents of every error-report log in the system should be identical. The MCUs and BIUs use this log to determine an appropriate isolation and an optional recovery action. System software can also access the log to maintain an error-history file and enact long-term recovery strategy that is based on the information.

Recovery at last

The process of recovery from an error is performed in three phases, which consist of the error-reporting sequence, a quiescent wait period, and a retry period. During the error-report sequence, all MCUs and BIUs flush their memory-bus pipelines and reset these buses to an idle state. MCUs appropriately terminate any transactions that were issued by a request in the pipelines. BIUs will reissue any memory requests that they had outstanding (on a retry basis) in the third phase of the recovery process. At the end of the error-reporting phase, each

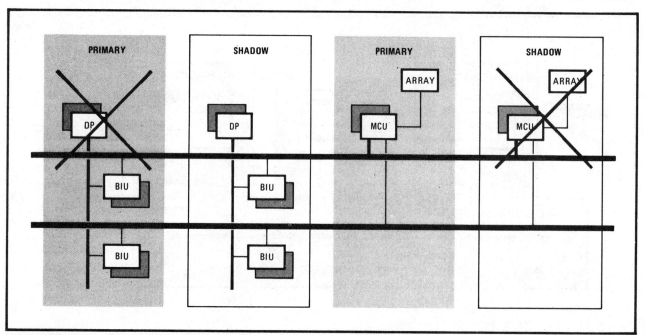

5. Togetherness. A system breakdown, such as a malfunctioning primary processor module and a broken shadow-memory module, is averted because the failed modules may be isolated and the surviving ones will carry on the operation of those modules.

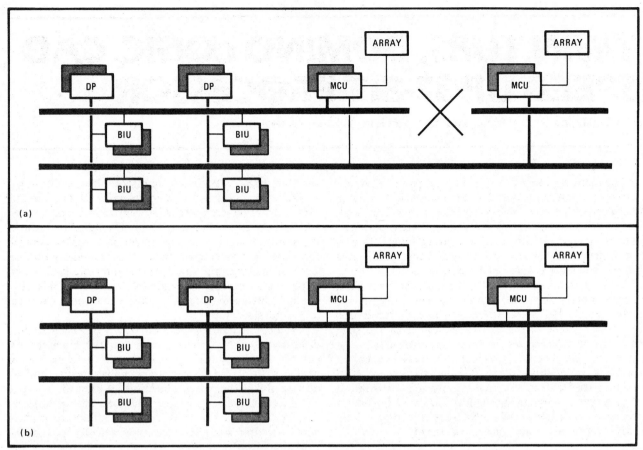

6. Take another bus. In the event of a permanent bus failure (a), a memory control unit can attach itself to its alternative bus (b). The bus interface units reroute all data that is attempting to gain access to the new bus, and the system continues to operate.

MCU and BIU in the system has logged a copy of the error report.

The quiescent wait period allows the entire system to settle down to a uniform state. At the end of this period, error confinement is complete. If the issued error report specified that the error was permanent, then the appropriate hardware isolation and automatic reconfiguration would have taken place, depending on the level of redundancy incorporated in the system configuration.

The third phase of the recovery process is the retry period. At this time BIUs retry outstanding access requests that were flushed from the bus pipeline in the first phase. Following this, normal system operation is resumed.

Classifying errors

Some error types are considered to be permanent immediately upon detection. An example of this is an FRC error between master and checker MCUs at the memory-array interface. In this case, the potential damage to data in the memory array may be indeterminate. However, most errors are considered to be transient when first detected and reported. These include bus parity errors, memory bus FRC errors, and ECC errors.

Recovery from transient errors like those caused by noise is performed simply in the retry period of the recovery process. If, however, the same error is reported again during the retry period, the new error report indicates a permanent fault. This error report begins another

recovery sequence, but this time a hardware reconfiguration takes place during the quiescent wait period. The failed hardware is isolated and replaced with its previously allocated hot backup.

The two most significant recovery mechanisms provided by the MCU and BIU are module reconfiguration and bus reconfiguration. As discussed, module reconfiguration depends upon forming logical modules consisting of a marriage of two master-checker modules (Fig. 5).

In the event of a permanent failure that entails module reconfiguration, a dispatching mechanism in the 432 notifies system software. Notification allows software to enact a different long-term recovery mechanism, such as allocating another spouse for the module or decommissioning the module and continuing operation with gracefully degraded performance.

Automatic bus reconfiguration requires a minimum of four memory buses but for simplicity two buses are shown in Fig. 6. In (a), each MCU is connected to each of the two memory buses. The MCUs, however, have a connection to an alternative bus. The X of the upper memory bus denotes a permanent bus failure. In this situation, the MCUs recognize a report of a permanent bus error. They then attach themselves to the alternative bus shown in black in (b), and the BIUs reroute all accesses initially destined for the malfunctioning bus to the backup. The system continues to run and perform its usual chores but with degraded memory-bus bandwidth as long as the faulty bus is isolated. □

TWIN TUBS, DOMINO LOGIC, CAD SPEED UP 32-BIT PROCESSOR

by B. T. Murphy, L. C. Thomas, and A. U. Mac Rae, *Bell Laboratories, Murray Hill, N. J.*

□ The nonstop increase in computer power that has marked the last three decades seems unlikely to slow in the foreseeable future. The emergence of very large-scale integrated circuits with submicrometer dimensions alone implies single-chip computers executing some 100 million instructions per second (MIPs) and thus performing on the same level as many mainframes (Fig. 1).

As the technology that yields the most MIPs per watt, complementary-MOS will feature prominently in the VLSI advance. Bell Laboratories had already recognized this power factor in the mid-1970s and from the start based its microprocessor design program on C-MOS. Its search for the best semiconductor process and circuit combination led first to the Bellmac-8 microprocessor and then the Bellmac-4 microcomputer and has found its most recent expression the Bellmac-32, a 32-bit microprocessor that exploits twin-tub C-MOS technology, domino C-MOS circuitry, and automated design.

Rising to 32 bits

The Bellmac-8 microprocessor, which became available in 1976, was primarily a software-driven design. As microcomputer systems had become more complex, high-level language programming called for an efficient compiler, and this in turn called for a microprocessor with a wider range of memory modes than was then obtainable. Both 8- and 16-bit capabilities were required. Because of these features, the control structure had to be unusually complex.

The result—the Bellmac 8—included an 8-bit arithmetic and logic unit, a 16-bit address-arithmetic unit (AAU), and a pointer register. All working registers were in main memory, and pointers could directly address 16 registers with overlapping stacks anywhere in main memory. This pointer structure made subroutine calls and returns, for example, efficient enough to exploit structured programming techniques properly.

The 8-bit ALU was implemented in hand-designed pseudo–n-channel MOS circuitry. Since the ALU was active only about one cycle out of every six, the use of a ground switch reduced power dissipation markedly. The high average fan-in made the pseudo–n-MOS more effective than static C-MOS in both speed and packing density.

In the 16-bit AAU, on the other hand, the simple address arithmetic being performed led to a low average fan-in and the unit was in continuous use, so that conventional C-MOS was chosen for this design. Pointer registers also used conventional C-MOS. Computer-aided design support for the data path was restricted to simulation of the hand-drawn logic, and the ALU was simulated

with Bell Labs' MOS timing simulator software (Motis).

The control selection was complex for its day, for the rich instruction set included several addressing modes and both 8- and 16-bit data types. Though microcoding, the simplest method of implementing complex control functions, was considered, the read-only memory needed was just too large and slow. A programmable-logic array implementation was more efficient, but even in this case the straightforward single-PLA approach would have led to a large, slow chip.

The approach finally chosen was a pipelined design using two PLAs—a main control PLA supplemented by another one dedicated to ALU control, with each PLA having multiplexed outputs to minimize its size and to achieve Bell Labs' speed objectives. Within the PLAs, a row of gates between levels eliminated near-redundancies. As a result, the PLAs could be efficiently packed with code that was generated automatically by system-level simulation programs.

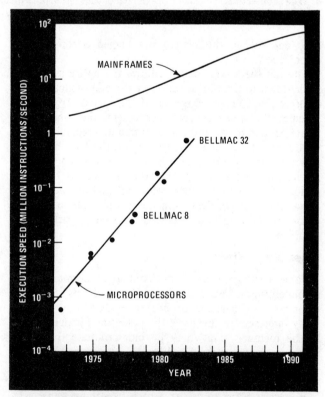

1. Approaching mainframes. As can be seen from the graph, the Bellmac-32 single-chip microcomputer is approaching the performance of a mainframe. In fact, if the two growth curves are extrapolated, they will meet some time later this century.

The overall chip layout used metal for bit lines and polysilicon for the control lines orthogonal to them. The control lines got their signals from the demultiplexing logic controlled by the main and ALU PLAs.

This design, first executed in 7.5-micrometer design rules in p-tub, latchup-free C-MOS technology, was later manually updated to 5-μm rules for higher performance and lower cost. Typical gate speeds for these rules were 7 to 30 nanoseconds, depending on gate function and load. Power dissipation at full clock rate is 0.5 W.

The Bellmac-4 microcomputer, which came out in 1980, had about the same complexity and used the same design techniques as Bellmac-8 microprocessor. However, it featured 4-, 8-, 12-, and 16-bit instructions operating under the control of a software-settable register, with four address modes for each of its two source and one destination operands. On-chip random-access memory and ROM were designed by hand, but the I/O control logic was built up from a mixture of PLAs that were automatically wired polycells. This was the first, or one of the first, uses of CAD tools in the design of any microprocessor or microcomputer.

The same circuit design techniques were employed for the Bellmac-4 microcomputer, except that they were implemented in the twin-tub C-MOS technology, which

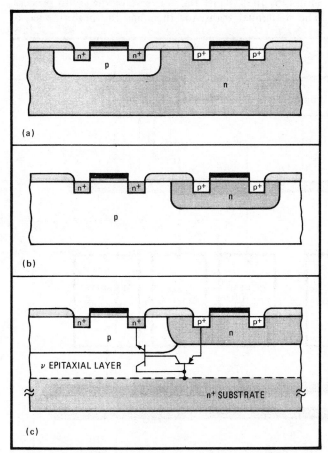

2. Twin-tub C-MOS. The traditional complementary-MOS process uses a p well in an n-type substrate (a). However, the same principle can be used to form an n-channel device in a p-type substrate (b). The best of both worlds can be had by using two tubs (c).

has higher switching speeds. Typical ALU gate delays using 3.5-μm design rules ranged from 3 to 12 ns. Employing a new format that can be technologically updated, the chip has now been shrunk to 2.5-μm design rules that lower gate delays to 2 to 5 ns. At the typical 10-MHz operating frequency, the time to add two 16-bit numbers is 8 microseconds and the power dissipation is 100 milliwatts.

A 32-bit microprocessor

The Bellmac-32 is a full 32-bit, single-chip microprocessor. Control logic, a 32-bit bus, and 63 I/O channels all fit on the same chip. Its instruction set and address modes are similar to those of today's minicomputers in the 1-MIP range. It was designed to support the structured C language under the Unix operating system, with virtual memory capability implemented in hardware.

All this called for a processor 10 times more complex than its two predecessors. In fact, when it became clear how large the chip would have to be, it at first seemed that the control logic and bus interface might better be put on two chips. But then, on the grounds that a 32-bit machine would most probably be used in systems with so much memory that it would dominate system cost, the decision was made to give chip performance precedence over chip cost.

However, the use of two chips would have hurt performance because of the long delay inherent in communication between them. Also, little savings in cost could be reaped unless the bus between them were narrow enough to prevent chip I/O from adding deleteriously to the size of the two chips. Furthermore, a product of this complexity and power would probably have a long lifetime during which its size could be reduced repeatedly as smaller design rules became feasible. So the final choice was a single-chip design in a format whose technology could readily be updated.

New ideas

Nevertheless, innovation was needed on many fronts before it was to be possible to manufacture this chip. In the 1978 planning phase that preceded actual design, several new approaches were selected. The development of the twin-tub C-MOS technology and domino C-MOS circuits was started, to meet the performance needs for this machine. Updatable polycells were developed to support the need for a rapidly correctable automated design of the random logic in the control section, while an updatable gate-matrix layout technique was designed to give a densely packed, high-performance internal bus structure. The modularization of the design used in the Bellmac-8 microprocessor was carried to a much higher level in a hierarchical, modular, top-down approach to the control section. Finally, chip-level logic and timing simulation were supported by automatic generation of component parameters from the mask data base.

Traditionally, C-MOS circuits have had slower switching speeds than n-MOS circuits, but in spite of this difference, they can still perform better chip for chip if the total number of gates in a chip is limited by power dissipation. In addition, C-MOS's longer gate delay is not a fundamental defect but a matter of technology choice and circuit configuration. With appropriate technology and circuitry, the power dissipation advantage of C-MOS can be combined with competitive and in some cases superior gate-level performance—even though the

n-MOS transistors within C-MOS chips have traditionally had slower switching speeds than those in purely n-MOS chips.

C-MOS circuits have a higher input capacitance but better drive capability than n-MOS when low fan-ins are involved. For high fan-in situations, other C-MOS circuit alternatives are available, however.

Some options

Figure 2a shows a conventional silicon-gate C-MOS cross section. The p-channel transistor is formed in the n-type wafer doped to give the right threshold voltage—about 1 volt. A p-tub is formed in the n wafer to accept the n-channel transistor. The p-tub doping therefore has to be much higher than the n-wafer doping in order to overcompensate it with some degree of control. This leads to higher drain and source capacitances and also a high back-gate bias effect. The last causes poor performance whenever the source voltage goes above ground potential—for example, in transmission gates or transistors in the serial string of transistors in NAND gates—causing the channel to pinch down and in the extreme case to pinch off completely.

This poor performance can be improved for the n-channel transistors by using an n-tub C-MOS technology (Fig. 2b) that is just the converse of the p-tub process. The n-channel transistor then has the performance of

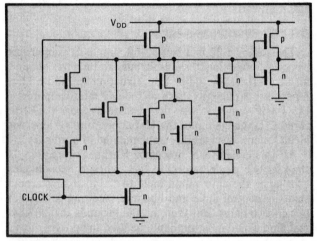

3. Like dominos. This form of dynamic C-MOS doubled the speed of the processor's arithmetic and logic unit. A low clock pulse biases all of the gate outputs and inputs to a logical 0. When the clock rises, logic signals cascade from the first gate to the last.

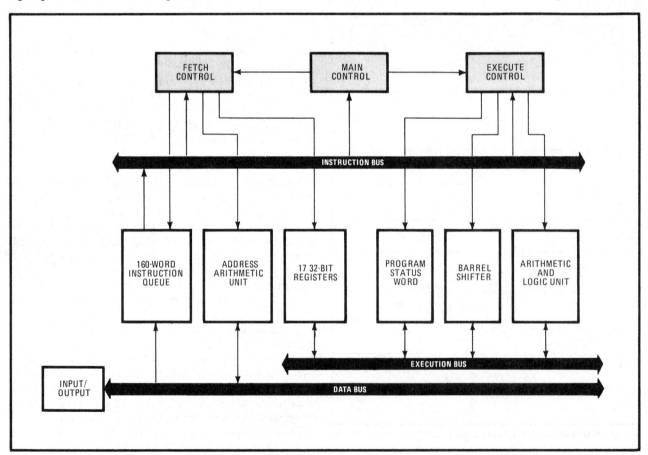

4. Parallel control. The Bellmac-32 has separate fetch and execution functions. The fetch control section has a separate address-arithmetic unit for address calculations and a 160-word-deep instructional queue. The execution unit features a barrel shifter.

that obtained in normal n-MOS technology, an important advantage. Unfortunately, the converse problem to p-tub C-MOS exists—the p-channel transistor has capacitance and back-gate bias problems.

The complete answer to the performance problem is shown in Fig. 2c—twin-tub C-MOS, in which, ironically, both types of transistor are formed in tubs; but in this case the background doping is very low, so that each tub can be implanted with the optimum dose for its corresponding transistor.

Finer design rules are easily accommodated in this twin-tub technology since such problems as punch-through are minimized by the ability to dope each tub separately. The structure also has the advantage of symmetry. The tubs are self-registered with respect to one another—wherever there is no n tub, there is a p tub, so that only one mask is needed for both tubs. (Twin-tub C-MOS, incidentally, is also being used for linear circuits, such as codecs, by the addition of another level of polysilicon to form capacitors.)

No latchup either

Traditional C-MOS technology also causes latchup because the parasitic pnp and npn transistors combined to form a latching pnpn device, usually when there are current surges in an input or an output. The surge current flows into the base of either the npn or pnp device, and once turned on, the pnpn transistor remains latched until the power supply is turned off. This effect can be eliminated by using an n$^+$ substrate as shown in Fig. 2c. The n$^+$ substrate forms a base contact to all of the parasitic pnp transistors. By connecting this substrate to the positive power supply voltage, it is possible to provide a low-resistance path across the base-emitter junction of the parasitic pnp transistors.

The corresponding solution for n-tub technology, however, does not work as well, since it calls for a p^{++} substrate that would have lower conductivity and cause more out-diffusion problems than an n$^+$ substrate. In the I/O circuits, additional protection is provided by surrounding the p-channel transistors with n$^+$ guard rings and the n-channel transistors with p$^+$ guard rings. The former gives additional contact to the pnp bases, the latter a contact to the npn bases. I/O circuits take up only a small proportion of the total area in a VLSI chip—4% in the case of Bellmac-4 microcomputer—and the guard rings are a small fraction of this area.

Another factor that has limited the application of C-MOS in the past was the relative complexity of the process. But if C-MOS wafer-processing costs have increased in the search for higher performance, n-MOS costs have risen even faster for the same reason. The days of the simple four-mask process have long gone, and depletion-mode n-MOS, with one chip containing three and even four different kinds of transistors implanted to give different threshold voltages, are now not uncommon. C-MOS is no longer the most expensive MOS process around.

With a correct choice of technology, then, the performance of conventional C-MOS logic circuits can be made competitive with those of n-MOS logic circuits. And with a correct choice of circuits, the situation can be improved even further.

The existence of opposite-polarity transistors within a C-MOS chip can be exploited in many ways other than for low-power dissipation. The p-channel device makes an excellent passive-load device, and since its source is grounded in that configuration, it does not suffer from back-gate bias effects. The pseudo–n-MOS circuit performs a similar function to that of a depletion-mode n-MOS circuit and has a similar performance, given a similar n-channel device.

Room for creativity

Dynamic circuits can be used for saving die area in C-MOS circuits just as they are in n-MOS, but here again the p-channel device gives additional circuit design flexibility. In PLAs the p-channel device is in this case being used as an active device with its gate under clock control. The p-channel device pulls up or precharges a word line and logical operations are performed on it. The n-channel transistors are controlled by a ground switch that is also under clock control.

Another form of dynamic C-MOS—domino C-MOS—is illustrated in Fig. 3. Here the p-channel pull-up devices and n-channel ground switch or pull-down devices are driven by a common clock line. Precharging occurs on the high-to-low clock-pulse transition. Discharging, under the control of the n-channel input transistors, happens as the clock signal rises.

The output inverter buffers the output signal and also ensures logic transmission without noise spikes or glitches. During precharging all circuit outputs—and hence, circuit inputs—are supposed to be low. When discharging begins, the first logic stage is activated, then the second, and so on (hence the name domino). If one of a circuit's inputs happens to remain high from a previous

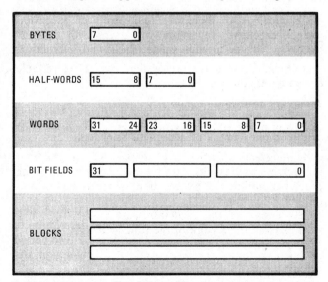

5. Data structures. The Bellmac-32 microprocessor is a byte-oriented machine capable of operating on 8-bit bytes, 16-bit half-words, and 32-bit words. The device is also able to work effectively with variably sized bit fields and with large blocks of data.

6. Compacted. This is just the ALU portion of the machine. It contains 20,000 transistors and took nine months to complete. Recently scaled down using 2.5-micrometer design rules, the ALU now operates at 8 MHz. Overall die size will be about 150,000 mil².

phase, it might generate a high-level output. However, the inverter makes certain that the inputs to the next stage remain low during discharging regardless of input conditions.

Use of domino C-MOS gave twice the speed of conventional C-MOS in the ALU module. Moreover, only a single clock line is required, whereas an equivalent n-channel MOS circuit would demand two. Additional transistors can also be added to make the circuit quasi-static and immune to charge-sharing effects.

A 32-bit architecture

The focus of this work on C-MOS technology was, of course, the Bellmac-32. It is the first chip ever to use domino C-MOS logic—in its ALU, its barrel shifter, and its AAU.

As the block diagram in Fig. 4 shows, the chip also includes two temporary registers, a barrel-shifter, seventeen 32-bit general-purpose registers, an instruction queue 160 words deep, and a program counter. All of these units are 32 bits wide. The 32-bit multiplexed data-address bus is split into two parts that communicate through the two-ported register set. This splitting provides faster operation of each part and allows parallel data transfers for increased throughput. I/O transfers are also 32 bits wide for wide-path communication with all peripherals.

The 32-bit machine is byte-oriented in its data structure (Fig. 5) and in its instruction and address coding. It supports three address instructions—separate addresses for each of the two source and the destination operands. Multiply, divide, modulo, subroutine call and return, and system call and return can each be executed with a single instruction. Also, there are four levels of execution: kernel, executive, supervisor, and user, with different access privileges in each mode. Privileged instructions are provided for operating system use, as is reliable exception-handling mechanism.

Design automation helps

Layout of the 100,000-transistor-site chip was finished within three months of receipt of final logic, and chip debugging took a further five months. Only three minor logic errors were found, with the remaining errors being problems introduced by the hand-stitched power and ground connections.

The design of the 20,000-transistor ALU took nine months from the receipt of the functional description to fully debugged and functional chips (Fig. 6). The period included the time needed to debug the new design and circuit tools.

The 32-bit ALU uses carry–look-ahead at the 4-, 16-, and 32-bit levels. Simulations predicted an add time of 124 ns with worst-case two-sigma limits on processing parameters for 3.5-μm design rules. Actual measure-

ments of delay on the same slice yielded 105 ns, as compared to a 98-ns prediction by the simulator—an indication of the latter's accuracy. Simulations of all portions of the data-address path showed that all would pass a 4-megahertz test with worst-case processing. Actual measurements of a number of chips showed that the typical frequency was in fact 6 MHz—none was as low as 4 MHz. The ALU portion of the machine has now been updated to 2.5-μm rules with a typical operating frequency of 8 MHz.

The control section of the Bellmac-32 is hierarchically organized. A main PLA distributes control to other slave PLAs, with demultiplexing logic passing the control signals to the bus interface and I/O sections of the machine. The first stage of the the hierarchical structure is instruction decoding. The second stage is carried out in a random-logic design using CAD-supported polycell layout with automatic signal wiring for all but the power and ground connections.

The chip area was 1.45 square centimeters in 3.5-μm design rules. Yield, though of course low for a chip of this size, fit the expected value based on an extrapolation from smaller chips. Also, although the yield could easily have been too low for it to be possible to distinguish between design and processing defects, this turned out not to be the case. Debugging proceeded quite well on chips with a single or even two processing defects. Enough defect-free chips were obtained for their code to be run in a single-board computer in order further to study the design and use of this machine.

The present chip has provided much valuable feedback on its design and technology, of which extensive use is being made to shrink it down to 2.5-μm design rules. The new version will have a clock distribution system that has been substantially improved for higher throughput. Also, more of the control logic is implemented in PLA

structures, and the remaining random logic is being implemented in the PLA style, rather than as polycells, for greater density and performance. The overall layout will occupy 1 cm².

The performance of the chip in a system is difficult to measure, as it varies with the memory speed and the instructions required for each application. Moreover, the MIP term is vaguely defined and hard to interpret, since a chip with a high MIP value may do well in one application program for which its instruction set is suitable but poorly in another for which it is not. Clock frequency alone is useless as a performance measure, since throughput depends on what the machine is designed to accomplish within a clock cycle.

Figure of merit

In view of all this, the performance objectives for the Bellmac-32 microprocessor were established by the software users in terms of throughput on seven user-defined benchmark programs. The throughput of the Bellmac-32 microprocessor was then defined as a percentage of an existing Western Electric minicomputer, whose performance on these same programs is comparable with a 1-MIP minicomputer when coupled with a memory system with average access time of 400 ns.

A major design consideration for a VLSI microprocessor is that its product life cycle is likely to be much longer than the interval between design rule changes, primarily because of the large investment in software and hardware needed to realize a design. Improvements in its operating speed and cost can be obtained by implementing the existing design with the new design rules, but it must be possible to do this quickly and for reasonable cost. This is now accomplished in the Bellmac series by means of designing all of the parts in a design-rule–independent way.

Appropriate CAD software calls out the actual design rules from a design-rule file and from them generates the mask and simulation data bases. Designs can then be implemented in silicon with state-of-the-art design rules and, as smaller rules become feasible, can be followed by rapid technology updates with a minimum of the agonizing effort that traditionally accompanies new layouts.

The above factors were basic considerations in the selection of a design methodology for the members of the Bell Labs microprocessor and microcomputer family. A typical microprocessor has three major parts—the data-address bus structure, the control logic, and the I/O logic—for each of which different methodologies are appropriate.

Fitting designs

The bus structure consists of several subsections that can be designed separately, each having a regular structure imposed by the bit-organized nature of the circuits. Thus its complexity is low, and it can be designed in a reasonable time. The control logic is much less regular, and a well-disciplined, machine-aided design approach is definitely needed. I/O, however, is highly modular and is the latest major section to undergo the transition from hand to machine design, mostly out of a desire to ensure that the technology can be updated.

The design methodology employed by Bell Labs has taken these factors into consideration and has evolved from family member to family member as the complexity and therefore the pressure to find faster and surer design techniques has increased. The design approach for the bus structure has consequently evolved from a hand-packed design to the use of gate matrix, which is a regular but hand-packed design done at a symbolic level, with machine generation and verification of the resultant layout and circuit.

Within the control section, the major control functions have been implemented as PLAs with multiplexed outputs to keep the PLA sizes within bounds set by performance constraints. The demultiplexing logic has been implemented with increasing levels of CAD support as its complexity has increased. In addition, increasing emphasis has been placed on modular design, so that individual modules could be handled as separate, less complex, designs. Inevitably, however, there is more interaction between modules in the control section and less regularity in intermodule communication than is the case in the bus structure.

The resulting problems are best handled with a top-down, hierarchical design. A module function, its approximate size and shape, and its I/O are defined, and wiring between modules is done automatically before the interior of the module is finalized. In this way, it is possible to keep track of long intermodule communication paths from the early phases of the design, preventing surprises in machine timing and wiring area. This methodology consciously emulates that of structured programming, which has been increasingly used in the last decade to ease the problems of development of complex software. □

16-bit bipolar microprocessor marches to standard instruction set

Microcode implements floating-point instructions on chip, while interrupt and fault handling serves real-time uses

by S. Mor, H. Hingarh, M. Vora, D. Wilnai, D. Maxwell, and T. Longo
Fairchild Camera & Instrument Corp., Palo Alto, Calif.

☐ Caught between the severe demands of high-speed applications and the need to implement an extensive set of standard instructions designed for real-time uses, microprocessor developers will generally balk at the notion of capturing so much functional capability as to satisfy both on a single chip. Yet a new 16-bit microprocessor, the F9450, combines a high-density bipolar technology with a microcoded architecture to meet that challenge and, in addition, fully implements a military-standard instruction- set architecture (ISA), MIL-STD-1750A. In order to do so on one chip, the F9450 combined Isoplanar integrated injection logic with very large-scale integration to pack 140,000 transistors onto 98,500 square mils of sili-

con (see "Putting a real-time squeeze on VLSI," opposite).

The chip's architecture was developed specifically for embedded computer systems. Thus, the F9450 is well suited to such applications as automatic flight control, inertial navigation, and industrial control, all of which require high-precision computation of rapidly changing variables. The needs of such real-time applications are met through the use of five major functional blocks in the chip: the data processor, microprogrammed control section, address processor, interrupt and fault processor, and the timing- and bus-arbitration unit, which generates internal and external strobes that are required for bus arbitration and central-processing-unit operation (Fig. 1).

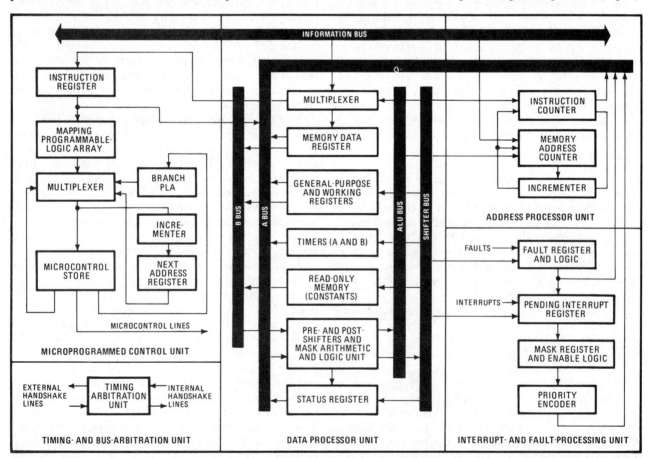

1. A chip in five parts. In the F9450 16-bit bipolar microprocessor, real-time processing is distributed over five functional blocks. On-chip floating-point operations are handled by microcode using a 17-bit arithemetic and logic unit located in the data processor block.

Responsible for all data processing in the F9450, the 16-bit–wide data-processor section includes 16 general-purpose registers, several working registers, two timers, and a read-only-memory section for holding bit patterns used in bit-manipulation instructions and floating-point over- and under-flow. Also 16 bits wide are two timers, called timer A and timer B, that are started, halted, loaded, and read using input/output instructions that may be accessed only in the supervisor mode of operation. Timer A operates at the timer clock frequency (100 kilohertz), while timer B counts at a tenth that frequency. When the timers overflow, the corresponding bits are set in the pending interrupt register in the interrupt-processor section of the F9450.

In addition to these registers and timers, a 17-bit arithmetic and logic unit keys all arithmetic operations, providing an extra bit for accommodating modified-Booth-algorithm overflows during multiplication. Handling a full range of data types from 8-bit bytes through 48-bit extended-precision floating-point values, the processor's instruction set includes a comprehensive set of instructions for arithmetic operations, including single- and dou-

ARITHMETIC EXECUTION TIMES (IN MICROSECONDS) OF F9450 16-BIT MICROPROCESSOR				
Operation	Single-precision integer	Double-precision integer	Floating point	Extended floating point
Register addition/ subtraction	0.2	0.8	4.5	5.75
Register multiplication	1.85	5.75	5.6	12.4
Register division	4.7	12.0	9.8	21.15
Note: System configuration is a 20-MHz CPU clock with a 0.2-microsecond bus cycle time; execution times vary linearly with CPU clock rate.				

ble-precision integer, single- and extended-precision floating-point, absolute value; a variety of multiply and divide instructions; and an extensive set of data-type conversion intructions.

More significantly for performance, the F9450 puts this comprehensive set of floating-point instructions on

Putting a real-time squeeze on VLSI

Getting the most out of a real-time microprocessor means squeezing the most functional capability into the least area. Isoplanar integrated-injection logic (I³L) is an advanced bipolar technology developed as an alternative to MOS technologies, aimed at achieving high packing density and low power-delay products at a low cost. The I³L-II technology used in the F9450 microprocessor is a 3-micrometer second-generation bipolar process that meets these goals.

As shown in the figures below, the basic I³L gate is a single complementary pair of transistors: a vertical transistor with multiple collectors acts as an npn inverter and a lateral pnp transistor serves as both current source and load. The thin n epitaxial layer acts as not only the grounded-emitter region of the npn inverter, but also as the grounded-base region of the lateral pnp transistor. Likewise, the base of the npn transistor, merged with the collector of the npn transistor in a single p⁺ region, occupies the space of a single multi-emitter transistor.

At a basic level, this technology provides a minimum gate delay of 2.5 nanoseconds, as well as a packing density of 535 gates per square millimeter, including power buses, routing wire overhead, and a 1,200-gate/mm² intrinsic density. As a comparison, n-MOS technology, such as that used in the 68000, yields 300 gates/mm². I³L-II manages this high packing density because of

the simplicity of designing with a single transistor and because of a number of layout considerations, including the absence of diffused, area-hungry resistors, the small number of contact windows required for each gate, and routing intercell wiring over unused base areas. These factors, in addition to the regularity of the logic, result in an extremely dense and highly optimized chip layout.

Using a modified bipolar Isoplanar process results in direct TTL interface capability, fast and dense conventional circuitry—such as programmable logic arrays, read-only memories, and random-access memories—and a scalable technology. In addition, oxide isolation, a self-aligned device structure, and ion implantation techniques have helped reduce transistor size. The process also yields improved dc gain and an optimized power-delay product. Since the device structure is self-aligned, it gives independent control of pnp and npn device characteristics. An added feature of the process is better performance over the complete military temperature range as well as an enhanced radiation tolerance of 10⁵ rads.

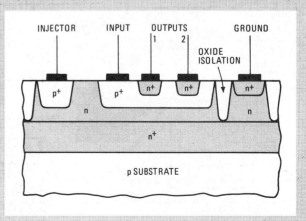

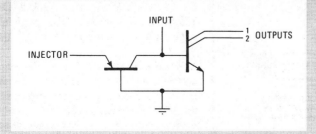

chip for the first time in the microprocessor arena. Although floating-point operations are handled by the microcode, special hardware—such as some of the working registers used as hardware shift registers—results in high-speed arithmetic operations (see table). Other circuits that boost floating-point performance include masks that strip the exponent field to enable efficient exponent processing and over- and under-flow detection hardware to speed up floating-point exception handling.

Floating-point numbers are represented in the F9450 microprocessor by a fractional 2's complement binary mantissa and a 2's complement unbiased integer exponent. The microprocessor employs a floating-point arithmetic scheme in which the results of every floating-point operation are normalized. In the 2's complement representation, a normalized floating-point number is one in which the sign bit of the mantissa is not equal to the bit next to it.

For control, a status register in this section contains flags, processor-state information, and address-state bits that are used for extended addressing with the F9451 memory-management unit and can double as segment pointers without the MMU. Furthermore, a configuration register defines the hardware state of the system to the CPU. This latter register is set during system initialization to indicate the presence of the MMU, the F9452 block-protection unit (BPU), coprocessors, or console.

Brains and brawn

If the data-processor section is the brawn of this workhorse, the microprogrammed control section serves as its brain. Using two levels of pipelining, this section governs all CPU operations. When new instructions enter the instruction register, a programmable logic array uses the bit patterns as input to generate the two pointers necessary for execution of the software routine and for generation of the effective address from the microcode ROM. Using the output from the PLA, the 50-K microcoded ROM generates three fields: a next-address field, a branch field, and a control field. The first two fields determine the subsequent microaddress, while the last controls the operation of all CPU components.

The address processor includes an instruction counter and a memory-address register for determining the address of all instructions and operands. Normally, the counter will contain the instruction address and the register will hold the data address. In branch instructions, the source for the instruction address is the memory-address register. An independent incrementer in this section provides instruction counter update that parallels data processor operations.

As with all modern microprocessors, the F9450 handles a variety of addressing modes. A particularly unusual and efficient mode accommodated is immediate indexed addressing. In this mode, an immediate operand is added directly to the contents of a register. In another, the immediate short mode, 4-bit operands are manipulated directly as positive or negative numbers. In accessing double-precision or floating-point numbers, both of which are 32 bits in length, the derived address (DA) and the location immediately following it (DA+1) are used. For 48-bit extended-precision floating-point values, DA, DA+1, and DA+2 point to three 16-bit words.

The F9450 addressing scheme is based on three entities: the 16-bit information bus, 4 bits of the address-state bus, and the data/instruction line (Fig. 2). If the MMU is not used, these lines make available 4 megabytes of directly addressable segmented memory space, organized as 2 megabytes for instruction space and 2 megabytes for data space. Each of these spaces is partitioned into sixteen 128-K-byte segments, using the four address-state bits in the status register as the segment pointer.

However, with the F9451 MMU the addressing range may be expanded up to 16 megabytes. The MMU translates the logical address into a physical address by mapping the data in 4-K-word pages. The mapping mechanism shown in Fig. 2 incorporates 512 page registers organized in 16 pairs of register groups—one for instruction memory space and one for data memory space. Each group contains 16 page registers for a total of 256 registers for data space and 256 registers for instruction space.

One of the 16 pairs of groups is selected by the four address-state bits. The selection of the group within the pair, in turn, is performed by the data/instruction bit. The page register within the designated group is selected by the four most significant bits of the address. Although in the current definition of MIL-STD-1750A only 8 bits of the physical page address are used, 11 bits of this

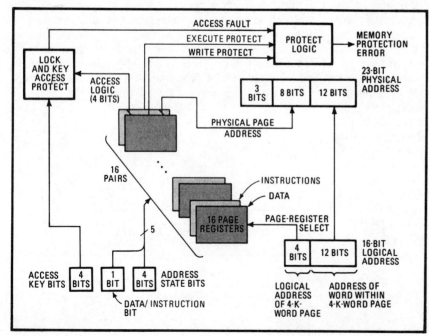

2. Memory in 512 parts. For memory management, the F9451 divides the address space into separate data and instruction spaces, each served by 256 16-bit page registers. The upper 4 bits of the logical address have the job of selecting the page register.

field are concatenated with the 12 least significant bits of the address to become the 23 bits of the physical address.

The MMU also checks for protection violations by comparing the access key with the access lock fields in the page register. This unit also examines the write-protect bit in the page registers if data is accessed or the execute-protect bit in the same register if instructions are accessed. If a violation occurs, the MMU activates the memory-protect error output. Page registers are read or written by means of privileged single-transfer, or XIO, instructions.

Likewise, the F9452 BPU may be used for write protection in the physical space. The protection is effected in 1-K-word blocks according to a lookup table accessible through XIO instructions. The BPU can be used with or without the MMU. It will protect both the CPU and direct-memory-access spaces, and will set the memory-protect error output if a violation occurs.

Real-time booster

For its use in real-time applications, the interrupt and fault processor is a vital section of the F9450. This section uses a pending-interrupt register to handle all faults and any of 16 external or internal interrupts. In addition, the section includes a mask register, enable logic, and a priority encoder. The fault register records external violations—such as memory-protect error, memory parity error—and internal violations—such as built-in test, privileged instruction, and illegal instruction. When a fault occurs, an interrupt will be generated, and in cases of major or unrecoverable errors, the instruction is aborted. Internal faults include timers and fixed and floating overflows.

In cases involving floating-point exceptions, a floating-point overflow-interrupt bit is set whenever the exponent of a result is greater than $7F_{16}$. Any result of an operation causing overflow is set to the greatest positive number ($7F\ F\ .\ .\ .F_{16}$), if the sign of the result's mantissa is positive. Conversely, if the sign of the result's mantissa is negative, the result of the operation is set to the greatest negative number ($7F\ 80\ .\ .\ .0_{16}$). A floating-point divide-by-zero operation will set the overflow interrupt bit.

On the other hand, a floating-point underflow interrupt bit is set when the operation produces an exponent less than 80_{16} and the result of any operation that causes underflow is set to 0. Both floating-point overflow and underflow interrupts may be masked.

High-level backing

High-level languages find direct support in the instruction set through instructions such as "subtract 1 and jump" for loop control and "compare between limits" for verifying, for example, that a subscript falls between declared upper and lower bounds of an array. In the compare-between-limits instruction, the contents of a register is compared with two different derived operands (DO_1 and DO_2). These operands reside in the derived address and the one following it. The condition-status (CS) field of the status word is used to report the comparison results. First, the boundary values are compared to ensure that the lower limit is in fact less than or equal to the upper limit. Then, if this test fails, the instruction

will terminate with the CS field set to a particular value:

If $DO_1 > DO_2$ then CS:=1000
else
  begin
    if $(RA) < DO_1$ then CS:=0001
    else if $DO_1 < (RA) < DO_2$ then CS:=0010
    else if $DO_2 < (RA)$ then CS:=0100
  end

The stack-manipulation instructions such as "stack instruction counter and jump to subroutine" and "unstack instruction counter and return from subroutine," as well as instructions that push and pop multiple registers, simplify procedure calls and context switching. In addition, the F9450 has a move-block instruction in which up to 64-K-word blocks can be moved in the memory space. Any pending interrupts are honored after each single word transfer is completed. The instruction counter points to the current instruction location until the last transfer is completed.

For reliable multiuser–operating-system implementation, the F9450 provides a privileged, or supervisor, mode set when PS = 0 in the status word. The instructions that handle I/O, interrupt and DMA processing, real-time clock manipulations, memory management, protection commands, and processor status-word modifications will be restricted to the operating system and, hence, to the privileged mode.

With this protection, user programs cannot destroy the operating system or other user programs. But when access to another user area is needed, the F9450 supplies an instruction called branch to executive (BEX). This instruction is an executive call that provides a means to

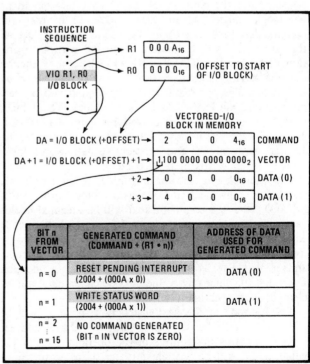

3. Instruction expansion. In order to expand a single explicit instruction into several executed instructions, the F9450 CPU uses a pair of registers as well as a block of memory to generate up to 16 commands for a vectored input/output transfer instruction.

jump to code in another address state, which may be another user or another process. It is typically employed to make controlled, protected calls to an executive using one of 16 entry points. The BEX instruction is handled as a part of the uniform interrupt scheme employed by the F9450.

Another important function of an operating system is process synchronization. Using an uninterruptible read-modify-write operation in its test-and-set-bit (TSB) instruction, the F9450 permits process synchronization through the use of a memory location as a semaphore. When a semaphore is 0, its corresponding resource is available for use, and a 1 indicates that the resource is in use. To avoid a situation wherein two processes try to modify that location simultaneously, an uninterruptible TSB instruction is necessary. With the TSB instruction, a bit is tested against a code set in the condition status register and subsequently set to 1. If the value of the semaphore was already 1, system software will normally queue the process on list of blocked processes until the resource associated with the list becomes available.

Smart input/output

For I/O, the F9450 incorporates a very unusual instruction set that uses two basic formats: XIO for single transfers and VIO for vectored multiple transfers. In the single-transfer case, XIO, the command can be taken directly from the instruction or calculated using an index register. The VIO provides an extremely flexible structure utilizing modern I/O processing concepts in which a pointer refers to a block in memory (Fig. 3).

With a VIO instruction, up to 16 commands can be generated on the basis of the contents of one of the registers and the contents of the DA+1 location in an I/O block starting at an address DA. In forming the commands, every bit (n) in the vector register DA+1 that is set to 1 will generate a command with an operation code equal to $(DA)+n*(RA)$, where n is the bit position starting with n = 0 for the most significant bit in DA+1. The command that is generated will operate on data location DA+2+i in the I/O block. The value i, initially 0, is incremented only if bit n in DA+1 is 1. Thus, for example, if only 5 bits in the vector register are 1, there will only be five consecutive data words for a total of seven words in the I/O block.

For example, as shown in Fig. 3, if an I/O block, starting at some location DA, has a vector register value of $C000_{16}$, the first command that will be executed in this case will simply be the one having an operation code equal to the value in DA. The instruction "reset pending interrupt" is the command associated with this op code, and it will use as its data the contents of location DA+2(+0). Since this value is 0000, interrupts will be cleared in the pending-interrupt register.

The op code of the next instruction (n = 1) will be $2004+000A\times1$, "write status word." Here, address DA+3 contains the address of the operand, so that the value 4000_{16} will be written into the status word. Since the rest of the bits in the vector register are 0, no further I/O commands will be executed from this block.

The VIO is a very powerful tool in I/O-processing applications and may be used for sending a block of commands to the same device, such as page registers in the MMU, the lookup table in the BPU, or I/O channel control registers. It can also be used for such applications as sending the same command to a series of devices—for example, resetting or initializing several devices, enabling interrupts on several devices, or reading status of several devices.

Self-testing on initialization

A comprehensive initialization sequence that includes an extensive built-in self-testing procedure is another feature of the F9450. Invoked by the reset signal, the initialization sequence starts with execution of the self-test, which extensively exercises the various sections of the CPU. If the processor passes the test, the normal power-up output, which is useful as a system-reset signal, is then set. Self-test failure is recorded in the fault register.

The F9450 also supplies direct support for debugging through a conditional breakpoint instruction that complements the extensive console operation of the microprocessor. On encountering a breakpoint instruction, the microprocessor first reads the configuration register to check whether a console is present. If no console should happen to be present, this instruction is ignored. On the other hand, if a console is present, the processor waits for input from the console.

Set at predefined I/O addresses, the console registers act as a powerful link to the F9450 for debugging operations, allowing the user to directly examine and alter general- and special-purpose registers in the F9450. Once the CPU detects a console request, it completes the current instruction, executes an I/O cycle to read the console command from the information bus at I/O address 8400, and then executes the console command. Typically, this involves addresses I/O 8401_{16} in order to enter console

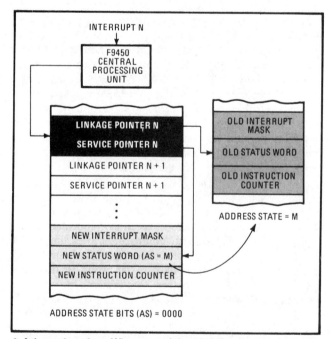

4. Interrupt vectors. When one of the 16 defined events interrupts the F9450, the CPU uses a pair of pointers unique to the particular event. The service pointer serves to retrieve the new register values, and the linkage serves to store the old ones.

data and 0400_{16} in order to write data to the console.

Real-time processing requires extensive fault handling, and the F9450 employs a very comprehensive scheme involving the fault register, interrupt processor, and the abort mechanism. The various faults and errors are handled at three levels of severity. Class 1 faults are unrecoverable errors or those with major implications for program execution. These errors will abort the instruction, be recorded in the fault register, and generate a machine-error interrupt (priority = 1) that cannot be disabled. They will also set the unrecoverable-error or major-error signals through dedicated pins on the package.

Although severe, class 2 errors have no fatal implications for program execution. These will be recorded in the fault register and result in a machine-error (priority = 1) interrupt after the instruction has completed execution. Class 3 errors are arithmetic exception cases and timer terminations. These are not recorded in the fault register but are fed directly to the pending-interrupt register to generate lower-level interrupts. The fault register records class 1 and 2 faults resulting from violations detected outside the CPU as well as faults that are detected internally.

The F9450 includes a 16-level priority-interrupt processor that uniformly handles externally and internally generated interrupts and the BEX software interrupt. All interrupts are latched in the pending-interrupt register, and those that are maskable can be masked by a special register.

The F9450 accepts nine external interrupts, power-down interrupt, five general-purpose user interrupts, and two I/O-level interrupts that may be used to expand the number of user interrupts. Once it enters the I/OL$_1$ or I/OL$_2$ interrupt handler, a register in the I/O space containing the highest-priority interrupt request in that channel

can be read into the CPU, which will then execute the service routine associated with that request.

By programming the interrupt-mode bit in the system-configuration register, the user can select edge-sensitive or level-sensitive recognition modes for all external interrupts except I/OL$_1$ and I/OL$_2$. Other interrupts handled by the priority processor are generated internally—for instance, machine errors, which reflect faults recorded in the fault register and cannot be disabled.

Enabled interrupts are acknowledged by resetting the acknowledged-interrupt bit in the pending-interrupt register and executing an I/O cycle during which the acknowledged-interrupt number is sent to I/O device 1000_{16}. After the vectoring sequence (see Fig. 4), the specific interrupt handler written by the user will begin executing. To return from interrupt, the load-status instruction is used. This instruction loads the values of status word, mask register, and instruction counter that were saved by the vectoring sequence.

A distributed future

As real-time system design grows in sophistication, distributed architectures are certain to gain increased application. The F9450 directly supports multiple-processor configurations through a special instruction and a flexible bus-arbitration design. The built-in function (BIF) is an escape code in the F9450 instruction set that makes it possible for instructions to be user-defined by means of an external coprocessor. The F9450 will send out to the external coprocessor both the command and the operand address defined by the specific BIF instruction. In this manner, up to four coprocessors are supported by the F9450's BIF format.

In the arbitration scheme, all bus users are considered as potential masters. In fact, any device can become bus master in an F9450-controlled system as long as it complies with the microprocessor's timing requirements. Once the bus is assigned to another bus master, the CPU will go to a high-impedance state.

In this scheme, for example, a DMA device could be treated as a master or slave by controlling the DMA enable output signal by its associated CPU through the XIO or VIO instructions. Because of the amount of circuitry included for this task on chip, external circuitry is kept to a minimum.

A typical system would have all bus masters running off the same CPU clock, including the external bus arbiter that controls system-bus accesses. The external arbiter samples the different bus requests, resolves their priority, and responds with the appropriate bus grant every CPU clock cycle. In a dual-CPU or CPU-DMA configuration, the arbiter can something be as simple as a single D-type flip-flop (Fig. 5).

When using the common bus, the F9450 can lock it by asserting its bus-lock output, locking out other bus masters. No other bus master can get onto the bus as long as the bus-lock signal is asserted, even if the requesting master has the highest priority and has already received a bus grant from the external arbiter. The processor uses this lockout technique when executing such instructions as test and set bit, for which it has to perform an uninterruptible read-modify-write operation. ☐

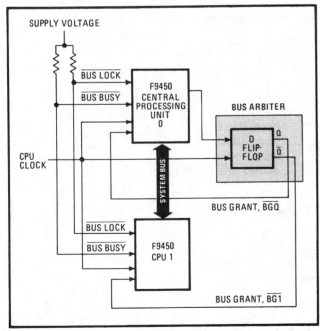

5. Easy judgment. With its extensive on-chip arbitration logic, the F9450 microprocessor is simple to use in a multiprocessor configuration. By sharing bus-lock and bus-busy signals, the CPUs need only a D-type flip-flop to handle bus arbitration.

Electronics/May 5, 1983

Microprocessor chip integrates a host of peripheral functions to simplify systems

With seven functional blocks on a single chip, the 80186 outperforms its compatible brother and yields compact microcomputer systems

by Kenneth Shoemaker, *Intel Corp., Santa Clara, Calif.*

☐ A well-furnished microprocessor that integrates many of the common peripheral functions greatly simplifies the design of microcomputer systems, as well as improving system performance. Such a chip is the 16-bit 80l86, which combines seven separate functional blocks into a very large-scale integrated circuit. Included with the central processing unit are a direct-memory-access unit, a timer, an interrupt controller, a bus interface unit, a clock generator and crystal oscillator, and a chip-selection and wait-state–generation unit (Fig. 1)

The 186 family actually consists of two microprocessors, the 80186 and 80188. The only difference between the two is the width of the external data bus: 16 bits in the 186 and 8 bits in the 188. Thus, except where noted, all 186 information in this article also applies to the 188.

The CPU shares its architecture with the 8086, 8088, and 80286 microprocessors and is completely object-code–compatible with the 8086 and 8088. This architecture features four 16-bit general-purpose registers, which may be used as operands in most 8- or 16-bit arithmetic operations. It also features four 16-bit pointer registers, which may be used both in arithmetic operations and in accessing memory-based varibles. Four 16-bit segment registers expedite simple memory partitioning to aid construction of modular programs and position-independent code. Finally, the architecture has a 16-bit instruction pointer and a 16-bit status register.

A wealth of operand addressing modes that simplify and enhance programming of the processor are possible with the rich memory addressing scheme. The 16-bit

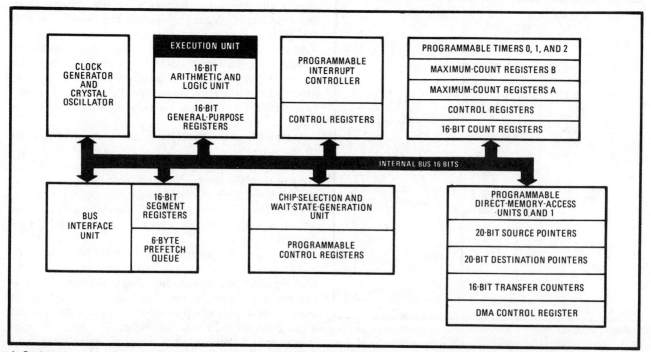

1. System on a chip. The 80186 contains a variety of common peripheral circuitry, making it almost an entire microcomputer. Integrated programmable units include a two-channel direct-memory-access unit, three timers with count registers, and an interrupt controller.

Hardware enhancements speed up the 80186

The enhanced central processing unit of the 80186 executes most instructions in fewer clock cycles than does the 8086. Some of the hardware enhancements made to the processor include modifications to the multiplier and divider, an address calculator, an arithmetic-and-logic-unit bit shifter, and additional hardware for string moving.

Multiply and divide. An additional bit-shifter is included in the 80186 to boost its multiplication and division to about three times the speed of the 8086. Thus any program that is limited by the execution speed of the multiply and divide instructions—for example, digital filter routines, matrix multiply routines, and graphics translation routines—will see a significant performance improvement.

Effective address calculation. The 8086 instruction set includes powerful addressing modes that access instruction operands. As a result, the processor must automatically and transparently calculate various register and immediate addressing values just to derive the memory address of these operands. The speed at which the 186 processor performs these calculations has been enhanced by adding dedicated hardware in the bus interface unit in order to gain from 1.25 to 3 times the 8086's speed, depending on which addressing mode is used.

Multiple bit shifting. The 80186 contains additional hardware in the execution unit that speeds the performance of multiple bit-shift operations by the processor. Thus individual bit shifts require one processor clock cycle in the 186 and four in the 8086.

String-move operations. The 80186 contains additional hardware enhancements in the bus interface unit that allows the string-moving instructions to operate at the full bus bandwidth of the processor, as opposed to the 8086's procedure, which inserts bus dead time after each transfer of the string instruction.

These additional hardware features enable the 186 to outperform the 8086 when running two benchmark routines. As defined in Intel's August 1981 "16-bit Microprocessor Benchmark Report," they are the X-Y graphics transformation and the bubble-sort routines.

The computation-intensive X-Y graphics transformation translates and scales a 16-bit–deep 128-by-128-word memory array. This type of routine would typically be used to translate the contents of a window in display memory to the often smaller viewport of the screen. A bubble-sort routine arranges an array of numbers in the proper order by comparing each adjacent pair of numbers and swapping them if necessary. When the processor goes through the array without swapping any pairs of numbers, the array is sorted. As the table shows, the 186 improves significantly on the 8086 for both of these benchmark routines.

BENCHMARK COMPARISON OF 8086 AND 80186			
Name	8086 performance	80186 performance	80186 improvement
X-Y graphics transformation	1.4 s	0.532 s	2.6 X
Bubble sort	1.14 ms	0.921 ms	1.2 X

segment value is shifted 4 bits to the left and then is added to an offset value derived from combinations of the pointer registers, the base registers, and immediate addressing values—three components that add flexibility in building operand addresses. If the addition of the segment value and the offset generates a carry, it is ignored. The result is a 20-bit physical address presented to the system memory, which can be as large as 1 megabyte. These physical-memory addresses are identical to those of the 8086.

CPU features

The 186 has a 16-bit arithmetic and logic unit, which performs 8- or 16-bit arithmetic and logical operations. For high-speed data transfers, the CPU uses string-move instructions for transfers from one area of memory to another and block I/O instructions for transfers to or from an I/O port and memory.

In the 80186, as in the 8086, instruction fetching and execution are performed by separate units—the bus interface unit and the execution unit, respectively. The 186 has a 6-byte prefetch queue, as does the 8086. Correspondingly, the 80188 has a 4-byte prefetch queue, as does the 8088. As a program is executing, instruction bytes are fetched from memory by the bus interface unit and placed in this queue. Whenever the execution unit requires another instruction, it takes it out of the queue.

Effective processor throughput is increased because the interface unit may continue to fetch instructions while the execution unit executes long instructions.

Although the 186 is completely object-code–compatible with the 8086, most of the latter processor's instructions require fewer clock cycles in the former because of hardware enhancements in both the bus interface and execution units (see "Hardware enhancements speed up the 80186," above). In addition, the 186 provides many new instructions that simplify assembly-language programming, enhance the performance of high-level–language implementations, and reduce object code sizes (see "New instructions are added to the 80186,").

The 186 bus structure is very similar to the 8086's. It includes a multiplexed address and data bus, along with various control and status lines. Each bus cycle requires a minimum of four CPU clock cycles along with the required number of wait states to accommodate the access limitations of external memory or peripheral devices.

With DMA on chip, many advantages accrue. A system built with this IC is greatly simplified, not only because a separate DMA chip is not required, but because the integrated unit shares the bus interface unit with the CPU. Thus DMA bus cycles are exactly the same as the CPU's, eliminating any need for external hardware to respond to two different types of bus cycles. Also, transfers through either of the DMA unit's two high-speed channels are performed at the full bus bandwidth of the processor—at 2 megabytes a second with an 8-megahertz part.

The integrated DMA unit will perform transfers to or from any combination of I/O addressing space and memory space by either bytes or words. Every DMA transfer requires two to four bus cycles: one or two to fetch the data to an internal register, and one or two to deposit the data. This arrangement allows word data to be located on odd boundaries, or byte data to be moved from odd locations to even locations. The necessary byte swapping is done automatically, so the system designer need not worry about routing byte data to the proper half of the 16-bit data bus.

The operation of the DMA channels is controlled by source and destination pointer registers, transfer count registers, and a control register, which are addressed through the 186's integrated-peripheral control block (see "Controlling the on-chip peripherals,"). For direct access to all memory or I/O devices in the system, each DMA channel maintains independent 20-bit pointers for the sources and destinations of the data to be transferred. Each of these pointers may address either I/O or memory space. Whereas the CPU randomly accesses memory in segments, the DMA unit sees memory as a linear array. The various channel characteristics are controlled by the bits in the DMA control register (Fig. 2).

After each DMA cycle, the pointers may be independently incremented, decremented, or maintained constant. This feature allows data to be read from an I/O device into a memory buffer (in which case the source pointer would remain constant and the destination pointer would be incremented after every transfer), data to be transferred from one memory block to another (in which case both the source and destination pointer would be incremented or decremented after every transfer), or data to be written from a memory buffer to an I/O device (in which case the source pointer would be incremented and the destination pointer left alone). For word transfers, the increment or decrement will be by two, since 2 bytes are being transferred.

Each DMA channel also maintains a 16-bit transfer count register that may be used to terminate a series of transfers after a preprogrammed number. It works by decrementing the register after every DMA transfer, whether the operation has moved a word or a byte, and it can count up to 65,536 transfers. The DMA control register will halt activity after the set number of transfers have occurred only if so programmed; thus it conceivably could perform an unlimited number of transfers with no CPU intervention.

The 186 includes a unit containing three independent 16-bit programmable timers. Timers 0 and 1 can be used to count external events, to provide waveforms derived from either the CPU clock or an external clock of any

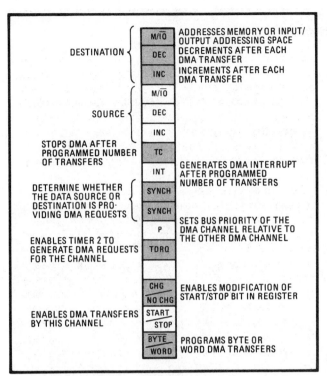

2. Controlling the DMA controller. Control of the integrated direct-memory-access controller is accomplished through a 16-bit control register. Combinations of the 15 control bits provide much flexibility in the timing and priority control of the two DMA channels.

duty cycle, or to interrupt the CPU after a specified number of timer events. Timer 2 counts only CPU clocks and can be used to interrupt that unit after a specified number of these cycles have been counted. It can also be used to give a count pulse to either or both of the other two timers or to give a request pulse to the integrated DMA unit—both actions taking place after a programmable number of CPU clocks.

Integrating a highly programmable timer unit with the CPU results in a standard timer-software interface shared with every 186 system. An example of how this feature could simplify system software is the replacement of the customary software timing loops with simpler code using the built-in timers.

A block of registers controls the timers. Each of these registers can be read or filled, whether or not the timer is operating. All processor accesses to these registers are synchronized to all counter accesses, meaning that the user will never read a count register in which only half of the bits have been modified. This setup simplifies the software interface with the timer.

Each timer also has a 16-bit count register incremented for each timer event, which can be a low-to-high transition on the external pin for timers 0 and 1, a CPU clock transition, or a time out of timer 2 that is sent to timers 0 and 1. Because the count register is 16 bits wide, up to 65,535 events can be counted.

Counting the most

Another useful timer register is the maximum-count register. Whenever one of the count values is equal to the value in the timer's maximum-count register, that register will be reset to 0 so that it can continue to be used by the processor. A maximum-count value of 0 implies a maximum count of 65,536.

Timers 0 and 1 each contain an additional maximum-count register. When both of these registers are used, the timer will first count up to the value in register A, reset to 0, count up to the value in register B, and reset to 0 again. When in this mode, the timer's output pin indicates which of the maximum-count registers is being used. Since the two maximum-count registers can contain different values, the output pin may be high or low for independently programmable periods of time. Thus output waveforms of practically any duty cycle can be generated. Also, because the processor has access to the maximum-count registers, the timer's high and low output times can be changed on the fly.

In addition, a bit in the timer control register is set and an processor interrupt is generated whenever the timer count reaches a maximum value. The timer control register (Fig. 3) also contains control bits that enable any of the timers so that it may count events, set modes on its input and output pins, and allow for continuous operation.

A programmable interrupt controller on the 186 makes hardware design simpler for an interrupt-driven system and also provides faster interrupt response. The controller arbitrates interrupt requests among all sources, both internal and external.

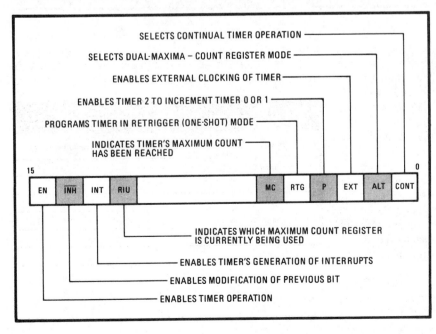

3. Counting and timing. The timing unit with its three counters and various counters is programmed through the timer control register. Ten control functions, including maximum counts, interrupt generation, and the use of external clocking, are available to the system programmer.

Controlling the on-chip peripherals

All the integrated peripherals within the 80186 microprocessor are controlled by sets of registers within the individual peripheral blocks they control. They are addressed, however, by the processor as an integrated-peripheral control block This set of registers fills the equivalent of 256 contiguously addressed bytes beginning on any 256-byte boundary of either the 186 memory or input/output addressing space (see figure).

Each of the integrated peripherals' control and status registers is located at a fixed offset above the starting location of the peripheral control block. Most of these registers may be either read or written by the 186's central processinng unit. In addition to the control registers for each of the peripheral units the 186 integrates, the control block contains a relocation register. This setup allows the block to be relocated within the processor's memory or I/O space. Since it is itself contained within the peripheral control block, any time the block's location changes, the location of the relocation register changes.

During system reset of the relocation register, the peripheral control block will be automatically located at the very top of the I/O space—addresses $FF00_{16}$ to $FFFF_{16}$. After a reset, the relocation register itself will be located at word location $FFFE_{16}$ in the I/O space.

The processor will run an external bus cycle for any memory or I/O cycle that accesses a location within the control block. Thus address, data, and control information will be driven on the 186 external pins just as if a normal bus cycle had been run. Any information returned by the external device will be ignored during a read. The processor generates a ready signal whenever any of the integrated peripherals is accessed. Any external ready signals are ignored whenever an access is made to any location within the control block. The processor will insert no wait states to any access to this block, except for accesses to the timer registers Access to a timer's control and counting registers will incur one wait state.

All accesses made to the integrated peripheral control block must be whole word accesses. Any write to the integrated registers will modify all 16 bits of the register, whether the operating system specified a byte write or a word write. This procedure holds for both the 80186 and the 80188: even though the 188 has an external 8-bit data bus, internally it is still a 16-bit machine. Word accesses performed to the integrated registers on the 188 will each occur in a single bus cycle with only the lower 8 bits of data being driven on the external data bus on a write.

```
INTEGRATED-PERIPHERAL
CONTROL BLOCK                    HEXADECIMAL
                                 ADDRESS OFFSET

RELOCATION REGISTER              FE16

                                 DA
DIRECT-MEMORY-ACCESS
CONTROL REGISTERS FOR
CHANNEL 1                        D0

                                 CA
DIRECT-MEMORY-ACCESS
CONTROL REGISTERS FOR
CHANNEL 0                        C0

                                 AB
CHIP-SELECTION CONTROL
REGISTERS                        A0

                                 66
TIMER 2 CONTROL REGISTERS        60
                                 5E
TIMER 1 CONTROL REGISTERS        58
                                 56
TIMER 0 CONTROL REGISTERS        50

                                 3E
INTERRUPT-CONTROLLER
REGISTERS                        2016
```

When acting as a master controller, it can be directly connected to as many as 18 external 8259A interrupt controllers. In addition, it can be configured as a slave to an external interrupt controller to allow compatibility with the 80130 that holds the iRMX 86 operating-system kernel, an 80150 chip that holds the CP/M-86 operating-system kernel, or the iRMX 86 real-time operating system. This slave mode is called the iRMX 86 mode.

Signaling interrupts

In its master mode, the integrated interrupt controller presents its interrupt signal directly to the 186 CPU, but in its iRMX 86 mode, the interrupt signal goes to the external controller whose own interrupt signal goes back to the CPU. The interrupt controller is set to the iRMX 86 mode with a mode bit in the integrated-peripheral control block's pointer.

The 186 can respond to an interrupt in two different ways. First, if the internal controller is in its master mode and is providing the interrupt vector information, the interrupt types associated with all the interrupt sources are fixed and unalterable (see table). In response to a CPU interrupt acknowledgment, the interrupt controller will generate the vector address rather than the

TABLE: VECTOR TYPE AND DEFAULT PRIORITIES FOR INTERRUPTS OF THE 80186 MICROPROCESSOR		
Interrupt name	Vector type	Default priority
Timer 0	8	0a
Timer 1	18	0b
Timer 2	19	0c
DMA 0	10	2
DMA 1	11	3
INT 0	12	4
INT 1	13	5
INT 2	14	6
INT 3	15	7

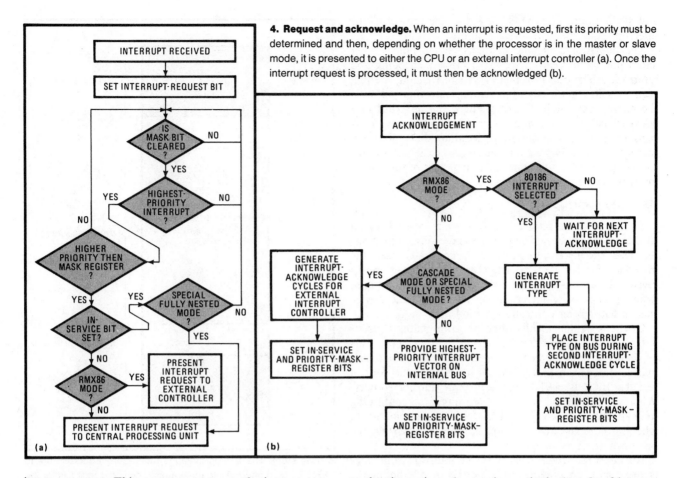

4. Request and acknowledge. When an interrupt is requested, first its priority must be determined and then, depending on whether the processor is in the master or slave mode, it is presented to either the CPU or an external interrupt controller (a). Once the interrupt request is processed, it must then be acknowledged (b).

interrupt type. This arrangement speeds interrupt response by about 50%.

Secondly, if the microprocessor gets interrupts from an external controller, which could be a master controller supervising several slave controllers in the system, or if the internal controller is in its iRMX 86 mode, the interrupt type will be sent to the microprocessor. During a first interupt-acknowledgment bus cycle, the external master controller determines which slave unit will be allowed to place its interrupt vector on the processor bus. During a second cycle, the processor reads the interrupt vector from the bus. This interrupt response is exactly the same as the 8086, so that the 8259A interrupt controller can be used as it would in an 8086 system.

Controlling the interrupts

The interrupt controller has a number of registers controlling its operation. This control scheme allows placing different interrupt sources at different priority levels, masking individual interrupt sources, polling interrupt requests, and ending interrupt generation. The interaction among the various interrupt-controller registers is shown in the flow chart of Fig. 4.

There is a control register for every interrupt source—a total of seven. These registers contain 3 bits that select one of eight interrupt priority levels and a mask bit to enable the interrupt. In the master mode, four of the registers serve the external interrupt inputs, two are for the two DMA channels, and one is for the collective timer interrupts. In the iRMX 86 mode, the external interrupt inputs are not used, so their control registers are assigned

to the timers in order to give each the benefit of its own control register.

The interrupt-request register contains 7 active bits, one for each interrupt control register. Whenever an interrupt request is made, the bit corresponding to the source of the interrupt is set. The bit is cleared automatically when the interrupt is acknowledged.

The mask register of the interrupt controller contains a mask bit for each interrupt source. These bits are identical to the mask bits in the interrupt control registers—modifying a mask bit in a control register will also modify it in the mask register, and *vice versa*.

The interrupt controller also contains a priority mask register that contains 3 bits indicating the priority of the current interrupt being serviced. When an interrupt is acknowledged, these bits are set to the priority of the interrupting device. This step prevents any interrupt of lower priority (as set by the priority bits in the interrupt control registers) from interrupting the processor. Therefore most interrupt service routines can be run with processor interrupts enabled. This feature is necessary for high-performance interrupt-driven systems.

Another important register that is part of the interrupt controller is the in-service register. A bit in this register is associated with each interrupt control register and is set when an interrupt request by the device associated with the control register is acknowledged by the processor. The bit is set when the CPU signals the end of the interrupt to the interrupt controller. This feature prevents a single device from providing multiple interrupt requests to the CPU before the latter has time to process any of the interrupts, thereby avoiding the growth of the interrupt stack beyond tolerable limits.

The interrupt controller contains both a poll register and a poll status register for using priority encoding and interrupt arbitration in a polled system. Reading the poll register will acknowledge the pending interrupt just as if the microprocessor had acknowledged the interrupt in a conventional manner, and in-service and priority mask registers are set appropriately. Reading the poll status register will merely transmit the status of the polling bits to the processors without modifying any of the other interrupt controller's registers.

Handling interrupts

To end a device interrupt, the program sends a signal to the controller by writing to the end-of-interrupt register. Then the interrupt controller automatically resets the in-service bit for that interrupt and the priority-mask-register bits, thus opening the door to further activity from lower-priority interrupts or from the same device that has just been controlling the bus.

Of the 4 significant bits of an interrupt status register, 3 bits show which timer is causing an interrupt. This capability is required because in the interrupt controller's master mode, the timers use a single interrupt control register. Bit 4 is used to halt any DMA transfer activity. When set, this bit prevents the DMA unit from continuing to hold the processor bus. This bit is set automatically when an nonmaskable interrupt is received, allowing the processor to respond quickly.

An interrupt-vector register in the interrupt controller is used only during operation in the iRMX 86 mode. Unlike the case with the master mode, the interrupt vectors associated with the various interrupting devices may be changed. The interrupt-vector register specifies the 5 most significant bits of the vector placed on the CPU bus in response to an interrupt acknowledgment, while the lower 3 significant bits are determined by the priority level of the device causing the interrupt.

Clock generator and oscillator, too

The 186 includes a clock generator and crystal oscillator, eliminating the need for a separate chip to perform these functions. The crystal oscillator can be used with a parallel resonant fundamental-mode crystal at two times the desired CPU clock speed—16 MHz for an 8-MHz part—or with an external oscillator, also at twice the microprocessor clock rate. The clock generator divides the clock input or oscillator output signals by 2 to provide the 50%–duty-cycle CPU clock. All timing parameters are referenced to this CPU clock, which is also available externally. The clock generator also provides ready synchronization for the processor.

The 186 includes integrated chip-selection logic, which can be used to activate memory or peripheral devices. Six output lines are used for memory addressing, and seven are used for peripheral addressing.

The six memory-addressing lines are split into three groups for separately addressing the major memory areas in a typical 8086 system: upper memory for system-initialization code, mid-range memory for program memory, and lower memory for interrupt vectors (Fig. 5).

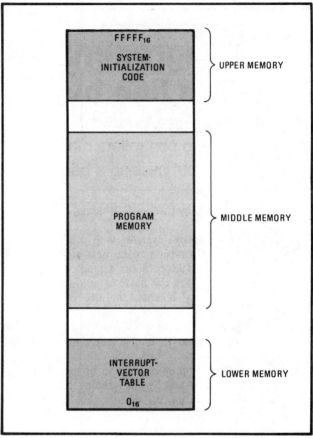

5. Tidy store. The system memory, running from address 0_{16} to $FFFFFF_{16}$, is organized into three areas: the upper region is for the contents of the start-up read-only memory, the middle one holds programmable start and stop locations for the program, and the lower area is used for the interrupt-vector table.

The size of each of these regions is user-programmable. The starting address of lower memory is fixed at memory address 0_{16}, while its ending address is determined by the block size selected. The ending address of the upper memory is fixed at $FFFFF_{16}$, and its starting address is determined by the block size. Finally, the starting address of midrange memory is programmable.

Each of the seven peripheral-selection lines addresses one of seven contiguous 128-byte blocks above a programmable base address in system memory or I/O addressing space. Therefore, peripheral devices may be either I/O- or memory-mapped.

An integrated wait-state generator allows a programmable number of wait states (0 to 3) to be automatically inserted whenever an access is made to the area of memory associated with any of the 13 chip-selection lines. This number of wait states is controlled by a set of programmable ready bits associated with these lines. In addition, each set of ready bits includes a bit that determines whether the external ready signals will be used or ignored. If this bit is set, the bus cycle will terminate, even though a ready has not been returned on the external pins. There are five sets of ready bits for independent wait-state generation for upper memory, middle memory, lower memory, peripheral devices 0 to 3, and peripheral devices 4 to 6. □

Highly integrated 16-bit microprocessor ups performance, aids design of work station

A personal professional work station, a typical application, is easy to build with the processor and a few other chips

by Kenneth Shoemaker, *Intel Corp., Santa Clara, Calif.*

☐ Microprocessor makers are bringing a new guest to the party, and system designers are celebrating. The manufacturers have been using the advent of very large-scale integration to produce processor chips with many more integrated peripheral functions than ever before, thus making it possible for designers of work stations and personal computers to obtain the highest possible performance with the greatest number of features at the lowest possible cost.

One such processor is the iAPX 186, also known by its part number, 80186. Besides its 8086-compatible central processing unit, it contains a direct-memory-access controller, an interrupt controller, timers, chip-selection and wait-state circuitry, and a clock generator, so that it suits applications where component count, board size, and cost are primary design considerations. The low cost of VLSI designs like the 186 makes it possible to expand upon the set of features commonly expected in work stations and personal computers. Today these systems typically include a 16-bit microprocessor, at least 64-K

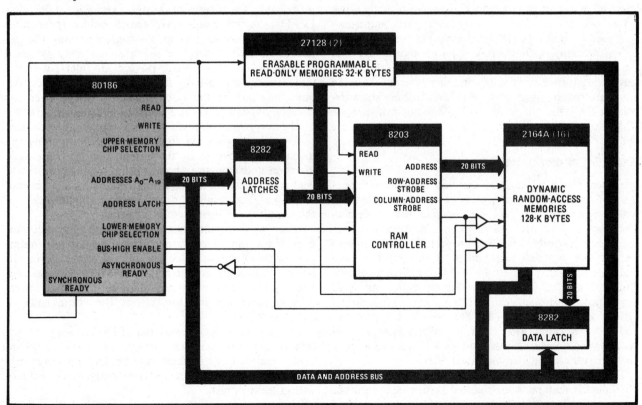

1. Memories. A typical memory subsystem for a personal work station's computer that is based on the 80186 microprocessor contains 16 dynamic random-access memory chips with their controller and two 27128 128-K erasable programmable read-only memories. Also part of the memory subsystem, but not shown here, is the memory portion of the 80150 CP/M 86 operating-system kernel, which is 16-K bytes of ROM.

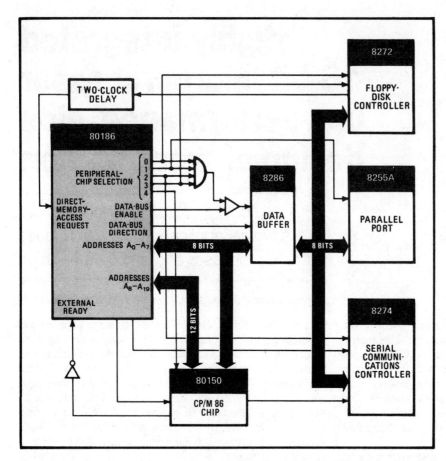

bytes of random-access memory, a couple of floppy-disk drives, one or two serial-communication ports, and usually a parallel input/output port driving a printer.

Compatibility with existing application software and the bulk of new software being produced is almost always a high priority in such computer systems. The 186 fills these requirements because it is completely software-compatible with the 8086 and 8088 microprocessors, which have been used in many recent personal computers and work stations.

Designing a work station

Typical of the systems that can take most advantage of the performance and cost benefits of the 186 is a personal work station for business use. Such a design demonstrates how much the design process is simplified with the highly integrated 186. The integrated circuits used to provide the complete capabilities of this work station include an 8-megahertz 80186, an 8274 dual-channel synchronous and asynchronous serial controller, an 8272 floppy-disk controller, the 80150 CP/M 86 operating-system kernel, an 8255A 24-line parallel-I/O port, an 8203 84-K dynamic RAM controller with sixteen 2164A-20 (200-nanosecond) RAMs, and two 27128 128-K erasable programmable read-only memories.

The 186 microprocessor bus is almost identical to the 8086 bus. It features a multiplexed address and data bus and various control and status lines. These include read and write lines, a valid-address latch signal, a data-bus–direction signal, and a data-bus–enable line. It also has three status lines used to differentiate the bus cycles. The

control and status lines may be connected to either a 8288 bus controller or a 8289 multimaster bus arbiter, which will be used in large 186 systems. The type of bus-exchange protocol in the 186 allows easy interfacing with the new generation of Intel peripheral devices, such as the 82586 Ethernet controller and the 82730 alphanumeric text coprocessor.

The 8-MHz 186 requires medium-speed memory and high-speed peripheral devices if it is to operate without wait states. However, it can be programmed to insert wait states automatically for simple interfacing with slower memory or peripheral devices. This provision simplifies system design when slow devices are used, since no external circuitry is required for adding wait states.

Because the 186 is really an enhanced version of the 8086, the functions of certain memory areas are predefined. The processor begins execution at location $FFFF0_{16}$, so this location will usually hold a nonvolatile-memory address such as an E-PROM containing the initialization code. Since the 186 uses the memory space defined by addresses 0_{16}–$3FF_{16}$ for an interrupt-vector table, this area is usually filled with RAM addresses. All other locations in the system memory can be used for operating-system code and users' application programs.

The integrated chip-selector and wait-state generator on the 186 supplies six signals for selection among the memory components in the system and for automatic insertion under program control of up to three processor wait states when an access is made to a particular memory device. The result is a considerable simplification of the circuitry for memory-chip selection.

In a typical memory system (Fig. 1), the chip-selection lines of the 186 select various memory banks. For example, the two E-PROMs, which include the power-on initialization code beginning at address $FFFF0_{16}$, are selected with the upper-memory chip-selection line. The lower-memory chip-selection line selects the entire bank of dynamic RAMs.

Though the E-PROMs and the 80150 memory do not require any wait states for proper operation, the RAM bank requires three of them for standard operation and additional time if a processor-to-memory access collides with a RAM refresh.

The reason for the three wait states, which slow down the interface, is the nature of the asynchronous 8203 RAM controller chosen for this design example. Much time is lost during every bus cycle to the memory bank

Interfacing with the 80186 bus

The 80186 single-chip microprocessor has a high-performance bus cycle with four clock periods, called time or T states. In performing a data transfer, different actions occur in each T state (see figure). Some devices may require additional time beyond the four-period cycle to drive the processor or to receive information from it. The additional time is obtained by inserting wait T states between cycles T_3 and T_4.

These wait T states may be inserted automatically by the integrated wait-state generator or by external logic driving the synchronous or asynchronous ready lines of the processor. The table shows the read access times for devices with various numbers of wait states connected to the 186 bus.

Another possible complication is bus contention after a read from a slow peripheral device. After the microprocessor performs a read operation from a device, it will drive the read-control line high. This step signals the external device to disable its data-output drivers. The 186 will then begin to drive address information onto the bus for the next T state no sooner than 85 nanoseconds after the read line has been driven inactive. If the external device cannot disable its output drivers within 85 ns, there could be bus contention between the 186 when it is driving address information for the next cycle and the external device when it is driving data information from the previous cycle. This problem is solved by placing a data buffer between the peripheral device's data lines and the microprocessor's bus.

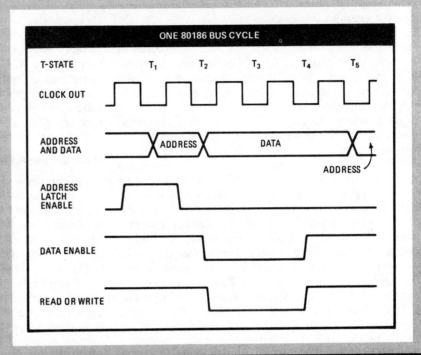

resolving the asynchronous signals from the processor to the RAM controller. Alternatively, a synchronous RAM controller such as the 8207 would yield higher performance if needed. The response time of the memory bank to accesses from the 186 would be much faster because fewer or no wait states would be required.

Since the 186 multiplexes both addresses and data over its external bus, addresses must be latched into external devices if they are to remain stable during a bus cycle. Few memory devices have such latches. A typical 186 system will require separate transparent address latches, which minimize the time between the arrival of a valid address from the processor and its presentation to memory. The address-latch signal from the 186 allows simple latching of valid addresses into external registers.

Although data and address information share the processor bus, performance is not penalized, since data and addresses are moved on the bus during completely independent time cycles. Also, the requirement for external address latches does not complicate system design because address information must go to a variety of memory and I/O devices that are likely to require some buffering anyway.

The 186's memory is arranged as 16-bit words; however, it can also be accessed as individual 8-bit bytes. This duality means that a memory write operation can modify either the entire word or just the upper or lower byte. To access each byte of a word separately, the system needs a mechanism to enable only the correct half of memory during a byte write. The 186 provides two signals to control writing to either half of memory or to both at once. Such a technique is unnecessary during byte reads, for both halves of the memory may be accessed and the unused byte discarded.

External ready lines are either automatically assumed to be ready or are ignored by the processor or are used to insert additional wait states after the integrated wait-state generator has inserted the programmed number of wait states. Because the wait-state generator can be programmed to ignore external ready lines, they need not be driven ready by devices that require a fixed number of wait states, such as E-PROMs, most static RAMs, and most I/O peripheral devices. The correct number of programmed wait states is always generated for these parts, thus simplifying the ready circuitry of 186-based systems.

Peripheral grouping

The 8274 serial-communications controller, 8255A parallel port, and 8272 floppy-disk controller in this design for a work station may be considered as a group because they are all addressed the same way. Since the external data bus is 16 bits wide, these 8-bit peripheral devices reside only on the bus's lower half, the even half. The sequential registers of the peripheral chips will reside at subsequent even addresses, 400_{16}, 402_{16}, and so on.

A sample peripheral system (Fig. 2) requires a data buffer like an 8286 or 8287 to prevent bus contention between the 186 processor and the peripheral devices (see "Interfacing with the 80186 bus," p. 145). The processor provides two lines to control the enabling of the buffer and the data direction. The data-bus–direction line is directly connected to the transmit line of the buffer, while the data-bus–enable line is joined with the peripheral-selection lines of the processor such that it is enabled only when an access is made to a peripheral device.

This interdependency is required because the data-bus–enable line is driven active during all bus cycles when data is active on the bus. If the peripheral-chip–selection lines were not factored into the buffer-enable control line, the buffer would drive the 186 bus during any read cycle, whether to the peripheral devices or to memory. This intervention would cause bus contention between the peripheral buffer and the memory system.

The 186's peripheral-chip–selection lines directly select the individual peripheral devices. These seven lines activate seven contiguous 128-byte locations above a programmable base address. This base address may be either in I/O space or in memory space, so that the peripherals may be mapped as I/O or memory under program control. In addition, whenever any of the peripherals is selected by the 186, the integrated wait-state generator will insert the required number of wait states to ensure that good data is written to or read from the device.

The floppy-disk controller uses the DMA unit on the 186 to provide high-speed I/O from and to the disk. The controller requests a transfer for every byte of data, and the DMA controller accesses consecutive bytes in memory from either the upper or lower half of the data bus, thus handling both the sequential access of 8-bit data from the disk and putting 16-bit data in the memory.

The 186 DMA controller does not return an acknowledgment signal. The DMA acknowledgment is just the writing or reading of data to or from the requesting device. The acknowledgment can be handled this way because every DMA cycle on the 186 will require two bus cycles—one to fetch the data, the second to deposit it.

An explicit DMA acknowledgment is required only when data is passed from an I/O device to the memory in a single bus cycle. Because the disk controller requires both chip-selection and DMA-acknowledgment signals, two of the 186's peripheral-chip–selection lines are dedicated to providing them. Whenever the processor wishes to read or write control information to the floppy-disk controller, it accesses the address corresponding to its chip-selection line connected to the controller's chip-selection line. Whenever the DMA unit needs to read or write data in response to a request, it accesses the processor's chip-selection line that is connected to the controller's DMA-acknowledgment line.

The integrated DMA controller can gain control of the

READ ACCESS-TIME REQUIREMENTS FOR 80186	
Number of wait states	Read access time (ns)
0	311
1	436
2	747
3	1,058

processor bus much more quickly than an external controller could. The result is better system performance, because fewer clock cycles are wasted during the bus transfer between the CPU and the DMA channel. However, this speed can cause problems with some peripheral devices that require a minimum time between the request for a direct-memory access and the DMA unit's acknowledgment. For example, the 8272 floppy controller requires 800 ns between request and acknowledgment, while the DMA controller can respond in as little as 625 ns. The problem is solved by inserting two clock cycles of delay between the disk controller's DMA request-line output and the DMA controller's request-line output.

Operating-system chip

This example of a personal work station based on the 186 uses the 80150 for its CP/M 86 operating-system kernel. This chip supplies the system with an additional interrupt controller and additional timers. Because the 186 bus is almost identical to the 8086 bus, the 80150 attaches to the 186 without any glue chips.

The 8274 serial-communications controller uses the timer unit on the 186 to provide the baud-rate clock for one of its serial channels. It uses the baud-rate timer on the 80150 to provide the clock for the other channel. Both clock sources can be programmed to deliver a continuous stream of pulses with the proper spacing for the required baud rate. However, different programming sequences are needed to initialize the two clock sources.

The acknowledgment line from the 80150 is connected to the external ready line of the microprocessor so that whenever any resource on the former is accessed, an external ready signal is returned to the latter. This return signal is not, however, required for accesses to the 80150's 16-K ROM or its integrated peripheral devices. The chip-selector and wait-state generator on the 186 can be programmed to ignore all external ready signals when accessing such a chip and to terminate the bus cycle regardless of the state of the external ready.

The system initialization code must set up the control registers of the microprocessor's chip-selector and wait-state generator. The only chip-selection line that will be active before being explicitly initialized by the CPU is the upper-memory selection line, and it will be active only during access to the top 1-K of memory space. When the the integrated chip-selection unit is used and the program jumps the top 1-K of the address space before the related registers are properly programmed, the system will not operate because the memory-selection line will not be driven active.

All that the initialization code (see table) need do is determine the number of wait states required for the various devices in the system and then insert the appropriate programmed values. After the chip-selection lines are initialized, the rest of the system may be initialized in any order the system designer wishes. □

8-bit microprocessor harbors 16-bit performance

Particularly when complex algorithms are applied to byte-wide data, the 8-bit 8088 is the next best thing to a 16-bit 8086

by Irving H. Thomae, *Dartmouth College, Hanover, N. H.*

☐ Anyone weighing a move from an 8- to a 16-bit microprocessor should consider the 8088. This recently introduced microprocessor combines the internal architecture of the 16-bit 8086 with an external multiplexed 8-bit bus. Though requiring two bus cycles to fetch a 16-bit word, it does not inevitably take twice as long as the 8086 to execute a program. In many applications — strongly mathematical ones in particular — the 8088 comes very close to the 8086's computational power.

The 8088's architecture is responsible for this ability. Unlike other 8-bit microprocessors, its architecture is identical to the internal workings of an existing 16-bit machine. More specifically, it is divided into an execution unit and a bus interface unit, just as in the 8086 (see Fig. 1).

A minor difference is that while the interface unit of the 8086 has a 6-byte queue, the 8088 has room for only 4 bytes. But by the time a demanding instruction has been executed, the next one will be ripe for execution anyway. Thus, especially for byte-oriented operand streams, the half-wide data bus is a moot point.

Another attractive 8088 feature is system-level compatibility, a characteristic that Intel Corp. has worked long to preserve. The multiplexed bus closely resembles that found on the purely 8-bit 8085, so that upgrading it to the 8088's hardware is smooth. Also, software originally intended for the 8080 or 8085 can be put through an Intel utility program called CONV-86 that has as its output 8086 (and therefore 8088) instructions. Thus, reworking an existing design for a more powerful family can be done piecemeal, with unconverted portions remaining intact.

A prerequisite

Aside from bus-multiplexing logic and the difference in the instruction queue length, the 8088 is identical to the 8086. Consequently, to understand the operation of the 8088 in general, it is essential to grasp what is unique about the 8086. The architectural philosophy behind the 8086 will therefore be compared with those chosen by Zilog Inc. for its Z8000 and Motorola Inc. for its

MC68000, the two other most intensively promoted 16-bit microprocessors. Some provisions unique to the 8086/8 will then be pointed out prior to outlining the specific merits of the 8088.

The more obvious similarities among the 8086, Z8000, and MC68000 include reasonably speedy hardware multiplication and division, string move and compare operations (planned but not yet implemented in the case of the 68000), expanded register sets, and provision for address spaces substantially larger than the (traditional) 64-K allowance of older 16-bit minicomputer and microcomputer systems.

However, there are also some significant differences

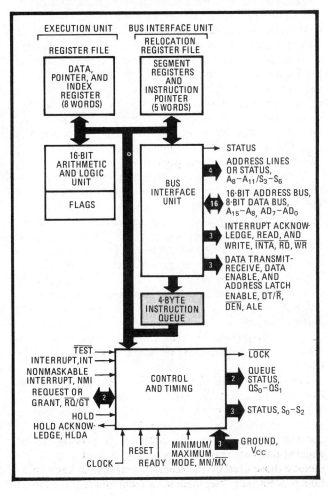

1. CPU in two. The 8088, like the 8086, is split into an execution unit and a bus interface unit. The latter contains an instruction queue, 6 bytes long in the 8086 and 4 bytes long in the 8088. The queue minimizes dead time between the execution of instructions.

151

Computer architecture: a working definition

A number of slightly different definitions of digital computer architecture can be found in current usage [*Electronics*, May 24, 1979, p. 112]. The one adopted here follows the philosophy of IBM as expressed by G. F. Blaauw: the architecture of a digital computer is that set of its attributes (such as registers, addressing modes, and instruction set) that are visible to the programmer. Issues such as the number and width of the buses or the level of integrated-circuit technology used to build the machine (implementation) may greatly affect execution speed of a program, but (in principle) object code that runs on the lowliest member of the 370 family will supposedly produce the same results when run on the most expensive. The machines are then said to be architecturally identical, despite differences in implementation.

It could be, and sometimes is, argued that since nobody in his right mind still uses assembly language (though many programmers admit to doing so), architecture should be defined at the compiler source-code level. Equivalence of the computational results is then much more difficult to verify, however. Also, for the user of microprocessors in original equipment, there are significant economic advantages in being able to regard blocks of object code—not source code—as stock components, usable interchangeably with different implementations of the same architecture.

between the 8086 and the other two, one of which is the maximum size of those address spaces. Motorola provides 24 address bits, Zilog has 23 (when a memory management unit is used along with the 48-pin version of the central processing unit), but Intel settled for 20 (see Fig. 2). Also, in the inevitable tradeoff between the number of general-purpose registers and the number of bits per instruction, Intel has favored code density to such an extent that for many applications, 8086 programs appear likely to require approximately 30% less memory than will Z8000 and MC68000 programs.

Another fundamental difference is the provision by Zilog and Motorola, but not by Intel, of hardware and instruction-set support for a supervisory operating state different from the normal state. There are two distinct stack pointers (normal and system) and certain classes of privileged instructions that can only be executed when the device is in the supervisory state. Attempts to execute privileged instructions while in the nonsupervisory state result in traps. Zilog's memory management unit (MMU) extends these protection concepts to memory accesses as well by allowing segments to be declared off-limits to normal-mode programs.

Such features support sophisticated operating systems intended for multiple users. They place the Z8000 and the MC68000 squarely in competition with high-end minicomputers, for applications in which one computer is used at various times (or in rapidly alternated time slices) for many different purposes. This, however, is a very different market from the dedicated-function applications on which microprocessors have so far made such an enormous impact, and Intel has chosen thus far not to enter it. When the end users of a microprocessor-based product will not in fact be writing programs, there may be no advantage to the added complexity (and input/output overhead) of such system-protection features.

The third issue in which clear differences are apparent between these three vendors' architectural philosophies is the size and use of the register set. The Z8000 has 16 16-bit registers, the MC68000 16 32-bit registers. In contrast, the 8086 family provides just eight 16-bit general-purpose registers, although this tally does not include those used by the memory-mapping or segmentation process (see "Segmentation techniques: the 8086 vs the Z8000,"). Each of the eight can be designated as a source or destination of almost all arithmetic and logical operations, as can any memory location.

On the other hand, Intel has also allocated unique functions to specific members of its general-purpose register set to a far greater extent than have Motorola and Zilog. The greater coding efficiency thus gained permits the 8086 to provide an extra level of array indexing at no penalty in code density.

To a programmer, one of the most appealing aspects of the 8086 architecture is the form of its two-operand instructions. All the register-to-memory operations (except multiply and divide) are fully symmetrical, in the sense that the result may be left either in any register or in the memory location referenced. Those addressing modes involving the use of a second (and sometimes a third) register to point to memory, however, can employ only specific subsets of the entire register set for that purpose.

Two 8086 registers (BX and BP) are designated as base registers, and two others (SI and DI) as index registers. The effective logical address is computed by summing any possible combination of a base, an index, and an 8- or 16-bit displacement. Omitting the first two, of course, is equivalent to direct addressing and all others are forms of register-indirect addressing.

Associating one implicit operand with certain operations, however, reduces the bit count assigned to operand specification, permitting those operation codes to occupy only a single byte in many cases. This of course is the advantage of designating one register as the accumulator, as Intel has traditionally done.

Two formats

In the 8086/8, therefore, most instruction types appear in at least two formats, one of which is completely general, while in the other the accumulator is implied as one of the operands. Even in encoding the general format, however, the indirect-addressing functions have been restricted to four of the eight registers. That makes code bits available for other purposes, such as specifying either word versions or byte versions of nearly all instructions, while still allowing the basic increment of instruction-word length to be 8 bits rather than 16.

The second major attribute of the 8086/8 family

visible to a programmer is an instruction set with a richer choice of available functions than preceding 8-bit CPUs have offered. While this is perhaps a consequence of having more code bits available, it is not really dependent on having a 16-bit machine *per se*, since the number of bytes involved in specifying an instruction together with its operands can vary from one to at least six in certain cases (such as move immediate word to memory with 16-bit displacement).

Of the wide variety of these new instructions, perhaps the most interesting to many potential 8088 users are the string operations, which use the source and destination index (SI and DI) registers for automatically-incremented indirect addressing. The scan and compare instructions, respectively, examine a string for a match to either a 1-byte or one-word pattern held in the accumulator or to the corresponding successive elements of a second string. Both memory-to-memory and accumulator-to-(or from-)memory moves are also available for copying or initializing blocks of storage. Normally, a string instruction will be preceded by the extremely useful repeat prefix, which specifies that the instruction will be repeated on successive memory locations, while counting down a block length that has previously been set up in the 16-bit CX register, until either the whole block is completed or a match (or nonmatch) has been discovered.

As an example, a comparison between two strings that might be written in PL/M as:

DO UNTIL A(I) = B(I) OR I = N
I = I + 1;
END:

requires only 2 bytes to encode: CMPB or CMPW preceded by REPEAT. The same looping options are also available for blocks of instructions that use LOOPZ and LOOPNZ. These are decrement-and-test conditional jumps that can be terminated by either the loop counter or the results of operations performed with the loop.

Another extremely convenient instruction, TRANSLATE (XLAT), accomplishes table lookup in one step. A data byte held in the accumulator is used as a pointer into a table, and the entry found there then replaces the previous data in the accumulator. This mechanism in addition aides sequential lookup operations, as might occur in working with a hierarchical data base. As the address of the first entry in a table is taken from the 16-bit BX register, these tables may be located anywhere in memory.

The arithmetic operations of the 8086/8 include built-in multiply and divide, available in 8-bit and 16-bit signed and unsigned versions, as well as data-adjustment instructions that facilitate binary-coded decimal and ASCII arithmetic. For BCD addition and subtraction, data may be stored as either one or two digits to a byte; for multiplication and division, data must be in one-digit-per-byte form.

While the accumulator is implied as one operand of the multiply and divide instructions, there are no restrictions at all on the other source operand—it may come from any register or from memory. The result, however, is left in the accumulator (extended into DX when a

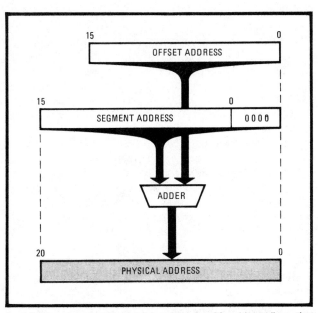

2. Address construction. Intel settled for 20 address lines that allow its 8086 and 8088 products to address 1 megabyte. To arrive at a physical address, a 16-bit effective address is added to the contents of a segment register that has been shifted up 4 bits.

32-bit product results). These operations are respectably fast, too: a 16-bit unsigned multiply takes 26.4 microseconds plus the operand-access time.

The increased internal word length has the most impact on arithmetic-intensive programs, where the data precision (particularly in multiply and divide operations) saves much programming effort relative to 8-bit processors. The input/output options have also been expanded. Besides the 8-bit immediate device code familiar to 8080 users, it is possible to input or output data through one of 2^{16} ports, as dictated by the contents of the 16-bit DX register.

It seems clear that programs written in 8086 family code may require many fewer bytes than if the same functions were written for older 8-bit processors, although the exact numbers would certainly depend on the type of program. While this remark is precisely as valid for the 8088 as for the 8086, the 8088 must obviously perform two bus cycles to access a 16-bit instruction or operand, so it is less obvious that execution speed will be improved. Nevertheless, in many cases, the 8088 will easily outrun a 5-megahertz 8085 or a Z80. To see why, it is necessary to consider briefly some 8086/8 characteristics that are properly described as implementational rather than architectural.

Implementations count

First, the n-channel 8086/8 parts are fast, with a standard clock rate of 5 MHz, and selected parts operate to 8 MHz. The basic 8086/8 bus cycle, however, is actually more leisurely and allows the use of memory parts with 450-nanosecond access times instead of the 350 ns needed to operate with the premium-grade 5-MHz 8085-2. In systems with large amounts of memory, the initially much higher cost of the 8088 CPU may therefore be partially offset by savings in memory costs.

The greatest increases in the rate of program execution, however, come from the internal subdivision of the 8086/8 into a main processor and a semiautonomous bus interface unit, which overlaps instruction fetches with execution. By filling a queue (as mentioned it is 6 bytes long in the 8086, 4 bytes in the 8088) with prefetched instruction bytes, the bus interface unit renders effectively unnoticeable the time involved in performing address relocations and frequently permits the CPU to operate in an execution-bound manner.

Both architecture and implementation, as the terms have been used here, affect the total performance of a system: the former through the efficiency of the typical byte of code or the work accomplished per instruction-fetch cycle; the latter through the rate at which instructions are executed. An equally important attribute of any modern computer family is support software, which ideally has little effect on the performance of a completed system but can completely dominate its design cost.

Similar system software

By having a common instruction set, the 8086 and 8088 also use the same system software. PLM-86 provides more data types than PLM-80 (signed 16-bit integers, pointers, and real floating-point types in addition to the unsigned 8-bit and 16-bit integers of PLM-80) and can directly handle somewhat more complex data structures, so that programmer's effort is reduced. The 8086 assembler copes with the sometimes bewildering variety of options for encoding an operation and its operand references in what might be called an optimizing manner, so that the assembly-language programmer need not be plagued by a host of different mnemonics for essentially the same instruction.

Viewed as a whole, the register structure and the instruction set of the 8086/8 scarcely permit calling it a 16-bit 8080. They represent an architectural design that is well-balanced in its own right. Nevertheless, all of the registers and instructions of the 8080 can be mapped onto the 8086/8. Programs written for the 8080, once translated into 8086/8 code, can therefore be used intact, with either 8-bit or 16-bit operands. The CONV-86 program performs the translation.

As of this writing, all of this support software is offered as a package intended for use only on Intel's development systems. The source code, being a significant development investment, is closely guarded. Customers who prefer to perform their compilations, assemblies, and other support functions on in-house minicomputers or time-shared mainframe computers will apparently have to either look to independent software houses for equivalent 8086/8 tools or buy more Intel development systems.

With this family portrait in mind, the specific merits of the 8088 can be more closely examined. From a hardware viewpoint, the 8088 is completely compatible with the 8085's partially multiplexed bus. All of the software advantages inherent in the 8086 family architecture can therefore be made available to existing 8085-based systems simply by substituting a new CPU board. Backplanes, input/output interfaces, and memory boards designed to work with 8-bit processors can

continue to be used, so that radically upgrading the software has only moderate impact on hardware costs.

As mentioned, when a 16-bit processor design is grafted onto an 8-bit data bus, two bus cycles will be required to fetch a 16-bit word. While this appears to imply that an 8088 will execute a program at half the speed of an 8086, that turns out to be a lower boundary. That is only partly because 25% of the operation codes in the 8086/8 instruction set use just 1 byte. There happen to be more instructions requiring 3 or more bytes than there are 1-byte instructions, but the queue makes these facts largely irrelevant.

By the time a reasonably complex instruction has been executed, the next one will have been fetched. (A queue of simple 1-byte instructions, on the other hand, is more likely to empty, so that the processor then becomes fetch-time–limited.) A program segment performing several multiply operations, as in a polynomial evaluation, will therefore run very nearly as fast on the 8088 as on the 8086 because bus access accounts for so little of the total execution time.

It should be pointed out, however, that the impact of the queue on execution rate is not always significant. Whenever a branch occurs (jump, calls, returns, etc.), all of the prefetched instruction bytes in the queue become useless, and fetch time becomes visible until—perhaps a few instructions later—the queue is again full. Since the 8086/8 bus cycle uses four 200-ns clocks, the next few instructions following a branch will be completed at a rate that is actually slower than that of an 8085-2, whose bus cycle uses only three clocks. Whether a given program as a whole will be completed more rapidly by the 8088 than by an 8085-2 depends on the instruction mix. Interpreters (which employ large numbers of calls) and simple control programs (those made up largely of conditional jumps) are not likely to run much faster on an 8088 than on an 8085-2; for those applications only the greater instruction set efficiency favors the 8088.

Because operands do not go through the queue (except immediate operands, which appear in the instruction stream), a program involving frequent memory reads and writes of 16-bit data will probably take almost twice as much time to execute on an 8088 as the same program working with 8-bit operands. Conversely, programs handling byte-oriented data execute on the 8088 at greater than 95% of the 8086's speed.

Where to use it

For what kinds of systems will the 8088 be most useful? The answer is different for existing system designs and for new ones.

Because the 8088 makes the 8086 family architecture and instruction set available on an 8-bit data bus, it becomes an attractive option to upgrade an existing 8080 or 8085 system design. The CONV-86 code-translator allegedly permits quick transplantion of 8080/5 programs to the 8088, where they may or may not run much faster because of the queue alone. As implied above, the greatest performance improvements are likely to be realized with programs that involve either large numbers of multiply or divide instructions or data-handling procedures supported by the table lookup and

Segmentation techniques: the 8086 vs the Z8000

The differing needs of dedicated and general-purpose applications show up in the 8086 and Z8000 microprocessor families even in their detailed philosophies of memory segmentation.

Intel has achieved significantly greater code density by two measures: having only four segments (code, stack, data, and extra), and defining a default reference segment for every memory access. Four correspondingly named segment registers hold the segment starting address. Although a single-byte instruction prefix can be used to override the default choice of segment register, normally no code bits are therefore needed in each instruction to designate the appropriate segment.

Physical addresses are computed automatically on the central processing unit chip by adding the logical address to 16 times the contents of the appropriate segment register. In allocating memory space, segment boundaries therefore start at multiples of 16 bytes. The address-translation process is transparent (invisible) to those programmers who do not alter the segment registers, and because of the instruction queue, it adds a very small cost in execution time.

Zilog, in contrast, has chosen to provide greater flexibility at greater cost. The memory relocation function requires a second 48-pin chip (the memory management unit, or MMU) and a different CPU package and introduces an extra but potentially useful step. When the logical address space exceeds 2^{16} bits, the instruction format must specify a 7-bit segment number. This will come either from a word of the instruction itself or, in the register-indirect addressing mode, from the register following that specified for operand addressing. This is used by the MMU to look up in its stored 128-entry table both the starting address of the segment and certain attributes, such as its total length and permissible accesses. The MMU therefore both maps logical addresses into the physical memory space and provides memory protection, but at the cost of a large chip and one added clock cycle per memory access. Because of the necessity to specify which of the 128 segments is involved in each access, however, programs written for the segmented (8001) version are incompatible with those written for the unsegmented (8002) both at the object code level and in register usage.

string instructions. Some recoding would be necessary to exploit the new instructions, and of course that effort should be focused on those modules the program is known to spend the most time executing.

Major performance improvements to a microprocessor-based product, even though mandated by pressure from competitors' newer designs, are often postponed because of the expense inherent in developing new hardware and new software simultaneously. Because the 8088 is compatible both with 8-bit data buses and (via CONV-86) with 8080/5 software, it permits the conversion to a more powerful family to be made in stages, with certain software or hardware modules continuing in use until their development cost has been recovered. If a product line will eventually require 16-bit precision, the 8088 eases that transition by allowing new software to be developed independently of hardware growth.

When a new product is about to be developed, unconstrained by existing hardware or software, the cost of the 8088 may be justified in several situations. In text-processing, data-communication, and arithmetic-intensive applications, the advantages are similar to those discussed just above. Whenever execution speed is a factor, moreover, both the queue and the architecture will be beneficial. Programs written from the start for the 8088 should also require somewhat less program memory space than earlier 8-bit machines needed.

There may also be cases where the natural word length is 16 bits, but the full execution speed of the 8086 is not essential. Each new random-access memory capacity is introduced first in a 1-bit width, and multiple-bit parts seem to lag them by one to two years. Certain sizes of total memory, therefore, can be implemented much more economically 8 bits wide than 16 bits wide. This is true now for 16-K-by-1-bit RAMs and will be even more true for 64-K-by-1-bit RAMs.

The 8088 has another advantage in the manufacture of a product line since different models offer a number of groups of options, where each option is supported by a different and rather complex mix of subprograms. Such situations often require that the necessary code blocks for different functions be linked and located anew for each model in the product line. Because the segmentation method used in the 8086/8 accomplishes program relocation simply by altering the contents of one segment register, the program code for each function option can be linked, located, and programmed into read-only memories with the same starting address—as if no other program modules were to be present. These modules can then be loaded into any convenient position in the 1-megabyte physical address space of the 8088. A short supervisory user-interface module then suffices to load the code segment register with the physical location of the function module selected by user input. The various program modules can therefore be inventoried as fully programmed ROMs that need not be modified as the software options present in different models are varied.

But perhaps the most valuable asset of the 8088 is the fact that because it is architecturally identical to the 8086, the same programs can be run on either CPU without modification. Two distinct levels of computer cost and performance are therefore available to the original-equipment manufacturer developing a broad product line, without duplication of software effort. Upgrading from a nonsegmented Z8000 system to a segmented one, in contrast, will require careful reexamination of programs. For applications that do not require sophisticated protection facilities, this may well represent the bottom line. □

Bibliography
J. McKevitt and J. Bayliss, "New Option from Big Chips," IEEE Spectrum, Vol. 16, 1979, pp. 28–34 (the Intel 8086).
B. L. Peuto, "Architecture of a New Processor," Computer, Vol. 12, 1979, pp. 10–21 (the Z8000).
"The 8086 Family User's Manual," Intel Corp., October 1979 (the 8088).

Handling exceptions gracefully enhances software reliability

The 68000 processor vectors to special routines upon encountering divide-by-zero operations and other exceptions

by Thomas W. Starnes, *Motorola Inc., Austin, Texas*

☐ The main task of any computer system is to execute instructions. Illegal instructions and other exceptions to this process often cause unpredictable behavior unless the processor's design takes them into account.

The 68000 is uniquely well defended against such eventualities. When confronted with bus errors indicative of some kind of memory failure or with undefined operations like divide by zero, it vectors to a trap—a known memory location containing the user-supplied exception-handling routine. Such a routine might, for example, notify the operator of an attempt to execute an illegal instruction and then let the machine resume its normal activities. This feature, which greatly increases the 68000's reliability, is to be found on few other microprocessors.

In addition, the 68000 is exceptional in its handling of multiuser environments such as swapping user programs in and out of main memory. These kinds of tasks are conventionally serviced entirely in software, with program swapping, for instance, being handled by means of an executive subroutine that is either periodically called by the operating system or vectored to by an external interrupt. But in the 68000, built-in hardware supports a privileged, supervisory level of operation that makes this exception processing much easier to implement.

Traps also count as exceptions. Besides being caused by undesirable occurrences within the processor, they may be called expressly by instructions or requested during the execution of certain instructions. Each type of trap is associated with a vector which points to a service routine. The old program counter and status register are restored after execution of the routine. Any task can call the trap and utilize the trap routine.

Finally, to ease software development, the 68000 supports a trace function, in addition to the usual single-step mode that utilizes the halt pin. Like the other new features, it aids the designer of sophisticated systems but may be left unused in less complex systems. Figure 1 shows the memory locations of all exception vectors.

User and supervisor levels

The 68000 operates at all times on one of two levels: supervisor or user. Operation at the supervisor level has certain privileges attached that are not permitted at the user level (Table 1). Programs other than those designed for system control execute for the most part at the 68000's user level. Operating system chores, such as task or context switching, should execute at the more privileged supervisor level. At this level of operation, the program's regular complement of instructions is available, allowing the operating system to vary the working environment of the microprocessor, service interrupts or act-on-error conditions caused by hardware or programs.

Whether the processor is at the supervisor level or at

1. Exception-handling vectors. All exceptions cause a vector to be fetched from this map and loaded into the program counter. The old program counter and status register are saved on the supervisor stack and are restored at the end of the routine.

TABLE 1: PRIVILEGES OF THE 68000's USER AND SUPERVISOR LEVELS		
	User level	Supervisor level
Enter level by	clearing status bit 'S'	recognition of a trap, reset, or interrupt
Function code output (FC2 =)	0	1
System stack pointer	user stack pointer	supervisor stack pointer
Other stack pointers	registers A0—A6	user stack pointer and registers A0—A6
Status bits available (read) (write)	C,V,Z,N,X,I_0-I_2,S,T C,V,Z,N,X	C,V,Z,N,X,I_0-I_2,S,T C,V,Z,N,X,I_0-I_2,S,T
Instructions available	all, except those listed at right	all, including: STOP RESET MOVE to SR ANDI to SR ORI to SR EORI to SR MOVE USP to (ea) MOVE to USP RTE

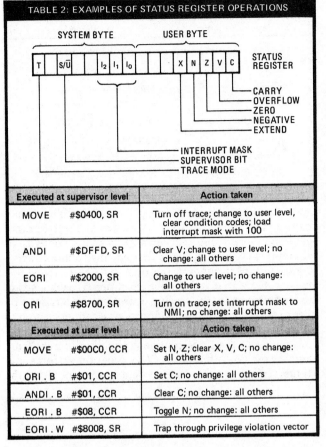

TABLE 2: EXAMPLES OF STATUS REGISTER OPERATIONS

Executed at supervisor level		Action taken
MOVE	#$0400, SR	Turn off trace; change to user level, clear condition codes; load interrupt mask with 100
ANDI	#$DFFD, SR	Clear V; change to user level; no change: all others
EORI	#$2000, SR	Change to user level; no change: all others
ORI	#$8700, SR	Turn on trace; set interrupt mask to NMI; no change: all others
Executed at user level		Action taken
MOVE	#$00C0, CCR	Set N, Z; clear X, V, C; no change: all others
ORI . B	#$01, CCR	Set C; no change: all others
ANDI . B	#$01, CCR	Clear C; no change: all others
EORI . B	#$08, CCR	Toggle N; no change: all others
EORI . W	#$8008, SR	Trap through privilege violation vector

the user level is determined by the S/$\overline{\text{U}}$ bit in the status register. Transition from one level of operation to the other is accomplished in a number of ways.

The processor will go to the user level from the supervisor level if the S/$\overline{\text{U}}$ bit is reset by a MOVE, ANDI (and immediate), or EORI (exclusive or immediate) instruction (Table 2). Conversely, the trap instructions are the only means of getting from the user to the supervisor level in software. For example, certain instructions can cause such a switch to the supervisor level if particular conditions arise during the instructions' execution. In addition, a bus-error signal or any of the other hardware traps will also force the processor to the supervisor level, as will the servicing of an interrupt request.

If the microprocessor is at the user level before an exception is processed, then it will normally return to that level once the routine is closed with the RTE (return from exception) instruction. This instruction also serves to reset the S/$\overline{\text{U}}$ bit.

Traps

There are 16 user-definable trap instructions that, when executed, always direct program control to a designated trap routine at the supervisor level. These software interrupts are useful for calling the operating system, simulating interrupts during debugging operations, signaling the completion of a task, or indicating that an error condition has appeared in a routine.

Two additional instructions—trap-on-overflow and check—examine operating conditions and cause a trap if those conditions are not satisfied. Trap-on-overflow

(TRAPV) will cause a trap if the overflow bit in the status register is set (V = 1). A single routine at the operating system level may then handle every overflow occurrence. The check instruction (CHK) determines whether a chosen register's contents are within the bounds of zero and a specified upper limit and, if it finds the register is outside of the designated bounds, initiates a trap. It may be used to verify that a stack does not overrun, that a string of characters will fit into the allocated space, that an entry into an array is within the dimensions of the array, or that a task does not access data outside its designated space. Failure to remain within bounds causes a call by the operating system to the check service routine.

The two divide instructions—DIVS, which is signed, and DIVU, which is unsigned—can also cause a trap. The attempt to divide a number (dividend) by zero (divisor) is detected before the operands are modified, and a trap is taken automatically. This turns program control over to the supervisor for alternative action.

The divide instructions may encounter one other situation that will divert the normal divide operation—an overflow condition during the division. When this happens, the overflow bit (V) is set, but the result is not written to the destination and the original operands are left intact. Instruction execution continues with the next instruction, though a succeeding TRAPV instruction could call the supervisor for special processing.

Undefined instructions

The attempt to execute certain instructions not implemented in current versions of the 68000 can cause one of two traps to occur. These instructions have op codes whose first 4 bits are 1010 (A_{16}) or 1111 (F_{16}) and are reserved for future enhancements to the instruction set. In anticipation of the expanded instruction set, the "line 1010 emulator" and the "line 1111 emulator" traps are provided to allow the user to imitate the operation of future instructions with macroinstructions. When specific op codes become available for the additional instructions, those can be included in programs. Currently, when an instruction op code is fetched whose first 4 bits are 1010 or 1111, a trap is made to the emulator routine—the "line 1010 emulator" and "line 1111 emulator." When the operation becomes available as a machine primitive, the macroinstruction routine can be eliminated.

There are other op codes that would otherwise cause problems but instead initiate exception processing. Those, for example, that neither decode into valid instructions nor fall into the line 1010/1111 category are considered illegal, and the attempted execution of one will result in a trap. This is a particularly valuable exception because it helps to catch incorrect machine code. Most microprocessors perform some unknown or variable operation when an undefined op code is fetched, inviting the destruction of program or data. Software integrity is improved by forcing an operating-system call to be made upon receipt of an invalid op code.

Unlike most instructions, which may execute at either the user or the supervisor level, privileged instructions, listed in Table 3, may execute only at the supervisor level. Privileged instructions are designed for system control; hence any instruction that modifies the entire status register is privileged. This privilege prevents a user-level program from turning on or off the trace feature, from changing the privilege level, or from changing the interrupt mask level.

The stop, reset, and return-from-exception instructions are also privileged. STOP suspends execution of instructions, loads the status register (including the interrupt mask), and awaits an external prompt (unmasked interrupt or reset). RTE is privileged, since all exception processing takes place at the supervisor level and hence the return instruction must also be on that level. Neither can RESET be used by a program operating at the user level, for this instruction holds the reset pin low long enough to initialize all devices tied to that line, which is clearly a supervisor operation. Any attempt to execute a privileged instruction while on the user level would be a privilege violation and would therefore result in a trap.

In addition, while operating at the supervisor level, the operating system can use both the supervisor stack pointer and the user stack pointer. That privilege allows it to change the user stack location in the course of switching from task to task.

To assist in program development and debugging, the

TABLE 3: PRIVILEGED INSTRUCTIONS	
Privileged instruction	Operation
RESET	reset external devices
RTE	return from exception
STOP	stop program execution
ORI to SR	logical-OR to status register
MOVE USP	move user stack pointer
ANDI to SR	logical-AND to status register
EORI to SR	logical-EOR to status register
MOVE EA to SR	load new status register

trace feature is provided along with the standard halt feature. The trace routine is written by the programmer and might print out register and memory contents or whatever debug operation is desired. Instruction tracing is initiated by turning on the trace bit (T) in the status register. Once that is done, the execution of each instruction is followed by the tracing operation. This is done by the trace trap vector, which directs program execution to the trace routine.

Jumping to the trace routine is slightly different from jumping to the other traps. The program counter and status register of the main program are stored on the

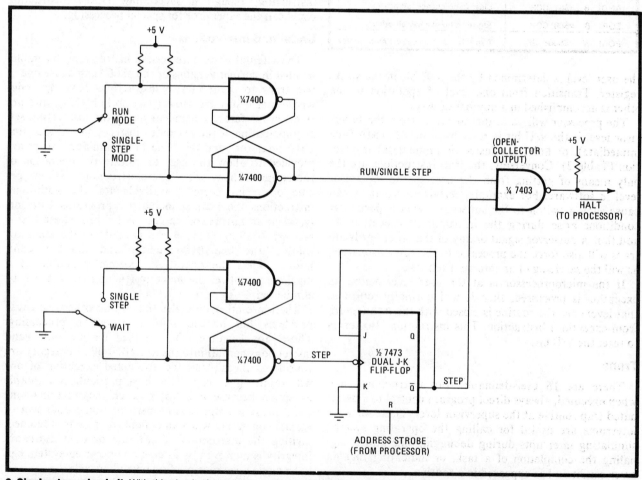

2. Single-step using halt. With this circuit, the operator can control memory accesses by stepping through them one at a time. Each time an address strobe from the processor is issued, it resets the flip-flop. If the upper switch is in the single-step position, then the processor will halt and remain halted until the lower switch is toggled. In this way the asynchronous buses can be exercised under manual control.

supervisor stack and the trace bit is turned off (T = 0), while the S/$\overline{U}$ bit is set to the supervisor privilege level. The trace vector is then fetched and loaded into the program counter.

The trace routine is terminated, as are all exceptions, with an RTE, which causes the processor to fetch and execute the next instruction in the main program. To turn off the trace function, the stack location containing the saved status register must be modified to reset the T bit. Then when the RTE instruction pulls the program counter and status register from the supervisor stack, trace has been disabled, allowing normal instruction execution to resume.

The $\overline{HALT}$ pin on the 68000 may also be used in evaluating a program's execution. With the circuit shown in Fig. 2, the processor can be halted after each bus cycle is completed.

By delaying the data transfer acknowledge, $\overline{DTACK}$, signal with intercepting logic (Fig. 3), the buses will remain asserted by the processor indefinitely. The buses and control signals can then be inspected. When the examination is complete, the intercepting logic allows $\overline{DTACK}$ to propagate through to the 68000, completing the bus cycle.

On every memory access, after sufficient time has passed, the memory or peripheral uses the 68000's asynchronous bus to send the processor a signal acknowledging the data transfer. Should an error be detected during an access, a bus error ($\overline{BERR}$) can signal the processor

that the bus cycle should be aborted.

The faulty memory accesses that prevent a bus cycle's completion may be due to any of several conditions. External circuitry to detect parity errors or—in more sophisticated systems—Hamming codes or other techniques detecting single- or double-bit errors might activate the $\overline{BERR}$. In the absence of a $\overline{DTACK}$ from a block of memory, a timer should flag the processor with a $\overline{BERR}$ after the access time of the memory has been exceeded. The timer also notifies the processor whenever an interrupting device is not responding to an acknowledge signal, resulting in a trap to the spurious-interrupt routine. The unitialized interrupt vector handles interrupts arriving from uninitialized peripherals.

Finally, memory management systems may decide that the memory access is outside of the memory or I/O space currently active and, if they take advantage of the function codes, that the access was not within the bounds of the space allotted to that type of program or data.

For example, the three function-code outputs on the chip provide information on the type of memory cycle about to take place and can activate the bus-error line if anything is out of order. The three pins (FC$_0$–FC$_2$) (Fig. 4) can be decoded to tell whether the processor is attempting to access writable memory or instructions and whether it is doing so while operating at the supervisor or user privilege level. They also may acknowledge interrupts for vectoring by device. By using a 74LS138 decoder, the type of access can be employed to partition

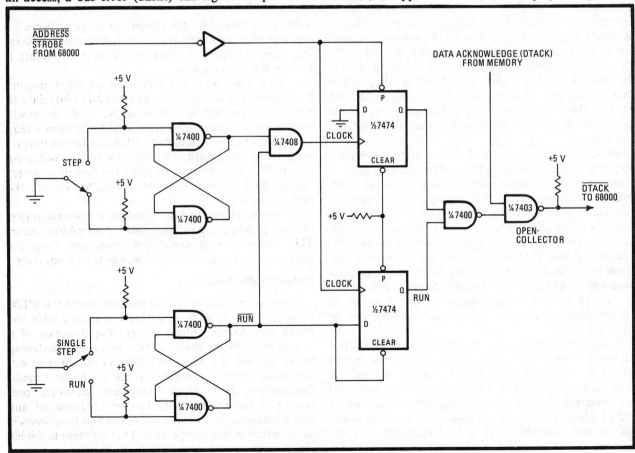

3. Single-step using $\overline{DTACK}$. Here the user can implement a single-step mode by delaying the data-transfer–acknowledge signal. In an error-correcting system, the upper manual switch might be replaced by logic that recognizes the proper bus behavior.

memory into blocks of supervisor code, supervisor data, user code, and user data. Data space is defined as being the memory locations containing variables, vectors, stacks, queues, strings, tables, lists, or any other type of data found separate from the instruction, and fixed (immediate) operands, which are found with the instructions using them. The failure of a memory access to remain within its allotted memory space can be indicated to the microprocessor using the bus-error ($\overline{\text{BERR}}$) signal.

Response to error

There are two forms of responses the 68000 might have to a bus error, depending on whether or not the halt line is asserted at the same time as $\overline{\text{BERR}}$. With both signals asserted, the 68000 will make an attempt to rerun the same bus cycle. The rerunning of the cycle will take place when the $\overline{\text{BERR}}$ and halt lines are released. Rerunning the bus cycle gives the memory system another chance to respond correctly. This type of bus error would be most useful for parity or other error-checking methods, in which noise or other extraneous signals might have caused the soft error.

When the $\overline{\text{BERR}}$ pin alone is asserted, the processor aborts the current bus cycle and initiates bus-error exception processing. Because a bus-error trap might be taken at any time, extra information is pushed onto the supervisor stack to ease recovery from the condition. Though currently the exact state of the processor cannot be retained to effect a complete recovery, sufficient information is stored to allow the operating system to determine the cause of the bus cycle failure. When a bus-error trap is taken, a copy of the program counter and status register is placed on the stack, as well as the op code being processed and the address on the bus at the time of the bus error. Also placed on the stack is whether or not an instruction was being processed, whether the access being made was a read or write, and the condition of the function codes when the $\overline{\text{BERR}}$ line was pulled.

From the information on the stack after a bus-error trap, the conditions leading to the error can be analyzed. Comparison of the address with the function codes might indicate that the wrong memory space was accessed. Further inspection of the address may reveal that the access was outside the range of the physical or active memory. Perhaps a virtual memory system needs to be reloaded. Possibly the section of memory accessed simply did not respond or is providing garbled data or instructions and should be deactivated and listed as bad memory. Maybe a stack or data space has grown out of its allotted block of memory and a new block needs to be allocated.

Examination of the op code may indicate that after the cause of the error is corrected, the instruction can be rerun—a possibility only if any operands or pointers used were all recoverable and if the condition codes did not affect the instruction execution, since it may not be known whether the condition code saved has been modified by the instruction. If it is determined that the instruction can be re-executed, further examination of the op code will indicate how much the saved program counter must be backed up. If data is lost, if the cause of

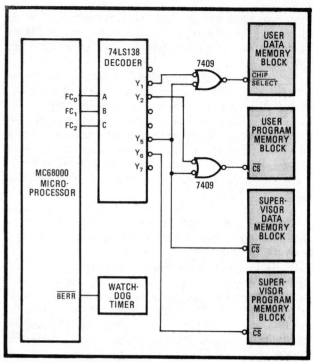

4. Simple memory segmentation. The function outputs are utilized here to separate memory into four areas. The "watchdog timer" notifies the processor of a bus error whenever an access is requested but a data-transfer–acknowledge signal has not been received within a reasonable time limit (say, 30 milliseconds).

a bus error cannot be determined, or if the software for one reason or another cannot continue normal processing, then the operating system will have to initiate a trouble call to an operator.

Current versions of the 68000 do not allow instructions, word (16-bit) data, or long-word (32-bit) data to be aligned on odd-byte boundaries; to do so would require an additional memory access to perform a read or write operation. Attempts to fetch or write an instruction, word or long word at an odd-byte address will cause a trap. This address-error trap lets the operating system realign data on even-byte boundaries or correct the program counter.

The same information saved during a bus-error trap is also saved when a trap is caused by an address error. This information is useful for recovering from the address error in much the same way as from a bus error.

Catastrophic halt

There are several situations that will cause the 68000 to discontinue all processing. These are the double bus errors and double address errors. The detection of a second error during the exception processing (including vector fetches) of a bus error, address error, or reset will shut down the microprocessor. When any of these conditions appear, the processor determines that correct processing is impossible, halts further execution of any operations, and, in a unique use of the halt line, drives it as an output to flag an operator. That response to double errors prevents the processor from running away and destroying data or other tasks when it knows the system has had a catastrophic failure. □

Electronics / April 24, 1980

16-bit microprocessor enters virtual memory domain

Central processing unit supports 24-bit addresses; memory management unit offers instruction-aborting facility vital to virtual memory systems

by Yohav Lavi, Asher Kaminker, Ayram Menachem, and Subhash Bal, *National Semiconductor Corp., Santa Clara, Calif.*

☐ The concept of virtual memory used to be the exclusive domain of mainframe computers. Now that the capabilities of high-end 16-bit microprocessors are approaching those of bigger systems, they, too, are finding virtual-memory–based designs necessary and desirable.

The latest of these advanced microprocessors, the NS16032 central processing unit uniformly addresses 16 megabytes. In addition, it fully supports virtual memory systems. When the device is used in conjunction with the NS16082 memory management unit, it enables the user to construct a flexible page-oriented virtual memory system that, with the proper operating system software, can address 16 megabytes of virtual memory.

The driving force behind virtual memory systems is the desire to increase storage size while making memory management functions transparent to programmers. Among the reasons for wanting large storage space is the current trend toward larger applications programs, as well as toward larger and more sophisticated operating

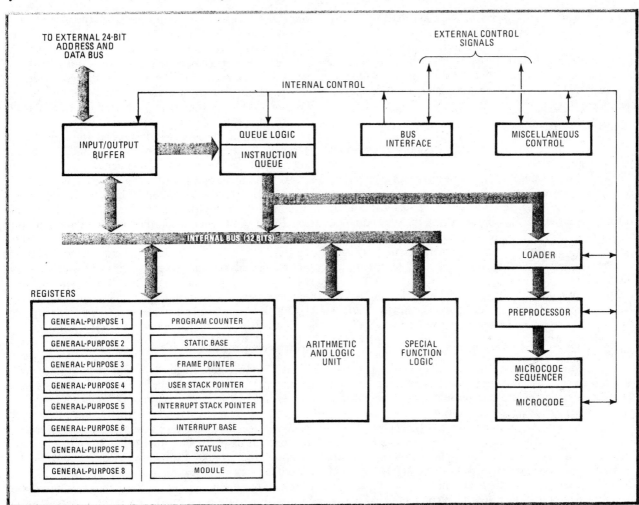

1. Big brother. The largest of the 16000 family of microprocessors, the 16032 central processing unit operates on 16-bit data but features 32-bit internal bus and general-purpose registers and a three-stage instruction pipeline. It uses 24-bit addresses to access 16 megabytes.

The virtues of virtual memory

Memory has been a problem from the time the Eniac computer was first switched on in 1946. Programmers realized almost immediately that managing it was a major overhead chore. One early solution was to allocate memory before a job was run, but the allocation would not be changed once execution of the program was started.

A more sophisticated approach was developed by a group of researchers at Manchester University, Manchester, England, in the late 1950s. Memory was divided into logical pages, which were then swapped between a peripheral drum memory and the main core memory as needed. In this way the system itself handled the housekeeping chores of memory allocation. The Atlas computer, completed in 1962, was the first to implement what later became known as virtual memory.

The first commercial computer to employ this type of memory management was the Burroughs B6500, introduced in 1966. But not until IBM coined the virtual-memory name and added it to the System/370 model 158 and 168 in 1972 did the idea catch on. Now it is widely used in the mainframe industry and on many larger minicomputers.

With virtual memory the user regards the combination of main and peripheral storage devices as a single large storage space. Consequently, the user can write large programs without worrying about the physical memory limitations of the system.

To accomplish this, the operating system software places some of the users' programs and data in peripheral storage. When they must be brought into main memory for execution, the system performs an operation called a page swap. Information not currently in use is removed from the main memory and returned to peripheral storage, making room for the new material. For efficiency, when the referenced location has to be brought from the peripheral to main memory, other locations likely to be referenced next are brought also.

Of course, the beauty of virtual memory is that the user, or programmer, does not have to be aware of this process. He uses one consistent set of addresses, called virtual addresses. The memory management hardware keeps track of where the information resides at any moment and converts, or translates, the virtual address to its real location in main memory. When the hardware finds the virtual address requested unavailable in main memory, it initiates a swap procedure.

---

systems software. Furthermore, business, teleprocessing, and communications applications require increasingly large data spaces. Efficient multiprogramming demands virtual memory. The continuing reduction in memory prices — both electromechanical and solid-state — makes it economically feasible to include a large virtual memories in a system.

Economical expansion

However, the solution for large storage requirements does not necessarily lie in physically large memories in the form, for example, of many random-access memory chips. Such a simple memory addition is not economical, especially since programmers will generally use all the available memory. This approach also makes it difficult to add new tasks to a system because it forces programmers to resort to memory management techniques, such as overlay memory structures, that limit programming efficiency.

On the other hand, a virtual memory scheme allows the expansion of storage quite economically since a significant portion of the memory can be less expensive than mass storage such as disk (see "The virtues of virtual memory,"). Also, it frees the programmer from worrying about the housekeeping details of memory management. That is especially important because software development costs represent an ever increasing portion of system development cost.

But a microprocessor chip — like any computer — needs dedicated hardware to support virtual memory system software. This special hardware, not available on current microprocessors, is now provided on the 16032 CPU and the 16082 memory management unit.

Before examining this special virtual memory hardware, it is useful to describe the basic 16000 architecture. The 16032 is the largest of the 16000 family of microprocessors, which also includes the scaled-down NS16008 and NS16016. (Although architecturally compatible, these parts do not support virtual memory and are instead intended as low-cost CPUs for small and medium-sized systems). These parts will be available in sample quantities by the end of the year or the first quarter of 1981 at the latest. The 16000 family's architecture supports a single uniform address space, and allows 32-bit addressing that can access 4 billion bytes of memory. In the initial offering of the 16032, however, only 24-bit addresses are implemented, which allows access to 16 megabytes.

Also supported in the 16000 architecture are 16 32-bit general-purpose registers and 17 special-purpose registers. Eight of the general-purpose registers are contained on the 16032 CPU chip, along with 8 special-purpose registers (Fig. 1). The other 8 general-purpose registers are contained on the special NS16081 floating-point mathmatics chip, along with the floating-point status register (see "Expanding the architecture through slaves,"). The rest of the special-purpose registers are in the memory management unit described later.

Addressing modes

Nine addressing modes are provided in the 16000 architecture, four of which are unique. Top-of-stack addressing allows manipulation or referencing of an operand on a stack by all instructions as in a stock machine. Relative addressing lets the pointer reside in memory rather than in a register. External addressing supports the 16000's software module concept (see "Modular software leaves room for growth,").
which allows the modules to be relocated without linkage editing. Finally, scaled indexing can be added to any of the addressing modes to index and address automatically by units of 1, 2, 4, or 8 bytes, providing easy addressing

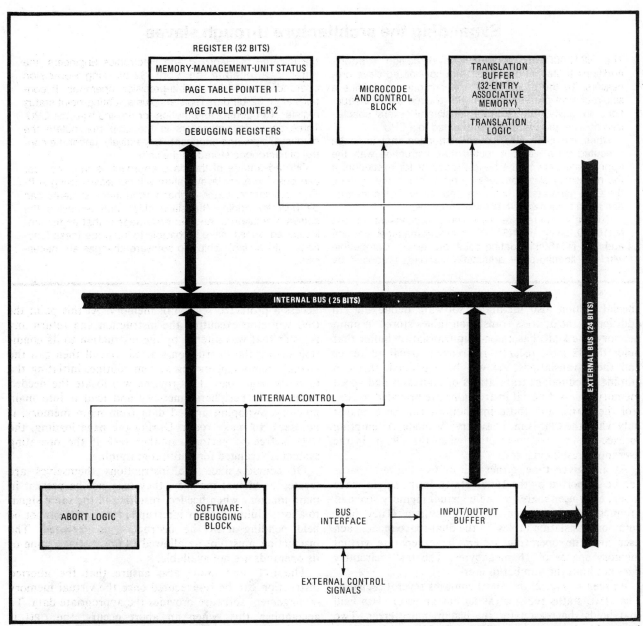

REGISTER (32 BITS)

MEMORY-MANAGEMENT-UNIT STATUS
PAGE TABLE POINTER 1
PAGE TABLE POINTER 2
DEBUGGING REGISTERS

MICROCODE AND CONTROL BLOCK

TRANSLATION BUFFER (32-ENTRY ASSOCIATIVE MEMORY)

TRANSLATION LOGIC

EXTERNAL BUS (24 BITS)

INTERNAL BUS (25 BITS)

INTERNAL CONTROL

ABORT LOGIC

SOFTWARE-DEBUGGING BLOCK

BUS INTERFACE

INPUT/OUTPUT BUFFER

EXTERNAL CONTROL SIGNALS

2. Memory specialist. The 16082 memory management unit handles virtual address translation and memory protection. A unique feature of this chip—vital to virtual memory schemes—is the abort facility that interrupts instructions on the CPU when needed data is not in memory.

of arrays of byte, word, double-word, or quad-word quantities.

Along with these memory-addressing features, the 16000 architecture includes over 100 basic instructions. This instruction set is symmetrical—any instruction can be used with any addressing mode and any operand length, including byte, word, and double-word. These instructions allow operations between memory locations as well as between registers, a feature that facilitates register allocation for compilers.

Internally, the NS16032 has 32-bit-wide data paths and features a pipeline organization. An instruction queue holds up to 8 bytes of instructions for decoding by a preprocessor before a microcode sequencer actually locates the microprogram necessary for executing the instruction.

The CPU chip interfaces with the outside world

through a 24-bit-wide multiplexed address and data bus. To facilitate the design of operating systems, the 16032 operates in two modes—user and supervisor. Privileged instructions for the operating system cannot be executed when the CPU is in the user mode.

To make this microprocessor into a virtual memory machine, the 16082 memory management unit (MMU) is paired with the 16032 CPU. The two could be conceived of as a single CPU that simply produces a physical memory address. Because of limitations in chip size, however, the MMU was fabricated as a separate chip that operates as a slave processor to the CPU.

The MMU shares the external multiplexed address and data bus with the CPU and can assume full control of this bus for fetching information from main memory tables.

The MMU contains the logic for doing the dynamic address translation as well as for memory protection. A

Expanding the architecture through slaves

The NS16000 architecture's novel design supports additions to its instruction set with specialized slave processors. To the programmer, the computer looks like a single central processing unit with a large set of instructions. In reality, the hardware consists of several specialized or slave-processor chips attached to a CPU.

When the CPU receives an instruction that is to be executed by a slave, it routes that instruction with the appropriate data to the slave processor for execution. If the necessary slave processor chip is not in the system, the CPU generates a software trap, allowing the instruction to be emulated with software routines.

Currently, there are two slave processors in the NS16000 family: the NS16082 memory management unit and the NS16081 floating-point processor. Compatible with the floating-point arithmetic standard proposed by the Institute of Electrical and Electronics Engineers, the latter can operate on both 32-bit single-precision operands and 64-bit double-precision operands. It contains eight 32-bit data registers plus a floating-point status register with control information for dealing with the CPU. Three separate processors in the chip manipulate the mantissa, sign, and exponent, respectively, under the control of microcode stored on the chip.

One advantage of the slave approach is that the user can build an entry-level system without slaves using software emulators. Later, higher performance systems can be built by adding the slave chips and removing the software emulators. Another advantage is that as technological advances make it possible to integrate these functions onto a single chip, no software changes are necessary.

special section also facilitates software debugging. In addition to the address translation tables stored in main memory, the MMU has an on-chip translation buffer that holds the 32 most recently referenced virtual addresses and their translations. As will be explained, this can eliminate redundant translations of addresses and speed memory access. Special instructions are provided to control the MMU, and those instructions can be executed only when the CPU is in the supervisor mode. Attempting to execute an MMU instruction when the CPU is in the user mode results in a trap.

At any given time, either one or two address spaces can be supported by the 16082 MMU. In the single-space mode, each user shares a single virtual memory space of 16 megabytes with the operating system. They have common translation tables. In the dual-space mode, each user and the operating system have separate virtual memory spaces of 16 megabytes. The MMU circuitry does not limit the number of users.

As seen in Fig. 2, the MMU contains several registers. The MMU-status register (MSR) has an error-class field that holds the reason for the last memory error. Two page-table base pointers (PTB1, PTB2) on the 16082 point to the starting location of the translation tables in physical memory used for user space and supervisor space. Other registers control the debugger portion of the MMU.

Aborting facility

The MMU's most significant feature, however, is the aborting facility that supports the virtual memory operation system. To understand its importance, it is helpful to examine the execution of an instruction in a virtual memory environment. After fetching and decoding the instruction, the CPU sends the virtual addresses of the operands to the MMU. The MMU examines each address to determine if it resides in main memory. If so, it translates the virtual address to a real, or physical, address and sends it to the memory.

If the necessary data is not in main memory, however, the MMU sends a signal to abort to the CPU. The MMU will also abort the memory access if the CPU is trying to access a protected section of memory. At this point the CPU will stop executing the instruction and return any register that was altered by the instruction to its condition before the instruction started. It will then call the virtual memory operating system routine, initiating the memory page load. This routine will locate the needed data on the peripheral memory and load it into main memory, swapping unused data from main memory, if necesary, to make room. During the page loading, the CPU is free to perform another task if the operating system is arranged for multiprogramming.

Of course, since the instructions themselves are treated as virtual memory, they may not be present in main memory when needed, resulting in the same signal to abort. Unlike regular interrupts, this signal cannot be held pending until the instruction is executed. The instruction must not be allowed to finish, since some of its operands are not available.

The CPU and MMU also ensure that the aborted instruction can be re-executed once the virtual memory management software provides the appropriate data. To accomplish this, when an abort occurs, the CPU is returned to the state it was in prior to the aborted instruction.

As a result of an abort, the program counter is automatically saved. The instruction will be retried when the page is loaded and the operating system performs a return-from-trap instruction. In addition, the condition codes in the processor's status register are affected by many instructions and therefore must be restored. Similarly, the stack pointer register, which is decremented or incremented when the top-of-stack addressing mode is used by an instruction, is restored. The program counter is normally incremented for the execution of the next instruction and must be decremented. Special hardware on the 16032 automatically restores these registers to their previous value.

Because the 16032 CPU instruction stream is pipelined, provisions must be made for the instructions in the pipeline when aborting takes place. The 16032 aborts only the instruction being executed, ignoring others.

Signals to abort generated while the instructions are

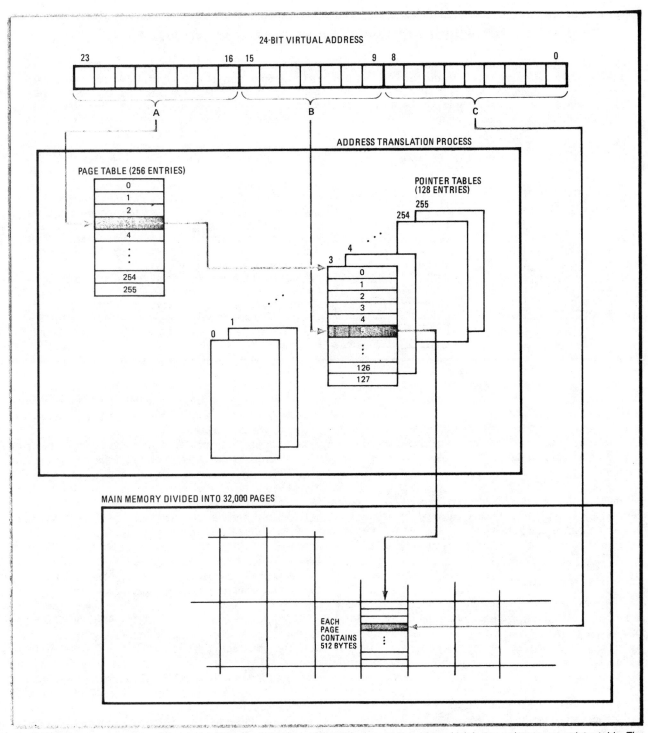

3. Virtual. The upper 8 bits (A) of the virtual address point to one of the 256-page table entries, which in turn points to one pointer table. The next 7 address bits (B) index an entry indicating a page in main memory. The last 9 bits (C), untranslated, locate a byte.

being prefetched are suspended until the instruction is about to be executed. This prevents instructions following certain program flow-control instructions, such as call, return, and jump, from generating an unnecessary abort state when they are not intended to be executed and may not reside in virtual memory at all.

The string type of instruction, in particular, requires special handling during an abort. Obviously it is not desirable to have a long string instruction repeated from the beginning if an abort occurs somewhere in the string.

The 16032 provides for the aborted instruction to be reexecuted from the point where the problem occurred.

Obviously the other major function of the MMU is to translate the virtual, or logical, address used by programmers and generated by the CPU into the real, or physical, address used to address the physical main memory. When the translation hardware finds that the virtual address is not in physical memory, it starts the abort process above.

For the purpose of virtual memory management, both

165

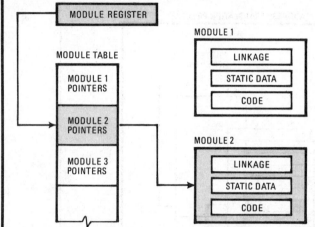
the logical and the physical address spaces are divided into 32,768 pages each with a fixed size of 512 bytes. It is the MMU's job to keep track of the logical addresses and their corresponding locations in physical memory. It does this by means of two sets of address translation tables, called page and pointer tables, stored in main memory.

The upper, or most significant, 15 bits (sections A and B) of the 24-bit virtual address represent the virtual address of a page and, once translated by the MMU, define a physical page of 512 bytes. The lower 9 bits are used to address a byte within this page and are not translated (Fig. 3).

Tables for translation

The translation is carried out by tables. The page table has 256 entries, each 32 bits wide. Thus, its total size is 1,024 bytes. Section A of the virtual address, which is 8 bits long, is used to index an entry of this table. The contents of this page-table entry, in turn, point to the beginning of one of 256 different pointer tables, which could also be stored in main memory. These pointer tables contain 128 32-bit entries each. Section B of the virtual address is used to index one of the pointer table entries, which points to the actual physical page.

Although at first glance this scheme appears to occupy a large portion of available memory space to maintain table entries, the overhead is actually very small. A maximum system of 16 megabytes of virtual memory will use one page table of 1,024 bytes plus 256 pointer tables of 512 bytes each, for a total of 132,096 bytes of mapping entries. But since a typical system would use a much smaller virtual memory size, it should be possible to reduce the amount of page table entries required. Also, the pointer tables may be paged in and out of main memory just like other parts of virtual memory.

The translation process starts when the MMU receives the 24-bit virtual address from the CPU. The first thing the MMU does is compare the upper 15 bits of the virtual address with the 32 entries in its translation buffer. This associative memory contains the most recently accessed virtual addresses with their translated physical addresses. Thus, if the address is in this table—as it is expected to be 97% of the time—the physical address can be available in only one clock cycle.

If the address is not in the translation buffer, however, the MMU refers to the page and pointer tables in memory and updates the buffer. This process takes 16 clock cycles. While the MMU is performing the translation the CPU is kept inactive, since the MMU must have access to the external bus to access its translation tables in main memory.

The MMU's pointer base registers (PTB1 or PTB2) are controlled by the operating system. These registers contain the starting address of the page table in main memory. The MMU then takes the top 8 bits of the virtual address, multiplies that number by 4, and adds it to the starting address to point to one of the 256 page table entries (Fig. 4).

Each 32-bit page-table entry contains a 16-bit page-frame number as well as 8 flag bits and memory protection information. The ninth bit in the entry is ignored, and the uppermost 7 bits are reserved for future use. Among the flag bits is a valid bit that signals unused or invalid page entries that are not present in physical main memory.

As for the referenced bit, it is set whenever a corresponding page is referenced and is used by the operating system to help determine the least needed page. The modified bit is used to alert the operating system that a page has been modified, and therefore its copy in peripheral memory must be updated before that page can be removed from main memory. The other bits in the entry

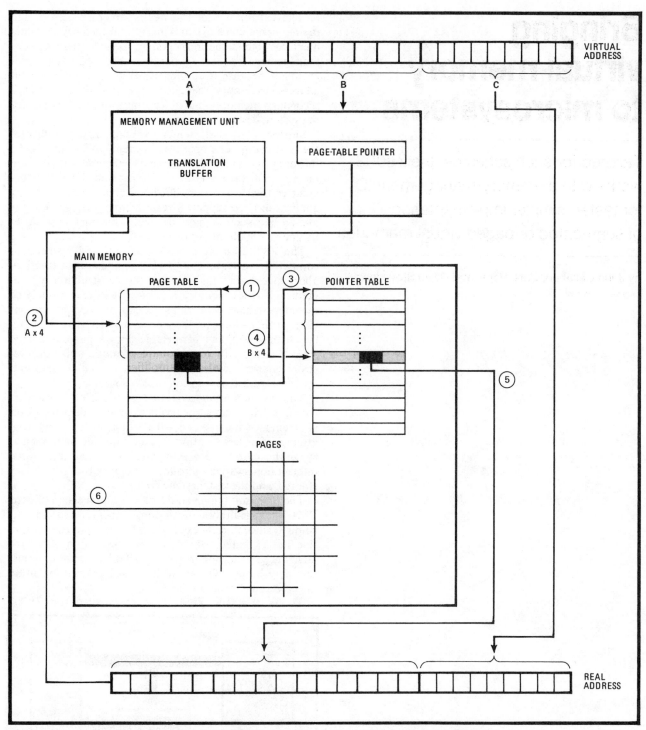

4. MMU at work. If a virtual address is not in the MMU's translation buffer, it uses its pointer base register to locate the page table in main memory (1). Multiplying virtual address section A by 4 locates an entry that points to a pointer table (2 and 3). Multiplying section B by 4 locates the correct entry (4), 15 bits of which become the upper portion of the physical address (5). The lower 9 bits (C) are untranslated.

are used to hold memory protection information.

This 16-bit page frame number is then used by the MMU to locate one of the 256 pointer tables in main memory. The MMU takes the second 7 bits of the virtual address, multiplies that number by 4, and adds it to the page frame number to locate one of the 128 entries of the pointer table. Each entry on this table is similar to those on the page table. The MMU now takes the 15-bit page-frame number and appends it to the unchanged lower 9 bits of the virtual address to create the 24-bit physical address of the information in main memory.

Obviously, if an address is already in the translation buffer, the translation can be completed much more quickly. For this reason, a replacement algorithm stored in the MMU replaces addresses in the translation buffer that have not been recently used with recently accessed addresses. The translation buffer, by the way, is invisible to the user. □

Electronics/June 30, 1981

Bringing virtual memory to microsystems

Tailored for such schemes, the Z8003
works with a memory-management IC
for faster, simpler implementation
of segmented or paged virtual memories

by John Callahan, C. N. Patel, and David Stevenson
Zilog Inc., Cupertino, Calif.

□ The capabilities of the newest microprocessors and their support chips are making virtual memory management possible at the microsystem level. Virtual memory management can be a boon for the applications programmer because it automatically maps a large logical address space onto a smaller main memory and a large secondary memory—but it can be a mixed blessing for the system designer to implement.

Support of virtual memory management complicates the host computer's operating system, which must swap the program and data fragments into and out of main memory, but the rewards of automatic memory management can be worth the additional complexity for many applications. To support virtual memory design, Zilog is adding hardware support of virtual memory schemes to its line of Z8000 microprocessors.

The Z8003 16-bit processor is pin- and instruction-compatible with the Z8001, but it adds an instruction-abort mechanism that aids in the construction of economical virtual memory schemes. With the associated memory-management chips, it can be used in systems (Fig. 1) that support either of the popular virtual memory schemes: segments of variable sizes or pages of a fixed size. It also facilitates the implementation of multiprocessor systems with a special status signal that aids synchronizing access to common resources.

The instruction-abort feature of the Z8003 is a vital part of solving the major problem in implementing virtual memory management—handling instructions that attempt to access locations resident outside main memory. In this case the processor must be halted, the desired information swapped into main memory from secondary storage, and the instruction retried.

The interrupt pin on standard microprocessors like the Z8001 is unsuitable for halting the processor in this context, since it is checked only after the current instruction has executed. But this check will often occur too late, since during the instructions faulty execution registers may be overwritten with nonsense, resulting in an uncorrectable error.

To fix this, the Z8003—at first called the Z9000

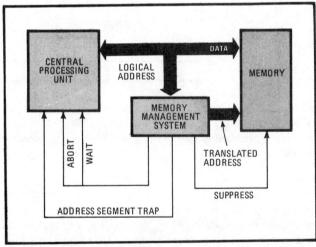

1. Virtual partners. Working with a memory-management chip, the Z8003 processor can implement a virtual memory setup. It includes an instruction-abort pin that facilitates the swapping-in of missing data or instructions to main memory from secondary storage.

—includes a pin located at the Z8001's reserved pin 33 that lets the processor be interrupted during execution. This new function leaves the processor in a well-defined state that allows software to recover from the aborted instruction. Software can then swap in the missing data or instructions automatically, without operator intervention and without the need for special code in the program.

Managing a hierarchy

Facilitating this swapping action is the key to implementing the storage hierarchy of a virtual memory, in which fast, but expensive, random-access main memory is supplanted by slower, but cheaper, storage like disks or tapes or bubble memories. This hierarchy can reduce hardware costs by accommodating very large programs and data sets in the secondary memory and moving them block by block to the main memory for execution.

However, managing the use of the memory hierarchy can be a considerable problem. It all boils down to determining what information should be in main memory at a given time.

The early solution for system designers was to use the technique of overlays—dividing a program and its data into logically coherent units (such as subroutines or records) and moving them in and out of main memory with software provided by the applications programmer. The major disadvantage of this scheme is the difficulty of tracing all control paths through a program and of laying out memory for efficient use.

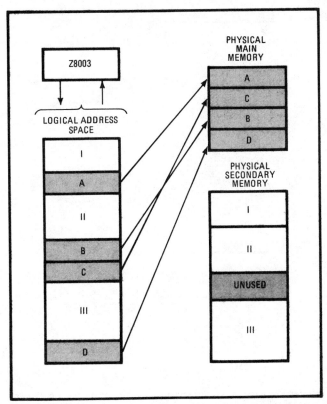

2. Logical mix. In a virtual memory system, the processor sees all its memory resources in a single logical address space, but only some portion of those resources physically resides in the main memory. Segments I, II, and III must be swapped in for use.

To complicate matters further, code usually had to reside in the same location whenever it was present in main memory. The result was that overlays could be difficult to construct and prone to subtle runtime errors, as well as being a time-consuming programming task.

A better solution is to automate this memory management task, resulting in a virtual memory system. It presents a programmer with a large, homogeneous logical address space of differing memory types, rather than with a large, heterogeneous physical address space.

In order to use a Z8003-based virtual memory management system, the programmer merely partitions the program and data into segments of whatever size is most convenient. The operating system may then automatically further partition the segments into fixed-size pages—in other words, a paged virtual memory is a variant of the segmented scheme.

As a program executes, unneeded portions of its code and data reside in the secondary memory, while the information most likely to be accessed is maintained automatically in main memory. When the program generates a logical address, the memory management system automatically translates it into a physical main-memory location. If the information is not in main memory, the processor is temporarily halted, the program suspended, and operating system software invoked to swap the desired information from secondary memory into main memory. After an updating of the translation mechanism, the program is restarted by reexecuting the uncompleted instruction.

Invisible mapping

As an example of such a setup, Fig. 2 shows a large logical address space, with only a portion of the locations accessible to the program actually residing in main memory. If the program generates an address in areas A, B, C, or D, the memory management system instantaneously maps the logical address into the appropriate main memory location. If, however, the program generates an address in areas I, II, or III, the instruction must be aborted and software invoked to swap out some data or instructions in main memory and swap in the required data from the secondary memory. With the new data in memory, the original program may reexecute the aborted instruction and proceed as if nothing unusual had happened.

Here the applications programmer is not involved with anticipating the need for new information as the program executes or with handling the transfer. Even more importantly, he or she need not know the memory characteristics of the system on which the programs will run. Freeing applications from limits on memory size greatly enhances the utility and portability of large, complex programs among different system configurations, regardless of their main-memory sizes.

The Z8003 generates segmented logical addresses—23 bits divided into a 7-bit segment number and a 16-bit offset—allowing external circuitry (becoming available as special-purpose integrated circuits) to implement virtual memory with variable-sized segments or with fixed-sized pages. So the choice of which type to implement is up to the system designer.

In order to fetch information at a given logical address in a segmented virtual memory, the entire segment containing that address must be in main memory before the program may continue executing. The Z8003 accommodates 128 segments that can hold between 256 bytes and 64-K bytes each.

In a paged virtual memory, each segment is subdivided into fixed-size pages (2-K bytes is a typical size). When information is fetched at a given logical address, only the page containing that address must be in main memory before a program may continue executing.

There are a number of tradeoffs between a segmented and a paged virtual memory. These will play an important part in the designer's choice.

For the Z8003, the software required to recover from an address translation failure is simpler and more efficient for the segmented virtual memory since fewer instructions require fix-ups before backing up the program counter. Also, the system tables indicating the location of logical segments in main or secondary memory are considerably smaller than those indicating the location of logical pages, since there are typically many more pages than segments.

But since segments are larger than pages, virtual memories in which the segments are divided into pages require less information to be transferred between main memory and secondary storage with each address translation failure. Thus they give better response time and throughput in multiuser systems. On the other hand, pages are usually larger than the minimum increment for segments (2 K versus 256 bytes), so the last page of a segment usually has unused space.

On the plus side, the fixed page size simplifies the allocation of the physical memory. In a segmented memory with its variable sizes, segments may have to be moved around in order to create a contiguous block of main memory large enough to hold an incoming segment. The single size of a page automatically creates contiguous blocks of the proper size in the main memory.

Software support

After the Z8003 attempts to reference a logical address not in the main memory and the current instruction is aborted, the addressed data or instruction should be brought into main memory and the aborted instruction should be restarted. To do this, the system designer must provide two pieces of software: a fault handler and an instruction restart routine.

The fault handler is invoked by the address/segment trap request and is responsible for saving information about the aborted instruction and for initiating a request that the data or code be brought into main memory. The designer must also ensure that the state of the aborted program (flag and control word, program counter, and register file) be saved and that another process be executed while the missing data or code is being fetched. Obviously, the fault handler must not generate a fault itself until all data about the aborted instruction and the program state have been saved.

The instruction restart routine must return the program counter to point to the aborted instruction. In addition, it must decode the instruction's operational code to determine if any of the registers had been modified before the cycle when the abort occurred (Fig. 3). For a small number of instructions, some registers will have been modified, so this routine must return these registers to their previous states. Which instructions require fixing of the registers and how to fix the registers depends upon whether segmentation or paging is used.

In either case, the system stack must always be in main memory so that accessing it will never cause a fault. Input/output buffers should always be in main memory so that I/O instructions will never cause a fault. Finally the program status area should always be in main memory, too.

Given these conditions, the following information must be available for restart of an instruction: the program-counter value during the initial instruction fetch cycle (signaled by a special code on the status

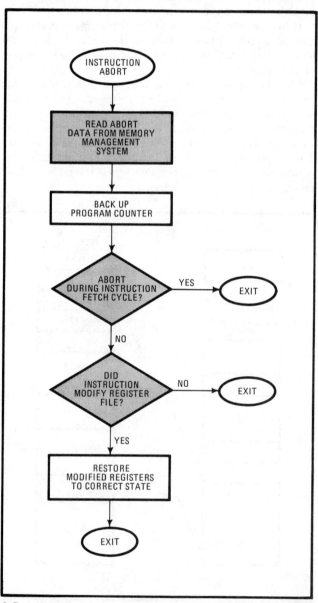

3. Reaction. Whenever the instruction-abort mechanism is activated, the system-level software must save the program's status, swap in the missing segment, restore registers that may have been modified, and retry the instruction by backing up the program counter.

170

output lines), the address that caused the fault, the state of the status lines during the aborted cycle, and (for paged memories) the data in a counter that records the number of successful data accesses made by the instruction before it was aborted.

Restarting instructions

To recover from an absent segment, an aborted instruction can simply be restarted after the segment swap by reloading the program counter value saved by the memory management system. There are 24 instructions for which registers may have to be reinstated to their original condition. The software fix required for these functions involves adjusting either a pointer register or a count register. For example, if a write is attempted to an absent segment during a push instruction, the stack pointer must be incremented by two before the instruction is restarted.

To recover from a page fault, an aborted instruction can simply be restarted after the page swap by reloading the program counter. On a paged scheme, there are 29 instructions for which registers may have to be reinstated in their original status. Aside from the updating of pointers (as for the segmented virtual memory), most of the complexity of the instruction restarts arises from accessed data crossing a page boundary while modifying a register used for the address calculation.

An example might be an instruction that loads four words into contiguous registers, using the contents of the first two registers to point to the data. If a page fault occurs after two data reads, the addressing information will be overwritten and must be recovered before restarting the instruction. Given the faulty address and the number of successful read operations carried out before the fault is encountered, it is a simple matter to restore the contents of the pointer register and restart the instruction.

Zilog's memory management unit, the Z8010 MMU, contains most of the circuitry required to implement a segment-swapping memory management system. It contains 64 segment descriptors, so that a pair can translate

addresses for all 128 segments a Z8003 can access.

The 8010 also automatically records the most significant 15 bits of a violation address, so only an additional 8-bit register is needed to record the low-order byte of the program counter. This register is updated at the beginning of each instruction (indicated by the instruction fetch-status that the Z8003 puts out) and is locked when a suppress signal indicates a missing segment or an access violation.

One bit in each segment descriptor can be used to indicate that a segment is currently outside main memory. Other bits provide additional protection, since segments may be marked as read-only, execute-only, or system-only.

The 8010 also records the accesses and writes to segments. This record can be used to determine which segments have been referenced and which of them have been modified.

Such data is useful in improving the performance of a virtual memory system. Segments that are frequently referenced should remain in main memory. Segments that have not been modified from their original state in secondary memory may simply be written over when swapping in new segments without writing the unmodified segment back into secondary memory. Thus the frequency of address translation faults and the amount of traffic between main memory and secondary memory may be minimized.

In addition to the 8010, Zilog will be offering another MMU that will add the hardware support for a paged virtual memory. In fact, no external circuitry beyond this paged MMU will be required.

Managing more processors

The Z8003 differs from the Z8001 in one other respect. It includes a feature useful in implementing software semaphores that synchronize access to critical resources in a multiprocessor environment.

During its test-and-set instruction, it puts out a special status code that in effect forms a read-modify-write data access. This signal can be used to lock out other processors from, say, accessing memory between the reading and updating of a variable.

In a two-processor system (Fig. 4) where each processor has access to a dual-ported random-access memory with a list of tasks to be performed, a RAM byte can be used to indicate when one of the processors is updating the list. For access to the list, a processor performs a test-and-set operation on this byte, checking to see if the other processor is accessing the list and setting the byte to indicate that it intends to access the list. It repeatedly executes the test-and-set operation in a loop until the other processor has finished, then updates the list and clears the byte (indicating the list is available to the other processor).

By using the test-and-set signal to lock out simultaneous accesses, the system guarantees proper synchronization of the two processors. It is impossible for both processors to read the semaphore byte simultaneously and to assume that each has exclusive access to the list—which could lead to both removing the same task from the list. □

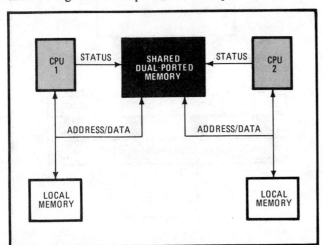

4. Multiprocessors. The Z8003 also implements a special instruction that locks out other processors trying to access a common resource, in effect performing a read-modify-write operation that is ideal for implementing semaphores for interprocessor communication.

Data compression shrinks microprocessor's control store

Eliminating unused storage areas squeezes space requirements yet does not slow 16-bit processor's operation

by Karl Guttag, *Texas Instruments Inc., Houston, Texas*

☐ Usually associated with communications, data compression can do more than speed the transmission of digital information—it also can shrink the size of the control store on a microprocessor. In the TI 99000, in fact, data compression yields a read-only memory only a quarter the size required by conventional storage techniques. Furthermore, this technique of microinstruction storage unites space saving with speedy retrieval, a combination that control-store schemes in other 16-bit processors have not been able to achieve.

Microprocessors such as the 99000, Intel's 8086, and Motorola's 68000 contain internal subroutines of primitive machine instructions, or microinstructions, that specify the flow of bits through the registers and data lines of the chip. Each such subroutine in these microcoded microprocessors in fact performs the necessary operations to complete execution of all or part of what is typically considered a machine instruction.

In a simple instruction, for example one that adds two values using an arithmetic and logic unit, several microinstructions are needed, which in turn may have to be handled by microinstruction subroutines:

- Fetch the data values.
- Add the values.
- Store the result.

The most straightforward way of executing microinstructions is to dedicate a bit in the microcode control-word register to each possible control line in the micro-

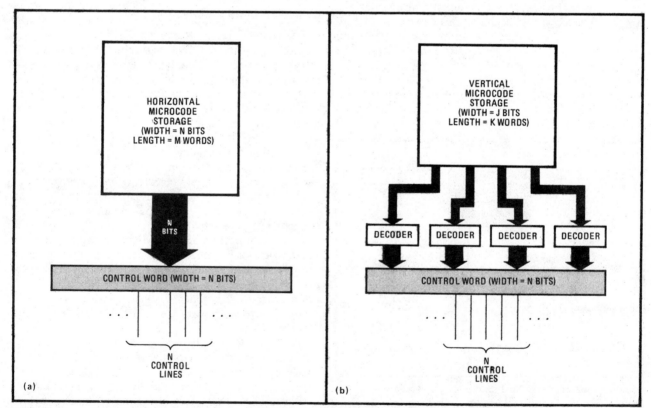

1. Microcode configurations. With horizontal microcode, the control-word register can be loaded directly from microcode storage, but at the cost of wide data paths from storage (a). With encoded data and a set of decoders, the same register can be loaded over narrower data paths (b).

| | ADDRESS | CONTROL LINES | | | | STATE NAME |
		1	2	3	4	
COLUMN 0	0	0	1	0	1	A
	1	1	0	0	0	B
	2	0	1	0	0	C
	3	0	0	1	1	D
COLUMN 1	4	0	0	0	0	E
	5	1	0	0	0	F
	6	0	0	0	1	G
	7	1	0	0	0	H
COLUMN 2	8	0	1	0	0	I
	9	0	0	0	0	J
	10	0	0	0	0	K
	11	0	0	0	0	L

2. Data array. In this 4-bit-wide data array, the 12 addressable states (A through L) are divided into three sections ($YSEL_0$ through $YSEL_2$). The control-line outputs ($CNTL_1$ through $CNTL_4$) determine process flow through the hardware elements of a microcoded processor.

processor (Fig. 1a). Then each word in the control store performs a set of operations, such as simultaneously turning on the output of two registers, latching the data into the inputs of the ALU, and activating the line to the ALU that performs the addition.

On typical 16-bit microprocessors, over 200 control signals are required and could cause the control store to be very large. The size of the control store can be reduced because the number of mutually exclusive operations is usually large. For example, the outputs from several registers sharing the same bus cannot all be activated simultaneously. Consequently, extensive amounts of microstorage may not used for a given output operation.

Encoded fields

The classic solution is to group the binary fields in the microword into encoded fields, possible when the set of circuit elements controlled by such a binary field has only one element to be selected at a time. For instance, two fields could be dedicated to the two operands that are delivered to the ALU each from one of a set of seven temporary registers. Because no more than two operands will ever be delivered to the ALU, separate bits controlling data transfer from each register is wasteful. Thus on a machine with seven registers that can each load either of two inputs of an ALU, 14 bits are required.

With encoding, however, only 6 bits are needed—two sets of 3 bits specifying which (if any) register loads each input. In this way, the width of the microcode word is reduced from a wide horizontal to a thin vertical structure (Fig. 1b), giving rise to the name of such an encoded microcode technique—vertical microcode.

The great advantage of vertical microcoding is a more reasonably sized microcontrol store—a fact that proved influential in its use in Intel's 8086 with its 21-bit microcontrol word[1]. However, the heavily encoded microcode word in the 8086 necessitated an extensive amount of random logic and programmable logic arrays in order to generate the final control signals for the processor. On the other hand, the use of local decoders allowed routing

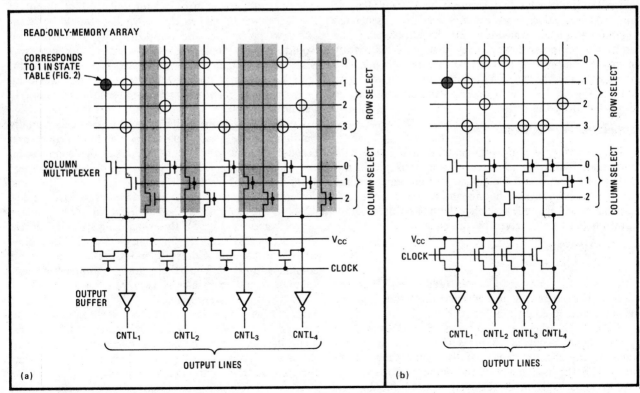

3. Squeeze play. In a read-only memory implemented with conventional techniques (a), some columns, tinted, do not contain any logical 1s. In the compressed ROM (b), these blank columns are eliminated, resulting in a smaller structure.

the encoded signals themselves about the chip, making the interconnection matrix smaller.

Recognizing the performance degradation entailed in the use of vertical microcode, Motorola, with its 68000, leaned toward a more horizontal approach[2]. It did not go all the way to a full horizontal microcode implementation, but decided to take the middle path, using a two-level approach in which an encoded 10-bit microword addresses 70-bit control microinstructions. However, the 70-bit control word needs considerable decoding before the full set of control signals can be generated.

Texas Instruments' microcode word on the 99000 is 152 bits wide and is almost totally unencoded, thereby allowing the fastest possible memory-processing cycle time—166 nanoseconds compared with 400 ns for the 10-megahertz 8086 and the 10-MHz 68000. By using a new compression technique, the 99000 winds up with a reasonably sized control store while still using an unencoded (horizontal) microcontrol word.

Column elimination

The key to this technique can be demonstrated by reviewing the application of the compression technique to a conventional unencoded ROM. A simplified ROM array of, for example, 12 words by 4 bits wide (Fig. 2) can be implemented directly with an unencoded scheme. The coding for each of these control-bit outputs is organized into three columns, or groups, of four rows, resulting in a ROM with an internal structure of four rows with three columns for each output (Fig. 3a). This ROM could be organized in a number of alternate ways, such as using six rows with two columns for each output.

Because the tinted columns in Fig. 3a will not discharge the input value to the output buffer regardless of the row-select value, those columns and their associated column-multiplexer transistors can be eliminated. The result is a compressed ROM array that produces a fully unencoded output. Thus, whenever a control signal is 0 for all states with the same column select in the state table of Fig. 2, the corresponding ROM column can be eliminated from the array.

Compression probability

However, when dealing with actual control ROMs with more than four rows for each output, it is much less likely that columns and their associated decoding transistors can be eliminated. The probability that a given column can be eliminated, assuming the bits occur randomly within the ROM is given by the equation:

$$\frac{(S-P)!(S-R)!}{((S-P)-R)!S!}$$

where S is the number of states (addresses), P is the number of occurrences of a given control signal in the memory, and R is the number of rows.

In the 99000, there are 256 states (S = 256) and the average signal occurred 18 times (P = 18). With this equation, the chance of successfully compressing a ROM varies with the assignment of the number of rows.

ROMs are usually made relatively square—roughly the same number of rows as columns—because this format helps to reduce the total amount of row-decoding and

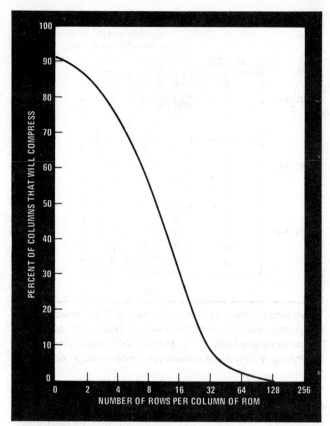

4. High stakes. Selecting the appropriate number of rows determines the probability that a column can be eliminated with the compression technique. This technique assumes a random occurrence of bits in the array, but in actual ROMs, the probability is better than shown here.

column-multiplexing overhead for a control-bit output. If the 99000 were designed this way, there would be about 128 rows per output and the probability of compression would be very low (Fig. 4). Actually, the processor achieves a minimally sized ROM with 16 rows per output (and 16 columns, in the worst case) because data compression more than adequately offsets the increases in overhead per bit.

The equation assumes that control signals occur totally randomly. This is not true for actual ROM arrays, and because they do not occur randomly, the compression can be better than that shown in Fig. 4. Although there are a number of ways to improve compression, the most powerful method is that of state-address assignment. Thus, in the example of a simplified ROM, more columns can be removed (Fig. 5). By exchanging state B (address 1) with state G (address 6), control line $CNTL_1$ is now all 0s for column address 0 and $CNTL_4$ is all 0s for column address 1. Thus there are two more removable columns, resulting in a fully compressed ROM.

Such state rearrangement is possible in the 99000 since each microword in the microprocessor contains a field that addresses the next state. Consequently, the microcontroller can jump between nonsequential ROM locations, as opposed to using a program counter to select the next address. This ability to jump anywhere in the control store directly supported state rearrangement for implementation of the compression technique.

The 99000's 256-state control store is 152 bits wide;

| | ADDRESS | | CONTROL LINES | | | | STATE |
	OLD	NEW	1	2	3	4	NAME
COLUMN 0	0	0	0	1	0	1	A
	6	1	0	0	0	1	G
	2	2	0	1	0	0	C
	3	3	0	0	1	1	D
COLUMN 1	4	4	0	0	0	0	E
	5	5	1	0	0	0	F
	1	6	1	0	0	0	B
	7	7	1	0	0	0	H
COLUMN 2	8	8	0	1	0	0	I
	9	9	0	0	0	0	J
	10	10	0	0	0	0	K
	11	11	0	0	0	0	L

5. Optimization. Rearranging the states in a control-state table lets even more columns be eliminated. In this example of state-address assignment, two additional columns can be eliminated in the final fully compressed ROM.

therefore, a noncompressed control ROM would consume 38,912 bits. However, after compression, the 99000 required only 9,792 bits, about the same as Intel's heavily encoded control store and one third that of Motorola's two-level structure.

In this way, the 99000 profits from the higher execution speed of a horizontal microcode word without suffering from its size disadvantages. Horizontal microcode also allows more control lines to be manipulated at one time, since every possible operation is simultaneously available. Thereby, throughput is increased even further. Also, because of its high-speed microcycle, only a single-level instruction-prefetch queue is required for performance that the 68000 could only achieve with two levels and the 8086 with three.

As it turns out, the compression technique works best on sparse data-storage applications such as unencoded control stores. Whereas most encoding schemes are rather arbitrary—the result of a great deal of trial and error—this compression technique is an automatic iterative algorithm. Its net result is fewer control-store bits without the additional random logic of encoded schemes.

Chip layout

With 16 rows per output in the 99000's ROM, the number of columns is large, even with compression, and so the memory array is relatively long. However, the use of a special strip chip architectural topology layout turns this into an advantage.

The SCAT approach [*Electronics*, Jan. 27, 1981, p. 107] works by running all data paths in one direction in metal and all control lines perpendicular to the data lines in polysilicon. The memory elements, registers, and ROM in this processor are only as wide as the data paths—16 bits for the 99000.

The reduced storage requirements resulting from ROM compression promote another space-saving tactic. When a microcode bit is supposed to control more than one area, it saves space just to duplicate it in the control

store in a position near the second control input, rather than route the signal across the chip. For instance, if a control signal is needed at both the top of the chip and the bottom, less real estate is used to duplicate the bit and its buffer rather than try to run a control signal all the way across the chip.

This tactic brings the length of control-signal lines to a minimum. Furthermore the 99000 has control store on both sides of the data elements so that the closest site may be chosen to store the microcontrol bit. This reduces the amount of silicon consumed by interconnnect even lower than methods that route encoded signals around the chip and use local decoders. The number of buffers needed is also smaller because only one buffer is required for each microcode bit, rather than the duplicated buffers needed for each level of a multilevel store plus those needed at the local decoder sites.

Because the compression technique can achieve a 4:1 compression ratio for unencoded bits, putting extra control lines into the control store costs less. The technique allows all control signals to be generated by the microcode word and not by random logic. Even if a control signal occurs once and only once for one state of one instruction, placing that control bit in the microcode word and compressing the state table is still more effective than a method that employs random logic and a special decoding scheme.

Microprogramming

Microprogramming a very wide control store has been considered a difficult task. However, the effectiveness of freely using control bits as needed—and letting the compression algorithm squeeze the ROM—is shown in the fact that the first pass on the 99000 instruction set was microcoded in only six man-weeks. Because relatively few rules were imposed, the microcode programmer need not be concerned with the internal architecture of the processor, because each microcode bit controls but one function.

The free use of control-bit field also opens the door to creating microcode for the 99000 with an ordinary text editor, rather than a microassembler. In fact, most of the software tools developed for the project were those that perform and evaluate the compression technique and its results. □

References
1. James McKevitt and John Bayliss, "New options from big chips," IEEE Spectrum, March 1979, p. 28.
2. Skip Stritter and Nick Tredennic, "Microprogramming implementation of a single-chip microprocessor," Proceedings of the 11th Microprogramming Workshop, December, 1978.

Fast on-chip memory extends 16-bit family's reach

When stored on the same chip as the microprocessor, frequently used routines will execute faster

by David S. Laffitte and Karl M. Guttag, *Texas Instruments Inc., Houston, Texas*

☐ In the years ahead, advances in very large-scale integration will either sink the systems designed today around current microprocessors—or bear them triumphantly into new application areas. To succeed, today's systems must be capable of stretching to accommodate increasingly fast and powerful VLSI chips as and when they arrive.

A new generation of 16-bit microprocessors under development at Texas Instruments is being designed to form the core of such evolutionary VLSI systems. The TMS 99000 series will, in addition, carry forward already existing designs based on the TMS 9900 family of microprocessors, microcomputers, and support chips, updating the 9900 architecture while retaining software compatibility with their predecessors.

The microprocessors in the 99000 series will employ the strip chip architectural topology first used extensively for the TMS 7000 8-bit microcomputers

Also their greatly optimized microcode, as well as instruction prefetching, will speed program execution. But perhaps their most distinctive feature will be what TI calls the Macrostore.

The Macrostore is a high-speed memory that can be addressed independently of main memory. Once a function has been placed in the Macrostore, it can be executed much faster than when located in the main system memory. Macrostore functions will be coded in assembly language but derive the speed with which they are executed from the faster on-chip memory—as little as 167 nanoseconds will be needed for each memory cycle.

The Macrostore memory occupies 64-K bytes, some of them on chip and the rest located off chip in fast random-access or read-only memories. It is designed specifically for frequently used operating system functions and for real-time functions that can be stored in firmware. Initially, the on-chip part of the Macrostore will consist of a 1-K-byte read-only memory, plus a 32-byte random-access memory that will serve as a high-speed register set (Fig. 1).

It will also be possible to use the Macrostore as a waystation to even higher performance by implementing the same functions in what TI is calling attached processors. Several standard functions will be offered in both the Macrostore and attached processors.

Users of the 99000 family will follow a design cycle in which the first step will be to emulate the desired function in normal memory. Once the program was debugged and verified, a production run could be scheduled to commit the program to the ROM portion of the Macrostore either on a 99000 processor itself or externally in a separate package. Alternatively, greater performance will be obtainable if the Macrostore is replaced by a dedicated attached processor.

TI plans to offer several standard solutions to common processing problems in specialized Macrostore ROMs. The 99110 will contain high-performance floating-point routines, and the 99120 will contain the kernel of TI's Real-time Executive, which supports the operating system of Microprocessor Pascal.

When operating in its standard mode, a 99000 processor will directly execute the op codes it has

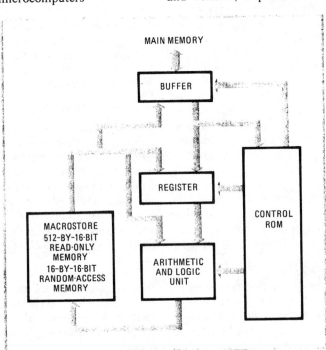

1. The Macrostore. Standard 99000 microprocessors will contain a separate on-chip address space called the Macrostore. Often used or time-critical routines can be stored there and will execute up to twice as fast as the same routines when they are kept in main system memory.

MAIN MEMORY

BUFFER

REGISTER

CONTROL ROM

MACROSTORE
512-BY-16-BIT
READ-ONLY
MEMORY
16-BY-16-BIT
RANDOM-ACCESS
MEMORY

ARITHMETIC
AND LOGIC
UNIT

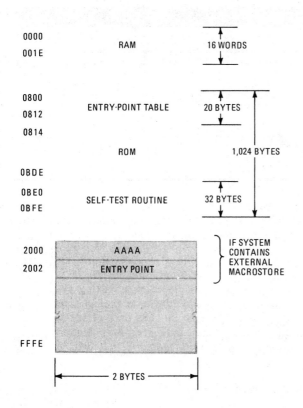

0000	RAM	16 WORDS
001E		
0800	ENTRY-POINT TABLE	20 BYTES
0812		
0814		
	ROM	1,024 BYTES
0BDE		
0BE0	SELF-TEST ROUTINE	32 BYTES
0BFE		

2000	AAAA	IF SYSTEM CONTAINS EXTERNAL MACROSTORE
2002	ENTRY POINT	
FFFE		

2 BYTES

2. Address map. The separate Macrostore address space uses the lowest 32 bytes as RAM locations that will ordinarily act as a high-speed register set. Programs may be kept in the ROM area with an entry point table indicating the starting address of each one.

in common with the 9900 series of devices as well as its new instructions. But when it recognizes an op code that is not defined, the Macrostore will become active. In this situation, the 99000 processor uses the same macroinstruction detection (MID) mechanism as the 9995 processor [*Electronics*, Dec. 18, 1980, p. 91].

Upon encountering an MID op code in the user's program in main memory, it will first interrogate its bus to determine if an attached processor is present to service the request. If none is present, it will check the on-chip Macrostore, and if that does not contain the routine, it will check the external Macrostore. If that search, too, should fail, it will trap to interrupt for conventional software emulation or illegal op-code error detection. Otherwise, it carries out a number of actions in the Macrostore.

Inside the Macrostore

First, the 99000 searches the entry point table in the on-chip Macrostore ROM to find the starting address of the appropriate routine. If found, it makes a context switch similar to a 9900's. The speed of this operation — a minimum of 14 machine states or 2.33 microseconds — has long been one of the hallmarks of TI microprocessors. Once the return address, or program counter (PC), the workspace pointer (WP), and the status register (ST) have been stored in the last three locations of the on-chip RAM, control is transferred to the Macrostore routine. Upon completion of the function, another context switch

returns control to the calling program in main memory.

The 99000 complete Macrostore address space is shown in Fig. 2, with the off-chip portion located above 2000_{16}. The first 32 bytes are high-speed RAM and are normally used to hold the 16 general-purpose 16-bit registers. The work-space register set may alternatively be located in off chip RAM, which must be fast if the high-speed edge is not to be lost.

Next, starting at 800_{16}, come 1,024 bytes of on-chip ROM. The Macrostore routines in this ROM are entered via an entry-point table that stores the address of each.

Normally, accesses to the Macrostore, whether on or off chip, will take place within a single machine cycle (167 ns with a 6-megahertz four-phase clock). However, users will be able to add external memory with longer access times very simply, by using the ready line to insert wait states.

There is no need for the main memory to be homogeneous. Fast bipolar chips may be used for time-critical segments, and less exacting routines may be located in cheaper, slower memories. That memory partitioning will enable systems designers to trade off speed for cost and the lower power consumption of MOS memories.

It is unnecessary to have large amounts of high-speed memory in order to take advantage of the 99000's high throughput. If frequently used sections of code are stored in fast memory, the average execution time of programs can be significantly reduced. It should be noted that relatively small caches, on the order of 512 words, can have 90% or higher hit ratios — the percentage of memory requests for information located in the cache. (Of the microprocessors in Table 2, only the 99000 is designed to exploit fast cache memories.)

The prototyping mode

Before committing to the large production runs necessary to mask-program the Macrostore ROM, a user will be able to emulate and debug that operation in a special prototyping mode. In this mode, external RAM and/or ROM replaces the internal memory. The same mode may even be used to start low-volume production, giving way to the on-chip ROM only when the volume demand makes that option cost-effective.

The prototyping mode is a pin-programmable function that maps the lower Macrostore ROM locations into an off-chip memory of the user's choice. In this way users will be able to experiment inexpensively with the 99000 processor to evolve custom forms that are particularly suited to their applications by only adding ROM — since the high-speed on-chip RAM is still available.

Other improvements

Figure 3 is a block diagram of the microprocessors in the 99000 family. Strip chip architectural topology (SCAT) lines up all register and memory elements in strips and passes all control and data interconnections over them, saving silicon and shrinking die size. Such a design gives the 99000 series a radically different die layout from the 9900 series.

Still, the processors in the new series will use the same 69 instructions as those in the old series, adding several new ones to bring the total to 85. The 4 operations that

TABLE 1: STEPS IN MICROINSTRUCTION SEQUENCE				
STEP NO.	OPERATION	STATE COUNT	MEMORY CYCLE	INTERNAL FUNCTION
1.	FETCH INSTRUCTION	4	FETCH INSTRUCTION	PROCESS PREVIOUS OPERANDS
2.	DECODE INSTRUCTION	1	WRITE RESULTS	DECODE INSTRUCTION
3.	FETCH SOURCE OPERAND	2	FETCH SOURCE	
4.	FETCH DESTINATION OPERAND	3	FETCH DESTINATION	
5.	PROCESS THE OPERANDS	4	FETCH NEXT INSTRUCTION	ADD OPERANDS
6.	STORE THE RESULTS	1	WRITE RESULTS	DECODE INSTRUCTION

were added to the 9995, including signed multiplication and division, are employed, but 12 others are completely new to the 99000.

Included in the 12 are 4 32-bit operations that can streamline floating-point routines: shift left, shift right, add, and subtract. There are also 3 new bit-manipulation instructions to set, clear, and test specified bits in the main memory space. Two stack manipulation instructions allow the 99000 to conveniently push and pop multiple stacks that can be located anywhere in memory. The remaining 3 new instructions are dedicated to communicating with the 74610 memory mapper, which expands the basic 64-K-byte address space to 16 megabytes using a segmentation methodology.

Besides the high speed of Macrostore accesses, a 99000 processor will use several other techniques for faster execution speeds. Whenever possible, op codes and operands are prefetched from memory while the processor is working internally.

Smarter pipelining

Unlike some other prefetching 16-bit processors, the 99000s will have some intelligence built into this pipelining process. For instance, branch instructions are often troublesome to a prefetching scheme since the next instruction need not come from the next location in physical memory. On 99000 processors, however, the microcode that executes all branch and jump instructions will inform the prefetching unit of the true next instruction location. In fact, only an interrupt will be able to cause the prefetcher to discard a prefetched item.

The prefetching scheme overlaps two successive bus cycles whenever possible, eliminating the time required to fetch an op code. For example, precessing an instruction to add involves the sequence of six steps outlined in Table 1. The prefetch mechanism recognizes that, while operands are being added (step 5), the memory bus is inactive and therefore can be used to prefetch the next instruction's op code. Then while the result of the current instruction is being stored, the prefetched op code is decoded. Thus all six steps are performed by the processor in only four machine cycles since in the first and fourth states both an internal operation and a memory bus transfer are made.

Microprogrammed

Microcode in a separate control ROM defines the operations that must be performed in order to execute each assembly-language instruction. The microinstructions specify the control signal states that manage the processor's arithmetic and logic unit, its internal registers, and its input/output operations. Each microinstruction is active for one machine cycle, or four cycles of the input clock. In fact, a microprogrammed processor is something like a computer within a computer. The smaller one consists of the microcode itself plus the mechanisms that apply a sequence of microinstructions to the control lines themselves. The length of time that a microinstruction remains active depends on the frequency of the processor's clock. For example, each microinstruction would last 167 ns for a 24-MHz input clock from which a four-phase, 6-MHz internal clock is derived.

Several microinstructions will be needed to execute a

TABLE 2: MACHINE CYCLES NEEDED BY 99000 AND OTHER MICROPROCESSORS TO EXECUTE TYPICAL INSTRUCTIONS				
Instruction and addressing modes / Microprocessor	99000	68000	8086	Z8000
Move register to register	3	2	2	3
Move memory to memory	5	10	29	20
Move register to register, indirectly autoincrementing each	9	6	18	20
Add register to register	4	2	3	4
Add memory to register	5	6	15	9
Jump relative	3	5	16	6
Signed multiply register to register	25	35	128 to 154	70
Signed divide register to register	34	79	165 to 184	95

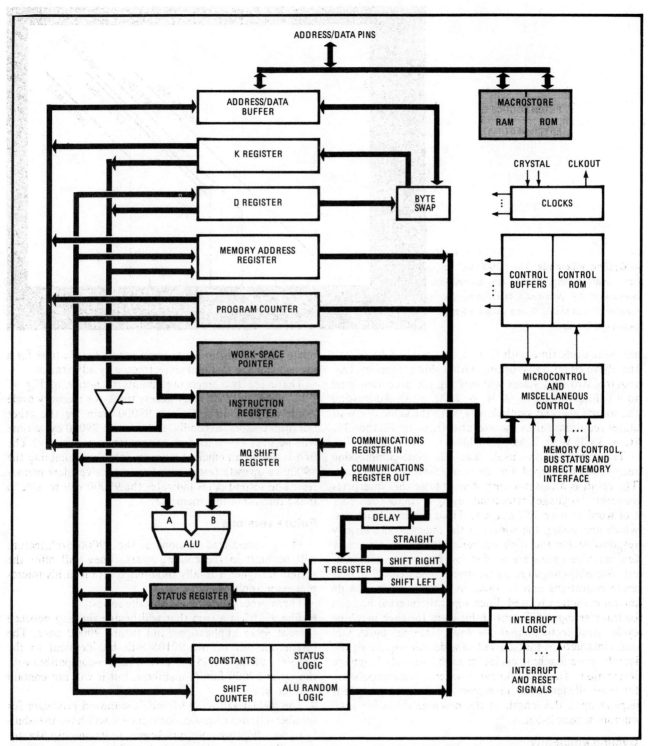

3. Internal architecture. Like its predecessor, the 99000 does not rely on an internal register set, but allows access only to the program counter, status register, and workspace pointer. The last of these indicates where in main memory the 16 contiguous registers are located.

single assembly-language instruction, and TI will make available a table listing the number of machine cycles and memory accesses needed for each 99000 family instruction. The total execution time, T, for any instruction may be computed from:

$$T = t_c(C + WM)$$

where

t_c = the machine cycle time

C = the number of machine states needed to execute the instruction and modify the associated addresses

W = the number of wait states per memory access

M = the number of memory accesses.

For example, when memory is accessed without wait states and both operands are in work-space registers, executing a move instruction (MOV) could take as little as 500 ns in a system operating at the maximum design clock frequency of 24 MHz. This would yield a 167-ns

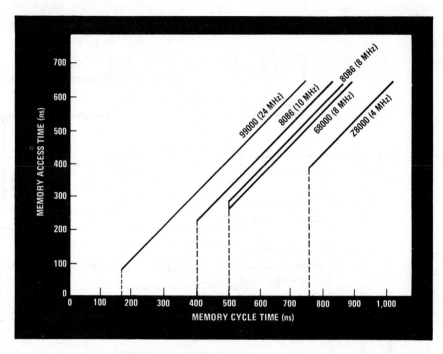

4. Cycling efficiently. The 99000 will accommodate a range of memory speeds as determined by processor clock rate and number of wait states. Some values are projected in this graph.

machine cycle time with C = 3, W = 0 and M = 3 in the above equation. Working with a slower memory that requires two wait states will prolong the execution time to 9 t_c intervals (C = 3, W = 2, M = 3). Addressing the source operand symbolically, with the same two wait states required, raises the execution time by another 3 t_c (C = 3 + 1, W = 2, M = 3 + 1).

The control ROM itself uses the code-compression techniques developed for all new 16-bit TI processors. The result is a faster-acting, denser ROM that interprets assembly-language instructions using a microcoded control word of over 150 outputs. These microinstructions, which are among the widest in the industry, are largely responsible for the high efficiency of the device—very few machine cycles are needed for it to do the commonest assembly-language instructions. The reason is that more operations can be done in parallel when a wide microinstruction is used. Each separate internal bus can be transferring a different 16-bit word for each machine cycle. Architectures that use fewer internal buses and microinstructions that are not so wide will require significantly more machine cycles for each assembly-language instruction. Table 2 compares several microprocessors for their efficiency in this respect. The execution speeds depend upon the length of the machine cycle for each microprocessor listed.

Cycling efficiently

The relationship between the memory access time— the time needed to fetch data from a memory location— and the memory cycle time—the time from the start of one memory cycle to the start of the next—is the factor limiting efficient use of memory. Generally, the memory access time is determined by the memory subsystem itself, while the cycle time is adjusted to fit.

Two methods are used to extend a microprocessor's memory cycle: either wait states can be added to the access portion of the cycles or the clock frequency can be adjusted to the processor. The curves in Fig. 4 show the average relationship between access and cycle time for a range of wait states and clock frequency adjustment.

There are two important points to notice in Fig. 4. First, for a given memory access time, the memory cycle time can be shorter for the 99000 than for the other microprocessors. Secondly, the shortest 99000 cycle time will be over twice as fast as the other processors'. The first is due to an efficient memory interface, enabling the 99000 to operate faster with less expensive, slow memories. The second point indicates the 99000 will be able to make full use of fast memories.

Future versions

Many specialized versions of the 99000 architecture will be built in the coming years. They will offer the system designer a totally modular solution to his microprocessor application.

Three processors will pioneer the series:

■ The 99105 is a part that will bridge the gap between current 9995 applications and future 99000 ones. The instruction set of the 99105 will be identical to the 9995's, and the 99105 device will be pin-compatible with the other 99000 family members, but it will not contain a Macrostore.

■ The 99110 will be the family's standard processor for number-intensive applications since it will have the ability to do a floating-point arithmetic in its on-chip Macrostore. This part will not only free the programmer from the need to write floating-point routines but will also reduce the time needed to the execute those functions.

■ The 99120 will be the standard processor for applications requiring intensive use of TI's Micropascal system function. Its on-chip Macrostore will contain the kernel of TI's Real-time Executive.

All 99000 devices will initially employ the scaled n-channel MOS technology called SMOS and use 3-micrometer or less design rules. They will be supplied in 40-pin packages that multiplex the data and address lines and will operate off a single 5-V supply. □

Electronics/September 22, 1982

Functional cells support 16-bit CPU to create alterable microcomputer

Extensive design-tool software draws hardware elements from library, creating custom single-chip systems

by H. Lyle Supp, *American Microsystems Inc., a subsidiary of Gould Inc., Santa Clara, Calif.*

☐ Frustrated by microprocessor chips that are either too general-purpose or too dedicated for their needs, micro-system designers are feeling an ever stronger urge to get their hands on the inner workings of these very large-scale integrated circuits. A new fully alterable micro-computer (AMU) gives them that freedom.

Complete with a library of standard hardware cells and software support for implementing systems, the AMU design procedure yields a device with the same degree of functional capability as a standard microcomputer chip yet with the specificity and efficiency of custom parts. Moreover, the process is in line with the trend toward increasing the productivity of the VLSI designer, which is expected to rise from the present level of 50 transistors a day to 10,000 a day by the end of the present decade.

This semicustom approach of combining functional cells with efficient computer-aided design tools seeks a middle ground between a pure custom product and a standard part: it unites optimized subsystem perform-ance with quick turnaround, low cost, and proven subsys-tem design. Dodging the potential risks and costs of a fully custom design, this method opens new markets and applications to the possibilities of a solution resembling a custom one. Though development costs and times must still be considered, they are much less significant. Turna-round times of two to three months and costs of less than $30,000 will be common by the mid-1980s.

A cellular architecture

At the heart of the AMU concept is a modular archi-tecture and structured approach for the independent design of stand-alone functional cells. Furthermore, a flexible interface allows the modules or cells to be quick-ly and efficiently integrated on one piece of silicon. The use of a complementary-MOS process is also integral to the AMU design concept, providing the flexibility to handle the greatest number of digital and analog func-tions while retaining low cost and high performance. Finally, as the backbone of the design methodology, CAD tools facilitate designing unique functional cells and

integrating them quickly into a single design (Table 1).

The AMU's library of standard functional cells has the architecture and—more importantly—the topology to help system architects implement their designs easily and quickly in silicon. Using the S9900 instruction set with hardware multiplication and division, a 16-bit central processing unit serves as the keystone in an alterable microcomputer system. This C-MOS micropro-cessor is well-suited for real-time process-control appli-cations needing low power and high computational abili-ty. Since the CPU functions as a logically cohesive unit, it forms a single functional cell in the AMU library.

Along with memory—combinations of a 4-byte ran-dom-access memory cell and a 64-byte read-only memo-ry cell—the CPU forms a core surrounded by the required special-purpose cells (see Fig. 1). While the CPU and memory core form a powerful microcomputer themselves, most special-purpose functions needing a dedicated microcomputer tend to be input/output-inten-sive operations, often with data paths that do not fit the usual 8-bit or 16-bit mold. With the modular design concept of the AMU, the designer may build up the required I/O data paths by cascading a number of more

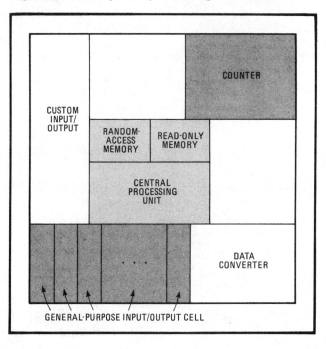

1. Configurable. Designers draw from a library of standard cells to build their custom system around a central core (shaded). Many kinds of input/output architectures can be constructed on the basis of the general-purpose input/output cell.

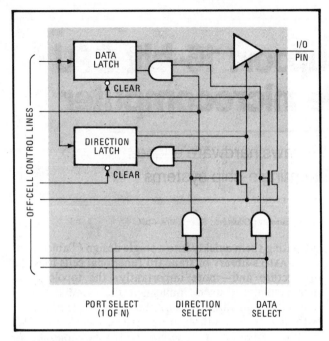

 itself shows the figure with labels:

DATA LATCH

CLEAR

DIRECTION LATCH

CLEAR

OFF-CELL CONTROL LINES

I/O PIN

PORT SELECT (1 OF N)

DIRECTION SELECT

DATA SELECT

2. General purpose. This basic design for a bidirectional input/output cell serves as a basic building block in constructing a custom 16-bit microcomputer. Computer-aided-design tools handle the linking of several such functional cells into larger blocks.

"primitive" functions to arbitrary sizes.

For example, the general-purpose I/O module (Fig. 2) is a single-bit bidirectional cell that may be repeated in the AMU system to form I/O paths of the desired width. Its ability to drive both C-MOS and TTL allows the designer to treat this relatively low-level design issue at the modular level by using this same cell for either interface function.

Other bricks

Besides CPU, memory, and general-purpose I/O cells, the library already includes another major cell—a versatile counter cell that can provide a variety of functions

having to do with system timing. Other major cells, such as a serial communications cell and several analog cells, will soon be added to the catalog of functional elements.

In addition, several minor cells are in the library. These include a clock generator cell, a clock driver cell, an oscillator cell, a data-pad driver cell, an address-pad driver cell, and a general-purpose–pad driver cell.

To reduce the risks perceived by the designer in creating a custom microcomputer, each functional cell is packaged separately. This setup makes it feasible to create a prototype that is functionally and parametrically identical with the circuit when all the individual cells are integrated onto a single piece of silicon.

CAD software

But the workhorse in using the library and designing new custom cells and in subsequent AMU integration is AMI's CAD Technology (Act) software system (Table 1) for MOS VLSI design. Using a common data base called Bolt, Act meets the challenge of design from logic design and simulation through mask layout to subsystem test. The cell structure supported by Bolt allows design engineers to manipulate function and custom cells and to describe the chip logic in hierarchical terms, preserving the structured methodology of the AMU.

Design follows an iterative process of logic description and evaluation through simulation until a satisfactory set of design specifications emerges. Act software gets to work at the top level in the design cycle with Simad, a simulator with assignable propagation delays that simulates the logic network behavior for logic design verification and also develops a functional test pattern for later use in testing the completed chip. For this purpose, Simad simulates both unidirectional and bidirectional MOS transmission gates, accounting for delays of different duration that may be assigned to the various gates.

In addition to the detail from Simad, designers learn critical path information from Path, the path analysis timing verification program. Path traces a design, searching for paths with a cumulative propagation delay exceeding specified limits. With this information, the design may be tuned to minimize sensitivities due to variations in the fabrication process. Actual layout of a custom function cell is done symbolically using Sids, the symbolic interactive design system. Once the actual layout is complete and the masks have been designed, the delay parameters are recalculated using capacitance values extracted from the layout. Path can be run again with this updated information to provide a more accurate picture of the delay of the design.

This iterative check on the design's performance is supported by two additional Act routines, called Delay and Capacitance. The Capacitance program extracts the capacitance parameters for each circuit node from the mask. Delay calculates even more accurate propagation delay values and maps these values back into the Bolt logic description.

TABLE 1: ELEMENTS OF THE ACT COMPUTER-AIDED DESIGN SOFTWARE		
Design area	**Element**	**Acronym**
Common data base	block-oriented logic translator (compiler)	Bolt
Logic design	simulator with assignable propagation delays	Simad
	PATH analysis timing verification program	Path
	register transfer language simulation	RTL
	propagation delay calculation from mask layout capacitance	Delay
Circuit design	circuit simulator	AMI Spice AMI Aspec
	switched-capacitor analysis routine	Scar
	pole-zero location analysis	PZSLIC
Mask design	topological layout planning aid for full custom plus automatic or interactive placement and routing of cells, both variable- and fixed-height	LPA/Cipar
	symbolic interactive design system for full custom mask design, including design-rule and continuity checking	Sids
	capacitance calculation from mask layout	Capacitance
Test design	test-pattern generator to format compressed test patterns	Testgen
	test-program generation	Testpro
	fault simulator	Faultsim

3. Design support. Revolving around a central data base, the design methodology for the alterable microcomputer is carried by a sturdy backbone of computer-aided-design software tools that handle design, layout, and subsequent circuit testing.

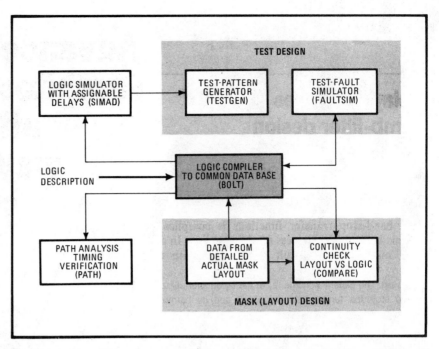

At the transistor level, AMI-Spice simulates the behavior of the circuit on the basis of process-technology parameters. For linear circuits there is a program called PZSLIC, for pole zero analysis, which performs a frequency-domain analysis of a proposed design. Another program, Scar, verifies the satisfactory performance of the switched-capacitor elements, of the kind used for analog-to-digital conversion. Thus the Act software forms a detailed picture of the performance of the proposed design. Once an acceptable circuit design exists and the logic description is in the Bolt language, the designer has all the power of the Act system to speed the rest of the design cycle (Fig. 3).

The mask stage

Moving a design to the mask stage has required months and even years of effort from layout artists in the past. Several software tools in Act relieve the designer of this burden.

At the upper level in AMU's hierarchical design strategy, several tools aid in construction of the chip. A program called LPA/Cipar (see Table 1) is first used as a layout planning aid to develop the chip plan—the allocation of silicon for the various cells—and to route the interconnections. LPA/Cipar efficiently places the variably sized rectangular blocks used in the AMU design and routes the connections between them.

LPA/Cipar can also pack the block shape for a custom-designed functional cell, ensuring its snug fit with other cells from the library during automatic placement. For functional cells constructed of more basic standard cells, Cipar is used to place and route the interior of the cell. Thus LPA/Cipar takes a validated logic description of a circuit from the Bolt data base and combines it with the chip plan to produce an error-free pattern-generator tape—used to cast the final design into silicon. Sids

supports the layout designer with creation of the cell mask design by graphically manipulating the cell design on a large-screen color cathode-ray tube. Besides checking continuity of the cell design, Sids checks conformance with the process design rules both on any single mask level and between mask levels.

Testing

Although this may seem to complete the story for chip design, Act goes one step further to complete production of a chip. Two test-program development tools, Testpro and Testgen, are used to create Fairchild Factor test programs and functional test patterns for the Fairchild Sentry test systems. In addition, the Fault Simulator, Faultsim, determines the quality of the functional test patterns. Moreover, since custom functional cells are supplied prepackaged, the system designer may construct the proposed system and test it in real time before casting it in silicon.

By providing the individual characterization of the functional cells in this way, the AMU approach resembles the modular methods used by software engineers. Just as software systems became so large that such techniques became the rule, large-system design demands a modular approach to increase designers' productivity and hardware testability and reliability. Thus, this intermediate design step helps ensure the functioning of the individual cells and their interaction through a set of well-defined inputs and outputs—just as in software modular programming—prior to committing to the fully integrated system.

Each cell is designed for implementation in a dual-polysilicon C-MOS process that may use either p or n wells. In the future, it will be possible to fabricate alterable microcomputers with a twin-tub C-MOS process. Furthermore, the fact that the design is fully static grants wide operating margin, consistent yields, and the ability to slow the operating frequency of the chips to zero without loss of any RAM data. □

TABLE 2: ALTERABLE MICROCOMPUTER FUNCTIONAL CELLS		
Cell	Size (mil²)	Typical power dissipation (μW)
Central processing unit	24,700	1,000
Single-bit general-purpose input/output	450	100
Counter	4,200	150
Random-access memory (4 bytes)	525	100
Read-only memory (64 bytes)	555	100
RAM/ROM (4/64 bytes)	1,080	200

Electronics/June 16, 1983

Advanced parallel architectures get attention as way to faster computing

by Tom Manuel
Computers & Peripherals Editor

Very large-scale integration, more funding could assist massively parallel designs in breaking out of the laboratory

The next act in the continuing drama of very high-speed computation will likely see the introduction of what is being called the fifth-generation computer, and it almost surely will represent a sharp break with the past. Novel architectures for parallel processing are being readied, mostly in university laboratories.

Four generations of computer electronics spanning less than 40 years are generally recognized: vacuum tubes, transistors, integrated circuits, and very large-scale integrated circuits. These generations have increased computer performance seven orders of magnitude while dramatically reducing the cost. Yet there is a need for a speed hike of up to three orders of magnitude in this decade to solve ever more complex problems in physics, aerodynamics, ballistics, meteorology, image and voice processing, knowledge processing, artificial intelligence, and other disciplines.

The common computer architecture in use today has not changed fundamentally in the 35 or so years since it was first developed by John von Neumann. But now there is a revolution afoot in large-scale computing, and the main strategy is to divide and conquer—to divide up the work among many processors and conquer the shortcomings in the von Neumann architecture.

In this classic architecture, a single processor is fed a single stream of instructions with the order of their execution controlled by a program counter (Fig. 1). At any one time, only one instruction of the program is being acted upon. In addition, almost all of today's programming languages faithfully follow this sequential model. This almost total reliance on machines and languages based on the von Neumann principles has led computing down a dead-end street, albeit a long one.

The stored-program von Neumann computer, also called a control-flow computer, has proved a powerful tool because of its very general nature. But the machine's serial nature is a major bottleneck for high-speed processing, relieved to some extent by such important refinements as fetching and decoding the instructions in a pipeline and the minimal use of multiple processors.

Indeed, the fact that computers have achieved dramatic advances despite a fundamentally unchanged architecture is due almost solely to the incredible effort and expense that have been, and are continuing to be, applied to electronics to make the machines run faster. But the restrictions inherent in sequential operation place fundamental limitations on how much longer this can continue.

To many researchers, the obvious answer is to go to parallel processing, to have many things happening at once (Fig. 2). However, in the words of John Darlington of the Department of Computing, Imperial College, London, "if we attempt to do this while still following the von Neumann model and, more importantly, are attempting to execute von Neumann–based languages that are inherently

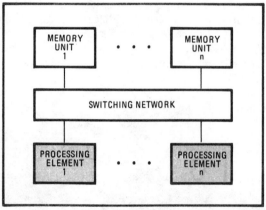

1. Traditional. Almost all computers now in use follow this traditional architectural model set forth by John von Neumann. Instructions are fetched, decoded, and executed one at a time under control of a single program counter.

2. Radical. Parallel architectures involve multiple processors, one or many shared memories, and a fast, interconnecting switching network. To achieve the most parallelism, various methods of program control are being tried.

sequential, we run into severe difficulties. Extensive coordination and communication is needed between processors to ensure that different parts of the program are executed in the sequence prescribed, and this soon outweighs the gains involved." These hurdles have stimulated research into parallel processing in radically new hardware and software architectures.

This extensive research has been going on for a long time, making what seems like frustratingly slow progress. And most researchers in the field and experts in industry admit that much more work has yet to be done. Research on advanced parallel hardware and software architectures deserves and needs more support and attention to fulfill its promise.

Designs for faster processing can be roughly divided into three groups. The first group contains those computers designed around an extremely fast single processor in a control-flow architecture. Many groups are hard at work on it. Some examples are recent developments in Josephson junctions, gallium arsenide circuits, and denser packaging, plus the U.S. Department of Defense–sponsored Very High-Speed Integrated Circuits (VHSIC) program and the British Very High-Performance Integrated Circuit (VHPIC) effort. This approach

to faster processing is primarily what the research departments of all the world's major computer companies are working on because clearly they need to retain compatibility with their existing systems.

The second approach is to use a few very fast processors and then enhance the control-flow architecture with pipelines, vectoring, and some specialized processors. This is the primary research direction at the supercomputer companies, such as Cray Research and Control Data Corp. in the U.S. and Hitachi Ltd., Fujitsu Ltd., and NEC Corp. in Japan. The same techniques, in fact, are being applied in high-performance microsystems.

The third option is to take a huge number of fast or medium-speed processors and arrange them in a parallel architecture and perhaps put several hundred of them on one wafer. This approach is primarily the research domain of the universities, with Inmos plc and General Electric Co. Ltd. in the UK, Nippon Telegraph & Telephone Public Corp. in Japan, and Denelcor Inc. in Aurora, Colo., being current commercial exceptions. One parallel architecture, data-flow, is very attractive conceptually. In the simplest terms, data flow is a concept for control of execution of computer instructions such that these are executed as soon as the input data they require is available; no program counter is used. The concept has been the basis of most parallel architecture research at many laboratories in the U.S., Europe, and Japan. A data-flow machine automatically exploits the parallelism inherent in problems because all instructions for which data is available can be executed at the same time—if enough processors are available.

A number of parallel architecture projects are in high gear in five countries. The rest of this special report will examine some of these research projects, country by country. The focus of the report is mainly on the hardware, but of course major overhauls of software to fully use the new parallelism are badly needed and are being studied. After all, multiple processors can do a job faster only if they all can be kept busy.

A plethora of projects in the U.S. try data-flow and other architectures

Many universities and three commercial companies are searching for novel ways to speed up computers

Perhaps the most fertile environment for research into advanced parallel architectures is in U.S. universities. A by-no-means complete list includes: work at the Massachusetts Institute of Technology; the Parafrase software and the Cedar machine projects at the University of Illinois; a reconfigurable array computer at the University of Texas; two projects at Purdue University; a unique project at the University of North Carolina; and New York University's Ultracomputer. Not all of these ideas may reach fruition, though, for funding is notably scarce. Some research is also under way at commercial computer makers, but this work tends to be honing of the von Neumann concept, rather than investigation of the data-flow and other parallel concepts.

The drag that lack of funding has induced in almost all university parallel-architecture projects is apparent at MIT in Cambridge, Mass., where Jack Dennis, the father of data flow, started a project in 1967 to develop a data-flow supercomputer and produce software

for it. An engineering model with eight processors is in operation. Dennis's team is ready to produce a design for a large data-flow machine that can be built in the next five years. What the project needs now is, first, some sponsors, then, more staff. To get the highest performance, fully custom very large-scale integrated circuits would be best, but it may be easier and quicker to start with gate arrays or standard cells, Dennis feels.

As for software, he says, "we know how we expect to structure programs and languages." A high-level programming language for data flow, a value-added algorith-

David Kuck

Daniel Gajski

Duncan Lawrie

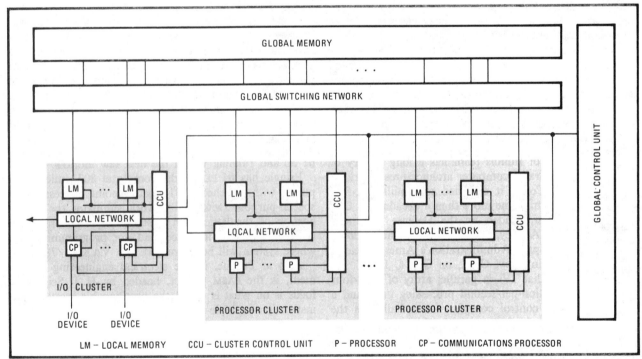

1. Cedar. The Cedar machine, with two levels of clustered processors, was designed by the team of Kuck, Gajski, and Lawrie at the University of Illinois. It will use von Neumann control within a processor cluster, but the clusters will be data-flow–controlled.

metic language called VAL, has also been developed.

Taking an different approach, with one goal being to save the multitude of programs written in Fortran, the Parafrase project at the University of Illinois, Champaign-Urbana, has for the past 10 years been working out the automated restructuring of ordinary Fortran programs for parallel, pipelined, and multiprocessor systems. Fortran is by far the dominant language of scientific computation, and there are many researchers who are not yet ready to scrap it. Parafrase has been tested and refined through measurements taken on 2,500 Fortran programs.

Out of this software work comes a hardware project called Cedar, a two-level multiprocessor design (Fig. 1). At the top level, processor clusters are interconnected by a global switching network, and control is handled by a global control unit using data-flow techniques. At the second level, each processor cluster has local memories and processors interconnected through a local network and controlled in a conventional von Neumann fashion with a cluster control unit. A prototype has been designed in detail and a schedule for its production worked out, but realization depends upon funding, which is being pursued.

The Cedar team, including principal researchers Daniel Gajski, David Kuck, and Duncan Lawrie, also expects that its work will ultimately lead to the development of a high-speed machine by a commercial company working in partnership with the university. Indeed, the schedule calls for early 1990 development of a multigigaflop machine capable of processing many billions of floating-point instructions each second.

Pioneering work

The University of Illinois team has a long history of experience with parallel computer architectures. Working with Burroughs Corp., it designed and built the first massively parallel machine more than a decade ago. One Illiac IV computer, funded by the Defense Advanced Research Projects Agency, was delivered to the National Aeronautics and Space Administration's Ames Research Center in Mountain View, Calif., on Oct. 4, 1972.

At that time, Illiac IV—a parallel array of sixty-four 4.5-million-instruction-per-second processing units and a Burroughs B6700 control computer—was hailed as the first of a new breed of computer architecture. But no more were built, largely because programming to keep all processors busy proved an overwhelming burden but also because of reliability problems with processors made from the electronic technology of the late 1960s.

2. TRAC. A model of the Texas Reconfigurable Array Computer is being held here by project leader Jack Lipovski. TRAC is a three-tier network of processors (top), switches (middle), and memories (bottom), capable of assuming a variety of configurations.

More up to date than Illiac IV and somewhat further along than Cedar is the Texas Reconfigurable Array Computer. A team at the University of Texas in Austin has a prototype of TRAC running now, and a Pascal compiler for the four-processor, nine-memory module prototype is also available (Fig. 2). The design of this engineering model can be easily scaled up to many processors and memories. Because it is based on dynamically coupling processors, input/output units, and memories in a variety of configurations using an intelligent, switching network that is called a banyan switch, TRAC can implement many different models of advanced architectures—that is, the configuration can be changed on the fly to suit the structure of the problem. For example, enhanced von Neumann architectures using lots of pipelining—the technique whereby different steps in the preparation and execution of instructions can be done simultaneously, as on a production line in a factory—and the non–von Neumann tree-structure and data-flow structures can all be formed and tested within this variable configuration.

Perhaps advancing the most quickly is the less-than-two-year-old project at Purdue University in West Lafayette, Ind. The Blue CHiP (for configurable highly parallel computer) project, headed by Lawrence Snyder, is a collection of homogenous processing elements (PEs) placed at regular intervals in a lattice of programmable switches (Fig. 3). Each PE is a computer with its own local memory. This architecture is targeted at wafer-scale implemention, but until that can be done, a computer that looks like a true CHiP machine is needed for further research. Such a pre-prototype system, built from conventional components and called Pringle, is expected to be up and running within the next few months.

Pringle has 64 PEs made from Intel 8031 microcomputers with attached 8231 floating-point processors. A special-purpose switching network simulates the switch portion of the lattice. An 8086 processor is used as a controller and I/O interface, and, for programming, the whole system will be connected to a VAX 11/780.

Also at Purdue, in the electrical engineering department, is the PASM project, headed by H. J. Seigel. Its focus is on what is called the partitionable-array single-instruction–multiple-data and multiple-instruction–multiple-data (SIMD-MIMD) computer, from which the name PASM comes. The machine could take several guises: it might be a shared-memory configuration or a distributed machine or a collection of clusters of shared-memory machines because it can be dynamically reconfigured—

somewhat like TRAC—into one or more machines.

At the heart of the system is a specially designed parallel computation unit and a high-speed intelligent network. To be built primarily for image-processing, pattern-recognition, and speech-processing applications, PASM is designed to function with a maximum of 1,024 CPUs. A prototype using 25 MC68000s has been designed, and funding to build it is being sought from the usual Government sources and industry. The 1,024-processor PASM "is a nice way to use VLSI when it comes to fruition," according to Seigel, who would like to take advantage of custom VLSI for the big machine. He and his team are working on a PASM operating system and also on a parallel C language.

A non–von Neumann computer that is not a data-flow machine is under way at the University of North Carolina at Chapel Hill. There Gyula Magó and his team have designed a binary tree computer—actually an inverted-tree configuration (Fig. 4), with processors at the leaves and resource controllers at the interior nodes and root. Expressions are stored in the linear array of processor cells, which include memory. The processor cells are directly connected to their immediate neighbors to facilitate data movement within the linear array. The resource controllers cooperate with their neighbors in a largely asynchronous fashion to achieve distributed control.

A computational cycle in the Magó machine consists of a number of waves of expressions and control information that sweep down from the root and are reflected upwards by the leaves. During the passage down and up the tree, the wave exchanges control and data information with the interior nodes and processor and memory cells along the way. A variable number of sweeps is required to execute a basic Magó machine cycle.

The Magó machine is a language-driven architecture, inspired by and implementing a formal functional programming (FFP) language. Computer scientist John Backus first proposed FFP languages in 1978 as a means of liberating programming from the von Neumann straitjacket. The machine's architecture implements FFP directly, meaning there is no need for an operating system nor for an intermediate language.

In an FFP language, expressions containing both program and data are applications, sequences of other expressions, or numbers (constants). An FFP expression is executed by reducing applications within it until only irreducible expressions (constants) remain. Only innermost expressions can be reduced, but all of them can be reduced in any order or all at once, providing the opportunity for parallelism.

Though not yet realised in hardware, this highly original architecture has been simulated with excellent results. The regular pattern of only two element types—processors and resource controllers—lends itself to VLSI implementation, and funding has been requested from the National Science Foundation to do just that. The chips would be designed and built at the university's Microelectronics Systems Laboratory.

Another as-yet unbuilt machine is the New York University Ultracomputer, a project under the direction of Prof. Allan Gottlieb. This highly parallel MIMD machine aims to combine hundreds or thousands of small, relatively conventional processing elements, all using a large shared memory. Processors will communicate with memory through a very high-bandwidth switching network, which executes a few operations vital to ultraparallel interprocess synchronization, in addition to its basic data-routing function

Hanging onto Fortran

Operating systems with structures suitable for efficient operation on this architecture have been studied, but no choice has been made yet. Also, there is a detailed design for a switching chip for the high-speed switching net. Simulations of scientific applications show that the machine can be programmed with relatively conventional techniques, such as a slightly extended version of Fortran, and still succeed in keeping the processor multitude busy all the time.

Nonetheless, the commercial supercomputer industry remains somewhat skeptical of the high utilization, or efficiency, of these massively parallel research architectures. At Cray Research Inc. in Minneapolis, Peter A. Gregory, vice president of planning and corporate development, articulates an "I'll believe it when I see it" point of view toward the massively parallel architecture projects of the universities. Such machines have "been a dream for 20 years," says Gregory, noting that they

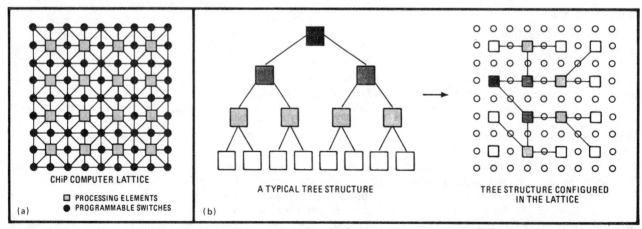

CHiP COMPUTER LATTICE

□ PROCESSING ELEMENTS
● PROGRAMMABLE SWITCHES

(a)

A TYPICAL TREE STRUCTURE

(b)

TREE STRUCTURE CONFIGURED IN THE LATTICE

3. Blue CHiP. Another type of configurable parallel computer is the Blue CHiP lattice of Purdue University. The lattice of processors and switches (a) is quite general; however, particular structures, such as a typical tree structure (b), can be set up by programming the switches.

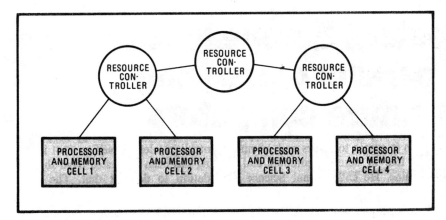

"always look very attractive" from a theoretical viewpoint. Except for very specialized applications, no such machines have been successful for real-world jobs, he observes.

The major problem "that's likely to sink you" with large numbers of small processors running in parallel involves the software and communications overhead in keeping all the processors properly synchronized and working efficiently on a problem, he says. Gregory points to his company's X-MP, a dual-processor machine planned for initial delivery this year, and the Cray-2, a four-processor supercomputer planned for first deliveries in 1985, as representative of pioneering work in the use of small numbers of very fast processors in parallel .

The maximum number of processors to which the multiple–large-processor approach can be extended "will take a few years" to discover, he says. "At the end of five years, we'll all have a better idea as to what are the limits to multiple processing and whether expanding those limits makes sense."

In the meantime, Gregory emphasizes, there is still plenty of mileage to be gotten out of building faster central processing units. Even on the dual- and four-processor X-MP and Cray-2 models to come, "we're not deviating from the fact that you've still got to have the fastest CPU," he declares.

At Control Data Corp., Minneapolis, senior vice president of research Lloyd M. Thorndyke takes a more moderate view. He agrees with the university researchers that conventional von Neumann architecture cannot provide the thousandfold performance improvement needed for large-scale computing. "It's very clear that we have to exploit parallelism, as well as development of faster processors," he says.

Maybe a merging

"There's more than one way to skin a cat," says Thorndyke. "While industry might approach the thousandfold goal from one direction, universities might approach it with creative architecture from another direction. Exactly which is the right direction is probably going to be distilled out of the two of them."

One of the problems that usually arises with massively parallel approaches is that "they tend to start to focus on very narrow application areas," Thorndyke says. The Advanced Flexible Processor produced by CDC's own Information Sciences Division is an example. That machine comes with software for linking up to 64 processors together for blazingly fast speed, but only for specific applications.

CDC, of course, is a big backer of cooperative research. Not surprisingly, then, Thorndyke says that university-industry-Government cooperation is essential in the development of massively parallel architectures and other innovations, though the method for that cooperation is yet to be worked out. "We strongly believe in cooperating and in not reinventing the wheel," he reiterates. On questions involving the successor to CDC's current supercomputer, the Cyber 205, Thorndyke declines to provide any detail. But he does make it clear from his comments that more than one processor will be employed.

The maverick in the commercial corral is Denelcor Inc. of Aurora, Colo. The architecture of its HEP system sits between von Neumann and data-flow. It is a multiprocessor with up to 16 process-execution modules (PEMs) and a shared memory. Within each PEM, cooperating programs, called processes, are highly pipelined to allow many of them to execute concurrently. "In order to get real speed from a massively parallel system, everything has to be parallelized, not just the computational hardware, but the input/output and all software," says Burton J. Smith, Denelcor's vice president of research and development. "This we have done with the HEP," he notes.

In the HEP-1, three of which have been delivered, everything but the Fortran language compiler has been parallelized, and a parallel compiler will soon be ready. An upwardly compatible HEP-2 with faster and more reliable processors that will allow configurations with more than 16 processors, is under development.

In HEP-1 there are two eight-segment loop pipelines, one for data and one for instructions, with each segment responsible for a different phase of instruction execution. Each PEM has its own program memory, general-purpose registers, and functional computation units much like conventional von Neumann machines. The PEMS and the large shared memory are interconnected by a very high-speed pipelined packet-switching network.

Synchronization and control of processes in the PEMs are handled by a concept Denelcor calls full-empty. One process can fill a data location and another can empty it, allowing instruction streams to wait for and demand data at a very low level in the system—the full-empty property is at every memory and register location in a PEM. Full-empty synchronization and control is very similar to data-flow control, but as scheduling in HEP is done by a program counter, the system is a hybrid between data-flow and conventional architecture.

Western Europe looks to parallel processing for future computers

Projects in West Germany, France, and Britain are testing advanced multiprocessor architectures

☐ Ever rich in inventive talent, Britain's computing community has a long pedigree in parallel processing. The chain of innovation extends from the distributed-array processor built by ICL plc to an early data-flow computer at Manchester University to the a process-oriented microprocessor due in 1984 from Inmos plc, Bristol. Moreover, the British tradition of innovation extends into software, with notable advances being made in operating systems and programming languages for parallel processing.

A likely goal is several hundred processors, such as Transputers, harnessed together in parallel on a single wafer to yield a system capable of 2.5 billion instructions per second (Fig. 1). This vision is Iann Barron's of Inmos. Though he is not suggesting that such a goal is achievable now, he does see it as a possible target.

Hardware push first

The earliest push towards parallel processing came from the hardware engineers. Machines like ICL's distributed-array processor or (London) University College's Clip-4 image processor are both attempts to break the von Neumann bottleneck between memory and processor. Both are single-instruction multiple-data machines (SIMD) in which an army of processors each execute a single broadcast instruction using locally stored data.

Both projects are alive and well. The Clip-4 is turning up in industrial vision systems, and the Hirst Research Centre, Wembley, Middlesex, of General Electric Co. Ltd. wants to harness it in medical and other imaging applications. ICL is developing a VLSI distributed-array processor to team with its Perq desktop work station, and Ferranti Ltd.'s radar operation plans a version for airborne surveillance.

Many problems do not have the regular data structure to exploit the SIMD machines efficiently. Therefore general-purpose parallel machines are needed. Manchester University's data-flow computer is such an attempt. It falls into the multiple-instruction multiple-data (MIMD) category of parallel computers. It will prove a useful test bed for fifth-generation computer languages, though it is primarily a hardware project.

In the early days, computer engineers did not know how to design parallel-processing systems in hardware, so they engineered them in software and called the result an operating system. The task of such a setup is to share a single processor among many applications and many users. Tony A. Hoare, now heading Oxford University's programming research group, was one of the first to struggle with the complexities of these systems.

In 1978 Hoare got together with Iann Barron, a former Elliot Automation colleague, when Inmos got under way with UK government backing. Occam Inmos's new language for parallel processing, is the distillation of Hoare's work. And Transputer is the chip designed to exploit the language efficiently.

Taking the chip approach

Another operating-system approach is exemplified by the work at Newcastle University, where the computer science department under Prof. Brian Randell has used Bell Laboratories' Unix operating system to give the von Neumann control-flow machine a parallel-processing facelift. The department is now implementing Unix's contextual addressing and nested-cell structure in hardware.

There are two chip projects under way. One is a fairly conventional 16-bit reduced–instruction-set microcomputer with instructions to support parallel processing. It has a small set of often-used instructions, combined with an

1. Tiny Transputers. The little, but very capable, microcomputer that is known as the Transputer is being designed by engineers at Inmos plc to be replicated all over a semiconductor wafer for subsequent interconnection right on the wafer.

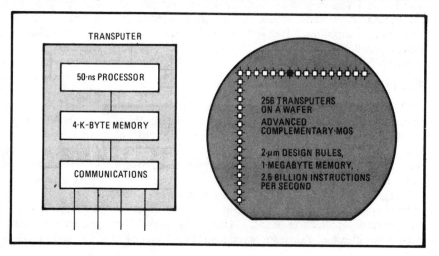

TRANSPUTER

50-ns PROCESSOR

4-K-BYTE MEMORY

COMMUNICATIONS

256 TRANSPUTERS ON A WAFER
ADVANCED COMPLEMENTARY-MOS

2-μm DESIGN RULES,
1-MEGABYTE MEMORY,
2.5 BILLION INSTRUCTIONS PER SECOND

architecture tailored to the efficient execution of this set.

The other chip, designed by Philip C. Treleaven, also at Newcastle, is a more radical design implementing a synthesis of the concepts found in conventional control- and data-flow and reduction architectures. A simple programming language called Basix, with concepts taken from Basic, Lisp, and Unix, is being developed by colleague Isabel Gouveia Lima to run on this hardware.

In Treleaven's view, "von Neumann [architecture] is probably a better starting point for parallel processing than some of the newer architectures such as data-flow and reduction. But what we need to do is decentralize the control flow. The model we are seeking to develop embodies the principles that can already be seen in modern operating systems like Unix."

Central to the Unix system is its concept of file store management realized as a hierarchy of variably sized files and directories. By selective naming, it is possible to address the files contextually. This extremely powerful concept frees memory from the limitations of a machine's 16- or 32-bit address space.

In another project, Newcastle has already exploited the Unix file-structure features in a distributed computing environment with its Newcastle Connection. This software add-on for Unix-based networks creates a distributed system indistinguishable to user or programmer from a uniprocessor system.

Also prominent in the British thrust towards parallel processing is a new breed of experts that are designing languages from a base of mathematical or logical theory without reference to the hardware on which they are to run. One such is John Darlington of Imperial College, London. His Hope language will run on his Alice computer which is to be built with a network array of Transputers.

Microtechnology can also mold computer architectures into faster configurations. One of the first to recognise the connection was computer theoretician Ivor Catt. He devised a complete wafer-scale technology and a computer architecture to go with it. Alone among UK manufacturers, Burroughs Corp., at its Cumbernauld facility, tried out Catt's ideas and demonstrated working systems.

Others are now coming up with architectures that could support wafer-scale integration one day. In particular, the University of East Anglia is devising a machine consisting of a regular array of microprocessor-like devices. Such computer arrays are to be compared with the systolic array, devised by H. T. Kung at Carnegie Mellon University in Pittsburgh [*Electronics,* June 2, 1982, p. 46]. In the systolic array, data circulating through parallel pipes of multiple processors gets some processing done on it at each processor stop along the way.

First the music, then the instrument, maintain the researchers at the Centre d'Etudes et de Recherche de Toulouse, France. Their decade-old project to study and design a SIMD single-assignment data-flow computer began with software. The team, led by Jean-Claude Syre, first designed a high-level parallel language. Then it wrote a compiler for the language along with a software simulation. When the simulation proved successful, a hardware prototype of the LAU (for single-assignment language) system was built.

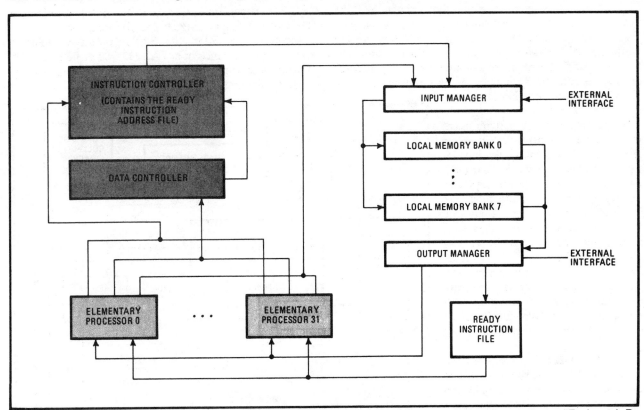

2. The French connection. The world's first working data-flow machine was the LAU system designed at Toulouse's Centre d'Etudes et de Recherche. The prototype has four processors, but a bigger machine could have up to 32 interconnected processors.

The architecture of the complete prototype is a multiprocessor data-flow computer with 32 identical 32-bit processing elements (Fig. 2) connected to six external buses. The central memory is eight banks of local semiconductor memory, with a total capacity of 32-K 64-bit words. The instruction controller unit implements dataflow control. To maximize parallelism, single-assignment programming seems to be the best for data-flow machines. Single-assignment languages are based on a rule that a variable may appear on the left side of only one statement in a program fragment. This allows the system to detect data dependencies in a program and therefore determine which instructions can be executed in parallel.

A four-processor prototype was constructed to evaluate the feasibility of the design. It is a slow machine built with third-generation technology. But it was strictly a research project not meant to be expanded into a commercial machine.

The team is continuing basic research on single-assignment parallel architecture. Improvements to the high-level language are planned, the main one being to allow data structures to be changed during program execution. Team members are now working with computer manufacturers on future developments in parallel architecture but can say no more than that at this time.

Buoyed by an annual infusion of about $4 million of government funding, West German universities are mounting several research efforts into parallel processing. The Ministry for Research and Technology backs several computer architecture projects, alone or in concert with other groups like the German society for mathematics and data processing.

A data-flow computer project is under way at the University of Frankfurt. It entails a multicomputer system with single-board microcomputers operating according to the data-flow principle. A custom-designed associative processor handles the data-flow control.

Probably the most activity is at the Technical University in West Berlin, at the laboratory for innovative computer systems. Wolfgang Giloi, who heads the group, says two data-type parallel architectures are involved. One is a general-purpose multiprocessor computer called Starlet and the other is a special-purpose microprocessor-array computer (MAC) for signal and image processing. Both apply the principles of object addressing and data typing; both are structured to distribute functions over a hierarchy of processors.

3. Deutschland Star. The vector-processing pipeline of the seven-processor Starlet data-flow computer at the Technical University of Berlin teams MC68000s with custom floating-point and reduced–instruction-set processors in the pipeline.

The two machines' architecture is called data-type because data-type objects are constructed and manipulated at the hardware level and the execution of complex operations on such objects occurs in the SIMD mode. Starlet and MAC differ, though, in the way they handle the typing. As a general-purpose machine, Starlet handles arbitrarily structured data objects user-defined as objects of abstract data types. In contrast, MAC handles just three machine-defined data types—vector, digital image array, and fast Fourier transform.

The first prototype of Starlet was working by September of 1981. A multimicrocomputer system (Fig. 3), it uses seven Motorola 68000 microprocessors. Also included are two types of custom processors: a fast TTL floating-point and fixed-point pipeline processor in the data processor, and three microprogrammable reduced–instruction-set processors in the three structure processors, which perform descriptor interpretation. The four 68000s not shown in the figure are three in the structure processors to do address generation and one in the data processor for pipeline configuration.

In October 1982, the Starlet team received a new grant from the West German Federal Government's Ministry of Research and Technology to develop a production model. All functional units will be repackaged on multilayer printed-circuit boards, and test hardware and software will be developed to support the manufacture and maintenance of the computer system.

For software, the group has developed and implemented a Pascal extension for parallel processing, called parallel Pascal. Giloi's group also developed a structured version of MIT's experimental abstract data-type cluster (CLU) language, and called it CLU-S but is considering ADA as the primary language in the long run.

According to Giloi, the Starlet prototype achieves twice the performance of a VAX/11 780 at half the cost. In array processing, the machine reaches a speed of up to 3 million floating-point operations per second.

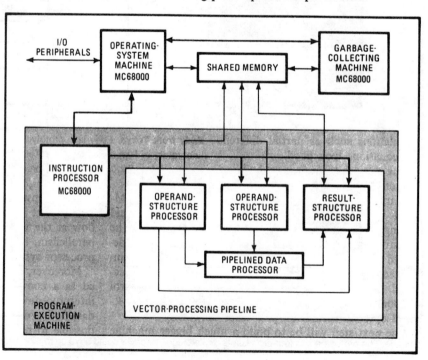

Japan is busy trying to make manufacturable data-flow computers

Two projects at the NTT laboratory and another at Tokyo University advance the data-flow concept

☐ Data-flow architecture has its adherents in Japan as well, with two important research efforts well launched at two institutions. At the Musashino Electrical Communication Laboratory of the Nippon Telegraph & Telephone Public Corp., two types of data-flow architecture are under study. In the electrical engineering department of Tokyo University, a data-flow project named Topstar has been under way since 1978.

Double-barreled research

Of the two NTT data-flow architectures, one is a highly parallel processor array for scientific calculations, while the other is an architecture designed to apply data-flow techniques to parallel list processing using the functional language Valid, also developed in the project. These teams are under the direction of Makoto Amamiya, a staff engineer at the Musashino lab.

Already built is a hardware simulator for the data-flow processor array. Eddy, as the simulator is called, uses 34 Z8001 microprocessors with 32 of them making up a 4-by-4 array. Each processing element consists of two microprocessors and is connected·to eight neighboring elements (see figure). Two processors are used as broadcast control units, which can move programs and data to and from the processing elements in a given column or row or to or from all processing elements at once. The Eddy experimental system is now running, and results with scientific calculations such as partial differential equations look good.

The project team is now building version 1 of the list-processing data-flow machine prototype, DFM-1, and is designing DFM-2. It is considering folding DFM-1 into DFM-2 and getting the latter up and running in about two years. The tentative configuration of DFM-2 is eight specially designed processors using multiple integrated circuits, embedded within eight 32-K-word memories for list-structured data. In addition, there will be eight control memories consisting of 8-K-word instruction and 32-K-word operand memories, plus three networks.

The next step will be to build a much bigger machine using very large-scale integrated circuitry. No target date

has been set, but it would be after DFM-2 is finished and has been evaluated. The big machine would consist of 128 or 256 processing elements each implemented with two or three VLSI chips.

The NTT researchers have also developed a high-level functional language, Valid, which has recursion plus parallel expressions. Pure Lisp and other functional languages have recursion but not parallel expressions, whereas MIT's VAL has parallel expressions but is not recursive. The team is now developing a cross-compiler to translate Valid language programs into the data-flow machine code. The next step will be to develop a self-compiler on the data-flow machine.

A composite approach characterizes the Tokyo Uni-

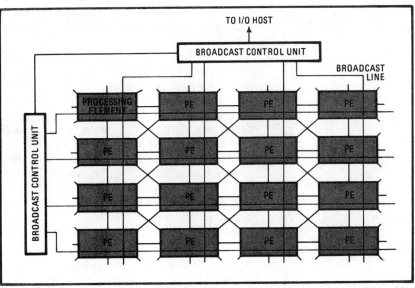

Eddy from Tokyo. Eddy is a prototype data-flow array computer built at the Musashino Laboratory of Nippon Telegraph & Telephone Public Corp. The basic processing element comprises two Z8001 microprocessors and is connected directly to eight neighboring PEs.

versity Topstar project. As a first step, it implements data flow at the procedure level and conventional control flow at the instruction level. Although it results in less parallelism, the dual structure is well-suited to a multiprocessor system using conventional LSI microprocessors.

Moreover, each procedure may be written and executed as a conventional program. However, all high-level interprocedure relations are controlled and executed as a data-flow program. Further off in the future, it should be possible to replace each conventional LSI processor with an instruction-level data-flow machine. ☐

3.
SYSTEM
MEMORY

Although most computer users count on the ability of a computer to manipulate data at high speeds, many do not often appreciate the close association between the central-processing unit and system memory. Mainframe computer designers have long used a number of tricks to bring this partnership even closer. Special high-speed memory, called cache, works as a very fast local memory to a CPU and buffers the exchange of data between a high-performance CPU and slower system memory.

However, for systems whose memory requirements are greater than their need for speed, computers can exploit memory-management methods that make a small amount of physical memory appear to be much more. These techniques combine some hardware with special software algorithms that shuffle data betweeen mass storage and system memory.

Still, with the tremendous advances in technology for very large-scale integration, designers are broadening the range of capability of memory chips. Besides producing a line of fast, dense chips in a variety of packages and word widths, memory engineers are bringing some of the intelligence of the CPU on to memory chips themselves.

The technical articles in this chapter highlight approaches to memory management used by the major chip manufacturers. Following this and a discussion of new integrated memory chips, the chapter winds up with a look at how memory is controlled and how errors are caught and corrected.

Microsystems exploit mainframe methods

Proven techniques protect tasks from illegal operations, remove present limits on program size and number of users

by R. Colin Johnson, *Microsystems & Software Editor*

☐ Now that multiuser capability is to be found on smaller and more widely affordable computers, memory management schemes reminiscent of mainframes are finding their way even into microsystems. The ultimate management scheme, of course, is virtual memory—the ability of a computer system to make its diverse kinds of memory, be they semiconductor, disk, or tape, appear identical to the programmer. Such a system takes care of swapping code and data into and out of main memory as they are needed by the programmer and in a manner transparent to him or her.

Memory management schemes make it possible for a system to run programs larger than its main memory by requiring only those portions of a program that are currently needed to be resident. In large multiuser situations, the response time at terminals can be greatly decreased if each user's complete program does not have to be resident in main memory. Instead, only the small fragments currently in use reside there, making room for many more users' programs. No long disk accesses are allowed either (only the short ones required to swap in fragments), making switching between tasks even faster.

However, the methods used to decide just which program fragments should be in main memory and which should remain in mass storage can become quite complex (see "Old programmers need new tricks,"). Ideally, the segments most likely to be used in the immediate future should be in main memory, but the solution to such a nondeterministic problem can at best be approximated. Also, the location and order in which segments are placed in memory can become a significant problem, especially if they are of varying sizes. Incoming segments must have contiguous free areas to be loaded into, and that could necessitate moving resident segments about to make room available to them (see "Swapping software for virtual memory,").

The payoff for fine-tuning a memory management scheme is worth it, though—the system's throughput is significantly increased. And, as semiconductor technology continues to breed ever faster processors and ever cheaper memory, schemes for managing these resources will continue to proliferate, particularly in 16-bit microsystems using special memory management large-scale integrated circuits.

One key issue in the management of a large semiconductor address space containing diverse kinds of information is protection. Users must be prevented from interfering with each other's memory areas by hardware that makes it impossible for them to do so.

However, to make protection possible, individual tasks must be subdivided into sections that hang together logically. For instance, code that has been developed using modular techniques can be easily divided into separate sections for the main program, subroutines, and functions. Also, the data used by the program should already be divided into various structures, like records, arrays, and strings, whose nature can be reflected in the way they are mapped into main memory. In addition, stacks that are subject to dynamic growth and shrinkage can be placed in special areas for the various users as well as one for the operating system.

Multiuser, and often even single-user jobs that use multitasking within a single program, demand this sort of separation. Also a necessity are hardware protection mechanisms that prevent code sections from being overwritten with data, stop attempts to use read-only areas for scratch-pad write operations, and generally raise the integrity of the total system by guaranteeing that unwanted operations cannot be performed. As a bonus, many of the hardware implementations allow users to share areas of memory, such as high-level–language compilers, without the need to keep copies.

Basic techniques

To manage memory at all, it is necessary to separate the addresses used in a program from those delivered to the memory system itself. The addresses in the program are termed the logical addresses, since they identify logically distinct pieces of information with a unique numerical quantity. They are not necessarily the actual semiconductor memory locations—those are the physical addresses. The physical address is what programmers have traditionally used in programs, being the actual bit patterns supplied to the address bus of main memory. The logical addresses must be translated into the physical ones by a hardware mechanism that recognizes the former, looks up its physical counterpart, and supplies that to the memory system.

To effect this translation, each memory segment or page is associated with what is called a descriptor—a hardware register that contains its physical address and protection status. The way in which this descriptor is accessed varies widely, as does its actual composition and layout. For instance, the operation code of the instructions might simply contain a field that indicates the descriptor to be used, whereas a more elaborate scheme might use an associative (content-addressable) memory that looks up the proper descriptor on the fly.

Mainframes often use several levels of look-up, involving several types of segmentation. There might be a user look-up table that identifies the processes accessible to that user; then each process may be segmented into its various data, code, and stack segments; each of those may in turn have associated with it a descriptor identifying its beginning address and length; and those may then be further subdivided into fixed-size pages. This four-level look-up may then be speeded up by a local cache memory that holds those pages currently in use.

On the microsystem level, however, a two-level look-up is the commonest, as is the use of software to perform many of the functions implemented in hardware by mainframes. In fact, the varying amounts of hardware and software needed to support a memory management system is one of the distinctive differences between approaches. At the least, hardware is needed to hold the addresses of the beginnings of segments or pages, and for virtual memory management the processor itself must have an abort-instruction function with which instructions that try to access information not yet in main memory can be restarted after it has been swapped in from mass storage. (This is an uncommon feature, however—it was not designed into any of the 16-bit microprocessors now in production, though most of the next generation will include this capability.)

Some implementations

The simplest form of memory management is called bank switching. It involves merely turning on one of many memory banks under software control. Usually an output port is dedicated to selecting one bank and disabling all others (Fig. 1). This scheme is the easiest to implement and is found on many existing multiuser microsystems. A copy of the operating system kernel is kept in each bank, and switching between users is accomplished by periodically interrupting the processor, which then branches to the system subroutine that actually writes the next user's number into the bank-select

GLOSSARY OF MEMORY MANAGEMENT TERMINOLOGY	
abort (instruction)	halting an instruction because its operands are not in main memory
address binding, address mapping, address translation	calculating the real physical memory address of operands from the logical address supplied by the processor
bank switching	wiring memory banks in parallel so that only one is active at any given time (under software control)
base address	the address of the first location in a segment or page of memory
content-addressable memory (CAM)	a memory bank in which the contents of each location are simultaneously compared with incoming data for matches
compaction	relocating programs in memory so that they and unused areas are contiguous
descriptor	a preformatted data set describing the location, access privileges, and status of a region of memory
dirty regions	regions of memory that have been modified since being loaded into main memory
dynamic allocation	the run-time reorganization of data storage to accommodate an executing process
hit ratio	the percentage of time that the information requested is resident in a cache memory
latency	the extra time delay introduced by a memory management unit into the path that the address lines take to main memory
logical address	the address used in programs to separate logically distinct values
offset	the number of locations from the base address to the desired information
page	fixed-size region of memory
physical address	the bit pattern applied to the address bus of real physical main memory
residency	the situation when information currently needed is already in main memory
static allocation	the load-time organization of data storage that then stands all the while a program is executing
swapping	exchanging information between mass storage and main memory

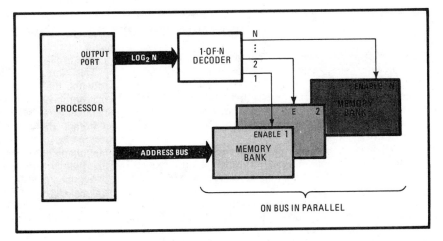

1. Switching banks. The simplest kind of memory management uses several banks of memory wired in parallel, only one of which is activated at any one time. An output port specifies the bank to be switched on, and an off-board decoder guarantees that only one bank will be active. This method is easy to implement but does not let users share regions of memory and often wastes memory space since users seldom fill their bank.

output port. But this form of memory management is very rudimentary—it wastes a lot of memory, does not support shared code or data, and does not allow programs any larger than normal to be run on the system.

A single latch can expand a memory system's address space (Fig. 2). The data in the latch serves as the upper bits of the physical address, which are often called the base address, and the logical address can then be appended as the lower bits, indicating how many locations past the base address the desired information is and hence called the offset. But this method still does not permit the use of shared code, requires that segments be located on boundaries as large as the banks are in the switching approach, and does not allow any oversize programs to be run.

A common extension of this method sequesters some of the upper bits of the logical address and uses them to select one of several base registers. This scheme is used by the MC6829 memory manager made by Motorola Inc. of Austin, Texas, as well as by the 74610 made by Texas Instruments Inc. of Dallas. Neither of these parts is as sophisticated as the LSI parts available for 16-bit processors like Motorola's MC68451 (Fig. 3) or National Semiconductor's 16082 (Fig. 4), but they offer an economical alternative to small-scale IC implementations. The 610 uses the upper 4 bits of a 16-bit address to select one of sixteen 12-bit base addresses. This address is then appended to the remaining 12 bits of the logical address to form a 24-bit physical address. Thus, a 16-megabyte address range is divided into 4-K-byte pages, 16 of which are accessible without reloading any base registers (Fig. 5).

The 6829 uses the upper 5 bits to select one of 32 10-bit registers to form a 20-bit address, thus dividing a 2-megabyte space into 2-K-byte pages. This method allows pages to be relocated in memory in a manner transparent to the programmer merely by reloading the base registers.

The approach can also be used to share code, eliminating the need to keep duplicates of often used pages, like those containing the operating system kernel—a necessity in the bank-switched method. The way to do this is to allow each task to have access to the same page in memory by loading one of the base registers with the same address every time a context switch has to be done between tasks.

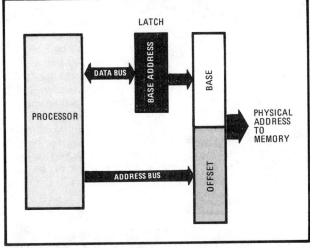

2. Expanding space. A external latch can serve to expand the available memory space if the data in the latch is used as a base address. The address coming from the processor is used as an offset (index) and is appended to the base to form a wider address bus.

If only one set of base registers is provided in a system, then a context switch requires that the base registers be reloaded with the locations of the new task's program and data. However, this overhead can be eliminated by using multiple mapping registers that are selected in the same manner that banks are—namely, writing a number into a dedicated location that enables one of many base register sets. Alternatively, the function code outputs can be used to select memory management units, so that separate ones can be used for system, data, code, and stack operations. The 6829 has four sets of 32 base registers for fast switching between four tasks, each of which has access to 32 unique 2-K-byte pages. Both the 6829 and 74610 can be selectively disabled, so that more than one unit may be used in a single system.

Any such method, though, introduces another time delay into the path that addresses take to memory. Called latency, it is the time it takes to decode the upper bits of the logical address and deliver the base address they select to memory. Latency can be minimized by using base registers that can be accessed quickly (the 6829, for example, introduces only 100 nanoseconds of latency); but it cannot be eliminated entirely unless the memory fetch cycles are performed in parallel with the

Old programmers need new tricks

When microprocessors first became available in the early 1970s, engineers designing logic with the relay ladder approach were hard put to convert that process into machine language programming. Even though the microprocessor was to perform the same function as the relay ladder, programming it had little in common with relay ladder design.

A similar phenomenon is occurring today—designing software for computer systems using the new memory management units is a task riddled with concepts new to the microsystem programmer (see glossary on p. 120). New items like segment descriptors, on-demand page-swapping algorithms, and virtual address translation make programming these systems a task that requires new methodologies.

At the lowest level there is the matter of loading and managing off-chip segment registers in such a way that memory is fully utilized. Segments or pages of memory must be allocated so that its use is optimized for the tasks to be performed by the microsystem in question. This process involves demand-swapping algorithms that keep track of which segments or pages of memory are being used the most (see "Swapping software for virtual memory,"). Then, when a new task is brought into the system, the least used region can be returned to mass storage, making room for the new one while affecting the performance of the rest of the currently executing tasks as little as possible. Also, there is the issue of memory protection: the flagging of individual segments or pages with access privilege information that prevents users from crashing the system or destroying other users' data.

This sort of real-time control of memory allocation requires the use of programming techniques new to the microprocessor software engineer. Still, it is not as if these techniques will have to be invented.

In fact, the answers to most of the questions a microprocessor programmer might have regarding memory management can be obtained from the mainframe industry. There are two reasons for this: extensive research and testing has already been done by it in the development of optimal algorithms for storage management; and the manufacturers of memory management chips are employing former mainframe people as designers.

Every major semiconductor manufacturer of a memory management unit has had experienced mainframe engineers on its memory management design team, and it shows. The methods employed are taken directly from those already in use on the bigger machines, albeit on a smaller scale. For instance, the use of a bit to flag regions of memory that have been altered since being loaded is taken directly from mainframe practice. However, the biggest machines track not only use, but also how many times a page has been used, so that swapping algorithms may decide which pages can be returned to memory while having the least possible impact on the total system throughput.

It is safe to assume that mainframes will continue to lead the way for microsystem development, too, since memory management designs will not be committed to silicon before being tested and proven in mainframes.

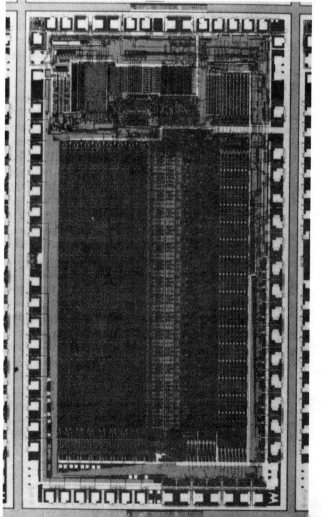

execution cycles, as in pipelined machines like Intel's iAPX-286 that prefetch instructions.

But there is one problem with only appending the offset to the base address—pages may be located only on boundaries equal in size to the page length. This can cause difficulties in systems that use large page sizes, since a significant amount of memory can be consumed by pages with unused portions. For instance, if Digital Equipment Corp.'s PDP-11 minicomputers, which use 8-K-byte pages, only appended their 13-bit offset to a base address, then the 11/34 could only be configured with 32 8-K-byte pages in its 256-K-byte address space, many of which would have unused portions.

One solution is to make the pages smaller, such as the 512-byte size of the 16082 from National Semiconductor Corp. of Santa Clara, Calif. But a result is that the page descriptor tables become quite large. The 16082 needs all of 128-K bytes to hold its page tables, so that they had to be made accessible only virtually (a two-level look-up scheme is used, with only 1-K byte of tables in main memory and the rest kept on a disk).

To alleviate these problems in the 11/23 and /34, however, DEC uses an overlapping add operation between a 12-bit base address and a 13-bit offset to produce a 18-bit physical address (Fig. 6a). This arrangement

3. Keeping it regular. The extreme regularity of Motorola's memory management unit (MC68451) is strikingly apparent in this die photo. It stores some sixteen 9-byte-long descriptors as well as containing several control registers for handling multiple-unit configurations.

allows pages to be located on 64-byte boundaries and also to be of varying lengths—for which reason they will hereafter be referred to as segments. The first step is the division of the 16-bit logical address from the processor into a 3-bit segment number and a 13-bit offset, the former selecting one of eight 12-bit base address registers. However, the 13-bit offset instead of being appended, is separated into fields so that its upper 7 bits are added to the 12-bit base and the lower 6 bits are appended to that result, creating an 18-bit physical address. This method produces variably sized segments of 64 bytes to 8-K bytes locatable on any 64-byte boundary.

The 8010 memory management unit devised by Zilog Inc., Santa Clara, Calif., uses a scheme that is modeled after DEC's (Fig. 6b), the primary difference being the number of bits allotted to the various fields. A 7-bit quantity selects the base address for 128 possible segments (64 base registers being provided on a single 8010). Also, the segment sizes vary from 256 bytes to 64-K bytes, and a 24-bit physical address is produced for a total space of 16 megabytes.

Intel Corp.'s 8086 also does an overlapping add operation on a 16-bit base and offset to produce a 20-bit physical address. However, its base registers are implied by instructions rather than being explicitly specified in the op code. In the 286, which is software-compatible with the 8086, the Santa Clara, Calif., company abandons this overlapping method, preferring to add a 24-bit base to a 16-bit offset for complete freedom to relocate on any byte boundary.

The other major 16-bit microprocessor manufacturer that has chosen the variably sized segment approach is Motorola. But its MC68451 memory management unit adopts a novel implementation. In place of an adder, it employs a special mask register that allows segments to be any size that is a power of 2 greater than 256 bytes. This is effected by masking the logical address that is brought on chip with a bit pattern stored in that segment's descriptor.

If the mask is all 1s, then the base address is completely masked out and the logical address is passed straight through, becoming the physical address; thus memory in effect becomes a single 16-megabyte page. At the other extreme, if the mask is all 0s, then 16 of the upper 24 bits of the logical address are masked out and replaced with the descriptor's base address, leaving only an 8-bit offset for a 256-byte page. In other words, the mask determines how many of the lower logical address bits will be used as an offset and thus how big the page is. This method has the advantage of replacing an adder, which is an iterative silicon-consuming module, by masking hardware, which is a single-logic-level array of AND gates, thereby making the part faster than it would be if an adder had been used (its latency is 130 ns).

Another distinguishing feature of the 68451 (and also of National's 16082 and Zilog's forthcoming Z8015) is its use of a content-addressable associative memory to select the base register. This method, used on many high-performance mainframes, requires an additional logical–base-address register for every physical–base-address register. When a logical address is applied to the memory management unit, it is simultaneously compared with all the logical–base-address registers and the one that matches it activates the physical–base-address register associated with it (Fig. 7). In this way, purely logical addresses can be used by the programmer, rather

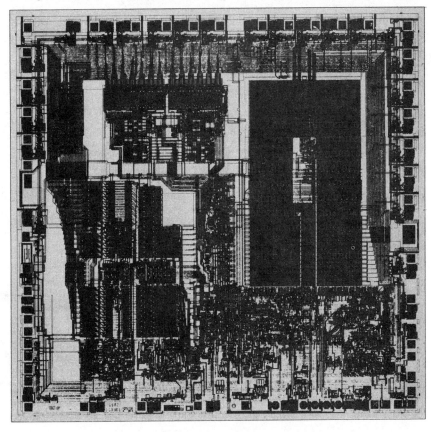

4. Die layout. This memory management unit from National Semiconductor, the 16082, is the only one from a major 16-bit microprocessor maker that fetches descriptors from main memory on its own. It is really a special-purpose processor in and of itself, as can be discerned from the photo. It is the first of a series of slave processors designed to work in a closely coupled configuration with its 16000 series 16-bit microprocessors.

Swapping software for virtual memory

Main-memory management involves a lot of support software to optimize the way programs and data are arranged in memory for maximum throughput. Usually it keeps three lists: an occupied-space list that indicates those portions of memory now occupied by programs and data; an available-space list that reveals which regions of memory have no significant information in them; and a directory of secondary-memory devices that shows the location of information currently being used by executing programs. With the aid of these three lists, main memory can be allocated and reallocated to programs competing for system resources.

Whenever a new task is brought into the memory system for execution, an unused region must be provided to load it into. If after checking the available space list, it is discovered that a large enough region is free, then the new task can be loaded directly into it without the need to swap any information out that is already there.

Many times, however, there will be more than one contiguous area available, requiring the software to choose between them. Two of the best accepted methods for doing so are called "best fit" and "first fit". The first checks the sizes of all available regions and chooses the one that is closest to the size of the task to be loaded. The other just takes the first available space that is big enough. Of course, the tradeoff is between the extra software overhead needed for checking the sizes and the

wasted memory that results from loading small tasks into big regions. The fine tuning of a memory managment system involves making just such decisions as to which method will work best in a given application.

On the other hand, if no space is large enough for the current task, then either a compaction must be done on memory, so that the regions that are available can be grouped together making room for the new task, or one or more tasks already in memory must be swapped back out to mass storage.

Coming up with an optimal replacement strategy in this situation can become an incredibly complex process. One of the simplest methods is a first-in, first-out policy that requires only that the swapping software track the order in which tasks were loaded.

Another more complex method swaps out the least recently used region. This can be accomplished by keeping an age-register count for each loaded task. Whenever a region is accessed, the age register is set to some predetermined positive number. Then periodically all the age registers are decremented by the computer system software, and the least recently used region becomes associated with the age register with the smallest value in it. However, other parameters must be taken into account, too—for instance, whether a region has been altered, since then it need not be swapped back into mass storage, being identical with the copy already there.

---

than those in which the upper portion is really a segment number. Many programmers prefer this method even though it involves yet another level of logic in the memory address path and obscures the problem of determining whether a mistaken address calculation was caused by an attempt to overflow the current segment or by an improper type of access (like trying to write a read-only area). The Z8015 directly supports 2,048-byte pages and

puts 64-page descriptors on line. Other sizes of pages can be hardwired in, and up to 4,096 page descriptors can evenly divide the 8-megabyte address space.

Intel's 432 also uses an on-chip content-addressable associative memory. However, it is not comparing logical addresses with its contents but instead uses what is called a nickname. This local identification number can be as short as 6 bits. Unlike segment numbers, which

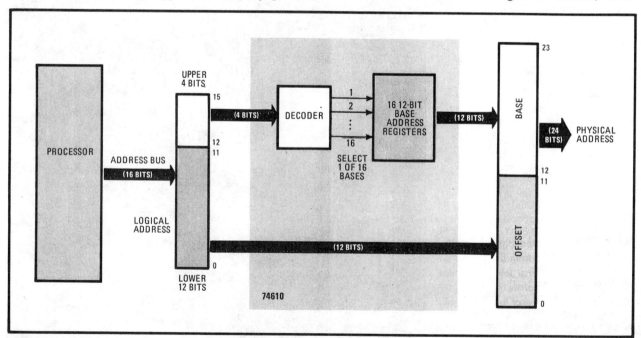

5. Only mapping. This memory-mapping unit from Texas Instruments may be used with any microprocessor with 16 address lines (like most 8-bit units). It expands such a memory space to 16 megabytes with sixteen 4-K-byte pages accessible without reloading any registers.

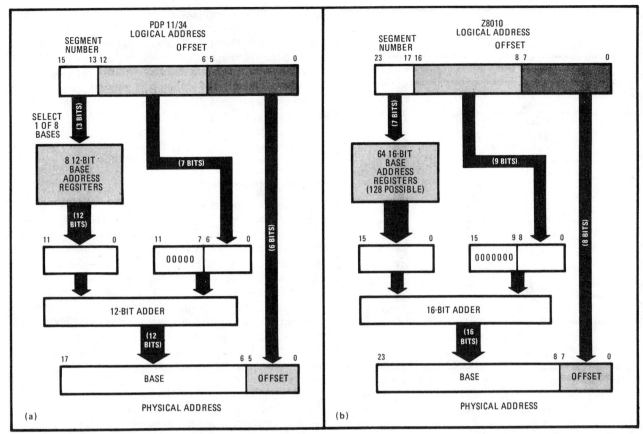

6. Copy a winner. The proven address-translation mechanisms of the PDP 11/34 minicomputer from Digital Equipment Corp. served as the template for the design of Zilog's Z8010 memory management unit. The only differences that are found are in the sizes of the bit fields.

indicate a specific descriptor register, it is written directly into the associative memory array, just as resident logical addresses are written into the 68451s and 16082s. If the nickname is present in the associative memory, then it activates the physical–base-address register associated with it. Otherwise, the required descriptor information must be located by means of a two-level look-up process. Two-level look-up schemes are popular because they allow a single segment or page to have different access privileges attached to it, depending on the path used to get there. For instance, the operating system will use a different path from the one users do.

Protection racket

But the logical into physical address translation is only half of the memory management story. Protection is the other half. Whether the system uses variably sized segments or a fixed-size page, hardware support protecting them against improper accesses is becoming mandatory, especially in large multitasking systems. A fully protected system stops users from inadvertently violating the operating system and causing a crash. It can also allow users to share code without letting anyone else overwrite it or even, for that matter, inspect it (this is the result of execute-only protection status).

The most common protection status possibilities attach a system-only, execute-only, read-only, code-only, data-only, or stack-only status to each segment or page. Also, several levels of access privilege are becoming popular, allowing code from various levels of operation

ranging from system subroutines to user applications to be protected from inadvertent mishaps.

These status indicators are held in the segment's or page's descriptor, along with the physical and possibly logical base addresses. These registers can become very wide and often include other status bits indicating current usage, such as whether the segment or page is present in main memory, whether it has been used recently, and whether it has been modified since being brought in from mass storage.

Each time a memory access is tried by the processor, the memory management unit checks to see whether the attempt violates any of the protection status bit fields in the descriptor and allows the access to occur only if all is found to be well. Also during the access, the current status bits are updated by the memory management unit so that the operating system may easily keep tabs on the status of each segment or page. This can greatly increase the efficiency of swapping operations (see "Swapping software for virtual memory,") since segments or pages that have not been modified (are not "dirty") need not be returned to mass storage because the copy that is already there must be identical. In addition, segments or pages that have not been used recently are flagged as prime candidates for swapping back to mass storage in the event that room is needed to bring in a new task.

Figure 8 shows the basic layout and definition of the 8-byte-long descriptors used on Intel's iAPX-286, the only 16-bit microprocessor to employ an on-chip memory management unit. The 286 approach uses only four

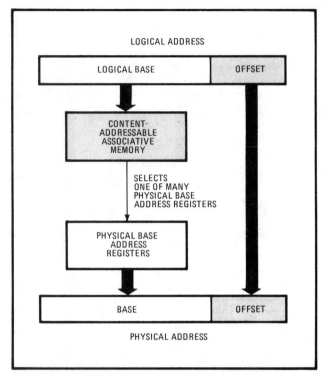

7. Memory associations. A content-addressable memory (CAM) can be used to activate a physical base register. The logical address put out by the processor and all CAM locations are compared simultaneously, activating the base address associated with a match.

descriptors so as to maintain compatibility with the 8086 (in fact, they are merely widened versions of the 8086's base registers). Thanks to the 24-bit base, segments can be located on any byte boundary in the 16-megabyte address space. The 16-bit limit field specifies the segment's length, and the access byte gives its privilege status. In addition to the normal access restrictions, the 286 also has four operating levels that are prioritized, so that access to segments may be restricted to tasks operating at the specified level or higher.

The 286 actually uses several different kinds of descriptors, each with slightly different layouts and definitions depending on the type of information that is contained in them. Also, the management and organization of system tables for these various types of segments will be supported by silicon subroutines.

The 68451's 9-byte descriptor (Fig. 9) has several unusual features in addition to the logical address mask that determines how many bits of the base address will be appended to the offset, thereby setting the page size.

One of the most prominent of these is the address space table, which holds an 8-bit task identification number for each of the eight possible combinations of processor access (as determined from its three-function code output), as well as a duplicate set for direct-memory-access requests. Then for each memory-access request the task number is masked by the segment's address-space mask, which then must match its address-space number for the access to be granted. This setup allows code and data to be shared by tasks.

For instance, suppose that operating system tasks are assigned an address-space task number of 10000000_2

and a user's segment has an address mask loaded with 01111111_2 and a task number of 00000000_2. Then the operating system will have access to the user's segments since after the mask operation ($10000000_2 \cdot 01111111_2 = 00000000_2$), the task number will match the segment number. Though this scheme is unusual and initially cumbersome, it does allow many more combinations of segment sharing than the others do.

There are 32 descriptors on a single 68451. Up to six of them may be wired in parallel, and with external buffering any number may be put on line.

Virtual transparency

Virtual memory refers to the property of a system that permits programmers to ignore the process of swapping. The system itself interprets logical addresses, bringing the information to which they refer into main memory without the programmer having to deal with the actual operating system calls that effect the swap. Virtual memories not only free the programmer from the task of managing storage, but in addition make programs independent of the particular configuration and capacity of the system used to execute the program. There are a number of tradeoffs involved here, especially as to how much of this activity should be handled in software or by hardware.

The total hardware approach is taken by National's 16082—the most ambitious memory management unit of all the LSI offerings. It lets the programmer use purely logical addresses with no embedded segment numbers. It uses a 32-entry associative memory to see if the requested logical address is referring to a page that is present in main memory. If the page descriptor is absent, the unit halts the processor and fetches the missing descriptor from main memory, a process that takes only about 3 to 4 microseconds if the page is already in main memory. Most other implementations require the processor itself to fetch missing descriptors—a much slower business. If the page is not present in memory and must be fetched from mass storage, then the instruction making that request is aborted, the missing information is brought in from disk, and the instruction is restarted.

The ability to restart instructions implies that the processor itself must have some special capabilities. The reason for this is that the instruction requesting the missing information is in the middle of execution when the discovery is made that a page is missing and its operands are not in main memory. Most processors do not recognize any external inputs while they are executing an instruction and will, therefore, go ahead and work with the erroneous data. The normal interrupt pin cannot be used to stop a processor that is encountering a page fault since it is checked only after each instruction has been executed, possibly leaving garbage in its internal registers.

This problem may be solved in one of two ways. Either hardware backup registers must be provided on chip to save the state of the machine, or the microcode that performs the execution must check with the memory management unit to make sure that the information is really present in memory before it begins work. The former method is used by the 16082, so that when an

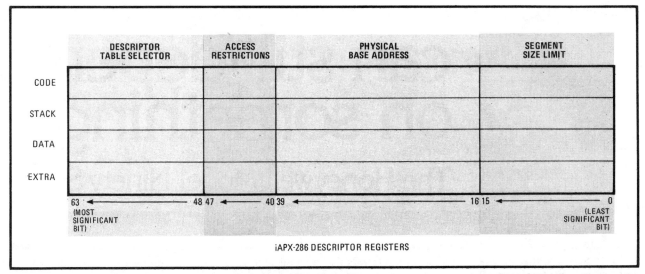

	DESCRIPTOR TABLE SELECTOR	ACCESS RESTRICTIONS	PHYSICAL BASE ADDRESS	SEGMENT SIZE LIMIT
CODE				
STACK				
DATA				
EXTRA				

63 ◄——— 48 47 ◄——— 40 39 ◄——— 16 15 ◄——— 0

(MOST SIGNIFICANT BIT) (LEAST SIGNIFICANT BIT)

iAPX-286 DESCRIPTOR REGISTERS

8. Widened. The four segment base registers of Intel's 8086 have been widened on the instruction-set–compatible iAPX-286 to accommodate the extra fields necessary to implement virtual memory management. Also, 24-bit base registers allow relocation on any byte boundary.

instruction is aborted, all the registers that could have been changed are restored to their former states by being reloaded with their back-up copies. This is also the approach being taken by some users of the 68000 but very clumsily. Since the present 68000 is not capable of restarting instructions, several users are employing a second 68000 whose only function is to back up its registers, which are then flushed out and reloaded into the main 68000 whenever a page fault is encountered. Motorola's memory management unit, however, does detect and signal page faults, and the company promises a new version of the processor that will have its own on-chip back-up registers sometime next year.

Zilog too, is redesigning its processor to handle page faults and calls the new one the Z8003 . It works with Zilog's new memory management unit, the Z8015, to provide instruction abort and restart capability. Some software is also needed to figure out which registers on the Z8003 may have nonsense in them and how to restore them.

Intel's approach to restarting instructions on the 286, however, is quite different. First of all, only instructions that load the descriptor registers are restartable—not just any instruction, as on the 16082, 68451, and Z8015. When one of the instructions that affect the segment registers is encountered, a new descriptor is fetched from main memory and loaded into one of the four on-chip segment-descriptor registers. At this time additional protection checks (other than the ones made with accesses that do not load segment registers) are carried out to ensure that the desired access is a legal one and the segment is actually present in memory. If it is present and access to it is legal, the instruction is completed, and later instructions will use that descriptor implicitly (that is, without having to specify it). If the segment is not present, then an interrupt is generated and software must fetch it from mass storage, update the descriptor table in main memory, and load it into available free space, possibly swapping out other data to make room.

As descriptors must be reloaded whenever a new segment is to be accessed anyway, all instructions need not

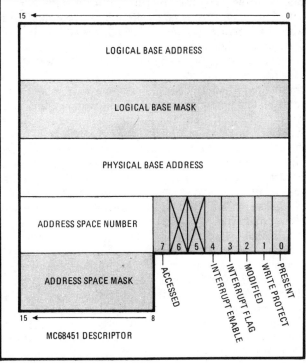

MC68451 DESCRIPTOR

9. Masking many. Both the page size and the memory-sharing capability of Motorola's 68451 memory management unit are determined by a masking operation. Pages may be any size that is a power of 2 greater than 256, and segments are easily shared.

be restartable—only those that load segment registers. This characteristic matches the 286's memory management architecture, which holds only four segment descriptors implied by instructions (code, data for global variables, stack, and extra for local variables). Since these descriptors will be reloaded fairly often, more software overhead is involved than in schemes that put multiple descriptors on line. However, the instructions that will most often be used will have only 16-bit offsets in the op codes, making programs shorter than those that use longer addresses. □

Memory protection moves onto 16-bit microprocessor chip

Hardware implementations of virtual-memory management and protection adapt this device to sophisticated multiuser, multitasking applications

by Peter Heller, Robert Childs, and Jim Slagev, *Intel Corp., Santa Clara, Calif.*

☐ The 16-bit microprocessor has won rapid promotion from its comfortable early jobs running simple terminals and instrumentation controllers to the more strenuous responsibilities of organizing multiterminal word processors and small business systems. But its success in a multi-tasking and -user role has brought with it pressures for memory-management and -protection hardware to increase system performance and to simplify system implementation.

In order to run a reprogrammable, multiuser, multi-tasking system, a 16-bit microprocessor needs higher throughput than it does for a single-task, single-user setup. It also needs to protect its operating-system software against its users and its users against each other. And it could support more users or more tasks if it had virtual memory. Moreover, both memory protection and virtual-memory management should be implemented in hardware, rather than software, so as not to compromise throughput.

Intel's iAPX-286 has been engineered with these requirements in mind. And it achieves its goal on a single chip without the need for cumbersome external memory-management units. Applications like financial transaction systems, in banks or for stock transfers, can benefit from the 286's ability to protect confidential data. Real-time process control systems can profit from its fast interrupt response time, automatic task switching, and ample address space. The 286 supports the needs of multiuser business systems and can serve as the host of a distributed-processing network by managing a number of work stations and local communications lines. It is also closely matched to the needs of telecommunications and data-communications systems like private branch exchanges.

In sum, the 80286 processor, together with its family of support circuits, offers performance and features previously available only from minicomputers. On-chip circuitry provides powerful yet flexible memory protection, completely controlling access to operating-system resources and isolating individual application programs and programmers from each other. A physical address space of 16 megabytes maps into a full gigabyte of virtual memory per task.

Also, the 80286 processor has six times the throughput of its predecessor, the 8086. Compared with the 29,000 or so transistors of the 8086, the 80286 has 130,000.

Lastly, to minimize software development costs, which can become very steep for complex applications, the 286 system is equipped to run high-level languages and has a complete set of software development tools. Its instructions are a superset of the 8086's, maintaining complete compatibility with software for the 8086 and 8088.

No forgetting

Large computer systems normally allocate portions of a sizable virtual-address space to multiple tasks or multiple users. To enforce the memory boundaries and also prevent unauthorized access to or modification of information stored, these systems use hardware support. The 80286 is the only microprocessor that has such a protection mechanism built into its own silicon.

The system designer may exploit the 286 protection mechanism in different ways to accommodate systems of varying complexity. One possibility is to split all memory between user and supervisor functions. But this traditional two-level system is seldom reliable enough for

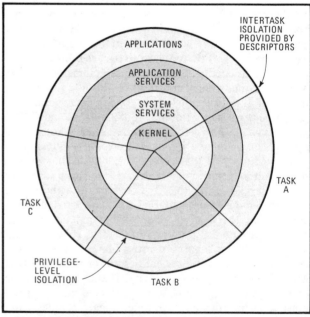

1. Lines of defense. Each task running in a 286 system can operate on any of four privilege levels. This form memory of protection is augmented by isolation between tasks. Hardware implements all forms of protection for higher performance and throughput.

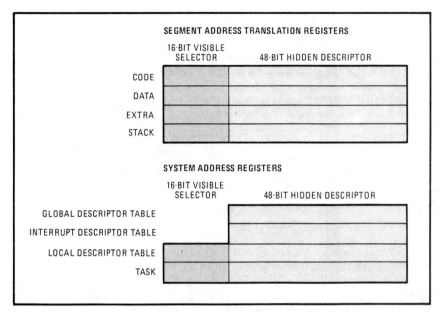

SEGMENT ADDRESS TRANSLATION REGISTERS

16-BIT VISIBLE SELECTOR   48-BIT HIDDEN DESCRIPTOR

CODE
DATA
EXTRA
STACK

SYSTEM ADDRESS REGISTERS

16-BIT VISIBLE SELECTOR   48-BIT HIDDEN DESCRIPTOR

GLOBAL DESCRIPTOR TABLE
INTERRUPT DESCRIPTOR TABLE
LOCAL DESCRIPTOR TABLE
TASK

2. Extended registers. The four segment registers of the 8086 are expanded with 48-bit descriptors on the 286. The 16-bit segment register selectors are virtual addresses that are mapped into physical memory via the descriptors containing access rights.

complex systems or flexible enough for customization.

The 286 instead has four hierarchical protection levels, creating a structured environment that promotes reliable system design. For instance, the programs written for each level can be smaller and easier to develop and maintain. Being in hardware rather than software, the protection mechanism also speeds operation and means there is no software overhead for these functions.

In terms of a processor's operation, memory protection levels may be more meaningfully described as software privilege levels. Whenever the 286 is executing a procedure, it is doing so at the privilege level assigned to that task. The task's position in the hierarchical organization of the system software determines its privilege level.

Therefore a task in the system may be executing at any of the levels depending on the procedure being executed. This allows the operating system to be structured as a set of protected procedures, which can be directly called yet are protected from the user.

The operating-system kernel—the most trusted soft-

ware—operates at the highest of the four privilege levels. The kernel is typically assigned the critical responsibilities of managing memory space, scheduling tasks, and handling intertask communications. A small, fast operating-system kernel takes the best advantage of the high-speed capabilities of the 286 and indeed may be treated as an extension of the actual processor.

Below the kernel comes the supervisor level. The supervisor manages input/output resources, allocates data buffers, and does more global job scheduling. Whereas the kernel serves as an extension to the processor, the makeup of supervisor programs depends more on the intended applications. Because they perform more complex tasks, supervisor programs are usually larger than those at the kernel level.

On the third level of privilege are application services. Programs located at this level are dedicated to the support of the application programs. File-control systems, job-control language processing, and application support utilities are all to be found here.

Least trusted software, such as unproven user programs, operates at the fourth or lowest privilege level to prevent interference with more trusted software.

The multilevel protection mechanism of the 286 is extremely flexible. System designers have the option of using two, three, or four protection levels for system software to provide the level of protection required in any system. By reserving a privilege level for operating-system extensions, they may customize systems without compromising the original software.

Controlled memory access is fundamental to the 286 protection mechanism (Fig. 1). Control of memory references must be strict and continuous to isolate operating-system software from destruction by user programs, as well as to isolate user tasks from each other. To this end, each task has controlled access to two areas of virtual memory, one public and one private as defined by the contents of two kinds of descriptor tables.

FOUR SEGMENT REGISTERS

SELECTORS
DESCRIPTOR
SEGMENT DESCRIPTOR
DESCRIPTOR TABLE

TABLE BASE ADDRESS
OFFSET
DESCRIPTOR TABLE REGISTER

(a)

INSTRUCTION   CACHE   ADDRESS UNIT

READ OR WRITE OP CODE TYPE
SEGMENT TYPE
PROTECTION HARDWARE

OFFSET WITHIN SEGMENT
SEGMENT LIMIT
DATA BYTE/WORD
DATA SEGMENT

SEGMENT BASE

(b)

3. Mapping mechanism. Descriptors are stored in main memory (a) until selected, whereupon they are loaded transparently into a segment register. Thereafter all access rights and protection modes are checked (b) in parallel with virtual-address translation.

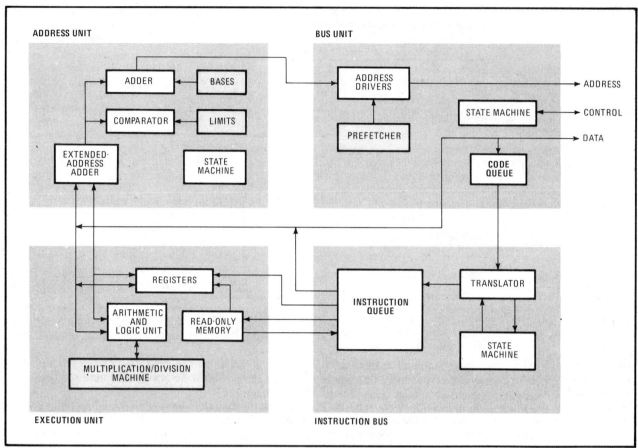

4. Pipelined operation. The four separate subunits of the 286 operate in parallel to address, fetch, decode, and execute instructions. Throughput is further increased over the 8086 by demultiplexing the address and data bus and by the use of improved microcode.

The global descriptor table lists those segments that all system tasks may access, subject only to privilege-level restrictions. A local descriptor table lists those segments available to only one task; as each task includes such a table as part of the description of its state, a typical 286 system will have many local descriptor tables. A register pointing to this table is automatically loaded, along with the other registers, during a task-switching operation.

The descriptor for each segment contains the base address and size of the segment and an access rights field. This field defines how the information in the segment may and may not be used. For example, code segments are always write-protected and may be read-protected as well, whereas data segments can always be read but may be write-protected if desired.

Other bits in the access rights field include the present bit and the descriptor privilege level. The present bit indicates whether the segment is present in real memory or whether it is located in secondary storage for virtual memory systems.

The descriptor privilege level is compared with the processor's current privilege level and, if higher, does not allow the program to gain access to the segment. Any attempted access to such a segment results in a protection fault.

The 286's flag register is similar to the 8086 in containing six arithmetic and three system status flags. Where it differs is in adding further system status flags—the nested flag and the 2-bit I/O privilege level flag. These new flags control protected I/O operations.

Altogether, the 286 has 17 registers. It has the same eight programmer-visible registers as the 8086 for general-purpose arithmetic and offset address computation to ensure compatibility with the 8086 and 8088 software base (Fig. 2).

Protective register structure

Four segment registers define the four segments of the virtual address space currently visible to the executing task. They are the code, data, extra, and stack segment registers. Wider versions of the 8086's 16-bit segment registers, the 286's 64-bit segment registers each contain a 16-bit selector and a 48-bit descriptor. Though a task utilizes only four hardware segment registers, up to 16-K segments are accessible to a single task. The hardware registers are reloaded each time a new segment is requested in a manner that is completely transparent to the programmer.

A selector is an index to a table of descriptors kept in external main memory. As before, the descriptor includes the base address of a segment, the segment length, and the specific access rights for that segment. The processor copies this descriptor information from main memory into the segment register where it is used for high-speed address translation and protection-checking operations.

Three descriptor-table registers are provided in the

Software simplifies 286 evaluation

When a new microprocessor was introduced in the past, customers had to wait until silicon devices were available to evaluate the chip. To avoid this delay, Intel has developed the iAPX-286 evaluation package for an Intellec series III microcomputer development system. It enables system designers to begin their development of 286 software before an actual processor is available.

Four evaluation programs with support libraries help programmers become familiar with the operation of the 286 instruction set and memory-protection mechanism. The demonstration program illustrates the architectural features of the 286 with an evaluation version of a multitasking operating system and a series of utility programs and can be used as a model for customers to develop their own operating systems.

The evaluation version of the 286 macroinstruction assembler translates 286 source code into an object file and a source listing. The evaluation builder accepts that object file and creates an executable task that may be debugged using the evaluation simulator.

The evaluation simulator contains a loader and a monitor/debugger. It provides built-in system functions for input and output as well. After loading a task into memory, it initializes the descriptor tables, the task-state segment, and the code- and data-segment registers. The symbolic debugger is also controlled by the loader program.

The simulator itself is an 8086 program that runs on the Intellec development system. It runs 286 programs, either normally or a step at a time, enforcing all of the 286 protection rules and executing all supported instructions.

Though the 286 evaluation package can familiarize designers with the operation of the 286, it does not provide the total support required to develop large systems. Intel's planned releases of development software include a full-scale macroinstruction assembler, a system builder program, a linker-binder program, a librarian program, and several high-level–language translators. PL/M will be the first high-level language to be offered for the 286, with Pascal to follow in 1982. Future high-level languages will include Fortran and other standard languages from the 8086 family. Hardware support will include in-circuit emulation and a single-board computer.

---

286. These registers point to the three active descriptor tables in main memory. The global and local descriptor tables contain descriptors for the segments accessible to a task. The interrupt descriptor table is used to vector interrupts.

A task register is the seventeenth and last of the set of 286 registers. It indicates the segment reserved to describe the state of the currently executing task and is used to save and restore the machine state automatically when one task is being swapped for another.

A gigabyte of virtual memory

Because all the 286's instructions refer to virtual rather than physical addresses, the operating system can relocate a program to any available segment of physical memory. This addressing scheme potentially gives every user access to a gigabyte of virtual memory.

A segment of the 286 is a portion of the virtual address space that may vary in length from 1 byte to 64-K bytes. This approach makes more efficient use of available memory space than would a page, which has a fixed length. The variable-length feature enables a segment to match the length of a procedure or data area exactly for more efficient swapping operations.

A virtual address on the 286 is composed of a selector and an offset. The selector is an index from the base address of a descriptor table to the desired location of the descriptor within the table. The offset is the byte location of the data within the segment (Fig. 3).

The process of addressing memory begins when a selector is placed in one of the segment registers. When the processor receives the new selector, it compares the access rights of the current task with the access rights indicated in the selector's associated descriptor while the latter is still in main memory.

When access is granted, the descriptor is automatically copied from main memory into the segment register and thus installed alongside the selector. Only the selector is visible to the program. The descriptor being used by the processor makes the absolute physical reference to memory.

At this point, the processor may access the code or data within the new segment. Subsequent accesses to that segment need specify only the desired offset, thereby minimizing the software overhead of managing and using the virtual-address space.

On-the-fly virtual-memory management is implemented through a present bit in each descriptor. If the operating system has marked a segment as nonpresent, a nonpresent fault initiates procedures to bring the segment into main memory. Once that segment is brought into main memory, the present bit is modified and the instructions loading the segment may be restarted.

Software compatibility

Software developed for either the iAPX-86 or -88 processors—the 8086 or 8088—can be run directly on the 286. The 286 even offers a mode of operation that will execute unmodified 8086 and 8088 object code. Called the real address mode, it greatly increases throughput but does not support protection or virtual-addressing features. The other operating mode, called the protected virtual-address mode, invokes the 286's memory-protection and memory-management hardware and is upwardly compatible with both 8086 and 8088 source code.

A system designed around 286 hardware can be used immediately with 8086 software, since the instruction set of the 8086 is a subset of the 286 instructions. Later, as operating systems are developed to use the full power of the 286, this system may be upgraded to operate in the protected mode without hardware modifications of any kind being necessary.

Virtual-address translation and protection checking operations are transparent to the 8086 application programs, which normally require only recompilation or reassembly to make them fully compatible with the 286 protected mode.

Most microprocessors must fetch, decode, and execute each instruction in serial fashion before starting the next instruction. Computing effective address values typically adds more steps and more time to this sequence. However, the 286 carries out these operations in parallel. Pipelining makes maximum use of the system bus by enabling one part of the processor to fetch instructions while other parts are decoding and executing previous instructions. In addition, the 286 can utilize available bus cycles to get as many as three instructions ahead of the processor's arithmetic and logic unit. As a result, the 286 provides much greater throughput than previous microprocessors, without requiring faster memory.

A pipelining plus

Instruction pipelining also makes it possible to detect invalid instructions before they can be executed and to check the protection attributes of a memory segment before granting access to that segment.

The 8086 provides two levels of pipelining. However, the 286 contains four separate logical units: the bus, address, instruction, and execution units (Fig. 4). These four units operate simultaneously so that memory accesses, address calculation and protection checks, instruction decoding, and execute cycles can overlap, partially accounting for the sixfold increase in throughput the 286 offers over the 8086.

The bus unit transfers information from its code queue to the instruction unit at a rate of 1 byte per clock cycle. The instruction unit then decodes and formats complete instructions and places them in an instruction queue to await execution.

The execution unit contains the working registers, the ALU, and the microcode read-only memory. The ROM defines the internal microinstruction sequencing, which executes instructions. As the microinstruction sequence for an instruction nears completion, the ROM generates a signal that causes the execution unit to take the next ROM address from the instruction queue. This technique

keeps the execution unit continually busy.

The address unit translates addresses at the same time as it checks access rights. This unit maintains a cache that contains the base address, the boundary limit, and the access rights for all virtual-memory segments currently selected for use by the executing task. By minimizing the need to read this information from memory, the explicit cache enables the address unit to perform its function in a single clock cycle.

The parallel operation of these four internal units enables the 286 to support virtual-memory management and to provide total memory protection without degrading its high-speed operation.

Another reason for its high speed is that the 286 microprocessor is equipped with separate data and address lines, as opposed to the multiplexed scheme of the 8086, thus doubling bus bandwidth and requiring a 68-lead package. This interface is highly optimized—pipelined bus cycles let successive bus operations take place at a rate of one bus cycle every two processor cycles—200 nanoseconds with a 10-megahertz clock.

Hardware supports of multitasking

In anticipation of multitasking environments, dedicated task-switching hardware has been included in the 286, which is the only microprocessor with this capability. This hardware automatically handles transitions between tasks to support task dispatch operations and to handle interrupts. The hardware-supported switching operation requires less than 18 microseconds at 10 MHz.

Most contemporary microprocessors require numerous instructions to save the state of one task and then recall the state of another. The task-switching hardware of the 286 lets programmers make transitions much faster and more easily using just a call or jump instruction or by an external interrupt.

All of the dynamically variable registers for an inactive task reside in a part of memory called the task-state segment. When a task switch is invoked, the processor automatically verifies all protection requirements before the switch takes place. After these requirements are satisfied, the hardware saves the state of the current task in that task's task-state segment and then loads the processor registers with new information from another task-state segment.

Nested interrupts are supported by a linkage word within a task-state segment. When these occur, the linkage word points to the previous task-state segment. The linkage then provides a return path to the task that was originally interrupted and eliminates all software overhead for these operations.

The 286 instruction set facilitates the implementation of sophisticated systems developed in modern high-level languages (see table). To the 8086 instructions, the 286 adds others that improve high-level language execution. These new instructions simplify handling stack operations, calculating and checking dynamic-array indexes, and executing procedure entry and exit commands in structured high-level languages. With privileged instructions that are accessible only to the highest-level priority, the kernel can set up or reconfigure the memory-protection parameters for the system. ☐

NEW iAPX 286 INSTRUCTIONS		
Instruction	Function	Comments
BOUND	Verifies that a variable's value is within a user-specified upper and lower bound. If the variable value is outside of the specified range, a bounds-exceeded exception is caused.	This is extremely useful for array index checking.
ENTER	Creates the stack frame required by most block-structured high-level languages for procedure calls (this includes allocating space for dynamic variables and maintaining stack frame pointers to previous stack frames).	———
LEAVE	The converse of ENTER deletes stack frames and de-allocates the stack space.	———
PUSHA, POPA	Pushes or pops all eight general registers.	These instructions simplify and speed up interrupt handling and high-level language procedure calls.
BLOCK I/O	Inputs or outputs a block or string of data using a single instruction.	———

Demand-paged memory management boosts 16-bit microsystem throughput

Associative cache returns most references within 100 ns, multiple breakpoint registers lend hardware support to debugging

by Gary Martin, *National Semiconductor Corp., Santa Clara, Calif.*

☐ Despite the expanded addressing capabilities of the newest 16- and 32-bit microprocessors, designers are forced by the cost, size, and power requirements of megabytes of semiconductor memory to settle for much less physical storage and to make up the difference by employing memory-management techniques. The NS16082 XMOS chip (Fig. 1) slips into those NS16000-based systems where increased memory is a requirement, lending high-speed hardware assistance in implementing demand paging—perhaps the most efficient technique for handling memory.

As a slave processor driven directly by the NS16032 central processing unit the NS16082 memory-management unit (MMU) undertakes memory mapping and protection. It also furnishes on-chip facilities for debugging and even helps in implementing virtual machines.

Although the 16-megabyte memory space now available frees designers from the severe limitations imposed by the 64-K-byte limit of earlier 8-bit machines, many are wondering how to take advantage of these new architectures while not significantly raising the price of end systems. Besides the size and power requirements of megabytes of semiconductor memory, original-equipment manufacturers and end users alike often simply cannot justify its expense, particularly in the cost-competitive low-end business market.

The solution, as pioneered by mainframe and minicomputer manufacturers, is the efficient management of semiconductor main memory using a hard disk to give the illusion of a much larger physical address space. A properly implemented memory-management scheme reduces the need for expensive main memory while permitting sophisticated system capabilities such as virtual memory, software protection, and even built-in debugging features.

Contemporary memory-management schemes are alike in some ways because they all attempt to meet the same functional goals. Each technique translates an address issued by the CPU into the address of the physical location of the information. Furthermore, each method protects address space so that programs cannot access or change sensitive data in, for example, the operating system.

Memory-address translation is often augmented by the capacity to detect invalid memory references and abort an illegal reference before any irrevocable changes are made, either in memory or in the CPU itself. This detection is the key element in an approach called virtual memory, in which the operating system swaps needed data into memory from fast-access mass storage. The two major memory-management schemes in use today are segmentation and demand paging.

Although it seems to be a natural approach to memory management, segmentation suffers from hidden problems that do not become apparent until an attempt is made to build a cost-effective high-performance system. Executing algorithms for segment replacement exacts a substantial overhead and can degrade system performance. Furthermore, the penalty for making a wrong decision is high since the entire segment must be swapped back if removed prematurely (see "The drawbacks of memory segmentation,").

On the other hand, the problems associated with unequal-sized segments are overcome by the demand-paging scheme, which divides virtual and physical address spaces into pages 512 bytes long. In this approach, the

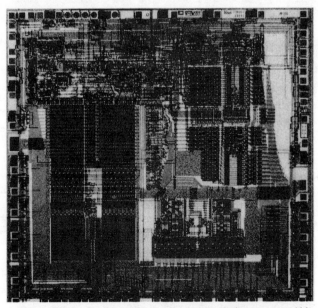

1. Pager. This single-chip memory-management unit uses an on-chip 32-entry content-addressable cache (lower left block) for high-speed translation of virtual addresses. For those 97% of all references that score hits in the cache, translation takes only about 100 ns. A reference not saved in cache takes 2 to 3 μs to translate.

fundamental swapping unit is a page of uniform size, rather than a segment of arbitrary size (Fig. 2). When a portion of code or data is needed, it is not necessary to swap out an entire program or data structure to free enough memory—any page will be sufficient. Dealing with pages greatly reduces the time spent in data movement. Swapping a 512-byte page or cluster of pages is much more efficient than swapping out some large segment, say, 100 kilobytes in length, for example. Furthermore, fragmentation of backup storage due to the scatter-

ing of segments of unequal size is eliminated.

Overhead is reduced as well, since the CPU does not have to search for an appropriately sized hole or segment to swap. If any hole is available, it must be the right size since all pages are the same length. Thus the replacement algorithm can concentrate on which page is the optimal to swap on the basis not of its size but of its history of usage. Hence, the penalty for making a wrong prediction is greatly reduced.

Multitasking systems benefit further from the demand-

The drawbacks of memory segmentation

Adopted by minicomputer manufacturers in the 1960s as a short-term solution to the memory capacity problem, segmentation divides the memory's address space into a number of blocks, or segments, of unequal length, as shown in the figure. The operating system uniquely identifies and describes each segment, assigning one or more to each program or task in the system. In fact, each program or task may be split into several segments—some for data and some for independent parts of the program itself.

Since the fundamental unit of swapping is the segment itself, the worst flaw in this approach occurs in resource allocation. When information contained in some segment is needed, the entire segment must be transferred from disk to memory, not just the smaller portion containing the data that is actually needed. As a result, any segment needed in memory must reside wholly in physical memory.

Thus when a segment must be swapped into memory, a hole of sufficient size must be available in physical memory to fit the segment. One implication of this restraint is that the maximum segment size that can be accommodated by a system is slightly smaller than the size of contiguous physical memory—under 1 megabyte in most microprocessor-based systems. This arbitrary limit on the size of programs or data in small systems in effect nullifies the advantage of the huge memory space of the new microprocessors.

Furthermore, the allocation of physical memory to segments severely degrades overall system performance. If a large data segment must be swapped out of memory to make room for another segment, the bus and disk must be tied up to transfer the entire segment.

Another limitation with this scheme that is felt on the system level involves the number of segments that may be active at once. Even if many segment descriptors are resident on board for high-speed translation, the system may be able to handle no more than a few tasks simultaneously. Each task will require at least one descriptor for its program and another for data. In fact, typical programs take four or five segment descriptors. Just as their associated segments must be loaded into memory, segment descriptors must be loaded be-

fore the program segment begins execution.

In some implementations of segmentation, segment descriptors can identify only those memory spaces that are a power of two in length—for example, 2-, 4-, 8-, or 16-K bytes. The number of bytes allocated to a segment in excess of those actually needed for the program or data structure is wasted space. A way around this internal fragmentation of memory is to add enough segment descriptors so that the granularity of the segment size is decreased. But the cost here is a waste of descriptor space. Matching segment size with the correctly sized hole in memory leads to another memory-allocation problem called external fragmentation. Before a segment can be swapped into memory, a hole of the right size must be found. When the holes between segments in memory are too small, the operating system must decide whether it should swap out a segment to create a large enough hole, wait for a program to terminate and release enough space, or crunch the existing segments to create enough room.

Few systems adopt this latter approach, called dynamic relocation. More typically, the operating system removes segments to create a hole of the right size. Since the segment swapped into this hole rarely completely fills the available space, a certain amount of memory will remain unavailable for use—too small for any segment. This external fragmentation problem extends to the use of space on the swap disk for similar reasons.

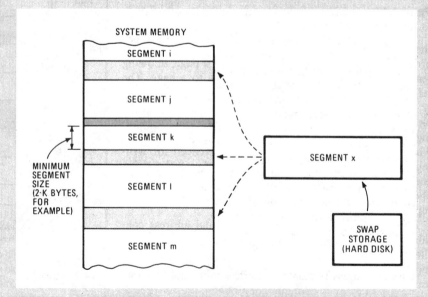

210

paging method. Since more programs may have some parts in physical memory rather than just a few having large segments resident, the number of active tasks may be increased without increased context-switching time.

Demand paging does waste a small amount of storage in some pages since the size of the fundamental unit is fixed. This internal fragmentation, found also with segmentation, is still minor when compared with external fragmentation in segmented schemes.

Associative cache

The NS16082 MMU aids implementation of demand-paged virtual memory through several independent hardware features (Fig. 3). Primarily, the MMU translates virtual addresses into physical addresses through an associative table containing references to the most recently used 32 pages. Since this translation method requires that each address reference be looked up in memory-based tables, its use would be prohibitive in high-performance systems without such high-speed cache. On the average, however, cache references account for 97% of all references and are accomplished within 100 nanoseconds. For the remaining 3% of the address references, the MMU needs only 2 to 3 microseconds to effect their translation into physical addresses. Thus, the weighted average translation time is 157 ns. There are no automatically inserted wait states to lengthen address translation time.

The additional translation time for approximately 3% of the address references accrues during an automatic MMU function called page-table lookup. When a reference is not in the translation cache, the MMU accesses a set of descriptors in memory through a page-table base register. The MMU then replaces the least recently used cache entry with the new reference from memory.

Address translation is controlled by page-table entries in physical memory. Each such entry controls the mapping of one page of virtual memory into real memory, telling the CPU whether that page is in physical memory or not. If it is in physical memory, the page-table entry contains the mapping, memory-protection, and usage information for that page.

Page-table entries

In the page-table entry, the valid bit indicates whether the entry may be used for address translation. The 2-bit protection-level field controls accesses to a page, allowing read and write, write, read, or no access to a page. The referenced bit indicates whether the page has been recently accessed. Since the referenced bit remains set until cleared by software, this bit provides a means for locating inactive pages. Another bit, the modified bit, is set whenever the corresponding page is referenced for writing. High-performance operating systems use the referenced and modified bits to make intelligent decisions about which pages are the best candidates for replacement.

As it enters the MMU, the 24-bit virtual address contains three fields of information that are used to map to the appropriate page. The high-order 8 bits are called the index-1 field, the next 7 bits are the index-2 field, and the low-order 9 bits are the untranslated offset. One of the two page-table base registers holds the physical address

of the level-1 page table. The contents of the 4-byte-long page-table entry contain status information regarding the corresponding page. If the protection level in the level-1 page-table entry denies access to the level-2 page table, an exception called an abort (1), occurs. The abort level associated with a particular address-translation error is reflected in a 3-bit translation-error–type field in the MMU. Thus, the MMU indicates an abort (1)—a protection-level error—by setting bit 0 in the translation-error–type field. If the valid bit in the level-1 page-table entry is 0, an abort (2) occurs. Only if no page fault is detected is the referenced field set in the level-1 table entry.

A similar set of validation and protection checks occurs as the access goes down to the level-2 stage. The physical address of the index-2 page-table entry is obtained by replacing bits 0 through 8 of the index-1 page-table entry with a number four times the index-2 field of the virtual address. At this point, if the protection level in the level-2 page-table entry denies access to the page, an abort (1) exception occurs. If the valid bit in the level-2 page-table entry is 0, an abort (4) exception occurs. However, if there is no fault, the referenced bit is set and, if the access is for writing to the page, the modified bit is also set. Finally, the physical address of the desired location is obtained by replacing the low-order 9 bits of the level-2 page-table entry by the low-order 9 bits of the virtual address.

Updating the record

To ensure that the translation-buffer cache reliably reflects the state of the page tables in memory, its contents are discarded whenever the page-table register is modified. But when a change is made to one of the page tables in memory, the cache must be updated by storing

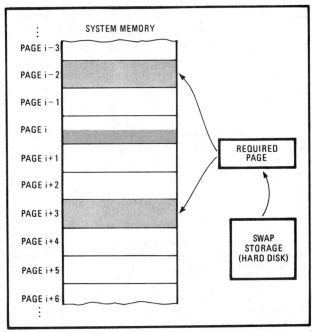

2. Always space. With demand paging, replacement algorithms need only be concerned with optimum replacement strategies and not with the size of the available memory slot since any unused page (tinted) is always the right size. Internal fragmentation (shaded) can occur since data or a program may occasionally need only a fraction of the page.

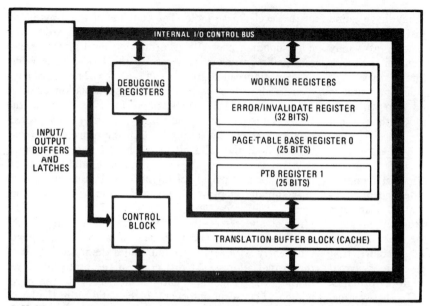

3. Multipurpose. Besides the high-speed cache block, the NS16082 memory-management unit contains a separate control block as well as a pair of blocks for debugging and address translation. Two page-table base registers allow two virtual-address spaces simultaneously.

the address of the affected virtual page into the error–invalidate-address register. This double-word register invalidates a reference in the translation buffer. Thus when an entry in a page table is modified, its copy in the translation buffer must be deleted by writing the address of the affected virtual page into this register.

With its two page-table base registers, the MMU is able to support two virtual-address spaces simultaneously, allowing for rapid switching and dispatching of tasks in a multitasking system. For example, one virtual-address space may belong totally to the supervisor, while the other may be held by the currently active task. In order to transfer control to a new task, the operating system need only replace the page-table register with the page-table address of the new task. The hardware then automatically invalidates only those cache entries that are associated with the altered page-table base register. With this technique, multiple virtual-address spaces are not difficult to implement.

Multiple virtual-address spaces are particularly advantageous whenever a high level of security is mandatory. The dual address space of the NS16082 permits the operating system and application tasks to share the available physical memory, while maintaining completely independent virtual-address spaces. The address spaces of tasks may share pages as needed—as within a common data

MEMORY-MANAGEMENT INSTRUCTIONS ON THE NS16082	
Instruction (all privileged)	**Description**
LMR	Load memory-management register
SMR	Store memory-management register
RDVAL	Validate address for reading
WRVAL	Validate address for writing
MOVSUi	Move a value from supervisor space to user space
MOCUSi	Move a value from user space to supervisor space

base—but they may also possess totally disjoint spaces for maximum system security. Instructions in the NS16032 CPU provide a mechanism for moving data between such disjoint address spaces (see table).

In a virtual-memory environment, a programmer may view all 16 megabytes of address space as available memory, subject only to any restrictions imposed by the operating system. The mapping procedure that converts virtual into physical memory addresses is transparent to application programmers. When the CPU attempts to access a part of a program or data structure that is not in physical memory, a memory-management exception—called abort—occurs and the instruction in progress is immediately terminated.

At this point, the CPU resets its state back to the one that existed just before execution of the offending instruction and reads the cause of the abort trap from the memory status register. After the exception service routine resolves the error condition—for example, by swapping in a needed page from disk—the instruction that gave rise to the trap is reexecuted from the beginning.

A pair of additional capabilities of the MMU—debugging and virtual machine support—prove particularly useful in the software development environment. Whether following sequential or nonsequential program flow while debugging a program, a programmer must be able to halt program execution when a specified address is accessed some specified number of times.

Breakpoint registers

Two registers in the MMU allow four different breakpoints to be selected either at specified virtual addresses or at specified physical addresses. For even finer control of program flow, the breakpoint-address registers can be designated to halt execution when the selected address is written to, read from, or when an instruction is fetched. These two hardware breakpoint registers supplement the software breakpoint in the CPU instruction set.

As additional hardware support, a pair of program-flow registers record the addresses of the last two nonsequential instructions—instructions to which program flow passes following an exception or a branch, jump, call, or return instruction.

For programmers needing a variety of systems, the NS16000 family supports implementation of virtual machines. These software entities give the programmer the illusion of having not only a large address space but also a completely independent computing system. In a virtual machine, every resource is described by a table in memory. The status of each input/output device, for example, is stored in these tables. Requests by user programs or by operating systems are satisfied by information from these tables, rather than from hardware in the physical machine. □

Microsystems can expand with virtual-memory management

Chip provides paged virtual-memory management, allowing larger programs and access for more users

by Jackson Hu, David Stevenson, and J.K. Tsai, *Zilog Inc., Cupertino, Calif.*

☐ Encompassing the capabilities of memory management, the Z8015 paged memory-management unit extends the reach of Z8000-based microsystems. The single-chip PMMU expands the memory space available to the Z8003, facilitates multiuser applications, and provides a variety of memory-protection mechanisms.

The prime role of the Z8015 is to manage main and secondary memory as a unified space so that the system user has a much larger address space than main memory alone can provide. Virtual-memory management, as it is called, begins by the PMMU's translating the logical addresses used in a program into physical addresses denoting the information's actual location in main or secondary memory (Fig. 1).

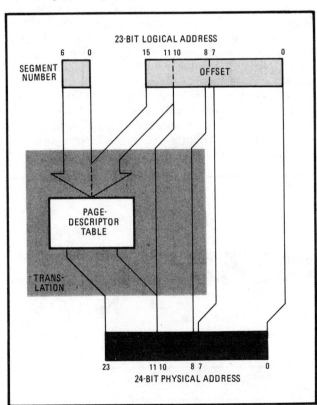

1. Get physical. The 23-bit logical address put out by the Z8003 microprocessor is divided into a 7-bit segment number and a 16-bit offset. The PMMU translates the upper 12 bits into the 13 most significant bits of the page's physical address.

Whenever a logical address refers to information outside main memory, the Z8015 alerts the Z8003 to suspend execution of the program and to fetch the relevant data from a mass storage device, swapping it for information that is not being used. Thus programs much larger than main memory can be run as a unit—and the memory management making that possible is transparent to the system user.

A virtual memory manager also can expand the number of nodes a multiuser system can accommodate by permitting only small portions of each program to be present in main memory at any one time. It also will defend the integrity of the information by denying any one user access to any other's segments of memory and by preventing such undesirable operations as writing into a read-only area.

Bringing virtual-memory management to the microsystem level requires some very specialized hardware to map a host of logical addresses into a necessarily smaller physical main memory. In a paged virtual-memory-management scheme, this process is further complicated since only program fragments of a fixed size—pages—are present in memory at any one time.

The beauty of the paged scheme is that it allows a program of any size to run on microsystems with widely varying memory sizes, because only a small portion of the program need be resident at any given time. However, the hardware to make this page swapping user-transparent can get very unwieldy.

The payoff for a good page-swapping design is worth it, though. In multiuser applications, more users can have needed portions of their programs simultaneously in main memory, thereby decreasing the response time at each user's terminal. Also, a paged approach can appreciably cut the overhead of the operating system's task swapping because information in memory need never be relocated in order to make a continuous block available for a large task.

One of the most important requirements for a virtual-memory-management scheme is the ability to abort an instruction attempting to access a page not present in physical memory. This capability requires special hardware in the microprocessor chip that can suspend action on such an instruction, like that included in the Z8003 processor. All the additional circuitry needed to implement a virtual-memory microsystem is provided on the Z8015.

The PMMU provides the basic capabilities for numerous system designs ranging from those with small physical memories but supporting an 8-megabyte virtual-address space to multiple-Z8015 systems that support large multiple-address spaces. In order to use a Z8003-based paged virtual-memory system, the programmer or compiler simply partitions the program and data into variable-sized modules called segments. For example, data and subprograms may be grouped into different segments for the Z8015 to handle.

Virtual paging

When the program is loaded into the system for execution, the operating system further partitions the segments into fixed-size pages. As the program executes, unneeded pages reside in the secondary mass storage, while the information most likely to be accessed next is maintained in main memory. If the needed information is not there, the program is suspended, and operating-system software is invoked to load the required page into main memory. The translation mechanism is updated to show the new page's presence, and the program is restarted by reexecuting the aborted instruction.

Occurring independent of the application software, virtual paging greatly enhances the portability of large, complex programs among different system configurations by freeing the programmer from the worry of sizing the program to make it fit the amount of actual memory space that is available.

The Z8003 divides its 8-megabyte address space into 128 segments of up to 64-K bytes each. It issues a 23-bit segmented address made up of a 7-bit segment number to indicate the segment and a 16-bit offset to locate any byte relative to the beginning of its segment. These segmented addresses, called logical addresses, are transformed by the PMMU into the physical addresses required for access to main memory.

The PMMU further divides each segment into as many 2-K-byte pages as are required. Each Z8015 in a system has internal registers to handle 64 pages. If more pages

are required, more PMMUs can be used, or the one unit's registers can simply be reloaded periodically. Pages are assumed to be allocated in memory on 2-K-byte boundaries, so that the starting location of each page always has the low-order 11 bits of the offset equal to 0.

Not all pages of a segment need be in main memory, and those that are need not be contiguous. The PMMU detects the absence of a page from main memory and initiates an instruction-abort request and an address-translation trap so that the operating system can fetch the required information and restart the program.

The Z8015 saves on chip all the information necessary to restart instructions. First of all, the logical address that caused the page fault is available in three address-violation registers. This address can be used to swap the required instruction or data page into main memory and to create a page-descriptor entry so that the executing program can access this information.

Also, the information can be used to reload the program counter in order to restart the instruction and to determine whether the Z8003's registers must be adjusted so that reexecution will perform correctly. Finally, a data read-write counter register keeps track of how many successful memory accesses an instruction had before the abort operation so that instructions like load-multiple can be restarted correctly.

Memory protection

The PMMU's memory-protection hardware greatly enhances the integrity of the computer system. For example, read-only-memory areas can be protected from write operations, and one user can be prevented from accessing another's code and data. The key to providing these protections is the chip's page-descriptor register, whose format is shown at the top of Fig. 2.

Each memory page is assigned several attributes (Fig. 2, bottom), such as read-only, and each processor memory request is accompanied by status information, such as write. The Z8015 compares the memory-request status with the page's attributes and in the case of an access violation generates instruction-abort, trap-request, and

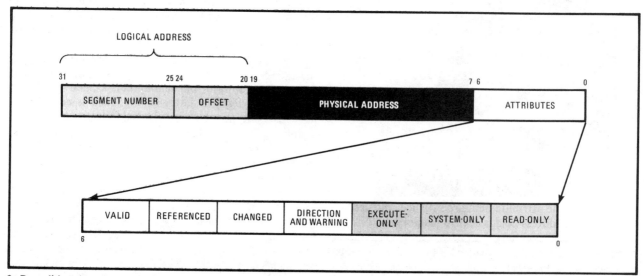

2. Describing descriptors. Each page has a descriptor (top) that indicates its logical and physical addresses and an attribute field (bottom) that holds its protection status. An associative lookup is done on the logical address to speed along translation.

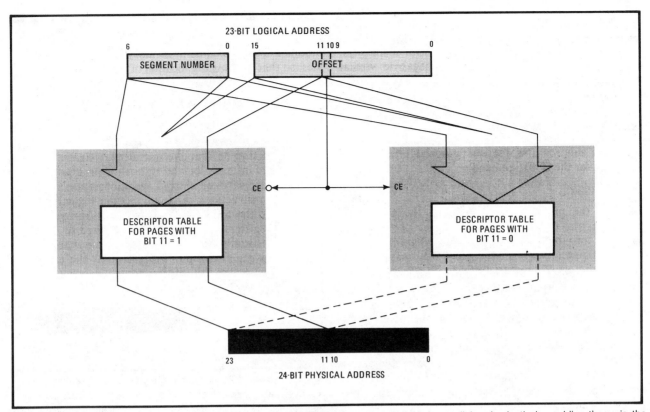

3. If 64 is not enough. More on-line page descriptors can be realized by wiring PMMUs in parallel and selectively enabling them via the chip-select input. Here an address bit is used to differentiate the PMMUs, but a control bit could separate, say, data from code.

suppress signals. The instruction-abort line signals the Z8003 to abort the offending instruction. The trap-request line informs the processor of a mismatch between status and attribute. The suppress line signals the memory to inhibit a store and thus protects the contents from erroneous changes.

Three access bits in the attribute field help prevent invalid accesses. The first of these, read-only, prevents writes to a page and is useful for programs that process data but should not modify the original copy. Another, system-only, prevents access by programs running in the user mode and is useful for protecting system tables when both the operating system and an application program share the same address space. The last, execute-only, prevents reads or writes except during instruction-fetch cycles and so prevents programs that execute a routine from making a copy of it.

When the PMMU receives a logical-address request from the processor, it compares the 7-bit segment number and the 5 most significant bits of the 16-bit offset number with the page-descriptor registers in a content-addressable translation table. It first checks the attribute field's valid flag, which shows whether the descriptor contains valid translation information (that is, that the page is in main memory). If the flag is valid and the 3 access bits of the attribute field are satisfied, the descriptor's physical-address field is sent to memory.

To form the 24-bit physical address, the Z8015 concatenates the lower 11 bits of the processor-originated logical address (indicating the location of the desired byte) to the 13-bit physical address from the descriptor. Because a page's base address always has the low-order 11 bits equal to 0, the PMMU stores only the higher-order 13 bits. For convenience, however, it transmits the 16 most significant bits of the translated address, the lower 3 of which pass through without alteration.

The other 2 bits in the descriptor's attribute field, the changed and referenced flags, are important aids in implementing efficient page swapping. The changed flag indicates that a page has been altered and hence should be copied to secondary storage before its main-memory location is used for another page. The referenced flag can be used to determine which pages have not been accessed recently and thereby can be removed from main memory when space is needed for an incoming page.

The Z8015 also contains a stack-warning facility, which indicates when more memory should be allocated to a stack that is about to spill over its allocated memory. Typically, the legal range of offsets within a segment is from byte 0 upward, but it may be specified downward from 64-K bytes. The latter arrangement is useful for a stack, because the stack-manipulation instructions cause it to grow toward lower memory locations.

When a stack grows to its limit, the PMMU notes the write request to the lowest allocated 128 bytes and generates a trap request. No suppress or abort signal is generated, so the write proceeds and the instruction is completed. However, the processor can use the write warning to allocate more memory to the stack.

Other control registers on the PMMU help configure the operating system to perform certain monitoring tasks that serve to improve the efficiency of the memory-management process. Among these registers are the multiple-page-table, user-mode–select, and fatal-condition flags, and the descriptor-address and descriptor-selection–counter registers.

The multiple-page-table flag indicates whether more than one table of pages is present—that is, that more than one Z8015 is in the system. If there are multiple PMMUs, the user-mode–select flag is used to enable the relevant PMMU to translate addresses in response to a user request.

The fatal-condition flag in the violation-type register indicates that a second violation occurred before the previous one had been serviced. It warns that a memory-access error has occurred in the trap-processing routine and typically indicates that the trap-handler routine has a bug and did not correctly handle the previous trap.

The descriptor-address register selects available page descriptors by pointing to one to be read from or written into. It has an automatic incrementing capability so that multiple descriptors can be accessed using the Z8003 special input/output read-write instructions. Further, the descriptor selection-counter register holds a 2-bit counter that indicates which byte in the descriptor is being accessed during the read or write operation.

Direct-memory-access operations from an external device may occur between instruction cycles and can be handled through the PMMU. The Z8015 permits DMA when either the operating system or an application program is running. For each memory access, the page attributes are checked and if a violation is detected, the suppress line is activated.

Because the memory-access request is from an external device rather than from the Z8003, the PMMU cannot issue instruction-abort or trap signals. The device requesting DMA should note the suppress signal and record sufficient information to enable the system to recover from the access violation.

Systems with multiple PMMUs

Although only one PMMU should be actively translating addresses at a given time, multiple units can be ganged to provide a memory-management system capable of handling more than 64 pages. Four approaches will provide particularly useful configurations.

In one approach, the chip-enable line can be used to select a particular PMMU from among multiple units to translate a page address. For example, if one Z8015 is assigned only logical pages with 0 in bit 11 of the logical address and another is assigned only those pages with a 1 in that bit, then address line AD_{11} can be used to select the appropriate chip.

In this case, there are 128 page descriptors on line, so 256-K bytes can be mapped without having to reload any page-descriptor registers. Figure 3 illustrates the address-translation activity of these two PMMUs for command cycles. AD_{11} is used to transfer control data and so must also enter the Z8015s as address lines.

Another use of the chip-enable line separates program pages from data pages. In a two-PMMU configuration, one translates addresses generated during instruction fetches, and the other handles addresses during data fetches. The processor generates special status codes to distinguish instruction from data fetches.

Several Z8015s can be used to implement multiple

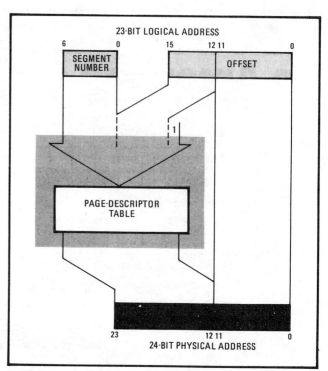

4. Fit the page. If 2-K-byte pages are too small for an application, 4-K-byte pages can be realized by hardwiring the least significant input to the PMMU high and always writing 1s into the least significant bit of the page descriptor's logical-address field.

translation tables in multiuser systems, with each user getting his own PMMU. Multiple tables can be used to reduce the time required to switch between users by assigning separate tables to each. The operating system can use the master enable flag in the mode register to activate the appropriate PMMUs through software.

A final approach employs two translation tables to separate system from user memory. This method uses the multiple-page-table flag in the mode register to indicate the system user. It uses the user-mode–select flag to indicate when the PMMU contains user-mode pages or system-mode pages. The system or user input line then activates the appropriate PMMU.

Changing page size

The PMMU directly supports 2-K-byte pages. However, it can be hardwired with some additional external circuitry to implement systems with larger or smaller pages. For example to implement 4-K-byte pages, AD_{11} should not participate in the translation process but be used directly as the MSB of the offset within a 4-K-byte page (Fig. 4). This can be achieved by setting the AD_{11} input to the Z8015 to be equal to the logical OR of the Z8003's status bit ST_3 and AD_{11}.

The least significant bit in the logical address field of each descriptor register must be set to 1. The AD_{11} input must be 1 during address translation but must equal the AD_{11} output by the Z8003 during command cycles to the PMMU; ST_3 can distinguish the two types of transactions.

To implement 1-K-byte pages, two PMMUs are used. The chip-enable input line is driven by AD_{10} from the Z8003 for one Z8015 and by $\overline{AD_{10}}$ for the other. This technique generates a 23-bit physical address. □

Chip set bestows virtual memory on 16-bit minis

Second-generation chips add support for coprocessors and multiprocessors as well

by Jan Beekmans,* Gerard Duynisveld,*
Claude Fernandes, Leo de Groot,* Louis Quéré,*
Frans Schiereck,* and Arjaen Vermeulen
*Philips Data Systems, Apeldoorn, the Netherlands,
and Fontenay-aux-Roses, France*

☐ The application of state-of-the-art MOS and bipolar custom circuitry to computer systems is boosting performance and the number of functions at a phenomenal rate. To protect its edge in system and software know-how over semiconductor houses, Philips Data Systems began a custom large-scale integrated-circuit design effort several years ago. It had the first building blocks by 1979: a 16-bit microprocessor (the SP 16C/10) and two bipolar circuits—one for bus arbitration (the SP16C/12) and one to support the interrupt system (the SP 16C/11).

But though this first generation was powerful, programs have become larger, requiring more addressable memory. Multiprocessing for multiusers demands virtual memory management, as well as strong memory protection. All this has led to a second-generation 16-bit processor—the SP 16C/20 instruction execution unit—and the SP 16C/23 memory management unit. This set supports virtual memory, dynamic code changes, and multiprocessor protocols, plus coprocessors for decimal and floating-point operations.

In addition, the new generation's instruction capabilities allow swapping of virtual memory into available physical space but do not restrict the swapping to fixed-size segments. By allowing segments to be of varying lengths, an entire task can be kept together.

Implementation

The SP 16C/10 was designed to execute a basic, 120-instruction set (called the primary, or P, set) using real, or physical, addressing. It was realized in static, depletion-load enhancement-driver n-channel MOS technology, initially with 6-micrometer minimum features, but now with 4 μm. The design is housed in a 40-pin package; the clock frequency of the 4-μm device is 4 megahertz. In that version, the shortest instructions take less than 2 microseconds. The processor works with both synchronous and asynchronous input/output interfaces,

* Temporarily at Signetics Corp., Sunnyvale, Calif.

supports direct-memory-access requests, and has a non-maskable interrupt input, along with four maskable ones. Its 16-bit data bus is multiplexed with the address bus. In its present version, the chip measures about 200 mils (5.1 millimeters) a side.

The addition of the virtual addressing scheme called for supporting an additional instruction class and led to a two-chip set for the new members of the computer family. Because the address translation is done in parallel with all instructions, it adds no appreciable delays to instruction execution. The block diagrams of the two new chips are shown in Figs. 1 and 2.

Complete compatibility

To preserve the vast investments of the last decade in system and application software, complete compatibility right down to the machine-code level is dictated. The best way to maintain compatibility and also add functions to an established computer line is to provide new instruction categories while incorporating more sophisticated address schemes, like support of virtual memory, into all instructions. Table 1 shows the four different instruction classes, including the two address schemes, along with the computer designed to execute them. All four classes are based on 16-bit-wide code and data.

Most of the 120 instructions in the P set have five different addressing modes: immediate, register, indirect, indexed, and indexed with indirection. Several data formats, including bits, bytes, words, and double words, are also supported. The set includes instructions like multiply and divide, 16 different shifts, and test and set or reset a bit, as well as 10 string-handling instructions that can move strings up to 64-K bytes long or search for a match with a specified character.

The D set acts on decimals up to 33 digits long and converts between the different formats currently in use for data processing. It comprises 22 instructions.

The F set covers floating-point instructions. Of the two addressing schemes—real and virtual—the real system is most widely used; here addresses directly indicate physical locations in main memory. Because the addresses are 16 bits wide in the real scheme and the smallest addressable unit is a byte, a 64-K-byte main memory can be addressed.

Virtual memory

In the virtual memory scheme, 32-bit addresses are handled in the program, whereas 24-bit physical addresses are computed. In this case, an extra instruction category, the V set, is added to support the wider addresses and the built-in protection mechanisms. Also, there are added instructions to support block-structured languages by implementing both a system stack, used for system parameters, and a user stack, for variables.

When instruction categories F and D are not being executed by hardware coprocessors, traps are generated to allow emulation of such instructions in software. There also are two privilege modes for instructions: system and user. Those instructions available only at the system privilege level control I/O operations, virtual memory management, and the system stack.

The segmented virtual memory management scheme

of Fig. 3 meets the requirement of upward compatibility with the existing computer line while serving the need for a well-protected memory space much larger than 64-K bytes. Simply enlarging the address space without any protection—making a linear address space of several megabytes—is inadequate for multiuser applications.

The address space

A virtual memory scheme with 32-bit addresses yields an address space of 4 gigabytes. The address space is divided into 65,536 segments, each ranging from a minimal 256 bytes to a maximal of 64-K bytes, allowing for convenient execution of older programs at the machine-code level by placing them in a single segment. Segments with flexible lengths are chosen over the simpler page-

based systems—where every page has a fixed length—because variable-length segments can each hold a complete software task.

Upward compatibility with the real addressing mode is preserved by dividing the 32-bit address into two parts—a 16-bit segment number and a 16-bit displacement. These are treated separately so that there is no overflow into an adjacent segment, which could destroy another user's program. When a user reaches beyond the end of his current segment a flag is set that is checked by the microprogram very early in each instruction's execution cycle, preventing illegal accesses.

A segment number signifies an entry in both the system context table and the segment index table. The system context table indicates the locations of the vari-

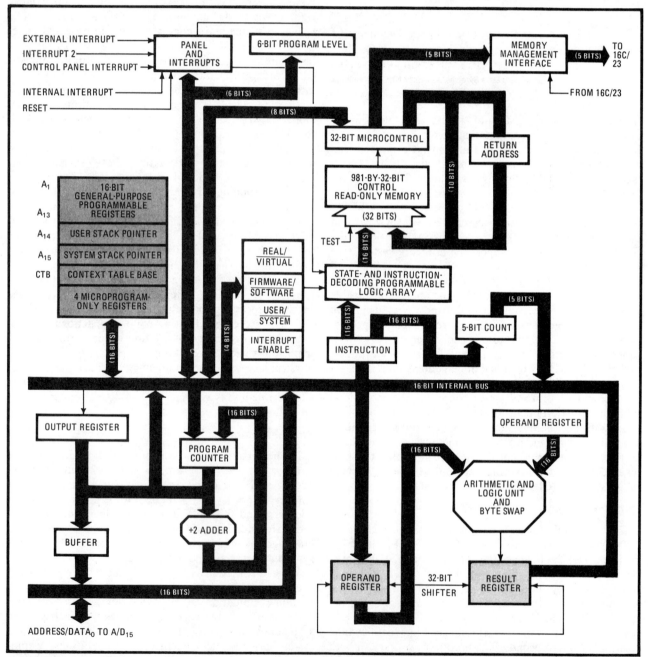

1. Inside the processor. The SP 16C/20 contains all the standard modules of a central processing unit, plus an interface to the SP 16C/23 memory management unit. It is fully microprogrammed and makes use of a programmable logic array to decode instructions.

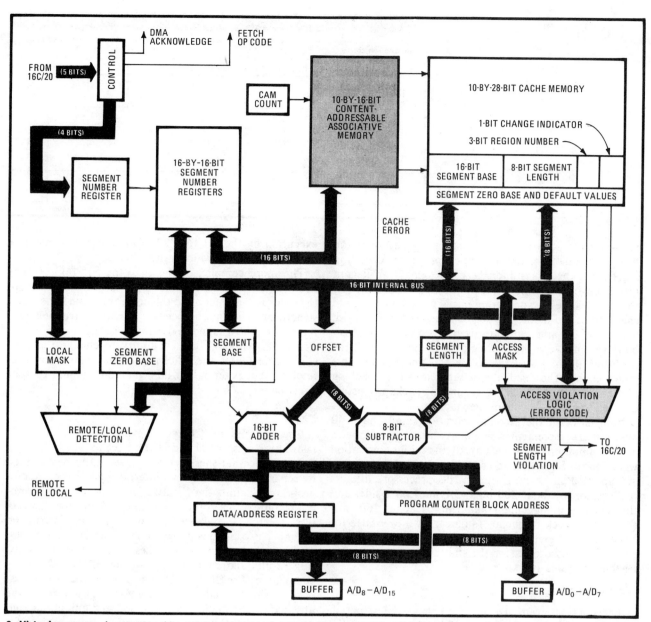

2. Virtual memory. A separate chip manages the virtual memory in parallel with the CPU's data calculations. The content-addressable memory and high-speed cache for descriptors keep protected address calculations from slowing down the processor.

ous parts of a user's program context. The segment index table holds the address of the segment descriptor, which in turn holds the address of the user's segment, as well as its length and protection status. These tables let users who by definition have different program contexts share the same segment without the need to copy it into different memory locations. The displacement and the first 16 bits of the segment descriptor (the segment base) form a 24-bit real address for the 16-megabyte on-line memory. The existence of segments is checked during the conversion through the tables, and the displacement is checked against the segment length. An abort trap is activated whenever one of those checks fails.

The protection scheme controls access to users' tasks being executed in the same virtual address space. Each task can be given different access rights to each individual segment (no access or read-only or read/write access). In addition, priority levels for tasks can either utilize 8

hierarchically organized task categories or 256 nonhierarchical ones.

A portion number is added on top of the segmented address scheme so as to group specific task segments. This scheme greatly eases the construction of the operating system's memory management function, which handles swapping between the 16-megabyte real address space (the on-line memory) and the 4-gigabyte virtual memory.

Not at home

Constructing a virtual memory space leads to requests for instructions or data that is not present in the on-line memory, causing a residence error. This type of error will occur frequently; depending on the execution speed of the instructions, the size of the on-line memory, and the regularity and size of the tasks, it will occur several times per second. Hence, a system must be able to

PHILIPS MINICOMPUTERS USING LARGE-SCALE INTEGRATED PROCESSORS

Instruction classes supported	Using 16C/10 chip (real addressing only)				Using 16C/20 and 23 chips (real and virtual addressing)			
	P-853	P-858	P-400	*	*	*	*	*
Primary	✓	✓	✓	✓	✓	✓	✓	✓
Floating-point		✓		✓		✓		✓
Decimal			✓	✓			✓	✓
Virtual					✓	✓	✓	✓

*Proposed only

recover from it without intervention by the operator. Early in an instruction's microprogram decoding sequence, a check is run for this error to make an elegant restart possible in case it occurs. The procedure slightly complicates the microprogram but is preferable by far to checking at the moment a segment descriptor is loaded, because of the inherent software overhead and the possibility that between the loading of the descriptor and the execution of an instruction in that segment, interrupts might change the residency of segments. The checking also eliminates the need for redundant backup registers to save the previous state of the machine.

Both chips in the second-generation family have 40 pins and are implemented in a dense n-MOS process with 3.5-μm minimum features. Layout and initial fabrication were done at Signetics, and second sourcing is now being set up at Philips in Europe. The processor, like its predecessor, is about 200 mils (5.1 mm) on a side, and the memory management unit (MMU) about 160 mils (4.1 mm). Clock frequency ranges from 6 to 9 MHz for selected parts, giving instruction execution times of less than 700 nanoseconds for the shortest, most frequently used instructions at 6 MHz.

Similar interfaces

The microprogram size for the enhanced instruction set increased from 360 words of 32 bits in the case of the SP 16C/10 to nearly 1,000 words of 32 bits for the SP 16C/20, owing mainly to its virtual memory capability and the requirement that instructions be restartable in case of a residence error. Because processors are members of the same 16-bit computer family, the interfaces with the interrupt system and their buses remain functionally the same.

Translating the logical into the real addresses in the virtual scheme and their inherent checks would normally slow down the processor significantly. Implementing a cache memory on the SP 16C/23 for 11 segment descriptors has fully solved this performance disadvantage. The associate memory checks for valid addresses and loads new descriptors into the cache under microprogram control in order to preserve speed. One of the 11 segment descriptors is always the one used to execute the programs written in the real addressing scheme of the SP 16C/10.

The checks on access rights and segment length are done on the SP 16C/23 in parallel with instruction execution by the SP 16C/20. Thus the virtual memory scheme does not slow down the processor.

The more complex of the two, the SP 16C/20, has about 60,000 transistors, over half of which are used in the read-only memory and the programmable logic array structures. The microprocessor has an instruction prefetcher that also supports dynamic changes in the operation code. Although the capability to change the code slightly decreases the efficiency of the instruction prefetch, it can potentially allow the construction of very dense codes.

Coprocessors, too

Since the SP 16C/20 and 23 execute only the P and V instruction sets, the D and F sets have to be emulated in software. So that these sets may eventually be executed by separate processors, two interfaces have been microprogrammed into the SP 16C/20—one to pass a program context to a coprocessor, in case a decimal instruction is fetched, and one if a floating-point instruction occurs. The context is passed in less than 20 clock cycles, after which the coprocessor takes over the task, transmitting results and context back to the SP 16C/20 at its completion. The SP 16C/20 detects a coprocessor's presence on the fly, and either a context is passed or, in the absence of the dedicated processor, the emulation routine is started. Because the computer line is mainly for business applications, priority is given to the decimal coprocessor, which is now being microprogrammed.

The P instruction set enables the construction of semaphores for a multiprocessor system. In addition, the basic interrupt protocol of the SP 16C/11 can support such systems.

Multiple processors

With this foundation, a multiprocessor system built of identical processors is envisaged. Each processor is placed on a separate printed-circuit board of the Eurocard size, with a part of the general-purpose memory on board. All these distributed memory chunks make up the total on-line memory. Whereas the local memory is addressed synchronously, the second category employs an asynchronous handshake to allow time for other processors to get off the bus and to support the use of memories having a wide variety of access times. To make this memory organization transparent to the system software, the SP 16C/20 and 23 have extra logic to take the

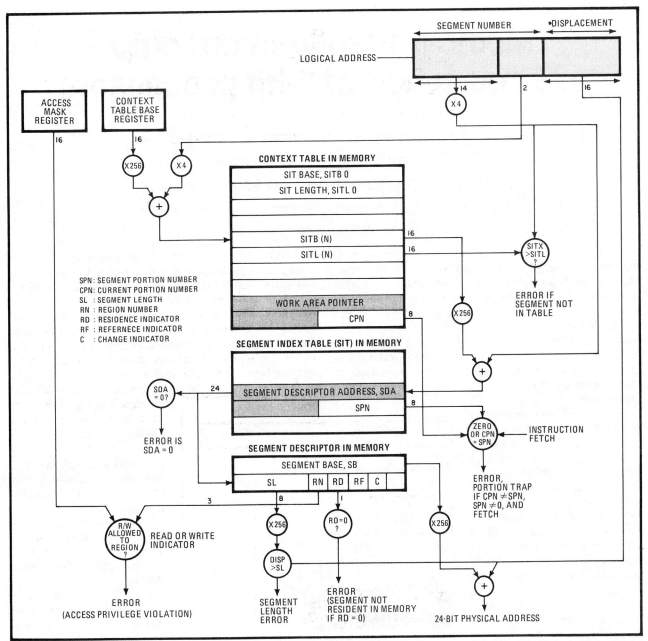

3. Logical to physical. The conversion of 32-bit virtual addresses into 24-bit real addresses is done in two steps. The logical address is used to locate the segment index table entry from the context table, and that entry in turn indicates the location of the segment descriptor.

memory partitioning into account. The idea is to have the processors accessing as much as possible their local (on-board) memory at full speed by a synchronous interface and to minimize the references to remote memory over the slower asynchronous system bus.

At the system level, the processor (or processors, in the case of a multiprocessor system), the on-line memory, and the I/O control units are connected by a system bus, which has as a physical form factor a 96-pin Euroconnector. A 28-pin bipolar device, the SP 16C/12, is designed to permit a bus master device—such as a central processing unit or direct-memory-access control unit—to request and gain control of the common system bus. The SP 16C/12 lets a bus master in a multimaster system communicate with other masters, as well as transfer data to common memory and I/O devices. The

chip is about 160 mils (4.1 mm) on a side and allows modular expansion to any number of bus masters. To maximize throughput, the bus allocation runs in parallel with the other functions on the chip.

To support an interrupt system with as many as 63 different interrupt levels, the SP 16C/11 was designed. It is realized in bipolar technology, measures about 170 mils (4.3 mm) on a side, and is housed in a 22-pin package.

The bus interface of the SP 16C/11 comprises only two lines: a clock for the interrupt system and one for the encoded interrupt information. This concept has many features in common with the interrupt structure of the proposed P-896 bus interface standard that the Institute of Electrical and Electronics Engineers is working on for modern 16- and 32-bit multiprocessor systems. □

Memory management chip extends reach of 8-bit processors

As well as boosting address limits to 2 megabytes, the MC6829 eases the handling of multiple tasks by providing separate register sets for users

by Edward J. Rupp, *Motorola Inc., Austin, Texas*

☐ Memory management is making its way into the 8-bit microprocessor world—and small wonder, for its benefits are as attractive here as in the realms of bigger processors. By allowing a larger memory to be divided into many fixed-size pages, a memory management unit can extend an 8-bit system's address limits beyond the bounds of 64-K bytes. The MMU—a subsystem in itself—can also promote the design of multitasking systems by easing control of swapping—the movement of tasks into and out of physical memory.

An MMU allows programs to be moved among the system's various types of memory with no need for code changes or even for program fragments to be in contiguous locations. Different tasks running on the system may all use the same logical addresses in their code, because the part handles the relocation necessary to prevent collisions.

Because it can translate different addresses to the same location, the unit eases sharing expensive peripherals and memory among processors. A shared memory makes economical use of read-only programs like language compilers and helps implement intertask communication via semaphores—flags residing in shared memory that synchronize the message passing.

On the microsystem level, however, a memory management unit built from TTL can become complex beyond the point of diminishing return. So a large-scale integrated-circuit implementation introduces reliability and is a cost-effective companion for a microprocessor. To expand the memory space of 8-bit microprocessors, Motorola has developed an MMU on a chip.

The MC6829 memory management unit is designed to be directly compatible with the MC6809 microprocessor. However, it will work with other 8-bit processors, too. It extends the addressing range of the 6809 to 2 megabytes and allows rapid switching between as many as thirty-two 64-K-byte memory maps.

The 6829 uses a simple paged mapping scheme converting 16-bit logical addresses from the processor into the 21-bit physical addresses delivered to memory (Fig. 1). Of the 16 processor address lines, five are fed directly into the MMU. They are applied to a 32-word mapping random-access memory, and the data outputs of the RAM become the upper bits of the physical address.

Four groups of 32 mapping registers each are resident on chip, although only one set is active at any one time, as controlled by the operating-key register. Each set is arranged as 32 words of 10 bits each, so that 10 mapped address lines leave the chip.

The 11 unmapped processor lines determine the page size of 2-K bytes. Combining the 6829's 10 output bits with the 11 unmapped bits gives a total of 21 address lines for the address range of 2 megabytes. It takes 110 nanoseconds to translate a logical address into a physical one.

The chip's resources are devoted to handling large memories in multitask environments—there is no provision for page protection, such as flagging read-only pages and generating traps when a write is attempted. Read-only areas could be created, however, by dedicating one of the upper address bits, like bit 20, to write protection. Also, the 6829 is not designed for transparent page swapping—the programmer must include instructions for loading mapping registers before page access.

The chip does provide a convenient means of setting up and changing the contents of its mapping RAM. In

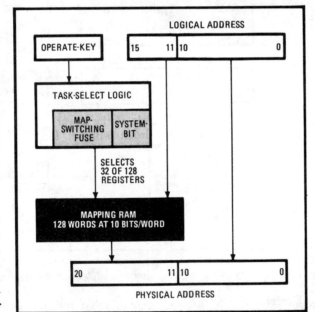

1. The physical translation. A 16-bit logical address is translated into a 21-bit physical address that gives 8-bit microprocessors access to 2 megabytes of memory. One MMU can handle four 64-K-byte tasks organized into thirty-two 2-K-byte pages.

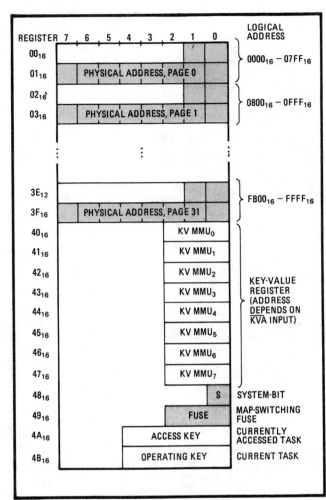

2. Register access. All the registers on the 6829 memory management unit are mapped into the host microprocessor's address space. The key-value registers differentiate MMUs that are wired in parallel, and the access-key register selects one of four tasks.

effect, it appears as a peripheral to the processor during such operations, specifically as 32 double-byte registers. Each of these registers controls the logical to physical mapping for one 2-K-byte page.

Multiple tasks

For multitasking, each 6829 contains enough mapping RAM to hold the addresses for four complete tasks, each of which may have direct access to up to 64-K bytes of memory on thirty-two 2-K-byte pages. If a task is larger, it can simply revise its memory map periodically, giving indirect access to the entire 2 megabytes. Eight of the chips may be present in any one system, which allows thirty-two 64-K-byte tasks to be maintained in hardware registers. Also, the chips may be wired in parallel, easing the design of a multiple-MMU system (Fig. 2).

If a system needs access only to large amounts of memory, a single chip can handle all accesses, though its mapping registers will need to be reloaded. If the goal is fast switching between many tasks, each of them can be assigned to a separate set of MMU registers in a multiple parallel configuration.

Task switching is accomplished by writing the task number in a special register (the operating-key). If that register's contents match those of the key-value register, then that MMU provides a mapped address; otherwise it stays off the memory address bus. During the power-up sequence, the processor initializes the key-value register for each part with a different value. With the exception of the key-value access pin, then, multiple MMUs may be wired in parallel (Fig. 3).

Task selection is controlled by the operating-key and the system-bit registers working with the bus-available and bus-state inputs. The 6809 generates the BA and BS signals directly, though other microprocessors may be adapted to the 6829 by generating these signals with external logic. The scheme for task switching may also change when using other processors.

Task 0 (usually assigned to implement the operating system) is the only one that has access to the registers on the MMU. This provision ensures that a register like the operating-key cannot be changed while its value is being used by a current task. In most multitasking environments, task 0 will contain the program that controls the mapping for all other tasks and will manage the hardware interrupts as well.

Mapping access

The operating system also must have access to the mapping RAM. To do this it uses the access-key register of the 6829. Writing a task number into the access key causes the contents of the mapping RAM for that task to appear in the first 64 bytes of the 6829's registers. The map may then be examined or changed as needed.

A typical operating system function (system call) is to transfer bytes between tasks, usually between the operating system task and a user task. A subroutine can do this easily by mapping a page of the task 0 map onto the appropriate user task page, with no physical movement of the data. The overhead for large memory transfers is only slightly greater than that of a nonmapped system (about two extra instructions per byte moved).

Software interrupts are an ideal way to handle such system calls because they cause automatic switching to the operating system, which can then perform the requested function and subsequently resume execution of the user task. The return to a task is accomplished by setting the operating-key register to the task number, clearing the system-bit (S-bit) and executing a return-from-interrupt (RTI) instruction (see table).

The S-bit controls the precise moment that the set of 32 mapping registers for a new task is activated. It must be cleared after execution of RTI, which is in task 0's memory and therefore is inaccessible to the new task. Since the instruction to clear the S-bit occurs before RTI, the clearing must be delayed a few cycles so that the processor can have the time to execute that instruction. The 6829 provides this delay with a 3-bit down counter called the fuse register. A value of n written to the fuse will cause an n-cycle delay in clearing the S-bit.

Direct memory access may also use the MMU. This is accomplished when the BA input is high, which temporarily overrides the value in the operating-key register and permits task 1 to be selected for mapping the DMA transfer address. BA = 1 implies that the processor has relinquished the bus to some other controller. By

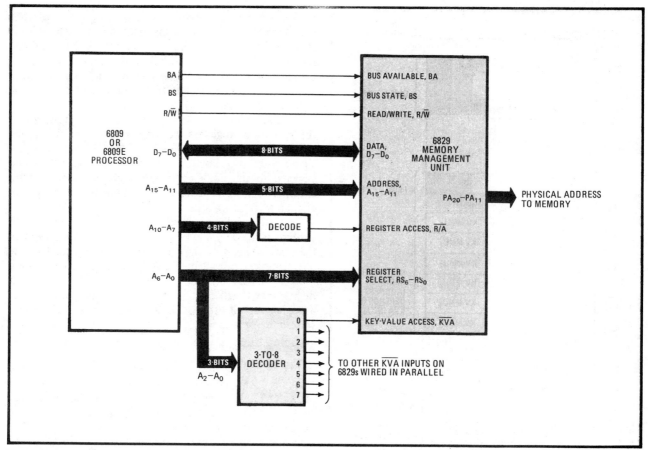

3. Memory marriage. The processor is married to the memory system by the MMUs. Eight can reside in a single system with all pins (except $\overline{\text{KVA}}$) wired in parallel. The $\overline{\text{KVA}}$ pin allows a unique value to be written into the key-value register on each chip separately.

switching to task 1 during these operations, the new bus controller has a completely separate 64-K-byte map with which to work.

Thus a DMA controller could transfer up to 64-K bytes without interfering with any other processor operations. Alternatively, parts of task 1 and other user tasks could be mapped together, allowing direct memory access into any task. The fuse register ignores DMA cycles in order to maintain synchronization with the processor.

The mapping delay, called latency, introduced by the MMU adds directly to the cycle time of the processor. The effect of this delay is to reduce the available setup time for the system peripherals and memory. The current design of the 6829 requires 110 ns to complete the mapping function and arbitrate among multiple MMUs.

The mapping starts at the very beginning of each cycle, but arbitration among multiple units cannot occur

until one quarter cycle later, since each of them must determine the state of the BA and BS inputs for the cycle. At this point, one of the parts will determine that it must supply a mapped address to the physical address bus and turn on its address lines, with all other MMU output lines remaining disabled.

Design choices

When building a system with the 6829, a number of choices are possible. One option is to build the system so that each task has its own set of MMU registers. This is probably the fastest and easiest approach, but it does limit the number of tasks that may be running on the system to a maximum of 32.

Another approach is to use a single 6829 and reload its registers at each task switch. This scheme uses task 0 as the operating system task, task 1 as the DMA map (if needed), and tasks 2 and 3 as the sites of the maps for the user task. The maps for the remaining tasks would be kept in memory and loaded as needed. Any number of tasks may be supported with this method. However, the overhead of reloading registers makes this approach relatively slow.

Alternatively, the designer could use multiple 6829s, treating their registers as a resource to be allocated among the tasks. When a task is ready to run, a free set of MMU registers is allocated and initialized for it. High-priority tasks could then remain in the registers, with little used tasks in external memory. □

SUBROUTINE TO SWITCH TASKS		
PROGRAM		**COMMENTS**
RETURN	ORCC #I + F	disable interrupts (enter critical section)
	STS OSSP	save current operating-system stack
	LDS SAVESP	restore user's stack
	LDA #1	cause map switch one cycle after write
	STA FUSE	write 1 to fuse register
	RTI	return to user task

Smart memories seek honors in proliferating small systems

For ease of use, dynamic RAMs and electrically erasable PROMs aim to look like static memories, while semicustom and associative types augur storage tailored to an era of special-purpose applications

by Roderic Beresford, *Solid State Editor*

☐ Before single-chip systems become routine, many generations of standard components have yet to come and go. Meanwhile, the drive to ever denser systems forces designers daily to question which functions should be integrated with which others, whether they have to make this decision implicitly, by selecting the products of the chip makers, or explicitly, by inventing a custom design themselves.

The most standard of the standard components are memory chips, and the easy assumption is that they will simply get denser and faster as the processing technology for very large-scale integration is put to commercial use. Of course, there are strong market pressures in that direction. Any part that strays from the beaten path with novel features risks narrowing its market and forgoing the high volumes it needs to be profitable.

Nonetheless, the once-sharp partition between memo-ry chips and logic continues to blur, thanks to the large amounts of support circuitry they can include these days for a relatively small overhead. For some time past, the devices have included address decoding and multiplexing as a matter of course. Now the commodity parts are also starting to acquire logic functions that make them easier to use or that optimize them for popular applications. The development is marked both in conventional serial computers and in novel memory architectures inspired by the capabilities for custom very large-scale integrated circuits.

But perhaps the biggest force for change lies in the changing nature of the end market. Most memory chips are now being used in small machines, rather than in mainframes or minicomputers. Clearly, the time is ripe for a fresh look at smarter memories.

The term "smart memory" is applicable to at least

225

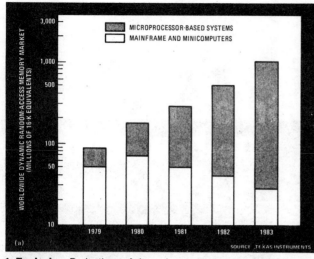
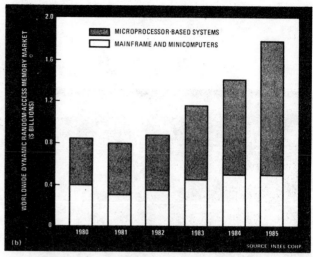

1. Explosive. Projections of dynamic memory consumption show a doubling in the total number of bits next year (a), with microprocessor applications accounting for all of the increase. Though dollar value will be increasing less rapidly (b), the trends are sustained.

three distinct creatures: a more convenient but otherwise conventional memory, a memory-intensive microcomputer, and a memory that, besides storing data, does something more, such as sort or associate its contents.

"Some so-called smart memories are not particularly intelligent, but simply more convenient," says Bob Proebsting, senior design engineer at Mostek Corp., Carrollton, Texas. "Does the chip do more than a perfect random-access memory would, or does it just come closer to that ideal?" Though ease of use may be the lowest grade of intelligence in memories, features that contribute to it are gaining popularity among users, and some appear to be headed for standardization. Prime examples include self-refreshing schemes for dynamic RAMs and electrically erasable programmable read-only memories that can be used like static RAMs. With a standard of ease of use to which other memory types aspire, the static RAM is itself being tailored for specific applications—a question of both convenience and performance.

The second breed, not a memory chip at all, nonetheless accounts for a lot of the memory bits sold. "People buy [single-chip microcomputers] for the kinds of things you buy a memory for; but instead of using them as just a memory, they will use them for intelligent functions, too," says Walden "Wally" C. Rhines, advanced development manager and assistant vice president of Texas Instruments Inc.'s Semiconductor Group in Dallas.

With the growth of libraries of standard logic blocks in the semicustom arena, the user of this type of smart memory will be able to turn away from these standard parts and customize a microcomputer or else call up a few thousand bits of memory along with predefined logic blocks in a semicustom design.

Finally, memories that do something more than just remember continue to intrigue designers and users alike. One area, cache memory, has already seen some entries and is likely to see more. Cache memory makes it faster to access the data currently most in use by storing it in high-speed buffers apart from the vast expanses of slower main memory. To date, it has mostly been found on larger machines, and potential single-chip cache memories face the problem of integrating a design that satis-

fies the needs of many more specific small machines.

In addition, if distributed microprocessing makes the impact it promises to, the door may be opened to further attempts at local virtual-memory chips for microprocessors. Further down the road, content-addressable memories—what some have called the ultimate intelligent memory—may be at the heart of data-base processors structured quite differently from present-day computers.

Dynamic RAM that does more

A familiar force stands in the way of dynamic RAM that does more, even if only a little—the extreme concern among memory producers over standardization of function and pinout that often seems to leave architecture a forgone conclusion as well. The nature of the memory market as a fiercely competitive commodity trade prohibits innovation for its own sake. Only a clear mandate from users can motivate a departure from the traditional product with a by-1-bit organization and multiplexed address inputs in a 16-pin package.

Nevertheless, two related forces are shaping a need for dynamic RAMs that do more, if only a little. At the next density level, 1-bit-wide 256-K parts would give small-system designers a big problem with the minimum eight-chip increment for byte-wide storage. Even today's 64-K increments are ungainly for many designs. Furthermore, giving the user a wider part would be only half the solution. In a system using fewer dynamic RAM chips than before, the cost of refreshing circuitry weighs more heavily and would wipe out the economic advantage that dynamic RAMs hold over static parts. Adding fuel to the fire are the predictions from every corner that the small-computer designer will be a very important customer three years from now.

Recent estimates show the dollar volume last year for all dynamic-memory chips to be split about evenly between the traditional users—mainframe and minicomputers—and smaller, microprocessor-based systems. By 1985, that mix may shift to as much as 75% to the smaller systems. Figure 1 shows some of these projections. Thus, a market of growing importance could be addressed by a smarter dynamic RAM.

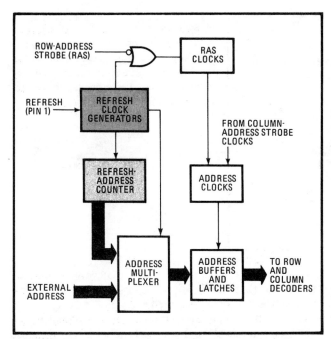

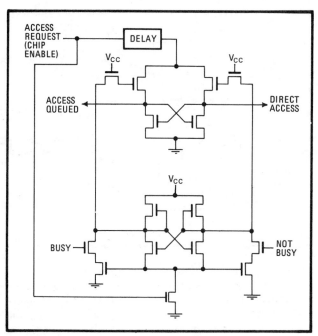

2. Triggered. A request signaled on pin 1 of a dynamic random-access memory by an external trigger starts automatically refreshing the row of cells indicated by the refresh-address counter. Motorola, for one, offers the extra circuitry on a 64-K-by-1-bit dynamic RAM.

3. Taking turns. This two-stage circuit arbitrates between an access request from the processor (chip-enable going low) and an internal refresh request (not-busy going low). Once the upper flip-flop receives the request, it is isolated from the steering inputs below.

"In the design of smaller systems, there is clearly a desire to trade the density of dynamic RAM for a part that is more modular and easier to use. In the past, that has meant by-8 static RAM," says Barbara Nelson, strategic marketing manager in the Memory Products division at Intel Corp., Aloha, Ore. Besides being simple to interface with a processor, the static RAM is popular for another reason: a designer can step through a program "manually" to pinpoint problems. No such slow-motion debugging is possible with a dynamic RAM that must be refreshed every 2 milliseconds. "Static RAMs enjoy a market essentially because of speed and ease of testing, both of the component itself and of the system it is a part of," affirms Wendell Sander, a consultant for Apple Computer Inc. of Cupertino, Calif.

Indeed, for a memory block size up to about 8-K, few would argue that static RAM is the only way to go. The present generation of 2-K-by-8-bit static RAMs, which first saw volume production last year, are addressing that market. On the other hand, above a block size of 64-K, dynamic RAM is almost certain to be more economical. In between, however, dynamic RAMs lose their advantage, as the cost of control circuitry is amortized over only a small number of chips. Here, it appears, is the place for a byte-wide dynamic RAM, particularly if it takes over some or all of the refreshing burden while still bettering static-RAM density.

Promoting dynamic RAM use in this small-system environment raises two questions. The first involves system partitioning: the control circuits that dynamic arrays require might be part of the RAM itself or a separate chip or set of chips. The second concerns the reorganization of the conventional by-1-bit part to give the user a more convenient memory increment, in either by-4-bit or by-8-bit versions. In a similar vein, a nibble mode, which gives a by-1-bit part the option of a 4-bit serial output, can also address this modularity problem.

Intel's Memory Products division will shortly announce the 2186, an 8-K-by-8-bit integrated RAM (iRAM) that simultaneously addresses both problems. Essentially, it puts a controller on a byte-wide dynamic memory chip. Rightly called an asynchronous self-refreshing dynamic RAM, the part appears to accomplish what previous pseudostatic devices—the synchronous self-refreshing RAMs—have not: namely, arbitration between external access requests and internal refresh requests. The significance of this achievement can best be understood in the light of past efforts at integrating dynamic-RAM control functions on the memory chip.

On-chip control

Last year, at the International Solid State Circuits Conference, Intel showed a 4-K-by-8-bit pseudostatic device with a pinout expressly tailored for Intel microprocessor buses   but the part was not pursued retaining that organization. Along similar lines, Zilog Inc., Cupertino, Calif., last year formally introduced the Z6132, also a 4-K-by-8-bit device. Again, the part is explicitly designed for use with the company's own processors.

Some present 64-K-by-1-bit devices also incorporate some refresh control. These parts integrate a counter, timer, and some additional logic for internally generating refresh addresses in response to an external trigger signal. Motorola Inc., Austin, Texas, uses pin 1 for the refresh-enable signal (Fig. 2). When this line is pulsed low, a refresh address is automatically latched into the row-address buffers and the address counter is incremented. If the enable signal is held low indefinitely, the memory continues in the extended-refresh mode to gen-

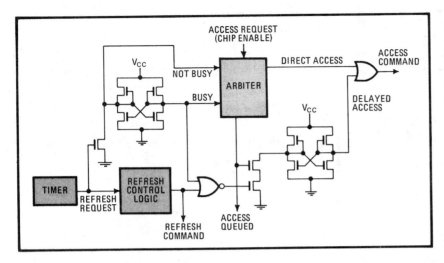

4. Sequencer. A timer periodically triggers a refresh request, which switches the busy and not-busy inputs to the arbiter shown in Fig. 3. If an access request collides with the refresh request, it is queued, and a handshake signal tells the processor to wait.

erate successive row addresses for refreshing.

This approach has its supporters and its detractors. Some other RAM makers have joined Motorola: Fujitsu Ltd. and Mitsubishi Electric Corp. offer the option, and Hitachi says it will introduce it in the third quarter of this year. Mostek, however, has scrapped the scheme after originally including it on its 64-K part. According to Mostek's Proebstring, "at the time, we had the feature, Motorola had it, and no one else did. Faced with multiple sources for 64-K RAMs and the small extra cost of automatic refreshing, we decided against it."

TI, which in fact holds a patent on it, does not offer the feature. Lionel White, dynamic RAM design manager at TI, explains some of the company's reservations: "One big hang-up with [the extended-refresh mode] is that under some conditions, the part does not look static. For example, when the processor comes out of the halt mode, all of the memory chips are asynchronously refreshing themselves and will have to be resynchronized. Another problem is that a simple refresh timer will run faster under best-case conditions—that is, high supply voltage and low temperature. If the design is to work under worst-case conditions, anything else leads to overrefreshing and a higher power dissipation."

At the 256-K level, of course, pin 1 will be used for the next–higher-order address line, and an alternative design must be used. A likely approach is the column-address before row-address strobe (CAS-before-RAS) scheme invented at Inmos Corp., Colorado Springs, Colo. Motorola and TI both say they are favoring it, as does Hitachi. In this scheme, the state of the column-address strobe is sensed as the row-address strobe is falling, that is, going active. If the CAS is low at that point, an internally generated refresh address is latched into the address buffers. Though Inmos has designed the feature in at 64-K, it formally entered the market just this month and is offering very fast, higher-priced parts.

So it seems likely that the extended-refresh mode will be abandoned, while the pulsed mode, what is now called pin-1–triggered refresh, will remain. "As many as half of the dynamic-RAM users are interested in automatic refreshing," says David Ford, strategic marketing manager for MOS memory at Motorola, "although those users typically need only small amounts of RAM and so

account for only about 15% of the unit volume. Part of the reason that number is so low, however, is that the feature was not second-sourced early on."

On balance, then, synchronous self-refreshing on an otherwise standard by-1-bit part offers a compromise between convenience and cost. Though more expensive, an asynchronous self-refreshing byte-wide unit such as Intel's iRAM is about as close to the static ideal as a dynamic RAM can get.

The iRAM described

The 2186 appears to hurdle the obstacles that hindered previous pseudostatic parts. First—and with obvious advantage—it departs from previous pseudostatic designs by using the standard 28-pin package, compatible with RAM, ROM, and E-PROM devices.

Because the 64-K array is dynamic, with the conventional transistor-plus-capacitor cell, it must be refreshed. Pin 1 of the 28-pin footprint, which is used for the high voltage in E-PROMs and is not going to be used in 8-K-by-8-bit static RAMs, provides a ready signal from the 2186. If a refresh is in progress when an Intel processor attempts to access the 2186, the ready signal is pulled low, telling the processor to wait. (Ready signals from many devices are simply wire-ORed to feed the processor input.) Though other processors have, in some cases, somewhat different protocols for wait-state generation, the interface requirements are minimal. For example, a single latch and several gates are needed to use 2186s with Motorola's 68000. (A companion device, the 2187, uses a synchronous pin-1–triggered refresh, similar to other automatic-refresh RAMs.)

Conventional logic circuits can monitor requests for refreshing (internal) and memory access (external). When a request for either is received while the other is being serviced, the request is simply queued and satisfied in its turn. The problem with such a circuit is that the two requests may occur virtually simultaneously, and some mechanism must guarantee a quick decision as to which request to service—it matters little which one is acted on, so long as one is acted on promptly.

The circuit that arbitrates such a decision, called an arbiter or synchronizer, has stirred some interest among circuit theorists and system designers during the last decade. The central issue is the response time of a bistable element—a latch—subjected to simultaneous conflicting inputs. A conventional cross-coupled inverter latch runs the risk of entering a metastable, or balanced, intermediate state when its inputs are nearly equal.

The arbiter used in the 2186 is shown in Fig. 3. The upper stage, basically a fast flip-flop, is required to latch into one of its two stable states within the time of the processor's address-latch-enable pulse. For an 8086 running at 8 megahertz, for example, that pulse width exceeds 50 nanoseconds.

The circuit operates as a transparent latch until chip-enable goes low, requesting a memory access. The circuit then isolates itself from its steering inputs (the busy and not-busy signals), and the outputs slew to one or the other of the possible states. By testing the circuit with an even distribution of input conditions, Intel engineers conclude that the probability of an arbitration error is on the order of one in thousands of years.

The overall diagram of the 2186's cycle-control logic is shown in Fig. 4. A temperature-compensated timer periodically initiates refreshing and pulls the not-busy signal low. The busy line is latched high, and if necessary, an external-access request is queued.

With an apparent technical success in the design of an asynchronous self-refreshing dynamic RAM, the commercial prospects for the part hinge on its position relative to the small-system designer's other two choices: static RAMs, or wider dynamic RAMs along with single-chip controllers.

On one side, the iRAM may be squeezed by 8-K-by-8-bit static parts. The extra circuitry required by the iRAM in comparison with a conventional dynamic RAM is enough to bring its price per bit up close or equal to that of current 16-K static RAMs. Its advantage, of course, is its greater bit density and, compared to n-channel MOS static parts, its lower power dissipation.

However, "with the iRAM fitting a standard byte-wide socket and making arbitration completely transparent to the user, it really competes with an 8-K-by-8 static RAM," points out Patrick Brooks, dynamic RAM strategist in Aloha. Indeed, Motorola's Ford notes that "we looked at an integrated RAM design a couple of years ago and dropped it in favor of an 8-K-by-8 static RAM program." Both Toshiba Corp. and Hitachi Ltd. in Japan have shown 64-K static RAMs

and Toshiba has begun supplying samples of them in the U.S. Their use of complementary-MOS technology and hence significantly lower power dissipation than the iRAM will perhaps make them worth the premium price they will likely draw initially.

Counterbalancing that, iRAM density should progress in step with standard dynamic-RAM density. Indeed, Yoshio Tominaga, a deputy chief engineer in Hitachi's memory IC engineering department, says that his firm is considering 32-K-by-8-bit and 32-K-by-9-bit pseudostatic parts because "it won't be possible to achieve this density with true static devices for another three years."

On the other side, self-refreshing byte-wide dynamic RAMs will face competition from the combination of wider parts and single-chip dynamic-RAM controllers, which together will offer a convenient and compact means of designing small to medium-sized memory sys-

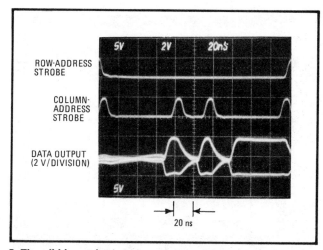

5. The nibble mode. A 4-bit serial output from a by-1-bit dynamic memory speeds access. This oscilloscope photograph from Inmos shows 20-nanosecond access times and a 40-ns cycle time for the nibble bits, which are selected by column addresses.

tems. Even without automatic refreshing, wider organizations will cost more than by-1-bit parts, because both chip and package are larger. The additional chip area relative to a 64-K-by-1-bit part is roughly 20% and 40% for by-4-bit and by-8-bit-designs, respectively.

Wider dynamic RAMs

First into the fray is TI, which recently announced its 16-K-by-4-bit dynamic RAM .

Other makers think TI is premature, but many see a wider dynamic RAM in their own futures. Hitachi and Fujitsu both say they will "soon make a decision" on the 16-K-by-4-bit part. Inmos plans to have samples of a fast by-4-bit unit ready next year. Motorola's Ford notes simply, "We have yet to see a cost analysis for by-4 or by-8 parts that would justify their development." Nippon Electric Co.'s semiconductor department manager, Shigeki Matsue, says it is readying samples of an 8-K-by-8-bit device that will include pin-1–triggered refreshing and will be available early next year.

At the 256-K level, makers and users agree on the need for a variety of configurations, including by-4- and by-8-bit parts. However, another option—the nibble mode—is likely to be widely available as well. Also invented at Inmos, the nibble mode is an outgrowth of the page mode generally available on dynamic RAMs. After addressing a given row, page mode allows reading from or writing to any column address without re-addressing the row. In the nibble mode, the process is sped up by loading just 4 consecutive bits into a shift register and clocking them out serially at high speed—typically 20 ns from the column-address strobe (Fig. 5). Inmos has the only 64-K RAM with the feature.

The chief advantage of a nibble-mode part over a by-4-bit 18-pin RAM is the savings in chip area and pin count. (Some memory makers lament the passing of page mode, which is supplanted by nibble mode and apparently holds some unique advantages in debugging a chip design.) Only a single output buffer is required, and the standard 16-pin package is retained. Fujitsu intends shortly to announce a 64-K part with the nibble mode

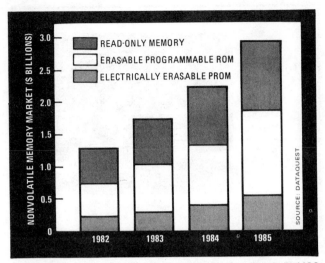

6. Nonvolatile growth. The worldwide market for nonvolatile MOS memories will nearly double in value by 1985. Alterable storage will see the highest degree of growth, with electrically erasable units reaching almost four times their 1981 level of consumption.

using the Inmos approach. Motorola and TI both expect to put it on 256-K parts. "It offers a good advantage at low cost," says Motorola's Ford. "A lot of dynamic RAMs go into video-refreshing applications, where the fast serial output is ideal." NEC says it will make a 64-K part with nibble mode if a standard emerges worldwide. At present, the Inmos proposal and another from Motorola and others are under review by the Joint Electron Device Engineering Council.

For small systems, then, wider organizations and nibble-mode parts will ease the modularity problems in coming generations of dynamic RAMs. Along with large-scale integrated circuits that do all the housekeeping for a dynamic-RAM system, the user will have another ready-made alternative to static RAMs. Single-chip controllers, which are available from several makers, succeed to varying degrees in interfacing with any processor with little additional hardware, introducing few wait states and allowing upgrading to denser chips as they come out. Nevertheless, with a single controller capable of supporting typically 90 chips and costing from $10 to $30, using one with, say, fewer than eight memory chips is bound to be a waste of resources.

In brief, there will likely be room for both integrated RAMs and integrated controllers in the booming small-systems market. The memory block sizes that would be most appropriate—based on present-generation components—for self-refreshing byte-wide dynamic RAMs are in the range between 8-K and 64-K.

If the dynamic RAM makers appear to offer a less than unified front regarding added features, the need to keep their commodities competitive underlies that caution. AMD's manager of product planning and applications for memory and interface products, Bruce Threewitt, summarizes that situation: "Memory products are the orphan of the industry. They are always the absorber of overhead costs and the vehicle for process development. Therefore, memories will continue to be the commodity items they traditionally have been. Only enough intelligence will be added to them to make the parts more widely used, which is clearly the case with EE-PROMs."

The relative novelty of electrically erasable programmable ROMs is one factor encouraging the development of intelligent parts: the markets are not entrenched because of the awkward requirements of the early entries in this area—multiple power supplies, long address- and data-hold times, and peculiar write pulses.

Gaining momentum

Driving interest even higher are visions of intelligent controllers and a variety of small systems that could adapt to a changing operating environment. The part that can make those visions real is an EE-PROM that readily interfaces with microprocessors. Based on recent successes in that area, *Electronics* and others have predicted annual growth in the value of the EE-PROM market to average around 40% to 1985 (Fig. 6).

In the case of EE-PROMs, intelligence means any or all of three nonmemory functions: a charge pump and associated circuits to generate a programming voltage from a 5-V supply; latches to capture address, data, and control signals when a write cycle is started; and control logic to automatically erase a byte location before writing it and to time the write cycle duration. With those additions, the once-ungainly EE-PROM becomes as simple to use as a static RAM and can be expected to penetrate microprocessor-based systems with ease.

One class of applications, typically needing a few hundred bits of nonvolatile storage, includes such niceties as channel selection in cable-TV tuners, settings for microwave ovens, and calibration of instruments and engines. Another, equally important, market will use dense arrays for control storage in microsystems, allowing remote software revisions and programs that learn. Early support for EE-PROMs comes from the military, which uses them instead of ultraviolet-light–erasable PROMs (E-PROMs) in flight- and fire-control computers.

Xicor Inc. recently introduced the first 16-K EE-PROM that puts all the needed support functions on chip . Wally Tchon, vice president for strategic planning at the Milpitas, Calif., firm, has hopes that EE-PROMs could also replace the E-PROMs as carriers of application software. "Although the only leverage the EE-PROMs have against E-PROMs is their cheaper package, in the long run that may be enough," he observes. E-PROMs now have more than a one-generation jump in density over EE-PROMs: the 64-K E-PROM market got off the ground last year. Whether Tchon's conjecture proves out or not, interest in the EE-PROM is growing among chip makers.

Another Silicon Valley firm, which was started by emigrants from Intel, Seeq Technology Inc. of San Jose, Calif., has also introduced a 5-V-only EE-PROM at the 16-K level and is working on 32-K and C-MOS parts. The one part of a smart EE-PROM that is not quite straightforward is its 5-V-only operation. Whereas the addition of a few latches and timing control for the write cycle is, if not trivial, fairly simple, the requirement for 5-V operation means an on-chip charge pump to supply about 18 V for altering the cells, and that pumped higher voltage can supply only small currents on the order of microamperes. Thus,

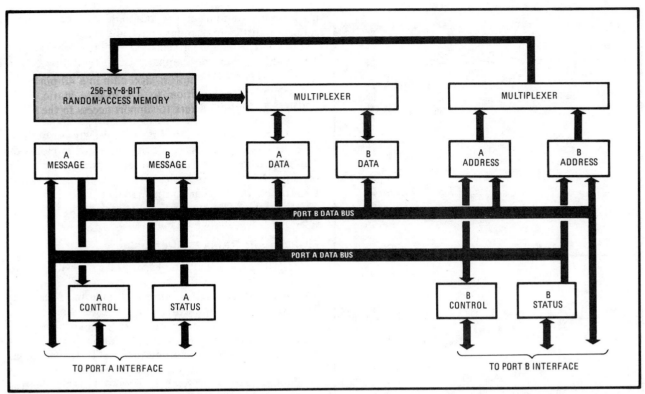

7. Mailbox. This interface chip, developed by Texas Instruments, lets two independent processors send and receive messages. The address registers point to blocks of the 256-byte memory. An arbitration circuit has control of access through the two ports.

care must be taken to eliminate dc-current paths from the high voltage to ground. A look at the data sheet for parts like Intel's 2816 or 2817 shows standby current consumption from the external 21-V supply on the order of milliamperes. Thus, 5-V-only operation means new cell and circuit designs.

In addition to Seeq and Xicor, Hughes Aircraft Co.'s Solid State Products division in Newport Beach, Calif., recently introduced a 5-V-only 16-K EE-PROM . Its C-MOS design is distinguished for its low power consumption, naturally, and also for its fast write time of 100 microseconds per byte—about 100 times faster than any other EE-PROM.

Other contenders in the EE-PROM market are also clearly headed for parts that are easier to use. Intel, whose vigorous EE-PROM marketing is widely credited with stirring user awareness, is unlikely to be left in the lurch by other 5-V-only efforts. For now, the firm offers the 2817, which requires outside the chip a fixed 21-V supply and a timing capacitor . Five-volt-only versions of the 2816 and 2817 from Intel are expected in the coming year.

National Semiconductor Corp. of Santa Clara, Calif., also has its eye on the market and notes the trend toward simple interface requirements. "EE-PROMs are definitely going toward an ease of use comparable to static RAMs'," says Andrew G. Varadi, vice president and group director of MOS integrated circuits. "In another year, National will offer a 5-V-only part, with latched data and address lines. Our 2816 and 9716 will be released this summer." The 9716 is a 16-K device similar to Intel's 2817.

Motorola recently described a 32-K EE-PROM at the

ISSCC and is now beginning to supply samples of it. Though not a 5-V-only part, it is the fastest EE-PROM commercially available, with typical access times of 90 ns. As Xicor's Tchon points out, "faster EE-PROM devices may find some eager users, for example, among minicomputer makers".

As for the future, EE-PROM producers and observers alike see rapid density improvements, faster access and write times, and eventually a shift to C-MOS.

In the shadow

The pioneering work at Xicor on shadow RAMs—static RAMs with EE-PROM backup arrays—is also being closely watched. "That market is just beginning to really develop," says Motorola's Ford. "For now, we are sticking to an approach, like Seeq, Intel, and others, that aims to develop dense EE-PROM arrays. But we are watching that segment, too."

The Novram, as Xicor calls it, today finds applications primarily in saving the state of a machine, be it a computer or a drill press, during a power failure. Typically, relatively small amounts of storage are required, so that the rather poor density due to their nine-transistor cell is not a severe drawback.

With higher density and faster access times, the shadow RAM would approach the ultimate memory: it reads and writes like a static RAM and remembers its contents without power. "Shadow RAMs at the 16-K level or denser would definitely have a market as writable control storage," says AMD's Bruce Threewitt. "To penetrate that market, however, will require access times in the 35-to-50-ns range." Access times now are 300 ns.

Merging static-RAM and EE-PROM technology, as is

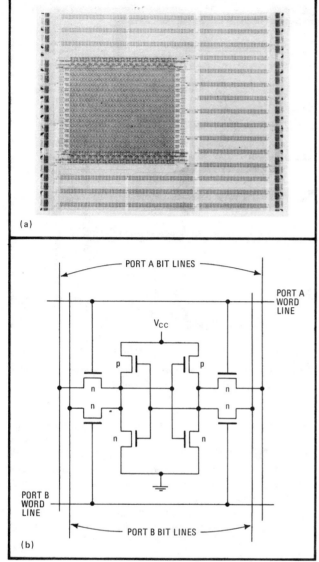

8. Custom RAM. Storage Technology adds a dual-port random-access memory to a complementary-MOS gate array (a) for applications in processors and controllers. The design (b) adds a second pair of transfer gates to the standard six-transistor C-MOS RAM cell.

done in shadow RAMs, could breed some other unique products. For example, the user of fast static RAMs often must decode chip-select signals or translate addresses off chip, stretching out the access time for which he has paid dearly. Adding a few bits of EE-PROM storage to a static RAM would be one way to produce a memory that could recognize its place in a memory map. A program could assign chips to particular subspaces of a large virtual address space simply by setting a few bits of EE-PROM.

Any attempt to make static RAMs even more convenient has to be limited to tailoring them to specific applications: the parts already set the standard for ease of use. One such niche has been opened up by the growth of multiprocessing, namely, the use of two or more inexpensive microprocessors or microcomputers instead of a single more capable and more costly system. Interfacing two processors at the board level takes either a maze of TTL and interconnections or, with some sacrifice

in flexibility, a first-in, first-out buffer or comparable stack of registers to pass data back and forth.

That niche led engineers at TI to develop the TMS99650, what the company calls a multiprocessor interface. The 22,000-mil² n-MOS chip in a 40-pin package contains, in addition to a 256-byte static RAM, registers and multiplexers to support access to the memory from two ports. The device resembles a dual-port RAM (Fig. 7), but instead of occupying 256 locations in each processor's address space, it is accessed in blocks of consecutive locations from pointer addresses stored in registers. "The part is basically a mailbox," says David Laffitte, engineering program manager in the semiconductor group. "One processor passes an address, telling the other where to pick up a message."

Fitting static RAMs to their tasks

As static RAM density increases, the parts will become more competitive with the programmable read-only memories widely used as control storage in processors. This control store application might foster static RAMs with output registers, for which PROM makers are finding a strong demand now. AMD, TI, National, and Monolithic Memories Inc. of Sunnyvale, Calif., for example, offer PROMs with this feature, which speeds execution by pipelining instruction fetches. For a writable control store, a static RAM might also integrate a serial input port, to bring in data from disks.

Though these and other niches will find some willing makers looking for a break from the low margins in commodity memory markets, most application-specific memories are more likely to come out of semicustom designs. "Memories will be moving onto gate arrays more," thinks National's Varadi, "rather than logic moving onto memory chips. Volume always goes down when you start adding specialized functions." The semicustom market is a more natural place for those developments, since the optimum system partitioning generally depends on specific systems.

Anticipating that coming trend, Storage Technology Corp., Louisville, Colo., recently developed a C-MOS gate array that incorporates a 40-ns dual-port static RAM (Fig. 8). The design was discussed in May at the Custom Integrated Circuits Conference in Rochester, N. Y. As senior design engineer Stephen Bowers points out, all processors and controllers require some type of register stack to hold source and destination data for the operands going into an arithmetic and logic unit. The implementation Storage Technology came up with uses a 128-by-9-bit RAM with two independent data and address paths, allowing two simultaneous accesses. (The RAM cell is also shown in Fig. 8.) The rest of the 30-square-millimeter chip leaves room for about 1,100 two-input NAND gates. Though the firm declines to describe the specific application for which the chip was designed, product marketing manager Ernie Stevens notes that it, or a chip like it, will be offered commercially in about a year. "I'm amazed there aren't more people getting into [hardware] macros for array logic," he says. "We have been looking in vain for a second source for some of the memory options under development."

As standard-cell designs begin to supplant the gate-

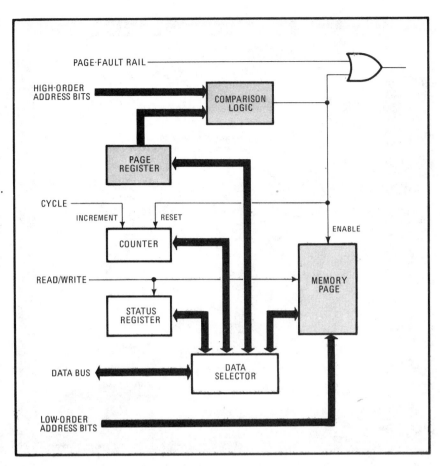

9. Virtually there. A proposed chip for distributing virtual memory in a network of microprocessors includes address-translation and page-fault–detection logic. The page register holds the number of the memory page currently stored; that number is compared with the high-order address bits.

array methodology, that situation will be changing. Zymos Inc., Sunnyvale, Calif., is among the early proponents of standard cell design.

The firm's libraries of predesigned cells include RAM and ROM arrays that can be expanded at the user's discretion. Continuing that line of reasoning, the company also added a 4-bit processor, stripped of all memory and input/output, to the libraries. The goal is a semicustom programmable chip, specified by the user.

The same aim has guided American Microsystems Inc. of Santa Clara, Calif., to the concept of an alterable microcomputer: a semicustom chip that lets users select the optimum RAM and ROM and I/O complement.

Though single-chip microcomputers and their semicustom derivatives are intelligent, the most legitimate claim to the name of smart memory is laid by a part that, like a conventional memory, is a dense and modular array of bits, but unlike conventional arrays, returns more than the data put into it. Though not yet a commercial reality, cache chips and associative, or content-addressable, memories are attracting growing interest among memory suppliers.

Association of bits

A cache chip would produce either the data requested or signals indicating that the data resides somewhere else. A common implementation of a cache stores the addresses of the data currently in the cache in a look-up table, or tag memory, so that they can be compared with incoming address bits to determine if the accessed data is in the cache or not. Putting an entire cache on a chip, even if technically feasible, is unlikely to satisfy the range of sizes and implementations now found. However, portions of a cache system have recently been integrated.

TI will formally introduce later this summer the TMS2150, what it calls a cache-tag memory. It is a fast static RAM (organized as 512 by 9 bits) with high-speed comparators and a parity generator and checker on chip. It will serve as a modular component of a cache memory system, namely, the address comparator. For example, at a memory access, the high-order address bits select a cache-tag location whose contents are compared to lower-order address bits. If there is a match, the data requested resides in the cache storage, which is then

accessed. According to TI, interest in the part has so far come from the minicomputer makers. As faster microprocessors penetrate the market, cache for microsystems may become commonplace as well.

Other memory makers are reviewing their options. "A cache-memory chip would address a good market, though it is a niche compared to the whole fast–static-RAM market," comments Intel's Nelson. "We continue to look at that area."

So far, virtual-address translation for microprocessors has not been approached with the design of smarter memories, but with centralized managers. These large-scale ICs, memory management units, absorb all the extra logic the memory system requires and are dedicated to a single processor, leaving the memory role to the familiar, standard parts. However, as in the case of self-refreshing dynamic RAMs, there may be good reason to consider virtual-memory chips for applications with small amounts of real main memory—for example, where distributed microcomputers share an expensive disk resource.

Professor Jack Lipovski of the electrical engineering department of the University of Texas in Austin, has researched distributed virtual memory for several years. His concept (Fig. 9) would provide an inexpensive and extendable virtual memory for microcomputers. Although it has yet to be cast as a single chip, Lipovski has used board-level implementations extensively. His main argument for including the logic for address translation and page-fault detection on each page of real memory is that it fits the system resources to the task. Specifically,

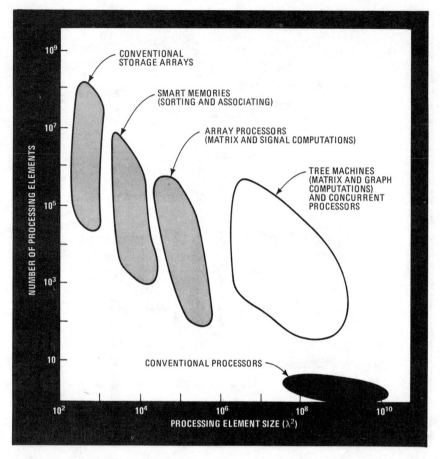

NUMBER OF PROCESSING ELEMENTS

CONVENTIONAL STORAGE ARRAYS

SMART MEMORIES (SORTING AND ASSOCIATING)

ARRAY PROCESSORS (MATRIX AND SIGNAL COMPUTATIONS)

TREE MACHINES (MATRIX AND GRAPH COMPUTATIONS) AND CONCURRENT PROCESSORS

CONVENTIONAL PROCESSORS

PROCESSING ELEMENT SIZE (λ^2)

10. Looking ahead. Charles Seitz of the California Institute of Technology outlines the ranges of feasible VLSI systems. Memories, both smart and conventional, and array processors embody hard-wired algorithms; the other machines are programmable.

spring, graduate Mark Johnson described one designed to replace the memory-management hardware used in the Nu personal computer developed at MIT.

Content-addressable memory is in fact commercially available, though in limited sizes. Companies such as Fairchild and AMD offer fast bipolar memories of this kind storing tens of bits. In principle, the technology is available to develop much larger models. According to Shigeki Matsue of NEC, the technology used for 64-K static RAMs can yield 16-K content-addressable memories. He says, "The design and fabrication of associative memory chips is no problem—absolutely no problem." What is in the way is the fact that "nobody now has computer designs that require associative memory." Clearly, a challenge is laid to their would-be users to demand such chips.

in the proposed virtual-memory chip, every page is accompanied by a page register, which is loaded by software with the page number when the page is filled. This register is compared with the high-order address bits, and, if a match occurs, the memory is enabled, and the selected location can be read from or written to. The result of the comparison is ORed with those from the other pages, so that if no match occurs, an interrupt signals the processor to bring in a new page.

To decide which page to banish when a new one must be brought in, counters are included on each chip. In every cycle, every counter is incremented, and if a page is accessed, its counter is reset. Then the highest count indicates the least recently used page, which is replaced by a new one. A bit in the status register indicates if the page has been changed, and therefore must be rewritten to secondary memory.

Though these cache and virtual-memory schemes do more than store data (they "know" what data they are storing), the memory arrays are still conventional and do not represent the ultimate in smart memories: a rudimentary processor in which each bit has associated with it some logic circuits to perform additional functions. The most readily useful one is the content-addressable memory, which can greatly simplify data-base manipulations. Typical search operations take a cumbersome route to what an associative memory is designed to provide—the address of specified data.

Content-addressable memory can also provide distributed virtual-address translation. At the Massachusetts Institute of Technology's VLSI Research Review this

Clifford Rodes, TI's static-RAM design manager, has this advice on what to ask for: "The component should be modular, that is, easily cascaded for any size memory system; it should allow for masking bits of the data field to allow flexible searches; and it should give an address output, not just flag that a match has occurred."

An eye on the future

Though that ideal content-addressable memory is obviously a way off, at least one company is hot on the trail of a commodity version. West Germany's AEG Telefunken recently secured rights to the recognition memory developed by Sydney Lamb of Rice University, Houston, and is gearing up to produce an integrated version .

These truly smart memories may be one member of a future class of special-purpose VLSI processors. The classification of machine architectures shown in Fig. 10 places smart memories in the context of other processing ensembles, as suggested by Charles Seitz of the California Institute of Technology in Pasadena. The zones outlined indicate ranges of distinct architectures as determined by the number of processing elements and their size (in terms of a lithographic feature size). Seitz points out that the performance tends to increase with the number of processing elements, whereas generality and programmability increase with the processor size. As VLSI-circuit designers move to exploit the technology by relying on regular arrays of identical, concurrently operating processors, system design shifts from the conventional serial computer to special-purpose ensembles.   □

Dynamic-RAM controller orchestrates memory systems

Up to 88 chips take their cues from an n-channel MOS IC that both housekeeps and supports error-corrected dual-port memories

by Jim Nadir and Mel Bazes, *Intel Corp., Santa Clara, Calif.*

☐ Designing a dynamic–random-access-memory system means balancing the goals of high performance, reliability, and versatility against the often contrary aims of economy, simplicity, and compactness. In the last five or so years, the advent of dynamic-RAM controller chips relieved designers of some of the onus of tending to the needs of dynamic chips: standard supportive integrated circuits brought together the counters, timers, multiplexers, and other elements needed.

But controllers diverged into two types. One bought the high performance to ride with fast memory systems at the expense of functionality, while the other took on more and more functions to do a complete but slower job. The 8207—an advanced dynamic-RAM controller—blunts the horns of that dilemma and also solves a variety of less severe design problems.

A dynamic-RAM controller is charged with making a dynamic memory system appear static to the host processor. At a minimum, therefore, the controller takes over refreshing the memory chips, multiplexing the row and column addresses, generating control signals, timing the precharge period, and signaling the processor when

data is available or no longer needed. But, beyond those local housekeeping chores, the controller can also go a long way to solving more global design problems, like sharing memory between two processors, not to mention detecting and correcting errors.

To realize this potential for a highly integrated solution, the 8207 has a dual-port interface and, when used with the 8206 error-checking and -correction unit, ensures data integrity in large dynamic-RAM systems. In addition to doing the jobs of refreshing, address multiplexing, and control timing, the unit supports memory-bank interleaving for pipelined accesses, overlaying RAM and read-only-memory locations, and initializing RAM.

The exact implementation of most of these functions is programmable, letting designers tailor their systems in detail. Systems containing up to 88 dynamic-RAM chips—whether 16-, 64-, or 256-K versions—in one, two, or four banks need only a single 8207 and no external buffering. Attesting to the high performance claimed, the 8207 mates dynamic RAMs having 100-nanosecond access times to the iAPX-286 processor operating at 8 megahertz without introducing any wait states.

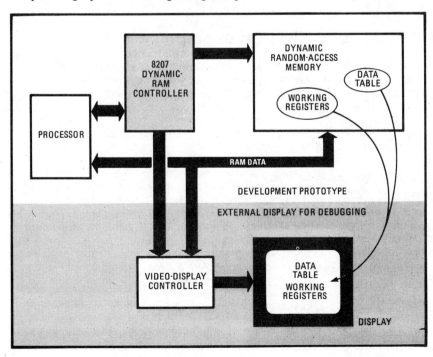

1. Window on a micro. One use for a dual-port memory shared by independent processors is the development system shown. Adding a video display to the prototype itself gives a window on the system memory.

To achieve that speed and include all those functions, the 8207 relies on a dense, high-speed n-channel MOS process (H-MOS II) and requires a chip some 230 by 200 mils in area. To meet the rigors of operation with even faster processors, novel logic and integrated-circuit designs are employed. Replacing the two-phase logic common in n-MOS ICs, single-phase edge-triggered logic simplifies logic and circuit design, precludes problems of clock-pulse overlap, and reduces the sensitivity to clock high and low times. Voltage-controlled capacitive loads form the delay elements that time critical output pulses, such as the address strobes, and compensate the output-switching delays for variations in power-supply voltage, temperature, and processing.

A low 20-ns setup time for input signals is achieved by cutting the RC delay of input-protection devices and moving the TTL-to-MOS signal buffering from the input pads to the pulse generators. A short 35-ns delay from input to output switching is achieved by triggering the output generators directly from the external clock, saving a buffer delay time. With the resulting high-speed performance and a high level of integration, the 8207 successfully attacks the stringent requirements of today's memory systems.

One system feature gaining popularity currently is the use of multiple processors operating on shared data to obtain higher performances and reliability. For example, a separate processor dedicated to input/output tasks frees the main processor for full-time data processing. Alternatively, multiple main processors can execute different tasks simultaneously. In all such cases, sharing a common memory space among the cooperating processors is the key to effective operation.

Unfortunately, when more than one processor accesses shared memory through a single bus, the limited bus bandwidth and the time spent in exchanging bus control slow down data transfers. Dual-port memory systems overcome this limitation by giving two processors access to a common memory through two independent buses. The 8207 includes a dual-port interface to simplify the design of shared memory systems.

Two-port memories can be used with multiprocessing or multitasking architectures. In the former, independent processors run independent programs, sharing only a common memory. Multitasking processors cooperate on different parts of the same task.

An example of a multiprocessing architecture is the dynamic video display (Fig. 1) that provides a window on a processor's memory. Centering the display over a data table, for example, immediately reveals how program execution affects the data, which aids in debugging programs. If a microcomputer is implemented with a dual-port memory—the second port for a dynamic video display—then the prototype itself can serve as a development and debugging system, reverting to single-port operation in the final version.

A dual-port architecture in a multitasking environment, on the other hand, adds a margin of safety to a shared-resource bus, such as Intel's Multibus. Although one of the biggest benefits of such a bus is the sharing of expensive peripherals among several users' programs, an intimidating problem is that a single program gone haywire can easily corrupt the entire system. A two-port memory, properly configured, circumvents this occurrence. Because each port has its own address, data, and control lines, problems on one side are confined by hardware to that side.

Port of call

As a general rule for multitasking architectures, one port of a two-port memory operates in a local environment, and the other port runs remotely, off the expandable shared-resource bus. The local processor is likely to require a synchronous port to reap the benefit of higher performance. Remote buses, in contrast, are usually configured asynchronously. Unless programmed other-

---

Dynamic-RAM controllers get in step

Synchronous and asynchronous signals have different requirements for interfacing with a controller. The terms synchronous and asynchronous are conventionally applied to dynamic random-access memory depending on whether it exists in a local or a remote environment, respectively. However, they more properly characterize the dynamic-RAM controllers, for the RAMs themselves need no clocks—the only restrictions as to the start of a memory access cycle involve ensuring that the refresh and precharge requirements are satisfied.

Because the controller decides both when to refresh and whether or not precharge and other timing requirements have been met, it does need a clock. Incoming commands can either always arrive with a fixed relationship to the controller's clock or have no particular relationship to it. The former are, of course, synchronous operations, the latter asynchronous.

The major difference between an asynchronous and a synchronous controller (or port of a controller, in the case of the dual-port 8207) is that the asynchronous controller must first synchronize the incoming commands to its own internal clock. From that point on, the asynchronous controller looks just like a synchronous device.

Whereas various techniques for synchronization are available off chip, on-chip synchronization is restricted to the resolution and sampling of states of a flip-flop. The incoming command is clocked into a resolving flip-flop. After a predetermined time, a sampling flip-flop reads the state of the resolving flip-flop, thereby synchronizing the command. Assuming that both flip-flops are triggered on the same edge of the controller's internal clock, the fastest that an asynchronous signal can be synchronized is one clock period. The slowest synchronization takes two clock periods; on the average, getting the signals in step takes one and a half clock cycles.

Because the processor typically requires four or fewer clock periods to complete a cycle, adding a cycle and a half for synchronizing increases the access time by approximately 25%. Synchronous controllers are therefore always preferred when the environment permits them, and local environments, such as single-board computers, generally do so.

wise, the 8207 configures one port synchronously, and the other asynchronously. For specific applications, both ports may be programmed as either synchronous or asynchronous (see "Dynamic-RAM controllers get in step,").

Whether the ports are programmed for synchronous or asynchronous operation, some mechanism must decide which processor will gain access to memory when both request it almost simultaneously. That mechanism consists of arbitration logic that controls access and always leaves one port selected. When a port is selected, its associated control and interface signals are passed directly to the RAM timing logic by the command multiplexer (Fig. 2). Both ports' command and control lines, after being synchronized, go into both the command multiplexer and the arbitration logic.

However, the arbitration logic enables the command multiplexer to pass only commands that appear at the selected port. At the same time as a command appears at a selected port, arbitration logic initiates the cycle-control logic that completes the timing of the RAM cycle that ensues. If a command appears on the unselected port, it will not get through the multiplexer to initiate a RAM cycle but will instead wait in the status-command decoder until the current command is completed, at which time the command multiplexer switches to the unselected port. The arbitration logic will then service this queued access request by starting a new cycle.

The arbitration logic examines all port requests, including the internal refresh port. The refresh-request port is subject to arbitration like the other two ports, except that it is always assigned a higher priority than an unselected external access port. Thus, refreshing can be delayed, at most, one RAM cycle.

While the current RAM cycle is running, the arbiter determines the next cycle to be initiated. Thus, the arbitration time of two or more simultaneous port requests is hidden by the memory cycle time. In other words, in cases where both a selected and an unselected port request access simultaneously, the arbitration time for the unselected port does not extend that port's access time, which is delayed by one memory cycle anyway. Only when an unselected port requests a free memory does the arbitration time slow access, because then the command must pass through the arbitration logic before a RAM cycle can be initiated. To minimize such delays in most cases, there are two arbitration algorithms to be selected by the user.

The first algorithm, intended for multiprocessing environments, automatically returns the arbiter to a designated preferred port, generally the higher-performance, synchronous port. Thus any command on the selected port generally has immediate access, whereas any command arriving at the unselected port must wait.

The second, or last-accessed-port, algorithm, which is applicable in multitasking environments, leaves the most recently accessed port as the selected port. This algorithm optimizes port selection for task passing in a multitasking environment. In task passing, the host processor sends a task to an execution processor; until the task is received, the execution processor seldom accesses memory. Conversely, once the task is passed, the host processor seldom accesses memory until the task is completed. Thus, the ports are used in spurts.

Because timely refreshing is needed to preserve dynamic-RAM data, a refresh request is always serviced on the next available cycle. The refresh algorithm, however, may be selected by the user. The options available are: no refresh, user-generated single refresh, automatic refresh, or user-generated burst refresh.

No refresh would be selected for applications like bit-mapped–video displays, where continuous, sequential access of all RAM locations itself refreshes every cell periodically. User-generated refresh modes allow the designer greater control over power dissipation, for example, in large memory systems. Automatic refreshing, in which the controller itself times the refresh interval and initiates the operation, lets the designer ignore the refresh requirements entirely. As mentioned, the refresh requests are subject to arbitration just like other access requests. However, once a burst refresh is selected, it remains active until completed.

Cleaning up errors

Ensuring data integrity is a major concern in large dynamic-RAM systems, particularly because of their susceptibility to soft errors caused by alpha-particle radiation. Various parity encoding techniques have been developed to detect and correct memory-word errors. The parity bits, called check bits when used for correction as well as detection, are stored in the memory array along with their associated data word. When the data is read, the check bits are regenerated and compared with the stored check bits. If an error exists, whether in the retrieved check bits or in the retrieved data word, the result of the comparison—called the syndrome—gives the location in the group of the bit in error.

Two drawbacks surface in the design of any memory system that is to be protected by error-correction circuitry. First, the memory-word width must be increased to store the check bits; second, extra time must be allotted for the error-correction circuitry to generate the check bits on write cycles, plus more time to regenerate and compare the check bits on read cycles. The 8207 provides several ways to minimize both problems.

Error-correction schemes require a smaller proportion of check bits to protect wider memory words. For example, an 8-bit word needs 5 check bits, for a 63% increase in memory. Put the other way around, 38% of the available memory would be dedicated to the check bits. Six check bits are required to protect a 16-bit data word—only a 27% overhead. Clearly, the wider the memory array, the more economical the error correction.

The 38% overhead necessary to protect such 8-bit–bus machines as the 8088 or 8085 makes error correction an unattractive proposition. However, if the memory width could be doubled, with the 8088 accessing only half a word at a time, the overhead would drop to 27%.

Reading a double-width word, checking for soft errors, and then sending the desired portion of the word to the processor presents no major problems, unlike writing to such an array. The check bits cannot be calculated from only a portion of the word—they must be calculated for

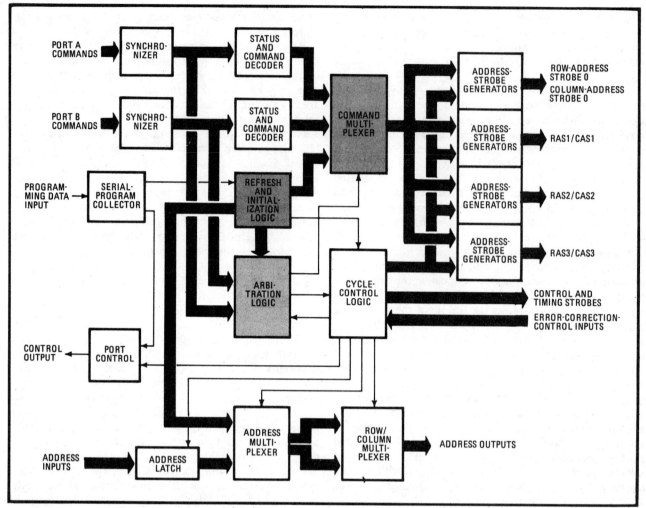

2. Arbiter's labor. Two external ports plus the internal refresh port can request access to the memory system at once. Arbitration logic decides which to service, based on programmable algorithms. High-speed logic design cuts the delay from input to output switching to 55 ns.

the entire word at once. Whenever the processor writes a partial word to memory, it must first read the entire word, check it, substitute for that portion of the word to be rewritten, and recalculate the check bits. Only then can the entire word be written to memory. The 8207, working in conjunction with the 8206 error-checking and -correction unit, contains mechanisms to expedite this potentially arduous process.

Whenever the 8207 performs a partial-write cycle, it initiates a read-modify-write cycle wherein the entire memory word is first read and latched into the 8206 (Fig. 3). After the retrieved data has been verified as correct, new data is supplied to the RAM, half from the processor and half from the 8206, which also generates the check bits for the entire new word.

Control signals—called byte marks—specify which portion of the new data word is coming from the processor and which from the 8206. The byte marks determine whether the processor or the 8206 drives the RAM data bus—for example, if the 8206 is driving one portion of the data bus, the processor is prevented from driving the same portion. The byte-mark signals simply disable the appropriate transceivers. If, on the other hand, the processor is driving a portion of the RAM data bus, the byte marks change the 8206 data outputs to inputs, allowing

the 8206 to read the data from the processor and calculate new check bits.

The ability of the 8207 to handle memories organized as one, two, or four banks allows tradeoffs between the cost and performance of an error-correction system. For maximum performance, memory would be organized in four banks, each 16 bits wide. In applications requiring error correction, but where maximum performance is not critical, concatenation of RAM banks into two banks of 32-bit words, or even one bank of 64-bit words, can make error correction very economical.

Holding to high performance

Even though the cost of error correction has thus been reduced to where it becomes an attractive solution, the problem remains of minimizing performance degradation. Tackling that challenge depends on the particulars of the configuration, such as whether the memory is to be used with a high-performance local processor, as system memory on a shared-resource bus, or is to be shared between a local high-performance processor and a shared-resource bus.

The method chosen to handle errors depends on the type of bus. Intel's Multibus is the kind that requires data to be valid prior to the issuance of a transfer-

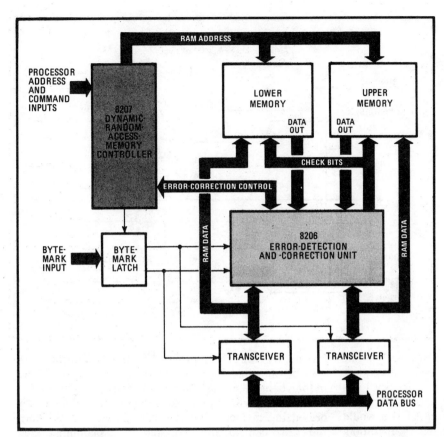

3. Teamwork. The 8206 error-correction chip joins forces with the random-access-memory controller so that an 8-bit–bus processor may utilize the 16-bit-wide memory that is more economical for error-correction schemes. Byte marks configure the data buses for partial-word transfers.

acknowledge signal, in contrast to the local buses of the iAPX-86, -186, and -286 processors. A local bus will usually be synchronous, with a single processor or coprocessor group attached to it; the processor characteristics are known, as is the processor's response to a transfer-acknowledge signal.

With Multibus and other shared-resource buses, the processor types that will eventually be connected are not known in advance, and the buses themselves are generally asynchronous. Hence the time between the transfer-acknowledge signal and data becoming valid is not known. Therefore, the rule with such buses is to acknowledge a transfer only when data is valid. (On some asynchronous buses, the acknowledgment is issued earlier to compensate for synchronization delay at the receiving processor.)

Two basic configurations for checking and correcting errors derive from these system considerations and the fact that it takes longer to correct data than to detect an error. One is for buses that connect to processors and coprocessors receiving a transfer acknowledge prior to data becoming valid, and the other for buses that connect to processors receiving a transfer acknowledge after data is valid. Both configurations are supported by the 8206–8207 team.

Buses among the former type of processors always get corrected data from the 8206, whether an error exists or not, and will carry a transfer acknowledge from the 8207 before data becomes valid on the bus. Though this means data is delayed for error correction on every transaction, the extra delay is immaterial, since it is hidden behind the processor's response time to the transfer-acknowledge signal. By the time the processor requires data, it is already corrected and on the bus. As a result, system performance is not degraded at all because of single-bit errors.

For buses among processors that receive the transfer acknowledge after the data is valid, the 8206 always checks for errors but does not routinely correct data. In this mode, RAM data passes through faster, because the 8207 will issue an acknowledgment sooner. If, however, an error is found, the 8207 will lengthen the cycle, command the 8206 to correct the data, and delay the transfer-acknowledge signal until the corrected data can be placed on the bus. For those buses with an acknowledge-synchronization delay, the 8207 can be programmed to issue the acknowledgment earlier to compensate for the delay.

Power-up problems

Another problem with memories protected by ECC circuits crops up when the power is turned on. At power-up, the data stored in memory is completely random; any attempt to read or perform a partial write will be aborted because the check bits will indicate multiple, and therefore uncorrectable, errors. For processors whose word width is the same as that of the memory array, the processor could simply initialize the entire memory array, taking some additional time and software. For memories whose word width is greater than that of the processor, however, initialization of the memory is not possible unless the error-checking or -correction circuitry is disabled by hardware, for example, by gating off the error flags.

The 8207 is equipped to deal with the initialization problem by itself. At system reset, the 8207 performs

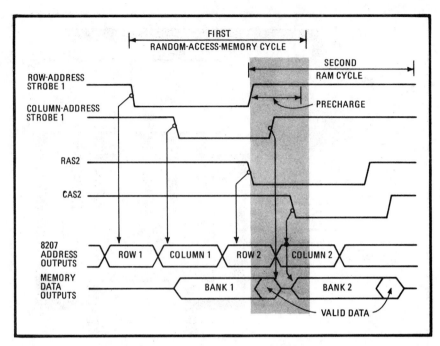

4. Interleaving. Overlapping accesses to different banks increases memory throughput. Once the column-address hold time is satisfied, the 8207 starts a second cycle, pulling the second row-address strobe low.

eight cycles on all banks at once to warm up the dynamic RAMs, a typical RAM requirement for stable operation. The chip then individually initializes all memory locations to 0, adding the proper check bits. Though all memory banks could be initialized in parallel, that would require more power than any other memory operation, calling for a heftier and more expensive power supply needed only at system reset.

One final problem associated with memories protected by error-correction circuitry stems from the fact that only data that is accessed by the processor is corrected. If the processor continually accesses one particular segment of memory, the rest of the array may be accumulating soft errors. The possibility of two soft errors accumulating in a word of seldom accessed memory now becomes significant—and not all double-bit errors are correctable in simple ECC schemes. The 8207 scrubs memories to clean up this problem. During each refresh cycle, one word of memory is read, checked for errors, and if necessary, corrected before data is written back to memory. Because scrubbing occurs during refresh cycles with a read cycle replacing a row-address-strobe–only refresh cycle, no performance penalty is incurred. Scrubbing rids the entire memory of errors at least once every 16 seconds, reducing the probability of two soft errors accumulating in the same word almost to nil.

Bells and whistles

All dynamic RAMs require a recovery period for precharging internal lines after each access. If the processor were immediately to reaccess the RAM, the controller would have to delay it until the precharge time was over. By automatically organizing memory into banks so that sequential addresses are in different banks, the 8207 is usually able to hide the precharge time of one bank behind the access time of another. That organization follows from using the 2 least significant bits of the address to select the bank. Of course, a break in the program flow, such as would be caused by a jump or call

instruction, raises the probability that the same bank may be immediately re-accessed. This probability is less in four-bank memories than in two-bank configurations.

Further performance advantages are gleaned by organizing memory into multiple banks. For example, the 8207 can speed throughput by pipelining cycles. Once the row and column addresses to one bank have been latched, the controller sends the row address for the next cycle to the next bank (Fig. 4).

The 8207's manifold features can be tailored to a given system with the use of a serial programming pin. This pin can either be strapped high or low to select one of two default modes or be programmed by means of a shift register. The external register is completely controlled by the 8207, eliminating any local processor support. Sixteen bits are shifted into the 8207 to configure up to nine different features. The bits are arranged in order of increasing importance; using a shift register with less than 16 bits permits just those features needed to be programmed.

Programmable features of the processor interface include the choice of arbitration algorithm, clock compensation, and preferred port. At the RAM interface, the user can specify fast or slow memory chips, indicate bank configuration, and select the optimal refreshing scheme. In anticipation of the next generation of 256-K dynamic RAMs, the 8207 can support a 256-row–1-millisecond refresh convention, in addition to the 128-row–2-ms one for current 16- and 64-K parts.

Helping facilitate system design is a self-programming processor interface. By decoding the command input pins at power-up, the 8207 automatically determines whether it is connected to the status lines of an 8086, iAPX-286 or to the command lines of the Multibus. Because the 8207 can directly decode the status lines of Intel microprocessors, it can anticipate the next memory cycle and start a new cycle before actually receiving a command. This extra pipelining enables the designer to specify slower RAMs then would otherwise be required.□

CORRECTION

Error detection and correction cleans up wide-word memory act

It simply is not possible to build equipment that generates totally trustworthy output data. Not that the designs are faulty—it is just that modern, complex electronics does so much, so quickly, that errors are sure to crop up.

But the designer and user of equipment do not have to live with them. If he or she is willing to bear the additional cost and design burden, coding techniques can be brought to the rescue. These codes can be either error-detecting or both error-detecting and -correcting. With more and more information being processed electronically, they have their work cut out for them.

For example, a mainframe computer, in one hour of operation at a calculation rate of one operation per microsecond, can do 3.6 billion chores. Putting this number into perspective is the fact that most people do not live 3.6 billion seconds—about 115 years.

It is clear, then, that even if errors occur only once every billion operations, this computer will produce errors every hour. The same statistics problem exists for mass-memory systems of all types: bubbles, 64- and 256-K dynamic random-access memories, and disks. Indeed, some of the sources of these errors are tinged with the exotic—for example, alpha-particle radiation emanating from substrate or package material and causing soft errors in RAMs.

Data-communications networks, too, have their fair share of error headaches. In addition to memory problems, the fiber-optic or satellite links that transmit and receive voice, data, and video signals at megabit-per-second rates are subject to all sorts of error-causing noise and pulse spreading from both internal and external sources.

There are several codes for sniffing out the bugs, and which one is selected depends on the number and kinds of errors expected. But all modern codes operate on one principle: some permutation or combination (or both) of the data bits, based on mathematical finite-field theory, is used to generate additional bits known as check or parity bits. Examination of the position in the encoded data word and value (1 or 0 in most cases) of these bits allows a certain number of data-bit errors to be detected and another number—usually fewer—to be automatically corrected.

There is, however, another penalty beyond design complexity and cost. The protection system has what is called a high bit overhead or decreased system throughput. For example, if the extended Golay code is used to automatically detect and correct three errors in a data word, 12 check bits are needed to verify the correctness of 12 data bits. Thus, as far as received voice, data, or video signals are concerned, half the received bits provide no useful information.

Of the many sophisticated codes now out, one of the newest is the Fire code, which can detect and correct bursts of 12-bit errors and is particularly suited for disks .

On the other hand, the best-known of the codes, the classic Hamming type, is particularly useful for semiconductor memories because it corrects 1-bit errors and detects 2-bit errors .

Even more arcane is the Orchard code, which is capable of detecting and correcting two errors in a data word with even fewer overhead bits than the Hamming code .

by Harvey J. Hindin
Communications & Microwave Editor

Fire code detects and corrects errors in wide words for large RAMs

New method flushes out 5-bit errors and repairs 4-bit errors; chip implementation uses shift registers and exclusive-OR gates only

by Ronald H. Sartore, *Synercom Technology Inc., Sugarland, Texas,* and David W. Gulley, *Texas Instruments Inc., Stafford, Texas*

☐ Now that millions of bits can be squeezed on a single printed-circuit board, the new architectures of large dynamic random-access memories, like the 64- and 256-K chips, require new concepts and circuit designs for detecting and correcting bit errors. As a result, the classic method of error detection and correction, the Hamming code, will no doubt be placed on the back burner as new error-detecting-and-correcting procedures are found.

One of these approaches, particularly suited for error detection and correction in wide-word memory systems, is the Fire code. This code can correct any error burst of 4 bits or less and can detect a burst of 5 bits or less. It is particularly suited to both the deep and wide RAM configurations like 16-K by 4, 64-K by 4, and 32-K by 8 bits that may soon become available from several vendors. Texas Instruments Inc. has come up with a 55-chip implementation of a modified Fire-code error-detection-and-correction circuit for such memories and is exploring its large-scale integration.

Though having more overhead than the Hamming code for certain RAM applications, the Fire code can be altered so that its overhead is similar. In addition, the number of memory components required for the Fire code is much less than for the Hamming code.

First used in magnetic-disk memories, the Fire code detects and corrects error bursts common to that type of large-scale storage. There is an analogy between error bursts in a magnetic memory and those in the words of a semiconductor memory organized around, for example, RAMs with a by-4-bit configuration. These RAMs can fail in bursts of 1, 2, 3, or 4 bits—the Fire code can provide suitable error detection and correction for them.

In contrast to a Fire code, the Hamming code is ideal for systems with by-1-bit–configuration RAMs because it handles their most common types of failures. These include multiple soft errors (caused by alpha-particle radiation) within a single device and the failure of an entire memory chip.

The Hamming code in by-1-bit–configuration systems is employed as a single-error–correction, double-error–detection code and thus is adequate in most cases. But, when it comes to chip memories with a by-4-bit configuration, the Hamming code has serious drawbacks. Though the code corrects for the most common failure in a system—the single-bit soft error—it compromises reliability by not correcting the second-commonest error—the hard failure of an entire device or a large portion of it.

When a circuit design involves wide-word (by-4-bit–configuration devices or wider) memory systems, off-the-shelf error-detection-and-correction devices are inappropriate because they are designed for by-1-bit–configuration systems. The Hamming code, which is the basis for these devices, offers no solutions. As Table 1 shows, hard bit-failures are caused overwhelmingly by the failure of a complete chip. However, the Fire code—suitably modified—is a scheme that is capable of detecting the malfunction or total failure of an entire device.

Failures in 64-K RAMs are ranked according to the specific error mechanisms leading to a device failure. A single soft error is the most common occurrence in a system (Table 2), followed by a single hard error. Most interesting, however, from the detection-correction–circuit-design stand-

TABLE 1: ERROR RATES OF 16-K AND 64-K RANDOM-ACCESS-MEMORY CHIPS	16-K	64-K
Soft errors (%/1,000 h)	0.10	0.45
Hard errors (%/1,000 h)	0.020	0.020
Hard error analysis (%):		
1 bit	25%	
Row or column	25%	no data
Whole device	44%	
Other	6%	

point, is the relatively low probability of compound errors like two hard or soft failures within a word. Because of the improbability of failures below rank 5 in Table 2, the correction chip's Fire code design can overlook these conditions, concentrating instead on single soft and hard errors.

Generator polynomials

Fire codes are described by polynomials known as generator polynominals. They are of the form $(x^n + 1)(x^c + \ldots + 1)$, where n and c are variables dependent on the individual RAM and the degree of protection desired. (The second polynomial has unknown low-order terms that can be determined only after the exponent c is established.) The number of bits the Fire code will protect, including the check bits, is $n(2^c - 1)$.

The error-detection-and-correction properties of the code are based on the mathematical characteristics of its generator polynomial. For example, if the code is required to correct any burst of 4-bit errors or less and detect any burst of 5 bits or less, the values of n and c must be chosen by mathematics-based rules.

Complex calculations for deriving the equation are rarely needed because the appropriate polynomial is usually available. For instance, 12 Fire-code bits are needed for a by-4-bit configuration, and the value of the exponent c is 4 while the value of exponent n is 8. (Only 11 bits could be employed, but the error-detection capability is accordingly reduced.)

The generator polynomial in this particular case is $(x^8 + 1)(x^4 + \ldots + 1)$, and the second polynomial must always have only 1 and itself as factors. Here, the polynomial is $(x^4 + x + 1)$, and the code protects a word as long as 108 bits $[n(2^c - 1) - (n + c)]$ from an error burst of 4 bits or less.

Hardware implementation

Once the final form of the generator polynomial is determined, the hardware design of the modified Fire-code logic is fairly simple. A right-shift register is constructed in which each bit from left to right is assigned an integer beginning with 1 and incrementing upward (Fig. 1). The resultant polynomial is then determined by multiplying $(x^8 + 1)$ and $(x^4 + x + 1)$. This procedure yields $x^{12} + x^9 + x^8 + x^4 + x + 1$.

An exclusive-OR gate is then inserted after each shifter bit that corresponds to an exponent in the polynomial. The last shifter bit, 12, feeds back into the exclusive-OR gate that combines this output with the incoming data to provide the input to the first bit and all the remaining exclusive-OR gates.

At this point, the serial hardware in Fig. 1 can be modified to represent a parity-generation matrix that is usually associated with Hamming codes. To design this

TABLE 2: BIT-ERROR PATTERNS IN RANDOM-ACCESS MEMORIES RANKED BY FREQUENCY OF OCCURRENCE		
Rank	Error pattern	Word failure
1	1 soft	single
2	1 hard	single
3	1 hard followed by 1 soft	double
4	1 soft followed by 1 hard	double
5	2 hard	double
6	2 soft	double
7	2 hard plus 1 soft	triple
8 insignificant errors	3 hard	triple
9	2 soft plus 1 hard	triple
10	3 soft	triple

matrix, the shifter is cleared and then seeded with a logic 1 at the data input during the initial shifts. The shifter states are then recorded and will indicate any shifter bits that are 1s.

Then the data input is returned to a logic 0; shifting and recording occurs until the shifter-bit pattern obtained repeats itself. The pattern must repeat on shift $n(2^c - 1)$ or earlier—if it does not, there is an error in the recording of the shifter bits.

The matrix that results from this procedure has $n(2^c - 1)$ or 120 states in a formation similar to that of a Hamming code. The check bits—those containing a single shifter bit within a 12-bit column—are produced by the parity generation of all bits that have a shifter bit in the same row.

Higher overhead

Twelve check bits can provide protection for systems of up to 108-bit word lengths. But this degree of protection is unnecessary because RAMs now in common use only have 64-bit words or less. As a result, compared with a Hamming code that requires just 8 check bits to protect 64 bits, the Fire code—using 12 check bits—has a higher overhead. However, this overhead is required in order to detect certain errors.

As set up, the Fire code protects a 4-bit word from any 4-bit error burst. But there is a large set of 4-bit error bursts that can span two 4-bit-wide memory devices. The 12-bit code can tolerate these bursts, but it may not be necessary for it to do so since the probability of such multiple-error occurrences is low. Thus if these sets are eliminated, the Fire code may be reduced to 8 check bits and will be able to protect 32-bit words.

To remove these sets, a by-4-bit device is mapped within certain boundaries of its 120-state generation matrix by using alternating sets of four entries—in this case, 1, 2, 3, 4 and 9, 10, 11, 12. Here, either the first 4 check bits generated (out of 12) are identical to the last four, or the middle four are not influenced (5, 6, 7, 8 and 13, 14, 15, 16).

However, two methods can reduce this code from 12

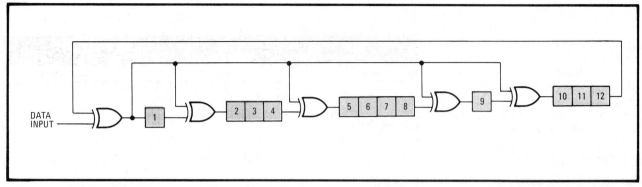

1. Hardware. Simple shift registers provide the basis for the implementation of Fire code error-detection-and-correction logic—involving in this case bursts of 4 and 5 erroneous bits, respectively. The register interconnects are algorithm-based.

to 8 bits by not using (always treating as 0s) alternating sets of four states from the generation matrix and by confining a by-4-bit device to just one 4-bit set. These methods are based on a 40-state generation table (Fig. 2) that is a subset of a larger 60-state table that can be derived from Fig. 1's shift register.

As a result, 4-bit error bursts not wholly contained within a device are unseen by the Fire code. The first method eliminates the middle four check bits by using only those clusters of 4 bits that do not have a shaded box for bits 5, 6, 7, and 8. The second selects those clusters of 4 bits in which bits 1, 2, 3, and 4 are duplicated by the shaded boxes for bits 9, 10, 11, and 12. TI is studying the implications of this procedure for error-correction codes and their implementation.

32-bit protection

It is clear that 8 check bits can protect a data field of 52 bits. But the most popular memory width below 52 bits is 32, so in actuality the code will protect 32 data bits with just a single check byte.

In this last case, the Fire code compares favorably in terms of overhead with the Hamming code, which needs 7 bits to protect 32. However, another advantage of the modified Fire code is the reduced amount of memory components needed for minimum-system implementation. For one design, the modified Fire code requires just 10 memory devices compared with the 39 needed by the Hamming code.

It is all well and good to design error-detection–correction circuitry, but to select the right type a designer must define errors that his system can tolerate. He must also know the types of error conditions that the system will produce. Failure predictions for error-corrected memory systems depend on two parameters: the number of RAMs in the system and the memory organization (the word or block size that constitutes an access).

Though the significance of component count is fairly obvious, memory-organization factors are often neglected and misunderstood. Because only several hundred soft errors will crop up in a system of millions of bits, the probability is extremely small that two such errors will occur within any one particular word.

To calculate this probability, the error rate for dynamic RAMs on a per-bit basis is required. This data has been obtained for worst-case measured values of both hard and soft errors for the 16-K TMS4116 and the 64-K TMS4164 RAMs. Measurements were made on RAMs

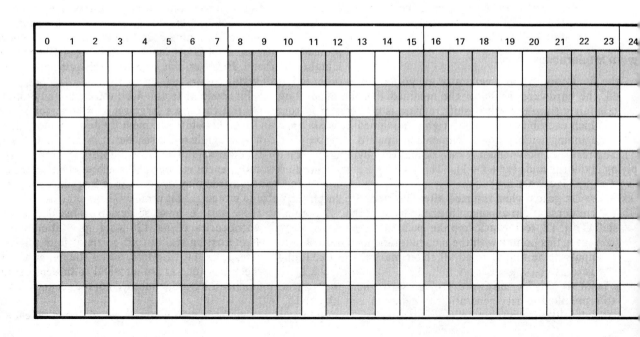

without a polyimide overcoat, which guards against soft errors.

From the test results, the probability of a single-bit soft error in a 16-K RAM is calculated as 6.11×10^{-11}. In addition, though a hard failure is at least 10 times less likely than a soft failure, the greatest probability for a specific bit failure is almost entirely due to the total failure of the device.

It is also possible to calculate failure-mode probabilities and error-correction priorities for large-scale memory systems for various error combinations. Unfortunately, the probability of a double-bit error caused by a hard failure is difficult because of the various RAM failure modes.

The probability of a single hard-bit failure in a 16-K RAM is the sum of three factors: the percentage of bit failures, row or column failures, and whole-device plus other failures. The 6% category of other failures in Table 1 should be included into the whole-device-failure category because these errors—timing drift, input/output leakage, and any parameter exceeding its specification—eventually lead to device failure.

In fact, the probability of a hard-bit failure is so heavily influenced by the failure of the entire device that the first two factors can be ignored as relatively small in the probability-determining equation. Once the single hard-bit failure is determined, it is also possible to calculate the probability of two hard errors within one word.

The effect of an entire-device failure is so pervasive that the appearance of two hard errors within a word indicates the complete failure of one component together with any failure of the remaining components composing that word. This often includes another device's outright failure. When this condition occurs, chip failure is not only word- but also device-dependent.

The most likely source of a 2-bit error within a single memory access is a component failure, which in addition increases the probability of a soft error. If a device contains a hard error, the system becomes vulnerable to a soft error, and thus a 2-bit error can be created in one word.

Memory organization

Various organization options and failure rates were analyzed for typical 16-megabyte memory systems with different architectures to help determine the codes that were needed for error correction in a wide-word memory system. Three types of memory systems were constructed: 16-K by 1, 64-K by 1, and 16-K by 4 bits. Moreover, both the 16- and 64-K systems were compared with a system implemented with 16-K-by-4-bit RAMs. Systems with different word sizes were also compared.

This study supplies interesting data to the memory-system designer who is concerned with errors. A soft error within a device is the most common system malfunction within a system, and 16-K RAMs show the lowest probability of such an error when compared with 64-K dynamic RAMs (both without polyimide overcoats). This difference is due to the larger geometry of the 16-K RAM and the resulting greater stored charge.

Thus, the 32-bit word data for 64-K-by-1- and 16-K-by-4-bit chips shows that a soft error will crop up about equally for both chips. Fortunately, soft errors can be easily tolerated and corrected, but only when the circuitry is designed with soft errors as the first priority.

In the hard-error category, the error rates on a per-bit basis for 64-K-by-1-bit devices is essentially one fourth that of the 16-K-by-1-bit chips. Among the reasons advanced for this result are the reduced power dissipation, reduced heat, and consequently lower junction temperatures of the 64-K devices. In fact, the 64-K-by-1- and the 16-K-by-4-bit RAMs show equal probabilities of a hard error for 32-bit-wide words. The larger devices have only one fourth the probability of a hard error when compared with the smaller (16-K) chips. This is important because a single hard error is the second most likely fault condition.

The situation for 16- and 64-K chips is reversed for the probabilities of a soft and a hard error within a single word. In this case, the 16-K device's probability of error is exactly one fourth that of the 64-K chip. Because the words are smaller in an 8-bit organization than in a 64-bit word, the probability of error in wide words is much greater—9.6 years versus 1.7 years before failure. In fact, the 16-K-by-4-bit organization is clearly superior to the 64-K-by-1-bit arrangement—3 years versus 327 days before failure. Two hard or two soft errors within a word have such low probabilities of occurrence that they hardly need be considered.

Though a 4-bit memory system has been described, use of two interleaved sets of the Fire code can provide fault tolerance for 8-bit-wide devices. This setup implies that a 64-bit memory word (eight devices) will have 16 bits of redundancy (two devices). □

2. Subset. This 40-state–generation table is a subset of a 60-state table, which, in turn, is a subset of a 120-state table. The Fire code's bit overhead may be reduced by eliminating those error combinations shown to be insignificant in Table 2.

27	28	29	30	31	C0	C1	C2	C3	C4	C5	C6	C7

Electronics/June 2, 1982

Nelson matrix can pin down 2 errors per word

48-pin, bipolar Schottky package handles 16-bit microprocessors and hard and soft errors in 256-K RAMs

by Mike Evans, *National Semiconductor Corp., Santa Clara, Calif.*

☐ With the arrival of 16-bit microprocessors on the system scene, the need for large main memories has grown. Likewise, the continued reduction in storage cost per bit for dynamic random-access memories, plus their coming 256-K capacity, has made it common for a system memory to contain many banks of high-capacity dynamic RAMs with 16-bit input/output for each bank.

However, the information written into dynamic memories may not be the same when subsequently read, giving rise to the need for an error-detection and -correction chip in addition to the essential RAM control circuitry. The DP8400, a 48-pin bipolar large-scale integrated-circuit chip implemented in Schottky logic for minimal time delay, answers such a need. Called an expandable error-checker and -corrector, this companion to National Semiconductor's DP8408 and 8409 dynamic RAM controllers detects and corrects one or two hard or soft errors—a capability not available with any other error-detection and correction circuit and due to the use of a modified Hamming code called the Nelson matrix.

Users of dynamic RAMs must carefully consider whether to incorporate error-correction capabilities into their systems. This consideration is equally valid for static MOS and bipolar RAMs, although these tend not to be used in large memories, in which errors tend to occur less frequently.

To help make such a decision, error-rate data is available from the dynamic RAM manufacturers. However, this data only covers RAM errors in a perfect test environment. In general, the data in a RAM will be incorrect by only 1 bit, as two errors occur infrequently. Most classic error-correction circuits will detect one or two errors. They will correct any single error, whether hard or soft (see "Errors hard and soft," below), but two errors in a data word are not correctable. Though two hard errors are unlikely in any one data word, two soft errors may occur at different times in the same two locations—often a pair that is seldom accessed.

To prevent such occurrences, memory "scrubbing" can be used to remove single soft errors before a second can occur. Scrubbing involves cycling through the memory, reading every location, and checking for errors. If an error has occurred, the erroneous data word is corrected and written back.

A deadly combination

But the combination of two errors that is the most troublesome is one hard and one soft error. Such an event can occur if a particular location or combination of locations develops a hard error. If a soft error now occurs at this address before the hardware fault is located and replaced, two errors are created. The error-correction circuit detects both errors but cannot correct them. The

---

Errors hard and soft

The data-bit errors that occur in most semiconductor devices are characterized as either hard or soft. Hard errors are those that will always repeat whenever a particular location or combination of locations is accessed, even when new data is written over previous erroneous data. An example of a hard error is an individual cell or group of cells that become permanently jammed in one state. Failure of a complete memory chip in a bank will also appear as a hard error. And, finally, if one bit of a memory buffer chip fails, this is interpreted as a hard error.

To understand how these errors affect a system, it must be noted that memory systems using dynamic random-access memories access a different dynamic RAM for each bit of data in any one data word. As a result, a cell group failure in one chip, or a total component failure, will introduce only one error into the data word.

The presence of a hard error can be determined by a simple test. Whenever the erroneous location is written to with a bit of the opposite polarity to the jammed value, the error is still present.

By contrast, a soft error can be removed by writing over an erroneous word. One of the most common causes of soft errors is alpha particles from packaging material containing thorium or uranium. These particles bombard the RAM's storage capacitors with enough energy to alter their charge. With enough change of charge, a subsequent reading of an affected cell can misinterpret the data. Most current dynamic RAMs are not as susceptible to this problem as past devices thanks to better cell design, better selection of nonradioactive packages, and the deposition of alpha-particle–absorbing layers on the chip.

Soft errors may also be noise-induced. For example, inadequate decoupling of a chip will cause soft errors, as will inadequate ground or voltage lines. A sensitive cell may even be affected by a neighboring data pattern, although manufacturers test the tolerance of each dynamic RAM to data patterns that are most likely to cause errors. Another kind of error occurs when a sensitive cell is seldom accessed. Occasional access creates an error, but regular use does not.

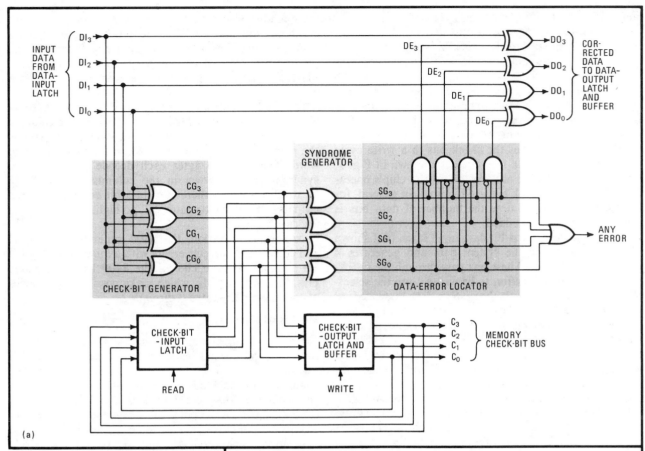

(a)

1. Bit generation. The DP8400 chip uses the circuitry shown in (a) to correct errors in a 4-bit data word from a dynamic RAM. Only standard gates and latches are needed to generate check bits in a write cycle and to correct errors in a read cycle (b).

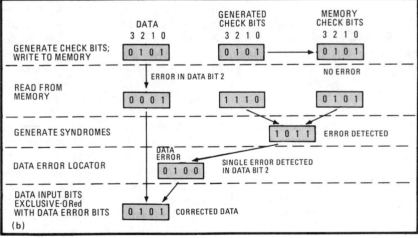

(b)

system now either crashes or, if the software and hardware allow, goes into an emergency routine.

It is this two-error case than can be reliably corrected by the 8400. The chip will not only correct any single error, it will also correct two errors in the same data word. In addition, provided one or both of the two errors are hard, the 8400 will correct both errors by complementing both of them (a 1 is made a 0 and vice versa)—a technique that needs no more memory space than single-error correction. Further, if the user cannot tolerate the risk of two soft errors in any data word, the 8400 can be optionally configured with additional check bits and circuitry to correct them both, using what is known as the double-syndrome–decode approach.

In addition to the double-complement and double-syndrome–decode error-correction· techniques, another option the 8400 carries for increased data integrity is byte-parity generating and checking. Thus, for example, if the processor is on a different printed-circuit card

from the memory, errors that might occur during data transfer between cards can be detected.

If the transmitting card sends a byte-parity bit for each byte presented to memory, the 8400 on the receiving memory card can be made to receive these bits. It then checks them against its own internally generated byte-parity bits to see if an error has occurred. If it has, the chip sets the corresponding error flag. When the memory card is read, the 8400 generates byte-parity bits on the same pins and supplies these to the receiving card to be verified in the same manner.

The 8400 has a 16–data-bit input/output port and an 8–check-bit I/O port (6 of which are used for applications with 16-bit microprocessors). The 16–data-bit I/O port sits on the memory data bus, and the 6–check-bit port connects directly to the check-bit section of memory. In other words, each memory location now contains 16 data bits plus 6 check bits.

The 8400 concept is expandable to beyond 80 data bits. In this case, each extra 16 data bits requires another 8400, but there is no need for more logic circuitry.

Both a circuit diagram and data-bit–flow diagram of how the 8400 generates the check bits in a write cycle and corrects errors in a read cycle are shown in Fig. 1, where a 4-bit example neatly explains the chip's operation. Here, only 4 check bits are required. In general, for error correction, each time the number of data bits is doubled, 1 check bit is added.

In a write cycle, the 4-bit data input latch (not shown in Fig. 1a) receives the system data and generates 4 parity, or check, bits. These bits pass through the check-bit output latch and buffer, to be written into the selected memory location with the system data, a procedure that delays every write cycle only 30 nanoseconds.

When these memory locations are subsequently read, the 4 memory data bits pass through the data input latch to generate 4 new check bits. The 4 memory check bits pass through the check-bit input latch and are fed into four exclusive-OR gates along with the 4 generated check bits. The outputs of these gates are called syndrome bits.

If there are no errors, the two sets of check bits will be the same and no syndrome bits will go high. If there is an error in the check bits, only the corresponding syndrome bit will go high. In this case, the data bits are still correct. If one of the data bits is in error, 3 syndrome bits will go high, and the syndrome word is unique for any one of the bits in error. Finally, the four AND gates decode which bit is in error and complement it out of the second set of exclusive-OR gates. The other three exclusive-OR outputs remain the same as the input bits, so the corrected word is now available to the system.

When the 8400 is being used with 16 data bits and 6 check bits, 16 AND gates decode the 6 syndrome bits to determine the data bit in error. Figure 2 shows the 8400's internal bit-correction matrix. A form of modified Hamming code known as a Nelson matrix, it has some unique double–soft-error correction features.

Basically, the matrix has two functions. Horizontally it describes the value of the generated check bits for any data word when being written to memory. Vertically it describes the syndrome word for any data bit in error

when read from the memory. In a write cycle to memory, a 1 in any row indicates that the data bit in that column helps generate the parity bit in that row. For example, the first check bit checks the parity of data bits 3, 6, 9, 11, 13, 14, and 15 and generates even parity for those data bits.

In a read cycle from memory, 3 or 5 of the 6 syndrome bits will go high for a single data-bit error. The columns represent the syndrome word so the data bit in error is the number at the top of the column for that syndrome word. The 16 AND gates each decode one of the 16 syndrome words shown in the columns of Fig. 2, to locate the error. If there is a data-bit error, one of the outputs of the 16 AND gates will go high, to complement the data bit in error.

In normal operation, the 8400 generates check bits and detects and corrects errors with a minimum of delay. To accomplish these chores, the 8400 has three mode pins, M_2, M_1, and M_0, which make possible eight modes of operation, designated 0 through 7.

Modes of choice

The most important two modes are normal write (mode 0) and normal read (mode 4), and for these, M_1 and M_0 are set low. Other modes are used for the double-complement–correction technique (modes 1, 3, and 5) and for diagnostics (modes 2 and 6). Mode 7 is used when the chip's operation is expanded to more than 16 data bits and faster correction times are required.

In normal operation, M_1 and M_0 are set low. While data is being written into memory in this mode, the data-latch–enable (DLE) control line must be kept high, the output-latch–enable ($\overline{\text{OLE}}$) and check-bit/syndrome-latch–enable (CSLE) lines low, and pin M_2 also low so that the 8400 is in mode 0. System data is presented to the data I/O port on pins D_0–D_{15} and enters the data input latch (DIL) where it connects to the check-bit generator.

In the next step, the six generated check bits pass through the check-bit output latch (COL) and are enabled (with M_2 low) onto the check-bit I/O port. A write operation to memory will now store the 16 data bits and 6 corresponding check bits in the selected location. To accomplish this the cycle is slowed down by 30 ns, which in most memory systems, is not significant.

In reading from memory, the DLE is set high to enter the memory data bits into the DIL, and CSLE is also set high to enter memory check bits into the check-bit input

			0	1	2	3	4	5	6	7	8	9	0	1	2	3	4	5		
			GENERATE CHECK BITS ———————————————————→																	
		0	0	0	1	1	1	1	1	1	0	1	1	1	0	1	1	1	0	
		1	0	0	0	1	0	0	1	0	1	1	0	1	0	1	1	1	1	
GENERATED SYNDROMES		2	1	0	0	1	1	0	0	0	1	0	1	0	1	1	1	1	2	GENERATED CHECK BITS
		3	0	1	1	0	0	0	0	1	1	1	1	0	1	0	1	1	3	
		4	1	1	0	0	0	1	0	1	1	0	1	0	1	0	1	0	4	
		5	1	1	1	0	1	1	1	0	1	0	0	0	1	1	1	0	5	

2. Two functions. The internal bit-correction matrix of the DP8400 shows the value of the generated check bits when a data word is written to memory and furnishes the syndrome word to locate any bit in error. The number of syndrome words is equal to the number of data bits.

3. Data flow. Double-error correction—one hard and one soft error in this example of a 4-bit data word—is obtained by the double-complement method. The flow of data- and check bits shown guarantees an error fix with 16-bit systems as well.

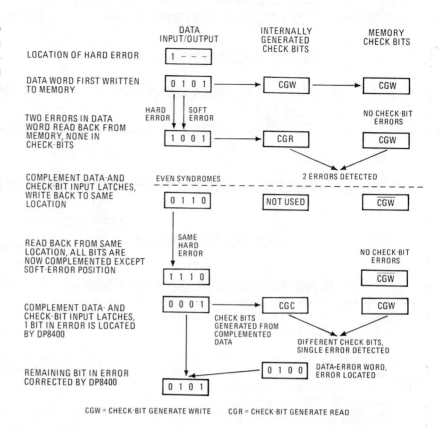

CGW = CHECK-BIT GENERATE WRITE   CGR = CHECK-BIT GENERATE READ

latch (CIL). M_2 is set high to put the 8400 in mode 4.

For fast 16-bit microprocessor systems, there are two possible approaches to correcting errors. The first introduces wait states into every read cycle to determine if an error exists. If no error is detected, the wait signal is removed and the read cycle continues. If an error in the data word is detected, then the memory must be disabled and the corrected data read from the 8400.

This procedure may seem the most logical approach, but in fact, it is too slow. The second approach involves disabling memory data after latching it in and then latching in output data from the 8400. The two sets of data are compared, and if no error has occurred, then the 8400's data word is unchanged.

If the error is a single data-bit error, the data-output latch (DOL) by now will contain corrected data. If there is no check-bit error, the COL contains the original check bits. Taking OLE high latches corrected data in DOL and correct check bits in COL. The memory is now disabled, so that corrected data can be transferred onto the data bus, and M_2 is then set low to transfer the contents of COL on to the check-bit bus. If the data-bit error was a soft error, writing to the same location of memory will remove it. The microprocessor can read the corrected data once the wait signal is removed.

Double complement

If instead of a single-bit error, a double-bit error is detected, it will still be correctable using the double-complement error-correction technique, provided one or both the errors are hard. A hard error is defined as an error that cannot be removed by writing opposite-polarity data back into the same cell or chip, and this condition is exploited by the chip to correct two errors.

In this process, when two errors are detected, both DLE and CSLE are set low to latch memory data and check bits into the 8400. Memory is now disabled, and the 8400 is set to complement the contents of DIL into DOL. Likewise, COL contains the complement of CIL. In other words, the complement of the read data is written back into the data portion, and the complement of the read check bits written back to the check-bit portion. In the case of two hard errors occurring in either the data portion or the check bit-portion or one in each, complementing the data will have now corrected these errors,

although all the other bits are still complemented. Since the complemented bits have been written back into the same location, the polarity of the hard bits in error is the same as it was when they were written the first time.

The memory location now contains all complemented bits, because the hard-error bits again complement the data written to them. The 8400 is now set to mode 5, DLE is set high, and information is read from the memory location. This complement-read mode for the second time complements both the contents of DIL and CIL and then performs a read operation.

The second complement of data and check bits re-creates the original data and check bits written to memory before the two errors occurred. No error is detected and DOL and COL now contain the original system data, along with the corresponding check bits that were generated. Both the errors have been removed.

One of each

Two hard errors are not likely, but may occur. The more likely 2-bit error condition arises when a hard error has developed but not been removed physically. If the situation persists, a soft error may well occur next to that location, resulting in two errors. Using a 4-bit example for simplicity, Fig. 3 shows the procedure for solving such a problem.

In this approach, two errors are detected, and complemented data and check bits written back into the same location to correct them, as with the previous example. But inside the memory, the hard-error position again complements this bit, as in the original write cycle. The

249

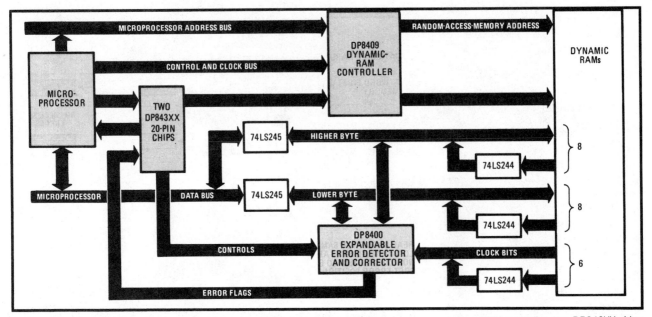

4. Full system. A 16-bit microprocessor system with a large dynamic random-access memory needs a RAM controller, two DP843XX chips, and auxiliary devices when it uses the DP8400 error detector and corrector. The chip pair is specific to a particular processor.

data and check bits are now all complemented, except for the bit in the position of the previous soft error.

In the next step the 8400 complements for the second time, leaving only 1 bit in error in the position of the original soft error. This may be among either the data or check bits. The error flags indicate which, but it does not matter, since the 8400 will correct the error as if it were a data bit, using its single-error–correction circuitry to do so. DOL will now contain correct data to be read by the system once the wait signal is removed.

The double-complement approach will therefore correct two errors if one or both are hard, and the error flags will indicate this. It does not matter whether the errors are in the data bits, check bits, or one in each. Before this routine is entered, the 8400 does not know the nature of the two errors, but at the end of the second complement, the error flags will still indicate two errors if both were soft and allow the system to crash.

If the system cannot tolerate two errors of this kind, then the 8400 may be configured with extra check bits and circuits to correct any two errors, including two soft errors. As noted before, this optional capability takes advantage of a feature of the Nelson matrix that allows use of the double-syndrome–decode approach.

On the boards

The 8400 is configured so that it is easy to control in most common applications. The port also has diagnostic capabilities that allow every on-chip gate to be exercised under microprocessor control. During this exercise, the memory check bits can be directly accessed from the data bus. This allows direct reading or writing of memory check bits to or from the microprocessor. A dedicated syndrome I/O port is also available for error-logging syndromes, if required.

Most memories contain dynamic RAMs and therefore need a dynamic RAM controller. A number of multiple-chip systems have been designed that allow control of the DP8408 or DP8409 dynamic RAM controller with the DP8400 (Fig. 4). In this configuration, each microprocessor requires a pair of DP843XX chips specific to it—the DP84320 and -21 for the 68000, for example.

Besides providing refresh capabilities for the DP8409, the two chips allow byte writing and single-error correction. To incorporate error correction into any 16-bit system, byte writing requires an extra operation, which usually slows down the write cycle. This is because the check bits in any location must be derived from both bytes. Such a procedure requires that, before writing, the location must first be read into the correction circuit. This circuit now outputs the unselected byte, while the microprocessor outputs the byte to be written.

In the next step the error-correction circuit generates new check bits that are derived from both bytes. The old byte, new byte, and check bits can now be written to memory. In other words, a read followed by a write operation is necessary. In speed-sensitive applications, this procedure can be reduced to one read-modify-write cycle. The same is true also with the 8400, and the two chips have been designed to carry out a read-modify-write, extending the write cycle by one clock period whenever byte writing is used.

The two chips also control correction by inserting one or two wait states (depending on the microprocessor) when memory is being read. If an error is detected, the two chips determine from the error flags the nature of the error. A double error causes an interrupt to the microprocessor to indicate uncorrectable data. Otherwise, for a single data- or check-bit error (or no error) the two chips disable memory and cause the 8400 to output its data. The wait signal is removed from the microprocessor so that it reads corrected (or already correct) data from the 8400. The 8400 is then disabled and a new cycle commences. □

4.
PERIPHERAL
CONTROLLERS

Without contact with external devices and physical processes, the speed and power of a central-processing unit is wasted. On the other hand, if required to perform all the functions entailed in dealing with external events, a processor can quickly become bogged down in details and become unable to execute the primary computational tasks of an application.

Consequently, just as mainframe designers turned to intelligent peripheral controllers, so are microsystem engineers making use of intelligent interface circuits to handle peripheral hardware like disk and magnetic-tape drives. Various methods provide designers with a wide range of alternatives for these interfaces. In addition, direct hardware support for interface protocols brings the needed simplicity of design, without sacrificing performance of the finished system.

Chips like those for control of direct-memory access are acting as servers for the CPU. The CPU merely requests a block of data from some source and returns to the major tasks at hand. These peripheral chips then come into play to acquire the needed data, load the data into system memory, and only then intrude on the activities of the CPU to notify it that the required data is ready.

Intelligent-peripheral interfaces

New interface systems conserve software,
but differences in system requirements foil search for
single intelligent-peripheral interface standard

by George Sideris, *Systems Integration Editor*

Once again, software is proving to be the tail that wags computer technology. Savings in software overhead, plus development and upgrading costs, add up to the major reason for the swing to intelligent peripherals. Microprocessors have accelerated the trend by making it practical to put the intelligent hardware in the peripheral rather than in an intervening controller subsystem. But to realize the potential savings, system integrators must resolve without delay some sticky questions concerning intelligent-peripheral interfaces. The series beginning in this issue of Electronics with the article that follows is intended to answer many of the questions.

Right now, intelligent peripherals allow most of the detailed peripheral-driving routines traditionally performed by host computers or controllers to be replaced with high-level commands. In the future, they should make systems almost device-independent—able to use new peripherals with little or no change in the original software design. The microprocessor will simply translate the commands into whatever new routines the new peripheral device requires.

However, although device independence was still a gleam in the eye of systems designers a few years ago, each manufacturer of intelligent peripherals had his own ideas about how to interface the peripherals with the host computer. Manufacturers of compact Winchester disk drives led the way with high-performance, byte-wide buses that expedite host-drive transfers of commands, status responses, and data. Compact drives were a natural starting point, because they were new and so were most of the systems using them.

Since the differences in interface architecture—in both command and hardware structures—could lock a system into one particular vendor's architecture, an effort was started up to standardize intelligent-peripheral interfaces. The goal of manufacturers and end users alike was an architecture that would allow intermixing not only of disk drives from different makers but of tape drives, printers, display and keyboard consoles, and other generally used peripherals.

The results of this effort are now emerging. A standard that would promote universal mutual compati-

bility is not in the cards—first, because system-integration needs are too diverse to stretch an interface standard across the gamut of system designs; and, second, because there is little agreement on which software costs are most important to save: the billions already invested in existing system software or the billions yet to be invested in new systems.

William Burr of the National Bureau of Standards, Washington, D. C., for instance, likens the issues to a "philosophical disagreement between Protestants and Catholics." Both sides agree on a fundamental need to connect computers to peripherals with an intelligent bus structure—but they disagree on whether bus control should be distributed or centralized. This issue led last year to a division in the American National Standards Institute committee (ANSI X3T9.3) then responsible for developing the standard interface.

Burr heads the "Protestant" move to another committee (ANSI X3T9.2) to come up with a standard for developing a peer-to-peer interface—one that allows the sender of data to control the bus, whether the sender is a peripheral or a processor. Named the Small Computer System Interface (SCSI), it is essentially the Shugart Associates System Interface (SASI), announced last year by Shugart Associates, a Xerox Corp. subsidiary in Sunnyvale, Calif. SASI, which is aimed primarily at microcomputer systems that may expand to multiprocessor systems, allows any combination of peripherals and processors to work together, up to a total of eight. However, there may be many more than eight peripherals in a system because any unit may interface with a group of peripherals. The standardized version, with a hardware option for larger systems and an enhanced command set, should be ready this fall.

The "Catholics" in ANSI X3T9.3, led by Gary Robinson of Digital Equipment Corp., Maynard, Mass., favor the more traditional hierarchical architecture, with a master host and slave peripheral units, each of which may interface a group of peripherals.

This design started out with a mainframe interface from ISS Sperry Univac division of Sperry Corp., Santa Clara, Calif. Now, much changed, the Intelligent

Peripheral Interface (IPI) has options that make it suitable for small computers and for small, slow peripherals. Yet it still offers compatibility with Federal Government mainframe interface standards (standards derived from the input-output–channel architecture of IBM's System 360/370 mainframe computers) and with the large computers' giant storage systems.

The second schism concerns what to do about existing software. The issue is not especially burning in the small-systems arena, but it was a major factor in the design of the ANSI IPI. To ensure that existing mainframe software would not become obsolete overnight—and thus prevent IPI's use on mainframes for years and years—the X3T9.3 committee put a migration path into the design. They divided the interface into hardware and software levels (physical functions and command or data transfer). This makes it possible to use any software, whether old or new, and to phase in new IPI-compatible peripherals and commands later. The hardware is now ready for use. It will also have high-level commands for new applications, but these are not yet standardized.

IPI's backers are counting on their design's software transparency to promote early use by peripheral manufacturers and to encourage the semiconductor industry to make it the basis for general-purpose interface chips. In fact, manufacturers of Winchester controller chips are startng to support both the SASI/SCSI interface and the IPI interface. A set of general-purpose chips that is adaptable to either one was recently announced by National Semiconductor Corp., Santa Clara, Calif. [Electronics, June 16, 1982, p. 117]. A semicustom chip set that is directly compatible with the SASI/SCSI design has been developed by Adaptec Inc., Milpitas, Calif., a recent spinoff from Shugart. What's more, several major semiconductor houses are expected to announce SASI/SCSI chips soon.

The article that begins this series describes the newest and potentially the strongest competitor among the proprietary standards: the Intelligent Standard Interface (ISI), developed by Magnetic Peripherals Inc., a drive-manufacturing subsidiary of Control Data Corp., Minneapolis, Minn. It will offer some competition to SASI/SCSI since it is suitable for small as well as large computers, but it will not compete with IPI in the IBM-compatible market, because it was not designed for that. However, ISI's most significant characteristic—a hierarchical, master-slave architecture—is expected to lead to an IPI-ISI confrontation in the original-equipment-manufacturer market.

ISI is off to a much faster start than IPI. Control Data has already started to introduce Winchester drives with a full set of high-level commands, and tape drives are on the way. Furthermore, to provide device independence, the same command format is applicable to the two types of drives and to other peripherals. Although now a one-company standard, ISI could become the third industry standard.

Smart link interfaces computer and peripherals

Implementing a new standard, control hardware promotes flexibility in peripheral setups while taking on tasks from host

by Bruce Johnson, Magnetic Peripherals Inc., subsidiary of Control Data Corp., Edina, Minn.

☐ A new system-integration facility, the Intelligent Standard Interface, will go into use this year on disk drives and in 1983 on tape drives. The same interface may also be used in the future on printers and other peripherals. The Intelligent Standard Interface—ISI for short—is so named because the intelligence minimizes peripheral-to-peripheral software changes. Added to the substantial advantages of hardware standardization and intelligent-peripheral operation, such device independence will ease many of the problems that systems houses face in the years ahead (see "What drives system integrators,").

ISI's hardware standard is a bidirectional, 16-bit data bus between a host adapter and up to eight intelligent modules, each interfacing with up to eight peripheral devices, plus the bus controls and protocols. The bus operates at data rates into the mainframe computer range. Built with microprocessors, the modules can easily be packaged with the peripherals (Fig. 1).

Command formats, status formats, and other generally required software elements have all been structured to promote such device independence without detracting from operational and diagnostic flexibility. This means, for example, that little or no change in host input/output software will be needed to replace today's disk drives with future drives. In fact, the same basic I/O software should be usable with tape drives and other peripherals. To be sure, some words in the software formats are device-dependent (disk and tape commands, for instance, are not identical). However, the way the host operating system handles the peripheral-driving software need not change, because the formats are standard and execution of device-dependent operations is delegated to the intelligent peripherals.

For the host, a major advantage of this partitioning is that high-level commands replace lengthy routines. Among the functions performed by Control Data Corp.'s new ISI-compatible disk drives are media-defect manage-

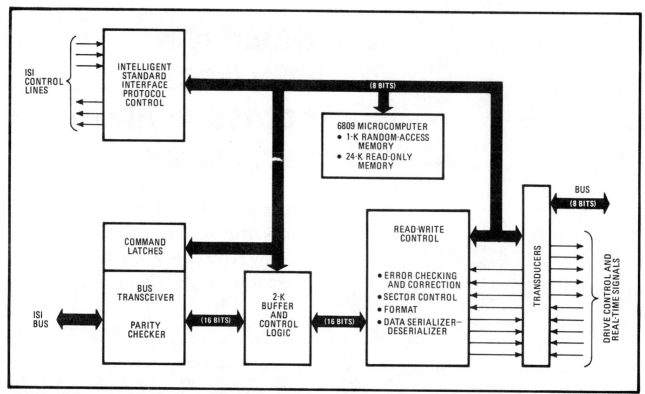

1. Slave number one. The first ISI slave unit is a programmable controller for two disk drives. Built with seven custom gate arrays, a 6809 microprocessor, and 24-K bytes of firmware, it can either be mounted on a drive or located as far as 10 feet away.

ment, error correction, data buffering, and diagnostics. Defect management, for one, involves routing accesses around sectors where media flaws would cause uncorrectable errors. Besides relieving the host of flaw-table maintenance and defect-management overhead, drive-level management will make future management techniques compatible with today's commands.

Some of the options

ISI's characteristics are the result of design goals that were set after numerous discussions with original-equipment manufacturers, as well as with CDC's own divisions. The design emphasizes performance, high-level I/O functions, and peripheral testability. The primary application range is from medium-performance minicomputers (which today often means higher-performance microcomputers) to high-performance mainframes. However, performance options make the design cost-effective in lower-performance systems.

The maximum data rate with fully interlocked, hand-shaked data transfers is 3 megabytes at a bus length of 15 meters. Because the bus transfers 2 bytes in parallel, the rate is easily reached with conventional semiconductor devices and low-cost twisted-pair or shielded cable. The 3-megabyte-per-second rate is comparable with a serial data rate of 24 megahertz. It is high enough for users to migrate from the OEM drives most generally used today with high-performance OEM computers (drives with a serial rate of 9.67 MHz) to drives with higher transfer rates.

Some cost-performance options are: data rate and unit selection and response times, buffer size, number of commands, and adapter design. The first three vary with

peripheral requirements and intelligent module design. CDC's first ISI-compatible drives are high-performance designs with intelligent interfaces that contain a 2- to 16-K-byte buffer and execute some 15 to 50 commands. The interlocked handshake allows adapters to range from sophisticated, high-performance direct-memory-access units to simple, programmed I/O cards. A dual-channel option supports redundancy in processsor data paths, improves system availability, and helps resolve contention in multiprocessing systems.

For testability, the status-reporting formats are designed to make it easy for the host system to determine when corrective action is required and to initiate the appropriate automatic (system) or manual intervention. Preferably, the intelligent module should not be a magical black box that leaves the host computer in the dark when problems occur—that is, the host has a right to monitor device operations, receive diagnostic information, and be told about any extraordinary delay in command execution. Consequently the ISI standard provides extensive status-reporting facilities at both the intelligent module and device levels.

Room for expansion

As many as 64 peripheral devices can operate as slaves within the ISI architecture (Fig. 2). The intelligent-module (IM) units are daisy-chained on a 50-pin cable containing the 16-bit bus (plus 2 parity bits) and six control lines. The adapter acts as the master, initiating peripheral operations, receiving responses, controlling the transfer rate, and, as an option, handling priority arbitration in multiprocessor systems. This setup gives the host control of functions such as checking selective

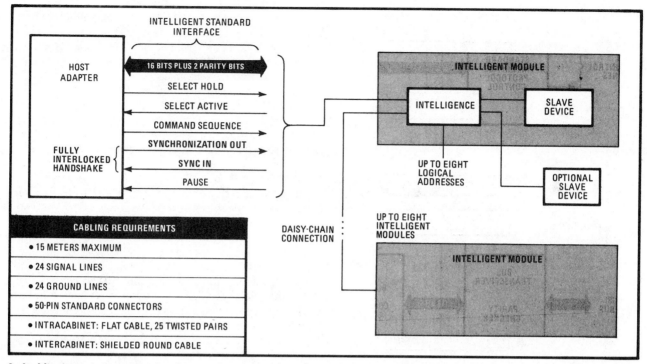

2. Architecture. Acting as the interface master, the host adapter in the facility controls up to 64 drives or other slave devices through intelligent modules. The modules are daisy-chained on a 50-pin cable and the overall link is a bidirectional 16-bit bus.

backup operations for errors, and it also saves the cost of replicating such functions in each of the IM units.

The bidirectional bus transfers control, data, or status words. These transfers are fully interlocked by the sync-in and sync-out lines—that is, the adapter and the on-line IM unit employ these lines to perform a handshake before each word is transmitted. Handshakes are also performed in an optional streaming mode that makes it unnecessary for the host to know the length of a data block to be transferred. The bus usually operates as a single I/O channel. The dual-channel option allows a single processor to have redundant parts or multiple processors to operate with a shared ISI subsystem. If one processor fails, another one can use the second channel to access data stored by the first.

Peripheral operations start with an IM-unit selection

process designed to verify that the right peripheral is selected. The adapter sends a unit-select address over the bus (using sync-in and sync-out exchanges for handshaking) and activates the select-hold line. The selected IM unit must respond to the select-hold signal by activating the select-active line. Both control lines must then remain active throughout the entire selection process to ensure interface integrity.

To verify that one and only one intelligent module was selected, the adapter logic can examine the lower 8-bit section of the data bus. During the unit-selection sequence, this bus section carries bit-significantly–coded responses from the IM units (that is, the individual bus lines designate which individual units are selected).

Before the command-sequence line is activated, all IM units can enable bit-significant busy and attention bus

What drives system integrators

Intelligent peripherals with standardized interfaces will not solve all the problems of system integrators. But they will make it easier to do the blending of software, hardware, manufacturing, and field support that is the *forte* of computer system houses.

As always, system integrators are driven by competition to keep on improving system cost-performance levels and maintainability. Today, however, they must upgrade existing systems and start up new markets faster than ever. Microcomputers, for example, have progressed to the point where a competitor can use a few boards to offer minicomputer- or even mainframe-like performance. Also, compact disk drives are close to the point of outperforming larger but older drives.

Yet the expertise needed to keep up is still hard to come by. This is where intelligent drives come in—they can automatically handle real-time control, formatting, error recovery, diagnostics, and other functions, so the system integrator can attack the problems at a much higher functional level.

Standardizing the intelligent-peripheral interface is the second part of the solution. That creates the volumes needed to develop large-scale-integrated controllers that can be optimized for each peripheral. The functionality of controllers has suffered in the past because of limitations on board size and cost, a problem compounded in most cases by the conventional approach of redeveloping designs for each specific computer bus.

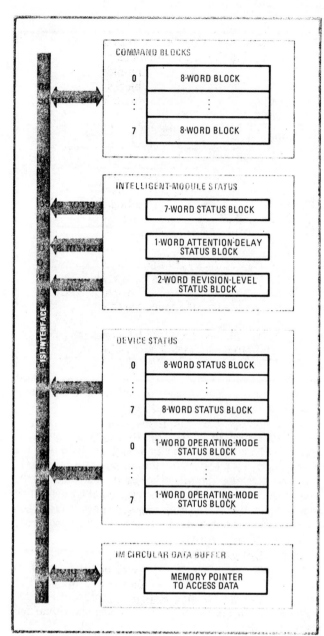

COMMAND BLOCKS

0	8-WORD BLOCK
:	:
7	8-WORD BLOCK

INTELLIGENT-MODULE STATUS

7-WORD STATUS BLOCK

1-WORD ATTENTION-DELAY STATUS BLOCK

2-WORD REVISION-LEVEL STATUS BLOCK

DEVICE STATUS

0	8-WORD STATUS BLOCK
:	:
7	8-WORD STATUS BLOCK
0	1-WORD OPERATING-MODE STATUS BLOCK
:	:
7	1-WORD OPERATING-MODE STATUS BLOCK

IM CIRCULAR DATA BUFFER

MEMORY POINTER TO ACCESS DATA

ISI INTERFACE

3. Programming model. In addition to taking care of its own status blocks, each intelligent-module (IM) unit can handle up to eight command and status blocks. The number matches the number of slaves per IM unit and also allows command queueing.

lines. The host adapter can thus scan the lines to determine the activity of all units, instead of running polling or status-reporting routines. Attention is comparable with an interrupt signal from peripheral to host. It can be asserted by an IM unit to indicate completion of a command, need for system intervention, and so forth. In the optional dual-channel mode, the upper 8 bits of the bus carry busy signals during the selection-response time, while the lower 8 bits carry the selection response. Since the busy state indicates a unit cannot respond, the host can immediately switch to another unit.

The host activates the command-sequence line to define the beginning of a new function and activates the line when that function should cease either temporarily or permanently. IMs use the pause line to let the host

adapter know that an information exchange must be temporarily stopped, usually because of a buffer-full or buffer-empty condition. Pauses do not lock up the interface handshake. The host adapter can back out of the handshake (if desired) to service other system needs and, after the pause line goes inactive, resume transfers with the unit that requested the pause.

If higher transfer rates are required in the future, an offset interlock or synchronous-transfer scheme could be added to the options. The pause function would then serve to slow down or halt the data transfer.

Commanding a transfer

ISI protocol requires that the first bus transfer after command-sequence activation be a single 16-bit function word. The function code defines bus direction and the type of information to be transferred in the subsequent message. Messages include command, status, or data-block transfers. They may be as small as one 16-bit word or as large as the total storage capacity of a disk drive. After the message block is specified by the function word, each sync-in or sync-out exchange increments the address to the next message word.

To minimize the amount of hardware needed to support these transfers, the command and status blocks are designed so the adapter can use the host computer's own DMA channel for transfers between the ISI bus and main memory, where the host assembles the blocks. Eight command blocks may be sent to an IM unit, one at time or all at once (Fig. 3 and 4a). This capability is what gives ISI architectural flexibility—it allows commands to be addressed to up to eight slaves on each intelligent module. Multiple blocks may also be used, for example, to queue disk commands and to complete optimal seeks.

The command block defines the command to be executed, the device number (if applicable), and, for disk accesses, the seek address. A block may be eight words long, but most commands require only three or four words and many only a single word (word 7 in Fig. 3a). The command parameter further defines the command to be executed. It may contain additional parameters of the command to be executed (for example, the number of disk sectors to be read or written). The host can store DMA address, stream address, or other additional information in the two spare-word locations. The spare words are not interpreted by the IM unit, but may be read by the host. To verify an IM unit's receipt of a command block, the adapter performs a wrap operation; that is, it immediately reads back the IM unit's command-register contents. This function is particularly useful for detecting programming errors and operating-system faults.

Disk primary and secondary seek addresses may be specified in cylinder-sector or in absolute-sector addressing modes. In the latter, sectors are numbered sequentially from cylinder 0, head 0, sector 0 to the last addressable sector. In this scheme, addressing is almost device-independent. Usually, only a primary seek address (words 5 and 6) is utilized. The secondary seek address is for complex operations. In a copy command, for example, it is used to define the starting address of the copy's destination (such as a backup drive).

An IM status block (Fig. 4b) contains a wealth of

	WORD 0	SPARE
	1	SPARE
	2	SECONDARY SEEK ADDRESS
(a) COMMAND BLOCK	3	
	4	COMMAND PARAMETER
	5	PRIMARY SEEK ADDRESS
	6	
	7	CONTROL; DEVICE NUMBER; COMMAND CODE

	0	NORMAL END; CHECK END; EXECUTION STATUS; SYSTEM INTERVENTION STATUS; MANUAL INTERVENTION STATUS; DELAY STATUS; DEVICE NUMBER; COMMAND BLOCK NUMBER
	1	SYSTEM INTERVENTION STATUS
(b) INTELLIGENT-MODULE STATUS BLOCK	2	MANUAL INTERVENTION STATUS
	3	ISI MODEL; DELAY STATUS
	4	TRANSFER COUNT RESIDUE
	5	DEVICE READY; DEVICE PRESENT
	6	COMMAND BLOCK ACTIVITY; DEVICE BUSY

	0	DEVICE IDENTIFICATION
	1	CURRENT SEEK ADDRESS
	2	
(c) DEVICE-STATUS BLOCK	3	
	4	
	5	DEVICE-SPECIFIC STATUSES
	6	
	7	

4. Software blocks. Although command (a), intelligent-module status (b), and device status (c) formats are standardized, the amount of information transferred varies with the operation. In many cases, the host sends only a single command word (word 7 in a) and reads only a single status word (word 0 in b). However, if a problem occurs, the module status block indicates the corrective action (intervention).

information that the host can either use selectively or ignore. The IM status block contains seven words of information about the progress or outcome of an operation. A summary (word 0) provides the conventional normal end and check end status, as well as pointer bits to system intervention, and manual intervention or delay status or both (words 1, 2 and 3, respectively).

In typical operation, the host system only needs to read word 0 following an attention signal to obtain the operational status. Additional words need only be read during exception conditions. To aid maintenance, intervention status words contain pointers identifying field-replaceable units. These pointers become valid after diagnostic routines are executed to identify which units should be replaced to correct a problem.

One half of the delay status word (word 3) identifies the unit (ISI model number) attached to the ISI bus. For disk drives, the transfer count residue (word 4) indicates how many data sectors were actually transferred between the IM unit and the slave during a command. The last two words (5 and 6) complete the IM status picture with information about unit availability.

The IM unit uses the device status block (Fig. 4c) to make device-specific information available to the host adapter via the bus. There are also smaller blocks used by the IM unit to report attention-delay status, revision-level status, and device-operating-mode status. Like command blocks, device status blocks can be sent in sequences up to eight blocks, to match the number of slaves per IM unit (see Fig. 3).

Intelligent-disk commands

CDC's new drives can be controlled in most applications through less than 15 basic commands. However, some models will support a superset of 50 commands. The superset provides additional error checking and diagnostics, supports the streaming mode, and supports inmmediate data transfers to the buffer.

The basic set is designed to minimize system software code. For example, the read and write commands operate with an implied seek and an implied data transfer. (Of course, specific seek and buffer commands are also provided). With operating-mode parameters, the system may enable automatic data correction, automatic sector reallocation, extended retry, and so forth. The system may also specify how much data should be in the buffer before the IM requires attention servicing. There are no specific commands for reading status—they are replaced by implied functions that are needed to terminate a command operation.

Copy and format are simply specified by the host, with no further intervention needed. The diagnostic command causes the unit to diagnose its functions, allowing this command to replace a large amount of system software. The salvage-data command allows the host to recover data if the IM unit cannot do so. Typically, the unit will make retries until errors are corrected and sends only error-free data to the host.

The new drives employ the latest run-length–limited codes to increase recording density. However, these codes also increase the possibility of error propagation because they merge code words on the recording tracks. Errors in one or two flux changes at code boundaries could cause data errors up to 8 or 9 bits long. Therefore, the IM units also execute state-of-the-art error-checking and -correction codes, which are optimized to detect and correct errors at rates that would stress the capabilities of conventional such codes.

Additional methods of ensuring long-term data integrity could be implemented with the command superset. To support predictive maintenance, for example, parameters such as disk rotational speed and operations such as retry and recovery could be monitored and catalogued on the disk. Analyzed periodically with system-maintenance software, this information would allow corrective action to be taken before failures occurred.

The storage densities and transfer rates of disk drives can be expected to more than double in the next three or four years. That will make new flow-management and error-correction techniques even more important than they are now. Yet, because these functions are handled by the IM units as part of normal command execution, the changes—like other changes that may come in device-dependent functions—can be expected to remain transparent to host operating systems. □

Intelligent Peripheral Interface updates master-slave architecture

Proposed ANSI standard depends on functional layering for microprocessor economy and mainframe compatibility

by I. D. Allan, *ISS Sperry Univac division of Sperry Corp., Santa Clara, Calif.*

□ A computer-to-peripherals interface standard that covers the requirements of new systems with intelligent peripherals and older systems that will one day have smarter peripherals has been drafted by the American National Standards Institute's technical committee X3T9.3. To accomplish this and other design goals, the committee's Intelligent Peripheral Interface (IPI) has a layered architecture that divides functions into physical and logical operations.

The new design can interface small or large computer systems with disk and tape drives, printers, and other commonly used peripherals. It operates asynchronously so that fast and slow peripherals can be intermixed on the same interface cable. Its logic functions are easily executed by microprocessors yet can be speeded up for mainframe computer applications. And being layered, it makes system design modular, easy to program, and simpler to implement.

As significant as all that, the physical layers are transparent to the logical layers. Software that operates dumb peripherals can flow over the same cable as commands for intelligent peripherals, so equipment vendors can offer users of older systems a migration path. IPI does not try to change the fact that most users cannot afford to abandon previous investments in software and hardware—often, they must upgrade to new technology

Computer interface standardization

Unlike many previous computer standards, the Intelligent Peripheral Interface was designed in an open forum by experts representing many manufacturers and users, rather than by a single company. This group—the American National Standards Institute X3T9.3 committee—has some 75 voting members and more than 100 observers. X3T9.3 also designed the Rigid Disk Interface for compact Winchester drives.

ANSI X3T9 subcommittees are also developing standards for a Small Computer System Interface (X3T9.2) and a Local Distributed Data Interface, for high-performance, local computer networks (X3T9.5). During the 1970s, the X3T9 committee focused on the channel interface between mainframes and control units. That work led to the establishment of Federal Information Processing Standard 60, now used with FIPS 61-62-63 to define the channel interface and operating modes of attached tape and disk drives.

X3T9.3 was formed in 1978 and first standardized disk-drive interfaces that had become *de facto* standards: the SMD (storage module device) drive interface and the SA1100 controller interface. These became the Storage Module Interface (ANSI X3.91-1982) and the standard Flexible Disk Interface (ANSI X3.80-1981).

During this period, compact Winchester drives were proliferating, but there was no dominant manufacturer to establish a *de facto* interface standard. Industry support existed for development of a new standard, so the committee invited all known and probable manufacturers of 8-inch drives to a meeting that was held in August 1979. Many doubted that a committee could produce a desirable standard, but it was agreed to make the effort. The starting points were the Internal Memories and BASF disk interfaces. About six months later, manufacturers began building the Rigid Disk Interface into new products. Now known as the popular ANSI X3T9/1226 interface, it will be designated as ANSI X3.101M-1982.

IPI's history is similar, but its scope covers tape drives and other peripherals as well as disk drives. This project was triggered by the pending development of intelligent peripherals—a product class that affects both software and hardware compatibility.

After the X3T9.3 committee established its design goals and entertained proposals, it selected in April 1981 the Sperry Univac Storage Control Interface as the initial working document. The current IPI design incorporates numerous ideas from other manufacturers of disk and tape drives, controllers, and computers, and also from systems houses and users.

In February 1982, it became apparent that small-computer manufacturers should have the option of using master-slave or peer-to-peer interfaces. The latter project, the Small Computer System Interface, was turned over to the X3T9.2 committee so that development of the alternate standards could proceed in parallel. Both committees have essentially completed their work on mechanical, electrical, and functional specifications, and work on command software is nearing completion.

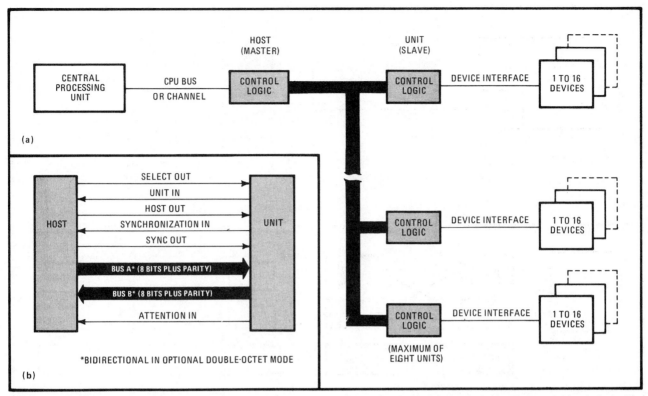

1. Master and slaves. Except for a division of bus-control logic between host and unit (a), functional partitioning is up to the designer. The unidirectional buses speed up command exchanges and save the cost of transceivers, but they can also join into one bidirectional bus (b).

in what are often agonizingly slow increments.

Layering also means that information being transferred on the bus, whether data or commands to be executed at the logical levels, have no effect on physical operations. Bus contents are completely transparent to physical-level functions (the interface system's basic mechanical and electrical functions). This transparency will facilitate the migration of older systems toward highly intelligent peripherals and more efficient software operations.

Today, manufacturers can start designing the new interface into equipment—test-beds have already been built; the components are readily available; and the semiconductor industry has begun to produce peripheral control chips usable in the IPI data path.

All that is needed for the control logic is an inexpensive microprocessor. Many manufacturers are already using interface standards previously drafted by the ANSI committee (see "Computer interface standardization," opposite).

Master-slave variations

The proposed IPI standard specifies a master-slave interface suitable for small or large computer systems. The standard defines a host (master) as the interface-control logic associated with the system's central processing unit and a unit (slave) as the logic associated with peripheral devices (Fig. 1). Up to eight units, each interfacing with as many as 16 peripheral devices, may be daisy-chained on a single cable, for a maximum of 128 peripherals to each host. The units may operate at different data rates, with a top speed of 6 megabytes per second.

A slave unit may either be integrated with the peripheral devices or drive them through an interface such as the X3T9/1226 (ANSI X3.101M) Rigid Disk Interface. Other than IPI control, overall system logic configuration is a designer's choice. For instance, the standard does not specify data buffering, buffer locations, or, for that matter, intelligent controllers for the peripherals. But the same microprocessor that executes unit control functions may also serve as a peripheral's intelligence.

In a low-end microcomputer system, there may be only a few slave units connected to the CPU bus through ribbon cabling and a bus adapter, so that the CPU acts as host (Fig. 2a). Although host control is centralized in a small CPU, distributing peripheral control to units with their own microprocessors would enhance overall performance. Typically, one slave unit will control high-speed peripherals like a Winchester disk drive and a backup tape drive, while the other controls slow devices such as consoles and printers.

In contrast, a mainframe computer would probably have several dedicated controllers as IPI hosts on its input/output channels and CPU bus (Fig. 2b). Dual-ported slave units, connected by coaxial cable, would be dedicated to one kind of device each, such as strings of disk or tape drives. Large-disk controllers could also be connected to perform outboard operations with the back-up tape drives.

Interface component classes

Four IPI configuration classes cover the range of applications (Table 1). The first three classes have ribbon cables and conventional 50-pin connectors. Class A is aimed at systems in which IPI hosts, cables, and units are

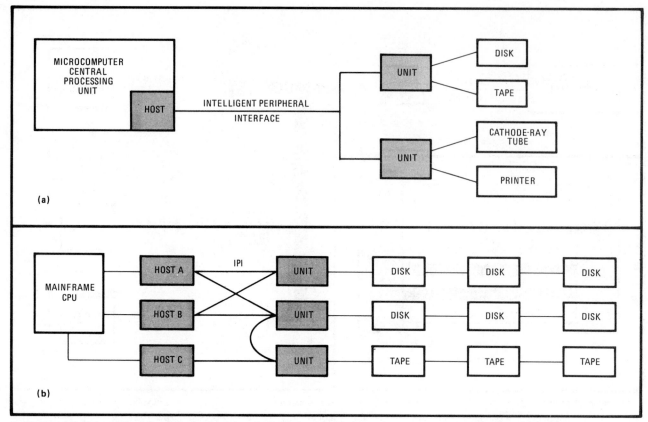

2. Mutt and Jeff. In small systems, the host is integrated with the central processing unit, and the units interface with peripherals generally used together (a). Multiple hosts and dual-ported units would be the choice for compatibility with mainframes (b).

contained within a single cabinet. Its cables and logic family are those of the ANSI X3.101M Rigid Disk Interface. Class B, for larger systems, has the same cables and logic family as Control Data Corp.'s Intelligent Standard Interface,

one of the interfaces considered by ANSI X3T9.3 in 1981. Class C, also for single-cabinet systems, offers electrical compatibility with class D.

Class D is suitable for large, multicabinet systems with cable runs to 125 meters (as in Fig. 2b). Its coaxial cable and 48-pin bulkhead connectors are compatible with Federal Information Processing Standard (FIPS) 60 for mainframe-computer I/O-channel interfaces.

The draft standard's mechanical and electrical specifications are compatible with commercially available, industry-standard logic families, cables, and connectors. Signal levels, logic states, and logic transitions correspond to the logic family choices (Table 2). All classes have identical protocols and commands at the physical level so that system integrators may interconnect classes through simple adapters. For instance, it is feasible to house a small cartridge-tape drive with a class A interface in the same cabinet as a large disk subsystem with a class D interface.

Two physical levels

Physical operations for all classes take place at two levels—0 and 1—with precisely defined functions. Executed by the interface-control logic, they include the common set of protocols, commands, and responses that are needed for basic operations such as unit selection and deselection, bus configuration, and data transfer. These functions are transparent to information that is being transferred on the buses.

Handshaking is accomplished by the host and units over the upper five control lines, along with synchronizing information transfer on the two buses. Units may also use the sixth control line to signal the host when they require attention.

Basic IPI logic is quite simple because operating states are defined by individual transitions of the upper five control lines. The five lines create 32 possible operating states, of which 12 are reserved and illegal, and six reset units. Thus, the logic need recognize only 14 states to execute all interface functions employed during normal system operations (Table 3).

At physical level 0, the buses are undirectional and carry exchanges between host and units. There are only five bus exchanges: out on bus A for the host to select units, issue bus-configuration commands, or request interrupts; and in on bus B for units to respond to selection or, after an interrupt request, to send radial addresses.

A host initiates unit selection by placing a 3-bit address on bus A and asserting the select-out line. (Alternatively, the host may address a device directly by setting bus bit 7 and placing a 4-bit address on bus A.) The unit places a status response on bus B and asserts the unit-in line. Besides a status code, the response includes unit-address and address-complement codes to verify correct selection. Next, the host places a bus command on bus A to define the bus for subsequent data transfers (at level 1) and asserts the host-out control line.

The small number of state transitions can also save computer-system overhead. For instance, unit selection and deselection require only four operating states (Figs. 3 and 4). This improves system performance when a host attempts to access a peripheral on a dual-ported unit that is busy to another port, a frequent occurrence in computer operations.

The interface exits from idle state with the normal level 0 selection exchange, but the unit status response indicates busy. So, the host releases bus A and negates the select-out line to initiate deselection. To return the interface to the idle state, the unit must release bus B and negate unit-in, so that all lines and buses become inactive. This ends the exchange, and the host can then begin another. Note also in Fig. 4 that the buses need be defined and stable only during states in which they carry a command from the host or a status response from the unit.

A status-response option named short-connect can save valuable time when a unit is busy. It lets the host know whether it should retry selection immediately or pass control back to software. In many systems, it takes several milliseconds for CPU operating-system software to select an I/O path. If the unit is able to determine that the operation to the other port will be completed soon, it posts the short-connect response, thereby saving the software overhead for new path selection.

At level 1, the buses transfer data with either handshaked or streaming operation. The buses may remain split to transfer bytes unidirectionally as in exchanges (single-octet mode) or be combined to transfer two-byte-wide information bidirectionally (double-octet mode). The unidirectional mode is the simplest and cheapest way to transfer data. Since bus directions are fixed, it requires only a line driver or receiver at each end of a bus line rather than a transceiver.

Although IPI hosts and units can drive long cables at mainframe data rates, speed is only one measure of bus performance. Others become important when slow and fast peripherals must be mixed on a small-system interface to save costs and when cable delays must be minimized in large systems.

Maximum data rates with interlocked handshaking are 1.5 and 3.0 megabytes for single- and double-octet modes, respectively. Streaming doubles the rates to 3.0 and 6.0 megabytes/s, respectively, by avoiding the handshaking turnaround time—which depends on cable length—of interlocked operation.

Setting the beat

In streaming, the sync lines carry multiple pulses simultaneously, instead of one at a time. The selected slave unit governs the sync-in pulse period while the host responds with complementary sync-out pulses. Optional unit logic counts the complementary pulses to ensure the numbers are equal when the transfer ends. A host can be designed to make the transfer method transparent. If sync-in pulse width is shorter than cable delay, the data streams; if not, transfers are interlocked.

Intermixing peripherals with a wide performance range is practical because the interface is inherently asynchronous and almost completely self-timing—that is, free of timing-dependent functions (Fig. 3). Timing relationships are specified at both host and unit connectors, with the operating states cross-referenced, and, as noted above, units can set their own transfer method as well as rate.

Splitting the bus into unidirectional sections at level 0 avoids the host-unit turnaround delays of conventional bidirectional buses. Instead of waiting through usual bus turnaround and settling times, a host can use bus A in rapid sequence because the unit responds on bus B. This may seem a minor consideration, but it becomes critical when, for instance, sizes of gaps in disk formats are dictated by cable delays (such as by the count-key-data specification of Federal standard FIPS 63).

The host can preset bus A with the next command in the exchange while anticipating the unit's status response on bus B. One status bit indicates if the unit failed in some way. If that status bit is not set, then the host can immediately initiate the next operation in the

TABLE 1: INTERFACE CONFIGURATIONS FOR DIFFERENT COMPUTER CLASSES				
Configuration class	Cable type	Connector type	Driver and receiver types	Maximum length (meters)
A (for single-cabinet computers)	flat ribbon	2-by-25-pin header	three-state and open-collector driver and TTL receiver with hysteresis	3
B (for larger single-cabinet machines)	twisted-pair ribbon		transceiver with open-collector driver and high-threshold receiver	15
C (for higher-performance single-cabinet types)	coaxial ribbon		open-emitter driver and receiver	5
D (for multi-cabinet computers)	coaxial cable	48-pin emi/rfi bulkhead		125

TABLE 2: INTELLIGENT-PERIPHERAL INTERFACE LOGIC LEVELS				
Interface		Internal		
Voltage level				
Open-emitter devices	Single-ended three-state and open-collector devices	Signal state	Logical state	Logical transition
high	low	active	1	assert
low	high	inactive	0	negate

TABLE 3: INTELLIGENT-PERIPHERAL INTERFACE OPERATING STATES		
Signal states	**Mnemonic**	**Definitions**
0 0 0 . 0 0	IDLE	Interface Is In Idle
. 0 1	RESETMST	Master Reset (Maintenance)
. 1 0		*
. 1 1	RESETMST	Master Reset (Maintenance)
0 0 1 . 0 0	REQINT	Request Interrupt
. 0 1	RESETSEL1	Selective Reset
. 1 0		*
. 1 1		*
0 1 0 . 0 0	DESEL	Deselect
. 0 1	RESETMST	Master Reset (Maintenance)
. 1 0		*
. 1 1	RESETMST	Master Reset (Maintenance)
0 1 1 . 0 0	INTACK	Acknowledge
. 0 1	RESETSEL2	Selective Reset
. 1 0		*
. 1 1		*
1 0 0 . 0 0	SELECTED	Selected
. 0 1		*
. 1 0		*
. 1 1		*
1 0 1 . 0 0	UNITEND	Unit Ends Operation
. 0 1		*
. 1 0		*
. 1 1		*
1 1 0 . 0 0	UNITACK	Unit Acknowledge
. 0 1	BUSCMD	Bus Command
. 1 0	HOSTEND	Host Ends Operation
. 1 1	BUSACK	Bus Acknowledge
1 1 1 . 0 0	XFRRDY	Ready To Transfer
. 0 1	XFREND	End Of Transfer
. 1 0	XFRST	Start Of Transfer
. 1 1	XFRRES	Respond To Transfer

```
| | |   | |
| | | SYNC OUT
| | | |
| | |  SYNC IN
| | |
| | HOST OUT
| |
| UNIT IN
|
SELECT OUT
```

*Undefined states that will initiate exception handling.

exchange by asserting just one control signal, host-out.

The physical design needs discrete logic only to recognize a reset condition, a precaution that allows a host to recover from a unit's failure. The remaining interface control functions are easily handled by conventional microprocessors or other programmable devices.

Inexpensive microprocessors are adequate to execute the logic functions for several reasons. First, since the design is timing-independent, changes in control-line states can be detected and the corresponding functions executed at a normal clock rate. Second, since data transferred over the bus is transparent, IPI logic need not interpret bus contents on the fly nor resolve issues like what to do when bad parity makes data invalid (although the same microprocessor might well handle such problems at higher design levels). Third, the small numbers of control signals, states, and bus exchanges reduce control program lengths. One IPI test-bed for low-end applications is based on a Z8 one-chip microcomputer with less than 300 instruction steps.

Furthermore, the ANSI X3T9.3 committee took extraordinary measures to prevent ambiguities in the method of programming functions. All functions are defined by precise terminology and master state tables and diagrams, from which sequences such as those in Figs. 3 and 4 are easily abstracted.

Clearing a migration path

The migration paths needed by older systems are created by defining logical operations that can evolve on top of the transparent physical operations. Here, layered-architecture principles apply, such as those in the International Standards Organization's Open Systems Interconnection model for computer networks. A computer-peripheral interface is not an open system, but IPI levels employ some of the layering principles to provide a suitable structure for equipment makers to build modular systems and choose migration paths.

Level 2—the lowest logical operating level—is device-dependent: operational commands (and responses) are oriented to specific devices attached to units. At level 3, commands become generic—they apply to an entire class of peripherals, not to particular device types. ANSI X3T9.3 is now reviewing command proposals at both levels. Higher levels, requiring knowledge of file structures and applications, are beyond the standard's scope.

At level 2, command repertoires such as those for drives with the ANSI X3.101M Rigid Disk Interface are applicable. The host is responsible for device addressing, command buffering, memory management, error correction and retry, detailed diagnostics, and so forth. At level 3, the unit is highly intelligent and can assume most, if not all, such duties. The unit would also support device-independent addressing structures in keeping with the

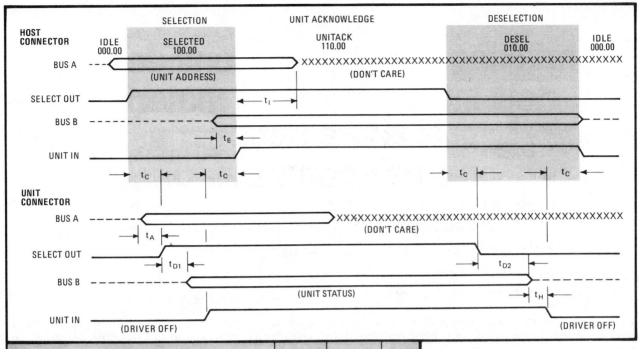

LABEL DESCRIPTION		MINIMUM	MAXIMUM	UNITS
t_A	HOST BUS A VALID TO SELECT RECOGNITION	50	–	ns
t_C	CABLE DELAY	–	SD	μs
t_{D1}	UNIT RESPONSE DELAY	0	SD	μs
t_E	UNIT BUS B VALID TO UNIT-IN RECOGNITION	50	–	ns
t_I	HOST BUS A VALID TO UNIT-IN HOLD	0	–	μs
t_{D2}	UNIT RELEASE DELAY	0	SD	μs
t_H	UNIT BUS B RELEASE TO UNIT-IN NEGATED	0	SD	μs
SD	SYSTEM-DEPENDENT (SEE VENDOR'S SPECIFICATION)			

3. Plenty of time. There are no critical timing specifications, another way of keeping the interface simple enough for microprocessors to control. This timing diagram describes the signal and state sequence for unit selection and deselection.

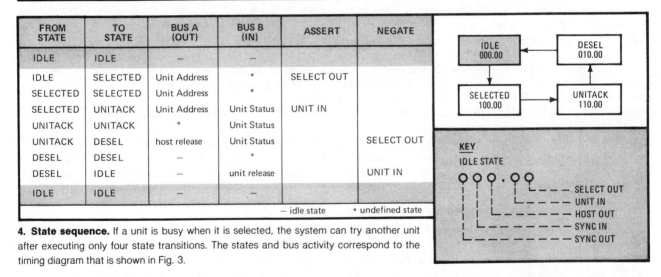

FROM STATE	TO STATE	BUS A (OUT)	BUS B (IN)	ASSERT	NEGATE
IDLE	IDLE	–	–		
IDLE	SELECTED	Unit Address	*	SELECT OUT	
SELECTED	SELECTED	Unit Address	*		
SELECTED	UNITACK	Unit Address	Unit Status	UNIT IN	
UNITACK	UNITACK	*	Unit Status		
UNITACK	DESEL	host release	Unit Status		SELECT OUT
DESEL	DESEL	–	*		
DESEL	IDLE	–	unit release		UNIT IN
IDLE	IDLE	–	–		

– idle state   * undefined state

4. State sequence. If a unit is busy when it is selected, the system can try another unit after executing only four state transitions. The states and bus activity correspond to the timing diagram that is shown in Fig. 3.

generic nature of level 3 commands.

Ideally, computer systems would continue host-driven operations at level 2 while level 3 is introduced on new systems. However in the real world, most computer products must migrate from old to new. The transition is slow and often painful, because operating-system software must be rewritten and entire systems reorganized. Consequently, mixtures of levels 2 and 3 may be needed for many years before only level 3 commands and truly intelligent units are in general use.

Since the purpose of standardization is to make such goals achievable, so the industry can grow compatibly, the IPI commands will permit different manufacturers to select different migration paths. The layered architecture does allow host-driven operations to continue—through emulation at level 2. Level 3 operations and new peripherals can be introduced on the same basic structure because changes at different levels have minimal or no impact on other levels. Likewise, new hardware technologies, such as fiber optics, can be introduced easily. □

Hosts share peripherals on small-computer bus

Proposed ANSI-standard interface for small systems
also has generic commands to speed peripherals replacement

by Henry T. Meyer, *Shugart Associates, subsidiary of Xerox Corp., Sunnyvale, Calif.*

☐ Several years in gestation, an official standard will soon be born for connecting intelligent peripherals to small computers and for programming the peripherals' operations. Already named the Small Computer System Interface (SCSI) by ANSI X3T9.2, the American National Standards Institute technical committee drafting the standard, it is based on the Shugart Associates System Interface (SASI). Like the latest implementations of SASI, SCSI will interconnect up to eight host computers and control units on a single daisy-chained bus (Fig. 1). Any of the host computers can access up to eight peripheral devices through each control unit.

Equally as important, sets of high-level, generic commands—commands for any type of peripheral in a class, such as disk drives—will allow peripherals to be mixed, interchanged, and upgraded without redeveloping host-system software. To make this prospect real, many companies have started or plan to produce SASI/SCSI-compatible products (see "SASI—already a *de facto* industry standard," p.   ). Moreover, the system makes detailed peripheral-driving routines unnecessary. The reduction in software overhead can approach 50% in applications requiring frequent peripheral access, permitting significant enhancement of existing host systems.

A full set of commands, already established for conventional disk drives, has been developed over the past three years. The SCSI version of the set will have ANSI nomenclature and be classified into standard, extended, optional, and vendor-unique commands (called controller-specific in SASI specifications). The extended commands are generic—they will operate any type of disk drive or any other type of random-access device. Generic commands for magnetic-tape drives were recently submitted to ANSI X3T9.2, and generic commands for printers will be submitted soon. Commands for host-to-host operations are in development. Communications devices such as video terminals and Ethernet local-network ports could be operated by the printer and random-access commands (Fig. 2).

Since its introduction as a Shugart disk-drive interface three years ago, SASI has become a mature system capable of supporting all three generally used methods of upgrading computer systems: replacing one generation of peripherals with the next, increasing the variety of peripherals, and adding extra host processors to the original single-processor system.

Looking to the future

To meet the first goal, the generic commands are designed to make hosts device-independent. That is, once a host computer's operating system has been programmed with the generic commands and connected to the interface bus through an adapter, changes in peripherals will not affect a host computer's software and hardware design. To be sure, the designer may change system software so that, for example, several hosts can share data file and program libraries stored on the same storage system. But even here the high-level commands will reduce software changes.

For example, the generic disk-drive commands will be executed by intelligent controllers for any type of moving-head disk drive, whether floppy-disk, Winchester or other rigid-disk drives, or future, laser-based, optical-disk drives. Underlying all command software is a sophisticated message protocol system, as indicated in Fig. 2. Together, the commands and messages offload all details of peripheral and input/output operations from the host to the interface system.

To support a mix of peripherals requiring different data-transfer rates, the interface operates asynchronously. With standard components, data rates range up to 1.5 megabytes per second over cable lengths to 15 meters, both of which are greater than the requirements of most small-business systems. Also, the interface offers 32-bit addressing to accommodate high-capacity storage systems. Moreover, it supports direct copy of data from one peripheral to another, such as from hard-disk to backup tape drives. For multiprocessor operations, it operates in true bus fashion, with priority arbitration distributed among host adapters and control units.

Architecturally, SASI is a general-purpose, local I/O bus rather than an interface designed for any specific

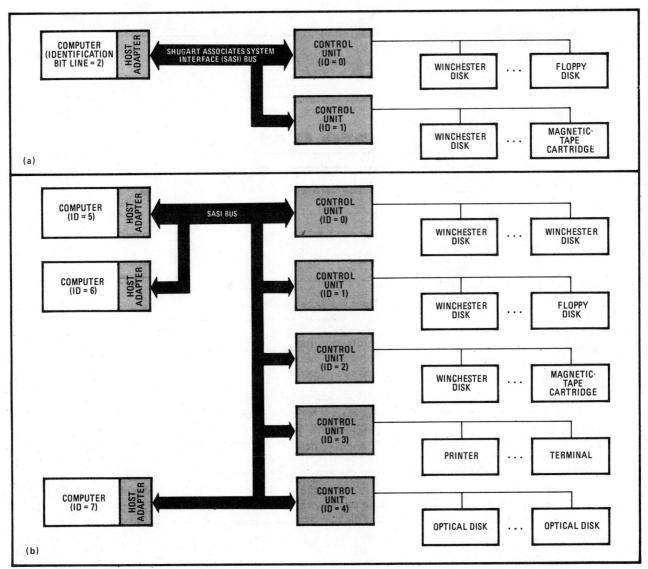

1. Expandable. The proposed ANSI standard is based on the Shugart Associates System Interface (SASI). Initially used as a single-host interface for disk and then tape drives (a), the system has bus arbitration so that multiple hosts can share a mix of intelligent peripherals (b).

type of peripheral. It can be implemented at several levels of sophistication. The highest level, known as the "full SASI" system, is being standardized, with lesser versions as options. Most early implementations had a single host and one or two controllers. However, those were only optional, upwardly compatible versions of the full system described here, for interfacing multiple processors and controllers. The full system has been dubbed a "peer-to-peer" interface by ANSI X3T9.2 members because it enables either type of bus device—a host computer or a control unit—to contend for use of the data bus, select another bus device, and initiate communications.

As well as being essential for multiprocessor operations, distributed arbitration maximizes overall system availability. Control units can disconnect while executing a command, then reconnect later to request another message or command or to transfer data with a host or another control unit. In the meantime, the bus is freed for use by another pair of devices. Likewise, combined operations can be performed, such as overlapped seeks

by disk drives. To maximize bus availability, control units may buffer as much data as desired. Buffer size is not specified, so that it can range from zero to any size the peripheral requires.

Such operations require not simply a connection from a host to a selected control unit, but management of the physical paths between different pairs of bus devices. To accomplish this, SASI employs an initiator-target communications concept (Fig. 3). The first initiator in any operating sequence is typically a host computer that wants a controller to execute a command, and the target is the controller that performs the function. Paths are managed with the message protocol.

To establish physical paths, initiators and targets use identify messages and bus addresses for indicating the logical unit number of a peripheral device that is to be addressed via a target control unit. An initiator sends an identify message after it selects a target, and the target sends the message after reselection, in order to reconnect to the initiator. Also, command, data, and status pointers are loaded by the initiator and moved by the target as

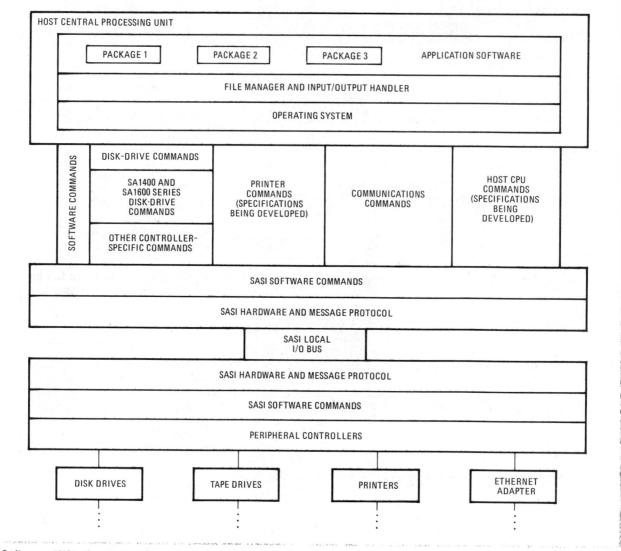

2. Software. ANSI will regroup command sets from Shugart into standard and extended, optional, and vendor-unique (controller-specific) commands. The host operating system drives peripherals with high-level commands; hardware manages the physical interface.

the basis for reestablishing paths and restoring previous states during disconnect-reconnect sequences. Initiators also send messages in order to reset the target to an initial state, to abort the current command, and to retry an operation if the initiator detected a retryable error (to correct a transmission error, since access retries are generally automatic).

Targets also send the following types of messages: disconnect, when the target will break the physical path and reconnect later to complete an operation; commands for initiators to save or restore pointers and to facilitate disconnect and reconnect; and command-complete messages. A linked-command-complete message enables the initiator to set up pointers for the next linked command. A similar message indicates that either a single command or a linked sequence has been completed.

Between interface operating phases, other messages can be sent. Either an initiator or a target, for example, may send a reject message to indicate that a previous message was inappropriate or not implemented. Either can also send messages to indicate that the previous

message had a parity error.

The interface cable (see table) contains a bidirectional, byte-wide (plus parity bit) data bus that serves to carry messages, commands, and data, plus nine control and handshaking lines. The spare and unused lines are grounded. For the single-ended option that is shown in the table, odd-numbered pins are grounded. For differential drive (plus and minus voltages), there are two pins for each signal and either common grounds or shield and ground.

Bus operations

All bus operating sequences start out in a bus-free phase. In systems without bus arbitration (Fig. 4a), the host computer is always the initiator. It first selects a target device by placing a target identification number on the bus (each data line serves as an ID bit) and asserts the selection control line. The target responds by asserting the busy line, then holds the line high until the cycle is completed. A cycle may end as soon as the target responds to a command, freeing the bus for selection of

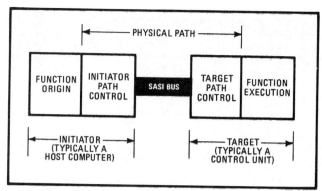

3. Hardware helps host. Connections between hosts and control units are established, disconnected, and reestablished with the aid of message-protocol communications between initiators and targets, so that physical paths can be managed largely by interface hardware.

another target, or it may continue through a series of linked commands and subsequent data transfers.

After selection, the target uses other control lines to request the initiator to send or receive a message, send a command, receive a status indicator, or send or receive data. It indicates the type and bus direction by controlling the states of the message, control-data and I/O lines (again using a data-bus line for identification). The I/O line indicates the direction of data transfer. During the data phase, for example, the host knows it may now read data from a peripheral if the I/O line is in the high state or, alternatively, write data to the peripheral if the I/O line is low. Each byte of information is transferred asynchronously with a request-acknowledge handshake.

In systems with arbitration (Fig. 4b), each host and

control unit has a user-assignable priority number (indicated by a specific data bus line) and logic for resolving bus contentions. Any host or unit may contend for the bus. An initiator is typically—but not necessarily—a host computer. As noted, paths are established and reestablished with the aid of identify messages.

When the bus is free, each host or unit that wants to use the bus drives its ID bit line on the bus and checks the bus to see if a higher-priority line is being driven. If so, it gives up the bus. If not, it proceeds to the selection or reselection phase and sends the identify message. The additional reselection phase allows a target to resume an initiator-target operation that the target previously interrupted. Then, it enters the command, data, status, or message phase to complete the operating cycle.

A command-complete message usually ends a cycle in both types of systems. To indicate that there will be more messages in full SASI systems, the initiator uses the attention line and the target responds by going to the message phase to transfer a message with the host. The final control line—reset—is an OR-tied signal to indicate a normal reset condition.

Black-box peripherals

SASI allows host computers to pass commands to a mix of nearly autonomous peripherals and to each other. Most commands have a basic 6-byte format, such as that for logical-block addressing (Fig. 5). Two longer command formats serve functions like extended addressing.

In effect, the generic commands convert peripherals to black boxes (see "Generic and optional commands in the SASI/SCSI scheme," p. 149). For instance, the inquiry

---

SASI—already a *de facto* industry standard

Although the Shugart Associates System Interface (SASI) started out as an interface for Shugart disk-drive controllers in 1979, it has now joined the ranks of *de facto* industry standards. Because they had that goal in mind, Shugart engineers designed a universal peripheral bus with high-level generic commands, rather than a conventional disk-drive controller interface.

The main idea was to cut the time needed to replace old peripherals with new ones—then as long as 18 months. However, to ensure that the interface design would have a usefully long life—at least 10 years—it had to accommodate future computer systems. Therefore, an architecture suitable for multiple-host, multiple-controller systems was designed. Although early versions connected only a single host to one or two controllers, the newest version has the full architecture.

Shugart first introduced single-host controllers for SA1000 8-inch Winchester drives, followed by controllers for SA800 8-in. floppy disks, SA4000 14-in. and SA600 5¼-in. Winchesters, SA400 minifloppies, and most recently, SA1100 8-in. Winchester drives. This summer, the SA1600 series of Winchester controllers implemented the full SASI architecture.

Meanwhile, other firms started using the SASI interface, usually on controllers for competing Winchester drives. Such manufacturers as Data Technology Corp. and OMTI Inc. led the way, followed closely by Scientific Micro Systems and Xebec Co., among others. Further, computer

manufacturers started building the bus connectors into small systems.

Shugart was asked to submit the design to the American National Standards Institute. Early supporters of standardization included the companies mentioned above, NCR Corp., Iomega Corp., and Adaptec Inc. In September 1981, Shugart submitted the design to ANSI X3T9.3, the committee working on peripheral interfaces. The committee initially declined the proposal because it was developing a standard for a large-system master-slave interface. Since the committee charter had not yet been approved, debate on the premature refusal of SASI followed.

The issue was resolved early this year by assigning development of the SASI-based standard to another committee, ANSI X3T9.2, while ANSI X3T9.3 continued work on the master-slave standard, the Intelligent Peripheral Interface. The SASI-based standard has firmed up in the ANSI X3T9.2 committee. It was renamed the Small Computer System Interface (SCSI), since ANSI policy forbids proprietary names.

Many manufacturers are now developing or have informed Shugart they plan products containing SASI/SCSI-compatible large-scale-integrated circuits. Plans for custom LSI controller chips have been announced by Data Technology, NCR, Iomega, and Adaptec, as well as Shugart. Also, semiconductor firms are working on general-purpose devices, such as LSI protocol chips.

and read-capacity commands can be executed automatically when the operating system is booted (loaded into memory) to determine how the system is configured. The first automatically determines what type of peripheral devices are on the interface bus. If they are conventional disk drives, the inquiry operation also determines whether the medium is fixed or removable. The capacity of storage devices is read back in blocks of data.

Another powerful command is request sense, which retrieves the status of operations in a target. The format-unit command automatically formats an entire disk for data storage. It can also be used to write the disk manufacturer's defect map on a spare track (if available) for automatic bad-sector reallocation by the controller. In conventional systems, the host must modify addressing according to the defect map (which identifies faulty media locations), forcing addresses to change when peripherals are changed. The write command transfers a specified number of blocks to a target device and the read command transfers a specified number to an initiator device. In new SASI disk controllers, error management and retries are performed by the target, so the initiator receives only good data.

These six generic commands are the most standard—manufacturers of controllers and peripherals will likely implement all to ensure that their products will meet device-independence requirements. The proposed SCSI standard also has a dozen optional commands.

A new optional command, copy, allows direct transfer of data between peripheral devices without involving the host computer. This command differs from previous commands in that it requires a controller that can act as both an initiator and a target on the SCSI bus.

The copy operation is initiated when the host computer sends the command to a target controller. That controller then reformats the command information to look like a normal read or write command (as it would normally be sent by a host computer). The controller then acts as an initiator and sends the read or write

SASI BUS AND CONTROL LINES (SINGLE-ENDED OPTION USING STANDARD 50-PIN CABLE)		
Signal	**Pin number**	**Function**
—DB (0)	2	data bus
—DB (1)	4	
—DB (2)	6	
—DB (3)	8	
—DB (4)	10	
—DB (5)	12	
—DB (6)	14	
—DB (7)	16	
—DB (P)	18	
—	20	not used
—	22	
—	24	
—	26	
—	28	
—	30	
—ATN	32	attention
—SPARE	34	(for future use)
—BSY	36	busy
—ACK	38	acknowledge
—RST	40	reset
—MSG	42	message
—SEL	44	select
—C/D	46	control-data
—REQ	48	request
—I/O	50	input/output
Note: All signals are low true. All odd pins are connected to ground.		

command to a second target controller. The data transfer required for the copy operation then commences between the two controllers. After the command has been executed, the second controller sends status information to the first controller. Then, the first controller sends status information back to the host computer.

Commands termed vendor-unique are specific to controller designs and thus strictly a designer's choice for

Generic and optional commands in the SASI/SCSI scheme

In the American National Standards Institute's standardized interface system, the following Shugart Associates System Interface commands will become generic—that is, standard, general-purpose—commands:

□ INQUIRY and READ CAPACITY: are generally used at start-up to identify all peripherals in the system and determine data-block capacities of disk drives.

□ REQUEST SENSE: provides a status report on peripherals, such as media changes, write-protect status, vendor-unique and diagnostic codes, nonrecoverable media or hardware errors, illegal requests, aborted commands, and so forth.

□ FORMAT UNIT: automatically formats a disk.

□ WRITE and READ: transfer specified numbers of data blocks to and from target peripheral devices.

The following commands are also being standardized, but equipment vendors need not design control units to execute them:

□ TEST UNIT READY: checks if unit is ready to run.

□ REZERO UNIT: rewinds tape or recalibrates disk drive.

□ RESERVE UNIT and RELEASE UNIT: enable one initiator to lock out others that are attempting to use a target device.

□ SEND DIAGNOSTIC and RECEIVE DIAGNOSTIC RESULTS: allow the initiator to send as much as 2^{16} bytes of vendor-unique test data to the target and get diagnostic results back for analysis.

□ VERIFY and WRITE AND VERIFY: verify a specified number of data blocks beginning at a specified address; the second command also writes data first.

□ SEEK: tells storage unit to position head arm.

□ SEARCH DATA EQUAL, HIGH, or LOW: three similar commands for specifying block area, number of blocks, and beginning block address of data searches. A search is satisfied when data in the block area is equal to, equal to or greater than, or equal to or less than the search argument, respectively.

Vendors may also use standardized command formats in order to develop unique commands tailored to special applications.

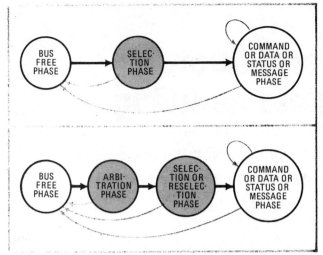

4. One at a time. Peripheral operating cycles can divide into phases with bus-free intervals. Single-host systems do not require bus arbitration (a). Systems with arbitration can have multiple hosts and control units that disconnect and later reselect hosts (b).

BYTE	BIT 7	6	5	4	3	2	1	0
00	GROUP CODE			OP CODE				
01	LOGICAL UNIT NUMBER			MOST-SIGNIFICANT-BIT LOGICAL-BLOCK ADDRESS				
02	LOGICAL-BLOCK ADDRESS							
03	LEAST-SIGNIFICANT-BIT LOGICAL-BLOCK ADDRESS							
04	NUMBER OF BLOCKS							
05	VENDOR-UNIQUE (VU)	VU	RE-SERVED	RE-SERVED	RE-SERVED	RE-SERVED	FLAG REQUEST	LINK

5. Command format. A typical format for control, data-transfer, and status commands includes peripheral-device address (logical unit number), logical data-block addresses, and control byte with room for an optional 2-bit, vendor-unique code.

increased command flexibility. Vendor-unique commands can be sent over the bus, but nothing will happen unless the controller recognizes them. SASI does not specify any such commands, but the proposed standard allows them to be used under operational codes not reserved for generic and optional standard commands.

Saving on software

Using high-level commands to delegate I/O and peripheral operating overhead to control units has two advantages. First, the host computer is more efficient. It executes less I/O software, requires less memory, is less likely to become bus-bound (tie up its internal bus in memory and I/O accesses), and can use the interface bus more often. Over 50% of CPU bus time is typically consumed in I/O operations like bus management, seeks to disk tracks, physical sector addressing, error retries, formatting, and other functions now performed by SASI logic. Saving this overhead means that less time will be needed to respond to terminal users, in network control, and in data-base management. In fact, control units can be designed to index, cross-reference, and back up distributed data bases without host intervention.

Second, and most important for competition in the original-equipment-manufacturer marketplace, changing the peripheral mix will not incur high development costs. With conventional interfacing, peripheral-driving routines must change to reflect changes in peripheral-device characteristics. In contrast, SASI's generic disk commands do not require alterations in the host system to change from floppy to rigid or optical disk, to increase disks per spindle, track density, or bit-packing density, to change error management, and so forth.

Shugart decided to design a device-independent system primarily because systems manufacturers and integrators were spending as long as 18 months to add the then-new compact Winchester disks to existing systems with floppy disks. The difficulty of keeping up with the state of the art with conventional I/O routines continually exposes existing systems to competition from new systems that have the advantage of starting out fresh.

SASI hosts and units are daisy-chained on conventional 50-pin ribbon cables, and some computer manufacturers have already built the 50-pin connectors into new designs. The single-ended option is for cables up to 6 m long, and the differential option for cables to 15 m. The first suits desktop systems in cabinets that meet the requirements for protection against electromagnetic and radio-frequency interference, and the second suits systems that must satisfy the requirements with cabling between cabinets.

The current maximum data rate of 12 megahertz (1.5 megabytes/s) was selected for a favorable tradeoff among costs of cabling and driver-receiver devices, cable lengths, bus-deskew timing, and handshaking turnaround timing. It is not an inherent limit and can be increased if desired. The physical, electrical, and timing characteristics were chosen for easy connection to the widest possible range of host-computer backplane buses. These buses include the S-100, STD, Unibus, Multibus, Versabus, Applebus, TRS-80, 8- and 16-bit Motorola, and others likely to be used in small systems.

An adapter card is needed to connect the SASI bus to the host bus. These cards have been made inexpensively with conventional logic because host bus-control applications are simplified by the way the control units operate the bus. The full SASI version requires only the addition of arbitration logic and the attention line. Since the interface adapts to almost any small-computer bus and will be an industry standard, adapter-logic chips built in large-scale integration can be expected soon.

In control units, the same microprocessor that executes commands can also handle most other peripheral control functions. There are already LSI control units for full-SASI systems—the new SA1600 series of Winchester drive controllers. Built with a microprocessor and four custom LSI drive-control chips, these have the same "footprints" as 5¼- and 8-inch drives and can be packaged with the drives. When the actual drive electronics are integrated in the future, the control units can migrate inside the drive. Other peripheral manufacturers have also been developing highly integrated SASI controllers. In addition, several semiconductor manufacturers are expected to announce stand-alone protocol chips soon. □

Electronics/June 30, 1983

Disk-storage architecture standardizes data handling

Host-resident device handlers, controllers, disk drives play together to accommodate state-of-the-art requirements

by Barry L. Rubinson and C. M. Riggle, *Digital Equipment Corp., Colorado Springs, Colo.*

☐ Tidying up the crazy quilt of software and hardware functions that make up the typical mass-storage subsystem, the Digital Storage Architecture partitions these functions into three independent layers that are linked with standard interfaces. Thus it is possible to make changes within one layer without affecting the others, an important consequence being the ability to mix and match hardware and software.

In effect, specialized functions are restricted to the relevant layer, and the necessary intelligence to perform them is distributed throughout the system. DSA joins the earlier central-processing-unit architectures and the Digital Network Architecture as part of an effort to standardize computer environments.

Within the DSA framework, commands and data are transmitted from layer to layer through the interfaces, in the form of message packets that themselves are defined by protocols. The various data-handling functions in interfacing layers, no matter how different in purpose and implementation, can communicate successfully because each accepts the applicable message protocols. Some products with this functionality are already available (see "Architecture defines disk products,").

There are three major functional and physical layers of DSA in a mass-storage subsystem (Fig. 1), which could be based on a disk, magnetic tape, or any other mass-storage medium. In the host layer, the computer runs users' application programs that make demands on mass storage. The controller layer's various functions ensure that the host layer is able to write or read data, without error, at its own speed, and when it wishes. The mass-storage layer receives the data, stores it as long as necessary, and makes it available to the controller on command.

The host layer uses two layers of software to accomplish input/output operations. What is called a mass-storage class driver, in response to requests from users' application programs, constructs message packets in the mass-storage control protocol (MSCP) in order to perform generic I/O functions, such as reading and writing. On the same level, a diagnostics and utilities class driver constructs message packets in the diagnostics and utilities protocol (DUP). The other sublayer, the port driver resident in the host, passes both MSCP and DUP packets along the bus between the host and controller.

The controller layer includes a port driver that receives messages from the host's port driver (or transmits messages to it). Two servers, one for MSCP messages and one for DUP messages, constitute the intelligence of the controller and, as such, define the functionality of the subsystem. There is also a driver that handles message traffic between the controller and storage device. For the midrange and high-end disk drive, these layers communicate by means of the Standard Disk Interface protocol over an SDI bus.

The disk layer consists of the SDI interface with the controller and the Digital Standard Disk Format, which describes how a disk is partitioned into logical areas. The disk drive, which includes one or more disks, performs a number of familiar functions, among them controlling head motion, accepting commands from the controller, reporting status to the controller, and, of course, reading and writing. The basic functions in a DSA disk subsystem certainly are not novel—they all have to be performed in some way—but there are significant differences from conventional subsystems in where they are performed and how they are related. In conventional subsystems, for example, the device driver in the host contains error-handling software and geometry data specific to a particular disk drive. It also includes bus- and register-handling routines specific to the particular bus

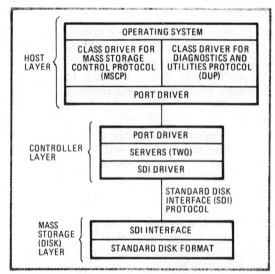

1. Tripartite. There are three major functional and physical Digital Storage Architecture components that cover mass-storage subsystems. These are the host, controller, and mass-storage devices, each of which is equipped with both hardware and software interfaces.

Architecture defines disk products

Advances in disk technology cannot be realized in working hardware without similar advances in other components of mass-storage subsystems. Higher area densities, for instance, require at least proportionately higher data-transfer rates and superior capability in handling their much greater vulnerability to media defects. At the same time, the computer industry's customers anticipate similar improvement in the reliability of mass-storage subsystems—zero data loss in the lifetime of a healthy disk drive is not considered an unreasonable expectation.

What has been the conventional approach in developing subsystems, however, has already shown itself to be a handicap to computer manufacturers implementing these advancements. The three main elements in disk subsystems—host-resident device driver, controller, and the disk drive itself—have been custom-designed for one other. A computer manufacturer therefore cannot independently design, say, a better disk drive or a user independently install a better drive. Both must invest, too, in compatible device drivers and controllers to make up a subsystem that works. Moreover, the functionality of succeeding models of controllers and drives, even from the same manufacturer, has not been consistent. The user has not easily been able to mix the old and the new gear and so has had to replace or add system and application software.

To overcome these constraints and better support future development of its own mass-storage products, Digital Equipment Corp. announced the Digital Storage Architecture. Development of DSA had been based mainly on two fundamental objectives, which in turn define a number of specific subsystem functions and performance requirements. The first was to establish a conceptual framework in which each component of a mass-storage subsystem could be fully independent and yet compatible with other components. The second, essentially an outgrowth of the first, was to provide an inherent flexibility that optimized performance of a mass-storage subsystem by permitting the introduction of new hardware technologies and design techniques without a complete reworking of the subsystem.

The first DSA products were the UDA50 (Unibus Disk Adapter) intelligent disk controller and three rack-mountable disk drives: the removable-media RA60 and the Winchester fixed-media RA80 and RA81. The microprocessor-based UDA50 links a PDP-11 or VAX host computer on Digital's Unibus data bus with as many as four of these disk drives. The controller, contained on two 8½-by-15½-inch boards in the host central processing unit's card cage, can handle data rates up to nearly 3 megabytes per second.

The RA60 provides 250 megabytes of formatted capacity per disk pack and an average access time of 50 milliseconds. The RA80 and -81 disk drives store 121 and 456 megabytes per drive, respectively, with average access times of 33.3 and 36.3 ms. Each drive is housed in an enclosure 10.5 in. high, and any three of them can be mounted in one cabinet, which occupies only 5 square feet of floor space. Maximum cabinet capacity (three RA81s) is 1,368 megabytes.

The UDA50 controller and RA60 disk drive embody the minimum functions defined for DSA products. More recently, the HSC50 hierarchical storage controller has been announced. The HSC50 interfaces to Digital's new high-speed CI (computer interface) bus and contains several additional sets of functions: tape input/output disk shadowing, and backup utilities.

and controller in the disk subsystem, respectively. Therefore, there must be a device driver in the host for every combination of controller, disk drive, and bus.

In a DSA subsystem (Fig. 2), on the other hand, one mass-storage class driver handles all message exchange between a given operating system and any mass-storage device of a specific class—disk or tape. The DSA disk-class driver contains no information specific to a particular controller or disk drive. Furthermore, with each controller and drive designed to understand the MSCP message protocol, only one class driver is needed for any number of controller or driver types that are active in a particular computer system.

The MSCP messages are independent of the communications medium, which is handled logically by the port drivers. Therefore, any DSA controller can be linked to a host computer through either the Unibus or CI (computer interface) communications bus, or any type of host bus that may be introduced.

In a similar way, DSA's standardization of the controller-to-disk interface leads to an independent controller and disk drive and independence of both those devices from the host. The disk drive itself contains a parameter table of all its own characteristics, such as geometry and retry counts for error handling. At start-up, this information is passed to the controller so that it may manage operation of that particular disk configuration. Controllers can simultaneously handle between 4 and 24 DSA disk drives having different characteristics.

In addition to relieving the host-resident driver of disk-specific data, the DSA controller and disk together provide the host with clean data—another advance over conventional mass-storage subsystems. In this case, "clean" means data for which all necessary error detection, correction, and recovery have already been done. The disk drive handles some positioner errors entirely by itself and performs certain error-recovery operations under direction of the controller. However, the DSA standard gives the controller the main responsibility, which is carried out by error-detection and -correction processes in the UDA50 and HSC50 controllers. With both of these controllers, the host is informed of error recovery by an error log but does not itself participate in the error-handling process.

Another function of the controllers, which also contributes to compatibility of layers in the DSA architecture, is matching the drive's speed to the host bus's speed. Some computer bus structures may not be able to sustain the very high data-transfer rates demanded by the higher disk densities. To achieve compatibility with minimal subsystem impact, the controllers perform multisector buffering.

Being able to mix and match class drivers, port drivers, controllers, and disk drives is valuable to both manufacturers and users of mass-storage subsystems. Both can then take advantage of advances in software and microprocessors and in electromechanical and chemical technologies, even though the improved controllers and disk drives that result are introduced at different times.

The Digital Standard Disk Format (Fig. 3), which applies to any type of DSA disk drive, ensures that the host operating system sees a fixed number of logical data-storage blocks throughout the useful life of the drive, whatever the number of media defects that develop in use. The logical-block area is about 98% of the total storage space, and the published capacity of the disk drive is the size of this host application area.

The host application area of the disk's recording surfaces is organized into sectors. With the DSDF protocol, each sector includes a data block of either 512 or 576 bytes (512 for PDP-11 and VAX computers, 576 for DEC-system-10 and system-20 machines), four copies of the block header (type code and block number), and fixed bit fields for error detection and correction codes. The host addresses sectors by sequential block numbers, from 0 to the disk capacity (the RA81 disk, for example, has 891,072 sectors with 512-byte data blocks).

Bad blocks, which are data blocks in host application sectors that have developed defects like holes, inclusions, or thin spots in their track space, must be retired and replacement blocks assigned to take over their stored data. The RA60 disk drive has 9,600 512-byte replacement blocks, and the RA81 drive has 17,612 replacement blocks, many times the number of bad blocks that are likely to develop in the useful life of the disk.

The process of detecting and replacing bad blocks is called revectoring and is handled by the controller, although the replacement tables linking the logical block and replacement block numbers are accessible to the host for diagnostic purposes. To minimize revectoring time, the first replacement block is available on the same track as the bad block (primary revectoring). After primary revectoring, replacement blocks from anywhere else on the disk can be assigned as needed (secondary revectoring), using the replacement tables.

Format control tables in the external-block area of the DSDF format describe the state of the recording medium, including whether it is formatted into 512- or 576-byte data blocks when the disk leaves manufacturing. The format also reserves space for diagnostic blocks (which may or may not be used) so that the controller can exercise diagnostic read and write logic without disturbing user data. Diagnostic space on the RA80 and RA81 Winchester drives and the RA60 removable-disk drive avoids storing user data temporarily on another disk while running tests. The host has no access to either the external or diagnostic blocks and so cannot inadvertently damage data in those areas.

An additional feature of the DSDF format is precession of successive tracks by an amount equal to the head switching time. Thus, the offset is zero on the RA80, which switches heads in only a few microseconds. On the

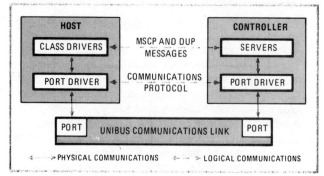

2. Free relationship. Logical communications between the host's MSCP and DUP class drivers and the controller's intelligent servers are independent of the physical communications that are handled by the port drivers in the host interconnection.

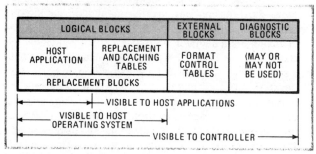

3. Quartet. The Digital Standard Disk Format partitions a disk storage device into four logical areas: the logical blocks (user area), replacement blocks, diagnostic blocks, and external blocks. Though all are visible to the controller, some are visible only to the host.

other hand, the RA60 has a multisector offset because it requires several milliseconds to switch heads.

Implementing DSA's functional definitions in Digital Equipment controllers and disk drives has been achieved through extensive use of more cost-effective hardware and application of new design techniques. In particular, the reduced cost of random-access memory and microprocessors has led to substantial, yet cost-effective, upgrading of disk-drive management functions in controllers and intelligent support for head-disk assemblies.

Optimizing performance

It has been possible to transfer optimization functions from the host CPU to the mass-storage subsystem, where real-time status information is more consistently available. This availability increases a DSA subsystem's throughput (number of host requests or data sectors per second), and its availability and data integrity.

The difference between the Unibus speed (or bandwidth) and rate of disk transfers is handled by sector buffers in the UDA50 controller's random-access memory. The sector buffers are loaded from the drive at the higher speed and, when the Unibus is available, are emptied over the bus at its speed into user buffers on the host. The number of sector buffers is selected—there are 51 in the UDA50 controller—so that they can handle all the data sectors transmitted to the host in response to most individual read commands. Although disk-to-controller transmission must halt whenever the sector buffers are full, this happens infrequently enough so that the

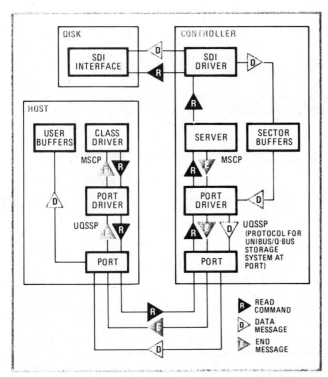

4. Trace the path. A message-flow diagram of a Digital Storage Architecture mass-storage subsystem shows how a read command initiated by an application program running on the host computer leads to receipt of the data that has been requested by the user buffers. An end message is sent by the class driver.

effect on throughput is actually rather negligible.

Another RAM buffer group in the UDA50 controller, called a command queue, stores as many as 20 I/O requests from the host. This arrangement helps to increase subsystem throughput by minimizing latency in receiving command messages from the host. In short, because the next command is always available in the controller itself, the subsystem need not wait for the next command from the host. More important, the command queue permits seek ordering, in which an algorithm running on the controller's microprocessor reorders commands to minimize seek time (seek ordering has been done, if at all, by the device driver on the host).

Among the ways in which a DSA disk subsystem's availability has been enhanced is radial interconnection between the controller and as many as four disk drives, in contrast to the conventional daisy-chain scheme. A drive can fail, or even lose power completely, without affecting operation of the other drives on the controller. In addition, dual-access logic on the disk drives permits each of them to be connected to two controllers, with automatic switchover in case of controller malfunction.

Radial interconnection, which would otherwise have been a good deal more expensive than daisy-chain connection, is cost-effective in DSA subsystems because the more intelligent controller can itself handle the necessary multiplexing task. Moreover, advanced integrated circuitry provides the logic for the three additional I/O ports with relatively low extra cost and board real estate. The key to this is use of a four-wire serial interconnection instead of a more conventional 56-wire interconnection.

The DSA architecture requires that each component diagnose itself and also be diagnosable by higher levels in the hierarchy. Equipped with self-testing, the controller and driver each monitor and report their own condition, specifically identifying most faults.

Better data integrity

The primary contribution of a DSA controller to high data integrity is error detection, correction, and recovery. Media defects have always been the predominant source of error in disk drives. As densities have increased, the corrupting impact of defects has been magnified, and so even more powerful data-protection capability is needed.

The vehicles for error handling in the DSA controller are stored with the data blocks in sectors on the disk. Four copies of the block number are recorded in the preamble of each sector during a write operation. In read operations, the controller compares the four copies and requires a match between any two copies to verify that the block number is correct. The block type field is verified, as well, by means of a Hamming algorithm.

Error-checking and -correction logic in the controller computes an ECC test from the data field or writes and adds it to the sector. On reads, ECC logic recomputes the test and checks the residue (a modulo 2 addition of the written and recomputed ECC test) to verify that the data field as received from the disk is correct. If not, corrections are made.

The controller also computes an error-detection-and-correction test and adds it to the postamble on writes. On reads, the EDC test is again calculated on the basis of the data field, whether or not data has been corrected, and compared with the write EDC test stored in the postamble. If the two tests do not agree, the controller attempts to recover the error(s) within whatever number of retries is specified for the particular drive. The EDC test also indicates logically corrupted data in sections that have been copied or replaced.

These error-handling procedures, with the help of other integrity-oriented functions built into controllers and disk drives, make it very unlikely that any error will not be recovered in a properly functioning DSA subsystem. If unrecoverable errors do occur (owing to hardware failure in the drive), they are reported in error-log messages.

Read a lot

The flow of messages through a DSA subsystem that accomplishes a disk read (Fig. 4) accurately reflects the three-layer segmentation of the DSA architecture. The end message reporting error-free completion of the read operation is generated in the controller's MSCP server and is transmitted to the class driver independently of the data transmitted to the host's user buffer.

In addition to MSCP and SDI, a third protocol, UQSSP (Unibus/Q-bus storage systems port), provides for transmission of the MSCP and DUP message packets between the port drivers and ports in both the host and the UDA50 controller. UQSSP specifies a ring buffer in host memory, from which the controller receives commands and to which it returns responses. This protocol also specifies rules governing how the host and controller interrupt each other. □

Very smart hard-disk controller offloads host microcomputer

A 16-bit machine capable of addressing an entire Winchester disk needs an I/O-processor–based controller to prevent crippling bottlenecks

by Hal Kop, *Intel Corp., Santa Clara, Calif.*

☐ The most important new trend in mass storage for microcomputers is the use of Winchester-technology drives. Far superior to floppy disks in both performance and capacity, they will upgrade existing floppy-disk–based systems and make a better match for the speed and megabyte-memory–addressing capabilities of third-generation microcomputers. But if the new drives are accessed by conventional controllers, the microcomputer will be distracted from its proper job—the execution of application programs.

Even the better of today's command-level controllers, such as those built around bit-slice processors, leave most of the work to the host processor. At Winchester drive speeds, that burden cuts heavily into system throughput. But the whole problem can be avoided by offloading the work onto a very intelligent controller built around the Intel 8089 input/output processor (see "The 8089 third-generation I/O interface."

With its two high-performance I/O channels, the 8089 IOP is a large-scale integrated version of the intelligent I/O channels used to unburden mainframes. In effect, the host computer has only to tell the IOP what records it desires. It can simply assemble disk-access parameters as a background operation while executing a related application program, dispatch a few setup signals to the channels, and return to executing the main program

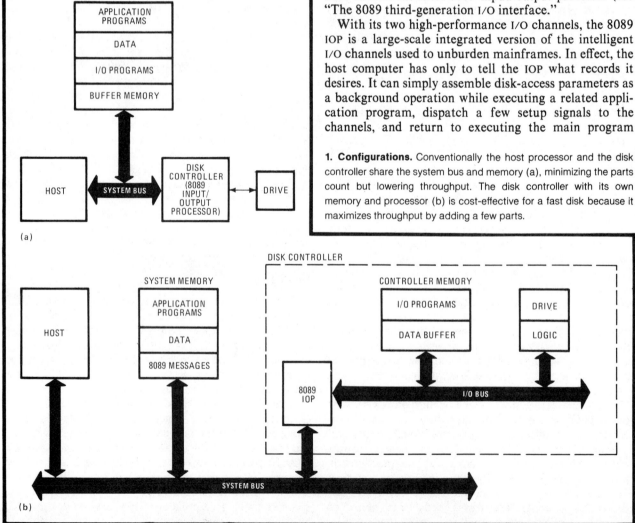

1. Configurations. Conventionally the host processor and the disk controller share the system bus and memory (a), minimizing the parts count but lowering throughput. The disk controller with its own memory and processor (b) is cost-effective for a fast disk because it maximizes throughput by adding a few parts.

The 8089 third-generation I/O interface

Since 1971, microcomputer peripheral controllers have progressed from TTL logic coupled to simple input/output ports, through single-chip programmable interfaces and controllers, to the specialized I/O microprocessor of today, such as Intel's 8089.

In the early designs, a host computer could handle only a few slow peripherals because it had to cope with input/output transfers at the bit level. The second-generation controllers allow data to be transferred in bytes or even blocks. However, the host is often interrupted for each byte transferred or has to halt while a block is transferred.

Intel's 8089 I/O processor raises I/O control to the next level. A member of Intel's iAPX 86 and iAPX 88 families of H-MOS microprocessors, the 8089 is normally used to execute the I/O programs of several peripherals for the host microcomputer.

Essentially, the host builds a message in memory to describe the I/O function to be performed and the 8089 IOP interprets the message and assumes all the device controller overhead required to make the transfer.

The two channels on the chip are designed to make direct-memory-access (DMA) transfers at high speed and also to manipulate and process data being transferred. These operations can all take place while the host is attending to other tasks. Transfers to and from system memory can also be made invisible to the host. As a result, the peripherals appear to transmit and receive whole blocks of data, instead of bits or bytes.

Each channel contains nine registers. They share a common arithmetic and logic unit, a common control unit, a common bus interface unit, and other logic on the 40-pin chip. With such an architecture the two channels may either execute entire I/O programs independently or execute individual I/O program tasks in a time-multiplexed manner—that is, concurrently or alternately, according to current priorities. If priorities are equal, executions are interleaved. There is no switching overhead, so different tasks can be performed in rapid succession.

The 8089 IOP has some 50 instructions. In addition to I/O operations, the set includes arithmetic, jump and call, logical, and other operations. The instructions most often used in the disk control applications are MOV and XFER.

The 8089 can be used in either of two modes: a local mode or a remote mode. In the local mode, a channel executing a task gains control of a local bus through the request/grant line on the bus interface unit. In the remote mode, an external Intel 8289 bus arbiter is needed to award control of the system bus according to system priorities. The lock line allows a channel task to retain possession of a system bus during an entire DMA block transfer. Each channel also has an I/O control section with DMA request, external termination, and system interrupt lines (DRQ, EXT and SINTR).

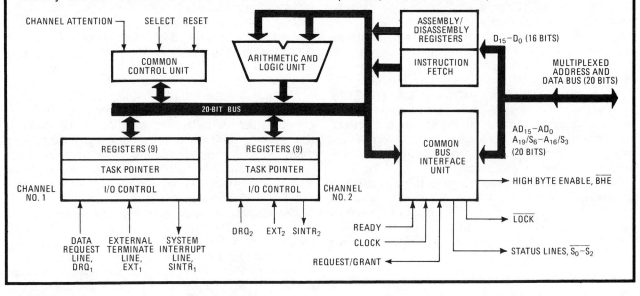

while the IOP finds the parameter information in system memory and handles all the disk-access details.

Such a hard-disk controller is also compact and flexible. The IOP replaces some two thirds of the components and occupies about a third the area ordinarily required when a bit-slice processor is used. Hardware and software can be fully modular and may be changed with little impact on the host processor design. Moreover, since only a fraction of the controller's I/O bus is needed for hard-disk control, the designer is free to add other control functions in hardware and software.

This 8089-based controller design was developed for systems using Intel's third-generation iAPX 86 and iAPX 88 processor families (based on 8086 and 8088 devices, respectively), but it is not restricted to them. The Multibus interface control signals and timing employed are also compatible with those used by the single-board Intel computers based on the 8080, 8085, and iAPX 86 and with equipment from other makers, since the Multibus is a *de facto* industry standard.

The 8089 IOP could be connected directly to an 8086 or 8088's address and data bus, as in the traditional configuration, so as to save system bus interface parts (Fig. 1a). For most disk-control applications, however, a remote configuration (Fig. 1b) is much more cost-effective since it maximizes system throughput at the cost of only a small number of additional parts.

With a conventional controller, the host microcomput-

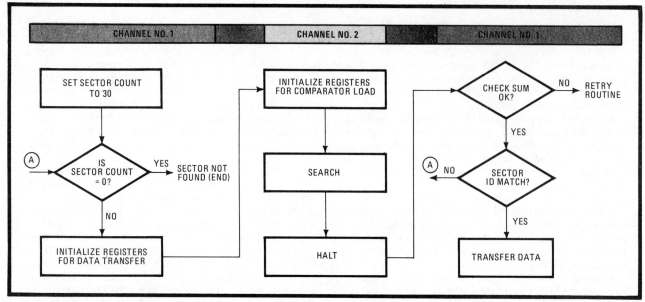

2. Two-channel operation. Control switches between the two channels of the 8089 during the search and transfer operation. Channel No. 1 initializes registers for the transfer, No. 2 performs the search, and then No. 1 checks the comparator and completes the transfer.

er executes I/O programs stored in system memory through the system bus. The host and its bus are engaged in detailed disk-handling operations a large percentage of the time during an access. This situation can create not only a lot of overhead but also bus bottlenecks, especially during periods of heavy I/O traffic.

The remote configuration fully resolves both difficulties. Since all the unchanging parts of I/O programs can be stored in erasable programmable read-only memory on the remote I/O bus, only the parameters of a disk access have to be obtained from system memory. These parameters are few—cylinder, head, and sector desired and memory address to start storing or reading the data. To obtain them, only a few system memory accesses are needed, and they can be made when the host microcomputer is not using the system bus.

Since data can also be stored in local buffer memory and transferred only when the host computer does not need the system bus, the host will have use of the system bus most of the time. As a result, it can execute application programs in parallel with the controller's execution of disk I/O programs.

Disk control requirements

To minimize the host's overhead, an intelligent controller should be able to perform all the basic disk control functions—formatting, seek, search, error-checking, buffering, and read/write transfer operations as a basis for randomly accessing files (see "Glossary of basic disk control terms "). More advanced capabilities, such as handling multiple drives, error-recovery operations, and data searches, would also utilize these basic control operations.

The drive type, of course, establishes specific requirements for the controller. If the controller cannot keep up with the transfer rate during search and data transfer or buffering operations, both performance and storage density will suffer.

However, speed during data transfers is not the only requirement. A microprocessor is designed to execute programs in sequence and must initialize registers at transition points between programs. But, while the microprocessor pauses to "change gears," the disk keeps turning. Since the microprocessor cannot control the reading or writing of data during these intervals, formatting gaps must be inserted within the sectors of data into which the disk track is divided—specifically a gap must be inserted between the header, or sector identification (ID), and the data block of each sector.

This gap has the job of providing time to enable or disable the drive's read-gate and write-gate signals. It also gives the controller time to tell from the header if this is the sector it wants before the data starts passing under the read/write head so that it can catch the sector on this revolution. In order to make the best use of the packing density of the disk, the controller must work very fast so that this gap can be kept short.

The amount of logic in a disk controller depends largely on how this problem is solved. In the 8089-based controller both I/O channels are used in an alternating mode to achieve speed while minimizing external logic.

The 8089 IOP's two channels effectively hide the time needed for register setup. They execute channel I/O programs independently or concurrently, handing control back and forth. One channel initializes registers for high-priority task, such as a DMA transfer, and then passes control to the other channel, which is programmed to do another part of the task.

Two-channel search

Figure 2 shows the two-channel flow of control during the sector-search and data-transfer part of the operation. At this point the seek operation has been completed and the read/write head is over the desired track. Channel No. 1 sets a sector counter register to 30, the number of sectors on the track. It checks the sector count and, if the count is not equal to zero, starts the search at the next sector to pass under the head. It does not have to wait to

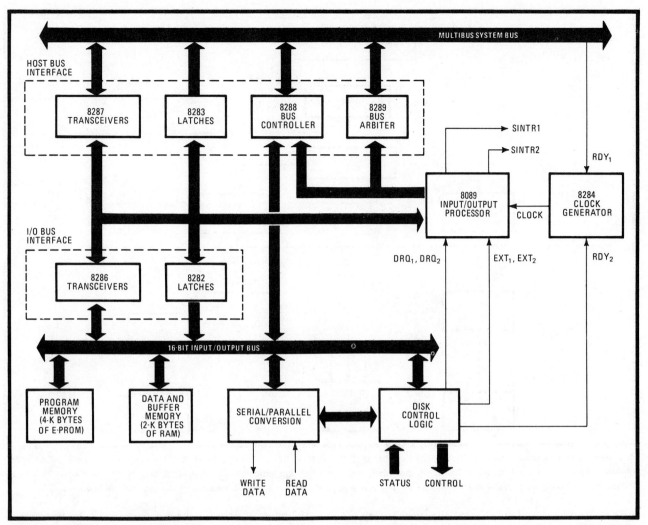

3. Controller hardware. Besides the 8089 input/output processor, the controller board contains its own I/O bus with program memory, data memory, serial/parallel conversion and disk control logic, and the components of the I/O bus and host bus interfaces.

start at the first sector on a track—it just counts off 30 sectors from wherever it happens to start.

The first channel does not actually make a data transfer at the beginning. Instead, it sets up its registers for the transfer and passes control to the second channel by sending it a channel-attention signal.

When channel No. 2 receives the CA signal, it wakes up, initializes registers for the comparator loading operation, searches for the next sector ID, and then halts. Next, with its registers already set up for a DMA transfer between the controller's local buffer memory and the disk, the first channel can immediately begin transferring data if the cyclic redundancy checksum of the sector ID is correct and the sector ID is the one desired.

If there is no header ID match, the sector count is decremented and the search operation is repeated on the next sector. There is now plenty of time for the channels to initialize their registers again because this is done while the unwanted sector data begins passing under the read/write head.

The program branches in Fig. 2 can be used to start a retry routine or other error-recovery processes. Since the 8089 IOP has the intelligence of a microcomputer, the system designer could implement more sophisticated error-checking and error-recovery techniques.

As an example, an 8089-based controller was designed for the Shugart Associates SA4008 drive, selected because it is typical of Winchester drives now being used in microcomputer systems. This drive has 1,616 tracks, four surfaces on 14-inch disks, and two heads per surface. Each track stores 18 kilobytes of unformatted data for a total of 29 megabytes.

With a high-density format such as 256 bytes per sector at 60 sectors per track, the formatted capacity is 15.4 kilobytes per track and 24.8 megabytes per drive. This controller design searches 30-sector tracks at 512 bytes per sector. Other formats would require only minor changes in software.

The drive has an average seek time of 65 milliseconds and revolves in about 20 ms, resulting in an average latency of 10.1 ms and a data-transfer rate of 889 kilobytes per second. Either I/O channel of the 8089 IOP can make DMA transfers at up to 1.25 megabytes per second at the standard clock rate of 5 MHz—more than fast enough for this disk.

The controller hardware configuration is shown in Fig. 3. During an access, the 8089 IOP interacts with two logic subassemblies on the I/O bus—specifically, the

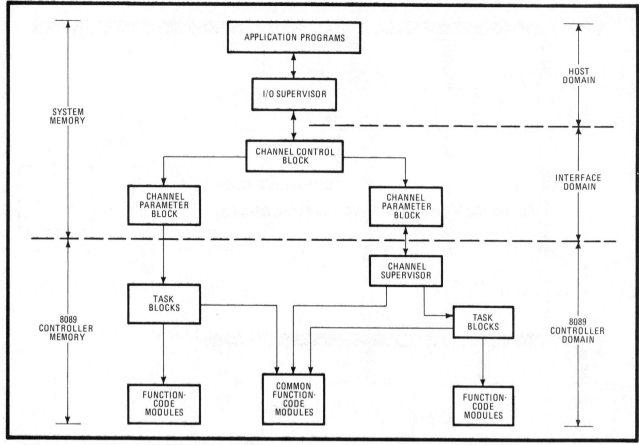

4. Software organization. Software for detailed control of the disk is in the controller's local memory. The host system software and controller-resident software communicate only in the interface domain, through the channel control block and the parameter blocks that are located in system memory. With a channel supervisor in use, one parameter block access is capable of starting multiple tasks.

disk-control logic and serial-parallel conversion logic.

The major components of the control logic section are the 16-bit comparator for the sector search operation and an 8253 programmable interval timer. The comparator is implemented with four 4-bit TTL comparators. The 8253 chip provides three software-configurable counter/timers used to synchronize cyclic redundancy check operations and to generate strobes.

The serial-parallel converter is implemented with two 8-bit TTL shift registers. Associated with the converter (but not shown) is a 9401 TTL CRC checker/generator device. The CRC chip adds CRC checksums to the header ID and to the data during writes, checks ID CRC checksums during read and write sector searches, and checks data CRCs during a read access.

Following a search operation, the controller transfers data between logical sectors and buffer memory. To write data, sectors are transferred to the track specified by the seek parameters, beginning with the specified logical sector. The data words are serialized and delivered to the drive. To read, serial data from the drive is converted into parallel and stored in random-access memory until the CRC check is completed.

During reads and writes, the data is double-buffered. For example, during a read, when 16 bits are received from the drive, the word is shifted into a 16-bit buffer, which is read by the 8089 IOP as a DMA operation.

A byte count terminates DMA when the entire block of

512 bytes of data has been transferred. The transfers to and from the disk are synchronized by means of the 8089's ready signal. If the CRC device detects an error, the controller retries the operation the number of times specified. Retries allow recovery from soft errors before the data block is transferred to system memory.

Like all controllers, this one requires a bus interface to the host microcomputer. The 8287 transceivers transmit and receive data information, and the 8283 chips latch address information. An 8288 bus controller and an 8289 bus arbiter coordinate Multibus access and protocol. The board also provides 4-K bytes of program storage space in the form of 2716 16-K E-PROMs, 2-K bytes of buffering and data storage in 2142 4-K static RAMs, and the interface to its own I/O bus.

The entire controller assembly fits on a 6½-by-12-inch prototyping board with wrapped-wire connections. This is about one third the size of a typical command-level controller built around a bipolar bit-slice processor.

All program and data communications take place via system memory. The only direct communications between the 8089 IOP and the host processor in a system are the control signals: channel attention (CA), select (SEL), and reset connected to the common control unit. The CA and SEL signals tell a specific channel to execute an I/O program, and, with RAM on the controller board, it is a simple matter to design the I/O programs to minimize system memory accesses.

There can be considerable variation in the software organization used for these communications. An example of a software hierarchy is shown in Fig. 4. Only the format of the channel control block is fixed, and one control block must be shared by both channels of the IOP. There must also be at least one parameter block for each channel. For instance, in a multiperipheral application, separate parameter blocks may be used for each peripheral so that the host only has to update parameters and not repeatedly assemble the blocks.

Three modules

Three types of software modules may be used in I/O programs for the controller:
- Task blocks for handling such tasks as seek, search, and data transfer.
- Function-code modules for such detailed functions as write, read, and retry (function-code modules may be designed to be called by one task block or to be shared by two or more task blocks).
- Channel supervisors that can be used to supervise multiple tasks without requiring the host's intervention.

The parameter block always starts with the address of the task block that starts the I/O program—such as the program for a seek—followed by function codes and variables for that operation. There are two ways the host can specify a continuing series of operations. It can extend the parameter block to provide a series of task block addresses and parameter sets, and the channel can then be programmed to execute the tasks in linked sequence. Alternatively, it may provide a task block address and multiple function codes and parameter sets. The task block can then be programmed to call the function code modules in turn. Likewise, a channel supervisor can be addressed to call task blocks.

After effects

These techniques allow the host to set up any number or variety of accesses as a background or low-priority housekeeping operation, dispatch the channels with a simple startup procedure, and return to main program execution. In effect, the host just requests the 8089 I/O

processor to read file X or write file Y.

The host starts up the IOP by sending CA and SEL signals to the channels. The channels read the command words, store the parameter block and task block addresses in their registers, and set the busy flags in the control block.

The host has three ways of determining the progress of disk accesses: it can poll the busy flags to see whether either channel is still active; it can read a status word written in the parameter block; or it can receive an interrupt from the channel completing the operation.

For this example, the 8089 IOP has only been programmed to illustrate the two-channel technique in straightforward read and write operations. But as a general-purpose device, it can handle many other storage operations. For instance, it could be programmed to manage the backup and recovery of data on backup peripherals such as floppy disks, tape cartridges, start-stop tape drives, and streaming-tape drives.

Input/output spooling is another possibility. Data from relatively slow I/O devices such as terminals could be read by the IOP and placed on disk or in local memory until the transmissions are finished. The IOP could then transfer the data at high speed when an application program needs the data. Conversely, data to be sent to slow devices such as printers could be assembled in system memory, transferred to disk, and then sent. Such operations could be handled as low-priority background tasks by the host microcomputer and the I/O programs.

Thirdly, the IOP could be programmed to implement high-level file systems that appear to application programs to be simple commands, such as open a file, read, or write. The IOP could search and update disk directories and maintain free-space maps. It could also implement hierarchical memory systems using high-speed and low-speed drives based on frequency of use, as for main storage and backup storage of critical data.

Finally, the IOP could increase the throughput of a multitasking operating system dramatically. The operating system could dispatch I/O tasks to the IOP, and the channels could be programmed to handle the highest-priority task automatically. □

DMA controller adds muscle to offload microprocessor

Chip's special flyby operation and chaining capabilities allow direct memory access with no processor involvement

by David Macmillan, *Advanced Micro Devices, Sunnyvale, Calif.*

☐ In line with the trend in system design to unburden the central processing unit of routine tasks, one new subsystem for the Z8000 microprocessor initiates direct memory access through a single chip, the AmZ8016. Boasting more muscle than other DMA devices, the controller employs two high-speed channels that allow a special transfer mode called flyby, a pattern-search capability, and self-initializing and chaining operations.

In the flyby transfer mode, one of the channels in the controller simply initiates the operations for data transfer between a peripheral and memory, for example. Once data is flowing, however, the controller is not involved in the transfer process. On the other hand, during a pattern search, a controller channel serves as the operating focal point. When the 8016 detects a match, it terminates the DMA transfer and points to the address of the matching word in memory.

Besides these capabilities, self-initializing and chaining operations allow the chip to handle control functions that would be managed by the CPU in conventional devices. By loading its own registers from a table in system memory, the controller can initiate a DMA transfer independently. Furthermore, since these tables may be linked into a chain, the 8016 is able to proceed through a set of sequential DMA transfers, all without CPU intervention.

Unlike CPU-orchestrated data movement, DMA techniques do not need to fetch an instruction from memory, decode it, and calculate an address in order to transfer data. Instead, DMA circuitry generates all the memory-address and -control signals needed to create a direct path between the data source and its final destination Thus the CPU is relieved of the burden of responding to interrupt requests from peripherals as they prepare to transfer data. By sharing the system bus with the CPU, the controller may load information into memory a byte at a time until a large block of data is assembled. Only then is the CPU interrupted to process data.

Manageable configuration

Sitting beside the nonsegmented Z8002 (Fig. 1), the 8016 delivers a single 16-bit offset address that corresponds to the processor's address. For extended addressing with a Z8001 CPU or a Z8010 memory-management unit—both use blocks of memory, or segments, to expand the address space—the chip produces extra address bits to mimic the output of the CPU and MMU (Fig. 2).

The controller may be positioned either beside the CPU in a logical-addressing space—so that addresses are translated by the MMU—or on the bus side of the MMU in a physical-addressing space—so that addresses pass directly onto the bus. When positioned beside the CPU, it delivers a 7-bit segment number and a 16-bit offset address identical to the Z8001's addressing format. In the alternative arrangement, the 24-bit address output follows the format of the MMU.

In many systems, the controller's position is determined primarily by whether the operating system's DMA drivers program data transfers with logical or physical addresses. In the logical-addressing space, the controller can take advantage of the address-translation and memory-protection features of the MMU. However, the MMU and the 8016 must be on the same card because of the MMU's timing requirements.

Although translation and protection are sacrificed in the physical-addressing space, the advantage of this ar-

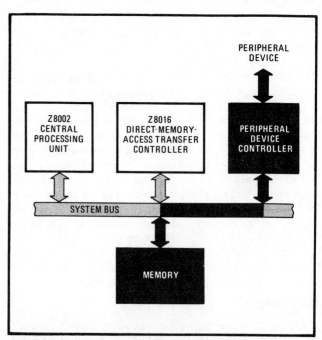

1. Laissez-faire. A direct-memory-access controller, like the AmZ8016, may set up a data transfer without a central processing unit. Through a special flyby mode, data may flow through a path (color) that does not involve the controller.

rangement is that the controller may be positioned anywhere in the system—even on a separate card. If a user wishes to program the controller in a physical-addressing space but keep it on a card separate from the CPU, the chip may be combined with its own MMU. For this arrangement, the controller would then be responsible for programming the translation tables in its MMU.

Multiple registers

Although the two channels have their own registers, the controller uses four general-purpose registers—master-mode, command, chain-control, and temporary—to manage its operation (Fig. 3). The 8-bit master-mode register sets the configuration parameters of the chip—whether it is in a logical- or physical-address space; how it will respond to an interrupt signal; and whether it will alternate or interleave its use of the bus with the CPU's.

By using the 8-bit command register, the CPU can initiate operations in the 8016, such as reset and software DMA requests. The 10-bit chain-control register, although not directly visible to the CPU, is loaded from memory when a channel initializes itself for the next DMA operation—the chaining process. Finally, a 16-bit-wide temporary register holds data during search operations. As the chip transfers data from a 16-bit bus to an 8-bit peripheral, it also uses this register to split the word into two bytes before sending the data to the device.

Both channels share these global registers; however, each channel also contains private ones (Fig. 4)—general-purpose registers that would be found in any DMA device and special-purpose registers that give the controller additional capabilities, such as pattern searching (see "Error correction with DMA").

In each channel, four different types of general-purpose registers specify transfer address, count, and type.

Two groups—address-register group A and group B—contain source and destination addresses for the transfer. Source and destination selection is specified through a bit in the channel-mode register. In addition, a third type, the operation-count register, holds the number of words to be transferred.

An important characteristic of the controller is that it may be reset without CPU intervention. For this reason, the address and count groups consist of a base register, which maintains the initial value of the DMA transfer, and a working register, which is updated as each word or byte is transferred.

In keeping with the controller's ability to handle logical- or physical-addressing space formats, each address register uses two 16-bit words for creating the appropriate address. The lower word represents the lower 16 bits of the source or destination address. The upper word contains addressing information and control bits—in an 8-bit segment field and a 7-bit tag field, respectively.

When the controller is used in the logical-address space, only the lower 7 bits of the segment field are used; the most significant bit is ignored. At the end of every transfer iteration when the addresses are incremented or decremented as needed, only the offset portion of the address is affected. Thus when a user programs a segment number, subsequent address manipulations do not cause that segment number to change. Consequently, the address will wrap around within the same segment when the offset address is decremented below 0 or incremented beyond hexidecimal value $FFFF_{16}$.

On the other hand, when the controller is located in the physical-address space, it must produce 24 bits of addressing information. In this configuration, eight segment bits are used along with the 16 offset-address bits. Furthermore, when the address is incremented or decre-

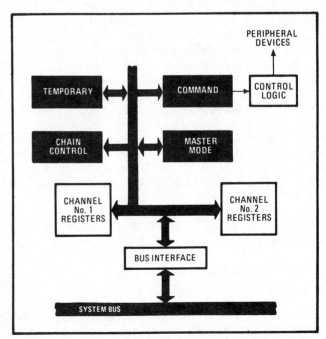

2. Alternate spaces. Depending on its placement before or after the Z8010 memory-management unit, the DMA controller can be configured to deliver a segmented address—a 16-bit offset plus a 7-bit segment signal—or a linear address of 24 bits.

3. Shared registers. For overall control of data transfer, the DMA controller uses four general-purpose registers that are shared by both channels. In addition, each channel contains a set of special-purpose registers to handle their separate operation.

281

Error correction with DMA

Direct memory access has traditionally been limited to data transfer between system memory and a peripheral device able to move data at high speeds. However, one unusual aspect of the AmZ8016 DMA controller is its ability to search as quickly as it can transfer data. In searching, the controller reads a word from the source and compares it with a bit pattern in one of its registers. Furthermore, a separate register specifies that some bits should be ignored in the comparison, restricting the search to certain fields.

Unlike traditional DMA activity, a search does not necessarily result in the transfer of data to a final destination. Instead, the controller reads data until some matching condition, set by the programmer, is satisfied. However, as with other DMA operations, the task can be terminated by other external events, like an operation count of 0 or an external end-of-process signal. Once the search stops, the address of the contents satisfying the search condition will be in register A or B, depending on which was selected by a bit in the channel-mode register. These search conditions include 8- and 16-bit matching, as well as 8- and 16-bit no-matching.

Stopping on a match is the conventional way to scan a list of bytes or words for a data pattern. Stopping on a no-match, however, might be used for memory testing. For example, after a block of memory has been initialized to some value using the controller, that same value is placed in the pattern register and a search operation is initiated by specifying a stop-on-no-match search. The 8016 then reads through memory, comparing each location with the bit pattern in its pattern register. A discrepancy, indicating a bad memory cell, would stop the operation.

Another useful application of DMA searching is in correcting dynamic memories through error-detection and -correction circuitry. If a location is not accessed for a long period of time, it may accumulate more than one error bit. Since most error-detection and -correction systems can detect multiple-bit faults but can correct only single-bit errors, infrequent access could result in uncorrectable mistakes.

To minimize the number of multiple-bit errors, many systems incorporate circuitry that periodically reads every memory location in the computer system, allowing the error-detection and -correction circuitry to fix single-bit errors in each location. The correction of single-bit errors restores the integrity of a word so that another bit error does not result in uncorrectable errors.

Microprocessor-based systems that use error-detection and -correction memory can emulate this error-correction capability of larger systems by using the DMA controller. By setting the mask register to ignore all bits during the search, the chip can be used to scan through a block of memory repetitively, reading from locations until the operation count goes to zero. With error-detection and -correction memory components, this action would cause each memory location to be scrubbed of faults.

---

mented, carries or borrows of bits move across the full 24-bit address.

Finally, the tag portion of the upper word in each address register specifies the type of address space—whether system memory, normal memory, or input/output—and the manner in which the space is to be accessed. One 2-bit-wide subfield in the tag field controls whether the address is incremented, decremented, or held constant for each transfer iteration. Another 2-bit-wide subfield selects the number of wait states that are automatically inserted each time the memory location or I/O device is accessed.

Since the separate source and destination registers contain these control fields, the type of DMA transfer may be specified independently for source and destination by the fourth register type, channel-mode. In addition, a pin on the 8016 allows insertion of hardware wait states with a conventional hardware-wait input. The mode register's two-word channel has 21 bits divided into subfields that specify the channel's operation. The operation field specifies both the type of access—transfer, search, or transfer and search—and the data's width—8 or 16 bits.

Data flyby

Two types of data movement are possible with the controller—flow-through and flyby. In flow-through transfers, data may move as quickly as 1.3 megabytes per second between any combination of memory and peripheral. During this two-step transfer, the controller first reads data from the source into its global temporary register and then moves it to the destination.

Providing up to 2-megabyte/s data movement, flyby transfer reduces the transfer cycle to a one-step operation. However, this method requires that the source or destination or both be a peripheral device, because a special flyby interface must be tapped.

In a memory-to-peripheral flyby transfer, the controller loads the source address onto the system bus and manipulates the bus signals as if executing a memory read. When the memory data is stable on the bus, the channel toggles its acknowledge-output pin, which is directly connected to a peripheral input pin that handles flyby data transfers. This signal serves to select the peripheral and to strobe data from the system bus into a register that is located inside the peripheral.

For example, in the AmZ8038 first-in, first-out buffer, all flyby transactions either enter or remove data from the end of the FIFO buffer. Since addressing information is not sent to the peripheral, the device must receive information about the internal registers to be accessed. Moreover, since the controller is driving the bus signals in the same way it would read memory, the peripheral must invert the read-write line of the bus to select the appropriate data-transfer direction once it receives the bus-acknowledge signal.

In a flyby peripheral-to-memory transfer, the operation is reversed. The 8016 sets the memory address on the bus—this time selecting the memory destination location—and then manipulates the bus signals as if writing to memory. When data signals are required on the bus

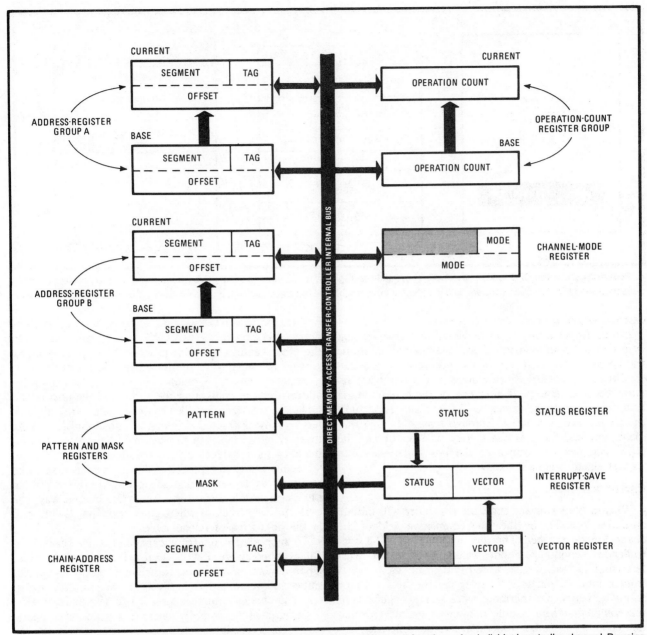

4. Separate registers. Multiple registers handle addressing, count, control, and interrupt functions of an individual controller channel. By using separate base and working registers, a channel may be restored to some initial state without intervention of the system CPU.

for writing into memory, the controller strobes the acknowledge signal to make the peripheral drive its data onto the system bus. Thus, as with memory-to-peripheral flyby, the DMA acknowledge signal serves as both a timing and a chip-select signal for the peripheral.

Because of its chip-select function, the acknowledge signal cannot be sent through the system bus to all peripherals. Instead, it must travel through a direct connection from the transfer-controller channel. Only those peripherals that are capable of transfering data at very high speeds, like the AmZ8038, will use flyby transfer.

When a peripheral toggles its DMA request line for a data transfer, the 8016 begins servicing the request. A hardware mask bit in each channel-mode register—loaded during initialization or by software command—allows the channel's request line to be masked out. But the chip

transfers data with this signal, either by single operations or on demand. A single-operation protocol performs one iteration of a transfer-type function for each DMA request pulse (or for each software request) issued to the channel. This mode will typically be used when the controller works with a byte-oriented peripheral, such as a serial communications controller.

On the other hand, demand operations keep data moving until an event occurs, and the nature of the terminating event depends on whether the DMA transfer request originated from hardware signals or software commands. When a software request is issued to a channel programmed for a demand operation, the channel will initiate transfers and continue moving data until either the operation count goes to zero, the specified match condition (a search or transfer and search) is met, or an

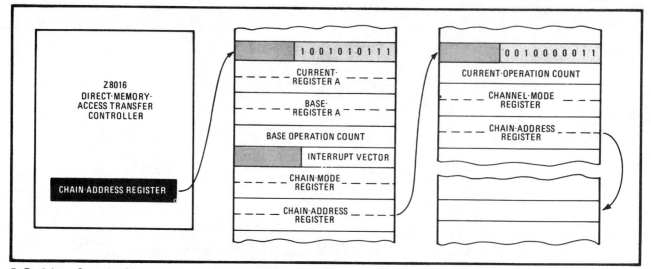

5. Bootstrap. Once the CPU loads a channel's chain-address register, a channel initializes its registers from a table in system memory. Subsequent initialization operations are able to occur independent of the CPU since each reload table contains the address of the next table.

external end-of-process signal is issued.

If a hardware DMA request is issued to a channel that is in demand-operation mode, the channel will continue transferring data until one of the previously mentioned conditions is satisfied. Furthermore, if the hardware request becomes inactive before one of these terminating conditions is met, the channel will stop transferring until the request becomes active. Through separately programmable options, the user can specify whether or not the 8016 will give up control of the bus when the DMA request signal becomes inactive.

End of transfer

When a DMA transfer ends, the controller will initiate an action specified by the 9-bit completion field of the channel-mode register. The user may program the controller for various operations: reloading its current registers from its base registers, self-initializing its registers from a table in memory, interrupting the host CPU, or taking no action. Furthermore, since separate subfields in the completion field handle the three possible termination conditions, the controller may execute different completion tasks for each type of termination.

The significance of chaining becomes apparent upon examining how the controller is initially programmed. Following system power-up or reset, the CPU programs each channel's chain-address register. This register points to a table in system memory that contains control information for other registers in the channel.

A channel will begin loading control information once the CPU issues a start-chain command and fetches the first word from the reload table in memory (Fig. 5). Because each bit in the reload word corresponds to a channel register, the first word—the reload word—specifies which internal registers need reloading. Once the reload word has been scanned and all registers with corresponding set bits have been loaded, the channel is ready for DMA. In addition, a software request bit in the channel-mode register allows two modes of channel transfer: immediately after chaining is over or after a software or hardware DMA request occurs.

If the bit associated with a register is 0, that register is not loaded, and the reload table has no value for it. On the other hand, when a bit is set to 1, its corresponding register is loaded with the data listed in the table.

Because one of the reloadable registers is the chain-address register containing the address of the next reload table, the transfer controller can execute a series of transfers by moving through a listing of reload tables. Linking together reload tables in this manner allows DMA without the need for constant CPU reprogramming. Furthermore, if required, the completion field in the channel-mode register may be set so that the controller interrupts the CPU once certain DMA tasks are over. In this way, the CPU can keep track of where DMA transfers have moved in the linked list of reload tables.

To support this interrupt capability, each channel includes a complete Z8000 vectored interrupt function. Upon issuing an interrupt, the channel stores its current status and vector information in an interrupt-save register. The channel can then proceed to reinitialize itself.

Consequently, when the channel starts a DMA operation, which results in a status change, it may do so without affecting the integrity of the information relating to the previous interrupt. At a later time, when the CPU responds with an interrrupt-acknowledge signal for the previous interrupt, the interrupt's status and vector information can be returned to the CPU, since the information has been preserved in the interrupt-save register.

Nevertheless, another interrupt could occur on the channel before the first is acknowledged. In this case, the channel will automatically release the bus so that the CPU can respond to the first interrupt by reading the preserved information from the interrupt-save register. Once the first interrupt-acknowledge signal is received, the second interrupt's vector and status information will be stored in the interrupt-save register, allowing the channel to proceed with a new task. This type of suspension allows the CPU to maintain control over the channel. As a result, the CPU may throttle down the activity of the channel so that DMA operations do not run significantly ahead of other processor activities. □

Winchester electronic functions fit on four high-speed chips

Data rates to 30 megabits per second and standardized design adapt chip set to high-performance as well as low-cost drives

by T. Stout, C. Carinalli, M. Evans, J. Jorgenson, J. Payne, and G. Tietz, *National Semiconductor Corp., Santa Clara, Calif.*

☐ During the past several years, Winchester hard-disk drives have multiplied the storage capacity and performance per dollar of countless computer systems. Nonetheless, all but the lowest-performance drives remain too expensive for many applications. At fault are their electronic subsystems and those in their controllers, which are both still being built with numerous high-performance analog and digital circuits.

A chip set just developed at National Semiconductor

Corp. attacks the problem by combining advanced large-scale integration technologies with a circuit design compatible with all major interface standards for hard-disk drives. The double-barreled solution was needed to meet (and in fact exceed) the performance requirements of state-of-the-art 14-inch drives without neglecting the needs of low-cost, compact drives.

Because the four chips are fabricated with advanced, oxide-isolation processes, the set can operate at a serial

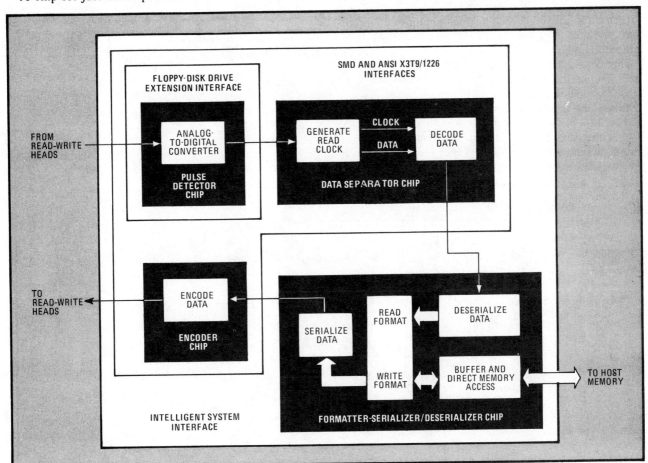

1. Winchester interfaces. Although the read and write data paths between a host system and a drive's read-write head can be viewed as continuous, they are actually divided into different functions according to the interface selected by the drive and controller designers. National Semiconductor's chip set is partitioned so it can be used with the industry-standard drive interfaces or in intelligent drive systems.

data rate of up to 30 megabits per second—a staggering speed by today's standards for drives made for the original-equipment manufacturer. In contrast, typical speeds are only 5 Mb/s today for 5¼-in. Winchester drives, 7 to 9 Mb/s for 8-in. models, and 10 to 24 Mb/s for 14-in.–disk drives.

Division of labor

The four LSI devices contain all the analog and almost all the digital functions generally needed across the standard drive interfaces (Fig. 1). To further ensure wide usage and low cost, they have been designed to accommodate the emerging standards for intelligent peripheral interfaces. Named for their chief functions, they are:

■ The pulse detector, which converts analog read signals into digital pulses.

■ The data separator, which generates a read clock and also decodes standard mfm data (mfm is the standard Miller or modified frequency-modulation form of run-length–limited coding).

■ The mfm data encoder.

■ The formatter serializer-deserializer, which does the read and write formatting as well as serial-to-parallel and parallel-to-serial data conversions.

The only other major component needed is a microprocessor to program formats and other variable functions. This processor is itself a design option—it could be a standard 8-bit, single-chip microcomputer in an intelligent drive or the central processing unit of a small computer system.

The chips' speed stems from their being fabricated by the same methods as are also used to produce high-

performance digital devices. Three make use of the advanced Schottky process, while the fourth member of the set employs a complementary-MOS process with two metalization layers called M²C-MOS (Fig. 2).

The pulse detector, data separator, and encoder all involve analog as well as digital circuitry, so they need bipolar transistors. The advanced Schottky process combines these devices with oxide isolation, which shrinks their geometries and parasitic capacitances, thus improving the speed-power product. The transistors' ion-implanted bases and emitters provide the chips with high-frequency response, and the Schottky barrier diodes shorten propagation delays. The typical gate delay is less than 1.5 nanoseconds, which falls to 1 ns for critical circuit functions.

The formatter-serializer/deserializer chip employs M²C-MOS. Also used at National to manufacture gate arrays, the process employs recessed oxide isolation, n-type wells, and self-aligned 2-micrometer gates. These features reduce transistor spacing, capacitance, resistance, and threshold voltage, bringing the propagation

2. Analog and digital. Since the analog functions on the pulse detector, data separator, and encoder call for bipolar transistors, they are made with a Schottky process (a). A complementary-MOS process (b) yields the all-digital formatter-serializer/deserializer chip. Both types have oxide-isolated transistors.

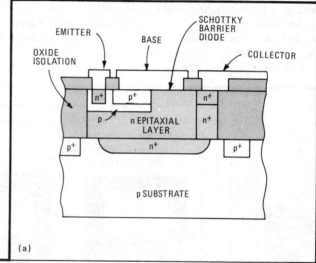

(a)

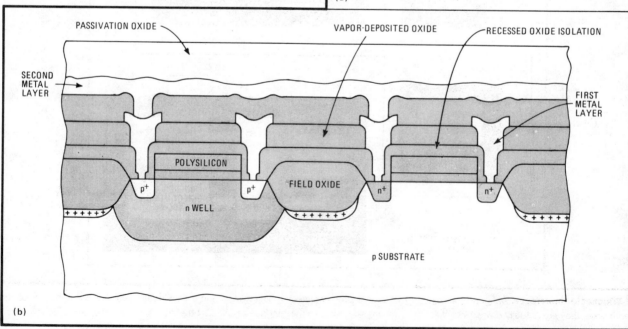

(b)

286

Pick a Winchester-drive interface

Today's original-equipment manufacturers generally use one of the following interfaces between Winchester drives and their controllers: the floppy extension, the Storage Module Device (SMD), or the American National Standards Institute's X3T9/1226. The first is an upgrade of the compact floppy-disk drive interface, and the other two were originally designed for hard-disk drives. Each has its pros and cons, as do the two new standards being proposed for intelligent system interfaces.

The floppy extension interface (a) is typically used on drives that employ low-cost head positioners, such as stepper motors, and have soft sectoring with the missing–clock-pulse type of address mark. Found on most 5¼-inch Winchesters and some 8-in. models, it reduces drive costs by minimizing drive functions and signal lines. However, the controller costs more because it must perform more functions. Also, the drive manufacturer cannot guarantee an error rate because the function that affects the rate most directly, data separation, is not in the drive. An economical solution would be to put the data separator and encoder in the drive and send nonreturn-to-zero data to the controller. Since NRZ is the type of digital waveform commonly used before encoding and after decoding, the chip set supports this option.

SMD, the traditional workhorse interface (b), is the standard for 14-in. drives and some 8-in. drives (particularly high-performance models, with heads positioned by servo-controlled, voice-coil motors). It is a very powerful design, suitable for mainframe systems, but also a costly one. All signals are carried on twisted-pair lines, so it requires a 60-pin cable, a 26-pin cable, and numerous driver, receiver, and terminating circuits. Cable A includes a 10-bit control bus that multiplexes cylinder addressing, head selection and some read/write control signals (the tag lines designate what the bus carries). The nine serial-data lines on cable B carry read and write data, read and write clock, servo clock, and miscellaneous signals.

ANSI X3T9/1226, also a daisychain design (c), can carry much more information on its control bus than SMD can. The adjoining handshake lines indicate whether the bus carries commands, command parameters, or other information. "Attention" is comparable to an interrupt, while "busy" indicates the drive cannot respond to a command. One major difference in the serial data path is that the new design combines the read and servo clocks.

Although this bus has not yet been formally adopted by ANSI, it is already popular on 8-in. Winchester drives and may become so on 5¼-in. units. An economical alternative to SMD, it requires only one 50-pin cable. As important, that 8-bit control port was designed for microprocessor-based control. However, it limits serial data rates to about 10 megabits per second, too slow for next-generation systems. The entrenched floppy extension and SMD interfaces will continue to win many design-ins.

An upwardly compatible, 50-pin interface is in the course of being defined by the ANSI X3T9.3 subcommittee for larger, higher-performance systems (d). Named the Intelligent Peripheral Interface, it will also be able to interface a variety of peripherals. It will have only six control lines plus a pair of data buses, each 9 bits wide—8 bits plus parity for command communications and data. The bus design will allow data rates ranging from 1.5 to 6 megabytes per second.

The floppy-disk–interface has evolved into the Shugart

Associates System Interface, or SASI, a byte-wide intelligent bus that interfaces host systems and control units (e). Now being standardized by the ANSI X3T9.2 subcommittee under a new name, the Small Computer System Interface, it will be a general-purpose host-to-controller interface rather than a controller-to-daisychained-drive interface. Designed for low cost, it has a maximum data rate of 1.5 megabytes per second (about 12 Mb/s in the serial paths) and fits into a 50-pin cable.

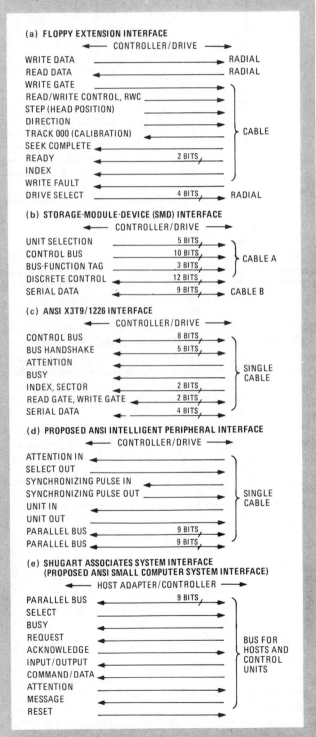

(a) FLOPPY EXTENSION INTERFACE

←—— CONTROLLER/DRIVE ——→

WRITE DATA	RADIAL
READ DATA	RADIAL
WRITE GATE	
READ/WRITE CONTROL, RWC	
STEP (HEAD POSITION)	
DIRECTION	
TRACK 000 (CALIBRATION)	CABLE
SEEK COMPLETE	
READY	2 BITS
INDEX	
WRITE FAULT	
DRIVE SELECT	4 BITS — RADIAL

(b) STORAGE-MODULE-DEVICE (SMD) INTERFACE

←—— CONTROLLER/DRIVE ——→

UNIT SELECTION	5 BITS	
CONTROL BUS	10 BITS	
BUS-FUNCTION TAG	3 BITS	CABLE A
DISCRETE CONTROL	12 BITS	
SERIAL DATA	9 BITS	CABLE B

(c) ANSI X3T9/1226 INTERFACE

←—— CONTROLLER/DRIVE ——→

CONTROL BUS	8 BITS	
BUS HANDSHAKE	5 BITS	
ATTENTION		
BUSY		SINGLE CABLE
INDEX, SECTOR	2 BITS	
READ GATE, WRITE GATE	2 BITS	
SERIAL DATA	4 BITS	

(d) PROPOSED ANSI INTELLIGENT PERIPHERAL INTERFACE

←—— CONTROLLER/DRIVE ——→

ATTENTION IN		
SELECT OUT		
SYNCHRONIZING PULSE IN		
SYNCHRONIZING PULSE OUT		SINGLE CABLE
UNIT IN		
UNIT OUT		
PARALLEL BUS	9 BITS	
PARALLEL BUS	9 BITS	

(e) SHUGART ASSOCIATES SYSTEM INTERFACE (PROPOSED ANSI SMALL COMPUTER SYSTEM INTERFACE)

←—— HOST ADAPTER/CONTROLLER ——→

PARALLEL BUS	9 BITS	
SELECT		
BUSY		
REQUEST		
ACKNOWLEDGE		BUS FOR HOSTS AND CONTROL UNITS
INPUT/OUTPUT		
COMMAND/DATA		
ATTENTION		
MESSAGE		
RESET		

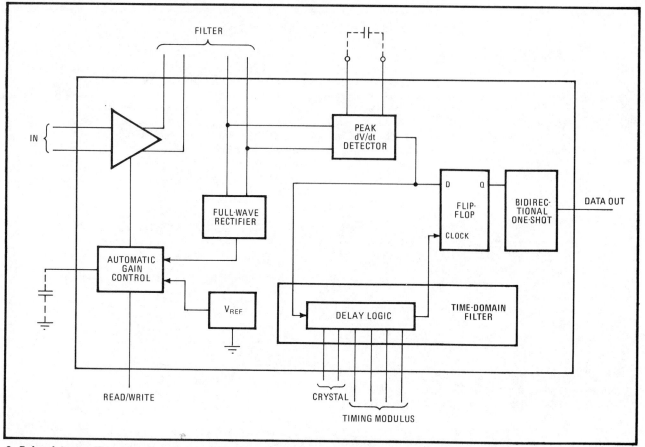

3. Pulse detector. This chip is the only one required for all the standard Winchester-disk drive interfaces. Automatic gain control manipulates signals coming from thin-film heads, while the time-domain filter deals with the relatively noisier signals from ferrite heads.

delays of typical internal devices down to 1.5 ns.

The chips' versatility stems, in large part, from the way data-path functions between the read-write heads and host-system bus have been partitioned among the four devices. All disk systems must perform certain well-defined functions to transfer data in the read and write directions.

To read data from a disk, the storage system must select a head and position it, convert the read preamplifier's analog output into a digital-pulse sequence, and generate a read clock from the pulse train. Next it must decode the data, group it into byte-wide blocks (deserial-

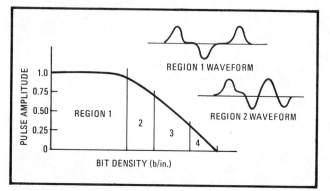

4. Noise suppression. Thin-film heads put out relatively clean read signals (region 1), whereas ferrite heads usually operate in region 2. Time-domain filtering with an on-chip delay line allows the pulse detector to cancel noise pulses in the region 2 mode.

izing), and strip off synchronization, addressing and error-checking information (formatting). Finally it must buffer the data and transfer it to a host system, usually by a direct memory access.

To write data, the process is reversed: DMA is followed by buffering, formatting (but now to access the correct sector and insert synchronization and error-checking fields), serializing, encoding, and head selection. The head's read-write driver then records the data in a series of magnetic-flux reversals on the disk track.

Most functions could be performed in the drive itself, in the controller, or even by the host computer. However, the dividing lines are generally established by interface standards. National's chips are therefore partitioned along the same lines. A drive manufacturer can use the chips shown on the drive side of an interface, in Fig. 1, while a controller or system manufacturer uses those on the other side (either could also use an equivalent conventional subsystem that meets the same standards).

The chip set is compatible with all three of the interfaces that are generally used today between Winchester drives and controllers: the floppy extension, the Storage Module Device (SMD), and the American National Standards Institute's X3T9/1226 (see "Pick a Winchester-drive interface ").

The pulse detector (Fig. 3) always resides in the drive. It converts the read preamplifier's analog output into raw digital data. At low recording densities, signal peaks are well-defined. However, as density rises, the wave-

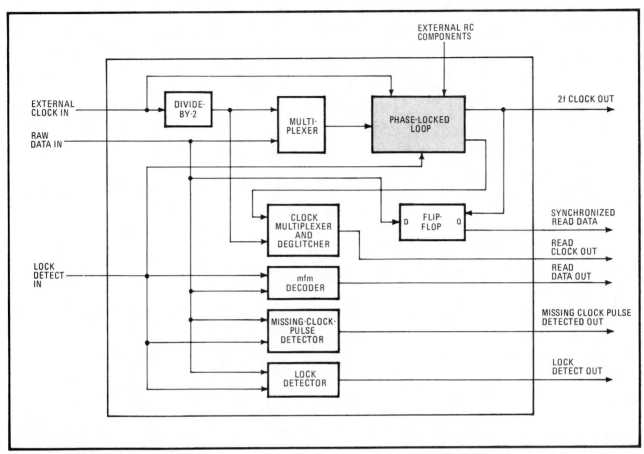

5. Data separator. After locking onto the raw data stream, this circuit generates a clock pulse and decodes data that uses the modified-frequency-modulation type of encoding. It also puts out signals that can be used by other types of decoders in non-mfm systems.

form moves from what is known as region 1 to region 2 (Fig. 4). In region 2, signal amplitudes drop because of bit interactions, the waveforms may not return to the base line, and the signal-to-noise ratio deteriorates. Drives that operate in region 1 are generally those with either thin-film heads or exotic run-length–limited encoding (such as the 2,7 RLL codes). Those using conventional ferrite heads and mfm are normally in region 2. The pulse detector is capable of working in both of these regions.

Region 1 detection requires automatic gain control and threshold comparison to discriminate signals from noise. Region 2 requires a form of time-domain filtering suitable for LSI. Such filtering normally needs an external delay line. However, the pulse detector does without such lines by producing high-resolution delays on chip with clock-gating circuitry.

The chip's region 2 mode exploits the fact that read noise pulses come in pairs and can be made to cancel each other out. A peak detector's output is delayed before driving a D flip-flop's clock input, while the undelayed pulse goes to the D input. The peak detector marks peaks by changing the pulse's polarity. If one signal pulse is followed by another, the flip-flop output will also change and force the bidirectional one-shot to generate a data pulse. However, if noise produces the clock input, the second noise pulse will cancel the first and no data pulse will be sent to the data separator.

The pulse detector is the only one of the four chips

placed in drives with the floppy extension interface. The data separator (Fig. 5) also goes into drives with ANSI and SMD interfaces. ANSI X3T9/1226 calls for a combined read and servo clock, so the circuit contains a clock multiplexer and deglitcher. SMD, on the other hand, requires separate clocks. But since an SMD controller ignores the read clock line when looking at a servo clock line, the same chip can be used with both interfaces.

The data separator generates the read clock pulse with a phase-locked–loop subsystem that acquires the data stream, delays the data signals to the half-window, and synchronizes the data output to a read clock pulse generated by the PLL. The PLL locks onto the data stream in less than 2 bytes at a high tracking rate, then switches to a lower, more stable rate that compensates for bit-shift distortion. Users can set the rates with two external resistors. The frequency source can be the servo surface or, in a stepper-motor drive, a crystal.

This chip also decodes data that was written in mfm, the code used in most hard-disk systems. To decode mfm data, the user simply ties the lock-detect output to the input. When a lock is detected, the phase pattern between clock and data pulses is frozen for decoding.

If the data separator detects an mfm clock-pulse violation when decoding mfm data, it produces a pulse that enables the formatter-serializer/deserializer chip to detect an address mark (in standard mfm encoding, a clock pulse is suppressed in the nonreturn-to-zero 10000 pattern to make it 100-0). The missing–clock-pulse

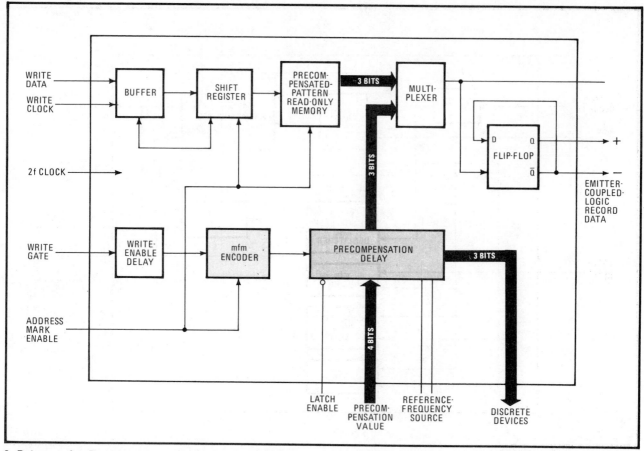

Figure labels:

WRITE DATA
WRITE CLOCK
2f CLOCK
WRITE GATE
ADDRESS MARK ENABLE

BUFFER
SHIFT REGISTER
PRECOMPENSATED-PATTERN READ-ONLY MEMORY
MULTIPLEXER
FLIP-FLOP (D, Q, Q̄)
WRITE-ENABLE DELAY
mfm ENCODER
PRECOMPENSATION DELAY

3 BITS
3 BITS
3 BITS
4 BITS
3 BITS

EMITTER-COUPLED-LOGIC RECORD DATA

LATCH ENABLE
PRECOMPENSATION VALUE
REFERENCE-FREQUENCY SOURCE
DISCRETE DEVICES

6. Data encoder. Besides encoding, the chip precompensates (changes) bit positions to facilitate pulse detection and obviate the need for delay lines. Track-to-track differences in precompensation can be programmed, minimizing read-signal distortion on the higher-density tracks.

detector makes the decoder compatible with the floppy extension interface as well as with the ANSI and SMD interfaces. (If there are no clock pulses in the data being decoded, the chips do not insert them.) However, an external decoder is needed for specialized RLL codes used to increase storage capacity.

A precompensating encoder

Built into the mfm encoder is a new precompensation technique that makes delay lines unnecessary and, for the first time, allows the amount of precompensation to be changed from track to track under microprocessor control. More precompensation is needed on the inner tracks, where density is highest, and little or none on the outer tracks. Precompensation shifts bit positions on the recording medium to reduce read-signal distortions caused by high-density recording.

Again, the design conforms to the ANSI specification while remaining compatible with the others. For example, it generates the missing–clock-pulse address marks used in the floppy extension interface. A signal from the formatter-serializer/deserializer chip (or equivalent controller circuit) indicates when a mark should be encoded. The encoder then looks for the 1000 NRZ bit pattern and suppresses the clock pulse normally inserted in it.

The on-chip buffering allows incoming data to be of arbitrary phase with respect to the 2f clock used for encoding. For precompensation, serial write data input is converted into parallel data, analyzed bit by bit with the

aid of the precompensation pattern stored in read-only memory, and delayed a programmable time after encoding. The delay section allows three precompensated positions: early (no delay), nominal (one delay unit), or late (two delay units). Then, the positioned bit feeds the TTL– and emitter-coupled-logic–compatible outputs for recording. Delay increments are externally programmable for 0 to 20 ns with a resolution of 2 ns. The precompensation value, which defines delay step functions, can be loaded and latched in by a microprocessor.

Formatting and serialization

Disk controllers contain the formatter-serializer/deserializer chip (Fig. 7) and an optional microprocessor. The former handles the data-path functions at a high data rate, while the latter performs other controller functions at a slower rate. The formatter chip's functions include sequencing the format fields, serializing and deserializing the data, buffering, and handling DMA.

Formatting adds extra fields to the data received from the host: a preamble for data-separation lock-on; a synchronization field to indicate the end of the preamble and establish the boundaries of data bytes; sector addresses; block addresses (called headers); error-checking and -correction fields; and various types of postambles and gaps. Since there is no standard format, it is user-programmable, along with operating modes such as single- or multiple-sector, read or write, and verify. The format can be loaded during system initialization and

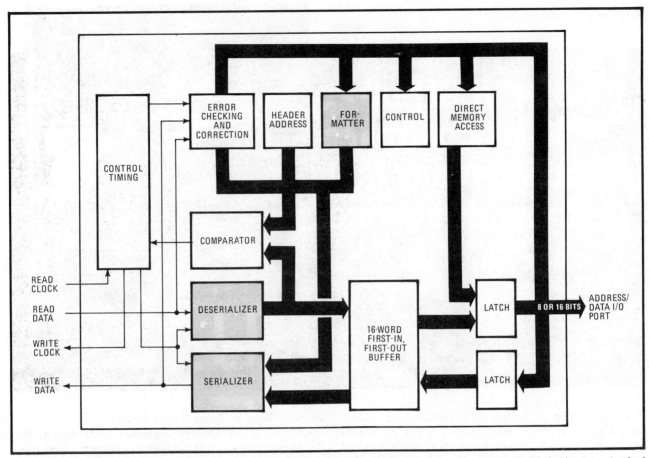

7. Formats and series. Essentially a single-chip controller, the formatter-serializer/deserializer device can be coupled either to a standard microprocessor or to a host computer for programming storage formats and other functions that vary from system to system.

the operating parameters changed as needed. On-chip registers can be accessed for status, error, and other operating information.

The serializer's output feeds the data decoder, and the data separator feeds the deserializer's input. During read operations, the comparator identifies header addresses and byte boundaries. The first-in, first-out buffer allows the chip to store 32 bytes of data—enough to prevent overruns when the system bus is not available for DMA transfers. All DMA controls are handled by the chip. For example, a counter provides an address field that can be strobed out of the input/output port prior to valid data. Parallel transfers can be 8 or 16 bits wide. This unique approach allows low-cost microcomputers to be built with only the formatter-serializer/deserializer chip, plus the microcomputer's own processor and memory.

Many diagnostic functions are built into the chip. For example, it handles cyclic-redundancy-check and error-checking and -correction calculations. Also, five control pins are available when external error checking and correction is required. A special interrupt signal notifies the processor when a sector matches but the header has failed, so that this type of error can be attended to immediately. The formatter-serializer/deserializer stores the last header read for subsequent access by the microprocessor. Moreover, the chip offers a duplex mode for read-after-write testing, sector interlocking for special microprocessor format-sequencing, and checkpoint interrupts during multiple-sector operations.

Intelligent disk drives—those that perform many of the traditional controller functions—have not been economical at Winchester data rates. Moreover, controllers have generally been made and sold as separate subsystems, so there is a built-in resistance to smart drives in the controller industry.

Getting smarter

Obviously, the chip set can be used to make today's drives intelligent at a more reasonable cost, particularly in fully integrated, desktop computers with only one Winchester drive. But intelligent system-interfaces will soon be needed in multiple-drive applications to boost data rates. Using cables for serial data transmission between drives and a controller becomes awkward at rates much beyond 10 Mb/s, but high data rates are easy to achieve if the cables contain byte- or 2-byte-wide parallel data paths.

The new intelligent interfaces anticipate this need, as does the chip set. Since the LSI devices can convert serial data into parallel (and parallel into serial) at serial rates of up to 30 Mb/s, they will allow the data buses of the new interface designs to carry data bytes at rates higher than required in most computer systems. Since the chips are compatible with the drive interfaces from which these standards are evolving and since they have a 16-bit data path on the host side, they will mate with the new interfaces with a minimum of external components or future modification. ☐

Bipolar VLSI builds 16-bit controller handling many fast peripherals at once

Special-purpose microprocessor has controller instruction set in microcode, manipulates three operands in one cycle

by Sunil Joshi, Deepak Mithani, and Steve Stephansen
Advanced Micro Devices Inc., Sunnyvale, Calif.

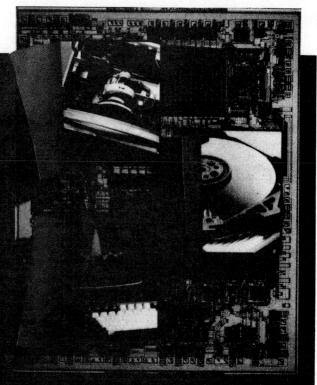

☐ In the last decade, peripheral controllers have evolved from little more than simple input/output ports into highly sophisticated dedicated processors that command the level of performance necessary for handling high data rates. They also must now provide intelligent pre- and post-processing of data to offload from the host computer the specialized tasks intelligent controllers perform.

Recognizing the need for such a processor, Advanced Micro Devices has combined its proprietary Imox processing technology with a bipolar circuit design of scaled emitter-coupled logic based on very large-scale integration to produce the Am29116 16-bit bipolar microprocessor. The largest and the most complex bipolar device ever produced, the 29116 has an architecture and an instruction set specifically designed for high-performance, intelligent peripheral controllers. The high performance is a result of its unique architecture, microprogrammable instruction set, and processing technology; its requisite high speed is achieved by designing the part in ECL with TTL-compatible levels at the pins (see "What is microprogramming?").

The instruction set of the 29116 has extensive data and bit manipulation capability to mask, rotate-and-merge, or rotate-and-compare, data in one microcycle — functions that are useful for field extraction, field insertion, and data alignment, which are frequently encountered in controllers. The architecture provides flexibility and parallelism in the data paths so that the device can perform in one microcycle a complex function that would take other processors several cycles to execute. One such feature is the barrel shifter, which rotates a 16-bit word by up to 15 places in one microcycle before the arithmetic operation is performed. The part also has an on-chip priority encoder and cyclic-redundancy-checking logic for specialized functions.

Created for a microprogrammed environment, the 29116 gives the user the flexibility to tailor the controller architecture for a specific application. MOS microprocessors, with their fixed architecture and instruction set, are limited in this respect. The performance is at least an order of magnitude higher than that of any available MOS device (see "Imox: a union of TTL and ECL ").

The 52-pin device has a microcycle time of 100 nanoseconds. In one cycle, the three-input arithmetic-and-logic unit operates on one, two, or three operands, while the barrel shifter is rotating one of the operands before it is used for an operation. The part also has a single-port register file that is 32 words deep by 16 bits wide and a dedicated accumulator to store temporary results. In this way, the advantages of both register-based and accumulator-based machines can be obtained (Fig. 1).

Bidirectional busing

The bidirectional 16-bit Y-bus is the primary off-chip data input and output port. The 16-bit D-latch at the input allows the data to be presented directly to the ALU, or be latched and used in the next cycle. This latch can thus be used as a pipeline for prefetching data while the ALU is performing a different function. It is also possible to bring data onto the chip on the Y-bus, perform some function on it, and then send it out again on the same bus without even having to store it.

The priority encoder generates a binary coded number, indicating the most significant bit in the operand that is a one. This special-purpose hardware module saves a significant amount of time, since a subroutine is ordinarily required to perform this often-used operation.

The status register is clocked with the ALU every cycle

and can even contain user-defined status bits whose function is defined by the microcode. Using microinstructions, it is also possible to provide a condition-test output based on the status. The bidirectional T-bus, when used as an input, exploits the device's parallelism further by allowing the user to select a condition for branching, while simultaneously executing an instruction in the ALU. The user can also select separate read and write addresses for the same instruction in both the byte and 16-bit word modes.

In addition to having full-carry lookahead across all 16 bits, the ALU executes all the conventional one- and two-operand instructions, such as move, complement, 2's complement, add, subtract, AND, NAND, OR, NOR, exclusive-OR, and exclusive-NOR.

Masking in a microcycle

Where the 29116 departs from convention is in its ability to operate on three operands simultaneously in a single microcycle. Thus a bit field can be selected from the two data operands with a masking operand all in a single microcycle.

The ALU produces three status outputs: overflow, negative, and carry. The zero flag, although not generated by the ALU, detects zero at both the byte and word level. The carry input to the ALU selects an input of 0, 1, or the stored carry bit from the status register, QC. Using QC as the carry input allows efficient execution of multiprecision addition and subtraction.

The condition-code generator contains the logic necessary to develop the 12 condition-code test signals. The condition-code multiplexer selects one of these test signals and places it on the CT condition-test output for use

by the microprogram sequencer. The multiplexer may be addressed in two different ways. In the first, a test instruction specifies the test condition to be placed on the CT output but does not allow an ALU operation at the same time. The second method uses the bidirectional T-bus as an input, which requires extra microcode but lets the controller simultaneously test and execute.

Specialized instructions

Immediate instructions are executed in two clock cycles. During the first clock cycle, the instruction decoder recognizes that an immediate instruction is being specified and captures the data on the inputs in the instruction latch. In the second clock cycle, the data on the instruction inputs is used as one of the operands for the function specified during the first clock cycle. At the end of the second clock cycle, the instruction latch is returned to its transparent state.

Since the 29116 is optimized for intelligent controllers, it has extensive bit manipulation instructions operating in either the byte or the word mode. These instructions allow operations such as setting, resetting, and testing of any particular bit without affecting the rest of the bits. Single-bit masks can also be created, such as a single 1 in a field of 0s or a single 0 in a field of 1s in a single microcycle. In addition, the instructions can generate memory addresses in powers of 2 by incrementing or decrementing a number by 2^n, where n can vary from 0 to 15.

The rotate-by-n instruction uses the barrel shifter with n specifying the number of bit positions the source is to be rotated. In the word mode, a specified number of bits are wrapped around over the 16-bit boundary; in the

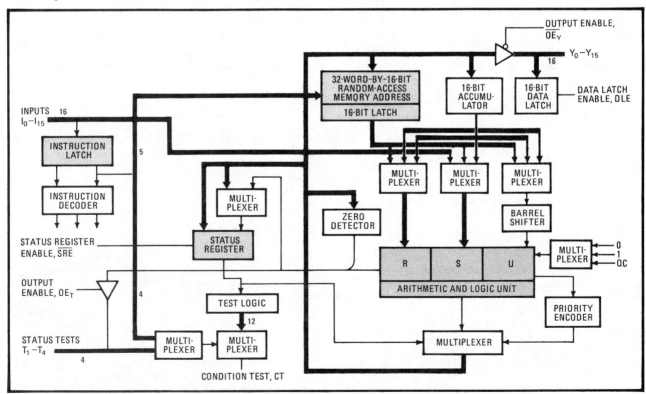

1. Novel architecture. The arithmetic-and-logic unit on the 29116 16-bit bipolar microprocessor has three inputs so that a masking operation can be performed simultaneously with another instruction. The barrel shifter and priority encoder further optimize it for control.

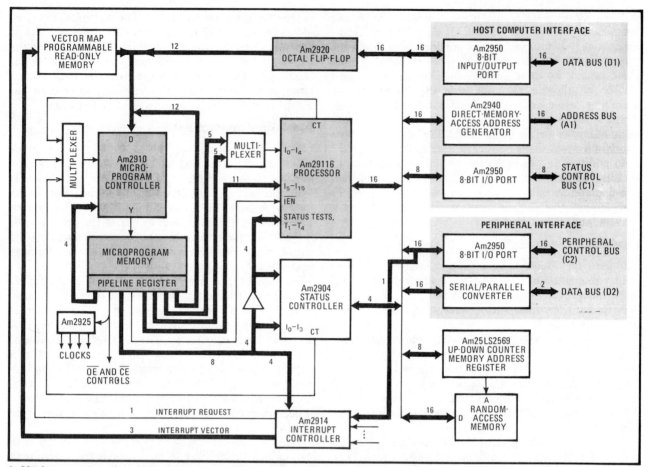

2. Maximum system. If the highest speeds are required, then the 29116 can be assisted by support chips from the 2900 family. However, a minimum system configuration can be realized by using only the shaded components, though system throughput will be slightly degraded.

byte mode, the bits are rotated around the 8-bit boundary of the least significant byte.

The rotate-and-merge instruction can merge two operands on a bit-by-bit basis, under the control of the mask as a third operand. Thus, in one microcycle, translation from one code to another, such as from ASCII to

hexadecimal, can be done with this instruction. This sort of operation would require at least three instructions with a conventional ALU.

The rotate-and-compare instruction compares a rotated operand with a nonrotated operand. A 1 at the mask input (third operand) eliminates that bit from the

---

What is microprogramming?

Most instructions execute a fixed sequence of steps to perform their function. This control sequence may be realized as a hardwired random-logic state machine that provides the necessary outputs for controlling the different functions. The disadvantage of this approach is that it leads to a design that is irregular and inflexible.

An alternative is the microprogrammed approach, where the control information is obtained from a regular structure, such as a programmable array or a read-only memory. A sequence of controls is obtained by accessing different words in the array. This access is usually obtained by cycling through consecutive words in the array until the instruction is completed. The action is performed by a sequencer that selects the microsubroutines that execute instructions.

Thus, a microprogrammed control mechanism consists of a memory and a sequencer. The memory can be a ROM, programmable ROM or random-access memory, and the information residing in it is referred to as the

microcode. The sequencer controls the order of execution of the microcode words. In a microprogrammed system, the output of that microcode memory, however it is stored, directly controls the machine's hardware. This memory in essence replaces the random-logic control mechanism of a machine.

The modularity of this scheme results in a design that is easy to upgrade or modify, since programming a PROM takes much less time than redesigning a random-logic state machine. In the same way that assemblers simplify machine language programming, programs called meta-assemblers can aid in the writing of microcode. A development system called System 29 aids the design of microprogrammed systems. It also contains a meta-assembler called Amdasm for assembling the firmware portion of a system. Using Amdasm, it is possible to write microcode using user-definable mnemonics and the other facilities provided by System 29 help in the development and debugging of this firmware.

comparison. The result of the comparison is loaded in the 0 bit of the status register. If the comparison passes, the 0 bit is set.

The 29116 can also prioritize a masked operand, which is ideal for performing n-way jumps as well as for normalizing numbers. The priority encoder accepts a 16-bit input and produces a 5-bit binary-weighted code indicating the bit position of the highest-priority active bit. If none of the bits is active, the output is 0. Such an operation requires a separate subroutine when carried out on conventional microprocessors.

Forward and reverse

For reliable data transmission, the cyclic-redundancy-check instructions permit generation and comparison of the CRC check bits using any 16-bit polynomial. Since the CRC code standard does not indicate which data bit must be transmitted first, the 29116 supplies both forward and reverse CRC instructions, each of which consumes only two microcycles per bit—perfect for bidirectional tape drives.

In the first cycle, the data bit is shifted from one of the registers into the link bit of the status register. During the second cycle, check bits are generated by executing either the CRC forward or reverse instructions. The result is stored back into the check-sum register.

The part also includes such niceties as exclusive-NOR sign extension for converting 8-bit integers into 16-bit ones and a single-bit shift directly on a register.

A typical system configuration for the 29116 consists of a host computer, memory, and peripheral controller interfaced through three buses. The peripheral controller and the peripheral devices are interfaced with a separate data bus, which may be either serial or parallel, and a control bus. Information on the control buses comprises status, command, and timing signals.

In a typical implementation of the peripheral controller portion of a system, the bidirectional interface to the host's data bus is via two Am2950 8-bit parallel I/O ports. Two Am2940 8-bit direct-memory-access address generators drive the associated address bus, and another 2950 interfaces with the bidirectional control bus. The interface to the serial peripheral data bus in this case is serial. The interface between these bus-interface units and the 29116 is a 16-bit bidirectional bus that connects to its Y port. A 256-word random-access memory for temporary data storage and a 12-bit interface to the microprogram controller connect to the D inputs of the AM2910 microprogram sequencer. The bus-control and clock-enable signals for these devices are generated by the pipeline register at the output of the microprogram memory.

The 29116, 2910, and the microprogram memory perform the data manipulation and routing; command and status generation and testing; and the timing-signal generation functions. This implementation minimizes the amount of hardware necessary to implement a controller, which is accomplished by sharing the instruction-inputs to the 29116 with the inputs to the 2910; by generating all the necessary test conditions within the 29116, which permits connecting the CT output of the 29116 directly to the condition code ($\overline{CC}$) inputs of the 2910; by performing all the necessary status manipulations within the 29116; and by using the same RAM address for reading and writing.

A tradeoff

Although the peripheral-controller implementation described above minimizes the amount of required hardware, it does limit the throughput. The architecture shown in Fig. 2 uses the same bus interface circuits but maximizes the throughput of the controller at the expense of additional hardware. In this implementation, the instruction inputs of the 29116 and the D inputs of the 2910 are driven from separate microcode bits, making possible simultaneous instruction execution in the 29116 and direct jumping in the 2910.

The multiplexer at the $\overline{CC}$ input of the 2910 allows conditions to be tested without loading the signals into the 29116. Four additional bits of microcode drive the T

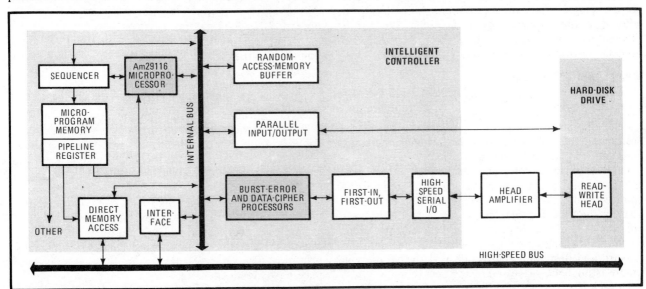

3. Typical application. The 29116 is ideal for controlling Winchester disk drives. It can handle up to eight such drives simultaneously and, with the addition of a burst-error processor and data-ciphering processor, it can be made very reliable as well.

Imox: A union of TTL and ECL

The Imox process is an advanced oxide-isolated structure developed by Advanced Micro Devices to address the reproducibility requirements of die sizes in excess of 50,000 square mils. It employs fully ion-implanted transistors, walled emitters, and two layers of metal interconnections. Assuming the same feature sizes, Imox can produce devices with less than half the base area and two thirds the collector substrate area of a diffused-isolation washed-emitter low-power Schottky transistor. Smaller sizes and inert isolation regions significantly reduce device capacitances and increase potential speed.

The approach selected was to combine an oxide-isolated device structure with emitter-coupled-logic internal and TTL input/output circuitry. The technique enabled engineers at AMD to pack the equivalent of over 2,500 TTL gates into 78,000 square mils of silicon, using 3-micrometer minimum features and an 8-μm metal pitch.

As with all large-scale integrated processes, Imox is a marriage of circuit and process approaches. The reason that the internal circuitry of the 29116 is implemented in ECL, while the inputs and outputs are all standard TTL levels with translators to the ECL interior, is because ECL possesses the ability to create dense structures with an excellent speed-power product through series gating.

The barrel shifter in the 29116 is an excellent example of how ECL can be applied to a complex LSI device. This function performs a selectable n-bit shift or rotate. It is the equivalent of 276 gates and is implemented with 526 components, consumes 92 milliwatts, and exhibits delays of less than 7 nanoseconds.

---

inputs of the 29116, permitting simultaneous conditional testing and execution of an instruction in the controller. In addition, the ALU status bits can be selectively loaded into the 2904 to reduce the number of cycles necessary to perform status manipulation.

By adding five additional microcode bits and a multiplexer at the I inputs of the part, separate source and destination addresses can be used in the same microcycle. For example, the contents of the third register can be added to the contents of the accumulator and the results can be stored in register 7.

In addition to supplying the basic oscillator and clock driver functions, the 2925 system-clock generator and driver lets the user dynamically alter the length of the microcycle and, thus, interface the 29116 with slower bus-interface and peripheral circuits. The 2914 handles high-speed interrupts from the peripheral controllers.

The 29116 functions as a superior disk controller because its bipolar technology enables it to perform at much higher speeds than MOS processors and, therefore, handle as many as eight Winchester disk drives simultaneously (Fig. 3). Its microprogrammability lets it be tailored to the requirements of a specific application. Efficient data movement and data compression is possible using instructions, such as rotate-and-merge.

Major application areas

The unit's bit manipulation instructions are useful for checking control and status bits. A microprogrammed system allows the controller to initiate a task such as positioning the disk head while performing other tasks until notified that the head is in position.

Fast response to interrupts as well as other speed enhancements can be designed in, using other 2900 bit-slice–family components. The CRC instructions can be used for the checking and generating the file header CRC bits; the CRC reverse instruction is included for systems (such as with magnetic tape) in which reading data in a forward and in a reverse direction is desirable to avoid time-wasting back-space and reread operations.

Graphics processors vary in complexity based on the performance required from them, but sophisticated image processors require very high-speed controllers.

The 29116 is well-suited for systems that include character and vector display or partition the screen into various regions that may need independent scrolling, cursor control, zoom and pan, scaling, and translation and transfer of data between various sections of the memory.

If the part is used for address generation, the arithmetic instructions using 2^n are useful. For example, in a windowing operation, there are certain bits in every horizontal scan that must be selected. The next line is displaced in the memory by a fixed address equal to the number of pixels in the horizontal line.

Thus, address generation is simplified considerably. In addition, vectors can be generated from the coordinates of two points to be connected can be done easily using algorithms that generate the intermediate points and require only additions and subtractions for interpolation.

Saving cycles

The rotate, rotate-and-merge, and other specialized instructions of the 29116 let the user perform the functions in one cycle that would take several cycles on conventional processors. For example, when a copying operation is performed on the display, a section of the area that was previously aligned with the 16-bit word boundary of the controller may no longer be aligned. The realigning may require rotation with a mask to leave the area outside the window unchanged.

Another excellent application for the 29116 is as a cluster controller that manages a group of devices requiring service on a statistical basis. These devices could be terminals or printers or specialized I/O ports. The controller can dynamically alter device priorities to assure a fast response to the active devices at the expense of the inactive ones.

The kinds of functions that a cluster controller may have to perform are data transfers between the devices themselves or between a memory and the devices, checking of device status, diagnostics, and assigning of service priorities. The priorities can be of different kinds and may be dynamically alterable. For example, when all devices are of equal priority, then a round-robin scheme can be used so that the device just serviced gets the last priority for the next service. □

All bubble memories look alike with a universal interface

Hardware and software combine to standardize board size, connection-pin assignments, signal timing, and protocols

by Joseph W. Slater, *Bubbl-Tec, a division of PC/M Inc., Dublin, Calif.*

☐ The complexity of linking magnetic-bubble memories to electronic circuitry is notorious. Worse yet, there are only four manufacturers of such memories—Intel, Motorola, Hitachi, and Fujitsu—none of which has a second source. As a result, a design for a magnetic-bubble interface that is not tied to a single manufacturer's memory is much to be desired since the circuitry and software involved could then be standardized. The Universal Bubble Interface is such a design.

This interface defines all hardware and software functions needed for mutually compatible bubble-memory systems. It sets board dimensions, connection-pin assignments, interface signal timing, and software protocols. To the user, all systems will, as a result, appear nearly identical, regardless of the bubble-memory device used. Bubble-memory systems built around this standard may connect with many host processors. The hardware interface requires only eight data and five control lines (one optional) to link up with any popular processor. (The optional line consists of an interrupt request that indicates when the memory system is ready for a new command.) The software interface has 10 high-level commands.

The interface is the center of the Generic-Bubble line

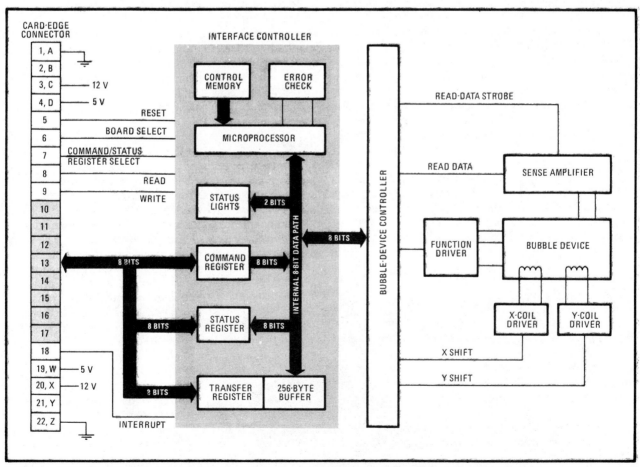

1. Universal Bubble Interface. A simple 8-bit parallel data bus plus five control lines are all that are required to interface with the universal bubble-memory system. Different manufacturers' bubble devices are transparent to the user, obviating the risk of relying on a single source.

2. Motorola's bubbles. The Universal Bubble Interface has been implemented for the bubble devices made by Motorola. The board measures 4.5 by 6.0 inches and has eight bidirectional lines connected to it that transfer data to and from the system.

of memory systems from Bubbl-Tec that can be used with any type of bubble memory. The line has a high-level command language, a simple hardware interface, self-test capability, and high-speed operation. In addition, all inputs and outputs are TTL-compatible.

The Universal Bubble Interface is implemented with an integrated controller that translates the bubble-specific hardware and software requirements into standardized signal lines and command sets. This is a practical approach because the storage capacity of all currently manufactured bubble-memory devices is the same (32- or 128-K bytes). The speed specifications are also very similar. Overall memory-system characteristics, therefore, vary only slightly when one bubble device is replaced by another.

The protocol handles data in a block size that can be defined by the user and is also capable of multiblock transfers. Interaction with the host processor is needed only for the transfer of complete blocks—byte-level attention is never required. As a result, this method can significantly increase the overall system operating speed compared with the other techniques of bubble-memory control, which often tie up the host servicing the bubble device.

In addition, board-level field maintenance of the system is easily carried out. The system can be put into a self-diagnostic mode that completely tests its operation either by closing a switch on the printed-

3. Other bubbles. Intel's bubbles have also been adapted to the standard, as have those manufactured by Hitachi, Fujitsu, and Motorola. Other magnetic-bubble devices will be adapted as they become available.

circuit module or by invoking a host-processor command. A light-emitting diode and an optional printout then indicate the system's status. If there is any trouble, the board-level memory system can simply be unplugged and replaced.

Typical implementation

A block diagram for a typical bubble-memory system using the Universal Bubble Interface standard is shown in Fig. 1. The major components of the system are bubble devices (with their attendant coil drivers, function drivers, and sense amplifiers), a bubble-device controller—often a 40-pin MOS integrated circuit—and an interface controller that uses a single-chip microcomputer. The host system interfaces with other equipment through a 44-pin card-edge connector having typical power requirements of 5 and 12 volts.

Figures 2 and 3 show two bubble-memory systems that use the interface standard. There are eight bidirectional lines for transferring data to and from the system. They also carry initialization parameters, for configuration, and error-report information.

The five input control lines all have low assertion levels. Use of the reset control line is optional because the quit command performs a similar function.

The host processor and the bubble-memory system communicate through a write-only command register, a read-only status register, and a bidirectional read-write transfer register. Commands are written by the host processor into the command register only when a done bit is set in the status register. The status register may be read at any time. The standard interface, therefore, can be addressed as two 8-bit read-write registers. One address is shared by the command and status registers and the other is used by the transfer register. In the host system, the two registers can be either input/output- or memory-mapped.

Buffered transfers

The transfer register is actually a buffer area in the interface controller to which the host processor is given access. Data is read from or written to the register in bursts that are up to 256 bytes long.

Commands are written by the host processor into the command register as a simple 8-bit number. The standard commands are shown in the table.

Bubble operations usually require a sequence of commands and data transfers. Data is stored within the bubble devices in blocks. The desired block size or storage space is specified by the configure command. The user can read or write from 1 to 256 contiguous blocks, starting at any block address, with just one command sequence.

When the done bit is set, a typical read sequence is started by issuing prepare (PREP). This command is written to the command register and is followed by 4 bytes that define the number of blocks and the first block address of the data to be transferred to the host processor. This 4-byte burst is then written to the transfer register.

After moving a burst of bytes from or to the transfer register, the host processor may then issue the burst-end (BEND) command to inform the interface controller that the transmission of data is complete.

Next, the read command is issued to start retrieving the bubble-stored data that was specified by the preceding prepare command. Once the read command is received, the interface controller reads the first designated block into the transfer register. The ready-for-transfer (XFOK) bit is then set, and the host processor proceeds to read the entire block from the transfer register. When the host has finished reading the block, it issues the burst-end command. The interface controller sees this command and then places the next data block in the transfer register. After receiving the last burst-end command, the interface controller sets the done bit. Writing is the converse of reading.

If the interface controller detects any uncorrectable error—like an uncorrectable data error—it will terminate the current operation and set the done and error bits. Upon detecting the error bit, the host processor can issue the report command to flush out an error report.

The report command causes the memory system to send a status burst to the user through the transfer register. An 8-byte burst is then returned to the host processor, consisting of an error code for the type of error encountered, a description of the system, the data-block size, and the block address where the error was detected. After reading the 8 bytes from the transfer register, the host processor issues the burst-end command to notify the interface controller that the register is free to receive data.

There are two other commands used in normal operation: quit and configure. Quit may be employed at any time to terminate an operation prematurely. Configure serves to select the operational data-block size. After issuing configure, the host sends 1 byte to the transfer register. The desired data-block size—64, 128, or 256 bytes—is encoded within the byte.

Error handling

This bubble-memory-interface technique eliminates the need for the host processor to waste processing time checking and repairing errors because hard– and soft–error-detection and -correction procedures are handled by the interface controller. For any block containing a soft error, the interface controller will do an automatic re-read. Hard errors detected during reading will be automatically corrected (when possible) and rewritten. Only uncorrectable hard errors will normally be reported to the host processor. An internal error-count log is maintained to keep tabs on reliability.

STANDARD COMMAND SET FOR UNIVERSAL MAGNETIC-BUBBLE MEMORY INTERFACE	
Command	Function
QUIT	terminates current operation
PREP	prepares memory system for data transfer
BEND	indicates end of burst to or from transfer register
READ	starts data movement from bubble memory to host
WRITE	starts data movement from host to bubble memory
REPORT	retrieves detailed error information
CONFIGURE	defines operational block size
ERRLOG	retrieves error information after self test
VERIFY	performs read-only self-test
TEST	performs write-read self-test

The last three instructions in the table are the self-test commands. Invoking the verify command or closing a switch on the system causes the bubble-memory system to begin a read-only (nondestructive) self-test procedure. In this mode, the interface controller tests the entire memory system, including its own control circuitry, and returns an error indication if it should find a fault. Every stored data block is repetitively read and checked for errors.

Use of this self-test technique greatly simplifies field maintenance because it isolates failures to a module level without test equipment. Normally, the detection of any error indicates that replacement of the memory module is warranted. This substitution can usually be done in the field by relatively unskilled personnel.

The test command starts a write-read test of the entire system—known worst-case data patterns are written throughout the bubble devices, then repeatedly read and checked. If errors are detected, on-board LEDs indicate that a fault has occurred, and a detailed error log is available to the host processor through the error-log (ERRLOG) command.

The error-log command allows the host to retrieve the results of either the verify or test commands. It operates like the report command and provides a count of the detected soft and the correctable and uncorrectable hard errors. The total number of blocks read during the test is also available to the host processor so that an error rate may be calculated.

For reliability purposes, an error log is also kept during normal operation. The host processor can periodically issue error-log to determine the number and type of errors encountered and the number of blocks that have been read since the error log was last cleared. The log is automatically cleared after it is read and also when the system is turned on.

In addition to complete bubble-memory systems based on this interface, Bubbl-Tec is offering a series of application notes that allow original-equipment manufacturers to design systems in accordance with the interface's standard. As a result, an OEM can act as his own second source. For large-quantity users, the firm will make available circuit schematics and pc-board artwork. □

5.
NETWORKS

Personal computers and work stations have turned what has been a computer age—dominated by large, expensive mainframe computers run by professional computer scientists—into an information age. Networks linking these small machines have become the focus of attention as buyers and sellers both guess at the leading technology. Several articles lead off this chapter with a discussion of systems integrators' approaches to tapping microsystems into the power of mainframe machines.

Networks illustrate the close alliance between hardware and software in a way that is perhaps unparalleled in other arenas of computer-system design. Systems designers draw on the talents of software engineers to create the most flexible approach to communications and on the skills of hardware specialists to build in the performance these systems require. These articles highlight the advantages and disadvantages of alternative approaches ranging from Ethernet to token-passing protocols as well as the dedicated chips designed to support these various methods.

Microcomputer and mainframe ally to bring offices new power

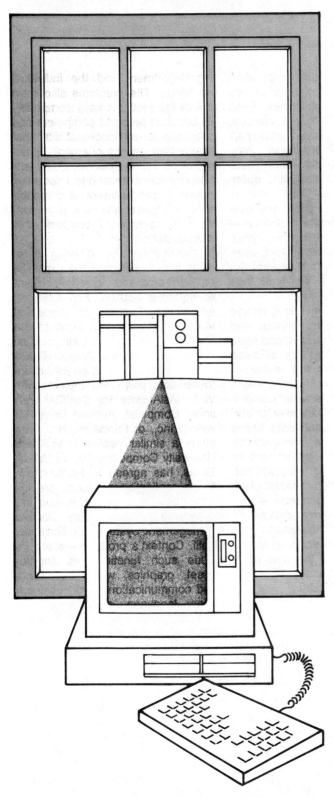

Communication between corporate personal computers and mainframes gives managers immediate access to data bases for decision making

by Harvey J. Hindin
Systems Integration Editor

History records that the first message Alexander Graham Bell sent on the telephone, in 1876, was a call directing his assistant to come into the master's laboratory. The message was insignificant, yet the call itself marked the beginning of the electronic office. Today, events of similar import are taking place—but between machines, not people. What Mr. Bell was to Mr. Watson, the mainframe computer is to the personal computer. They too are now communicating, and in a quicker and more sophisticated way.

"Quick" and "sophisticated" are the watchwords of the dozen or so firms that in the last six months have introduced software to link personal computers and mainframes. In the next six months a dozen more plan to do the same. What spurs all of them on is a common recognition that access to the corporate data base is just as important to managers as is access to desk telephones.

The physical creation of two-way links between communicating machines is no trivial matter, but the required hardware is well within the state of the art. As for the software, however, it is not even clear what functions it should have. Indeed, software design is what distinguishes one new product from another.

These differences reflect the uncertainty of the would-be market leaders, none of whom knows what most customers really need or want. Each vendor therefore addresses the market it knows best, and a wide variety of products is available. On one end of the scale are terminal emulators that allow managers to look at information from the corporate data base but to do absolutely nothing else with it. On the other end are products that download data from mainframes to personal computers, manipulate and change it at the managers' desks, and uploaded it back to the mainframes, where it is incorporated into the corporate data base.

Several products lie between the extremes of "don't touch" and "do as you please." Some let application programs be developed with the same software on personal computers and mainframes. Others download mainframe data to personal computers and let it be used in integrated application programs where managers perform "what if?" experiments. Still others take the

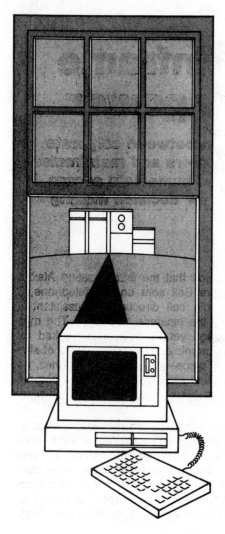

best personal-computer application programs and redesign them so they can run on mainframes. Even within the same product classes, the variation is endless. Certain personal-computer application programs that use mainframe data even sport English-like query languages.

Much information about the new products is vague. Many of them—even among those already introduced—are still in flux. In fact, even the articles in this report present the latest, not the final, views of their authors.

The new technology has spawned problems of corporate politics, and they make the technical problems even harder to solve. One of these political problems is the matter of control over the proliferating multitudes of corporate personal computers. The traditional caretaker of corporate mainframes and data bases has always been the management-information–systems department or the data-processing department. Some of these departments claim that if outside managers can access and—far worse—change data bases without restriction, their integrity will be subverted. Most vendors uphold this view by arming the new products with access control, file locks, passwords, and the like.

Another political problem is the responsibility for buying corporate personal computers. A firm can easily spend a fortune on personal machines that need expensive but redundant software to talk to one another or to mainframes. Of course, they can deal with this problem by compiling lists of approved hardware and software.

The problems of security and purchasing are not rooted only in the conflict between the data-process-

ing department and the individual managers. The problems also grow out of the fundamental incompatibility between personal computers and mainframes—an incompatibility that stems from their fundamentally different operating systems, query languages, communications interfaces, memories, and powers of computation. Only clever and expensive software is capable of resolving this incompatibility.

One popular way of trying to resolve it is to combine the expertise of mainframe and personal-computer software houses. For example, Informatics General, in Woodland Hills, Calif., has gotten together with VisiCorp, of San Jose, Calif., and as a result, Informatics' Answer/DB, a program for accessing an IBM mainframe data base, will interact with Visi's VisiAnswer for the IBM Personal Computer. Applied Data Research Inc., of Princeton, N. J., has made a similar deal with VisiCorp. University Computing Co., of Dallas, Texas, has agreed to let its mainframe application programs provide inputs to the MBA personal-computer program designed by Context Management Systems, of Torrance, Calif. Context's products—which include such functions as spreadsheet, graphics, word processing, and communications—do not use a query language, and communications can be downloaded only.

Another way of dealing with the problem of incompatibility calls for mainframe specialists to devise their own personal-computer software. Cullinet Software is taking this tack in its effort to link its new relational–data-base–management system for IBM mainframes to the IBM PC. The Westwood, Mass., firm is also getting interface information from Apple Computer Inc., of Cupertino, Calif.,

"Integration products include everything from emulation packages to full-blown systems for up- and down-loading."

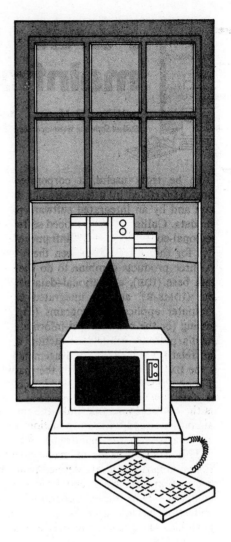

in order to develop software for Apple's Lisa personal computer.

Other contenders abound. Intel Corp., of Santa Clara, Calif., has a multiuser hardware and software link that connects the company's mainframe data-base–management system to its personal-computer application software. McCormack & Dodge, of Needham, Mass., has linked its financial–data-base–management system to personal-computer software from Lotus Development Corp., of Cambridge, Mass. And Ryan-McFarland, of Rolling Hills Estates, Calif., has designed a Cobol-based software-development system that allows identical applications to be worked up and run both on mainframes and personal computers. Traditional office-automation vendors are getting into the integration market, too: for example, Harris Corp., of Melbourne, Fla., is giving its office-automation computers data-base access to several different mainframes.

Of the various technologies for connecting the personal computer to the mainframe, terminal emulation is the oldest. It has been available for years but fails to create true integration, since all that users can do with the information they get is stare at it. But this limitation is rapidly disappearing. Software is being written, for example, to take data from emulated terminals and use it as input to integrated application-software packages that run on personal computers. The integration can go further still, in fact. Management Science America Inc., of Atlanta, Ga., has even built a data-base query language into its personal-computer programs.

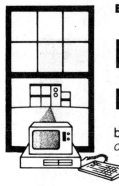

Electronics/August 11, 1983

Partitioned software joins mainframes to personal units

by William G. Nisen
Cullinet Software, Westwood, Mass.

☐ To be truly useful, a corporate personal computer must be fortified by a two-way link to a mainframe data base and by an integrated software package that can use the data. Cullinet has developed software not only for the personal-computer and mainframe ends of the link but also for the interface between them.

Three products combine to do the job: an information data base (IDB), a relational–data-base–management system (IDMS/R), and an integrated package of personal-computer application programs (Fig. 1). The data-processing (or the management-information–systems) department's production and transaction data are handled by the relational–data-base–management system (Fig. 2). It is the IDB software that links the manager at the personal-computer end with a production- or transaction-oriented data base at the mainframe end.

This IDB is a cache of management-oriented information summaries that are derived from the production and transaction data bases and from data bases outside the company—Dow Jones, for example. IDB's relational architecture lets managers use it with nonprocedural—English-like—languages, and it is accessed though a person-

al computer, which runs an application-software package comprising spreadsheet and query, a relational–data-base–management system, business graphics, document processing, electronic mail, and mainframe communications.

Users can choose among three communications options: a coaxial-cable connection (both local and remote), IBM 3270 terminal emulation (through a protocol converter), and asynchronous communication (through teletypewriter emulation). Just as important, IDMS/R and IDR support a variety of IBM mainframe-software environments, including the various Operating System/Virtual Storage (OS/VS) and Disk Operating System/Virtual Storage Extended (DOS/VSE) operating systems; the Basic Direct, Basic Telecommunication, and Virtual Storage Access Methods (BDAM, BTAM, and VSAM); all major Teleprocessing (TP) monitors; and the Basic, Virtual, and Telecommunications Access Methods (BTAM, VTAM, and TCAM). Cullinet decided that the mainframe software—the IDB—and the management-information–systems department should control access to and manage the corporate data resources. The IDB therefore has all the follow-

1. First things first. Cullinet's IBM PC code is written in C with some 8086 assembler code. About 256-K bytes of RAM and one double-density drive will do the job for most managers. Requirements for Apple's Lisa are just a 3270 communications option with LisaTerminal.

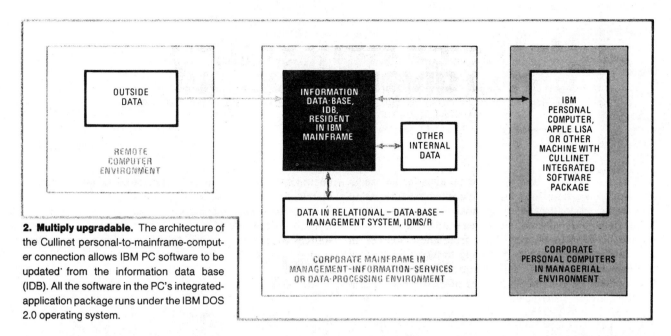

2. Multiply upgradable. The architecture of the Cullinet personal-to-mainframe-computer connection allows IBM PC software to be updated from the information data base (IDB). All the software in the PC's integrated-application package runs under the IBM DOS 2.0 operating system.

ing: an integrated-data and catalog area, security and access controls for end-user information, data-query support, a user-oriented view of data, on-line access for personal computers, and a 3270 terminal interface.

The IDB must also provide an easy interface with the production and transaction data bases. As a relational data base, it can create, edit, add to, read, and erase data tables; maintain a catalog of data entities; and provide data security and access control. Finally, the IDB interfaces with a family of Cullinet mainframe software products, such as the Application Development System.

Two data structures

The new data-base–management system, IDMS/R, which works with the IDB and with the package of integrated applications, combines network (tree-type) and relational data structures—an approach that has several virtues. One system, for instance, can meet the needs both of production and end-user applications, so it is no longer necessary to compromise or to purchase two systems. Moreover, IDMS/R incorporates both kinds of data structures and therefore eliminates the need to duplicate information, use different data-base technologies, or apply different methods of implementation.

Wherever the data may have been first defined, it can be accessed directly and used either in production or by end-users. And IDMS/R is fully compatible with older, nonrelational versions of IDMS, so existing data-base applications run without modification. IDMS/R makes all this possible because instead of providing a simplistic relational view of network data, it directly supports the storage and maintenance of relational tables that apply the full range of relational operators.

The IDB not only gets information from the IDMS/R but also stores files created in personal computers. These files—documents, messages, or graphs—can later be retrieved and mailed to other users. Moreover, Cullinet will make it possible to create files in personal computers and to update the IDMS/R—under the data-processing department's control.

When all the parts are ready, the IDB will be the center of a personal-computer support system, which will allow complete two-way communication between the personal computer and the mainframe. Already, the IDB can act as a central information source and unite a multitude of personal computers into a network by accessing data from data bases and outside sources, summarizing it, and sending it to personal computers.

Giving host mainframes control over personal-computer networks might have generated many problems—for instance, the proliferation of data bases or portions of them. Proliferation tends to make data redundant and perishable, to undermine its integrity, and to complicate efforts to transmit it without errors. Access to data and data security can both become more difficult.

The IDB deals with data proliferation because it was written as an application program that runs under IDMS/R: it stores each piece of data (on the mainframe) independently of every other piece, so all the data can be combined in any way. Therefore it is unnecessary to keep two similar but not identical data bases.

Data redundancy is not itself the problem—data integrity is. The IDB maintains it by letting data-base administrators construct procedures that access the data bases and massage and store the data in the IDB, which also provides file checks to ensure that data is current and correct. Data transfer is easy and routine: error-detection and -correction, data-flow–control, and transmission-control software see to it that data moves reliably between the mainframe and the personal computers.

Finally, the centralization of corporate personal computers promotes control of data access and security. Passkeys that distinguish among "eyes only" read, copy, append, modify, erase, and view provide for access control. Data security is provided for by well-established ownership rules and passwords for signing on, by restricting the times and places of access to the data base, by establishing sensitivity thresholds to track unsuccessful attempts to log on or break in, by encoding data, and by establishing activity logs that track access to data.

Electronics/August 11, 1983

Net helps work station talk to diverse computers

by James S. Lutz
Harris Corp., Melbourne, Fla.

☐ Harris Corp. had three fundamental aims for its executive work station. It had to provide integrated access to mainframes and thus to electronic-information sources, both through local and wide-area communications. It had to be capable of using data from these sources in application programs. Finally, it had to incorporate easy-to-use word processing. These requirements shaped the development of Harris' 9000 series of distributed, multi-functional, and clustered work stations (Fig. 1).

The 9000 provides several kinds of access to all of a company's mainframes. The simplest method permits the work station to emulate the industry-standard IBM 3270 terminal and use its Systems-Network-Architecture–based Synchronous Data Link Control (SNA/SDLC) protocols to create interactive access to a data-processing host (Fig. 2). Data received from host computers can be converted automatically into text and included in reports and memos.

Companies whose host computers cannnot support a 3270 terminal, as well as companies that have two or more mainframes, can form a gateway access to as many as four host computers by linking the Harris MIND series of distributed data-processors to a token-passing local network. The processor supports communications protocols for mainframes produced by IBM Corp., Burroughs Corp., Sperry Univac, Honeywell Inc., and Control Data Corp. thus giving work stations access to most possible corporate data bases.

The 9000 helps executives analyze such data by accommodating personal-computing software application programs written for Digital Research's CP/M-86 operating system—spreadsheets, for example. Finally, its easy-to-use word processor (with a menu-driven interface) can incorporate the data into documents. Throughout document processing, it has at least two levels of help messages.

Cost-effective

Harris knew that most companies already had word-processing equipment but needed a cost-effective way of giving work stations access to it. The 9000 can therefore transfer documents to and from various Wang and IBM word processors through appropriate Binary Synchronous Communications protocols, which permit documents to be accessed from local and remote word processors. With little or no loss of text structure, transferred

documents are automatically translated to and from the Harris document format. Other wide-area communications protocols are planned such as interactive teletypewriter, to provide access to such outside information sources as the Dow Jones News Service.

Timely service

An executive work station must be responsive if it is going to help executives analyze more data in less time. Therefore, for the 9000's main processor, Harris decided to use the Intel 80186, a 16-bit microprocessor that integrates functions formerly performed by peripheral chips.

The 80186 microprocessor permits the 9000 to use system and application software written in a proprietary, high-level language similar to Pascal, and this propri-

1. Easy to use. Work stations that Harris uses for connection to mainframes may be grouped in clusters or, as shown here, standing alone. Features include 15-inch-diagonal screens with 33 lines and a 108-key typewriter keyboard with 14 programmable keys.

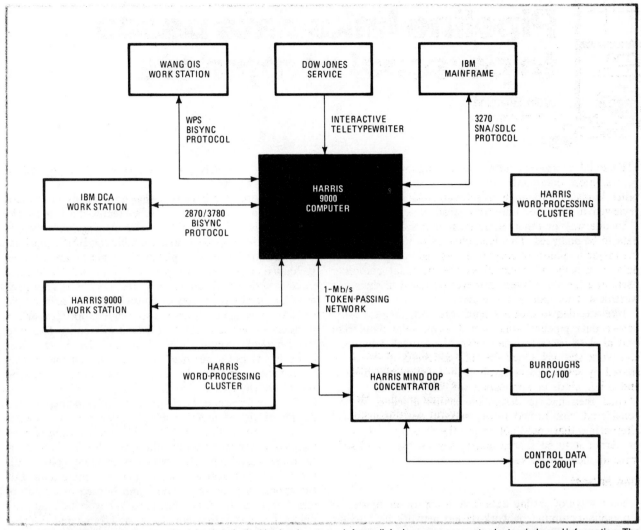

2. Flexible. Local and wide-area communications in the Harris micro-to-mainframe link give users access to electronic-based information. The 9000 provides decision makers with the benefits of access to data bases, much as the production process has already benefited from them.

etary language makes possible a modular software design that promotes the efficient addition of software as needs evolve. Yet the 80186's processing power also helps the 9000 operate quickly enough to be a clerical work station and a nonclerical one, as well.

Intelligent peripheral-controller cards—which make it unnecessary for the main processor to handle input/output for communications, disk drives, and printers—also contribute to the present and anticipated performance of the work station, with its 1 megabyte of random-access memory. As many as 12 work stations may be attached to a cluster that shares the disk storage handled by the peripheral-controller card. Sharing allows documents to be accessed by any user in a cluster and still provides security on a document and part-of-document basis. Each cluster also has floppy-disk storage for documents and personal applications.

The entry-level product of the 9000 series is the 9010 standalone word processor, which also serves as a multifunctional work station integrating word processing, communications, and computing functions. It can handle 1 megabyte of RAM and 16 megabytes of floppy- and rigid-disk storage as well as its own letter-quality printer.

Different clusters may need to share documents, too—a fact that helped shape Harris's design for the 9000's communications scheme. Analysis showed that a 1-megabit-per-second, baseband, local network could connect up to 32 clusters. This proprietary network uses the token-passing logical-ring–physical-bus protocol developed by the IEEE's 802 Local Network Standards committee. A large-scale–integrated token-passing controller chip supports the token-passing access protocol and reduces both the software load on the devices attached to the network and the cost of the connection.

Harris chose token passing, a deterministic protocol not dependent upon propagation delay times, rather than Ethernet or one of the other collision-detection–based networks, because it lends itself to later migration to a broadband local network that may extend further than a baseband link. In fact, either the present baseband link or a later broadband one may be used as a bridge link, to permit hierarchical interconnections among department or "work group" networks. Executives will then have access to many document-storage areas spread throughout the network. Thus, they will be able to work with increased efficiency.

Electronics/August 11, 1983

Pipeline links data bases to personal computers

by Jim Rutledge
Intel Corp., Austin, Texas

☐ Personal computers proliferate throughout large companies, most commonly for use with spreadsheets and other kinds of data-analysis software. Data can now be reviewed in hours or minutes instead of weeks.

In one way or other, users must themselves enter the data to be analyzed. This fact, obvious in itself, points to the major weakness of corporate personal computers. For data is usually as personal as the personal computer itself, and the spreadsheet, however powerful in theory, is worthless if its data is not correct.

Intel decided to create a hardware and software product—a data pipeline—that would move valid data from central data bases into networks of personal computers and work stations. Once the data got there, it was to be shared by several users involved in creating spreadsheets and other kinds of application software (Fig. 1).

Intel then had to design the actual pipeline. It first considered, but turned down, several existing technical alternatives that could not ensure the security of the data or permit it to be shared among several users and software application packages.

One is best

Four ways of getting data from a central computer to a personal-computer or work-station network have so far been devised. The most fundamental is just to copy (or dump) the data into a storage medium compatible with both systems. Among the most commonly used media are tape, floppy disks, and removable hard-disk devices. After the storage medium is copied at the host computer, it is carried and loaded—by hand—onto the distributed system—an unwieldy procedure subject to a myriad of security problems.

Because this kind of data sharing depends on human intervention, it has been called a "tennis-shoe" network. Time delays, the lack of true data sharing, and possible security failures made it unacceptable for Intel's pipeline.

File-controller–type application programs are another technique often used with personal computers, frequently in conjunction with tennis-shoe networks. The data goes onto a central storage device controlled by a fairly simple software package that serves user requests for files. When it receives such a request, it downloads entire files into the personal computer's local storage. In many cases, however, users do not need an entire file, so the process is inefficient and costly. Besides, the data cannot be shared by the users.

The third method of distribution is embodied in the design of the standard packages that permit personal computers to emulate an IBM 3270. Such packages have inspired announcements of others, which will allow users to access mainframe data-base–management systems directly from personal computers and thus share data. But the approach adds to the cost and burden of corporate mainframe and communications networks. And the unique computing powers of the mainframe and the personal computer go unused.

Intel eventually chose a method of distribution that lets users extract data as they need it from a mainframe data-base–management system. The extract software downloads bulk data into multiuser systems (Fig. 2) where it is manipulated by application packages and

1. Extras. Intel's personal-computer-to-mainframe connection, shown in a typical installation, offers more than mere data-base access. Users can implement spreadsheets, menus or forms, word processing, graphics, and project-management tools.

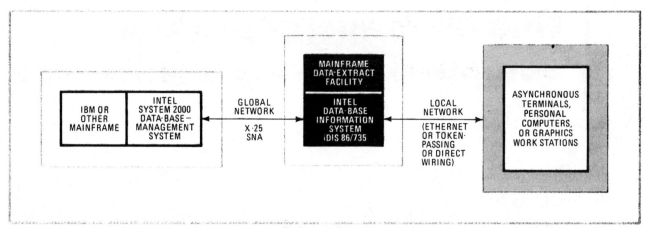

2. Pipeline layers. The 2000's data-base–management software acts as a gateway to IBM mainframe data. Once Intel's data-extracting software selects nonrelational data, it is sent over a global network. The downloaded, now relational, files are shared among two or more users.

accessed by an SQL-type (English-like) query language.

The data pipeline comprises four layers, with the top layer at the mainframe and the bottom one at the local network. The layer below the mainframe is the network-communication capability, which provides for bulk downloading of data and for on-line access to the mainframe.

The next layer down, the extract capability, allows users to construct requests for subsets of mainframe data. To do so, they need only follow a set of menu-driven prompts. The lowest layer in the mainframe–to–work-station connection is the local network. Here, local communications facilitate the sharing both of computing power and of data.

All users of Intel's Database Information System, the iDIS 86/735, can share the data. To aid in the sharing, the iDIS hardware includes a 35-megabyte Winchester disk, 765 kilobytes of random-access memory, support for five terminals, two lines for communicating with the host, and a printer. At both access and record levels,

security is provided by the SQL-like relational language.

Data can be shared because it is automatically converted during extraction from the mainframe's hierarchical data-base–management system into the relational structures that the SQL-like language requires. As the data structures are modified, the data files are converted (enabling sharing of data by multiple work stations and personal computers) into the file format of Microsoft Xenix, which is derived from Bell Laboratories' Unix operating system.

These conversions and the pipeline's design free users from worry about file conversions. The most recent corporate data for their integrated packages of software applications—spreadsheets, word processing, electronic mail or agenda, forms or menus, and others—will always be available and entered, and they can forget about data structures. IBM, Control Data, and Sperry Univac machines with different operating systems can interface with Intel's iDIS 86/735, most of whose system software is written in C.

How Intel opens up its spreadsheet

Only if software packages from separate vendors have well-defined interfaces can they become building blocks in more powerful systems. Or, as Microsoft Corp.'s Mark Orsino (p. 116) puts it, such packages must be "open" to be integrated into a single system.

Consider, for example, the way Intel's iDIS data-base information system embeds data-base commands in a spreadsheet. When managers prepare these documents, they may need data kept in a remote data base. Each time they prepare the spreadsheets, they must retrieve the latest data automatically. Intel's spreadsheet (Microsoft's Multiplan) does so with a novel file format. The manager starts by creating a spreadsheet model with static data and data-base directives, including a data-base name, a command to retrieve data, and details about the locations that will receive it. The directives go into one of the spreadsheet cells as "alpha" text.

The spreadsheet is saved as a "model" file, and a software utility program processes it. Microsoft describes

this formatting as a SYLK, for SYmbolic LinK file format. In the SYLK format, records of text written in the American Standard Code for Information Interchange define the spreadsheet's entire contents. The utility program locates all the SYLK file's directives and retrieves data from the mainframe data base.

The result is a spreadsheet file that contains both the newly acquired data and the spreadsheet's original contents. Once the model has been saved, the utility creates an up-to-the-minute spreadsheet whenever the manager calls for one, and it can be viewed or printed with the Multiplan application program.

The open iDIS system and defined software interfaces come with a bonus, too: a iDIS terminal can be accessed by an IBM Personal Computer through a terminal-emulation program and can also retrieve data from a mainframe through iDIS data-extract software, can prepare a spreadsheet model and a final spreadsheet, and can transfer it to the PC. —**Jack Dorman,** *Intel Corp., Austin, Texas*

Electronics/August 11, 1983

One file-transfer protocol serves all personal computers

by James Dow
Microcom Inc., Norwood, Mass.

□ So many different personal computers and work stations have surfaced that their protocols for communicating with mainframes urgently need standardizing. The only such hand-shaking software available so far has been geared to specific situations or specific personal computers. Also, many of the protocols fail to treat the machines as anything more than dumb terminals. In contrast, the Microcom Networking Protocol (MNP) is suitable for file transfer by most personal computers to most mainframes, and it utilizes the personal computer's intelligence.

MNP has the support of Apple Computer, GTE Telenet, VisiCorp, and Victor Technologies, among others in the industry. Perhaps even more important, from the standards point of view, MNP is an expandable, layered protocol that conforms to both the International Standards Organization's Open Systems Interconnect model for computer communications and the National Bureau of Standards' specifications for message formatting. The MNP protocol is available for a one-time license fee.

Everyone benefits

An industry-standard file-transfer protocol is much more than just a convenience for the users of a personal computer. Manufacturers of hardware products will no longer have to research and develop their own protocol techniques. Also, they will find the marketability of their products heightened by numerous new uses that should open up for them in conjunction with other computers—

mainframe, mini-, or personal. Likewise, software producers will save on protocol development. Even vendors of networks and data-base services stand to profit from the resulting increase in network traffic in graphics information, spreadsheet templates, and software updates, as well as electronic mail.

Far away

Nonetheless, it is the personal-computer users who have the most to gain from file-transfer standardization; for by enhancing communications with mainframes it will guarantee these professionals the timely data that is essential to rapid decision making.

The largest single segment of the personal-computer-to-mainframe communications market (see "Who connects?") is made up of people who are at least several miles away from the mainframe they wish to access, access it only on occasion, and require no more than moderate amounts of data. Establishing a connection through a local network is impractical because of the distance. Polled, leased-line networks, IBM 3270 terminal emulations, and protocol conversions are uneconomic because of the high cost of the communication lines, line drops, and interface equipment.

The majority of users in this category currently gain access to a mainframe by having their personal computers emulate dumb terminals and by using either the public switched telephone network (for direct connection to the host) or a public data network (without direct

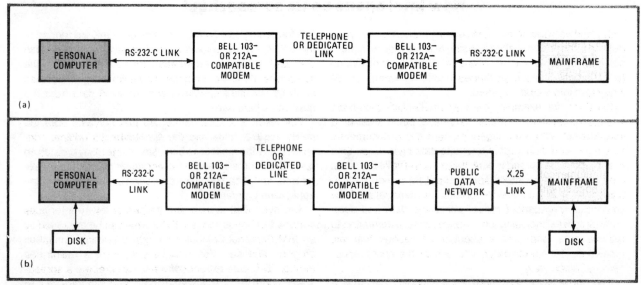

Fits right in. The Microcom file-transfer protocol handles either a direct link between communicating computers (a) or a packet-switching link (b). The protocol software can be resident in the computers or the modems and has been proposed as a standard.

connection to the host), such as GTE Telenet, Tymnet, or Compuserve's network. Either way, communication generally occurs at rates of 300 or 1,200 baud (see figure).

Because the personal computer is forced to act as an unintelligent terminal and not as a computer in a network, it is usually limited to transmitting only 7-bit ASCII data or text files. No provision is made for error control, data transparency, or end-to-end file transfer—all of which are needed in the sort of reliable communications network described by the ISO seven-layer model.

These limitations have been the catalyst for the development of numerous custom asynchronous protocols that do exploit the machines' intelligence in order to provide some of the required services. Unfortunately, most of these asynchronous protocols have been developed for a single application. Therefore, the protocol developed by vendor A for file transfer will rarely, if ever, be compatible with the protocol developed by vendor B, whose machines also must transfer files to the same host mainframe. Clearly, too, a mainframe cannot be expected to support even a small percentage of the many protocols that are available.

Inside the protocol

The Microcom networking protocol makes short work of this confusion by providing reliable flow-controlled, transparent data transfer on point-to-point connections both as a stream of bytes and as files. Equally important, it defines a minimal virtual file that is essential to the transfer of data between dissimilar computer and operating-system architectures.

As the ISO model requires, the first and bottom layer of the protocol is the physical layer—the actual hardware connection to the transmission medium. For this layer the R-232-C standard was chosen because of its widespread use on every size of computer.

Also, as the ISO model requires, the second (or link) layer of MNP provides data transparency, flow control, and error control. Data transparency is provided by software through which this layer and those above it can detect the beginning and end of what are known as protocol data units. MNP accomplishes this chore by framing, or marking, the beginning and end of each protocol data unit sent.

On byte-oriented machine architectures, a byte-stuffing technique is used. Where more powerful bit-synchronous hardware interfaces and synchronous modems are provided, the MNP switches to the more efficient Synchronous Data Link Control (SDLC) framing known as start-and-stop-flag, zero-bit insertion.

Reliable data transfer is achieved through the use of positive acknowledgment, error correction via a 16-bit cyclic redundancy check, and retransmission where necessary. The flow of data is controlled by a credit allocation (assigning a fixed quantity of memory per data transmission) or by a sliding window scheme (allocating as much memory space as needed).

Skip one

The ISO session layer (the ISO network layer is not used) creates a full-duplex connection between communicating devices. At the session level a message is exchanged identifying the communicating-device type, the file operating-system type, the application program, the source address, and the destination address.

In the event that the two device types and operating systems are identical, the session is a "native" one. But in the case of personal-computer-to-mainframe communications, where the devices and operating systems are dissimilar, the session is virtual and files are transferred in a virtual-file format.

The top, or application layer (equivalent to ISO layer 7), provides file-manipulation and -transfer services. At this layer the communication initiator gives his or her password and identifies the file's action type (its purpose), transfer mode, and name. He or she also handles the file's type, record length, source, and destination.

Now the two computers can start to communicate. What has happened is that the implementation of the physical, link, session, and application layers has resulted in an orderly creation of transparent data-transfer connections between the two highest-level users—the application programs on the personal computer and those on the mainframe.

Who connects?

How often, for how much data, and from how far away—the answers to those questions define the best way of linking a personal computer to a mainframe from which it needs to access data. Ideally, if the two machines exchange data frequently and in volume and are less than several thousand feet apart, they should be linked by a local network, such as Ethernet, Omninet, or some form of the IEEE 802 standard. But in the real world, few mainframes have local-network interfaces, so instead they use dedicated terminals and communications links.

If the personal computer is more than several thousand feet away from the mainframe but the other factors are unchanged—large amounts of data are frequently accessed—the most practical access method is often through the IBM 3270 terminal (or terminal emulation) using the Binary Synchronous protocol of IBM's Systems Network Architecture (SNA). This is usually done with a polled, leased-line network and with synchronous modems.

Such emulation-based communications, if properly implemented, will be invisible to the IBM mainframe. For most users of personal computers, on the other hand, the leased-line drops, the high-speed modems, and the specialized software needed for their use are expensive, and many minicomputer and other vendor application programs were not written to support the 3270 terminal.

The largest class of personal-computer or work-station user—many miles from the mainframe, with a low to moderate frequency of use, for moderate amounts of data—is best served by a telephone-line link to the mainframe and a standard protocol.

Electronics/ August 11, 1983

Open-architecture design unites diverse systems

by Mark S. Ursino
Microsoft Corp., Bellevue, Wash.

☐ By tradition, most computers are designed to be "open," capable of addressing many different needs. That flexibility confers great freedom of choice on the end user, of course, but it also forces system integrators to unify a wilderness of machines, networks, protocols, and operating systems. Usually, this system integrator must confront architectures with varying degrees of openness, embodied in a jumble of components—including communications logistics (like physical connections and protocols), data sources (such as data-base–management systems and files), and data applications (like accounting and productivity tools).

The magnitude of the problem convinced Microsoft that no single, magically clever package will solve it. After all, how likely is it that a single vendor could maintain strong relationships with all the vendors involved? The real solution will require all those—including in-house data-processing departments—who build software products to assume a share of responsibility. They will all have to build open architectures into the software they produce, and they will all have to generate apppropriate interfaces among the components they control. One part of Microsoft's share of this solution, SYLK (for SYmbolic LinK), will be discussed later, at the end of this article.

Physical communication between machines, and the passing of data between different operating systems, are two fundamental aspects of the integration problem. But even the physical connection between machines is hardly a trivial problem. And the tight coupling of mainframe systems and their communications hardware is an additional complication. So the burden of establishing the connection falls on the personal computer's operating software. What's more, mainframe systems tend to be wired to protocols sponsored by the mainframe manufacturer, and this too puts the burden on personal machines.

Fortunately, all the popular 16-bit operating systems for personal computers were developed by independent software vendors. Instead of the very specific operating systems of the mainframes, personal computers support a wide variety of architectures and can therefore communicate, without rigid predispositions, through integrated device drivers.

The problems of integration have also been simplified a bit by the communications level—in essence, message passing—permitted by classical operating systems. This simple mechanism allows personal-computer communications protocols to operate in tandem with device drivers.

Computer communications divide between two generic forms: telecommunications and local networks. General operating systems can interface with both forms. Whichever of them may be chosen, the operating system's

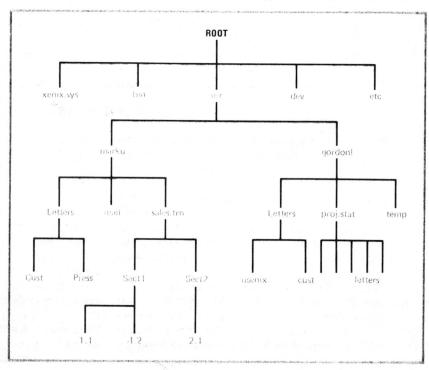

Tree structure. A typical hierarchical directory has a root and branches as shown. A directory, file, or peripheral on a network can be addressed by tracing a logical path through the tree branches. No knowledge of the network's architecture is needed, and both machines and users can change locations without disturbing the directory.

services should be defined at a level basic enough to eliminate the need to assume anything about the form's characteristics—even its performance. And the dynamic nature of the distributed information and resources in these networks means that they must be designed to allow logical addressing of data and services (see figure), independent of physical network address or the characteristics of a computer or a network (see "Where are you?" below).

A trio of classes

Integrating systems of differing functionality requires network services to be divided into three classes, set up as upwardly compatible layers to allow transparent networking between dissimilar systems and to avoid resort to the simplistic and inadequate—though normal—file-transfer and virtual-terminal protocols.

The first of these three classes, basic services, is the highest common factor. Basic services are so fundamental to computers that almost any machine can be given the protocol to join a network. There are no options, and all implementations provide all services. In effect, basic services consist of the facilities provided by a generic or pseudo operating system.

The second class, familial services, defines an extended functionality that is possible among operating systems of the same species. MS/DOS, Bell Laboratories' Unix operating system, and Xenix (and other Unix look-alikes and derivatives) are similar enough, architecturally, to be integrated at this level. Familial services allow these operating systems to merge files by supporting family-specific file-system operations, such as changing the files' protection "mode," altering the directory structure by adding and deleting directories, and accessing files on remote computers.

Finally, identical operating systems and identical extensions to different operating systems can have more functionality than operating systems of the same family. The third class of proprietary services—implementation-specific network extensions—takes advantage of hardware or software peculiar to a specific product.

Application integration

Integrating the application programs of mainframes and personal computers is even more difficult than integrating communications and system software. These days, the most celebrated form of program integration involves lashing up the productivity tools of personal computers to corporate data-processing resources or to commercially available information services. But this very limited definition of application-software integration solves only one limited problem.

Much work is being done to define "sockets" in personal-productivity tools and general application programs. These sockets provide a known and manageable interface that allows third parties to integrate applications from other vendors without modification. Mainframe data-base products have more or less been defined this way, since the data-base vendor must provide for the easy migration of data from oddly assorted application software into the data base.

Systems based on personal computers or work stations are following suit, at least in the sense that they are capable of reading and writing user-definable fixed-format records so as to load data from "foreign" sources. For example, data-base and application products generally incorporate a report writer that can also be used to provide this general interface.

The problem is harder with visually oriented productivity tools, like VisiCalc and Multiplan. Such visual tools interface with users more successfully than do applications that lack graphic displays; they give the data more meaning by presenting it, for example, as a function of position on a display. Of course, such data can always be dumped off as ASCII text and used in a text-only machine or application. But the user then loses the natural association of names, formulas, relative positions, and formats that describe the properties of the data and give it meaning. This diminishes the data's value to the application and creates a strained and unnatural association between packages.

Microsoft, for its part, has achieved a more intimate integration of its productivity tools—both among themselves and with "foreign" software—by defining a data interchange format called SYLK. The format not only dumps data but also adds extra properties that tell "reading" applications what it means. The format is designed for ease of generation, ease of parsing, and storage.

SYLK files, for example, can completely represent a Multiplan worksheet (like a program to build a cash-flow forecasting worksheet), so a program can generate one from a general-ledger chart of accounts. The resulting forecasts can then be "forwarded" for tracking to a budget-control system.

Where are you?

The most generally accepted way to provide an addressing interface is to extend the user and application file system. Since both the MS/DOS and Xenix operating systems have tree-structured (or hierarchical) directories, they can be pictured as an upward extension of the file system as it would appear on any machine. In other words, above the machine's top (or root) directory would be a network root.

Directories, files, and peripherals on any machine in the network can be addressed just by using the appropriate file system "path"—not the physical path that the system must travel, which is subject to architectural changes, but the logical directory path, which changes only as specified by a user or an application. The network file system removes the issue of network software and does so in a way that is general enough to allow networked applications to be developed without prior knowledge of the machines, communications mode, or media involved. Questions of file integrity, security, privacy, and reliability are resolved similarly. Thus, the end user has a uniform method of computer system control.

Electronics/August 11, 1983

Cobol compiler fits micros and mainframes

by Glenn Embrey
Ryan-McFarland Corp., Rolling Hills Estates, Calif.

☐ Since companies, like people, have their own styles of using personal computers, there is probably no single, most effective way of integrating these machines into an organization's data-processing operations. Instead, companies should be given a tool with which to evolve their own solutions. So Ryan-McFarland has developed a Cobol-language compiler that produces identical source and object code on many different processors and different operating systems.

Once all computers in a company speak exactly the same language, many data-handling scenarios become possible. For example, most companies see the Ryan-McFarland Cobol product primarily as a means of giving their data-processing departments greater control over personal computers. Other firms, however, view it as a way of offloading some mainframe tasks—they discover they can develop more software more quickly by using personal computers in place of the overburdened mainframe, uploading programs into it only when they are complete and debugged. Still other companies find the product turns personal computers into training stations for beginning programmers, who no longer deplete mainframe resources.

Many possibilities

The same Cobol compiler, known as RM/Cobol, is available for IBM mainframes, as well as for most popular desktop systems. Consequently, identical application software will run on all these systems (to date 18 processors and 35 operating systems) without any code having to be rewritten. Such program portability is often difficult for mainframe specialists to grasp, accustomed as they are to the major changes usually required in application software when it migrates to a different operating system, let alone different hardware.

This approach also means software development for all the different machines in a company can be done on a single machine, under a single operating system. In effect, the use of personal computers can be managed and controlled by a single resource—ordinarily, a company's data-processing or management-information–systems organization. An application program can be developed on the company's mainframe, by mainframe personnel, in Cobol, the language in which most business programmers are most highly trained. The application is then downloaded with either a modem or a direct link to all the personal computers or work stations throughout the business. The identical code will run on all the machines.

Source or object?

When it makes sense to protect an application from revisions by its users, only the software object code is downloaded. When more flexibility is preferable—for example, to allow a user to customize a report format—the source code itself can be downloaded.

In much the same way, identical data files can be downloaded to personal computers throughout the company. Though such computers cannot usually read mainframe files, because of file structure differences, these files can be rewritten by a mainframe utility into a format compatible with a personal computer and then downloaded.

Clearly, the firm's data-processing department can control what files are available to the rest of the company, can protect the mainframe files from unauthorized updates, and can ensure that all departments have access to the latest figures. This approach is also flexible enough to accommodate transferring data back to the mainframe, if this is desirable.

Independent instructions

The software technology of putting identical languages on a wide variety of computer environments is based on the use of machine-independent instruction sets tailored to very specific tasks. Fundamental here is the fact that the RM/Cobol compiler software consists of a number of modules, 70% of whose code is machine-independent. None of this 70% needs to be changed when the compil-

Small no longer

The size and complexity of Cobol programs that are capable of running on personal computers make their "small system" designation a misnomer. A case in point is a planning, scheduling, and control system for manufacturing, developed by Key Systems Inc., of Marathon, Fla. The 400,000 source-code lines of Key's mainframe package were developed by RM/Cobol on an IBM Personal Comput-

er with only 56-K bytes of random-access memory.

Mainframe RM/Cobol is also being used on an IBM mainframe at Tandy Corp., in Fort Worth, Texas, for inventory and account applications. Once the application has been tested, it is turned into TRS-80–executable object code by a mainframe utility program and downloaded via Telenet to TRS-80 model 3s and 4s in Tandy's stores.

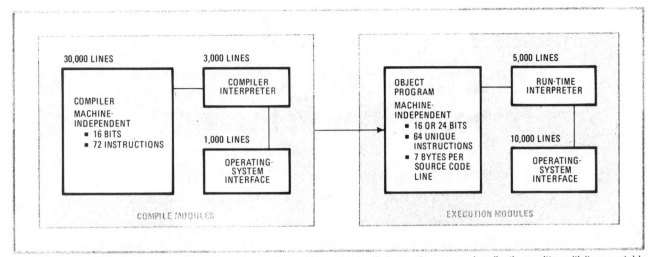

30,000 LINES	3,000 LINES		5,000 LINES

COMPILER MACHINE-INDEPENDENT
- 16 BITS
- 72 INSTRUCTIONS

COMPILER INTERPRETER

OPERATING-SYSTEM INTERFACE

1,000 LINES

COMPILE MODULES

OBJECT PROGRAM MACHINE-INDEPENDENT
- 16 OR 24 BITS
- 64 UNIQUE INSTRUCTIONS
- 7 BYTES PER SOURCE CODE LINE

RUN-TIME INTERPRETER

OPERATING-SYSTEM INTERFACE

10,000 LINES

EXECUTION MODULES

Portable. The RM/Cobol compiler is written in machine-independent, task-specific instruction sets, and applications written with it are portable at the source- and object-code level. Source code is compiled by a compiler module in conjunction with a compiler interpreter and operating-system interface. To be executed, the object code thus created requires a run-time system in a specific computer's machine code.

er is reconfigured to function on a different computer.

RM/Cobol can be put onto a new environment quickly, not only because so little of it needs to be changed, but also because the part that remains the same contains the scanning and translating algorithms of the compiler. Therefore, implementing the compiler on different machines is a rather straightforward task that does not require the man-years of work ordinarily needed to develop a distinct compiler.

Typically, the compiler module itself comprises 30,000 lines of code, all of it machine-independent. The module works in conjunction with two much smaller modules, usually totaling fewer than 5,000 lines of code, which are written in the assembly language native to the target machine (see figure).

Chief of three

The first of these modules, the operating-system interface, performs those compiler functions that depend on the operating system. These functions include allocating memory to data-base tables, reading a source record, writing an object record, writing a listing line, and loading a task-specific compiler overlay. The second module is the compiler interpreter. It handles data-management routines as well as interpreting each of the instructions in the compiler module.

Working together, these three modules compile source code into object code. The object code itself also includes machine-independent instructions. Thus, it can be moved from one machine to another without any alteration (or recompilation). In other words, an application can be run on any machine that supports the language.

Before the application object code can be executed, it requires two more modules, both written in the host machine's assembly language. The first is the run-time interpreter. It contains the implementation of the object-code instruction set and handles the instruction set's underlying data decoding and sequencing. Usually consisting of 3,000 to 6,000 lines of code, its size depends primarily on the input/output capability of the operating system. In some cases, nothing less than an entire in-dexed file manager must be included.

The second module is the run-time operating-system interface. It helps the operating system execute a Cobol program, and its functions include sequential, relative, and indexed input/output operations. The entire module can be quite small if the system file manager supports Cobol input/output in its entirety.

Minimal disadvantages

Traditionally, portable object code entails much slower program execution than does nonportable code. However, the Ryan-McFarland compiler minimizes this effect because its task-specific instruction sets are very compact. For example, the object code that represents a typical move statement requires only 4 bytes (16 bits per instruction). In contrast, a typical machine-language implementation would take about 10 bytes: a 3-byte branch-and-link instruction followed by a 2-byte argument A, followed by another 3-byte branch-and-link instruction and a 2-byte argument B.

On the average, the object code for each line of source code uses about 7 bytes, including instructions, data descriptions, variable storage, and literals. In contrast, typical mainframe versions of the Cobol language generate 25 to 35 bytes per source line.

Because of its compactness, the object program executes with much greater efficiency than do most pseudo-code technologies, such as the p-system that is currently in vogue. These approaches do not tailor their instruction sets to the tasks required and consequently suffer from poor execution speed.

One segment at a time

RM/Cobol's compactness, coupled with its segmentation feature, allows sophisticated and large application programs to run on personal computers. Segmentation aids in this endeavor because it permits portions of a program to be designated as nonresident in main memory until the moment they are executed. Once executed, a segment is replaced by the next nonresident segment needed. □

Local networks will multiply opportunities in the 1980s

As local-net concepts spring up, OEMs and chip makers will benefit if they can sort out all the possibilities

by Harvey J. Hindin, *Communications & Microwave Editor,* and Tom Manuel, *Computers & Peripherals Editor*

☐ Local networks will provide two boons for the data-communications industry in this decade, and it is difficult to say which is the more important. They will allow small businesses to reap the benefits of data-generating and -receiving machines that communicate with each other and with those at remote sites. For large companies, local nets will take some of the data processing and communications out of the central corporate facility and put them at the departmental level, where they will be tailored to specific needs.

Local networks will also have an impact on the factory. Manufacturing management-information systems will be able to be linked with automated production systems. Separate local networks for the major computerized activities of a business—production automation, manufacturing information systems, and office automation—can be linked with corporate data-processing systems to enhance the speed and accuracy of the flow of information among them. The individual local nets will be extended into hierarchical networks linking all the information resources within a business and also tying into public information nets.

These benefits mean new opportunities will open at a rapid rate for original-equipment manufacturers. Some of these OEMs have already gotten on the bandwagon with either the local network itself or transceivers and interface gear for data-generating and -receiving equipment. Others, less ambitious, are content to supply the needed coaxial cable and small computers that can operate either in a stand-alone or local-net mode.

A lot of work remains, however. For example, the opportunities for the chip manufacturer are great. The most obvious new chips will set up Ethernet networks—these are being designed by Intel and others. Nor are other local networks being ignored. For example, Datapoint has developed a special chip to interface gear to its Arcnet. But these two undertakings are only the beginning of the opportunities for chip makers.

Unlike the integrated circuits hooking up mainframes in the older architectures such as IBM's point-to-point, Systems Network Architecture, local-net chips need to work with a bus structure. Thus the kinds of data-communications controller, interface, and other such chips that are needed vary widely from those designed in the past. Today these requirements are met by medium-scale ICs. Tomorrow they will be met by one-chip large-scale ICs.

High entry costs mean that most of these chip requirements will probably be met by the traditional vendors. Yet, new suppliers might gain entry by designing a chip in conjunction with an equipment supplier who wants to make such an IC compatible with local networks.

Other opportunities abound in communications software. Thus IBM's already-announced 16-bit Personal Computer—if included in local networks much like the Apple 8-bit machines are included now—will need a lot of communication software. The same requirement holds for Tandy Corp.'s soon-to-be-announced 16-bit personal computer. Tandy has already set up its 8-bit TRS-80 model 2 machine to be compatible with Datapoint's Arcnet. The firm is sure to try to make similar local-net arrangements for its 16-bit machine if it is to compete with IBM and Apple and others in the office-automation markets.

Electronics/January 27, 1982

Many makers unloose a flood of local nets

This survey of the equipment available will orient the would-be network designer

by Kenneth J. Thurber and Harvey A. Freeman
Architecture Technology Corp., Minneapolis, Minn.

☐ Only four years ago just a gleam in a researcher's eye, today local computer networks are the up and coming technology in communications and are probably the fastest-growing segment of the computer industry. Over 100 companies now produce the hardware trappings for the local network, potentially one of the most pragmatic system concepts to emerge from a decade of thought on the subject of distributed processing.

The 1970s was the era of experimentation with distributed systems, which replace a mainframe computer and several terminals with multiple small computers. The 1980s will see their practical implementation in the form of the local network and its hierarchical system extensions. The concept is huge enough to dominate the marketplace in applications from office-automation to factory-management systems.

Though not precise, a workable definition of a local network is one where all the stations—computers, terminals, and other equipment (system nodes)—are located in a small geographic area—for example, within a radius of two miles. Typically, such a network is owned by a single organization and so tends to be more specialized than a widely scattered one. For example, the local

network may be installed on a single floor of an office building and form the basic hardware and software structure for an office-automation system. Alternatively, it may be the basic element of a factory-automation system that collects data, monitors plant security with television cameras, and at the same time manages the energy usage in the building.

Figure 1 illustrates a typical local network that is used for office automation, showing the variety of equipment it may contain. Single ownership means that functions may be specialized, but this individuality also implies that the system may have to interface with others that are most probably dissimilar.

The short distances involved mean that communication among devices on the network is limited to the designated local area, unless the system is also connected into a long-distance network. Studies have come up with the information that the communication among co-workers in a business environment occurs within a distance of 5 miles approximately 60% of the time and over distances of 500 or more miles less than 10% of the time. Thus the local restriction of the network would in most cases have little detrimental effect.

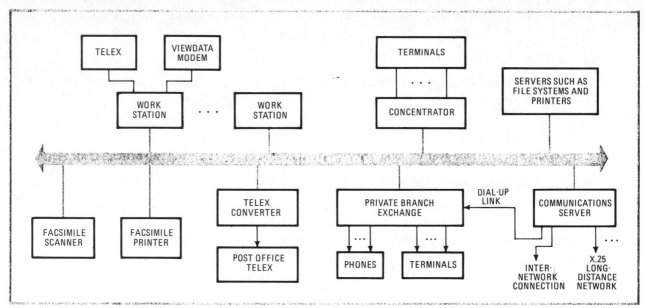

1. Hooking up the office. This could be a typical local network for an office of the future. The local-network bus connects a variety of office equipment. The PBX, communications server, and telex converter provide access to the world beyond the proprietay local net.

Usually, networks are implemented using packet switching. That mode of operation is ideal for the bursts of traffic that customarily occur in configurations with many terminals.

Local networks can be variously categorized. The definition developed thus far is by K. J. Thurber and H. A. Freeman[1]. There are other suggested definitions and readings. For instance, D. D. Clark gives a detailed overview of the subject and reviews a particular system[2]. A. Franck and P. C. Patton not only survey the subject, but also illustrate developments in the area of large-computer local networks[3].

The article by I. W. Cotton[4], like Thurber and Freeman's, is important because some researchers feel that the term local network necessarily implies a system such as Xerox Corp.'s Ethernet. Rebutting this, Cotton and Thurber and Freeman show more varieties than just this packet-switched local network—for example, networks built upon circuit switches (private branch exchange technology) and such concepts as input/output channels and computer bus structures.

With the strides being made in PBX technology and its capabilities for the integration of voice and data and the advances in large-scale integration and bus structures, the less esoteric technologies demand equal attention. PBX makers such as Datapoint, InteCom, Rolm, Mitel, Northern Telecom, IBM and Nixdorf in Europe, and others offer data communications along with voice

Stars of the constellation

The proliferation of local-network concepts is not letting up. Close to 120 companies are either building or about to embark on a project in this field and there is an impressive base of local-network systems already installed. For example, Datapoint Corp. of San Antonio, Texas, reportedly has over 15,000 installed bus interfaces in over 1,500 Arcnets worldwide.

In contrast, however, Sytek Inc. of Sunnyvale, Calif., has just recently begun to produce and deliver bus-interface hardware and has entered the emerging market for radio-frequency–based local networks with a product called LocalNet. Until recently, Sytek had concentrated on systems design—now it is actually building sophisticated products. Printer Terminal Communications Corp. of Ramona, Calif., provides a wireless local network known as Local Area Data Distribution (LADD).

Because of this wide range of companies and products, only a representative sample, as follows, will be used to illustrate baseband networks. In the baseband technique, digital pulses are put directly on the cable without a carrier frequency, whereas in broadband schemes, a high-frequency carrier is modulated.

There are three levels of baseband local-network systems, categorized by performance and hardware complexity: the low-performance area at less than a megabit per second, the midperformance range between 3 and 10 Mb/s, and the high-performance nets at 50 Mb/s. Examples in each of these performance ranges are: in the low-performance, low-cost range, the Nestar ClusterBus; in the mid-range, the Xerox Ethernet, the Network Systems Corp. Hyperbus, and the Ungermann-Bass Net/One; and in the high-performance range, the Network Systems Hyperchannel.

Again, the wide variety of equipment and the attendant design goals impede comparing local network systems in a meaningful way unless there is a specific design problem against which to trade them off. Subtle differences that are not obvious at first glance and that nonetheless can radically change the system capabilities prevent sweeping comparisons.

The Clusterbus from Nestar Systems Inc., Palo Alto, Calif. (Fig. 2), is known as the Cluster/One model A, and it provides the designer with the ability to physically connect up to 64 Apple II computers.

The ClusterBus is a baseband contention-channel design, with parallel transmission of bytes over a 16-wire cable at 240 kilobits per second. The key

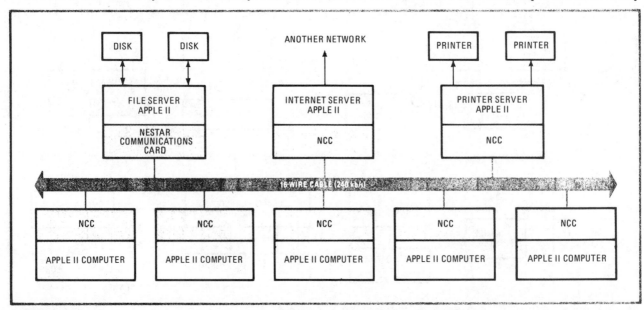

2. Bushels of Apples. The Nestar Cluster/One model A 240-kilobit-per-second local network connects as many as 64 Apple II computers together. It uses 16 parallel wires, either in a flat cable or as packaged, twisted pairs, transmitting data 1 byte at a time.

element of this system is an interface card that plugs into a peripheral slot on the Apple II—using the computer's power supply—which converts it from a stand-alone personal computer into a local-network work station.

Nestar sells a disk system designed to replace the floppy disks used on Apple II computers and to allow each Apple II station to work with the equivalent of 255 floppy disks. With the disk system the user receives a file server, and an electronic mail system is an option.

Corvus Systems Inc., San Jose, Calif., offers Omninet, a twisted-pair, 1-Mb/s baseband carrier-sense multiple-access (CSMA) network for the Apple personal computer, the Digital Equipment Corp. LSI-11, and, in the second quarter of this year, for the IBM Personal Computer, the Xerox 820, the Nippon Electric Co. PC-8000, the Commodore PET, the Zenith Z89, the TRS-80 models I and II, the Superbrain, and S-100 bus personal computers [*Electronics*, Aug. 25, 1981, p. 125]. Also, Tandy Corp., located in Fort Worth, Texas, is using Datapoint's Arc-net technology to offer local networks for its TRS-80 personal computer.

The Xerox Ethernet (Fig. 3) is a joint specification with Digital Equipment Corp., Maynard, Mass., and Intel Corp. of Santa Clara, Calif. It is a 10-Mb/s baseband CSMA network that specifies the two lowest levels of the International Standards Organization open systems interconnection reference model.

Ethernet is the backbone of Xerox's office-automation strategy. The company offers a low-cost license for it, 95 of which have been purchased in the U. S. and West Europe, with another 300 being negotiated. In December 1981, Xerox published its higher-level Network Systems protocols, which covers levels 4 through 6 of the ISO OSI reference model. Intel will be putting the Ethernet interface circuitry on a chip that is slated to be available sometime this year.

The Network Systems Hyperbus (Fig. 4) is a product planned by Network Systems Corp., Brooklyn Park, Minn., that is aimed at the midperformance range with its Bell System T2 speed of 6.312 Mb/s. The Hyperbus, sure to compete formidably with Ethernet, is designed to be compatible with multiple protocols including X. 25, IBM's Systems Network Architecture, and Synchronous Data Link Control, and to interface with RS-232-C channels and IBM 3270 and compatible terminals. Hyperbus uses a hierarchical addressing concept that will give it a substantial advantage over systems like Ethernet in hierarchical-network implementations. The system entered beta test at a site with 20 nodes in mid-1981 and is scheduled to be available for purchase in quantity by the middle of this year.

The Ungermann-Bass Net/One (Fig. 5), currently available, is also designed to compete in the mid-range. It performs at 10 Mb/s, is Ethernet-compatible, and is also targeted for the RS-232-C and IBM 3270 markets. Additionally, the system is specifically designed to evolve along with Ethernet and track its design changes as closely as possible. As it now stands, the system allows for the connection of up to 16 RS-232-C ports to an adaptor and has been widely installed.

Of particular interest is Net/One's installation at the U. S. Military Academy at West Point, which has Prime, Univac, and Terac equipment and a variety of terminals. A system model is being developed at West Point that will provide a tool for design of Net/One installations. Although the current product closely follows Ethernet, the design has been modularized to allow for alternative media and media-access techniques such as broadband and token rings.

In the high-performance area, the only available system of local-network components is the Network Systems Hyperchannel. Hyperchannel provides the user with the ability to connect to most of the popular mainframes, but it is complex and thus costly. An adaptor for the channel costs about $40,000, though with it the user can connect to four independent channel trunks.

The hardware technology exists—though it would hardly be cost-effective—to connect every terminal in

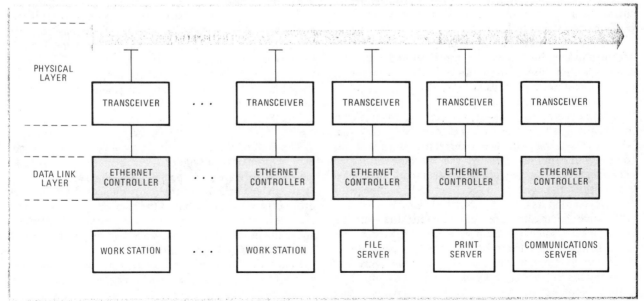

3. Ethereal. The Ethernet local network, developed by Xerox Corp. and supported jointly by Xerox, Intel Corp., and Digital Equipment Corp., forms the basis for Xerox's thrust into office automation. Ethernet specifies the protocols for the two lower layers of a layered architecture.

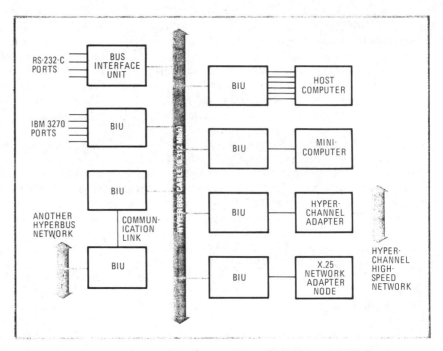

4. Variety. The Hyperbus local network now under test has been designed for compatibility with many existing protocols such as the international standard X. 25, RS-232-C, IBM Systems Network Architecture and 3270, and various minicomputer systems. The design embodies hierarchical addressing.

the world and, under some suitable performance constraint, find a clear pathway for their communication through many levels of networks of varying lengths.

Networks of networks

The future of network architecture is tending toward just such a hierarchy of networks, if on a smaller scale, and Fig. 6 shows a conceivable version. The concept is based on the premise that high volumes of communication are local and that communication among devices is inversely related to their distance apart. A hierarchy allows for economies of scale by limiting high-volume communications to the local level. With cost-effective devices that allow terminals to connect into the network, the local network can muster the aggregate capabilities that justify its connection to a larger, more capable system. Besides proving itself on a cost basis, the hierarchical configuration lines up with its user's structure, traffic patterns, and technology.

The system boasts other important benefits as well. In addition to simplifications in complexity and cost, subsystems within the hierarchy can be updated or changed with minimal material impact.

Local networks and hierarchical networks are ideas that developed by building on one another, an encouraging progression that generates the hope that future such innovative systems and their interrelationships will also come about. In fact, already, the movement to local networks and the emergence of personal computers have given rise to the concept of local networks composed of personal computers.

Personal computers are very capable and versatile devices, with some rather persuasive advantages over large systems. For example, the smaller computer is dedicated to an individual, so that the hardware and software can be custom-tailored to suit needs and capabilities. Nonetheless, there are cost problems with such devices—the personal-computer user may desire a letter-quality printer that not only is expensive but most proba-

bly will seldom be used by a single individual. Address space and on-line information storage are often limited.

The personal-computer network can resolve some of these problems. For example, the computers can share a printer and perhaps a large disk. In turn, if such features are provided from the network, then it may be possible to simplify the individual work stations. Clearly, the proper design and integration of a set of personal computers into the local-network configuration should allow advantageous use both of personal computers and of a large pool of expensive resources.

Such a system, from Nestar, has been applied in a number of dissimilar environments: schools, where it is used to transmit files to elementary-school children learning to program on Apple II computers (a highly rugged environment); in real-estate firms; and in diverse consulting houses.

An advocate of the local-network system for personal computers, Architecture Technology Corp. has designed a system using Nestar's hardware and software. It plans to develop the network over a period of time into a test-bed for internetworking, or linking, two or more networks and for interfacing equipment from different sources with the network.

Fighting through the maze

The field of local networks is growing so fast that the biggest problem a designer faces is matching a specific piece of hardware to a specific goal. The selection is not at all obvious because of the many choices. Further, very little software is available to the user off the shelf. There are a few standard drivers for some specific I/O systems and some other pieces of software, but as yet the designer must really design the entire system.

In addition to such technical selection issues there are a wide variety of political issues. For example, no standards exist. The Institute of Electrical and Electronics Engineers, however, is trying to rectify this situation with its IEEE standard 802, which today consists of a

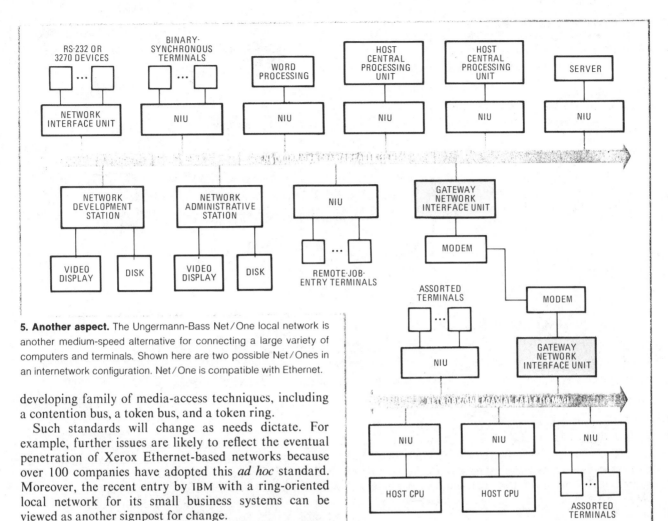

5. Another aspect. The Ungermann-Bass Net/One local network is another medium-speed alternative for connecting a large variety of computers and terminals. Shown here are two possible Net/Ones in an internetwork configuration. Net/One is compatible with Ethernet.

developing family of media-access techniques, including a contention bus, a token bus, and a token ring.

Such standards will change as needs dictate. For example, further issues are likely to reflect the eventual penetration of Xerox Ethernet-based networks because over 100 companies have adopted this *ad hoc* standard. Moreover, the recent entry by IBM with a ring-oriented local network for its small business systems can be viewed as another signpost for change.

With the explosion of concepts, just keeping track of the various vendors becomes a challenge. However, the problem is compounded in that computer, PBX, and office-equipment manufacturers and the communications companies all see the design of local communication systems as the key element in their entry into the potentially lucrative market for the office of the future. The state of the art is changing so fast that related information is outdated after six months.

However, some detailed fundamental questions remain unanswered—key design problems like choosing baseband versus broadband (rf) transmission; the effect of the backoff algorithm; the transaction vs file-transport nature of the systems; and the design of gateways.

Many local-network approaches make use of baseband-transmission schemes. Rf schemes have their proponents, because they promise to spare bandwidth by allowing multiple signals to be sent on a single available cable such as a cable TV system. A deterrent, though, is the relatively high cost of the rf modem, which bucks up the whole system's price.

Further, because the broadband network must be engineered as a total system, the initial installation and changes are expensive and difficult. Maintenance costs also are higher than those for baseband systems because the broadband type requires frequent balancing and the baseband, none. The Sytek system, though, proves that a cost-effective wideband system is in fact possible—one

of the Sytek interfaces is available for $1,000, about the same as a comparable Ethernet part.

Another broadband network—Wangnet—was recently announced by Wang Laboratories Inc. of Lowell, Mass. However, just as it is difficult to compare baseband equipments, their differing capabilities prevent a fair comparison of wideband networks. It is safe to say, though, that the rf and baseband technologies will both be viable for the near future.

When two or more stations try to transmit on the cable at the same time, a data collision occurs and none of the transmissions can be used. The stations must wait and try again later. There are a number of schemes by which each of the stations can determine its waiting time—since there is no controlling station in collision-detection networks of this type, all stations must decide when to make a second attempt and of necessity must not all try again at the same instant.

It is possible and even easy to design a backoff algorithm that is quite efficient for light to medium loads on the net. However, design of a good one for heavy loads can be quite difficult. Like any good system design, a local-network setup will address the complete spectrum of issues associated with the use of the system during those periods that are most heavily loaded.

As an example of a backoff algorithm, the Ethernet

6. Future link. A hierarchical network for the future might look something like this, if designed for the communication links required by an organization. Different communications technologies are used where they are most cost-effective.

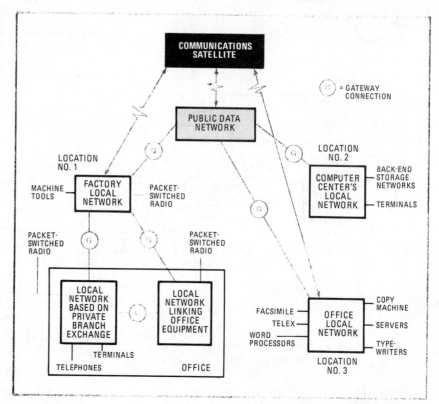

standard is one that appears to work well over a wide range of loads. The Ethernet backoff time is a random interval generated by a binary exponential algorithm. The interval is adjusted in proportion to the number of collisions that have occurred for the current transmission—as the number of collisions increases, so does each successive waiting time.

When a collision occurs, each station's Ethernet controller generates a new random retransmission interval based on the updated collision count. The retransmission intervals are multiples of what is called a slot, that is, the maximum time between starting a transmission and detecting a collision, or one end-to-end round trip on the cable. Each controller begins transmission of each new packet with a mean retransmission interval of one slot. In every instance when a transmission attempt ends in a collision, the controller waits for a random interval with a mean duration that is approximately twice that of the previous interval.

Many local-network products are designed for on-line terminals that produce a high volume of interactive traffic. But, once installed, the networks seem more suited for large-file traffic, and so manufacturers must consider designs that are transaction-oriented. The user should note when selecting a design that the cable used with the system can meet the required traffic loading.

Many players

Since systems are being designed by so many manufacturers, gateway devices will have to be provided to link one local network to other proprietary local and geographically distributed networks. Some of these systems can be quite complex, so the matter of gateways should be one of the early design considerations, to minimize design and manufacturing costs.

As the technology of local networks begins to stake a claim on the market, the concept is being embraced by the major mainframe and minicomputer companies. The office-equipment group led by Datapoint's four-year-old ARC (Attached Resource Computing) system and Xerox's Ethernet, along with the competitive products from Wang, Digital Equipment Corp., Prime, A. B. Dick, and others, is fast becoming a battleground for the medium-performance local-network system. The entry of independent manufacturers such as Nestar, Corvus, 3COM Corp., the Destek Group, SDSystems, and Interlan Inc. is both enriching and heating up the competition, no doubt spurring the technology's advance.

Because of the meteoric growth in local networks—from $100 million in 1981 to possibly over $5 billion in 1991—the market will not thin out for yet some time. The current demand and the potential market size dictate that there can be unabated growth for two to three more years before the initial shakeout.

The comers of this burgeoning technology are the network hierarchies with local networks as the cornerstone. The emergence of practical systems with the integration of satellites, microwaves, and other long-haul mechanisms into interconnected local networks will cause the expansion of the technology to increase at a far faster rate than the original researchers envisioned. □

References
1. K. J. Thurber and H. A. Freeman, "Architecture Considerations for Local Computer Networks," Proceedings of the First Annual Conference on Distributed Computing Systems, IEEE Computer Society, October 1979, pp. 131–142.
2. D. D. Clark, et al., "An Introduction to Local Area Networks," Proceedings of the IEEE, November 1978, pp. 1,497–1,517.
3. A. Franck and P. C. Patton, "Some Architectural and System Implications of Local Computer Networks," Digest of Papers, Compcon 79 Spring, IEEE Computer Society, February 1979, pp. 272–276D.
4. I. W. Cotton, "Technologies for Local Area Computer Networks," Proceedings of the LACN Symposium, May 1979, National Bureau of Standards Publication (ed. R. Rosenthal and N. B. Meisner), pp. 25–45.

Electronics / January 27, 1982

Microcomputer software meshes with local nets

CP/M-based line of operating systems expands to meet needs of varied local-network configurations

by Thomas A. Rolander, *Digital Research Inc., Pacific Grove, Calif.*

☐ Microcomputer operating systems are expanding in power and capabilities, just like the hardware they control. From their inception in modestly endowed single-user environments, this software has grown to serve a cluster of users sharing an inexpensive microcomputer and the expensive peripherals that can hang on it. The next step was an operating system for a network of microcomputers that shares memory resources and other peripherals, and beyond that are variants that run other network configurations.

A prime example of the growth of these operating systems is the family offered by Digital Research. It includes the single-user CP/M, which stands for control program for a microcomputer. There are currently more than 200,000 microcomputers using CP/M in over 3,000 different hardware configurations. More than 400 original-equipment manufacturers are using CP/M-based operating systems.

The next step in the evolution of these operating systems was to develop MP/M, a CP/M-compatible multiprogramming monitor. It enables multiple users to share expensive peripherals, as well as allowing each user to perform more than one task simultaneously, such as editing, compiling, and printing. However, MP/M does require a communal central processing unit. Thus the next evolutionary step is CP/NET, which stands for a control program for a network. It combines single-user slaves executing CP/M with masters executing MP/M to manage the shared resources.

The entire family of operating systems from Digital Research is portable—each system is divided into an invariant portion that is the same in every application and a variant portion that is customized by the user. The invariant part is sometimes called the logical portion because it maps the data structures onto an arbitrary disk, console, and printer. The variant part is often labeled the

physical portion because it contains the device drivers for each configuration.

CP/M is a monitor and control program for microcomputer systems, providing a general environment for program construction, storage, editing, assembly or compilation, program debugging, and application-program execution. An important feature is that it can be easily altered to execute on nearly any 8080, 8085, Z80, or 8086 or 8088 microcomputer configuration. As a single-user operating system, CP/M is quite small and fast and requires very little overhead.

Four parts

There are four parts to the CP/M configuration (Fig. 1). The invariant portion is called the BDOS, for basic disk operating system, and the variant portion is called BIOS, for basic input/output system.

The BDOS has a single entry point at absolute memory location 0005_{16}, which provides application programs access to a number of system functions including console, printer, and disk operations (see Table 1). It should be noted that the disk read and write operations are particularly simple because they operate on fixed-length, 128-byte sectors on up to 16 disk drives, each of which may hold 8 megabytes with an independent file directory on each drive. Examples of such mass storage devices are minifloppies, single- or double-density floppies, and hard disks.

The BDOS implements disk-allocation strategies that provide fully dynamic file construction while eliminating the possibility of lost and doubly allocated blocks. Thus files do not require space to be preallocated to them, and they can be extended at program-execution time to contain any number of records, up to the size of any single disk.

The BIOS portion provides the primitive operations necessary for access to the actual console, printer, and disk drives resident on a

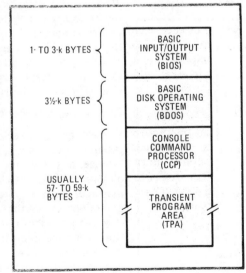

1. Memory configuration. In CP/M, the BIOS portion contains the code that is hardware-specific, BDOS has the disk routines common to all CP/M systems, the CCP communicates with users' terminals, and the TPA holds users' programs.

In the figure:
- 1- to 3-k BYTES — BASIC INPUT/OUTPUT SYSTEM (BIOS)
- 3½-k BYTES — BASIC DISK OPERATING SYSTEM (BDOS)
- USUALLY 57- TO 59-k BYTES — CONSOLE COMMAND PROCESSOR (CCP) / TRANSIENT PROGRAM AREA (TPA)

TABLE 1: CP/M OPERATING-SYSTEM COMMANDS	
Command	Description
Search	look for a particular disk file by name
Open	open a file for further operations
Close	close a file after processing
Make	make the specified new file
Delete	remove the specified file and free the disk space
Rename	change the name of a particular file
Read	read a record from a particular file, sequential or random
Write	write a record to a particular file, sequential or random

TABLE 2: MP/M ADDITIONAL FACILITIES
multiterminal support
multiprogramming at each terminal
support for bank-switched memory and memory protection among banks
concurrency of input/output and processor operations
interprocess communication, mutual exclusion, and synchronization
ability to operate in sequential, polled, or interrupt-driven environments
system timing functions, including the time of day
logical-interrupt system utilizing event flags
selection of system options at system generation time
dynamic system configuration at load time
spooling list files to the printer
scheduling programs to be run by data and time

particular system. The interface with BIOS is provided through jump vectors, located at its beginning address, which identify a sequence of 17 subroutines. CP/M can be customized for any particular hardware environment by replacing this BIOS portion.

The third part of CP/M, the console command processor, provides the user interface between the console and the operating system. The CCP reads from the console and processes commands. Some of these commands are termed built-in, because they are a part of the CCP program. Other commands, called transient, specify programs to be loaded from disk and executed, such as editing and debugging routines.

The last segment of CP/M is called the transient program area. The TPA holds programs that are loaded from the disk and executed by the CCP. During program editing, for example, it holds the machine code for a text editor and the data areas. Similarly, programs created under CP/M can be debugged and executed by loading and running them in the TPA.

The MP/M operating system is an upward-compatible version of CP/M with a number of added facilities. Compatibility was essential in order to let the large existing base of CP/M software run with little or no modification.

From the perspective of the user, MP/M is simply a

multitasking CP/M system. It contains a priority-driven real-time multitasking nucleus that provides process-dispatching, memory-management, and system-timing functions. In general, these added facilities (Table 2) are transparent to the user, though a number of system functions have been added.

The BDOS used by MP/M has been taken directly from CP/M and is executed as a serially reusable resource through a mutual-exclusion queue that controls access to the code. This approach achieves two goals. First, the corresponding disk drivers can be taken directly from CP/M, requiring modification of only the busy-wait loop for I/O completion. Second, simplicity and size advantages were gained by avoiding a reentrant disk-file system. In fact, MP/M is comparable in size to several other single-user microcomputer operating systems.

To BDOS, the MP/M configuration adds two parts (Fig. 2): XDOS, for extended disk-operating system; and XIOS, for extended I/O system. The XDOS contains the MP/M real-time nucleus for multitasking. The nucleus contains the process dispatcher, queue management, flag management, memory management, terminal handler, command line interpreter, and time-base management routines. The system calls are summarized in Table 3.

Queue management

XDOS provides several essential functions in a multitasking environment, notably queue management. In essence, a queue is a memory-resident first-in, first-out disk file. Queues can be used for the communication of messages between processes, to synchronize processes, and to provide mutual exclusion.

MP/M simplifies queue management for both application programs and system processes by treating queues in a manner similar to disk files. Queues can be created, opened, written to, read from, and deleted.

The command-line interpreter, contained in XDOS, processes commands passed from the console. The CLI reads the header record of the program to be executed, determines the program size, loads and relocates the program into the best-fitting memory segment, and then

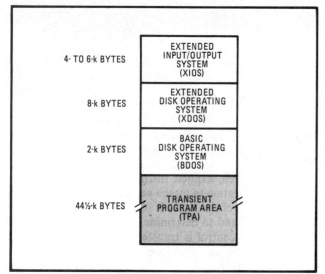

2. Multitasking configurations. The MP/M multitasking operating system adds to the CP/M memory-space configuration XDOS, which contains the real-time nucleus. It also extends the BIOS basic input/output system, renaming it XIOS, for extended I/O system.

TABLE 3: MP/M ADDITIONAL SYSTEM SUBROUTINES	
Name	Description
Rel—mem—rqst	relocatable memory request
Poll	poll specified device
Flag—wait	wait until specified flag is set
Flag—set	set specified flag
Make—queue	make the specified queue
Open—queue	open a queue for further operations
Read—queue	unconditionally read a message from a queue
Cread—queue	conditionally read a message from a queue
Write—queue	unconditionally write a message to a queue
Cwrite—queue	conditionally write a message to a queue
Delay	delay for a specified amount of time
Term—process	terminate a process
Create—process	create a process
Set—prior	set process priority
Attach—cns	attach console
Detach—cns	detach console

creates a process to execute the program. The XIOS part provides the primitive operations necessary to access multiple consoles, printers, and disk drives. Also, it performs device-polling, interrupt-handling, and memory-management functions that support bank-switched memory. The interface with the XIOS is provided through jump vectors, beginning with 17 jump instructions identical to those in the CP/M BIOS and continues with eight more jump instructions. MP/M can be customized for any particular hardware environment by replacing the XIOS portion.

Although MP/M achieves the goals of multitasking and

MP/M-86 aims at commercial use

MP/M-86, the version of MP/M developed for the 8086 and 8088 microprocessors, was designed by a Unix buff, Frank Holsworth, who used his experience with that Bell Laboratories-originated operating system to design his own. He believes that MP/M-86 is "safer and more convenient to use in business environments, since the files are not linked together—avoiding greater information losses during system crashes—and the user interface is friendlier to nonprogrammers."

Unlike Unix, MP/M-86 is built around a shared file system, which features file and record lock-out to enable concurrent access of a common data base by multiple programs. The file system also includes features such as password protection at the file level. This protection gives selected users the ability to modify sensitive data while a broader class of users can only read it. With archive flags and times of last modification and last access included in the file system, incremental backups are easily accomplished in this operating system using standard utilities.

Like Unix, MP/M-86 has a multitasking environment that allows a single user to run more than one program at a time. This feature has been improved to allow a user to start a program, let it run for a while, and at any time, place it into the background. The appearance of a prompt then allows a subsequent command to be typed.

of sharing expensive peripherals, it also shares the CPU resource. CP/NET allows the sharing of expensive peripherals, as in a multiuser system, while maintaining the advantages of an unshared CPU.

Thus CP/NET allows separate microcomputers to share and transfer disk files, to share printers and consoles, and to share programs and data bases. It consists of microcomputer masters running MP/M and slaves running CP/M. The masters are hosts managing the communal resources that can be accessed by the network slaves.

The design approach of separate I/O modules has been carried through to CP/NET. It is network-independent: all network-dependent code for the slaves has been placed in the slave network I/O system (SNIOS), and all network-dependent code for the master has been placed in the network interface process (NETWRKIF) module. Logical messages that are passed to and from SNIOS or NETWRKIF are transmitted over the network between masters and slaves using an arbitrary network protocol.

CP/NET configurations

Figure 3 illustrates possible CP/NET configurations. The interprocessor message format permits multiple CP/NET masters so that, if the hardware capability exists, more than one master can be present in a net.

The slave portion of CP/NET is divided into two modules: SNIOS and the network disk-operating system (NDOS). The hardware-dependent SNIOS defines the low-level interface to the NDOS that is necessary for network I/O. Although a standard SNIOS is supplied by Digital Research, explicit instructions are provided for field reconfiguration to match nearly any network.

The purpose of the NDOS is to intercept all CP/M BDOS function calls and to determine if the operation is local, in which case control is transferred to the BDOS. If the operation is to be done on the network, the NDOS forms the appropriate logical message and sends it to the master via SNIOS.

The simple message format used by CP/NET for processor communication includes some packaging overhead plus the actual message itself (Fig. 4). The packag-

3. Network configurations. CP/NET can be set up to support the star (a), the ring (b), or other configurations, the only difference being the manner in which messages are transported. Any hardware network media will work with CP/NET.

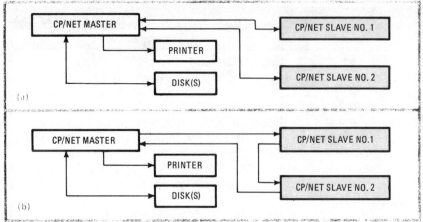

4. Message format. Messages are sent around a CP/NET system using a fixed header format followed by a message of variable length that can be either data or commands or a mixture of both. The header defines the message's destination as well as its contents.

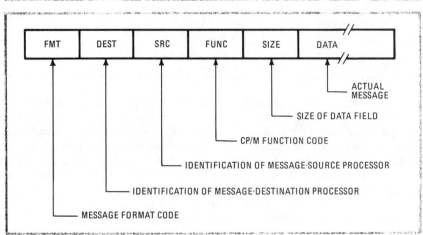

ing overhead consists of a message-format code, a CP/NET destination address, a CP/NET source address, a CP/M function code, and a message size.

The message format does not contain a cyclic redundancy code or any other error checking as a part of the packaging overhead. The user-written SNIOS can add the error checking when it actually places the message onto the network and then test it when a message is received from the network. This function is intentionally left to the user, avoiding redundant error checking where standard interface protocols, both in software and hardware, may already provide error checking.

The network interface processes, part of the user-written NETWRKIF module, perform the actual I/O for the CP/NET master. Typically there is one network interface process per slave that is supported by the master.

Queues are used to pass messages between the interface processes and the slave-support processes. The slave-support processes are provided for the CP/NET master in the form of a resident system process.

In CP/NET, the MP/M master manages resources that are considered public to the network. On the other hand, the slaves executing CP/M have both access to the public resources of the master and their own local resources that cannot be accessed from the network.

This choice of architecture guarantees the security of the resources of the slave while still permitting resources of the master to be shared among the slaves. The distinction between masters and slaves is also based on the ability of the MP/M masters to respond to the network

asynchronously in real time, whereas the CP/M slaves perform sequential I/O and are not capable of monitoring a network interface in real time.

CP/NET is the first of a family of network operating system products from Digital Research. The second is named CP/NOS and is intended for applications in which the slave microcomputer has no disk resources and is therefore unable to run CP/M.

Extensions to the family

CP/NOS consists of a bootstrap loader, which can be placed into a read-only memory or programmable ROM. It is a skeletal CP/M containing only the console- and printer-interface functions, and the logical and physical portions of the CP/NET slave. At the user level, CP/NOS provides a virtual CP/M system to the slave.

A slave microcomputer could consist of simply a processor, memory, and an interface to the network. Thus, a cathode-ray-tube display with sufficient random-access memory could execute CP/M programs, performing its computing locally while depending on the network to provide all disk, printer, and other I/O facilities.

A third network operating system, called MP/NET, provides the capability for MP/M systems to share each other's resources on the network. With MP/NET, there is no distinction between a master and a slave because all the nodes on a MP/NET can manage shared resources, as well as initiate network messages. Thus MP/NET provides a symmetrical network where all the nodes have equal opportunity. □

Electronics/September 8, 1982

Token-passing protocol boosts throughput in local networks

Explicit handoffs from one node to another end contention; refinements to control procedures add operational efficiency

by John A. Murphy, *Datapoint Corp., San Antonio, Texas*

☐ As competing protocol proposals for local networks jockey for position in the lengthy proceedings of standards committees, one local-net concept that dates to the mid 1970s is out in front in the marketplace. The Arcnet networking protocol used with the ARC multiuser system is found in more than 4,000 installations worldwide.

The protocol can take much of the credit for this popularity. Arcnet combines the advantages of token-passing network control, highly refined by years of development, with those of a baseband communications system. What's more, implementation is considerably eased because Arcnet includes automatic configuration and transmission procedures that unburden the host system.

Local nets and the distributed processing architectures they serve ideally couple resource sharing and functional stability so that the loss or addition of a node can occur with no noticeable interruptions of service to other nodes. Arcnet (Fig. 1) settles comfortably into this design through the use of a contention-free token-passing protocol that guarantees network access to each processor within a known time period.

Each node has an opportunity to send data, and then it explicitly passes control of the net to another node. Because this pass-along is always to a designated node, there is no competition for control of the network. Also, considerable safeguards against error conditions ward off a breakdown of the pass-along scheme.

End to guesses

Thus Arcnet eliminates the guessing game that system designers play through computer simulations of protocols such as carrier-sense multiple-access to determine expected access time. CSMA and its derivatives such as CSMA-CD (CSMA with collision detection added) need to listen to the broadcast line first before trying to send. In busy systems, two or more nodes can find the line clear, but when they send, their data packets collide.

The traffic jam becomes more common as the distance between nodes increases, because cable delays between nodes make it more difficult to determine if the cable is really free. The added sophistication of CSMA-CD allows

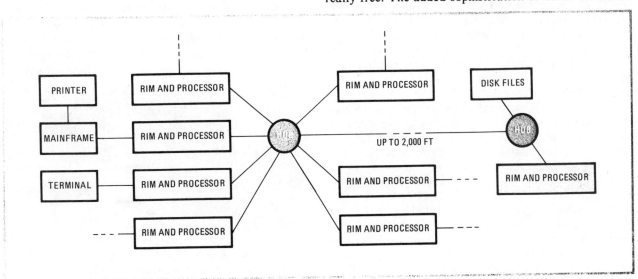

1. Free form. Arcnet allows any arbitrary topology as long as no loops are formed, no resource interface module is farther than 31-microseconds (about four miles) from any other interface module, and cabling between hubs does not exceed 2,000 ft.

327

a node to try again if packets have collided in transmission. Still, each node is required to compete for the control of the broadcast line, so contention on the line eventually becomes so great that data throughput actually decreases under heavy loading conditions.

With token passing, on the other hand, each node is successively allowed—or, more significantly, guaranteed—its turn at exclusive control of the cable. This total lack of contention between nodes ensures that efficiency is always high—the actual throughput rate of the system depends on the configuration of the system, such as the number of nodes in the local network.

Ever since its inception in 1976, Arcnet has been built around the notion of a resource interface module (Fig. 2) that contains considerable intelligence to manage the sharing of resources efficiently. Based on a microprogrammed controller, the interface module centralizes all the Arcnet protocol control firmware in a single n-channel MOS circuit (Fig. 3). The additional memory, interface circuitry, and bus structure complete the functional architecture of this key component.

Although the first breadboard interface modules used the CSMA scheme, the design soon adopted the token-passing protocol, in which each node is assigned a unique address. Only one unit can be considered master of the network at any given moment. Once in control of the network, the master sends out what traffic it has waiting for transmission.

Once its traffic was transmitted, it passed control to a new master by sending a special control packet—a token—to the node with the next sequential address. If it then heard no activity during the time required for a signal to make a round trip through the system, the master would try to pass control to the node with the next higher address. However, if the master detected any activity on the line, such as the start of a data packet from another node, polling, or even an attempt by a new node to join the system, it relinquished control.

Network stars

As a token-passing scheme, the initial implementation of Arcnet was similar to BRAM, the broadcast-recognizing access method, which has been promoted as an alternative to CSMA. However, Arcnet's scheme is active—each node is explicitly polled—whereas BRAM uses a passive scheme for scheduling—each node counts off a particular time interval from the time it last detected traffic.

In a large, high-speed system where the time to pass the token from one node to the next is much less than the round-trip propagation time of the system, Arcnet spends proportionately less time passing control. Using the BRAM protocol, the proportion of time spent passing control grows with the system, because the maximum round-trip propagation delay of the network is included in the particular countdown value used by each node. With no such configuration-dependent delays, Arcnet takes only the time needed to send a short message to the next node in the network.

Furthermore, it imposes less severe requirements on clock accuracy and stability. BRAM clocks must stay in synchrony for a period of time on the order of the

maximum propagation delay times the maximum number of nodes. Arcnet clocks need to stay in synchrony only for the duration of the maximum propagation delay.

If traffic is very light, BRAM networks see no activity for long periods of time, whereas Arcnet exhibits a regular and predictable pattern of transmissions. Although this may seem to be a dubious advantage for Arcnet, the regular and predictable activity aids rapid configuration of the network when a node enters or leaves the system.

Optimizing the protocol

Several additions to the protocol optimized Arcnet, completing its evolution to its present form. Rather than simply sending control to the next address in the system, the polling method was modified so each node remembers the address of the node to which it last passed control. Consequently, the network maintains a list dispersed throughout the system of all the active nodes. Since no time is spent waiting for responses from unused nodes, this refinement greatly speeds polling.

Excluding broadcasts, all transmissions on the network must be acknowledged by the receiving node. A further important improvement in the Arcnet architecture moved this acknowledgment function from the jurisdiction of the host processor into the firmware of the interface module.

Completing the evolution of the protocol, a packet called the free-buffer enquiry eliminates loss of data packets when a node transmits before the recipient has time to allocate buffer space. Such a problem can easily occur in a large network where a major flow of traffic goes between many users and few servers, such as disks and printers. Now, before attempting to transmit data, a node sends a free-buffer enquiry to verify that there is room in the receiving node's buffer. If the receiving node signals a lack of space, the transmitting node simply passes control to the next designated node, trying the transmission again the next time it becomes master.

In both Arcnet and BRAM-based systems, the ratio of throughput to overhead increases as the traffic on the network increases. Whether the only traffic is the token (0% utilization) or all nodes transmitting data upon becoming master (100% utilization), the time required to pass a token remains constant. This characteristic

2. Connections. Hooking into Arcnet through a Datapoint processor (on the right) becomes a simple operation through the use of the resource interface module (on the left). In later models, a single chip replaces most of the RIM circuitry and fits within the processor.

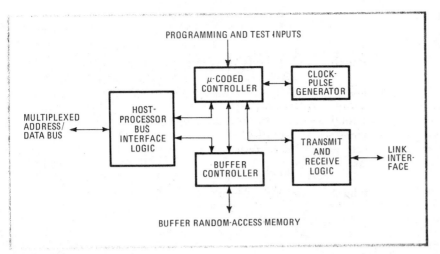

3. RIM chip. All the control firmware for the Arcnet link protocol resides in a single n-channel MOS circuit, the resource interface module (shaded area). Additional memory and interface circuitry is all that are needed to hook into an Arcnet.

explains Arcnet's high efficiency, unlike CSMA systems' decline after some optimal value.

Providing that the rules of the protocol itself can be met, Arcnet imposes few restrictions on the transmission medium. The architecture is limited, however, by a few constraints. For one, only a single path may connect any two nodes to ensure that a message arrives at a node only once. Also, the time for a signal to pass between any two nodes must not exceed 31 microseconds. Within these relatively minor limitations, token-passing protocols such as Arcnet may be implemented using any number of communications facilities, including broadband and baseband coaxial cable systems.

In a broadband cable system, a number of different communications services are frequency-multiplexed through the cable and associated amplifiers. Thus several totally independent Arcnet systems might share the line with a number of unrelated communications services, such as low-speed terminal connections, voice traffic, and even video transmissions.

All communications services in a broadband system pass through a central point called a headend. Since the services transmit and receive on different frequencies, the headend is the site where a transmitted signal is detected and retransmitted on the receive frequency associated with that communications service.

This capability to combine a number of different services on the same cable is an extremely attractive feature of broadband systems. However, the complexity and high cost of the components—including transmitters and receivers, bidirectional line amplifiers, and the headend equipment—is a serious drawback. Laying out the cable itself is a critical phase in developing a broadband system. All of the taps that will ever be required in a given run of cable must be present when the system is first installed.

Simplicity and low cost are advantages of a baseband system, which uses a single base frequency for all communications but essentially accommodates only one service. Furthermore, in a contention-free baseband system such as Arcnet, the amplifiers need not be bidirectional because only a single node is transmitting at a time. In fact, the amps are generally signal regenerators because the only signal that will be transmitted is a stream of data bits. Thus they actually improve signal quality—

unlike more general-purpose amps in broadband systems, which inevitably degrade it.

Both baseband and broadband systems suffer a common disability: tapping the line can introduce spurious signals on the line due to reflections at the tap. Reflections are the echoes that bounce back when a signal hits an impedance mismatch in a cable.

These mismatches are electrical rough edges that exist anywhere a tap is connected to the cable. Because the reflections from a number of different taps can accumulate and eventually overpower the real signal, the quality of the connections can limit the number of nodes tapped into the bus.

Differing solutions

In most broadband systems, the solution is a directional coupler that passes signals along from the headend, but heavily attenuates those (reflected) waveforms moving on the transmission frequency toward the headend. Arcnet found its own solution, however.

That problem, as well as some fault isolation and routing problems, is circumvented by using a central hub connecting with several nodes through a length of coaxial cable. The cable itself is carefully terminated at each end. This termination and the lack of any intermediate taps results in signals with no reflections.

The only point of connection for a node with the Arcnet is through the hub—effectively an amplifier with a number of ideal taps all contained in the same box. These taps are ideal in the sense that they have no insertion loss and no tap loss, yet suppress reflections even from unterminated lines. Thus any one of the ports of a hub may be connected to an Arcnet node, to another hub, to an unterminated length of coaxial cable, or even to nothing at all.

Each port of a hub consists of a line driver and receiver identical with those in the resource interface module. In its idle state, the hub enables all the receivers until one begins receiving a transmission. At that point, the hub disables all other receivers and feeds the transmission from the active port to the transmitters driving all the other ports. To provide protection against reflections from unterminated lines, the hub does not return to the idle state until any possible reflections cease—about 4.9 μs for 2,000 feet of RG62 coaxial cable.

4. Formats. Preceeding any one of the five possible messages on an Arcnet network is an alert burst composed of six unit intervals of mark. The remaining characters are transmitted using an 11-bit unit—two marks, a space, and the 8-bit character.

KEY:

ALERT BURST = 6 UNIT-INTERVALS OF MARK	SOH = ASCII START OF HEADER
EOT = ASCII END-OF-TRANSMISSION CHARACTER	COUNT = NUMBER OF DATA BYTES IN PACKET
DID = DESTINATION IDENTIFICATION	CRC = CYCLIC REDUNDANCY CHECK
SID = SOURCE IDENTIFICATION	ACK = ASCII ACKNOWLEDGE
ENQ = ASCII ENQUIRY	NAK = ASCII NEGATIVE ACKNOWLEDGMENT

Centralizing the location of the cable taps in a dispersed computing system may seem counter-productive at first glance. But after due reflection, the advantages emerge. Both initial and supplemental cabling within a site are simplified, because cables may be distributed from centralized tap locations with no need to consider any critical spacings such as required by the cable-tap hardware.

Only the cables themselves need be installed behind walls or ceilings. Extra cables may be laid for future expansion or for purposes of equipment mobility without adding the cost of unnecessary taps. In fact, since telephone systems tend to use the same topology, Arcnet cables may be routed through those existing raceways and conduits.

The standard Arcnet interface is to a baseband system using low-capacitance RG62 coaxial cable. The data is transmitted as a stream of bits using a unique coding scheme. A mark is coded as a 200-nanosecond bipolar pulse—positive for the first 100 ns immediately followed by an identically shaped 100-ns negative pulse.

Symbols built out of combinations of these bipolar pulses and spaces, then, can be transmitted with little residual charge buildup—as with monopolar pulses—resulting in a system with virtually no intersymbol interference. Transformer couplings to isolate cable sections and matched filters to capture the mark pulse further improve the reliability of the network.

Rules of the game

Arcnet's physical elements fit within the constraints of the net's electrical functions and limitations, such as reflections. Yet the definition of Arcnet combines this physical framework with a fixed set of operating principles that totally defines the performance of the network from its logical recognition of a new node down to the format of an individual piece of data. Thus the system designer starts his or her work with a welcome handful of well-defined rules.

The working unit of information in this serial asynchronous system is an 11-bit word transmitted at a 2.5-megabit-per-second rate. As in most communications systems, Arcnet imposes a limit on the maximum propagation delay through the system. No two nodes may be more than 31 μs apart. Taking into account the transmission medium and intervening electronics, this 31 μs translates into a distance on the order of four miles.

Idling in a spacing or no-signal condition, the bus becomes active with an alert burst—six unit intervals of mark (signal)—that introduces each of the five possible transmissions (Fig. 4). Each 8-bit character in the rest of the transmission is then preceded by two unit intervals of mark and one of space, thereby completing the 11-bit working unit.

In any case, the receiver must validate all incoming transmissions through a series of checks:
- Each character must be preceded by at least one mark and exactly one space.
- The character following the alert burst must be one of five particular control characters.
- If the transmission is a data packet, the cyclic redundancy check must succeed.
- The transmission must contain the correct number of characters, as delineated in Fig. 4 (1, 3, or 8 to 260).
- Finally, at least nine spaces must follow the last character.

In Arcnet's token-passing scheme, the address or identification assigned to each node or resource interface module in a system is a critical aspect. For each node, this identification is a unique value from 1 through 255; ID 0 is reserved to indicate a system-wide broadcast to all active nodes.

The key to smooth system operation is the continual passage of the token around the system. Each node must pass it to the node with the next higher ID (NID) in the system. A node receives the token when it has accepted an invitation-to-transmit message that contains its own ID. The receiving node then becomes master, sends a data packet if necessary, then sends an invitation to transmit to the node whose address is NID—a value determined during system reconfiguration and stored in the node sending the invitation to transmit.

System reconfiguration is signaled whenever the line has been idle for 78 μs—ordinarily the maximum delay between transmissions. Whenever any node detects that the line has been idle for 78 μs, it recognizes that system reconfiguration has begun. After first resetting the NID value in its storage register to its own ID, the node starts a timeout clock equal to 146 μs times the quantity 255 minus its own ID. When this time-out period expires with no line activity, the node sends an invitation-to-transmit message to the node with the next higher identification. This time-out expires first for the node with the highest ID in the system, so it is the originator of the token.

Checking for response

After sending an invitation to transmit, this node listens for a free-buffer enquiry, a data packet, or an invitation to transmit. If it detects no activity after 74 μs, it increments the value of NID and tries again. On the other hand, if it hears any activity before the 74 μs elapses, it releases control of the line.

In this way, invitations to transmit will be sent to all possible IDs during system reconfiguration. A node passing the token, however, will have saved as the NID value the address of the node that actually assumed control in response to the former's invitation.

System reconfiguration will occur only when a new node is brought on line or an active node misses the token due to line errors. Thus, during normal operation, control is passed directly from node to node without wasting time sending invitations to IDs of nodes that have been turned off or disconnected. The time that is required for system reconfiguration is a function of the number of nodes in the system and the highest ID among them, typically falling between 24 and 61 milliseconds.

In a decentralized network like Arcnet, a node that desires to join is obliged to initiate system reconfiguration on its own. The best way to do this is for the new node to destroy the token. This action causes the current master to release control and the intended new master to pass up its chance at assuming control. When a node is first powered up or if it has not received the token after approximately 840 ms, it transmits a reconfigure burst—756 repetitions of eight marks and one space.

This signal destroys the circulating token, terminating all activity on the line. That is, this burst is longer than any other type of transmission and will interfere with the next invitation to transmit, thereby preventing the next node from recognizing the invitation, accepting the token, and assuming control of the line. Similarly, the line activity from this signal causes the node that is trying to pass the token to release control of the line. Thus, the node in control relinquishes it, and no other node picks it up. The token has been destroyed, initiating a system reconfiguration.

Sizing down

Removing a node, on the other hand, does not require a system-reconfiguration cycle. When the node that had been trying to pass the token finds that there is no response from the deactivated node, it will simply increment the NID value and send another invitation. Just as in system reconfiguration, this sequence ends when the token is passed to the next active node—that is, to the NID of the removed node.

An Arcnet node is physically connected to a processor and logically connected to the network through a status register, a command register, and some number of 256-byte memory buffers. Unaware of any of the details of token passing, the processor need only be concerned with transmitting and receiving messages.

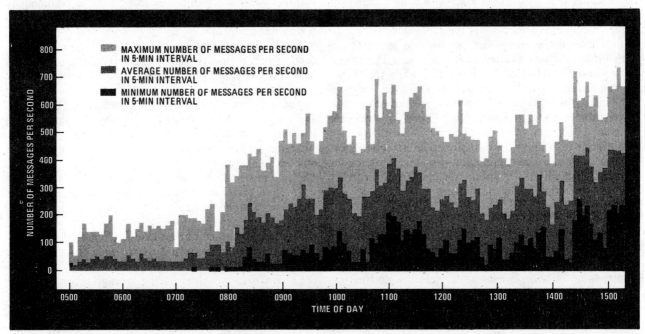

5. Performance. In an actual Arcnet installation with about 175 nodes active at any time, the message traffic is unimpeded, running along at over 400 messages per second during peak hours, with about the same token-trip time as the no-traffic value.

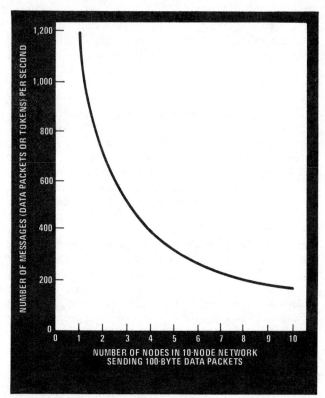

6. Throughput. In a theoretical network of 10 nodes, message throughput rates remain high. Even when all nodes are sending 100-byte data packets followed by a token pass, Arcnet's token-passing protocol guarantees that each node gets to send traffic.

To transmit a message, the processor writes the ID of the destination node, the number of characters in the data packet, and the data packet itself into one of the buffers. Once these housekeeping functions are performed, the processor simply commands the interface module to transmit the contents of the buffer. By convention, the first byte of the data is a code identifying the source system, useful when systems with entirely independent data formats share the same network.

Two bits in the status register provide the network with information on the transmit operation. The transmitter-available (TA) bit becomes false when the transmit command is given and returns to true when the node has finished its transmit sequence. At this time, the transmitted message acknowledged (TMA) bit indicates whether the destination node acknowledged the packet.

To receive a message, the processor issues a command to enable reception into a particular buffer. (A separate bit enables reception of broadcasts into the node.) Another status bit, receiver inhibited (RI), becomes false when the receive command is given and does not return to true until a packet has been received.

When a node receives the token, it checks to see whether it has a packet to send—whether TA is false. If TA is true, the node simply passes the token to the node whose value is NID. Otherwise it tests the destination identifier (DID) in the transmit buffer.

If this identifier is 000, the packet is a broadcast and is sent with no further action. If the DID code is not 000, the node sends a free-buffer enquiry to the destination node and waits the usual 74 μs for a response. If the

response is an acknowledgment, the node sends the packet; otherwise it passes the token to the node whose value is NID and waits for its turn to retry the free-buffer enquiry. If the node receives neither an acknowledgment nor a negative acknowledgment—that is, the 74-μs time-out expires—it sets TA and passes the token.

After sending a packet, the node again waits up to 74 μs for a response. If it receives an acknowledgment, the node first sets the TMA status bit and then TA and passes the token along. If it times out waiting for an acknowledgment (packets never go unacknowledged), the node simply sets TA and passes the token.

Careful listener

When a node receives a free-buffer enquiry, it tests its receiver-inhibit status bit. If it finds RI is true, the node responds with a negative acknowledgment; otherwise, it sends back an acknowledgment.

Upon receiving an start-of-header signal, indicating the start of a data packet, a node writes the source identification into the receiving buffer, then checks the first destination identifier. If this byte is 000—indicating a broadcast—the node ignores the rest of the packet if the status bit authorizing reception of broadcasts is disabled. If broadcast reception is enabled or if the first identifier is the node's own ID, the node writes the rest of the transmission into its receiving buffer.

After loading the transmission into the receiving buffer, the node will ignore it if it fails the cyclic-redundancy or length-validation checks. If the destination ID indicates a broadcast, the node simply sets the RI status bit. If it is the node's own ID, the node sends an acknowledgment before setting its RI bit. If it is neither 000 nor the node's ID, it ignores the packet.

From a performance point of view, an important characteristic of a local network is the time a given node may have to wait before it is able to send a message. In a token-passing scheme, this waiting time is bounded by the time required for the token to pass through all the nodes in the network.

Out of several possible sequences of events that can occur when a node receives the token, a simple token pass and a message plus token pass comprise the majority of cases. A token pass alone requires about 28 μs, neglecting propagation delay. A message takes about 113 μs plus an additional 4.4 μs per byte of data, again ignoring propagation delays.

At the high end of the spectrum in terms of size, the Arcnet system in the Datapoint Research and Development department has about 175 nodes active at any time. It supports two totally independent operating systems and a wide variety of applications including program loading, word processing, printer spooling, and program development.

The traffic load seldom falls below 400 messages/s during peak business hours (Fig. 5), yet less than 2% of the nodes send messages on the average token trip. The time required for a token trip, therefore, remains very close to the no-traffic value. On the other hand, a theoretical network of 10 nodes still handles 172 messages per second if all 10 nodes were sending 100-byte data packets through the network (Fig. 6). ☐

Electronics/October 6, 1982

Dual-chip sets forge vital link for Ethernet local-network scheme

Four chip sets each implement inexpensive interface between node and net; two provide the basics of linking, and the others offer enhancements

by Harvey J. Hindin, *Communications & Microwave Editor*

☐ Long trumpeted as a solution to the need for a mass-market local-network standard, Ethernet is about to realize that promise. Making this possible are four dual-chip sets, each of which will implement an inexpensive link between a work-station node and the transceiver that feeds into the Ethernet.

Such very large-scale integrated circuits will drastically cut the cost of an Ethernet connection, which at the moment requires 100 or so medium-scale ICs on several printed-circuit boards. The cost of the MSI implementation is a healthy percentage of the price tag of a typical office work station, and although it has not deterred the installation of high-end Ethernets, it has been a barrier to widespread use.

Summarized in the table below and discussed in the four articles that follow this one, the new chip sets each comprise an encoder-decoder and a microprocessor peripheral known as a controller. Interestingly enough, most of them are the product of alliances between chip

makers and systems houses, alliances foreshadowed by the beginnings of Ethernet, which was originated by Xerox Corp. with subsequent participation by Intel Corp. and Digital Equipment Corp.

In Japan, Fujitsu Ltd. is acting as a silicon foundry for chips that were designed by Ungermann-Bass Inc. of Santa Clara, Calif. This chip set is based on Ungermann-Bass's MSI implementation of the Ethernet link, which the company has used in a number of local nets.

Down the road in Santa Clara, Intel took the solo route to a controller chip that handles Ethernet specifications, which makes Xerox and DEC happy. However, many of the IC's key parameters are programmable to handle local nets similar to Ethernet but with different packet sizes and data rates—and this does not make Xerox and DEC so happy.

Meanwhile in San Jose, Calif., the designers at Seeq Technology Inc. worked with the firm of Silicon Compilers Inc. of San Francisco and another local-network

ETHERNET CHIP·SET COMPARISON						
Development team	Controller name and/or part(s) number(s)	Encoder-decoder name and/or part(s) number(s)	Controller fabrication process[1]	Controller pin count	Encoder-decoder pin count	Additional features[2,3]
American Micro Devices Inc. Digital Equipment Corp. Mostek Corp.	Lance (local-area network controller for Ethernet): Am 7990 (AMD) MK 68590 (Mostek)	SIA (serial interface adapter): Am 7991 (AMD) MK 3891 (Mostek)	n-channel MOS	48	24	direct memory access, diagnostics, buffer and network management
Intel Corp.	82586	ESI (Ethernet serial interface): 82501	H-MOS	48	20	programmable parameters, direct memory access, diagnostics, buffer and network management
Seeq Technology Inc.	EDLC (Ethernet data link controller): 8001	not yet available	n-MOS	40	—	—
Ungermann-Bass Inc. Fujitsu Ltd.	DLC (data-link controller): MB 61301	MB 502	complementary-MOS	64	24	—

Note: 1. All announced codecs are bipolar devices.
2. Intel's chips are geared to its microprocessors, though others can be accommodated with a hardware and software overhead; the remaining chip sets handle most 8- and 16-bit microprocessors.
3. Over and above the requirements of the Ethernet specification, which corresponds to layers 1 and 2 of the International Standards Organization's open systems interconnection reference model.

house already implementing Ethernet, 3Com Inc. of Santa Clara, to come up with its own version of a controller, this one based on a programmable logic array. Seeq's encoder-decoder IC is still under development, but the controller was introduced at Wescon [*Electronics*, Sept. 8, 1982, p. 48].

Unfazed by Intel's go-it-alone style, DEC of Maynard, Mass., has gotten together with Advanced Micro Devices Inc. of Sunnyvale, Calif., and Mostek Corp. of Carrollton, Texas, to come up with another two-chip set. AMD and Mostek will second-source each other and, in turn, will be second-sourced by Zilog Inc.

Only the results count

What has emerged from all this effort are ICs that, at the least, perform the layer 1 (encoder-decoder) and layer 2 (controller) functions of the International Standards Organization's open-systems interconnection reference model as they apply to local networks of the Ethernet type. Seeq and Ungermann-Bass have opted for chips limited to performing these functions.

The Intel chips, like those offered by AMD and Mostek, have memory- and network-management capabilities that are not specified by the Ethernet rules. Their makers claim these capabilities will be flexible enough to be useful to the systems integrator whose job it is to set up the work stations and buses that connect to Ethernet. For example, buffer management, they say, has nothing to do with the as-yet-unstandardized higher ISO layers as others claim, but merely helps the system integrator implement the higher layers, whatever they may turn out to be in the long run. For their part, the competing chip

companies may admit that the Intel or AMD-Mostek ICs are capable of more functions, but they say that the designer does not need or want them on chip. Others say that Intel is trying to set its own standards for buffer management, but these are not universally accepted and require a full commitment to Intel architecture and parts—a step potential customers may not want to take.

Intel has opted to make the most versatile chip of all—but at a price. Unlike the ICs available from the other manufacturers, which will work with almost any microprocessor, the Intel controller is best suited to its maker's processor line. It can work with other processors—but the question is whether it will be cost-effective for the original-equipment manufacturer to add the necessary extra chips and software. Intel claims that the adaptation can be readily done, but clearly the company has opted for an all-Intel chip solution to the Ethernet connection problem.

Optimized for Ethernet, Intel's 82586 controller chip also is designed to accommodate most other general-purpose carrier-sense, multiple-access collison-detection protocols for local networks. For example, by using the configure command, alternative frame formats to those specified for Ethernet can be set up. Lower data rates and different network distances than specified for Ethernet also can be handled.

Other programmable parameters include preamble length, address length, cyclic-redundancy-check algorithm (either 16- or 32-bit), and minimum frame length. Furthermore, the chip's link-management mechanism is programmable for different network topologies and traffic patterns. For example, interframe spacing and slot time are programmable, as are the maximum number of retries after a collision. Prioritization of messages can be implemented using a built-in linear priority mechanism.

None of these features is possible with the simpler Ethernet chip sets working alone. With this flexibility, Intel says, the 82586 can be used in a variety of CSMA/CD applications, including the interconnection of intelligent modules in a bigger system in what is known by the company as a serial-backplane arrangement. Xerox is already using such a scheme in one of its xerographic copier systems.

Put it to work

The Ethernet chips are being put right to work by OEMs. For example, 3Com has taken the Seeq IC it helped develop and will soon announce an interface for the popular IBM Personal Computer. In fact, with a single unit price of $950 per Personal Computer for an entry-level Ethernet capability that includes protocol and application software, 3Com has breached the price barrier to hooking up personal computers to nonproprietary, 10-megabit-a-second local networks like Ethernet.

3Com's EtherSeries is initially aimed at professional users. The entry-level EtherSeries product is called Etherlink and consists of the controller-based board with an on-board 3Com transceiver, cable, and diskette-resident software. Etherlink supports two or more Per-

Ready to use. The Mostek emulator for the Ethernet chip set is built on two double-width Eurocards that are housed in a structural foam cabinet. It is available with or without a dc supply. A microprogrammable bit-slice design assures the emulator's future modifiability.

Ethernet in brief

Ethernet is a 10-megabit-per-second, packet-switched communications scheme for local networks. It can span 2.5 kilometers with a theoretical maximum of 1,000 nodes. However, because it is intended for office-automation applications, the maximum number of nodes, or work stations, is likely to be in the hundreds.

Ethernet was invented at Xerox Corp.'s Palo Alto (Calif.) Research Center, which has several patents on the network access algorithms. Xerox licenses other firms to use these algorithms, and several hundred of them have chosen to do so. For most of these firms, Ethernet is a *de facto* standard, although the local-network standards committee of the Institute of Electrical and Electronics Engineers has been working on a very similar set of rules.

The Ethernet packet format consists of a 64-bit preamble, a 48-bit destination address, 48-bit source address, 16-bit type field, from 46 to 1,518 bytes in a data field, and a 32-bit cyclic redundancy check bringing up the rear. The variable widths of the packets accommodate both short status and command packets and long data packets. All packets are spaced 9.6 microseconds apart at a minimum, a timing appropriate for a node to receive large packets back-to-back.

The shared coaxial cable in an Ethernet is a passive medium with no computer performing centralized control. Thus access to the channel by nodes wishing to transmit is set up by the nodes themselves. They use a statistical procedure in which each station checks the cable to see if it is clear. If it is, the node proceeds to transmit. Otherwise,

it waits an arbitrary amount of time and tries again. Such an access scheme is called contention arbitration.

Ethernet is equivalent only to layers 1 and 2, the physical- and data-link specifications, of the seven-layer reference model for open-systems interconnection formulated by the International Standards Organization. As with any communications net, an Ethernet must implement the other five layers so that its messages may leap such barriers as different hardware at the nodes, different high-level languages and application programs, and different communications codes. One solution, of course, is to restrict the options so that each node is like any other, but Ethernet licensees around the world are at work on less restrictive alternatives.

A typical Ethernet architecture as accommodated by the two-chip sets described in the following four articles has a transceiver attached to the net's spine—a coaxial cable weaving its way from work station to work station. Attached to the transceiver is the encoder-decoder chip, which, in the main, handles the layer-1 functions. Attached to the codec is the controller chip, which mostly handles layer-2 functions.

Both chips are connected to each other and to the transceiver with multiple signal lines. They also may be connected to a local microprocessor and local memory, or in very simple networks, the work station's processor will provide the necessary control. There are also connections to internal and node buses, the latter being useful for direct communications between work stations.

---

sonal Computers in moving files between their disks and sharing a printer. Thus, each Personal Computer becomes, in effect, a network station.

Etherlink also serves as the link to EtherShare—a 16-bit microprocessor-based file server with a 10-megabyte hard disk that can support up to 20 Personal Computers. EtherShare will provide information sharing, centralized software bootstrapping, optional tape backup, and printer and mail services.

3Com is negotiating with Apple and other personal-computer firms to provide similar Ethernet boards for their products. Further complicating the alliance picture, DEC is one of these firms. So it may be possible for the user to have a DEC computer using a Seeq chip instead of either Intel's (DEC's Ethernet specification partner) or AMD/Mostek's (whose chips were developed with the aid of advice from DEC).

System integrators planning to provide products based on the new chip sets do not want to wait for actual ICs to begin their complicated, expensive, and time-consuming design work, and they certainly will not work from currently available hardware on pc boards that do not represent exact, final chip functions.

Recognizing this problem, both Mostek and AMD have taken steps to solve it. For example, an Ethernet emulator from Mostek provides the system designer a head start. The product (see photograph) not only provides a pin-for-pin emulator of the final chip set to be available

from Mostek and AMD, it also supplies some additional software flexibility that allows inclusion of specialized network monitoring and diagnostics.

According to Mostek's Hersh Parekh, product planning manager for the board and development-systems department, "an emulator design based on the 'Blue Book' [specifications] alone would not allow the user to properly evaluate the software tasks associated with the VLSI chips." What Parekh means is that any distributed system built around the low-cost chip set will require higher layers of software (layers 3 through 7 in the ISO model) to establish the virtual circuits required for communications between nodes. Much of the software written for any emulator not tied to a specific chip set will need to be discarded or, at best, significantly altered.

Not to be left out of the emulator fray, AMD has entered into an agreement with Associated Computer Consultants of Santa Barbara, Calif., for the development of its own hardware emulator. Both emulators provide the same base-line functionality—after all, the AMD and Mostek chips were jointly developed—but there are some customer-convenience features that are different in both systems. For example Associated Computer's Brian McGann, director of the local-net center, says that emulator software will be made available on disks or tape to exercise the Ethernet interface. The AMD emulator differs from Mostek's in being a pc board on legs for bench-top use.

335

Controller chip shares tasks in buffer, net management

by Vernon Coleman
Advanced Micro Devices Inc., Sunnyvale, Calif.
Thomas Ermlovich
Digital Equipment Corp., Maynard, Mass.
and James Vittera
Mostek Corp., Carrollton, Texas

Implementing the Ethernet protocol is only the beginning of the tasks assumed by a two-chip set designed by AMD and Mostek with the cooperation of DEC. As well as being the heart of the interface between a work station and the transceiver that links directly with the network's coaxial cable, the set handles certain buffer- and network-management functions.

Essentially, all of these tasks are performed by one of the chips, the Lance, for local-area-network controller for Ethernet. The other, the SIA (serial interface adapter), provides Manchester encoding and decoding and the interface with the transceiver's cable.

The Lance and SIA integrated circuits are designated Am7990 and Am7991, respectively, by AMD and MK68590 and MK3891, respectively, by Mostek. Each IC is plug-compatible with its counterpart from the other firm; and all will be further second-sourced by such firms as Zilog Inc.

Designed in n-channel MOS technology, the Lance packs the equivalent of 4,000 gates, 1,000 bits of random-access memory, and 12,000 bits of read-only memory into a 48-pin dual in-line package. It performs the link-level Ethernet functions, such as network access in the carrier-sense, multiple-access protocol with collision detection (CSMA/CD), direct memory access, interfacing with the host processor, and network management

through the use of extensive error reporting.

The Lance and the host processor communicate through buffers in memory with the buffer-management scheme handled by the Lance. The error reporting provided in the Lance allows inputs of such network-management parameters as access difficulty, abnormal-signal interference, and source-dependent frame errors.

The network designer has a wide choice of on-board microprocessors for use as a subsystem controller, because the Lance interfaces with both multiplexed and nonmultiplexed data buses using a minimum of external logic. For multiplexed buses (Fig. 1), a byte or word control signal compatible with such microprocessors as the 8086 family does the job. For nonmultiplexed buses (Fig. 2) used on such microprocessor families as the 68000, the Lance furnishes compatible upper and lower data strobe signals. Other standard microprocessors such as the LSI-11 and Z8000 may be likewise be accommodated as the on-board microcontroller.

Encoding and decoding

The SIA is a 20-pin bipolar IC providing Manchester encoding and decoding of the serial bit stream that must be put on the Ethernet cable. It interfaces the TTL signals of the Lance with the differential emitter-coupled logic of the transceiver.

Coupling an Ethernet node to the network cable requires a transceiver. Commercially available board or module transceivers can be used with the Lance and the SIA. What's more, a monolithic transceiver in an early phase of development at AMD should significantly lower the cost of this part. It will have the traditional driver and receiver responsibilities and collision-detection and circuit-testing capabilities, but it will contain other features. For example, a fault in the transceiver output-control chain can cause a "babbling" transmitter, bringing down the network. The transceiver IC will be built with internal intelligence that will detect such a

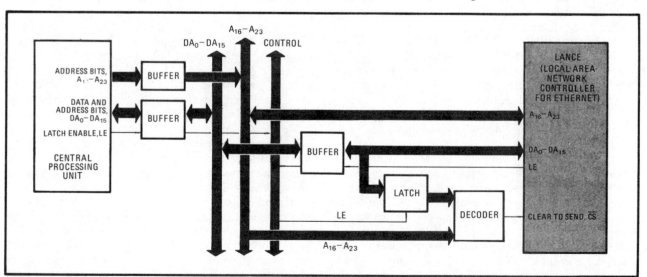

1. Multiplexed buses. The Lance chip implements its link-level Ethernet functions with a minimum of external logic. For multiplexed microprocessors such as Intel's 8086, a byte or word control signal is furnished by the controller.

condition and immediately remove its node from the net.

Ethernet is a send and receive half-duplex system, so a node must function in either a transmit or receive mode at any time. As a CSMA/CD system requires, the node ensures before transmission that there is no preexisting signal on the coaxial cable. To do this, the Ethernet CSMA/CD network-access algorithm is completely implemented within the Lance, as is the exponential binary backoff algorithm prescribed in the Ethernet specifications to handle bus access.

In the transmit mode, the chip initiates a DMA cycle to access data from a buffer memory. It prefaces the data with a preamble and synchronization pattern and then calculates and appends a 32-bit cyclic redundancy check.

The packet is transmitted serially to the SIA where the Manchester encoder creates differential signals to drive the transceiver cable. These differential signals are coupled through the transceiver cable and transceiver onto the Ethernet coaxial cable.

Getting the word

When a signal is present on the cable, the transceiver receives it and transmits it to the SIA for decoding by the Manchester decoder. A phase-locked loop that synchronizes with the Ethernet preamble enables the decoder to recover clock and data from the encoded signals. These two signals are supplied to the Lance as the TTL signals called receive clock and receive data.

In addition, the SIA creates the carrier-present signal while it receives data from the cable. This indicates to the Lance that data is on the cable. Then the CRC is calculated and compared with the checksum at the end of the packet. If the calculated CRC does not agree with the packet CRC, the chip sets an error bit. Ethernet packets can be received using three different destination-address schemes, known as physical, logical, and promiscuous. Recognizing a physical match is a simple decoding of the 47-bit physical address.

The logical address scheme is somewhat more complicated, for there are two types. The first is multicast addressing, useful for sending packets to all of a particular type of device simultaneously. A good example of this is sending a packet to all file servers or all printer servers. The second type is the broadcast address in which all nodes on the network receive the packet.

The last class of operation is the promiscuous mode, in which the Lance accepts all packets on the coaxial cable regardless of their destination address. The promiscuous mode is useful for system monitoring and implementing gateways to other facilities.

The Lance is designed to simplify the user's task of interfacing a micro- or minicomputer-based work station or terminal with an Ethernet local net. For example, it has a byte-swapping option to accommodate various 16-bit processors. Also, a programmable interface allows the Lance either to use a daisy-chain bus-priority scheme or to work directly with bus-priority-access devices.

To further the economy of implementation of the Ethernet connection, the Lance can share the system bus with other peripherals. This sharing feature is possible because the Lance must request use of the processor's data bus in order to transfer data. A maximum of eight 16-bit words can be transferred per bus request with each transfer occurring over 600 nanoseconds. Such an implementation assures other peripherals adequate time to access and perform useful bus operations without necessarily requiring the Lance to be isolated by additional memory buffering.

DMA for buffer management

The Lance has on-chip DMA, which facilitates buffer management for storing received packets and queuing packets to be transmitted in a 24-bit address space. To control the transmit and receive operations, the DMA capability makes use of what are known as descriptor rings, a bookkeeping scheme that tracks the location of the data defined by that address space. With the Lance, as many as 128 frames awaiting transmission may be queued on a descriptor ring.

Each descriptor ring holds, among other information, a 24-bit pointer to a data memory buffer and an entry for the length of the buffer. A variable length for the data buffer is essential for an Ethernet. The size of frames is, in typical applications, bimodally distributed between short frames of 256 bytes and extremely large frames (the Ethernet maximum is 1,518 bytes). Since 80% of the frames are short, the variable–buffer-length scheme requires only a third of the memory that would otherwise be needed.

Data buffers can be chained or cascaded to handle a long packet in multiple data-buffer areas. With this linking, the Lance looks ahead and searches the descriptor rings to determine the next empty buffer, so that it can chain buffers or handle packets back to back. As each buffer is filled, the host processor sets an "own" bit, which allows only the Lance access to the buffer. The

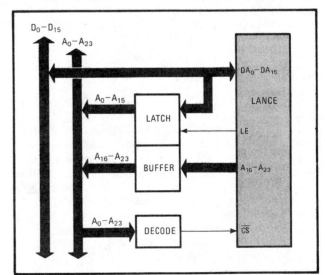

2. Nonmultiplexed buses. Lance also handles nonmultiplexed buses like those used on Motorola's 68000 microprocessor. For this architecture, the chip furnishes upper and lower data strobe signals.

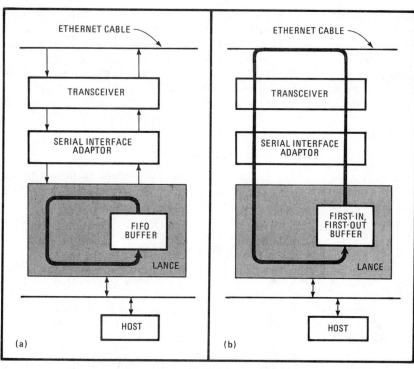

(a)

(b)

3. Checkup. The Lance can check itself with a local loopback test (a). It also can check the link to the Ethernet with an external loopback test in which it sends a packet to itself (b). In both, the cyclic redundancy generation and checking logic is tested.

of the reflection, it is possible to estimate the approximate distance to an open or short.

Extensive error reporting on the Lance enables system problems to be analyzed and resolved quickly, thereby enhancing system reliability. Errors are classified as either system- or frame-related, and frame-related errors are further separated into transmit and receive classes.

System-related errors are stored in the Lance and read out on command from the microprocessor. There are several forms that these errors can take. For example, babble is a transmitter timeout error, indicating that the transmitter has been on longer than the time that is allowed by Ethernet specifications.

A collision error indicates that the collision-detection output from the transceiver failed to activate within the required 4 microseconds after the end of the Lance-initiated transmission. The missed-packet error signal is set when the chip loses a packet because it does not own a receive buffer and its internal buffer has overflowed.

Checking the frames

Receive and transmit frame-related errors are loaded into a designated descriptor to be processed later by the CPU. Receive frame-related errors include framing error, CRC error, overflow, and receive-buffer errors. If the framing-error signal is set, the frame did not end on a byte boundary. The CRC-error signal announces that the received CRC was incorrect, and the overflow signal indicates that the Lance's internal buffer has lost incoming data. The receive-buffer error signal is set when the Lance cannot find a free descriptor in which to place received data while data chaining.

Major transmitted frame-related errors are underflow, transmit-buffer error, late-collision error, loss of carrier, and retry error. The underflow signal indicates that the Lance has truncated a message because of late data arrival from external memory. The transmit-buffer error signal is set when, in the process of transmission, the chip runs out of buffers in external memory. When a collision is detected after the slot time of the Ethernet cable has expired, a late-collision error is indicated. Loss of carrier is set when the carrier-presence input to the Lance goes inactive during a chip-initiated transmission. A retry error signal reports that the transmitter has failed in 16 attempts to transmit a message due to repeated collisions on the cable.

Lance clears the own bit when the task associated with that buffer is complete, and this action allows only the host central processing unit access to the buffer.

To enhance system integrity, several diagnostic capabilities not required by the Ethernet specifications are built into the Lance. These capabilities include loopback testing, CRC logic checking, time-domain reflectometry, and system error reporting.

Loopback may be performed either inside the Lance or externally (Fig. 3). For its part, internal loopback is performed by loading data into the internal FIFO buffer of the chip, connecting the buffer's output to the input, and then reading the data out. External loopback requires that the data stored in the buffer be transmitted onto the coaxial cable and then back into the Lance. In effect, the IC is addressing a frame to itself.

Checking the CRC logic

In both internal and external loopback modes, the cyclic redundancy generation and checking logic is also tested. The generation is tested by disabling the checking logic, looping back an agreed-upon data pattern, and checking the generated CRC pattern against one stored in the processor's memory. Likewise, the checking logic is tested by disabling the generation logic and appending a software-generated CRC to the loopback frame. The next step is looping the data and checking the software-generated CRC with the Lance's checking hardware.

In addition to identifying such points of failure between the processor and the coaxial cable, the Lance locates faults on the cable using its time-domain reflectometry function. With TDR, the chip senses reflections caused by a discontinuity in the cable. By measuring the time between the initial transmission and the reception

System-level functions enhance controller IC

by Robert Beach and Robert Galin
Intel Corp., Santa Clara, Calif.
and Alex Kornhauser, Moshe Stark, and Dono Van-Mierop
Intel Israel Ltd., Haifa, Israel

Beyond any single new feature, it is the integration of major system-level communications functions onto a single chip that makes the 82586 local area network communications controller a true next-generation communications controller for high-speed local nets. Such functions as on-chip control of direct memory access, buffer-memory management, programmable network parameters, and diagnostics will allow designers to quickly implement cost-effective and reliable Ethernet and local nets using similar other carrier-sense, multiple-access protocols with collision detection (CSMA/CD).

Combined with the 82501 Ethernet serial interface chip and readily available transceivers, users will have a complete implementation of the Ethernet physical and data links. Although other Ethernet controller integrated circuits will also handle the fundamental implementation of these two International Standards Organization layers, the 82586 goes beyond them to offer programmable network-management capabilities that permit users to optimize the controller's operation for a variety of local networks and to gage the net's health.

In fact, Intel's goal in designing the 82586 is to serve, not only the Ethernet user, but any net that uses some form of CSMA/CD. Therefore, many of the IC's facilities are programmable for nets with different maximum lengths and data-transfer rates from those found in Ethernet.

A major role for the controller IC is to act as an intelligent interface with the host central processing unit, reducing its workload and saving memory space. The chip may be viewed as a parallel processor (on the right in Fig. 1), fetching and executing commands from the host at the same time it is receiving data through its serial-interface circuitry and storing it in buffer memory.

1. Peek inside. Intel's H-MOS data-link-control chip has both parallel and serial interfaces and four-channel direct-memory access. It can operate in a multiplicity of local networks because its key parameters are programmable.

Communications between the host's CPU and the 82586 is by means of a shared memory. The only hardware interconnections are the interrupt line the controller uses to get the CPU's attention and the channel-attention line the CPU uses to get the 82586's attention.

Part of the shared memory is reserved as a bidirectional mailbox. One section of the mailbox holds instructions from the CPU to the controller, such as start, abort, suspend, and resume, plus pointers to a list of commands for execution by the parallel processor and to the received-frame area. The second section holds information the 82586 is sending to the CPU, such as status data (idle, active, no receive resources available, and so on) interrupt bits (command completed, frame received, for example), and accumulative tallies (such as cyclic-redundancy-check errors).

As well as a mailbox, the shared memory holds the list of commands prepared by the CPU that serve as the program for the 82586. The linked-list approach makes it possible to form a circular linked list used for repeated execution or a linear queue of commands.

The final section of the shared memory is the received-frame area. All the host CPU need do is identify the area by preparing two linked lists: one of frame descriptors and one of buffers with their descriptors.

Each frame descriptor has a forward pointer. The first descriptor is referenced by the mailbox and the last one is marked with an end-of-frame bit. The buffer descriptors are essentially the same for both the receive and the

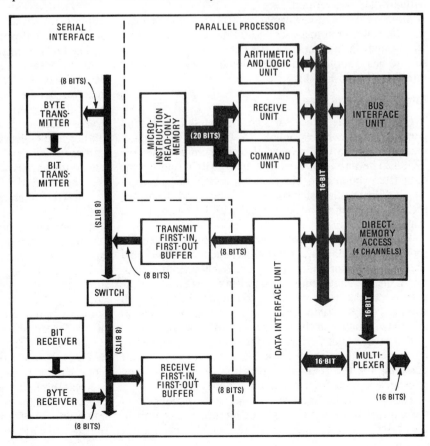

2. Partners. The bipolar 82501 Ethernet serial interface chip provides Manchester encoding and decoding, noise filtering, transceiver drive signals, and collision detection as it works with the data-link control chip and the network transceiver.

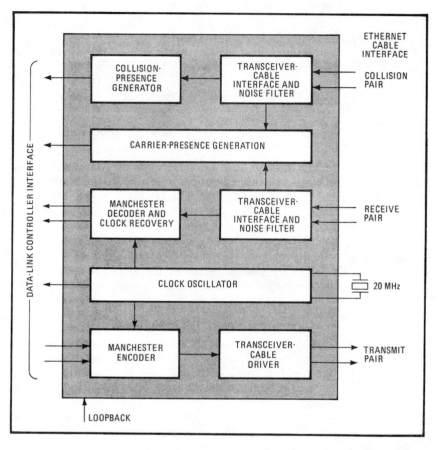

transmit processes; however, the receive descriptors include a field that specifies the size of the empty buffer and an end-of-list bit.

The 82586 fills the buffers upon reception of frames and reformats the free-buffer list. Receive-buffer chaining improves memory use significantly. Without it, the host must allocate blocks of memory under the assumption that each frame will be the maximum size (1,518 bytes for Ethernet). Successive transmission may fill the buffers, even though the actual frames are far less than the maximum in size, and the controller may receive a burst of several frames but have no room. Usually, the tradeoff in buffer chaining is the processing overhead and the time for buffer switching. The 82586, however, performs the buffer chaining without CPU intervention.

Made in the high-performance MOS (H-MOS) process, the controller chip has over 56,000 devices and fits in a 48-pin dual in-line package. Besides the parallel processor, it has another major functional block, the serial interface (left in Fig. 1).

Internal architecture

On the parallel-processor side, the bus-interface unit generates bus-control signals to transfer data, commands, and status between shared memory and the 82586. The data-interface unit is a switch routing the data from the system bus to the transmit first-in, first-out buffer or the internal parallel bus and from the receive FIFO buffer to the internal parallel bus or to the system bus.

The direct-memory-access logic is an address generator that performs DMA transfers between the 82586 and the shared memory. Commands are fetched from memory by the command unit, which also writes status information to the memory. The command unit has full control over the DMA unit, loads the starting pointers and byte counts, and then triggers the DMA start.

The receive unit performs tasks for the receive memory operation similar to those that the command unit performs for the command operation. Both units fetch microinstructions from a shared read-only memory.

The transmit buffer regulates the traffic flowing from the parallel processor through the data-interface unit to the byte transmitter. After executing the commands

coming from the transmit buffer, the byte transmitter sends status information back through the receive buffer.

The bit transmitter serializes and encodes data, generates the frame-check sequence, and transmits the data. It also controls the modem-like handshake. The bit receiver handles preamble stripping, address matching, error-flag generation, received-frame delineation, and frame-check sequence testing. It deserializes the information and delivers it in bytes to the byte receiver, which compares the destination address with the various possible address types. Then, if the address matches, it transfers the received data to the receiver buffer.

The controller interface is not complete without the 82501 Ethernet serial interface (ESI) chip. The 82501 is implemented in bipolar technology and is designed to handle the serial transmission and reception of 10-megabit-per-second packets to and from the transceiver.

The 82501 (Fig. 2) provides clock generation for itself and the 82586 controller, retiming and Manchester encoding of the transmitted data stream, driving of the transmit signal line to the transceiver, and noise filtering of the receive and collision inputs. What's more, it handles timing recovery and Manchester decoding of the received data stream and supplies receive-data, receive-clock, carrier-presence, and collision-presence signals.

Because of its four on-chip DMA channels, the 82586 can receive back-to-back bursts of frames, provided the minimum interframe spacing of 9.6 microseconds (for the 10-Mb/s Ethernet) is met. In addition, the pipelining

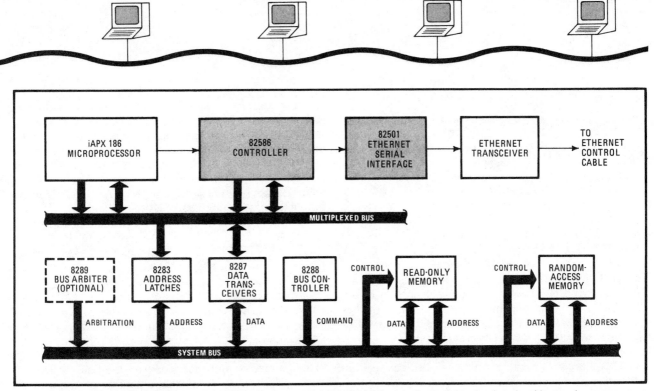

3. Complete system. A typical Ethernet local-network controller includes the Intel controller and encoder-decoder chips, a microprocessor, a transceiver, and auxiliary logic to connect the system to the work-station bus.

of the operation of the Ethernet interface and the host interface, plus the concurrent processing units, contribute to its performance.

The controller can operate with high-performance system buses, yet it is highly tolerant of system-bus limitations. The minimum data-transfer rate required to sustain a bit rate of 10 Mb/s is 1.25 megabytes/s. The 82586 is optimized for an 8-megahertz bus whose transfer rate is 4 megabytes/s, leaving considerable bandwidth for overhead and CPU processing.

Software diagnosis

Data-communications networks can be very complex because of their distributed and asynchronous nature, so it is hard to pinpoint a failure. The 82586 was designed with recognition of this problem and includes a set of features for improving reliability and testability.

All of these functions are performed under software control. They do not require any diagnostic hardware or any modifications. The chip offers such services as the monitoring of transmitted and received frames, support for statistics gathering and diagnostics of the entire network, diagnostic support for its node, and a means of testing its own operation.

In addition to the status information sent to the CPU after each transmission or reception, the chip also tallies the number of frames with CRC errors and alignment errors, as well as the number of frames lost due to DMA overrun or lack of empty receive buffers.

The 82586 also has mechanisms to collect statistics about the behavior of the entire network, as well as a means to locate problems in it. For example, the status of every transmitted frame provides network activity indicators, such as transmissions deferred because the channel was busy, the number of collisions experienced before the frame was transmitted, or no frame transmit-

ted because of an excessive number of collisions.

The controller chip can be configured into a promiscuous mode, which means it captures all frames regardless of address. Such a mode is, for example, useful in implementing a monitoring station.

Each 82586 is also capable of determining whether there is a short or open circuit anywhere in the network (using time-domain reflectometry). The chip can even determine the distance of a short or open circuit from the controller, an important aid in finding the fault.

To support testing of both the software and hardware of the work station, the 82586 can be configured to an internal-loopback mode in which it is disconnected from the network and any frame transmitted is immediately re-received. This routine will indicate problems in the chip or the station.

What's more, an external loopback configuration permits users to test all the external logic between the 82586 and the link itself. This chip also checks the correct operation of the carrier-sense and collision-detect signals from the transceiver for every frame transmitted.

In order to check the operation of the chip itself, there is a dump command that causes the chip to write its internal registers to memory. For parts of the chip that cannot be checked from the outside, such as the random-number generator, a diagnose command triggers a self-test procedure that exercises any inaccessible counters.

An Ethernet node can be designed using the 82586 in conjunction with Intel's 16-bit iAPX 186 microprocessors (Fig. 3). The two chips have identical bus timing and control requirements. Thus they may share the same address latches, data latches, and bus controller.

Moreover, as an option, a bus arbiter can be used to enable designers to build a multisystem node. In this application, the 82586's system clock is driven by the iAPX 186's internally generated system-clock output.

Design latitude broadens link-controller chip's appeal

by Stan Kopec and Dane Elliot
Seeq Technology Inc., San Jose, Calif.

Design latitude is the name of the game with the Seeq 8001 Ethernet data-link controller (EDLC). The very large-scale integrated circuit provides the basic data-encapsulation and link-management functions of the Ethernet protocol. However, it does not implement any data-buffer or -management functions, allowing the system designer to make the appropriate performance-cost tradeoffs in choosing ICs to perform these tasks.

Depending on the complexity of the network, the 8001 EDLC [*Electronics*, Sept. 8, 1982, p. 48] can operate under direct control of its node's central processing unit, most likely in a work station, or it can work with its own microcontroller to offload the host CPU. In fact, the designer is given a wide range of options on system configuration—including choices for the 8001's buffer memory, which again depends on the net's configuration.

Symmetrical structure

The IC's generic bus structure, with independent channels for data and for command and status signals, is compatible with virtually any host microprocessor or minicomputer. The interface with this processor supports both polled and interrupt-driven systems and is simple and symmetric. In fact, the chip's entire architecture is highly symmetrical, permitting implementation with a programmable logic array for control structures.

The chip's external first-in, first-out buffer structures provide 16 bytes each of receive and transmit frame buffering. Because the command-status port is separate from the data port, checking the status or writing into the command register does not interrupt the data flow.

The 8001 provides all the functions needed to communicate with an Ethernet network. These include error checking, cyclic redundancy generation and checking, retransmission interval calculation, and address matching. Thus the work station's CPU need not worry about the overhead associated with Ethernet communications but can view the 8001 as just another parallel port. In a 40-pin dual in-line package, the EDLC will be joined by an encoder-decoder IC that will take care of the serial interface with the Ethernet.

To gain breadth of exposure in structured VLSI design and system-level application, Seeq collaborated with two firms. Silicon Compilers Inc. participated in a joint pursuit of the early functional definition and design strategies for the chip. 3Com Corp., which will make Ethernet board-level products and networking software, provided input on the use of the 8001 in a standard product (see p. 90).

The block diagram (Fig. 1) shows the EDLC's three primary sections; the transmit and receive modules, and the interface with the CPU. Because the transmit and receive processes are essentially the inverse of each other, many similarities arise in the internal data-path and control structures. Such redundancy results in an economy of design effort when it is carried throughout the definition and design process for a gate-array implementation using structured VLSI design techniques.

The bit processors handle serial-to-parallel conversion or the reverse. They also take care of generating or checking the 32-bit cyclic redundancy codes that are appended to each Ethernet frame.

The transmit parallel-to-serial conversion is handled by a parallel-load shift register, while the receive serial-to-parallel conversion is accomplished by a parallel-read shift register. These are essentially the same functional blocks, and one shift register cell serves both purposes.

The CRC modules in each section are identical, except that the receive unit must compare the final-frame CRC with a constant to determine if the frame was correctly received. In contrast, the transmit generator must append the CRC to the end of the transmitted frame. However, the 32-bit shift register and exclusive-OR taps in both CRC modules are identical—another example of economy of design.

The transmit and receive byte processors also have many functional blocks in common. For example, both employ byte counters to determine when critical events in frame transmission and reception have occurred, and these counters are identical save for their widths.

Almost all the control structures on the chip, and those in the byte processors in particular, are realized in

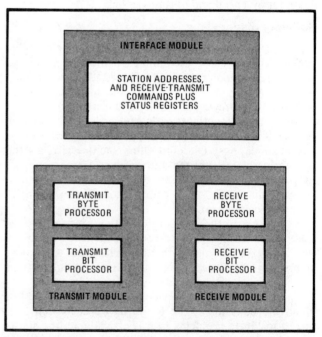

1. Three sections. The 8001 may be considered to have three modules: the transmit and receive sections and the interface with the controlling processor. The controller can be the system CPU, or it can be a dedicated microprocessor in more complex setups.

PLAs. Composed of optimized basic cells, these structures vary in size according to their system functions. By placing the control functions in these structures, logic design and verification is considerably easier, critical speed paths are minimized, and logic changes may be made much more easily.

On chip, all parallel data communications is accomplished through two 16-byte FIFO buffers, which are identical except for the direction of data flow. The buffers' operation is asynchronous to allow data clocking to and from them at any time.

Control commands from the processor are handled by transmit and receive command or status register pairs, which are similar in format and identical in structure. Each command register is accessed by a write operation, and each status register is accessed by a read operation. Both transmit registers occupy one address, and both receive registers occupy another.

For virtually all status bits reporting frame-reception or -transmission conditions, there is a command bit that will enable an interrupt in the corresponding bit position in the status register. Therefore the designer is not confronted with a large set of register formats.

The parallel data interface of the 8001 and the host uses a byte-wide bidirectional data port. Access to this port is controlled by strobe and ready-flag signals in both the receive and transmit directions. For transmission, these signals consist of the transmit-write strobe and the transmit-input ready flag, and for receiving, they are the receive-read strobe and the receive-output ready flag. Strobing of the port in a given direction is permitted only when the appropriate ready flag is high. This port is connected internally to the two independent FIFO buffers, which provide sufficient data buffering to handle any direct-memory-access latency or timing variations.

Processor interface

The 8001 command-status interface with the processor consists of an 8-bit port with address A_0-A_2, three control signals, and the receive-status and transmit-command bits. The first six locations in the address space are occupied by the controller's station address, which is loaded with the 48-bit station address. The controller is programmed to receive frames that have as their destination address the value programmed into the station-address register.

Besides the station-address registers, the controller's address space has the transmit and receive pairs of command and status registers. Bits in the receive command register can specify a variety of address-matching modes during frame reception. Thus they respond to all addresses, respond to no address, or respond to a correct station-and-broadcast address or station-multicast-and-broadcast address.

Some implementations require only the minimal capabilities in a controller subsystem. Such a system would be one in which low volumes of data and short frames will be sufficient to service the node.

In such a configuration, the host CPU provides the subsystem control and the shared memory. Major system chips required besides the EDLC are a transmit receive buffer memory and a DMA controller.

This setup uses a shared memory space, in which access to the CPU's memory is arbitrated between that chip and the DMA controller. Access to the buffer memory is available only to the DMA controller, but the CPU indirectly controls that access by means of its programmed control of the DMA unit's operation.

In this example, the DMA controller is assumed to have four channels, allocated to handle 8001-to-buffer, 8001-from-buffer, buffer-to-CPU, and CPU-to-buffer transfers. Transfers to and from the 8001 are assumed to be synchronized by the DMA request and 8001 ready flags for each direction.

Avoiding latency

Microprocessor access to the 8001 command-status interface is provided by simply connecting the command-status bus to the CPU. This gives the processor access to the Ethernet without bus-arbitration latency. Bus arbitration is assumed to be performed in a hold–hold-acknowledge technique. Hold is activated only when cycles to the CPU bus are required. A positive hold acknowledge in response will activate the bus transceivers and address buffer, effectively tying together the CPU system bus and the controller command-status bus.

To initiate a frame transmission, the CPU first constructs a frame buffer in its memory. It then loads a byte count and starting address to a DMA channel and enables it. Usually, transfers between CPU and buffer are of a lower priority than transfers to and from the 8001, but, at some point the entire frame is loaded in the buffer.

When the entire frame has been transferred to the buffer memory, the CPU enables a second DMA channel to initiate transfers to the 8001 from the buffer. The transfer of the first byte to the EDLC's transmit buffer initiates the Ethernet transmit cycle. Next the 8001 sends a preamble to the Ethernet and begins transmitting the serialized data stream. The DMA channel continues to place bytes into the transmit buffer in a synchronized operation.

If a collision occurs during transmission, the 8001 automatically transmits a jam pattern and begins the backoff interval. It also issues a transmit-retransmit signal that reinitializes the DMA channel so the same buffer contents may be retransmitted when the backoff interval is satisfied. It also flushes any remaining bytes from the internal transmit buffer. The first transmit bytes are reloaded to the transmit buffer as soon as the transmit-ready signal is active, so retransmission onto the Ethernet can occur as early as possible.

Frame reception consists of the CPU initializing DMA channels to handle the 8001-to-buffer and the buffer-to-CPU-memory transfers. When a frame with a valid address is received, the transmit-ready pin goes high, triggering the transfer from 8001 to buffer. When this transfer is completed, a second DMA channel may be started to transfer data from buffer to CPU memory. The

receive-ready signal serves as the request input to the DMA controller.

If the frame is found to contain errors upon completion of reception, the receive discard pin goes high to indicate a bad frame. This signal may be used to automatically initialize the DMA channel so that the bad data may be overwritten by data from the next frame.

Extended capabilities

The 8001 can also serve in an extended subsystem in which tasks are offloaded from the system processor by an on-board microprocessor. Such systems are characterized by large amounts of data traffic and a desire to dedicate all system-processing capability to the application task.

In such a configuration (Fig. 2), the buffer space is a two-port random-access memory. This setup eliminates the need for the two DMA channels to move data from the buffer to the shared CPU memory. The on-board microprocessor resides on one port of the buffer memory to act as a high-level frame composer and Ethernet communications manager.

A typical sequence consists of the system CPU developing a communication request and placing it in the dual-port RAM. The on-board processor then constructs an appropriate frame to be sent on the Ethernet. This frame is placed in the buffer and the DMA channel is enabled.

Upon completion of a frame transmission or reception, the 8001 interrupts its on-board controller CPU, which then checks the 8001's status and has available in the buffer any received frames. In the next step of the process, the controller CPU processes the received frame for the system processor and offloads it from any data-reformatting tasks. To minimize system interaction and loading, all messages between the system and on-board CPUs travel through mailboxes in the RAM.

The benefits of this two-port RAM configuration are particularly important in a multitasking environment. The system CPU need only construct a high-level request for a file known to exist in the network. The controller CPU then takes the file name and constructs a broadcast-addressed frame containing a file query.

When the controller CPU receives the required file, it places it in the dual-port RAM for the system CPU after stripping any extraneous transport fields. The result is much greater throughput for the system CPU and a modular system design with fewer potential conflicts.

2. Sophisticated setup. In a complex Ethernet, the 8001 data-link controller will operate with an on-board microcontroller and dual-port random-access memories, one to serve the microcontroller and one to act as a transmit-receive buffer memory.

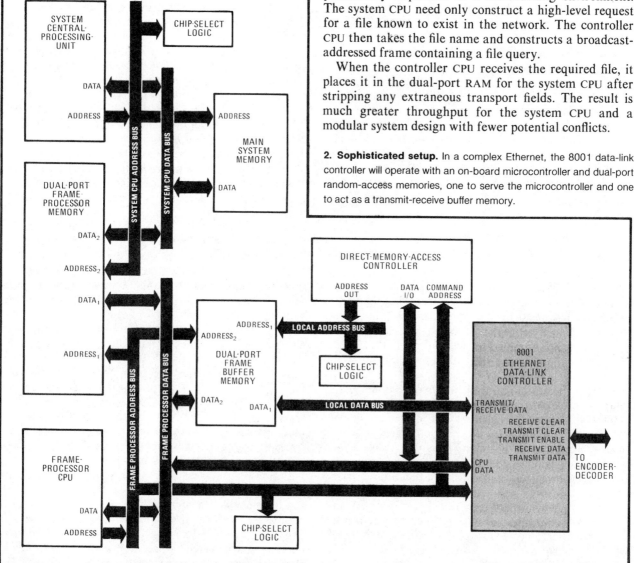

Link-controller IC combines versatility and flexibility

by Allen B. Goodrich
Ungermann-Bass Inc., Santa Clara, Calif.

Recognizing that different Ethernet implementations can meet the standard's specifications yet vary greatly in other important aspects, Ungermann-Bass in cooperation with Fujitsu Ltd. has developed a versatile two-chip set that meets the standard's specs while offering the designer maximum flexibility in realizing the other facilities. The two integrated circuits, the MB61301 data-link controller (DLC) and the MB502 encoder-decoder (Fig. 1), will suit a broad spectrum of applications.

For example, an Ethernet interface node for a terminal or a personal computer requires drastically different design tradeoffs than for a mainframe controller handling computer-to-computer traffic or large numbers of multiplexed circuits. Thus the two ICs integrate only the strictly specified parts of the Ethernet approach, leaving open the detailed interface with the node's processor. As different interfaces become standardized and as higher-level protocols are agreed upon by major vendor communities, they, too, can be committed to silicon.

In particular, system design using the 61301 and 502 gains flexibility in buffer management and interface control, as these are highly dependent on the particular application and environment. Except for providing signals to indicate retransmission after collision and to discard packets after erroneous reception, packet-buffer management is left to the system designer as required by the application.

A second architectural decision was to provide the 61301 DLC with the capability of transmitting and

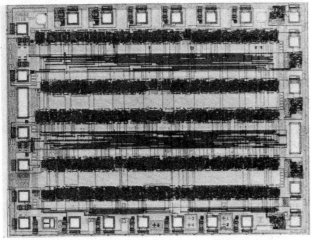

1. Manchester formatting. Developed by Ungermann-Bass and built by Fujitsu, the MB502 encoder-decoder chip converts non-return-to-zero code to Manchester code and vice versa. It performs Ethernet's layer 1 protocols with bipolar technology.

receiving packets at the same time. This allows important features such as efficient communication between devices at the same node (especially broadcast or multicast communications) because special filtering code in the transmission software is not needed for delivery to the receiving software.

In addition, a simultaneous transmission and reception capability permits more thorough diagnostic functions, such as loopback tests. Also, because the transmit and receive byte streams are distinct, systems needing extensive buffering can treat each byte stream as an independent event.

Another basic architectural decision was to keep the data paths separate from the control paths. The 10-megabit-per-second data rate specified for Ethernet is high relative to most microcomputer systems. Thus it requires some special handling of the byte streams to accommodate the required 1.25-megabyte bandwidth or the possibility of a 2.50-megabyte bandwidth in the case of a node's transmission to itself during self-testing, broadcast, or communication between devices on the same node. So separating the special requirements of data handling from the usually simple system timing requirements reduces the complexity of all interfacing.

The final architectural decision was to defer as many design decisions as possible to the system designer. For example, all three buses—transmit data, receive data, and control—may be tied together by three-state enable signals. Each bus has the signals required to implement a complete extension of the Ethernet timing requirements to a buffer-management chip. Alternatively, a controlling processor manages the buffer by using internal status indicators instead of the actual signals of the byte-stream interfaces.

The controller's design

Implementing layer 2 of the International Standards Organization's open-system network interconnection reference model, the DLC design is based on an existing Ethernet controller implemented in medium-scale integration that has been in volume production since July 1981. As mentioned, the algorithms and state diagrams exist in the Ethernet specifications for the signals on the coaxial cable, but no such simple definition of specs exist for the node interface. The 61301 design uses the MSI implementation's proven interface because silicon could be produced quickly with no interface problems. For example, provisions for packet-flow control and testing are already specified and proven in the existing design.

For this chip, complementary-MOS technology was chosen for its low power consumption. The architecture is based on a gate array for several reasons. For one, logic conversion is simplified because designing with a gate array is similar to MSI design. In particular, the fact that gate arrays may be easily configured to perform macroinstructions makes conversion simple.

Another reason for the use of gate arrays is that complete simulation before fabrication may be achieved by the design team. The geometry of a gate array is

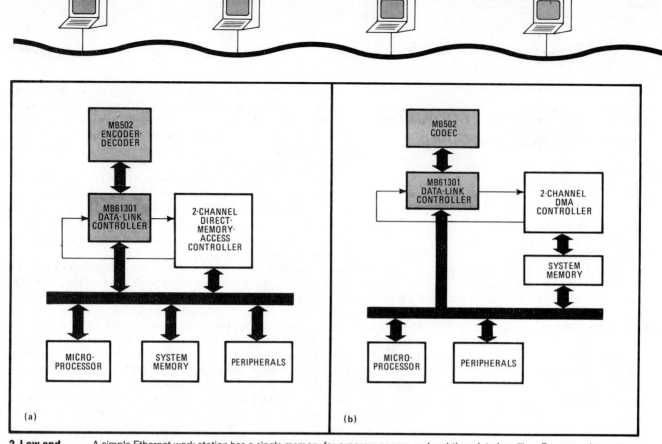

2. Low end . . . A simple Ethernet work station has a single memory for program access and real-time data handling. For many data rates, a single-port memory is adequate (a), but for higher rates a two-port memory may be needed (b).

fixed; as such, extremely reliable simulations are possible during design.

Also, gate arrays have a short fabrication cycle. The process time is less than that needed for fully custom designs, and the data base of the associated computer-aided design system makes changes easy.

Finally, the gate-array approach minimizes the penalty paid for adaptations. For example, any changes in the data-link level required in order to conform to the local network standards being drafted may be quickly accommodated in the Ungermann-Bass approach.

The C-MOS IC is configured as two principal sections— a transmitter and a receiver. Each section provides asynchronous buffering, provisions for byte-parity preamble generation or stripping, cyclic redundancy generation or checking, and conversion between serial and parallel data or vice versa. In addition, the transmitter provides contention resolution by means of the Ethernet-specified binary exponential backoff algorithm. For its part, the receiver provides various modes of address filtering.

The DLC chip has its architecture set up to optimize hardware and software interfacing in the Ethernet link. For example, the length of the receive first-in, first-out buffer (6 bytes) allows the reception of 10-byte packets (6 data and 4 CRC) for diagnostic purposes. The CRC is always tested and stripped from incoming packets. Also, for diagnostic purposes, a test bit inhibits the CRC accumulation in the receiver so that new packet data will be used as the test data.

There are other DLC features that make life easier for the network designer. A set of pins, controlled by the node's processor, gates the receive and transmit status bits in order to generate interrupt signals from such important events as packet transmission and reception and errors of various types. What's more, a time-domain reflectometry function in the transmitter measures the distance to a fault on the Ethernet coaxial cable.

Also, a status bit is cleared at the start of each transmission and set at the end if the receiver successfully receives a frame. This feature reduces software overhead since the receiver can still perform address decoding. Because the DLC is full-duplex, the receiver is active during transmission and will have the correct status for the packet being transmitted. Therefore, the software can be told after transmission that a copy of the transmit buffer should be made available to the receive function before release of the buffer.

Make the connection

The DLC chip has five groups of pins: power, control, receive, transmit, and transceiver. Its package is a 64-pin grid array, chosen to allow for the separate data paths for the control, transmit, and receive groups. The four power pins are broken down into two each for power and ground—a standard arrangement.

More novel is the design of the control group. Nineteen of these pins provide a byte-wide microcomputer interface port, including eight for data and four for register. To gate these, there are seven pins, a number that minimizes the number of external gates required for decoding and control.

There are also five special-function control pins, including a reset input for refresh, a receive interrupt output, and a transmit interrupt output. The others are

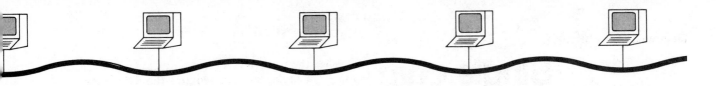

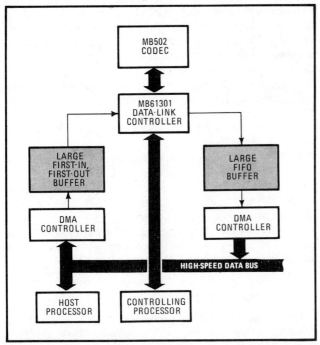

3. . . . and high. For a high-data-rate computer hooked up to an Ethernet, large first-in, first-out buffers may be needed to provide the mode with adequate bandwidth to do its tasks.

an output intended to control power to the transceiver by external switching and an output resulting from reception of a frame of a particular Ethernet type. The latter pin is intended for use as a remote reset function.

The transmit pins handle 8 data bits, a parity bit, and a last-byte flag, plus two byte-control signals that are the interface to a 2-byte asynchronous FIFO buffer. In addition, two packet-control signals are available for use in buffer-management tasks.

Incoming signals

The receive group of pins also includes the 8 data bits, a parity bit and a last-byte flag, plus three byte-control signals, which include a three-state output enable. Only one signal, discard, is required in the packet controls, because the last-byte flag indicates successful packet reception.

The transceiver pin signals are shared between the DLC and encoder-decoder IC. The transmit data is non-return-to-zero form and carries an enable signal with it. It receives its clock from the encoder chip. The receive data is accompanied by an enable (carrier detect) and a clock. A collision signal is received from the encoder-decoder chip.

The 502 encoder-decoder chip implementing the ISO layer 1 is a reversal of the DLC in that its external interface is specified without the algorithm being described. As in designing the 61301, an existing MSI design, in this case 10K emitter-coupled logic, was the best starting point for producing the decoder. However, a gate array is not feasible because of the Ethernet coaxial cable's voltage requirements, the multiple volt-

age levels required, and the internal speed requirements. As a result, a full custom design was appropriate, and a direct design translation was done from MSI to LSI in order to minimize the risk and decrease the design time.

The basic function of the 502 is to convert between Manchester and NRZ data. Beyond this function, there are two others: to serve as the interface with the baseband transceiver and to handle the signal distortion found in long cables with many taps.

Serving as interface

For transceiver interfacing, the encoder-decoder IC can send and receive for either dc- or ac-coupled amplifiers. To do this, the receiver adjusts the voltage threshold between the idle and active states while the transmitter maintains a 0-volt differential in the idle state.

To handle distortion, the 502 has a dual-bandwidth phase-locked loop, which can acquire phase in eight bit times or less. It can handle up $\pm 15\%$ waveform distortion during the preamble of the Ethernet packet and $\pm 20\%$ thereafter.

The encoder-decoder has a signal pin to put it in a loopback mode, in which it ignores inputs from the cable and tests the complete encode-decode path. It has five groups of signals: power, data-link, oscillator, cable, and controls in a 24-pin standard dual in-line package.

Most of the pin functions are straightforward. Thus, single power and ground pins are all that are required; and, in the oscillator group, three pins are used for direct connection of a crystal and a resonant circuit. The eight data-link group signals between the two chips were described earlier. There are also six pins in the cable group, and these interface directly to the three signal pairs of the transceiver cable.

In the control group of pins, two provide for a timing capacitor used to control the transmit pair to allow for ac-coupled transceivers. The last three pins are used for testing. Two of them also have other defined uses. For example, reset may be tied high, and dc link tied low to inhibit all ac-coupling provisions on input and output. The third pin is left open and used only for testing.

System interfaces

A typical low-end Ethernet interface has a single memory used both for program access and data buffering (Fig. 2a). A standard one- or two-channel direct-memory-access controller can support network access and be intelligent enough to supervise retransmission of discarded frames. Because the data rate of the network may be excessive for the bus protocols of some microcomputers, dual-port memory (Fig. 2b) may be a better design option.

Figure 3 shows a typical high-end use as would be found on network controllers for high-performance computer systems. The supervising processor may be the host processor or an intermediate processor resident on the controller board, as used here. In this design, the FIFO buffers provide network bandwidth and the elastic frame buffering to absorb peak traffic. □

Single chip encrypts data at 14 Mb/s

Three on-board write-only registers ensure key security under standard microprocessor or bit-slice control

by Dave MacMillan
Advanced Micro Devices Inc., Sunnyvale, Calif.

☐ When the U. S. government wants to protect sensitive data from prying eyes, it requires the data to be enciphered according to the National Bureau of Standards' data-encryption standard (DES). With the Am9518, a microprocessor peripheral chip from Advanced Micro Devices, this code can now be implemented at 14 megabits per second—fast enough to encrypt or decrypt on the fly as data is read from or written onto disk. Moreover, this rate is high enough to accommodate most telecommunications systems without the need for buffers. The resultant savings in memory and interfacing circuitry is considerable for both computer and communications applications.

High encryption and decryption speed is not the only feature of the 40-pin n-channel MOS chip (Fig. 1). The 9518 (and the AmZ8000 microprocessor family's identical AmZ8068) supports bidirectional, half-duplex operations at its top speed. Furthermore it contains three write-only key registers for enhanced security and can be configured in any of the three encryption/decryption modes recommended by the NBS

Telecom and data storage

Called the data-cipher processor, or DCP, the 9518 is intended for two markets: telecommunications and data storage. In telecommunications applications, it will usually be controlled by a standard microprocessor. In data-storage applications, it will encipher data as it is passed to (or from) a tape or disk drive and will be controlled by the tape or disk controller. Most of these tape and hard-disk controllers are based on microprogrammable bit-slice logic designs. To simplify system design in these applications, the 9518 has a special microprogrammed interface (called the direct control configuration), in addition to a standard microprocessor interface.

As part of the latter, there are two additional interface options. To attain this flexibility, the DCP uses three ports: a master port, a slave port, and an auxiliary port. The master port is bus-compatible with the Z8000 microprocessor and has an address-strobe ($\overline{\text{AS}}$), a data-strobe ($\overline{\text{DS}}$) and a chip-select ($\overline{\text{CS}}$) input, in addition to eight bidirectional address/data lines. The slave and auxiliary ports, with eight data lines, are subsets of the

---

Why a single data-encryption chip?

In addition to the usual reasons of lower power consumption, a smaller space requirement, increased performance, and easier system design for a one-chip instead of a multichip encryption and decryption scheme, there is another little-known rationale unique to the data encryption standard. Although the Government's regulations specifying the DES requirements are still being developed, it is likely that all DES equipment will have to be able to verify that it is operating correctly using one of two approaches as chosen by the system designer.

The first requires that whenever the DES device is not actively enciphering real data, test data must be pumped through it and compared with the expected output to verify correct device operation. This approach demands of both single- and multiple-chip encryption devices the almost full-time support of a microprocessor, in addition to special test software.

The other approach is to operate two DES devices in parallel and compare their outputs. With a single-chip device, the implementation of this approach is straightforward and requires minimal board space and overhead. On the other hand, DES devices using multiple chips for enciphering and a handful of interface components to connect to the system, the space requirements are formidable, and the user is forced to take the first approach.

Thus, with a single-chip device, the user can select either approach to best fit his space, speed, and cost constraints.

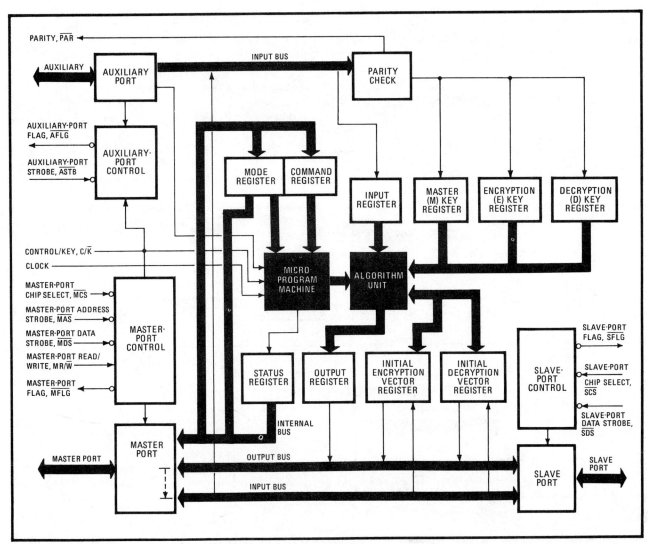

1. Versatile. The n-MOS Am9518 peripheral device can be controlled by a standard microprocessor or bit-slice processor for either telecommunications or disk-drive applications, respectively. For security, its key registers are write-only.

Z8000 bus interface. The interface flexibility results from the way these ports can be configured.

The most straightforward interface configuration is the master-port–only interface (Fig. 2a). In this mode, all commands and data are passed between the host microprocessor and the DCP through the master port. The encryption and decryption keys (described below) may be entered through either the master or the auxiliary port. In contrast, the master key may be entered only through the auxiliary port. The use of the separate auxiliary port to enter key data, perhaps directly from a keypad attached to the port, means that hardware separates data being enciphered from key data. Such a separation eliminates the possibility of a software error's jeopardizing the security of the keys.

In the second microprocessor-based interface (Fig. 2b), both the slave and the master port are used to pass data, although all commands pass through the master port only. In this mode, the DCP behaves like a bidirectional, half-duplex pipeline. The user selects which side (either the slave or the master port) is to handle encrypted data and which side is to handle clear data. The DCP can then be programmed either to encrypt,

accepting data from the clear-data side and passing it on from the encrypted-data side, or to decrypt, passing data in the opposite direction.

The architecture of the DCP is highly pipelined, so that the user can enter one 8-byte block ·of data while a previously entered block is being enciphered and while a third previously coded block is being read out. This pipelining yields enciphering rates of more than 14 Mb/s.

As is the case with the master-port–only configuration, hardware separation between the clear and the encrypted data enhances system security. For example, in an application like a telecommunications concentrator, separate microprocessors might be used on the clear- and encrypted-data sides to provide high throughput and to ensure that the two types of data never mix. Also, as with the master-port–only configuration, the user may enter encryption and decryption keys through the master port or, for enhanced security, encryption, decryption, and master keys through the auxiliary port.

The third possible interface applies to systems with a bit-slice processor. The DCP may be configured for such designs by applying a high signal to its control/key

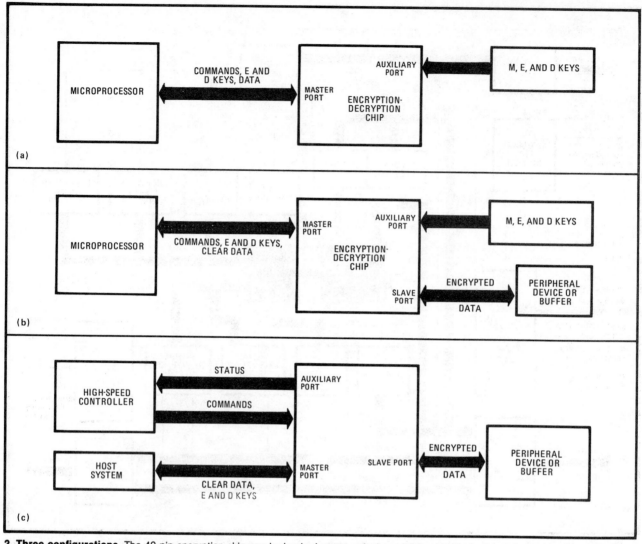

2. Three configurations. The 40-pin encryption chip can be hooked up as a single-port (a) or dual-port (b) device under time-multiplexed control or as a dual-port device under the management of a high-speed controller (c). All configurations are bidirectional and half-duplex.

(C/$\overline{\text{K}}$) pin. The auxiliary port is now reconfigured from an address/data multiplexed control to a direct control that interfaces directly with the bit-slice controller (Fig. 2c). Three of the port's signals are inputs, used to tell the DCP what operation to perform (encrypt or decrypt, load keys, start/stop). These lines may come directly from microcode memory.

In addition, status lines come out to indicate the state of the DCP. These outputs would typically be connected to the bit-slice sequencer for conditional branching based on the DCP's status. In the direct control mode, as in the microprocessor mode, data is passed via pipelining into the master port and out of the slave port or vice versa, depending on whether encryption or decryption is being performed.

Three modes

The DCP takes care of the three NBS-required enciphering modes by selecting from a 2-bit field of its mode register. These modes are known as the electronic code book (ECB), the cipher block chain (CBC), and the cipher feedback (CFB). Any enciphering option can be used with any of the interface options discussed earlier. The electronic-code-book mode (Fig. 3a) is a straightforward implementation of the DES: 64 bits of clear data in, 64 bits of coded text out, with no cryptographic dependence between blocks. It will be used mostly in disk applications, because the disk's need for random access and independence between data blocks is important.

The cipher-block-chain mode (Fig. 3b) also operates on blocks of 64 bits but includes a feedback step that chains consecutive blocks so that repetitive data in the plain text (such as ASCII blanks or runs of 1s and 0s) does not yield repetitive coded text. This approach also allows the data receiver to detect fraudulent data insertions and deletions. It will be widely used in telecommunication applications because of its message-tampering protection.

The cipher-feedback mode (Fig. 3c) is similar to the second in that it includes the logical linking of blocks required for detection of message insertion or deletion. Unlike CBC, however, it is byte-oriented, encrypting 8 bits of data at a time.

The DCP also contains three features that must be added to other encryption chips using external logic or host system software if they are desired. These are

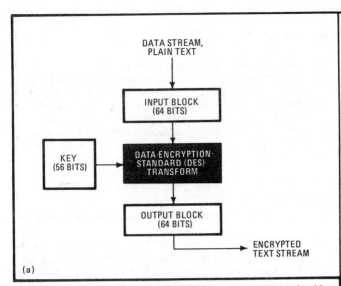

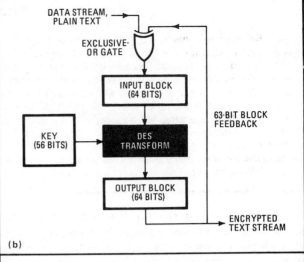

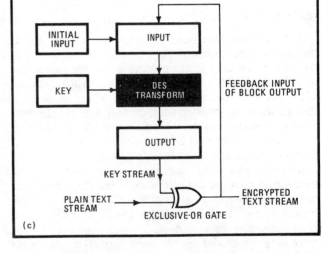

3. Three modes. The master, auxiliary, and slave ports, each with eight data lines, allow the 9518 to support the three enciphering modes specified by the National Bureau of Standards: electronic code book (a), cipher block chain (b), and cipher feedback (c).

initializing vector registers (one for encryption and one for decryption) that specify the initial data sequence used in the feedback loop for the CBC and CFB modes, a write-only master key register, and two write-only session key registers.

Whereas the initializing vector registers are straightforward in design and implementation, the master and session key registers bear explanation. The master (M) key register permits implementation of a multiple-key system. In this arrangement, a single master key, common to all DES devices in the system, encrypts session keys for transmission to remote DES equipment and decrypts session keys received from such equipment. The M key register may be loaded with clear data only through the auxiliary port.

The session keys

The two session key registers are an encryption (E) key register for encoding plain text and a decryption (D) key register to decode enciphered text. These keys may be loaded through either the master or the auxiliary port. In some telecommunication environments, E and D keys will be transmitted from a user at a terminal to the host computer. To provide security for the transmitted keys, the key data will be enciphered using the M key.

When the host computer receives the encryption and decryption keys, it decodes them using the master key. All subsequent communication between the host and the user uses the E and D keys. To support this type of interchange, the DCP has provisions to receive an encrypted E or D key, decrypt the key information using the M key, and store the decrypted E or D key in the appropriate key register. Because the entire operation is done on chip, the host will never see clear E or D keys. Thus the system is highly secure.

Although in most systems the same key will be used for encryption and decryption, it is not a DES requirement. Because of its separate registers, the 9518 can work easily in systems employing separate encryption

and decryption keys. The use of separate keys is readily accomplished, since the time-consuming reloading of the key register when changing from encryption to decryption and vice versa (required for DES devices with one key register) is eliminated.

The NBS standard specifies that each key byte must include a parity bit. Therefore, as a validation procedure, a parity-checking circuit is activated on the chip whenever the host central processing unit enters any E, D or M key in clear or encrypted form. The output of the parity detection circuit is connected to a parity (PAR) pin (see Fig. 1 again) and the state of this pin is reflected in the DCP's status register. In addition to the PAR bit, the status register has a latched parity (LPAR) bit that is set to 1 if the status-register PAR bit goes to 1. Once set, the LPAR bit is not cleared until a reset occurs or a new load-key command is entered.

The 9518, however, goes one step further than is required to ensure data integrity by adding an abort sequence. Because of the complex nature of the encoding processor, considerable internal checking is needed for internal consistency, and an abort will be generated if basic operating rules are violated. For example, writing a command into the command register before a previous command is completed triggers an abort.

Data encryption: a future market?

Over the next few years, the U. S. government will pass regulations requiring the use of encryption devices that conform to the National Bureau of Standards' data-encryption standard on all nonmilitary Government archiving of data on disks and tapes, as well as in data communications. These regulations, which are being drafted by various Federal agencies, will be significant for any computer manufacturer who wishes to sell his equipment to the Government. Their impact is also well appreciated by the semiconductor manufacturers, as shown by the dozen or so DES-compatible encryption chips of varying capabilities that are currently available for evaluation.

Although few pieces of computer equipment now have encryption capabilities, as the regulations are developed and the communications protocols are made final, manufacturers will start to include DES devices in their products. In addition, "black boxes" will be developed with encryption capabilities to fit older products. Initially, most firms will simply have an extra-cost socket for these devices. Then, as the use of the data encryption standard spreads to industries concerned with confidentiality, they will become a regular part of most computer equipment.

The 9518 is faster than any other DES device sold today. This feat was accomplished by processing a complete 64-bit data word in parallel, rather than serially, as many other devices do, and by using a pipelined architecture, as mentioned earlier.

Up to speed

As noted, the three-stage pipelined architecture allows the user to simultaneously put a 64-bit input on one 9518 port while the chip is enciphering a previously entered block and while the user is reading out (from a second 9518 port) a previously processed data block. Although data is transferred into and out of the two 9518 data ports in bytes, it is internally assembled into a 64-bit word. This word is processed in a 64-bit parallel fashion, instead of a bit or byte at a time.

Because processing can occur while data is being transferred into and out of the 9518, the chip can be internally manipulating data 100% of the time. In a typical system design exploiting the pipelined architecture, a direct-memory-access device, such as the 16-bit AmZ8016 (operated in the byte mode) or the 8-bit Am9517/Intel 8237, is used to transfer data fast enough to keep the 9518 operating at its maximum rate, with control pins conveying the hardware DMA requests.

Since two data ports are used for pipelined operation, it is easy to design the 9518 into disk-based computer and telecommunications systems. The designer need only determine where in the data path through the system he wishes the enciphering to be performed. The 9518 is then inserted at this point. One port is configured to handle clear data and the other port to handle encrypted data, as explained.

The flexibility of this architecture has been enhanced by making each port interact with the system by means of the standard Z8000 bus protocol. Further convenience is accomplished by allowing the user to dynamically program the direction of data flow and to define which port is the clear-data and which the encrypted-data port. Internal safeguards have been included in the logic to ensure that reprogramming of the chip cannot cause clear and encrypted data to appear on the same port of the device.

It must be remembered that a pipelined architecture is not ideal for all systems. There are some applications where the user may wish to place the encoding device on a separate bus rather than in the middle of a data path.

In that case, an interface for two ports is undesirable because it requires extra address decoding. Such a single-port requirement, usually found in systems designed for minimal cost rather than maximum performance, can be implemented with the 9518 by programming it to operate in its single-port mode, thus deactivating one of the two data ports. Data can still be read from and sent to the device while it is actively enciphering, as in the pipelined mode. However, there is some loss of overall performance, because data cannot be read from and sent to the device through the single port fast enough to keep it enciphering all the time. Encryption is so fast that it must occasionally halt to wait either for new data to be entered or for data already processed to be read out.

Slice that bit

Both the pipelined and the single-port mode accept commands from a microprocessor through one of the three ports. In some disk and telecommunications systems, however, the controlling computer may be built from bit-slice components.

In a bit-slice design, issuing commands to a peripheral device usually takes many instructions and tends to be slow. To facilitate use of the 9518 in bit-slice systems without significantly affecting system performance, a special bit-slice interface has been included. This interface lets the user control the 9518 by directly manipulating the voltage levels on certain pins, instead of by writing into an internal command register.

Since a bit-slice architecture is chosen to maximize performance, the designers of the 9518 decided to require that in a bit-slice system, the device must be used in the dual–data-port configuration. One port then handles clear data and one encrypted data, as in the pipelined mode. In other words, a bit-slice single-port configuration does not make sense in a bit-slice environment because of its reduced performance.

The dual-port configuration lets the internal enciphering processor work at full speed and, in addition, makes possible novel configuration possibilities. For example, the 9518 can be included within the data path of a bit-slice arithmetic and logic unit. The bit-slice control inputs on the chip can be driven directly from microcode memory and the status output lines can go directly to the microsequencer to control microcode branching. This design can have directly executable macroinstructions for encryption and decryption. □

6.
MATH
AND SIGNAL
PROCESSING

Once the sole domain of large batch-oriented systems, "number crunching" has infiltrated smaller systems. In keeping with this trend toward small, powerful systems, semiconductor manufacturers are turning out special-purpose chips that augment the inherent math-processing muscle of a central-processing unit. For example, the pair of articles that lead off this chapter recount a major breakthrough in floating-point processing—dedicated chips that handle math operations in record time using a standard format.

Besides these purely mathematical operations, however, designers are finding an increasing need for hardware support for more general problems in digital signal processing. Other articles in this chapter describe special-purpose chips for this important, yet complex arena of applications. Still, this type of hardware support requires an accompanying systems-level approach to signal processing. The final article in this chapter presents a modular method for making digital signal processing systems that combine powerful performance with the flexibility needed for a wide range of applications.

ALU, multiplier chips zip through IEEE floating-point operations

Pipelined multiplier crunches 32-bit multiplications at 5 megaflops;
separate ALU chip handles addition, subtraction, and normalization

by Bob Woo, Lyon Lin, and Robert E. Owen, *Weitek Corp., Santa Clara, Calif.*

□ Once confined largely to batch processing on mainframe computers, floating-point computations are migrating to smaller systems for such applications as seismic processing, medical imaging, and model simulation. To date, however, system designers hoping to exploit the precision and dynamic range of floating-point processing have been forced to use either fast but expensive array processors or low-cost but slow coprocessors—or even to build their own hardware subsystems.

Now, though, an attractive alternative arrives in the form of a pair of chips (Fig. 1) capable of churning out 5 million 32-bit floating-point operations a second in the standard format proposed by the Institute of Electrical and Electronics Engineers and designated IEEE standard 754. Among the choice of arithmetic functions possible, those most frequently encountered in high-performance systems are add, subtract, multiply, and floating-point–to–integer conversion. Functional partitioning of the chip set separates these functions roughly equally into a multiplier and an arithmetic and logic unit. (The less frequently used floating-point division can also, if needed, be performed in a two-step algorithm with a multiplier and ALU.)

Using a standard 3-micrometer n-channel process, the WTL 1032 multiplier and WTL 1033 ALU fit on dice measuring respectively about 300 by 290 and 305 by 225 mils on a side. Smaller than most floating-point coprocessors, these sizes ensure high-yielding commercial parts, not just captive-user technology show pieces. As for other practical considerations, the low power dissipation of 1.5 watts typical of each chip reduces cooling needs and also permits use of smaller packages like the 68-pin leadless chip-carrier, among others, in addition to the usual 64-pin dual in-line package. Also, the pinout common to both chips provides circuit-board layout advantages regardless of whether the chips are paralleled or cascaded as multiplier and accumulator.

These new floating-point components and the IEEE standard are attractive not just for new floating-point applications, but also for more established real-time control and signal-processing applications that till now have been forced to settle for integer arithmetic. In such applications, the arithmetic precision must also be high—20 to 24 bits—to maintain stable operation and provide the high signal-to-noise performance possible with digital solutions. Speed is of course not just a convenience but a vital necessity to the correct operation of such real-time applications. Often processors are arranged in parallel or cascaded together in order to furnish the needed processing power.

Integer deficiencies

In typical real-time systems today, dynamic range and precision have had to be restricted because of the use of an integer implementation. At that, only 16-bit parts have been available with the speed or any of the size and cost benefits of very large-scale integration. The severe performance compromise that such a situation causes hurts all the more because it is common practice to simulate and develop the systems first of all on floating-point array processors.

Transporting this type of system to a manufacturable solution then often involves extended development time and painful redesign of the algorithms in order to recover lost performance. The IEEE single-precision floating-point format with its 24-bit integer significand and 8-bit exponent—providing a dynamic range of over 1,500 decibels—satisfies the high-precision requirements and wide dynamic-range needs of these real-time applications.

For all applications, compatibility with the IEEE standard can improve the transportability of working solutions and speed the availability of products. Floating-point arithmetic does require more operations and take more time; however, in almost all interactive and real-time applications, data is processed as vectors, so that pipelining can be exploited to maintain the high data throughput that has previously been achieved by means of integer arithmetic.

Standard environment

Although the standard defines a complete programming environment, the choice between hardware and software functions is left to the implementor. Integrated circuits like the 1032 and 1033 contain only basic arithmetic functions, so that they cannot be said in themselves to conform to the standard for those functions, but rather to be merely compatible with it. Nevertheless, they must contain the complementary hardware functions if they are to implement the entire standard. In general terms, compatibility means using the standard's format, its special values, its arithmetic, and its methods for handling exceptions or errors.

In the format specified for single-precision 32-bit values, a variety of entities are defined (Fig. 2). Besides zero and unique representations of plus and minus infinity, the standard defines a range of bit patterns that do not represent numbers at all. Such a so-called not-a-number (NaN) can be used for communication. It should be noted that the most significant bit of the significand—called the hidden bit since it is not physically represented—is always 1 except when the value represented is 0 or a denormalized (or underflowed) number, in which case the hidden bit is always 0.

Arithmetic operations are defined for all values except for NaNs. Retaining denormalized-number arithmetic yields a gradual loss of significance for underflowed results. All numeric results are calculated to the highest possible precision and then rounded to the precision of the format. Even the methods of rounding and handling representations of infinity are specified. In each case, a default method is given, as well as options desirable in certain applications—for example, rounding options used in format conversions.

Rounding to the nearest number, or nearest even number if it is a tie, is specified as the default rounding procedure in the IEEE standard. This option will be preferred for most applications because of its decreased bias in the resulting values, but rounding toward 0 or plus or minus infinity may be selected.

Valid and invalid

Only normalized floating-point numbers are considered valid by the standard, and any denormalized (underflowed) number must be flagged as an exception. However, these denormalized numbers must be preserved and the arithmetically correct—though perhaps misleading—result produced. This is called gradual underflow.

When the ALU chip performs this arithmetic, it normalizes the numbers by allowing the biased exponent to roll under or wrap around, treating it as a 2's complement negative number. After the ALU operation is complete, the result is denormalized and flagged. These additional steps are easily done with the existing significand shifters and exponent incrementers and decrementers needed for normalized floating-point addition in the ALU.

These functions, though, are not needed for normalized floating-point multiplication and are not used enough on denormalized values to justify their inclusion on what is already the larger multiplier chip. Rather, denormalized operands for the multiplier are flagged and returned to the ALU, where they are normalized with a

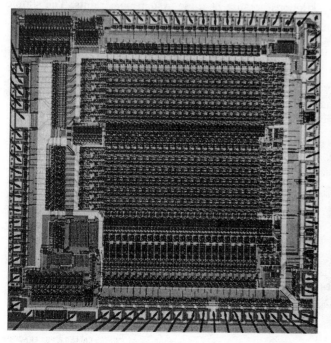

1. Megapower. Using a standard 3-μm n-MOS process, the WTL 1032 (left) handles 5 million floating-point multiplications a second in its 300-by-290-mil² area. Its companion chip, the WTL 1033 ALU (right), manages additions and subtractions at the same rate within its 305-by-225-mil² size. Each chip dissipates only about 1.5 W.

negative exponent. These wrapped numbers, with wrapped-around exponents, are then returned to the multiplier. This is a time-consuming procedure and one that in many real-time applications is not necessary. In these cases, substituting 0 for the denormalized operand produes a valid result of 0, and processing proceeds. This option is included in the multiplier and is invoked by choice of the fast mode of operation in its mode register.

Errors and exceptions

Additionally, the format specifies a uniform detection and treatment of errors or exception conditions. Invalid numbers and operations that arise in floating-point arithmetic are detected as exceptions and must be handled in either of two ways, according to the standard.

Case one, the default case, must flag five separate conditions and produce specified results. These exceptions include invalid operands, underflow, overflow, inexact results, and division by 0.

Each of these exceptions must result in certain default numerical results, like infinity at overflow or denormalized numbers at underflow. For data-path components, flagging the exceptions in a status register and returning the correct default result is all that is necessary. The four standard exceptions that apply to these chips (division by 0 does not apply) are output in a 3-bit status format. An additional exception handled by the multiplier is denormalized input. This exception detects the denormalized operands, which must be returned to the ALU unless the fast mode is enabled.

In the second case, user-written software routines must be able to attempt recovery of data as it existed before the exception occurred. NaNs can be helpful in this recovery process. Exception-detection logic must be present in the data path so that default results may be generated and exception flags set. Since the actual handling of the exception trap is defined by the designer, only the simplest control structure in the chips is desirable for maximum flexibility and speed.

Speed is an important requirement of most interactive applications. For high-resolution shaded graphics displays, systems churn through many millions of floating-point operations a second. Such megaflop rates are needed to maintain system response times at a level acceptable to the display user working with normal multi-operation commands. Simulations are similarly demanding because of the large number of data points and the fine resolution required to generate the needed results.

All logic is static, so any clock

2. Formats. Floating-point operations and fixed-point conversions find support in the WTL 1032 and 1033 chip set. In compliance with the IEEE single-precision floating-point standard, five basic entities are defined, including special nonnumerical values.

rate from dc up to l0 megahertz may be used. Propagation time through a pipeline stage is a maximum of 200 nanoseconds. Thus, two full 32-bit input operands can be loaded and one 32-bit result unloaded every 200 ns, keeping the pipeline full. This corresponds to a 5-megaflop rate for each chip. Total latency time from the entry of the most significant operand word on the chip to the delivery of the least significant result word is a maximum of 1.1 microseconds. In a special flow-through mode, the total latency period undergoes a reduction to 900 ns.

System effects

These high individual component speeds become high system data rates in a variety of different data-path configurations. In a more limited-function real-time signal processor, like those used for communications, the ALU and multiplier are more often placed in a serial pipeline. But in programmable array processors, the ALU and multiplier are likely to be paralleled on two data input buses and one output bus connected to registers or memory. With 32-bit-wide buses and with the individual microprogramming of each chip commonly used, such a configuration produces a 10-megaflop pipelined rate. This same 10-megaflop rate may, moreover, be multiplied by splitting the data samples among two or more pipelines—a feasible solution because of the small size of the arithmetic elements in this case.

More conventional central processing units are likely to configure the ALU and multiplier in parallel also, but on one or at most two buses. The buses may be limited to 16 bits. The floating-point elements may not be the primary arithmetic elements, and they are unlikely to function simultaneously as in the array and signal processors. Instead, they often work in concert with a register file on multiple-step algorithms, such as square root, in addition to just add and multiply. Data rates fall from a maximum of 5 megaflops into the range of hundreds of kiloflops because of these system constraints. The simple

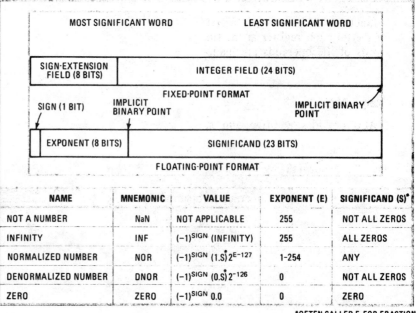

| MOST SIGNIFICANT WORD | LEAST SIGNIFICANT WORD |

FIXED-POINT FORMAT

| SIGN-EXTENSION FIELD (8 BITS) | INTEGER FIELD (24 BITS) |

SIGN (1 BIT) · IMPLICIT BINARY POINT · IMPLICIT BINARY POINT

FLOATING-POINT FORMAT

| EXPONENT (8 BITS) | SIGNIFICAND (23 BITS) |

NAME	MNEMONIC	VALUE	EXPONENT (E)	SIGNIFICAND (S)*
NOT A NUMBER	NaN	NOT APPLICABLE	255	NOT ALL ZEROS
INFINITY	INF	$(-1)^{SIGN}$ (INFINITY)	255	ALL ZEROS
NORMALIZED NUMBER	NOR	$(-1)^{SIGN}$ $(1.S)2^{E-127}$	1-254	ANY
DENORMALIZED NUMBER	DNOR	$(-1)^{SIGN}$ $(0.S)2^{-126}$	0	NOT ALL ZEROS
ZERO	ZERO	$(-1)^{SIGN}$ 0.0	0	ZERO

*OFTEN CALLED F, FOR FRACTION

direct controls of loading and unloading, function selection, and mode of operation on the 1032 and 1033 accommodate all of these configurations while providing near optimum performance (Table 1).

Common architecture

In the 1032 multiplier and 1033 ALU, two input operands and a single output result allow the data paths and control structure of the chips to be identical (Fig. 3). Each array is separated into three segments with nearly the same propagation time, and each segment is isolated by its own pipeline register. Furthermore, the array's function register and status are pipelined, so that these values propagate through the chip along with the associated data values.

All ports—both input and output as well as data and control—are buffered with registers on the chips. These registers, combined with three-state TTL outputs and a no-load mode of operation, ease the use of the chips in parallel bus architectures. Although the two 32-bit operands and the output result are time-multiplexed through the 16-bit ports, the clocking of input and output registers at twice the pipeline rate make this time sharing invisible. In cases where some operation is performed using a constant, bus traffic may be reduced by maintaining the constant in one of the operand registers while loading the other operand individually. Repeated multiplication or addition by a constant is a common vector operation in many high-speed applications.

Pipeline registers raise the continuous data rate through the arithmetic array logic, but at the cost of an additional clock delay for a single data value to propagate through them. This increased latency can be eliminated by using the flow-through mode in which the pipeline registers are transparent to data movement.

The status register is pipelined along with the data path so that the status at the output applies to the data concurrently at the output. The status remains constant for the two clock periods for unloading the least and most significant words of the result.

The function of the array is determined by the contents of the function register at the time the most significant words of the operands are loaded. The function is pipelined through with the data, so that it may change without all data first being unloaded from the pipeline.

Multistage ALU

The ALU provides addition and subtraction for the most useful combinations of signed and unsigned operands. Additionally, as Table 2 shows, there are the normalizing and denormalizing operations. The multiplier's only operation is multiplication, but there are four combinations of wrapped and unwrapped operands possible in its IEEE mode. The ALU array in Fig. 3 is shown in the pipeline mode with registers following each stage, all other logic being combinatorial.

Processing starts in stage ½ of the array with the loading of the most significant words of the operands. First the hidden bit is inserted by testing the exponents. If an exponent is 0, the hidden bit is a 0; otherwise, it is

a 1. For two operand functions, apart from format conversions and wrapping and unwrapping, the significands must be aligned so that bits of equal weight are operated on together. This alignment begins by selecting the operand with the larger exponent. All eight of the exponent bits are compared and the result stored in a register at the start of stage 1 to indicate if operand A is larger or smaller. If only one operand is used, an appropriate constant is loaded into the B exponent register.

At the beginning of stage 1, both 33-bit operands are complete and any invalid operand for the arithmetic operation can be detected and flagged. The larger and smaller exponents are selected by multiplexers, and the smaller is subtracted from the larger. The result is the number of binary places by which the smaller operand's significand must be right-shifted for alignment with the larger operand's significand. The smaller significand is then right-shifted, while the larger is complemented if that is required by the selected arithmetic function. For single operand functions, the constant entered earlier in the smaller exponent can produce a desired shift as, for example, in conversion to integer format.

At this point, the two properly aligned significands are added and the 28-bit sum stored along with the expo-

TABLE 1. CONTROL OPERATIONS FOR WTL 1032 MULTIPLIER AND WTL 1033 ARITHMETIC AND LOGIC UNIT			
L_1 L_0		Mnemonic	Load operation
0	0	NOP	No loading
0	1	LAB	Load operands A and B into array
1	0	LA	Load operand A only into array
1	1	LMODE	Load MODE register from F and U input registers

U_1 U_0		Mnemonic	Unload operation
1	X	DAB	Disable output register's three-state outputs to high impedance state
0	X	ENB	Enables output register's three-state outputs
X	0	UMS	Unload most significant word from array into output register
X	1	ULS	Unload least significant word from array into output register

F_3	F_2	F_1	F_0	U_0	Mnemonic	Mode operation
X	X	X	X	0	FLOW	Data flows through array without pipeline registers
X	X	X	X	1	PIPE	Data is clocked through three pipeline registers in the array
X	X	0	0	X	RN	Round to nearest number, or even number if a tie
X	X	0	1	X	RZ	Round toward zero
X	X	1	0	X	RP	Round toward positive infinity
X	X	1	1	X	RM	Round toward minus infinity
X	0	X	X	X	AI	Affine infinity (sign preserved)
X	1	X	X	X	PI	Projective infinity (sign ignored)
0	X	X	X	X	IEEE	Treats denormalized operands according to IEEE standard (WTL1032 only)
1	X	X	X	X	FAST	Replaces denormalized operands with zero (WTL1032 only)

nent, sign, and status in the pipeline register at the end of stage 1. The sum is composed of 1 bit for possible overflow, the 24 bits of the format, a guard bit, an additional lower-order bit for rounding, and what is called a sticky bit. The sticky bit is the logical OR of all lower-order bits below the round bit and is used in rounding operations.

Stage 2 initially complements the sum if this is re-quired by the combination of function choice and the sign of the sum determined in the previous stage. The resultant value in general will not be normalized at this point—that is, its most significant bit will not be set to 1. Its significand may have overflowed its original 24 bits because the two operands were of the same sign, or the value may be quite small with just a few lower-order bits set because it happened to be the

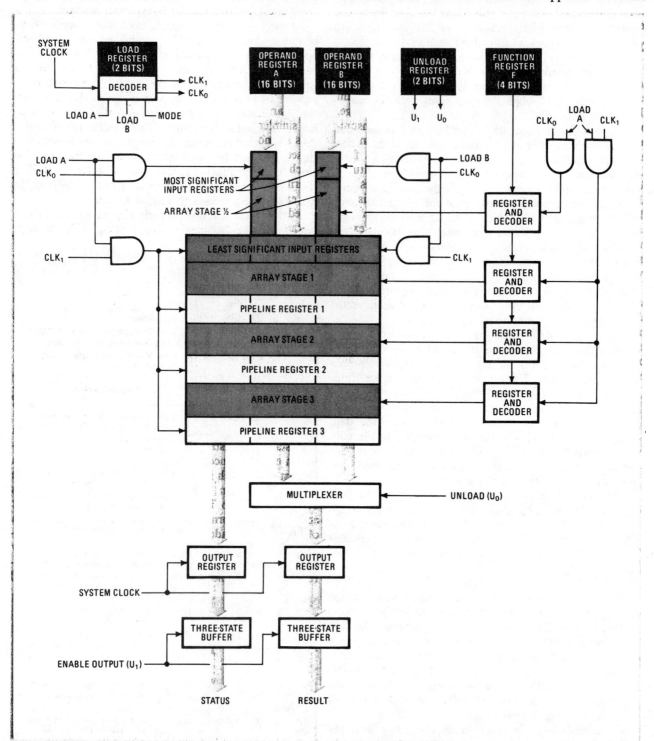

3. Single form. Both the 1032 multiplier and 1033 ALU chips use a common architecture to handle their separate functions. The shaded area is the pipelined multiplier in the 1032 and the pipelined ALU in the 1033. In the flow-through mode, the pipeline registers (color) are transparent.

difference between two nearly equal numbers.

To comply with the standard, all results must be returned normalized or at least as a denormalized number with the smallest possible exponent. The first step in the process of achieving either of these goals is to determine the location of the most significant bit that is set to a binary 1. This step is done with priority encoding logic, which returns a number equal to the displacement of the most significant bit set from the leftmost bit position.

Displacement matters

This displacement is the number of left shifts necessary to normalize the number plus the decrease in the binary exponent that must accompany the shifting to maintain the same value. The exponent is subtracted in this stage, but the displacement is stored for the more time-consuming shifting to follow in stage 3. Any underflow in the exponent as a result of decrementing generates a flag. Under this condition, the original exponent is substituted for the displacement to the shifter. This produces the shift necessary for a denormalized number, which is the desired result for a two-operand function. Under the same condition, too, the value 0 is entered for the exponent. For the wrap operation, the underflowed exponent is the desired 2's complement representation of the correct negative exponent and is retained.

With the proper amount of left shifting determined, stage 3 can complete the normalizing in its multiple-bit shifter. If the normalized 27-bit significand cannot be truncated to the 24 bits of the output format without changing its value, then it must be rounded. The sticky bit is used in this determination since it represents any exactness that has already been lost in truncation. The selected mode of rounding is accomplished with a simple adder, and the inexact result flag is set. Upward rounding of the magnitude can generate an additional higher-order bit. This, plus any previous growth, is shifted out in the rounder and the exponent incremented accordingly. Incrementing the exponent can produce overflow, which sets the exponent overflow flag.

At this point in the array, the calculation is complete, and any exceptions have been detected and flags set. The additional operations that are done at this time are for format conversions. Also, the exception flags are encoded and all output significands are reduced to 23 bits, with the most significant once again becoming hidden.

Multiplier pipes

The array of the floating-point multiplier is conceptually simpler than the ALU. Since the normalization functions are not required here (Table 3), the array's stage ½ is used only to expand the 8 exponent bits to 9, based on which of the operands have wrapped exponents, and to determine the value of the hidden bits. The expansion of the exponents makes explicit in 2's complement (and biased 127) form the negative exponent of wrapped operands.

The complete operands are loaded at the beginning of stage 1 and are tested. Denormalized operands, in addition to setting the invalid operand flag, also set the denormalized input flag signaling for their return to the ALU if operation is in the IEEE mode. Exponents are added in multiplication, and this proceeds after testing with the bias removed from one of them. Any exponent overflow or underflow values are preserved in the 10-bit sum. The sign bits of the two operands are masked off, and the output sign determined in a simple exclusive-OR operation. This relatively simple sign and exponent handling take little time compared with the multiplication of the significands.

The 24-by-24-bit significand multiplier extends across both stage 1 and stage 2. It uses an area-efficient combination of Booth encoding and carry-save adders except in the last row, which is carry-look-ahead. A full 48 bits are registered between the two stages and produced at its output. This step is necessary to maintain the 24-bit accuracy of the format, for there can be no simplification of the matrix of adders. After the final addition, however, the result is reduced to 28 bits including the sticky bit—a reduction that preserves enough precision for correct rounding, which follows in stage 3. □

F_3	F_2	F_1	F_0	Mnemonic	Operation
0	0	0	0	WRAP A	Conversion of a denormalized A operand to one normalized with negative (wrap-around) exponent
0	0	0	1	UNWRAP A	Conversion of a normalized A operand with negative exponent to a denormalized one
0	0	1	0	FLOAT A	Conversion of 24-bit integer to 32-bit normalized floating-point number
0	0	1	1	FIX A	Conversion of 32-bit normalized floating-point to 24-bit integer
0	1	0	0	A + B	Floating-point addition of operands A minus B
0	1	0	1	A − B	Floating-point subtraction of operand A minus B
0	1	1	0	− A + B	Floating-point addition of operands minus A plus B
0	1	1	1	ABS A + ABS B	Floating-point addition of operands |A| plus |B|
1	0	0	0	A − B ABS	Absolute value of floating-point subtraction of operands A minus B
1	0	0	1	A + B ABS	Absolute value of floating-point addition of operands A plus B

F_3	F_2	F_1	F_0	Mnemonic	Operation
0	0	0	0	A · B	Multiply normalized floating-point operands A times B
0	0	0	1	WA · B	Multiply wrapped (negative exponent) operand A times operand B
0	0	1	0	A · WB	Multiply operand A times wrapped operand B
0	0	1	1	WA · WB	Multiply wrapped operands A times B

Making mainframe mathematics

by John Palmer, Rafi Nave, Charles Wymore, Robert Koehler, and Charles McMinn, *Intel Corp., Santa Clara, Calif.*

☐ Ongoing advances in very large-scale integrated-circuit processing now permit a complete floating-point mathematics subsystem on a single silicon substrate. The 8087 numeric data processor is designed to function as a tightly coupled coprocessor to a general-purpose 8086 or 8088 microprocessor. Its specialized architecture is derived from experience gained in fitting much larger machines with similar mathematical capabilities.

As with mainframe computers, dedicated data types, instructions, and registers are fully integrated to enhance the performance of the hardware and untangle the design of software. The evolution of numeric-processing support for mainframes and minicomputers is spotted with gradual and often haphazard extensions imposed upon otherwise general-purpose hardware; the 8087, in contrast, represents one of the few attempts to rigorously analyze in advance the hardware and software needs for numeric processing.

This planning was expedited by the work of the Institute of Electrical and Electronics Engineers, which has proposed a standard for floating-point arithmetic. Therefore, unlike most prior implementations, the 8087 conforms to a detailed specification for numeric operations (see "The 8087's roots,").

The 8087 typically offers a hundredfold improvement in throughput over calculations done entirely in software subroutines executed by the 8086 or 8088. The new chip also offers enhanced precision through a 64-bit internal data path, an 80-bit register stack, and a 68-bit arithmetic and logic unit.

In many ways, though, raw speed and more bits are easily arrived at—scaling down devices can account for both, in fact. Even the 8087's single instruction for calculating trigonometric functions and logarithms, raising numbers to powers (exponentiation), and finding square roots do not warrant the careful attention that must be given, especially with number crunching, to possibly undesirable exceptions that are bound to crop up in the course of the computations. Here the 8087 really shines, with its high degree of immunity against overflow, underflow, and errors due to the rounding of intermediate results. This degree of immunity makes the 8087 applicable in the most demanding kinds of application—for instance, accounting, which requires exact

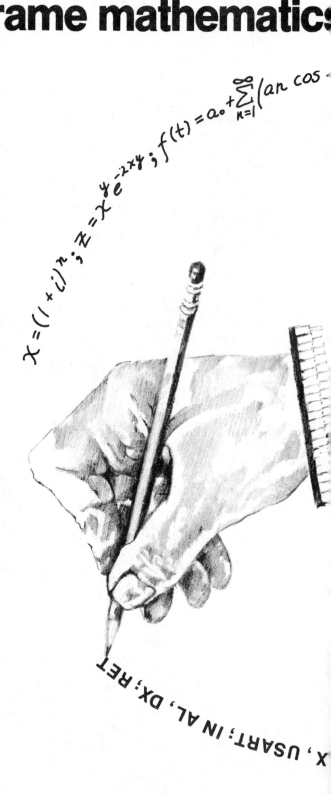

cessible to microcomputers

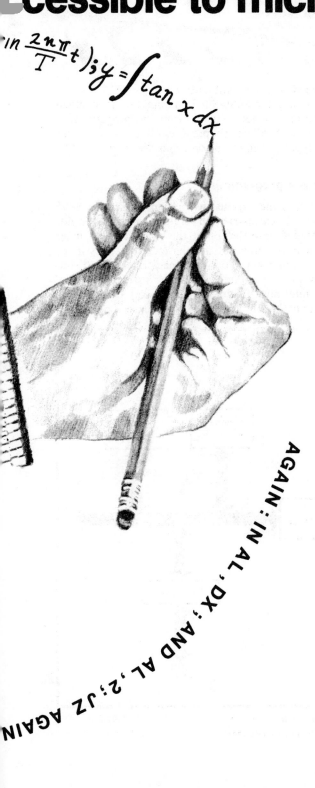

$$\sin \frac{2n\pi}{T}t\,);\, y = \int \tan x\, dx$$

AGAIN: IN AL, DX; AND AL, 2; JZ AGAIN

results with no rounding over a wide range (as large as 18 decimal digits).

The 8087 is the result of high-performance silicon-gate MOS technology (HMOS), which packs the die with scaled-down 4-micrometer transistors. On-chip substrate biasing yields faster and more reliable operation. With HMOS, the entire mathematics processor is about 109,000 square mils, containing the equivalent of over 65,000 devices (Fig. 1). This includes the internal register stack, comprising more than 700 bits of random-access memory, and a microprogram section that contains over 30,000 bits of microcode. The 8087 operates from a single 5-volt supply and is housed in a standard 40-pin ceramic package.

The coprocessor concept

As noted, the 8087 is specifically designed to operate as a coprocessor with the 16-bit 8086 (or 8088) microprocessor. A coprocessor extends the capabilities of the central processing unit to which it is attached; specifically, coprocessing is a special case of multiprocessing, one in which both processors execute from a single instruction stream. Figure 2 shows a typical configuration.

In the 8087-8086 combination, both processors operate in unison. They monitor the same instruction stream and execute selected instructions from it. For example, while the 8086 deals with memory segmentation, calculating the addresses of operands in memory, the 8087 can go off and perform complex arithmetic and logic operations that would otherwise have to be computed by the 8086 with software subroutines.

The 8087 can weed out its own instructions as they appear on the local bus that it shares with the 8086. When one of a particular set of escape instructions appears, the 8087 automatically recognizes it as its own. The 8086 calculates the memory address for the initial operand, if any, and puts that on the bus. The 8087 latches this address, reads the operand, and begins to execute the required numerical operation, leaving the microprocessor free to process nonnumeric commands. The 8087 takes control of the bus only when necessary, to load and store operands.

The 8087 and microprocessor communicate over the control lines shown in Fig. 2. The request/grant line is used by the 8087 to obtain control of the local bus for

1. Made for math. High-performance MOS technology puts the 8087's 65,000 devices on a single chip measuring 330 mils on a side. The device's register stack comprises the equivalent of 40 16-bit registers, and a microcode section stores over 30,000 bits.

data transfers. The queue-status lines synchronize the fetching and decoding of instructions by the two devices. The 8087's busy signal informs the 8086 or 8088 that it is executing an instruction, and the latter's wait instruction tests this signal to find out when the 8087 is ready to execute subsequent instructions. Finally, the 8087 can interrupt the 8086 or 8088 if it detects an unmasked exception. Typically, the interrupt request is routed via an 8259A programmable interrupt controller.

This type of coprocessing increases system throughput because no overhead is incurred in setting up the 8087 for a computation and because the 8086 does not have to wait for results from the 8087. Indeed, the 8087 can be viewed as an architectural extension of an 8086 or 8088—it in effect extends the register resources and instruction set of the CPU. Figure 3 shows the register

pool of the 8086-8087 combination.

Programming the 8086-8087 combination is identical to programming a lone 8086. From the programmer's standpoint, the 8087 simply provides 68 new instructions and data types (seven in all) on top of those provided by the 8086.

Coprocessor programming

Table 1 lists the various instruction classes the 8087 can execute. Each instruction has one or two operands that are loaded onto the top of the stack from an inner stack element or directly from the local bus lines if the operand is in memory. To bolster performance and simplify software, the common, or core, instructions (add, subtract, multiply, divide, and compare) can directly manipulate both memory- and register-based operands.

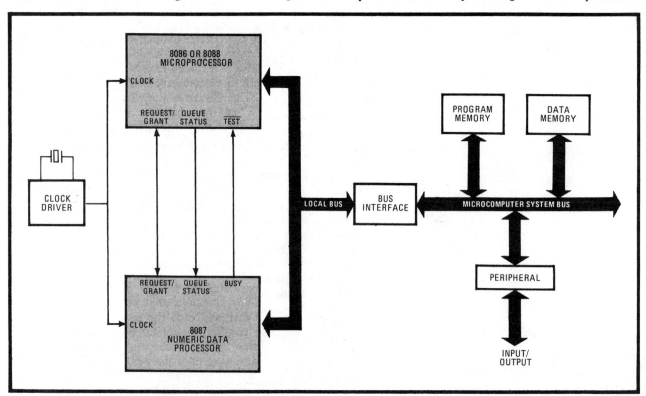

2. Coprocessing. The 8087 works with an 8086 or 8088 microprocessor through a tightly coupled form of multiprocessing called coprocessing. Both general-purpose and specialized processor eye the same data stream and perform the functions they do best.

The 8087's roots

In the mid-1970s, Intel embarked on expanding the computational capabilities of microprocessors from simple addition and subtraction of integers to an array of widely useful operations on real numbers. In 1977, the company adopted a standard for representing real numbers in a floating-point format. The floating-point arithmetic library (FPAL), the first product to use this standard format, is a set of subroutines for the 8080 and 8085 microprocessors. These routines perform limited standard functions on 32-bit single-precision real numbers; an FPAL multiplication takes about 1.5 milliseconds. The next product, the iSBC 310 high-speed math unit, implements the FPAL in hardware on a single card and reduces the single-precision multiplication time to about 100 microseconds.

The 8232 is single-chip arithmetic processor for the 8080/8085 family. The 8232 can operate with 64-bit double-precision real numbers; 32- and 64-bit multiplications take about 100 and 875 μs, respectively.

In 1979, a working committee of the Institute for Electric and Electronics Engineers solicited proposals for a standard for minicomputer and microcomputer floating-point arithmetic. The standard used by FPAL, the iSBC 310, and the 8232 was presented to the committee and subsequently expanded upon. This standard is designed to meet, among other things, the requirement that programs be portable, that is, that algorithms can be run on any machine complying with the standard and numerically identical results will be obtained. The standard also sets forth requirements designed to provide a high degree of safety and reliability for numeric computation. Standard data formats are established, and rules for rounding and precision control are specified. Most important is the requirement that devices satisfying this standard monitor their own activity and, in a prescribed manner, notify the program when numerical results are in error. This process has become known as exception handling.

The 8087 extends Intel's standard for numerics. It implements on a single chip the proposed IEEE standard, including all its options for single- and double-precision calculations. In addition, the 8087 provides many functional extensions to the proposed standard. It is compatible with previous Intel numeric products, and programs written for the 8087 will be transportable to future products that conform to the proposed standard. As the figure indicates, the 8087 provides over 10 times the speed of the 8232 and a hundredfold improvement over the FPAL; it performs 32- and 64-bit multiplications in about 18 and 27 μs, respectively.

Programs are written in ASM-86, an assembly language common to the 8086, 8088, and 8087. ASM-86 provides directives for defining all 8087 data types, plus additional mnemonics for all new 8087 instructions. The fact that some instructions in a program are executed by the 8087 and others by the 8086 is usually of no concern to the programmer.

PL/M-86, Intel's high-level language for the 8086 and 8088, can be used to program the 8087, too. PL/M-86 provides access to many 8087 facilities—again, without requiring that the programmer understand the details of the 8086-8087 combination. All 8086 and 8088 addressing modes may be used to access 8087 operands, thereby enabling convenient processing of numeric arrays and other structures in memory.

Figure 4 is a block diagram of the 8087. Data arrives via the local bus lines on the left. Operands for computations come in on the 16 address and data lines marked AD_0–AD_{15} and are held in the operand queue. The operands are converted into an intermediate format called temporary real as they are loaded into this register stack. This format affords more accurate results even when using double-precision operands.

Register resources

The 8087's substantial register bank comprises eight 80-bit registers, equivalent to 40 16-bit registers. These registers may be used as an ordinary push-down stack, but they can also be addressed explicitly by the program; that is, references can be made to any of the eight registers at any time, not simply to the top one or two. This feature makes programming more flexible because intermediate results can be tucked away in unused portions of the stack—and retrieved later—without additional memory references.

The stack may also be used for passing parameters to and from subroutines. Various routines can call the same subroutine without having to observe a convention for passing numeric parameters held in dedicated registers. As long as the stack is not full, each routine simply loads the parameters onto the stack and calls the subroutine.

Associated with the stack is a 3-bit pointer called top, and with each stack element a 2-bit tag field (Fig. 5). The stack elements are numbered relative to the pointer; ST(i) is the ith element from the top of the stack. The tag field is used to detect uninitialized stack elements and to designate special values (like zero) for exception-handling routines written by the programmer and for internal microcode optimization. The values represented in this stack are in the temporary-real format. They have 64 bits of fractional precision and a range of over $10^{\pm 4900}$ (15-bit exponent).

The lower block in Fig. 5 consists of a status word, a control word, a word containing the eight tags for the stack elements, the instruction address pointer, and the data address pointer. The status word stores the busy flag (which drives the busy signal), some condition codes, the top pointer, and the following exception flags:

I invalid operation
D denormalized operand
Q division of nonzero by zero
O overflow
U underflow
P inexact

The 8087 provides ample mechanisms for dealing with these exceptions that might arise during computation. The sophisticated programmer can write specific exception-handling routines and thus control the detailed behavior of the machine. In this case, the user would unmask exceptions and perform interrupts to exception-

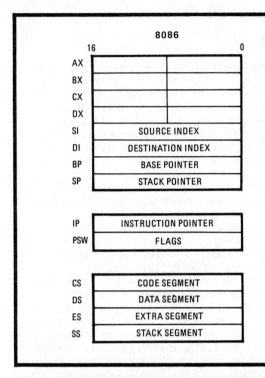

8086

	16	0
AX		
BX		
CX		
DX		
SI	SOURCE INDEX	
DI	DESTINATION INDEX	
BP	BASE POINTER	
SP	STACK POINTER	

IP	INSTRUCTION POINTER
PSW	FLAGS

CS	CODE SEGMENT
DS	DATA SEGMENT
ES	EXTRA SEGMENT
SS	STACK SEGMENT

8087

	79	0
R1	EXPONENT	MANTISSA
R2		
R3		
R4		
R5		
R6		
R7		
R8		

FLOATING-POINT EXECUTION UNIT STATUS
FLOATING-POINT EXECUTION UNIT MODE

3. Pooled resources. The 8087 can be viewed as an architectural extension of an 8086 or 8088. As such, each chip contributes its registers to a general fund. The 8087 adds eight 80-bit registers plus status and control words to the already healthy 8086 file.

TABLE 1: PRINCIPAL INSTRUCTIONS OF THE 8087	
Class	**Instruction types**
Data transfer	load and store (for all data types), exchange, free
Arithmetic	add, subtract, multiply, divide, subtract reversed, divide reversed, calculate square root, scale, increment, decrement, use remainder, round, to integer, change sign, absolute value, extract mantissa or exponent
Logical	compare, examine, test
Transcendental*	calculate tangent, arctangent, $2^X - 1$, $Y \cdot \log_2 X$, $Y \cdot (\log_2 X + 1)$
Constants*	$0, 1, \pi, \log_{10} 2, \log_e 2, \log_2 10, \log_2 e$
Processor control	load control word, store control word, store status word, load environment, store environment, save, restore, set interrupt-enable, clear interrupt-enable, clear errors, initialize

*Combining these instructions in very simple routines provides all the common trigonometric, inverse trigonometric, hyperbolic, inverse hyperbolic, logarithmic, and power functions.

handling routines. Alternatively, the 8087 will automatically handle exceptions on chip, relieving the programmer of the need to write and debug such routines. Thus, general applications programmers benefit from the 8087's precision and safety, whereas traditional machines would require familiarity with numerical analysis techniques and exceptions.

The control word in Fig. 5 consists of exception masks and control bits. For the seven exceptions having flags there is also a mask that, if reset, allows an interrupt to be generated. But if the mask is set, it suppresses the interrupt and causes the 8087 to execute an on-chip exception-handling routine. These default procedures are designed to handle a vast majority of situations that

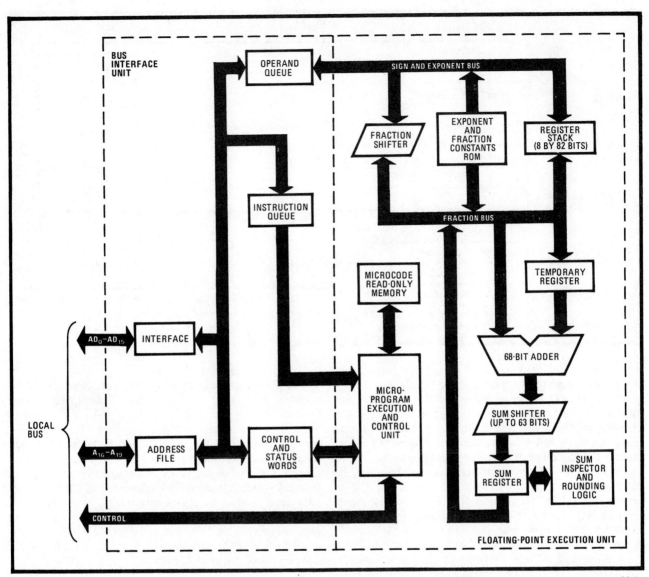

4. Sectioned off. Like the 8086, the 8087 is split into a bus interface unit and an execution unit. Data from a 16-bit local bus is converted into a temporary real format and processed by a 68-bit arithmetic and logic unit. Results are then converted back into the original data type.

come up. It is recommended that most users mask for all exceptions except invalid operation.

The control bits in the control word specify the level of precision as well as the actions to be taken for rounding and for infinite results. Precision control regulates the rounding process to one of three ranges: real (24 bits), long real (53 bits), and temporary real (64 bits). Control of precision is particularly useful when the programmer wishes to simulate other machines that might have less internal precision available than the 8087. Infinity control chooses between affine and projective infinity.

Rounding control selects one of four approaches: unbiased round to the nearest representable number, round up, round down, and round toward zero. The P (inexact) exception is especially important, since it notifies the programmer whenever the results of a computation are being rounded. Therefore, results that must be exact can be guaranteed as such.

Rounding control is also useful for interval arithmetic. Calculations can be carried out, for example, by always rounding up, then rounding down. Two sets of results are

obtained, with the true result in between. Thus, even when some rounding is inevitable, the 8087 can still make guaranteed statements by specifying bounds, or intervals, within which the exact result exists. Interval arithmetic has other applications, too, in which the user analyzes the effects of various types of uncertainties, errors, and other variations in the input data.

Completing the description of Fig. 5, the instruction and data pointers hold the address of an instruction and the data it refers to, if any, respectively. In the event that an exception generates an interrupt, this information is available to the programmer for use in the exception-handling routine.

Temporary-real format

The 8087's architecture includes an extended intermediate format called temporary real that affords the user significant advantages. As mentioned, the chip manipulates both single-precision 32-bit real and double-precision 64-bit operands, and as a result of temporary real, the commonly supplied system functions are accurate to

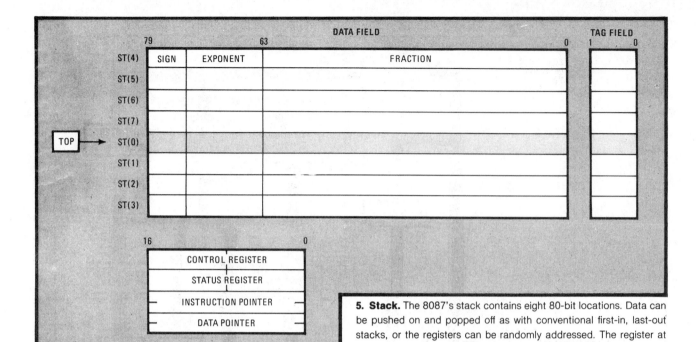

		DATA FIELD		TAG FIELD

5. Stack. The 8087's stack contains eight 80-bit locations. Data can be pushed on and popped off as with conventional first-in, last-out stacks, or the registers can be randomly addressed. The register at the top of the stack is singled out by the top pointer.

double precision. That is, if x is a long-real value, then e^x, ln x (the natural logarithm of x), and the tangent of x, and so on, will all be accurate to within less than one unit in the last place of long-real precision. In fact, because of their delicate hardware implementations, these functions will be more accurate—to within a few units in the last place of temporary-real precision.

The true test of temporary real comes, however, in calculating the most demanding function in the 8087's repertoire, x^y. In performing this function, as many fraction bits are lost to rounding as there are bits in the exponent of y; for instance, if x and y are in the double-precision format, then $z = x^y$ will lose about 11 bits. This loss would introduce significant error in a function that is crucial for many commerical calculations, including those for interest rates. However, with the 8087's temporary-real format and logarithmic functions, x^y (with x and y both temporary real) is accurate to about one unit in the last place of long-real precision. Besides ensuring accurate calculations of rates of return, the 8087 with temporary real guarantees that integral values of the arguments of x^y yield exact results: 2^3 equals 8, not 8.00 . . . 01.

Finally, the temporary-real format provides the means to construct accurate mathematical, statistical, and commercial libraries of functions. The user of these libraries supplies data in real or long-real formats and receives results with identical precision. The library uses temporary-real variables to perform the calculations and thus protects not only against roundoff errors, but also against intermediate overflows and underflows. (Most overflows and underflows occur on intermediate calculations, since the input and output variables are usually within reasonably narrow ranges.)

Performance claims for most libraries are "in the absence of overflow and underflow." But by judiciously using temporary-real variables, either overflows and underflows will be of no consequence or the user will be provided with a necessary and helpful warning.

The 8087 can operate on integer, binary-coded-decimal, and binary floating-point numbers, for a total of seven data types (Table 2). Regardless of data type, operands are converted without rounding into the temporary-real format as they are fetched from memory. All internal computations are done in the temporary-real format. Only when the result is about to be returned to memory is the data converted back into the format of the data type desired by the program. The conversions to and from temporary real are entirely transparent to the programmer. This automatic conversion also allows mixed-mode arithmetic, in which operands and results need not be of the same data type.

Easily emulated

One major advantage of the 8087's being so closely coupled with the 8086 is that a software emulator can be built easily. In fact, Intel provides such an emulator of 8087 hardware that runs on an 8086 or 8088. It generates trap routines that are substituted for the 8087's escape instructions. The use of these routines allows 8087 software to be written and executed while prototype hardware is still being developed. Then, when prototype hardware is ready, these same programs will run 100 times faster than the emulator. Table 3 gives an idea of the 8087's performance. Execution times for several 8087 operations are compared with those for equivalent operations executed in software on a 5-megahertz 8086. The software equivalents are the assembly language procedures for the 8087 emulator.

The hardware preparation required to add an 8087 to an existing 8086- or 8088-based system is an easy one, too. The 8087 uses the same clock generator and system bus interface components (bus controller, latches, transceivers, and bus arbiter) as the processor it supplements. Thus the 8087 itself is the only additional chip required for extensive high-performance numeric-processing ca-

TABLE 2: DATA FORMATS OF THE 8087

	Range	Precision	Most significant byte ·············· Format
Word integer	10^4	16 bits	I_{15} ... I_0 2's complement
Short integer	10^9	32 bits	I_{31} ... I_0 2's complement
Long integer	10^{19}	64 bits	I_{63} ... I_0 2's complement
Packed binary-coded decimal	10^{18}	18 digits	S — D_{17} D_{16} ... D_1 D_0
Short real	$10^{\pm38}$	24 bits	S E_7 ... E_0 F_1 ... F_{23} F_0 implicit
Long real	$10^{\pm308}$	53 bits	S E_{10} ... E_0 F_1 ... F_{52} F_0 implicit
Temporary real	$10^{\pm4,932}$	64 bits	S E_{14} ... E_0 F_0 ... F_{63}

Integer: I
Packed BCD: $(-1)^S (D_{17} \ldots D_0)$

Real: $(-1)^S (2^{E - bias})(F_0, F_1 \ldots)$
Bias = 127 for short real, 1,023 for long real, 16,383 for temporary real

TABLE 3: EXECUTION TIME FOR ACTUAL AND EMULATED 8087 INSTRUCTIONS

Instruction	Approximate execution time (μs)	
	8087 (5-MHz clock)	8086 emulation
Add or subtract magnitude	14/18	1,600
Multiply (single precision)	18	1,600
Multiply (double precision)	27	2,100
Divide	39	3,200
Compare	10	1,300
Load (single precision)	9	1,700
Store (single precision)	17	1,200
Calculate square root	36	19,600
Calculate tangent	110	13,000
Raise to the appropriate power	130	17,100

pabilities in such a system.

The transparent software and simple hardware interface of the 8087 make it extremely easy to add numeric support to existing products like board-level computers. Intel is following this simple course in adding numeric support to existing 8086-based iSBC 86/12 single-board computers. As an option, a plug-in module will be provided. The user simply unplugs the 8086, plugs in the module (which has the 8087 on it), and then plugs the 8086 into the module.

A wide range of applications will benefit from the 8087's combination of high performance and software support. For instance, small, accurate, and reliable inertial navigation systems can put the 8087 to work. Its built-in trigonometric functions speed up and simplify the derivation of positional information, such as bearing and acceleration data.

The 8087's ability to accept decimal operands and produce exact decimal results up to 18 digits long greatly simplifies the programming of business data-processing applications. Financial calculations that rely on power functions, like $(1+i)^n$ for compound interest, will take advantage of the 8087's exponentiation instructions. Business-oriented languages like Cobol also benefit from the 8087's accuracy and rounding.

In real-time process control situations, the 8087's extended precision and speed enable it to handle a wide dynamic range without loss of precision. Finally, the direct numeric support for the 8087 available in all 8086 high-level languages makes software cost-effective. □

Electronics/February 24, 1982

Microcomputer with 32-bit arithmetic does high-precision number crunching

Single-chip processor's separate data and program buses combine
with 200-ns multiplier and barrel shifter to enhance throughput.

by K. McDonough, E. Caudel, S. Magar, and A. Leigh, *Texas Instruments Inc., Houston, Texas.*

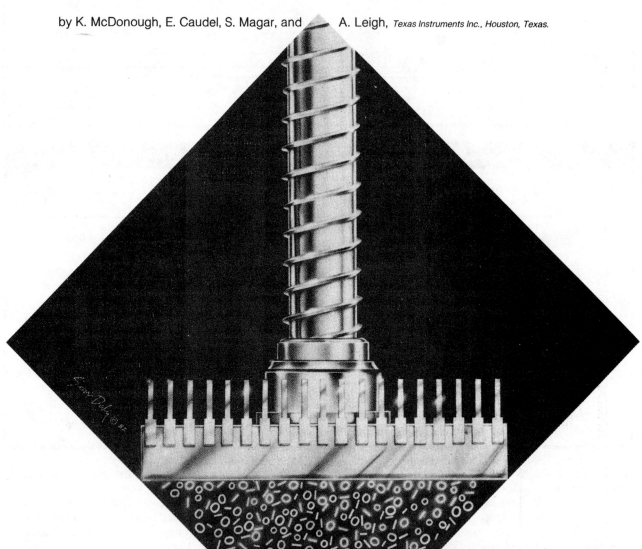

☐ Racing headlong at a rate of 5 million instructions per second, the TMS320 single-chip microcomputer is the first of a family of very large-scale integrated processors aiming at taking over computation-intensive functions. Up to now very few microcomputers have been fast enough to process the thousands of high-precision data values that signal processing and other high-throughput applications require each second. The 320, however, with its 32-bit arithmetic offers a single-chip solution to this problem. Applications include digital filtering, signal handling for telecommunications modems, data compression for linear-predictive-code speech analysis and synthesis, speech recognition, fast-Fourier transforms, and high-performance control applications. Underlying the 320's superior computational capability and high speed is a modification of what is called the Harvard architecture that supports separate program- and data-memory spaces. Unlike the more common von Neumann architecture, this configuration permits fetching information from both program and data memory in parallel; thus, the execution cycle of an instruction overlaps the fetch cycle of the next instruction in a pipelined manner.

In the 320, modifications on the conventional Harvard architecture include a special feature that allows crossovers between the program and data memories, providing program branches based on data-manipulation instructions and data values embedded in program segments. For example, an address can be computed and a jump made to that address, thereby basing program branching on data values. In the other direction, constants in the program memory can be read into the data path, and data can be written back to external program memory. In a strict Harvard architecture as originally envisioned, the two memory spaces never mix.

The Harvard architecture has been further enhanced by incorporating as much parallelism as possible into the 320. This goal is achieved by allowing the subunits to operate on different operands simultaneously. Also the subunits themselves have been optimized for speed, rather than for low power consumption or small size. For instance, the multiplier consumes a large part of the die area, but it can form a 16-by-16-bit–to–31-bit result in a single microcycle of 200 nanoseconds. Likewise, the barrel shifter can shift an operand from 1 to 15 bit positions in a single cycle.

What is more, the arithmetic and logic unit itself does double-precision operations automatically—it is a 32-bit unit. Also, several special-purpose registers are included that can increment and decrement themselves, relieving the processor of that task. To develop programs for the 320, software is provided on the AMPL (for Advanced Microprocessor Prototyping Laboratory) development system, which also includes full emulation support.

On the surface, the 320 (Fig. 1) looks much like a general-purpose microcomputer. However, it is optimized for high-performance number processing. A 20-megahertz crystal input accounts for the 5-million-

instruction/s rate—200-ns execution times for 90% of the instructions. At its input and output terminals, the chip accepts and delivers 16-bit digital data, but internally the 320 is TI's first 32-bit microcomputer. The 32-bit ALU prevents loss of precision when performing calculations on data derived from analog signals.

High-speed arithmetic is based around 16-bit signed, 2's complement numbers, but all results of arithmetic operations are carried out to 32 places in both the ALU and accumulator. In addition, the ALU handles Boolean logic operations on 16-bit data—functions that allow the 320 to serve in controller applications.

Adding further to arithmetic performance is the 320's 16-by-16-bit parallel multiplier, which performs a multiplication—producing a 32-bit product—and accumulation in just 400 ns (see "High-speed multiplier takes a big bite,").

Multiplication time alone is 200 ns with another 200 ns required to latch the result. This feature, more than any other, allows the 320 to handle signal-processing applications efficiently.

Memory also by design plays a major role in the 320's architecture. The on-chip program memory consists of 3-K bytes of mask-programmable read-only memory (organized as 1,536 16-bit words). Up to 5-K bytes of additional external memory can also be accommodated, and in a special mode called system emulation, the entire 8-K-byte program space is external. Data memory consists of 288 bytes (organized as 144 words of 16 bits) of high-speed on-chip random-access memory, representing the largest internal RAM space on a single-chip microcomputer to date.

1. Memory-intensive. The die layout of the TMS320 reveals the regularity of Texas Instrument's approach to building microprocessors. Almost all interconnections run over active devices on a separate mask level. The multiplier (bottom, left) can form a 32-bit result in only 200 ns.

By processing analog signals with digital techniques, most of the voltage, temperature, and noise problems encountered in the analog-signal environment are eliminated. Moreover, at high frequencies, it becomes increasingly difficult to design inductors and capacitors with sufficient component tolerances to maintain the accuracy and precision of the analog signals. A digital processor requires no such precision components.

However, it does require analog-to-digital and digital-to-analog converters to interface it to the analog world, and their characteristics must be tailored to a specific application. For example, a speech application can

High-speed multiplier takes a big bite

High-performance devices like the TMS320 call for hardware multipliers, since very high numerical throughput is required for applications such as signal processing. A fully parallel 2's complement 16-by-16-bit multiplier is incorporated in this new microcomputer so that multiplication can be achieved in one instruction cycle—200 nanoseconds. However, the inclusion of a multiplier, which devours power and chip area, makes the design of a high-performance microcomputer even more challenging. The key to a power-thrifty and small multiplier is the proper combination of four factors: an algorithm, its implementation, its logic approach, and its layout.

The multiplier on the 320 combines a Booth's 2-bit algorithm, feed-forward and ripple carry adders, static and dynamic logic, and strip layout in order to achieve the performance, power, and chip area desired. The multiplicand is decoded using the algorithm in order to control the eight levels of carry feed-forward adders.

The feed-forward carry scheme in these adders significantly enhances the multiplication process. The way these carriers work is that each level of adders calculates its sum with the partial product fed forward to the next level.

When all the levels of the static array settle, producing the final product, it is applied to a 31-bit row of dynamic carry-ripple adders, which perform the final evaluation and produce a 31-bit product in 2's complement notation. The 31 bits is then sign-extended to obtain a 32-bit product. Booth's algorithm reduces the number of adder stages to virtually half the number otherwise required.

The feed-forward carry adders in the multiplier array have been implemented in static logic—depletion-load gates. The carry ripple adders, which provide the final result, are implemented in dynamic logic. The dynamic array is precharged while the static array is evaluating its data. This combination achieves the desired speed at the required power levels.

The strip-layout approach—lining up the data and control contact points into strips for interconnection from above—has been used to lay out the multiplier. The slow speed signals run in polysilicon in one direction while the high-speed 32-bit data bus is embedded in the multiplier cells running in metal perpendicular to the slow lines. The integration of the 32 bus lines into the multiplier cells significantly reduces the size of the multiplier.

---

require 16 bits of dynamic range but only 8 bits of linearity, whereas a modem needs less range but a greater amount of linearity.

So the 320's designers decided against building converters on chip, but rather opted to develop a family of special support integrated circuits suited to particular applications. Already, analog peripherals are under development for speech-compression and modem applications. Relegating specialized functions to support ICs allows the 320 to be optimized for its primary task—high-speed signal processing and fast calculations.

As mentioned, the basic advantage of the Harvard architecture is that it allows the 320 to fetch instructions and data in parallel. With its high-speed on-board RAM, the 320 reads data into its ALU, performs a computation, and places the result back into the accumulator, all in a single 200-ns cycle. On the following cycle, the result can be returned to memory as the next instruction is simultaneously fetched from the on-chip ROM.

On the other hand, by abandoning the strict Harvard architecture, the 320 permits more flexible operations within its memory space. For example, data tables can reside within the program space, allowing a system designer to make tradeoffs between the amount of table and program space needed for a specific application.

By comparison, conventional signal-processing computers have separate ROM tables with fixed-size storage areas. In such cases, if an application uses just a small amount of table data, most of the table space is wasted because of its dedicated nature.

To support high-speed computation and program execution, the 320 maximizes throughput with parallel operations that can execute a complex instruction in a single cycle. The system designer can control almost every machine state, each of which requires but a single cycle, without resorting to a cumbersome microcoded instruction set. The more complex commands of micro-

coded instructions usually require 5 to 10 machine cycles for execution. The 320's simpler, single-cycle programming is also five times faster than assembly language, which often requires even more cycles to perform an equivalent operation.

To allow constants to be embedded in instructions, the 320 includes what are commonly called immediate instructions. In such an approach, a portion of the instruction word is dedicated to data and the instruction need not reference data memory to obtain the desired information. This tack significantly speeds up high-performance table-manipulation operations.

While most of the 320's instructions can be performed within a 200-ns cycle, program-control instructions like branching and calling require two cycles, with one of them fetching the new branch address. The branch instruction allows jumps anywhere within a 24-bit address space, facilitating future expansion of the 320's memory space to as much as 16 megabytes.

The on-chip ROM can store those routines that are both heavily used and invariate over many applications. The external ROM's function is to store the information required by a specific application. One example of how to use this storage flexibility is in automotive applications: program and data for different engines is stored in external ROMs, while the algorithm for manipulating any engine is placed in the on-chip ROM.

Hardware features

The 320's internal functions (Fig. 2) are organized around two buses, one a 16-bit program bus and the other a 16-bit data bus. In addition, a bus-interchange module provides for data exchanges between the two.

To provide for memory expansion, the 12-bit program counter's outputs are routed to pins, as well as addressing the internal memory space. Conventional processors have a separate register to supply addresses to memory,

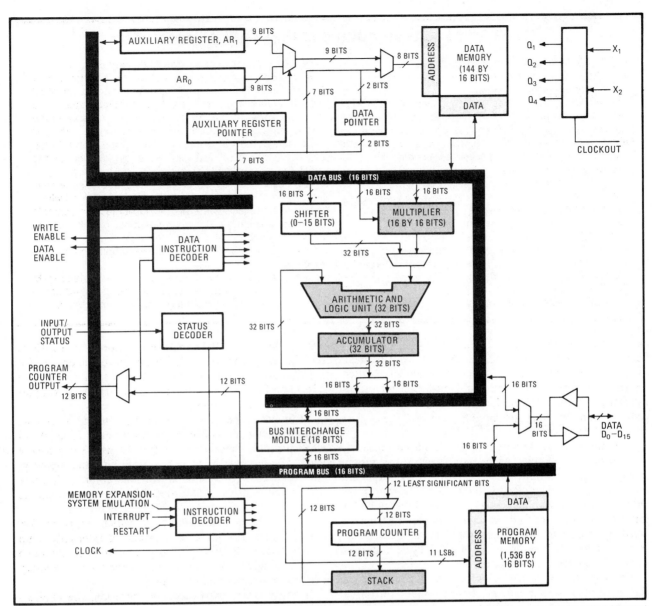

2. Harvard on a chip. Two separate internal buses, one for data and one for instructions, are the hallmark of what is called Harvard architecture. Many parallel operations can thus be performed by the separate subunits contained on the TMS320 chip.

but the 320's program counter itself always does that job. Its contents are automatically incremented, as is traditional, but can also be loaded from the accumulator with a special instruction or automatically from program memory in the case of branches and jumps.

During subroutine and interrupt calls, the program counter's contents are saved in a separate register stack. A 4-by-12-bit register file, the stack saves the counter's current contents by pushing them onto the top of the stack when a call instruction or an interrupt is executed. Successive call instructions keep pushing the counter's current contents onto the top of the stack. Up to four nested subroutines can be accommodated before an overflow occurs. However, no recovery mechanism is provided for overflow or underflow.

A subroutine is terminated by the execution of a return instruction. This action pops the stack, returning the contents at the top to the program counter. The program then continues from the point it had reached

before the last call. For example, each subroutine initiated by a call instruction or interrupt must be terminated by a return instruction.

Two 16-bit auxiliary registers, designated AR₀ and AR₁, can be used for loop control and indirect addressing of the data memory. Both registers support automatic incrementing and decrementing operations in parallel with memory and arithmetic operations. The auxiliary-register pointer determines the selection of an AR as the source for an address. Thus, it is always pointing at one of the registers.

When the 320 executes an indirect memory reference instruction, one of the ARs is used to address the onboard data RAM. In parallel with such an indirect operation, the unused address bits in the operation code are available to increment or decrement the AR and modify the address register pointer. In addition, the ARs are on call as temporary storage registers at any time.

In the 320, arithmetic functions are always performed

Transparent refresh mimes static-RAM performance

The TMS320 utilizes a novel sequential refreshing technique, transparent to the user, that creates the illusion of a static random-access memory. A conventional cross-coupled latch with transfer gates is used as the basic memory element. This is the circuit used in all static RAMs. In those parts, the required load resistors are implemented with polysilicon resistors or depletion transistors—the 320 instead uses sequentially clocked enhancement transistors to refresh stored logic-1 levels. This approach uses fewer components compared with polysilicon resistors and less area compared to depletion loads. In each case, an additional mask level over the number required for the transparent refresh cell is needed.

The refresh mechanism of the RAM relies on the fact that a logic-1 level stored in a cell is automatically refreshed when its row is addressed. The clocked loads of each RAM cell are turned on sequentially, with one complete row being refreshed each complete clock cycle. Each row is therefore refreshed every n clock cycles where n is equal to the number of rows in the memory.

Also, a cell is refreshed whenever a row is addressed by an instruction. In this case, a 1 level in the cell is refreshed from the precharged bit lines. A row address causes the voltage on the bit lines to charge the capacitance in the cell. Since the bit-line capacitance is many times the cell capacitance, the row address results in the 1 level in the cell being refreshed with very little degradation of the precharged 1 level on the bit lines.

In order to achieve fast access times, a sensing latch is connected across the bit lines. The latch, controlled with a delayed final-phase clock signal, duplicates the contents of the cell being read. Once a row address has allowed the bit lines to settle sufficiently, the delayed clock fires the sensing latch, which is capable of discharging the bit lines much faster than the cell.

These techniques result in a 144-by-16-bit static RAM with an access time from a decoded address of 40 nanoseconds and a power dissipation of only 95 milliwatts.

---

on signed, 2's complement numbers. The processor's barrel shifter performs a left bit shift of from 0 to 15 places within a single cycle. Left-shifted data is 0-filled on the low-order bits, with the high-order bits sign-extended to form a 32-bit input to the ALU. A data word coming from memory to the ALU always passes first through the shifter.

The multiplier has separate input and output registers. The former is 16 bits wide and provides temporary storage of the multiplicand. The latter is 32 bits wide and holds the product of a multiplication. The multiplier value comes either from data memory or is a 13-bit immediate value derived directly from an instruction word. A special feature incorporated in the multiplication instruction inhibits interrupts for one cycle to permit saving the output register contents.

The key to high-speed arithmetic performance with the multiplier is parallelism. For example, during a single machine cycle, the input register can be loaded with a new value in parallel with accumulation of a previous result. Concurrently, the data can be moved to the next RAM location. These parallel operations are very useful in auto-correlation functions.

Status check

The accumulator's status is monitored when an updating instruction is executed. Conditions monitored include an over- or underflow, and contents less than, greater than, or equal to 0. An accumulator-overflow mode, enabled by a status register bit that is under program control, allows a saturated accumulator result for signal-processing calculations. If it is reset—no saturation—unmodified results are loaded into the accumulator from the ALU. When it is set, results are set to the largest or smallest representable value of the adder upon over- and underflows, respectively, before being loaded into the accumulator. The largest or smallest value is determined by the overflow sign. This feature models the saturation process inherent in analog systems.

The first two chips to be available in the 320 family will be the TMS32010, a microprocessor version with no on-chip ROM for use in program development or for small-to-medium-volume production, and the TMS320M10, a 3-K-byte mask-ROM version to support high-volume production.

With both, the 288 bytes of data RAM, of course, remain on chip, and off-chip memories must have 100-ns cycle times to execute at the full 20-MHz performance level. The separate address bus, data bus, and memory-control lines are optimized for operation with these high-speed static RAMs and bipolar programmable ROMs.

The 320M10 microcomputer, which supports 3-K bytes of internal ROM, can be expanded externally to up to 8-K bytes of program memory. This version offers two memory configurations selectable by the ME-SE (memory expansion-system emulation) pin.

In the memory-expansion configuration, the application program can execute strictly from internal ROM by addressing word locations between 0 and 1,525. If the program addresses locations above 1,535 (1,525 to 1,535 are reserved for device testing), the instructions are fetched from external memory.

The system-emulation mode allows bypassing the internal ROM for program development with access to a full 8-K bytes of external memory. Once the 3-K kernel is debugged, it can be burned into the internal ROM.

The ME-SE pin also allows dynamic switching of the memory configuration to allow the chip to support self-emulation. The user program resides in external memory and the emulator support is in on-chip ROM. Switching the level of the ME-SE pin causes a nonmaskable interrupt, allowing a transition between memory spaces. Since the external memory interface runs at the same speed as the internal program memory, it allows real-time development of user programs.

To provide for this expansion, 12 output pins are assigned for addressing external memory. These pins are the buffered outputs of the program counter. Moreover, a strobe-output signal is generated during every machine

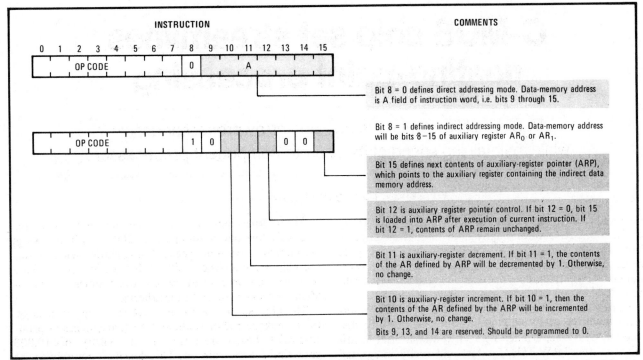

3. Formatting. Two basic instruction formats are supported by the TMS 320. With the direct addressing format, the data memory address is contained within the instruction. For indirect addressing, the data's address is contained within one of the auxiliary registers.

state to indicate an external memory reference.

The high-speed, on-chip RAM, organized as 144 words of 16 bits each, forms the 320's data memory (see "Transparent refresh mimes static-RAM performance,").

The size of the data memory is adequate to compute a 64-point complex fast-Fourier transform while maintaining system-linkage variables and constants for other functions.

A page of data memory

The data memory is addressed directly by the contents of the A field of the instruction word. The 7-bit A field is capable of directly addressing 128 words, which constitutes a page. To address the full 144 words requires the use of the data-memory page pointer. This 2-bit pointer will permit the expansion of data memory to four pages, or 1-K byte, in the next version of the 320. This pointer typically indicates the page storing randomly accessed control variables, while tabular data is addressed by the two auxiliary registers. The instruction set is defined to allow data-memory expansion to 256 pages or 64-K bytes in future versions.

The design of the data memory allows a word to be copied to the next higher address from its present location in one machine cycle. A special instruction mode—data-move—allows this operation to occur in parallel with the standard arithmetic functions. This instruction is extensively used in convolution calculations.

The 320 supports both direct and indirect addressing (Fig. 3). In direct addressing, the data word is derived from the data-memory address defined by the A-field of the instruction word. In indirect addressing, the data word is derived from the data-memory address specified by the contents of one of the auxiliary registers. In turn, the register is specified by the contents of the auxiliary-register pointer.

A 3-bit port address is implicit in both input and output instructions and is multiplexed onto the 3 least significant bits of the external memory-address output lines. This feature provides addressing capability for up to eight peripherals. The remaining higher-order bits of the ROM address outputs are held at logic 0 during these instructions. The 320 can perform such input/output operations at a burst rate of 40 million bits a second over the 16-bit parallel bus.

The 320 provides for a single interrupt level through a separate pin. The interrupt address is at location 2_{10} in program memory. When an interrupt occurs, the current contents of the program counter are incremented and loaded into the top of the stack, and program execution begins at the interrupt vector location (2_{10}).

The reset function is a special case of an interrupt. It requires an active low level on an external pin to implement the function. When the reset pin goes low, the data-enable, write-enable, and address strobe lines are forced inactive asynchronously, while the data bus is placed in the high-impedance state. The program counter is cleared synchronously after the next complete clock cycle. The reset pin must be maintained low for at least five clock cycles.

The self-emulation capability that is built into the chip's architecture is utilized by the AMPL development system. This mode assumes that the user's program memory space is external and the chip is programmed with emulator code. The development system then dynamically switches between the two memory spaces. □

Electronics/February 10, 1982

C-MOS chip set streamlines floating-point processing

VLSI simplifies scalar, vector, and array processor design
while maintaining speed of its discrete-component predecessors

by Frederick Ware and William McAllister, *Hewlett-Packard Co., Cupertino, Calif.*

☐ Numerical processors with both speed and a variety of functions have traditionally been built from discrete small- and medium-scale integrated circuits or gate arrays. The resultant unit has been expensive, power-hungry, and physically cumbersome—and also less reliable than designs using large-scale integration.

Commercially available LSI chips designed for numerical calculations unfortunately have fallen into two distinct classes. One, typified by such combinatorial multipliers as the TRW-16HJ, is fast and easily integrated into many processor designs, but it can process only low-precision fixed-point data. The other class, consisting of recently announced coprocessor chips, like Intel's 8087, can handle a wide range of operations and data types, including floating-point, but is slower and attaches only to specific microsystem buses.

Now, Hewlett-Packard has developed a three-chip set of floating-point processors that combines both the speed and design flexibility of combinatorial multipliers and the variety of functions and data types handled by coprocessors (see table). With this set, HP computer and instrument systems will be able to attain mainframe floating-point performance at what amounts to microcomputer prices.

The set of floating-point processors consists of one IC for addition and subtraction, another for multiplication, and a third for division. This partitioning was necessary so that each of the three distinctly different floating-point operations could be optimized. In addition, the chips employ combinatorial logic in their data paths for high performance, and if only a single chip had been used, the resulting circuit would have been too large to be economically manufactured with currently available MOS processes.

Each chip has identical pin assignments and interfaces with a general data-bus structure that will fit a wide variety of applications. On-chip control and sequencing capabilities are kept simple to give the chip set maximum flexibility.

All internal logic is static complementary-MOS for relatively low power dissipation (200 to 400 milliwatts per chip at maximum speed). Using static logic also lets the chip set interface easily with a variety of clocking schemes and operate at system cycle times as fast as 80 nanoseconds—over 12 megahertz.

The chip set is housed in a 64-pin plug-in package. Each package occupies about 1.5 square inches of printed-circuit board, resulting in a density of 10,000 gates/in.^{2} for the chip set. This density is roughly one to two orders of magnitude greater than that of an implementation in discrete SSI, MSI, or gate-array components with comparable performance.

All input and output voltage levels are designed to be TTL-compatible, although the chip set may also interface directly with 5-volt C-MOS and n-MOS systems. All output pins can be put in the high-impedance state, eliminating the need for external multiplexers. The 32-bit fixed-point and 32- and 64-bit floating-point formats used are those of the HP1000 minicomputer family.

Figure 1 is a block diagram of the elements of the floating-point adder chip, which performs addition, sub-

COMPARING DEDICATED ARITHMETIC PROCESSORS			
	TRW MPY-16HJ	Intel 8087	HP 1AE7/H4/H7
Data formats			
Fixed-point	16-bit	32- or 64-bit	32-bit
Floating-point	—	32-, 48-, 64-, or 80-bit	32- or 64-bit
Decimal	—	64-bit	—
Operations	multiply only	multiply	multiply
	—	add/subtract	add/subtract
	—	divide	divide
	—	square root	—
	—	trigonometric	—
	—	logarithm/exponent	—
Internal delay	100–200 ns	20–40 μs	400–600 ns
Number of data pins	48	16	48
Data-bus frequency	16 MHz	5 MHz	12 MHz

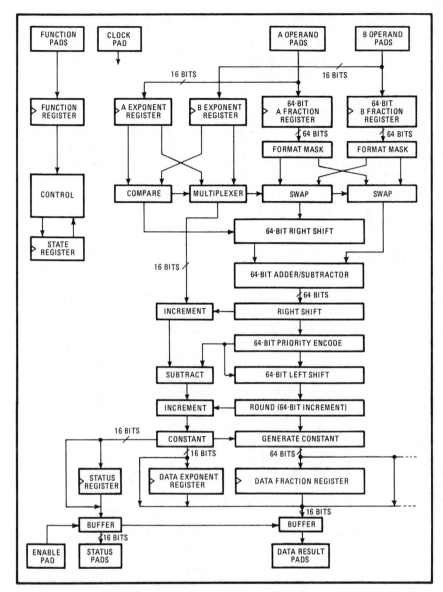

the resultant fraction is priority-encoded and shifted left by that amount so that it is normalized. Also, the amount the fraction is shifted left is subtracted from the resultant exponent.

The resultant fraction is then rounded to the desired precision and again checked for overflow. If overflow occurs, the exponent is incremented and a constant is generated to replace the fraction. The exponent is checked for both overflow and underflow, and if either has occurred, a constant is generated for both the exponent and fraction of the result. The final result is then unloaded from the chip at a rate of 16 bits at a time.

A pipeline register through which status and results may optionally be passed can be used to overlap the load and unload cycles for one function sequence with the wait cycles of another. Thus, two sets of operands and results can be processed simultaneously by the chip. Applications that can use this overlapped mode of operation include vector instruction execution, signal processing, and graphics processing.

The floating-point multiplier chip (Fig. 2) is operated in the same manner as the floating-point adder chip. As with the adder chip, a pipeline register may be optionally used to overlap two operations. The only difference lies in the combinatorial data-path logic of the multiplier.

traction, and conversion between the supported data types. A typical sequence in a synchronous system consists of load cycles, wait cycles, and unload cycles. Two or four cycles are required for loading operands and unloading results since all data buses are 16 bits wide and the data formats use 32 or 64 bits. When the two operands and the function code are loaded into edge-triggered input registers, they propagate asynchronously through the combinatorial data-path logic.

Leading exponents

First, the exponents are compared and their difference found. Then, the fraction with the smaller exponent is prealigned (shifted right) by an amount equal to the difference of the exponents.

The operand fractions are then added and, if they are of the same sign, checked for overflow. In the event of an overflow, the resultant fraction is shifted right by 1 bit and the resultant exponent (the larger of the two operand exponents) is incremented.

If the operand fractions are of opposite signs, cancellation of leading significant bits could occur. In this case,

Floating-point multiplication

The multiplication technique employed on the chip is based on a Booth's algorithm. Pairs of multiplier bits are encoded into a set of signed digits, permitting the number of adders used to be reduced. Each adder cell for the Booth technique requires a total of 24 C-MOS devices—16 for the full adder and 8 for the associated multiplexing logic. A 56-by-28-bit array of these adders is used—the floating-point fraction size is 56 bits—resulting in about 38,000 devices for the array.

The first step in the data-path logic is to mask the operand fractions and perform a modified Booth encoding on one of them. The encoding operation reduces the number of multiplier bits by one half. The two operand fractions (one encoded) then pass to the multiplication array, and the partial products are accumulated.

The resultant fraction is rounded to the desired precision and checked for overflow. If overflow occurs, the sum of the operand exponents is incremented, and the fraction is shifted right once. The resulting exponent is then checked for overflow or underflow, and if either occurs, a constant is generated for both the resultant fraction and the exponent.

Floating-point division

Unlike the addition and multiplication chips, the division chip uses a technique that is partly combinatorial and partly synchronous because a combinatorial data path for a floating-point divider is too big to fit on a single chip using currently available C-MOS processes. Combinatorial division could be performed with fifty-six 56-bit adders, but synchronous division requires only ten 56-bit adders and is faster than the combinatorial technique.

Despite this choice, the internal delay of the divider chip is still three to four times that of the adder and multiplier chips. However, since division is an infrequently used instruction—only about 5% to 10% of floating-point operations involve division—greater delay times for this function can be tolerated.

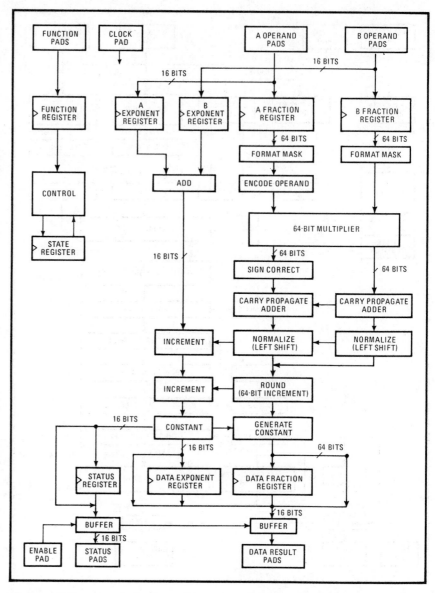

In the divider chip (Fig. 3), the divisor (B) and dividend (A) are loaded and one cycle is used to conditionally negate them so that the divisor ends up negative and the dividend positive. The dividend is clocked into the remainder register, and combinatorial logic is used to create seven integral multiples of the divisor.

At this point, the hardware is ready to begin generating quotient bits. The seven divisor multiples are subtracted in parallel from the remainder. Then, the seven signals from the subtraction array are encoded to form three quotient bits. These bits represent the largest multiple of the divisor that can be subtracted from the remainder without forcing the remainder to go negative.

The encoding logic then selects the smallest positive remainder, which is clocked back into the remainder register. The above sequence is repeated to generate enough quotient bits for the desired precision, plus guard bits for normalizing and rounding.

Once the last quotient-bit cycle has occurred, the remaining data-path logic is purely combinatorial. First, the resultant quotient fraction is normalized with a shift to the left. Then, the quotient fraction is rounded to the

desired precision. The quotient exponent is checked for both overflow and underflow. If either has occurred, then a constant is generated for both the exponent and fraction of the quotient.

Because of its high performance and simple interface requirements, the chip set is being designed into a variety of HP products. The most fundamental of these, as well as the one for which the chip set was originally defined, is the execution of scalar floating-point instructions in microprogrammable minicomputers.

Sitting pretty

In such a scalar processor, the floating-point processor chips sit in parallel to the primary data path, which handles fixed-point addition, subtraction, and shifting operations. The chips get operands and send results to the same subsystems as the primary path—cache, main memory, or register files.

A scalar processing operation begins when a floating-point instruction is fetched and sequencing control is transferred to the appropriate microroutine. Two operands, read from memory or register files, are loaded

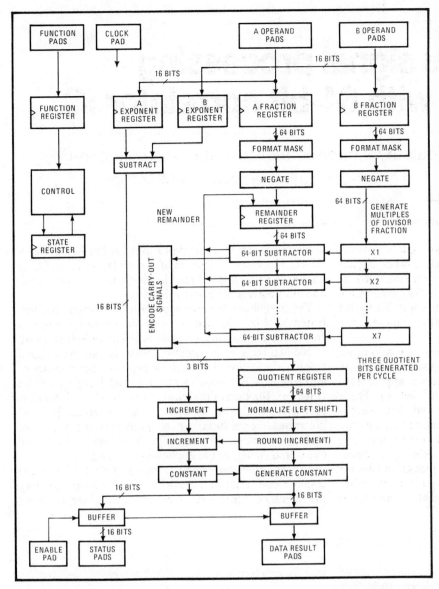

Figure blocks (labels):

FUNCTION PADS · CLOCK PAD · A OPERAND PADS · B OPERAND PADS

FUNCTION REGISTER · A EXPONENT REGISTER · B EXPONENT REGISTER · A FRACTION REGISTER · B FRACTION REGISTER

16 BITS · 16 BITS · 16 BITS

CONTROL · SUBTRACT · FORMAT MASK · FORMAT MASK

NEGATE · NEGATE

STATE REGISTER · NEW REMAINDER · REMAINDER REGISTER · 64 BITS · GENERATE MULTIPLES OF DIVISOR FRACTION

64 BITS · 64 BITS

ENCODE CARRY-OUT SIGNALS · 64-BIT SUBTRACTOR · X1

64-BIT SUBTRACTOR · X2

16 BITS · 64-BIT SUBTRACTOR · X7

3 BITS · QUOTIENT REGISTER · THREE QUOTIENT BITS GENERATED PER CYCLE

64 BITS

INCREMENT · NORMALIZE (LEFT SHIFT)

INCREMENT · ROUND (INCREMENT)

CONSTANT · GENERATE CONSTANT

16 BITS · 16 BITS

BUFFER · BUFFER

16 BITS

ENABLE PAD · STATUS PADS · DATA RESULT PADS

3. Divide and conquer. This chip is the only synchronous component in the set. With 35,000 devices resting on a 217-by-290-mil die, it uses 10 adders, three 64-bit incrementers, and a separate data path for exponents to yield results in 2.4 microseconds.

vector instructions can be supplied with a rich set of parameters that allows complex loops to be specified.

The design of a homogenous, pipelined processor for vector processing uses a number of identical floating-point chips operated in an interleaved manner. Each chip of such a structure can provide 2 million 32-bit floating-point operations a second of processing bandwidth. A maximum of three interleaved chipsets can be used because the data buses can support a maximum of 6 million operations per second. However, an arbitrarily high processing bandwidth may be achieved by increasing the number of bus sets.

Multiple sets

A vector processor with three chip sets could perform inner product operations at about 12 megaflops, could fit onto one or two medium-sized pc boards, and would have a manufacturing cost of about $2,000 to $3,000. Tightly coupled to its host system, such a processor could provide the host with outstanding vector floating-point performance, permitting a wide variety of computation-intensive applications currently running on mainframe computers to be moved onto a host minicomputer so equipped. The A700 processor, the new top-of-the-line computer in the HP 1000 series, is just such a unit in that it combines scalar floating-point arithmetic with the firmware and high-speed registers necessary to do vector processing.

It is possible to use the processor chips as simple building blocks for high-performance custom processors. Another specialized application of the chips would be as a custom hardwired fast-Fourier-transform (FFT) processor, which could be built using 10 monolithic processors—6 adders and 4 multipliers.

Such a system would have an overall processing bandwidth of about 20 megaflops (32-bit) and a manufacturing cost of about $2,000 or $3,000. It could also fit onto one of two medium-sized pc boards.

The FFT unit could be interfaced with a general-purpose minicomputer or a specialized test instrument. It would provide a price-performance ratio for signal and image processing (with floating-point data) that is currently unattainable. It would also be modular enough to be easily paralleled with identical units for even greater absolute processing bandwidth. □

into the appropriate floating-point processor. The system waits an integral number of microcycles for the result to be generated, and the result is written back to memory or the register files.

The performance of the chip set as a scalar processor involves about a 750-ns delay for 32-bit addition and multiplication and a 1.3-microsecond delay for 64-bit. These figures include the internal delay and load-unload time of the chips but not the time used for instruction fetching, operand fetching, and result storage required by the external system. In a high-performance minicomputer, these system operations will typically be overlapped with the adjacent machine instructions, so in fact, the machine instruction time for scalar floating-point operations will approach the values given above.

Vector processing

Vector instructions allow loop operations to be specified in a single machine instruction, thus reducing the control and addressing overhead otherwise required. The hardware to perform overlapped operand fetching, execution, and result storage is easily provided. In addition,

Digital signal processing hits stride with 64-bit correlator IC

Chip generates 7-bit output for error-correction, data synchronization, and other auto- and cross-correlation tasks at 15-MHz clip

by John Eldon, *TRW Inc., LSI Products Division, San Diego, Calif.*

☐ Correlation, or the comparison of two signals to determine their similarity, has become yet another signal-processing function whose design has been simplified by very large-scale integration. The TDC1023J monolithic digital correlator compares two 64-bit words bit by bit and produces a 7-bit digital output that indicates the number of bits in agreement.

Design engineers will find that this digital-output, one-chip version of a classic, multicomponent circuit can be used in most cross- and auto-correlation applications (see "The fundamentals of correlation," below). These include error correction for computers and their peripherals and interference reduction in communication systems; pattern recognition for image processing; bit, word, and frame synchronization for telemetry, video, and computer systems; and time-delay measurements for instrumentation, radar, and sonar systems. In other words, code correction, data synchronization, and time-

delay measurements are major uses for the 24-pin, bipolar 1023J, which is capable of a correlation rate of over 15 megahertz—a speed that is adequate for many cross- and auto-correlation applications.

The simplest correlation process performed is illustrated in Fig. 1a, where an 8-bit reference word is correlated with an incoming signal. The reference word, stored in a register, is compared with the incoming signal at each clock time. For each clock pulse, the number of agreeing bits is shown in decimal and binary notation (Fig. 1b). Maximum correlation occurs when all 8 reference bits match the respective incoming signal bits. As illustrated, correlation can be performed between two real-time signals, two stored signals, or one real-time and one stored signal, as the application requires.

The simplest implementation of digital correlation employs one serial-in, parallel-out shift register to store the reference signal and a similar shift register to accept

The fundamentals of correlation

Correlation of a stored and an incoming signal involves three basic operations: time shifting (delay), multiplication, and integration (summation). The shifting is performed first, followed by the multiplication and finally by the integration steps.

Multiplying the stored and incoming signals satisfies the logical definition that the correlation value should be +1 whenever the waveforms are identical. A positive correlation results from two signals of like sign, whereas a negative correlation occurs for signals of opposite sign.

Performing an integration after multiplication averages the product and aids in rejecting any noise that enters the correlator on the incoming signal. The closer the integration time is to the total time period of the signal, the greater the accuracy of the final average will be and the better the noise rejection.

Mathematically, correlation between two functions x(t) and y(t) is given by:

$$R_{12}(\tau) = \lim_{T \to \infty} \frac{1}{T} \int_{(-t/2)}^{(+t/2)} V_1(t) \cdot V_2(t+\tau) dt$$

Here, $R_{12}(\tau)$ refers to the correlation between two signals $V_1(t)$ and $V_2(t)$ with relative time offset, τ, which is determined by multiplying $V_1(t)$ by $V_2(t+\tau)$ and then taking the integral of the product. If both $V_1(t)$ and $V_2(t+\tau)$ are

periodic with common period T_0, the expression becomes:

$$R_{12}(\tau) = \int_{(-T_0/2)}^{(+T_0/2)} V_1(t) \cdot V_2(t+\tau) dt$$

Correlator applications can employ either cross-correlation or autocorrelation techniques. Cross-correlation is a bit-by-bit comparison between two real-time, delayed, or stored sequences. In contrast, in autocorrelation, one of the sequences is a time-delayed, exact replica of the other sequence.

Cross-correlation applications include the detection of differences (errors) between two data sequences and the determination of the time delay between two similar signals such as radar transmission and its returning reflection. Moreover, they also enable the multiplexing of data among several users, recognition of specified patterns in a data stream, and synchronization of a decoding process with an incoming data stream.

Autocorrelation is most useful in identifying periodicities within a data stream and as a time-domain alternative to spectral analysis and the associated time-domain–frequency-domain transformations. It can also be used to extract a periodic signal from its random noise background, since the signal correlates well with itself, but poorly with the random interference.

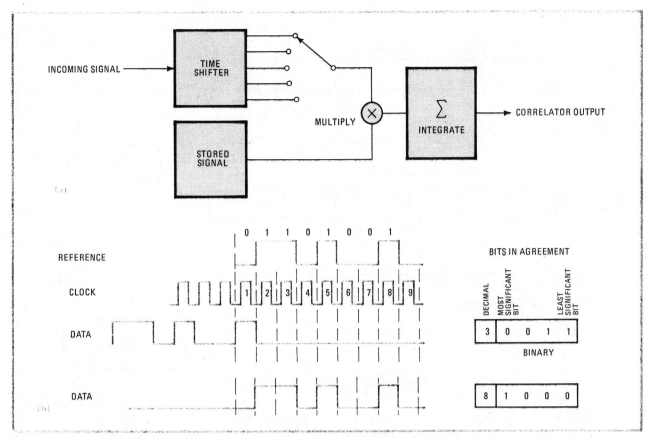

1. Bit by bit. In a correlation circuit, corresponding bits of a reference word and an incoming signal are compared to determine which are in agreement (a). The number of bits that are in agreement may be indicated by a decimal or a binary output (b).

the incoming signal (Fig. 2a). The reference word and incoming signal are compared by exclusive-NOR gates whose inputs are obtained from corresponding bit positions of the two registers. A logical 1 output from an exclusive-NOR gate indicates that both inputs are equal. The outputs of all the exclusive-NOR gates are applied to a summing network whose 7-bit output indicates the number of bits in agreement.

Either of two summing networks may be employed. An analog-output type provides a voltage or current that is proportional to the number of bits that correlate. A digital summing network, most useful in the applications discussed later, provides a binary count of the number of bits that correlate.

Bit by bit

Correlation is performed in the 1023J by serially shifting the reference word into an independently clocked 64-bit register (called the B register) and then serially shifting the incoming signal into the independently clocked 64-bit A register (Fig. 2b). By making load R a logical 1, the reference word is copied in parallel into the R latch. The user can then load a new reference word into the B register while correlation takes place between the A register and R latch.

Bit-by-bit comparisons between the A register and the R latch are made by the exclusive-NOR gates, whose outputs are applied to a digital summer through enabling AND gates. The output of the digital summer is a 7-bit binary word representing the number of bit positions in

the A register and R latch that are in agreement during the current A-register clock cycle. Since the digital summer is pipelined for the maximum data throughput rate, the updated correlation level appears after a delay of three summer clock cycles and still permits 15-MHz real-time correlation.

The designer may select bit positions where no comparisons are to be made by using the mask register. This is done by inserting a 64-bit serial word into the register with logical 0s in the bit positions indicating no comparison. Since the outputs from the register are applied to the AND gates that also contain the outputs from the exclusive-NOR gates, masked bits are prevented from reaching the digital summer.

Either a true or an inverted binary output can be selected from the 1023J using the invert control line and seven exclusive-OR gates that receive inputs from the digital summer. The gate outputs are then applied to seven three-state output buffers controlled by the time-shifted signal. A logical 1 on the time-shift line disables the buffered outputs by placing them in a high impedance state. When the output buffers are enabled and the invert signal is a logical 1, the outputs are inverted.

Establishing a threshold

If desired, a correlation threshold can be established in the 1023J by using the 7-bit independently clocked threshold register. To accomplish this, the time-shift control line is first used to disable the output buffers. Then, output lines D_0 through D_6 are used to load the

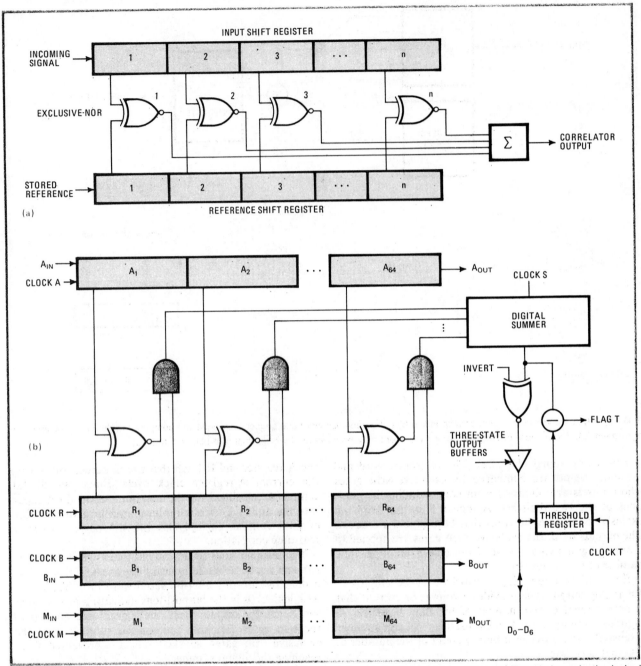

2. Many parts. Shift registers, exclusive-NOR gates, and a summing network make up the basic correlator (a). Three independently clocked 64-bit shift registers and one 64-bit latch store and shift data while comparisons are made by 64 exclusive-NOR gates (b).

desired binary threshold number into the register in parallel. Thereafter, the threshold flag will become a 1 when the binary number from the digital summer equals or exceeds the number in the register.

The output of the 1023J, designated S, is the total number of agreements between the bits in register A and those in latch R, not the number of agreements (positive product elements) minus the total number of disagreements. If desired, the statistically rigorous correlation coefficient, R, can be computed from S, since R = $(2S-M)/M$, where M (often 64 in practice) is the number of bits under comparison, or the number of logical 1s in the masking register. Under this equation, a correlator output of S = 32 with M = 64 bit positions enabled actually corresponds to zero (random) correlation between two data sequences.

When a correlation code longer than 64 bits is required, chips may be cascaded in series, as when the A_{out}, B_{out}, and M_{out} lines from each device are connected to the corresponding input of the next device. A binary adder is used to sum the outputs of the correlators. If a threshold flag is required, external integrated-circuit equivalents of the threshold register and threshold magnitude comparator must be used. The maximum number of correlators that can be added is limited by the loading and speed of such external circuits.

Error-correction techniques employed in computer and communication systems to ensure the error-free transmission of data are a major application for the 1023J. This procedure requires the use of expanded codes that contain extra bits beyond those absolutely required to convey information.

The improvements possible with expanded codes can be observed by first looking at a maximum-efficiency unexpanded code like ordinary binary numbers. In the binary system, each code is separated by only 1 bit from its neighboring code. Thus, a single 1-bit error transforms one allowable code into another unintended code.

In coding terminology, the binary system is said to exhibit a 1-bit distance between codes and the number of tolerable simultaneous errors is zero. For example, if the code 1110 is transmitted but 0110 is received, there is no way to detect the error.

Expanding for redundancy

Expanding a 4-bit binary code into a 7-bit code produces a redundant system that can correct single errors and detect up to two simultaneous ones. This expansion increases the number of possible code combinations from 16 (2^4) to 128 (2^7), but only 16 are valid codes. In this case, the true codes can be chosen to differ by at least 3 bits from all other correct codes. With this distance, each single-error code can be unambiguously associated with a particular code. The digital correlator is, of course, not limited to this code, and a variety of others can be accommodated.

The 1023J can readily be used in a system that employs a 7-bit expanded code. This arrangement involves a trial-and-error process wherein the incoming signal is compared with the 16 possible correct codes that are stored in memory. First, the incoming 7-bit signal is loaded into the B register and copied into the R latch. Then, the library of correct codes is sequentially applied to the A register, which compares each of the 16 possible correct codes with the incoming signal that is stored in the R latch. In this example, a correlation threshold of 6 is established in the T register to flag only perfect or nearly perfect correlations. The correlation flag threshold is set at the user's discretion.

Going by the clock

The system can operate at a fixed rate, clocking in a new data word after each full cycle through all combinations stored in the memory. Alternatively, the threshold flag can also restart the B register clock. In such a system, a new data word is clocked in as soon as a high correlation is reached, in effect short-cycling the system.

As described, the system is usable for single-error codes. If a relatively high error rate is anticipated, an even longer code expansion must be employed to increase the system's error tolerance. Using a carefully designed enhanced code, double-, triple-, or higher-order errors can be accurately corrected. In fact, the maximum number of simultaneous errors that can be corrected will always be less than half the distance between codes. However, because longer codes necessitate transmitting useful information at a slower rate, there is a tradeoff between a code's efficiency and its error tolerance.

Which code is used depends on the application at hand.

If higher data handling speeds are required in such an error-correction scheme, the incoming data stream can be applied to two or more correlators. If two correlators are used, each correlates the incoming data segment with only half of the possible correct codes contained in the memory. When one correlator registers an acceptably high level of correlation between the incoming data stream and one of the stored correct patterns, it feeds the contents of its A register serially to the output.

Explicit instructions

If fewer than 64 bits are required by the error-correction system, the masking register may be used to instruct the correlator to ignore the bits where no comparison is desired. It is done by masking the first $64 - N$ bits, where N is the number of bits of code. The last N bits in the register are then compared with the incoming word sample. When a high correlation is obtained, the correct signal occupies the last N positions of the A register and can be shifted out serially.

Although test patterns can be read sequentially into the A register without any spacing between words, synchronization data must inform the correlator when a new word is in position for testing. If this is not done, an unsynchronized comparison between an incoming signal segment and pieces of two sequentially stored patterns could trigger a false agreement.

The concept of code expansion can also be used to reduce the number of errors encountered in a high-noise or a high-interference environment. For example, a specific 64-bit code and its complement can be assigned to the binary values 1 and 0, respectively. Then, instead of a simple sequence of 1 and 0, a much longer serial sequence, consisting of the desired combination of expanded codes for 1 and 0, is transmitted. The resulting message contains the intended information, plus redundancy that permits detection of errors in the transmission and reception of the data.

Error detection is readily accomplished at the receiving end of a data transmission using only two receiver correlators—one holding the code for a 1 and the other holding a 0, to reconstruct the intended message. Then, whenever an expanded code version of a 1 or 0 is received, the appropriate correlator sends a 1 or 0 message to the output, where it can be transmitted to the remainder of the system.

Getting into sync

Synchronization of data frames, words, or bits is another common application for correlators. In frame synchronization, a correlator identifies the start of each new frame, or major group, of information. In word synchronization, the beginnings of individual data words are detected. In contrast, bit synchronization involves aligning individual bits of incoming information with the receiver's bit-by-bit clock.

A system can achieve and maintain frame synchronization only if the incoming data stream is interrupted periodically by a specific start-of-frame pattern. This pattern, transmitted at the beginning of each new frame, tells the receiver that a new frame will immediately enter

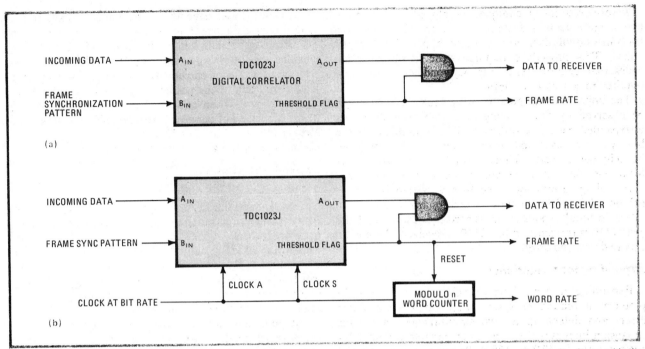

3. Synchronization. Frame synchronization is accomplished by comparing the pattern embedded in the incoming data stream with the pattern loaded in the B register (a). Word sync may be derived from frame sync with a modulo n counter operating at the system's bit rate (b).

the input register and must be handled accordingly. For example, in a video system, the start-of-frame pattern tells the receiver to return to the start of its vertical and horizontal scan. In a nonvideo application, such as a data filing system, the frame synchronization pattern can denote the beginning of a new group of data. This might be the data file for a particular individual.

Frame of reference

In a frame synchronization system, the B register of the 1023J is preloaded with the standard synchronization pattern, while the incoming data stream is shifted through the A register (Fig. 3a). When a frame sync pattern embedded in the incoming data stream aligns exactly with the stored sync pattern, the correlator's threshold flag goes to a logical 1, instructing the receiver to start handling a new frame of data. The start-of-frame pattern must be long and unusual enough to prevent false synchronization. However, this means that a percentage of the total data stream is unavailable for transmitting useful information.

The receiver-correlator system operates continuously, with the correlator producing a flag value of logical 1 as it receives each successive frame sync pattern in the incoming data stream. The rate at which these high outputs are generated is the frame rate of the incoming data. As long as its scanning system is reset at this rate, the receiver remains synchronized with the incoming data and continues to distinguish one frame or group of data from the next.

When presented with a data stream comprising a series of individual words, a system must decide where one word ends and the next begins. One technique for separating words in a continuous bit stream is to insert a start-of-word marker pattern at the end of each word and before the start of the following word.

The 1023J correlator in the receiver system can be programmed to identify the start-of-word marker. In operation, the correlator puts out a high correlation value whenever it encounters a start-of-word signal, which is analogous to the frame synchronization signal described earlier. If the data vocabulary and start-of-word marker are carefully selected, the correlator's output reaches isolated high values at the word rate with much lower correlation levels. If the signal-processing system is programmed to begin handling a new word at each correlator output, it remains synchronized for words with the incoming data and successfully distinguishes between individual incoming words.

The start-of-word marker code must be carefully selected to minimize the possibility of false triggering by data or noise, rather than the true synchronization pattern. Such low-error synchronization patterns are described in the literature on shift-register sequences, Barker codes, and spread-spectrum signal-theory.

Although the procedure can yield accurate word synchronization, it will be inefficient if the markers occupy a significant percentage of the total data stream. Clearly, if the number or length of the markers can be reduced, then more data can be sent.

Marking off the words

If the data words are organized into fixed-length frames and a frame synchronization marker is included, word synchronization can be derived from frame synchronization (Fig. 3b). If there are always N words per frame, then the word rate is N times the frame rate. The frame-rate output pulses of the frame synchronization correlator can be multiplied upward to produce the needed word synchronization pulses. Given a fixed word length, word synchronization can be established with a recirculating counter, operating at modulo n, where n is the number of bits per word. In this case, the counter is reset at each frame pulse, after which it continues cycling through its states, returning to its word-start position every n cycles. If it abruptly shifts or gradually drifts out of a word synchronization, the counter readjusts automatically at the start of the next frame.

Correlator-based systems can determine the time delay between two similar patterns of bits, such as a transmitted sonar or radar signal and its returned reflection. In these cases, the two signals appear similar in shape and bit pattern, but exhibit a relative time shift of $2D/V$, where D is the distance between the antenna and target and V is the velocity of propagation (the speed of light in radar and of sound in sonar). Conceptually, this technique involves the shifting of one signal relative to the other so that the shifting just compensates for the time delay between the two signals.

Measuring time delay

Using the 1023J, the B register can be loaded with the original, or transmitted, signal at the same time as the A register is loaded with the delayed, return signal. The two registers are clocked together so that the time delay between the signals appears as a displacement in their relative register positions. After both registers are loaded, the output of the correlator is monitored while the A register continues to be clocked. This process loads progressively later return signal bits into register A, while shifting the delayed pattern across the underlying signal stored in register B. As a result, the number of bit shifts required for acceptable correlation multiplied by the signal's bit time yields the total time delay between the two signals.

For this system to function properly, the code must be long enough not to trigger on false correlations. For example, a code such as 10101010101 would be unsuitable for time delay measurements because all shifts of 2N bits (where $N = 1, 2, 3, \ldots$) would yield high correlations and produce ambiguous results. In contrast, a code that repeats only once every 500 characters would be much more likely to provide an unambiguous measure for signals with a time delay of less than 500 bit times.

Nonrecurring codes

When a nonrecurring code, such as a single burst of information, is employed in a time delay measurement, the length and pattern of the transmitted code are subject to limitations. Under ideal circumstances, the only objective is to measure distance to a target, and a simple isolated pulse (a single positive bit surrounded by negatives) can be transmitted.

The returning reflection of this signal contains a similar isolated pulse, delayed by the round trip travel time between the antenna and target. However, this alignment test is relatively insensitive, having a total correlation score of 62/64 when the transmitted and received pulses are misaligned, versus 64/64 for perfect alignment. In the presence of noise or interference, the return signal can contain one or more false positives, which can reduce the perfect alignment correlation and generate other relatively high correlations.

Longer codes can be used to improve the accuracy and sensitivity of the time delay measurement. Particularly suitable are the Barker codes, which are characterized by longer correlations with time-shifted versions of themselves. Although a longer pulse code cannot improve the 64/64 correlation score for perfect time-alignment in the presence of noise, it greatly reduces the chance of a burst or random noise causing high correlation. For a given level of interference and bit errors, increasing the length of the Barker code tends to reduce the frequency and magnitude of false correlations and enhances the accuracy of the range measurement system. The Barker codes available offer suitable error rates and sensitivity for these applications.

Spitting image

To recognize periodicities or patterns, the 1023J can be used to compare a single data stream against a time-delayed replica of itself. First, the signal is loaded simultaneously into the A and B registers. Then, when the registers are full, the B register pattern is held, while the incoming signal continues to be clocked in sequentially through the A register. This simulates a steadily increasing time shift.

Periodicities in the data stream will generate high correlations, which appear periodically as the A register contents slide past the B register. These correlations and the number of bits between sequential high correlations correspond to the period of the repeating pattern. For example, the data sequence 100100100100 exhibits a high correlation for every delay of 3N bit times, when $N = 1, 2, 3, \ldots$ Although this example is obvious, there are others that are subtle and can cause system problems if they are not spotted.

Random noise can make such periodic signals harder to detect by reducing the contrast between periodic correlation peaks and the low residual correlations between them. However, a digital correlator can still identify signal periodicities in the presence of surprisingly high levels of random noise. If $S(m)$ and $S(m+n)$ are the original and time-shifted versions of the pure signal and $N(m)$ and $N(m+n)$ are the corresponding additive noise values, then the correlator performs the sum:

$$R(n) = \sum_{m=0}^{63} [S(m) + N(m) \times S(m+n) + N(m+n)]$$

where m and n are indexes representing discrete steps in time. In this example, the sum runs arbitrarily over 64 values only because this is the bit length of the 1023J.

The function being summed comprises the four terms $S(m) \times S(m+n)$, $N(m) \times N(m+n)$, $S(m) \times N(m+n)$, and $N(m) \times S(m+n)$. If the noise is truly random, it does not correlate significantly either with S or with its time-shifted self, and only $S(m) \times S(m+n)$ contributes significantly to the overall sum, $R(n)$. However, when a short sample is considered in a noisy environment, the noise can interfere significantly, masking a pattern of periodic high and low correlations. To overcome higher noise levels, longer correlation sequences are used to increase the signal's integration gain. A single 64-bit correlator can provide up to 18 decibels ($10 \log_{10} 64$) of signal enhancement, and two units in the series can supply twice as much, or 21 dB. □

Microprogramming enhances signal processor's performance

Pipelined architecture separates interface, control, numeric processing to complete 20 million complex multiplications a second

by Steven H. Chin and Charles W. Brooks, *Westinghouse Electric Corp., Baltimore, Md.*

☐ Demands on the performance of signal-processing systems promise to become ever tougher in the 1980s as the need grows for ever securer communications, more reliable target recognition by radar and sonar, and image-processing systems with increased capability. But microprocessors lack the necessary speed, while hard-wired circuitry of course lacks flexibility in algorithm implementation.

To date, perhaps the most economically feasible solution has been the use of a numerical coprocessor in combination with a standard microprocessor, such as the 8087 teamed with the 8086. But even here performance is not satisfactory at frequencies over 100 kilohertz. The modular software-programmable processor (MSP²) suffers from no such limitation.

Using high-speed semiconductor technology, chip-carrier packaging techniques, and an innovative processor architecture, the MSP² delivers the needed performance and flexibility along with the support software to make it work. Emitter-coupled-logic gate arrays and ECL 10K logic are behind the high multiplication speed of the MSP²—20 million complex multiplications a second—while the microprogrammable processor gives system designers the freedom to make alterations in control or processing flow later on.

Extending across a number of design levels, the modularity of the MSP² means segregation of control from signal-processing functions at the top level and judicious placement of hardware elements in the system at a lower level. This architecture ensures that future performance enhancements of the MSP² can be effected by simply substituting new chips rather than redefining the architecture. Thus, the end of the decade can bring an MSP² with twice the throughput without requiring any change in the functional organization of the system.

Distinct functional blocks.

The MSP² separates the three primary functions of a signal processor into distinct blocks. They are the control interface module, the processor-controller module, and the signal-processing module (Fig. 1). Each section is totally responsible for a particular share of the workload. Thus the communication path between the host computer and the internal storage in the MSP² lies in the control interface module, while control flow and numerical calculations are handled in the processor-controller and

signal-processing modules, respectively.

In a current system with a PDP-11/34 host computer, 16 twisted-pair bidirectional lines between the control interface module and the host carry all the program data and control words required to operate the MSP². This bidirectional bus, known as the communication interface bus (Fig. 2), uses a standard handshake for word transfers. Then in any transfer of program data, the host computer controls the direction of movement by means of a read-write signal to the control interface module's control logic.

Although this module is a critical path between the host computer and the functional power of the MSP², the other two modules are the brawn and brain of the processor. The processor-controller module uses a programmable read-only memory, timers, a memory-address generator, and several distinct storage areas to orchestrate the overall function of the MSP² as it executes signal-processing algorithms.

The PROM controller decodes instructions from a microprogrammed ROM to monitor the control-interface-module commands and to coordinate its function with the processor controller. Timekeepers in this component work with the memory-address generator to move data into and out of the signal-processing unit.

Memory-address generation

Working in a close supporting role with other components of the processor-controller module, the memory-address generator provides four identical address-sequence generators for accessing data memory. Associated with each memory-address generator is an offset memory that supplies the initial address or offset used along with one of the six possible addressing modes to create the actual address of the data. To list the six:

■ Straight count starts from an initial offset value and increments by one at each clock tick until the instruction is completed.

■ Complement count, on the other hand, decrements from an initial offset value at each clock tick until the instruction is completed.

■ Increment count starts from an initial offset value and adds an increment value at each clock tick until the instruction is completed. The converse mode may be obtained by using a 2's complement for the increment value, in effect decrementing at each clock tick.

- Bit-reverse count reverses the significance of the count—that is, the least significant bit is considered the most significant. The number of bits reversed in this way is controlled by whatever value is loaded into the bit-reverse register.
- Bit-twist count starts from an initial offset value and counts up just as in the straight count. A bit-twist number, loaded into the bit-twist register, determines which bits are twisted, or interchanged.
- The fast-Fourier-transform bit-twist count also starts from an initial offset value and generates the address sequence necessary to perform the calculations for the fast Fourier transform.

As two of the the major storage areas of the processor-controller module, the macro memory, as it is called, contains the microcoded algorithm, and the control memory stores the signal-processing-program parameters. Using the contents of these memory sections, the module's third major storage area—the micro memory—is responsible for selecting the next instruction from the macro memory for execution. Micro memory uses this macro instruction to select the appropriate group of micro instructions from its own local 256-word micro store. In addition, the micro memory issues control signals for the memory-address generators plus the data memory and the arithmetic unit in the signal-processing module. In fact, the control signals are derived directly from the individual 16-bit microinstruction retrieved from the 256-word storage area based on the macro instruction and retained in a local holding register. Each

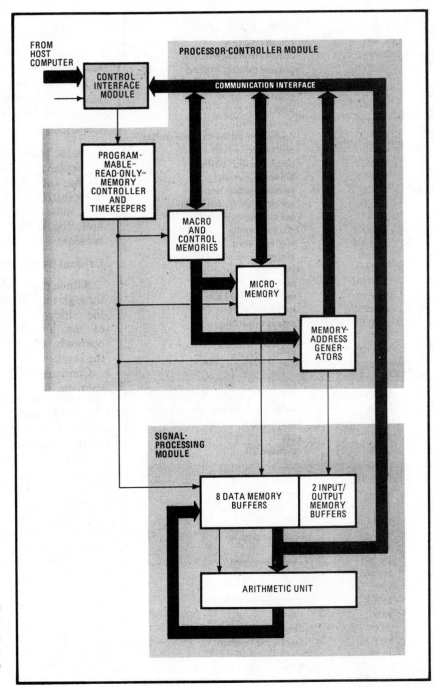

1. Troika. Three functional units manage interface handling, process flow control, and numerical computation in this modular software programmable processor. The current ECL gate-array implementation achieves 20 million complex multiplications a second.

SIGNAL-PROCESSING INSTRUCTIONS AVAILABLE ON THE MODULAR SOFTWARE-PROGRAMMABLE PROCESSOR	
FFT	
FFT	fast Fourier transform
WFFTS	weighted first-stage FFT
Filter	
POLE1	one pole
P1Z1	one pole — one zero
ZERO1	one zero
Arithmetic	
ADD	real add
ARMPY	accumulate real multiply
CADD	complex add
CLRM	clear memory
CLRM1	set memory to 1
CMPY	complex multiply
CMPYC	complex multiply conjugate
CMPYR	complex multiply recursive
CMPYX2	complex multiply X2
CNTH	count threshold
DET	detect
DETSQ	detect squared
DPACC	double-precision multiply accumulate
DPADD	double-precision add
DXMPY	double-precision multiply
FLMPY	full-length multiply
MADD	complex multiply add
MADD3	complex multiply add multiple
RCMPY	real-by-complex multiply
RMAXV	maximum vector
RMAXW	maximum word
RMINV	minimum vector
RMINW	minimum word
RMPYAC	real multiply add
RMPYC	real multiply conjugate
RRMPY	real-real multiply
SCALEV	scale determinator
SUB	subtract
VALID	valid
Logical	
AND	AND
CCOMP	conditional 2's complement
NOT	NOT
OR	OR
XOR	exclusive OR
Control	
BOND	branch on no data
BP	branch on pause
CLRP	clear pause
CP	conditional pause
HALT	halt
INCRO	increment register
JUMP	jump
LOI	load offset immediate
MOVE	move data vector
NOP	no op
REP	repeat
REPI	repeat and increment
SETP	set pause
UBT	branch on tag

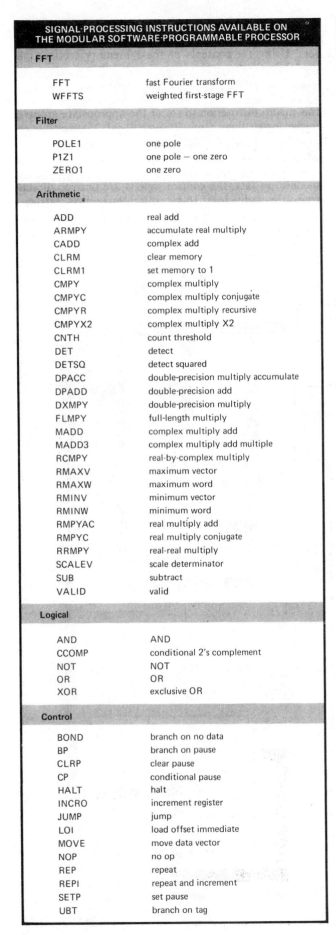

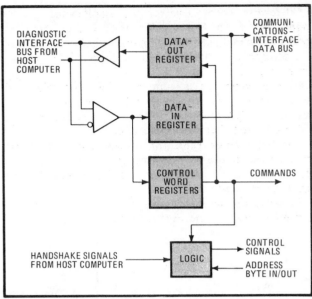

2. Communications. All interface functions are handled by the control interface module using a standard handshake procedure. This detail of the communication interface bus shows one of 16 bidirectional lines connecting the MSP² with the host computer.

bit in the holding register is decoded and distributed as a particular control signal.

Thus the micro memory sequences through a series of microinstructions (see table), decoding them to control data movement from data memory into the arithmetic unit, the numerical operations within that unit, and subsequent transfer of results from it into data memory.

Critical performer

Although the other two modules key process flow through the MSP², the signal-processing module contains the critical performers in the system. Under supervision of the processor-controller module, it stores data operands, performs operations on the data, and stores the result.

Consisting as it does of three major components—data memory, input/output memory, and arithmetic unit—this module further demonstrates the modular architecture of the MSP². Data memory stores operands and results under control of the memory-address generator and the processor controller. An I/O memory section uses half of its double-buffered organization to transfer data between the signal-processing module and an external memory; the other half is treated as one of the data memories.

Directly under control of the processor-controller module, the arithmetic unit (Fig. 3) is the workhorse of the MSP². Besides addition, subtraction, multiplication, and division, it performs more complex operations such as FFT calculations by virtue of its microprogrammed control. Thus, an arbitrary set of more complicated operations can be stored in macro memory and executed as functions within a larger microprogram.

Critical to the MSP²'s high throughput rate is the signal-processing module's 50-nanosecond instruction execution time and its ECL gate-array implementation. Four high-performance 16-bit multipliers and eight

3. Powerhouse. In the arithmetic unit, the crossbar multiplexer routes data through the required processing elements during the instruction cycle. Microprogrammed control enables the unit to perform fast Fourier transforms and other complex operations. Shaded areas are gate arrays.

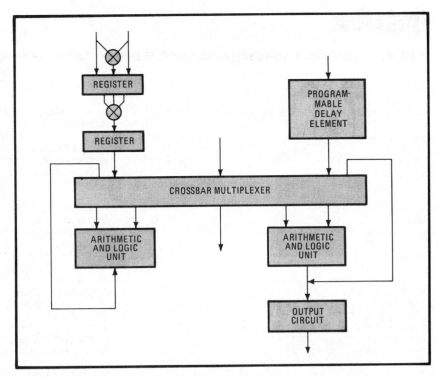

arithmetic and logic units—the site of simple arithmetic and logic functions—in the arithmetic unit ensure that even 16-bit complex operations, such as complex multiplication $(a+bj) \times (c+dj)$, may be performed within a single cycle of the 20-megahertz clock.

Pipelined architecture adds a further margin of performance with the overlap of data fetching and instruction execution. Thus the next set of operands are loaded into the signal-processing module's registers by the processor-controller module while the arithmetic unit is occupied with doing the calculation. After the calculation is complete, the processor controller can immediately initiate the next instruction, or calculation, with no time lost between instructions waiting for data movement to complete—hence the direct translation of the 50-ns instruction-execution time into 20 million multiplications per second.

Within the arithmetic unit, however, a special multiplexer allows the data to determine program execution for some instructions. For example, in an absolute-value instruction, the sign of the incoming data will determine whether the arithmetic unit must negate the value. For these data-dependent instructions, the multiplexer manipulates the data based on input flags—like the sign and overflow flags—to create the appropriate output.

Finally, a programmable delay element in the arithmetic unit helps synchronize data flow through that unit, while an output circuit section scales the results or generates over- and under-flow bit patterns as needed.

Software support

Although some systems analysts have in the past expected microprogrammed architectures to solve their design problems, the difficulty of implementing such systems has often proven too formidable. The MSP², on the other hand, is supported by a full software development set, which includes a simulator, language translator (or cross-assembler), loader, and debugger.

In the course of algorithm development, the simulator enables the designer to verify the logic and to develop test cases for subsequent validation of the completed hardware. Using a set of Fortran-callable subroutines, the simulator mimics the MSP² by showing the expected condition of the major registers following execution of each instruction. Once confident of the algorithm, programmers employ the language translator—or cross assembler—resident on the host computer to implement it as a microprogram.

Using the binary files generated by the translator, the MSP² loader places the microprogram into the appropriate memories and registers in the MSP² hardware. At this point, the debugger allows interactive examination and alteration of the contents of the programmable signal processor, as well as providing the ability to modify and control the processor's execution sequence.

The MSP² currently uses proven multiwire development boards because of the ease of changing wiring and replacing chips. But it will eventually be implemented with leadless ceramic chip-carriers when anticipated applications in airborne or marine systems demand high package density and lower weight. Unlike dual in-line packages, such carriers use space efficiently even as pin count increases. Lighter in weight than a DIP, they also have uniform and shorter conductor lengths. The short leads reduce parasitic resistance, capacitance, and inductance, thus increasing the operating bandwidth from 500 MHz to 4 gigahertz for those systems that make use of ceramic chip-carriers.

Ceramic substrate materials are being developed that are compatible with leadless chip-carriers in manufacturing, thermal, and mechanical aspects. The temperature coefficient of expansion of these ceramics matches the carriers' and thus makes the substrate immune to cracking due to thermal cycling during soldering. □

INDEX